Books by Lillian Hellman

PLAYS

The Children's Hour (1934)
Days to Come (1936)
The Little Foxes (1939)
Watch on the Rhine (1941)
The Searching Wind (1944)
Another Part of the Forest (1947)
Montserrat (an adaptation, 1950)
The Autumn Garden (1951)
The Lark (an adaptation, 1956)
Candide (an operetta, 1957)
Toys in the Attic (1960)
My Mother, My Father and Me (an adaptation, 1963)
The Collected Plays (1972)

MEMOIR

An Unfinished Woman (1969)

EDITED BY LILLIAN HELLMAN

The Selected Letters of Anton Chekhov (1955)
The Big Knockover: Stories and Short Novels by Dashiell Hammett (1966)

The Collected Plays

The Collected Plays brings together for the first time all of Miss Hellman's work for the theatre, and supersedes any previous editions and collections. For this edition she has made numerous small revisions and emendations in each of the plays: the texts as given here are henceforth to be regarded as definitive.

Lillian Hellman

The Collected Plays

Little, Brown and Company–Boston–Toronto

LIBRARY OF CONGRESS CATALOG CARD NO. 79-175482

FIRST EDITION

T 04/72

Published simultaneously in Canada
by Little, Brown & Company (Canada) Limited
PRINTED IN THE UNITED STATES OF AMERICA

Copyright information and acknowledgements begin on the following page.

Contents

The Children's Hour 1
Days to Come 71
The Little Foxes 131
Watch on the Rhine 201
The Searching Wind 267
Another Part of the Forest 325
Montserrat 405
The Autumn Garden 461
The Lark 547
Candide 603
Toys in the Attic 681
My Mother, My Father and Me 753

Publisher's Note

The Collected Plays brings together for the first time all of Lillian Hellman's works for the theatre, and supersedes any previous collections and editions. For this edition Miss Hellman has made numerous small revisions and emendations in each of the plays: the texts as given here are henceforth to be regarded as definitive.

The Children's Hour

For Dashiell Hammett
with thanks

The Children's Hour was first produced at Maxine Elliot's Theatre, New York City, on November 20, 1934, with the following cast:

(*In the order of their appearance*)

PEGGY ROGERS	EUGENIA RAWLS
MRS. LILY MORTAR	ALINE MC DERMOTT
EVELYN MUNN	ELIZABETH SECKEL
HELEN BURTON	LYNNE FISHER
LOIS FISHER	JACQUELINE RUSLING
CATHERINE	BARBARA LEEDS
ROSALIE WELLS	BARBARA BEALS
MARY TILFORD	FLORENCE MC GEE
KAREN WRIGHT	KATHERINE EMERY
MARTHA DOBIE	ANNE REVERE
DOCTOR JOSEPH CARDIN	ROBERT KEITH
AGATHA	EDMONIA NOLLEY
MRS. AMELIA TILFORD	KATHERINE EMMET
A GROCERY BOY	JACK TYLER

Produced and directed by
HERMAN SHUMLIN

Settings designed by
ALINE BERNSTEIN

Scenes

Act One

Living room of the Wright-Dobie School
Late afternoon in April.

Act Two

Scene 1. Living room at Mrs. Tilford's.
A few hours later.
Scene 2. The same. Later that evening.

Act Three

The same as Act One. November.

Act One

SCENE: *A room in the Wright-Dobie School for girls, a converted farmhouse about ten miles from the town of Lancet, Massachusetts. It is a comfortable, unpretentious room used as an afternoon study-room and at all other times as the living room.*

A large door left center faces the audience. There is a single door right. Against both back walls are bookcases. A large desk is at right; a table, two sofas, and eight or ten chairs.

It is early in an afternoon in April.

AT RISE: *Mrs. Lily Mortar is sitting in a large chair right center, with her head back and her eyes closed. She is a plump, florid woman of forty-five with dyed reddish hair. Her dress is too fancy for a classroom.*

Seven girls, from twelve to fourteen years old, are informally grouped on chairs and sofa. Six of them are sewing with no great amount of industry on pieces of white material. One of the others, Evelyn Munn, is using her scissors to trim the hair of Rosalie, who sits, nervously, in front of her: she has Rosalie's head bent back at an awkward angle and is enjoying herself.

The eighth girl, Peggy Rogers, is sitting in a higher chair than the others. She is reading aloud from a book. She is bored and she reads in a singsong, tired voice.

PEGGY. "It is twice blest; it blesseth him that gives and him that takes: 'tis mightiest in the mightiest; it becomes the throned monarch better than his crown; his sceptre shows the force of temporal power, the attribute to awe and majesty, wherein . . ." (*Mrs. Mortar suddenly opens her eyes and stares at the haircutting. The children make efforts to warn Evelyn. Peggy raises her voice until she is shouting*) "doth sit the dread and fear of kings; but mercy is above . . ."

MRS. MORTAR. Evelyn! What are you doing?

EVELYN (*she lisps*). Uh — nothing, Mrs. Mortar.

MRS. MORTAR. You are certainly doing something. You are ruining the scissors for one thing.

PEGGY (*loudly*). "But mercy is above. It . . ."

MRS. MORTAR. Just a moment, Peggy. It is very unfortunate that you girls cannot sit quietly with your sewing and drink in the immortal words of the immortal bard. (*She sighs*) Evelyn, go back to your sewing.

EVELYN. I can't get the hem thtraight. Honeth, I've been trying for three weekth, but I jutht can't do it.

MRS. MORTAR. Helen, please help Evelyn with the hem.

HELEN (*rises, holding up the garment Evelyn has been working on. It is soiled and shapeless and so much has been cut off that it is now hardly large enough for a child of five. Giggling*). She can't ever wear *that,* Mrs. Mortar.

MRS. MORTAR (*vaguely*). Well, try to do something with it. Make some handkerchiefs or something. Be clever about it. Women must learn these tricks. (*To Peggy*) Continue. "Mightiest in the mightiest."

PEGGY. " 'Tis mightiest in the mightiest; it becomes the throned monarch better than his crown; his sceptre—his sceptre shows the force of temporal power, the attribute to awe and majesty, wherein—"

LOIS (*from the back of the room chants softly and monotonously through the previous speech*). Ferebam, ferebas, ferebat, ferebamus, ferebatis, fere—fere—

CATHERINE (*two seats away, the book propped in front of her*). Fere*bant.*

LOIS. Ferebamus, ferebatis, fere*bant.*

MRS. MORTAR. Who's doing that?

PEGGY (*the noise ceases. She hurries on*). "Wherein doth sit the dread and fear of kings; but mercy is above this sceptred sway, it is enthroned in the hearts of kings, it is an attribute to God himself—"

MRS. MORTAR (*sadly*). Peggy, can't you imagine yourself as Portia? Can't you read the lines with some feeling, some pity? (*Dreamily*) Pity. Ah! As Sir Henry said to me many's the time, pity makes the actress. Now, why can't *you* feel pity?

PEGGY. I guess I feel pity.

LOIS. Ferebamus, ferebatis, fere—fere—fere—

CATHERINE. Fere*bant,* stupid.

MRS. MORTAR. How many people in this room are talking? Peggy, read the line again. I'll give you the cue.

PEGGY. What's a cue?

MRS. MORTAR. A cue is a line or word given the actor or actress to remind them of their next speech.

HELEN (*softly*). To remind *him* or *her*.

ROSALIE (*a fattish girl with glasses*). Weren't you ever in the movies, Mrs. Mortar?

MRS. MORTAR. I had many offers, my dear. But the cinema is a shallow art. It has no — no — (*Vaguely*) no fourth dimension. Now, Peggy, if you would only try to submerge yourself in this problem. You are pleading for the life of a man. (*She rises and there are faint sighs from the girls, who stare at her with blank, bored faces. She recites with gestures*) "But mercy is above this sceptred sway; it is enthroned in the hearts of kings, it is an attribute to God himself; and earthly power doth then show likest God's when mercy seasons justice."

LOIS (*almost singing it*). Utor, fruor, fungor, potior, and vescor take the dative.

CATHERINE. Take the *ablative*.

LOIS. Oh, dear. Utor, fruor, fung —

MRS. MORTAR (*to Lois, with sarcasm*). You have something to tell the class?

LOIS (*apologetically*). We've got a Latin exam this afternoon.

MRS. MORTAR. And you intend to occupy the sewing and elocution hour learning what should have been learnt yesterday?

CATHERINE (*wearily*). It takes her more than yesterday to learn it.

MRS. MORTAR. Well, I cannot allow you to interrupt us like this.

CATHERINE. But we're finished sewing.

LOIS (*admiringly*). I bet you were good at Latin, Mrs. Mortar.

MRS. MORTAR. Long ago, my dear, long ago. Now, take your book over by the window and don't disturb our enjoyment of Shakespeare. (*Catherine and Lois rise, go to window, stand mumbling and gesturing*) Let us go back again. "It is an attribute to —" (*At this point the door opens far enough to let Mary Tilford, clutching a slightly faded bunch of wild flowers, squeeze cautiously in. She is fourteen, neither pretty nor ugly. She is an undistinguished-looking girl*) "And earthly power doth then show likest God's when mercy seasons justice. We do pray for mercy, and that same prayer doth teach —"

PEGGY (*happily*). You've skipped three lines.

MRS. MORTAR. In my entire career I've never missed a line.

PEGGY. But you did skip three lines. (*Goes to Mrs. Mortar with book*) See?

MRS. MORTAR (*seeing Mary sidling along wall toward other end of the room, turns to her to avoid Peggy and the book*). Mary!

MARY. Yes, Mrs. Mortar?

MRS. MORTAR. This is a pretty time to be coming to your sewing class, I must say. Even if you have no interest in your work you might at least remember that you owe me a little courtesy. Courtesy is breeding. Breeding is an excellent thing. (*Turns to class*) Always remember that.

ROSALIE. Please, Mrs. Mortar, can I write that down?

MRS. MORTAR. Certainly. Suppose you all write it down.

PEGGY. But we wrote it down last week.

(*Mary giggles.*)

MRS. MORTAR. Mary, I am still awaiting your explanation. Where have you been?

MARY. I took a walk.

MRS. MORTAR. So you took a walk. And may I ask, young lady, are we in the habit of taking walks when we should be at our classes?

MARY. I am sorry, Mrs. Mortar, I went to get you these flowers. I thought you would like them and I didn't know it would take so long to pick them.

MRS. MORTAR (*flattered*). Well, well.

MARY. You were telling us last week how much you liked flowers, and I thought that I would bring you some and —

MRS. MORTAR. That was very sweet of you, Mary; I always like thoughtfulness. But you must not allow anything to interfere with your classes. Now run along, dear, and get a vase and some water to put my flowers in. (*Mary turns, sticks out her tongue at Helen, says* "A-a-a," *and exits left*) You may put that book away, Peggy. I am sure your family need never worry about your going on the stage.

PEGGY. I don't want to go on the stage. I want to be a lighthouse keeper's wife.

MRS. MORTAR. Well, I certainly hope you won't read to him. (*The laughter of the class pleases her. Peggy sits down among the other girls, who are making a great show of doing nothing. Mrs. Mortar returns to her chair, puts her head back, closes her eyes.*)

CATHERINE. How much longer, O Cataline, are you going to abuse our patience? (*To Lois*) Now translate it, and for goodness' sakes try to get it right this time.

MRS. MORTAR (*for no reason*). "One master passion in the breast, like Aaron's serpent, swallows all the rest."

(*She and Lois are murmuring during Karen Wright's entrance. Karen is an attractive woman of twenty-eight, casually pleasant in manner, without sacrifice of warmth or dignity. She smiles at the girls, goes to the desk. With her entrance there is an immediate change in the manner of the girls: they are fond of her and they respect her. She gives Mortar, whose quotation has reached her, an annoyed look.*)

LOIS. "Quo usque tandem ab*ut*ere . . ."

KAREN (*automatically*). "Abu*tere*." (*Opens drawer in desk*) What's happened to your hair, Rosalie?

ROSALIE. It got cut, Miss Wright.

KAREN (*smiling*). I can see that. A new style? Looks as though it has holes in it.

EVELYN (*giggling*). I didn't mean to do it that bad, Mith Wright, but Rothalie'th got funny hair. I thaw a picture in the paper, and I wath trying to do it that way.

ROSALIE (*feels her hair, looks pathetically at Karen*). Oh, what shall I do, Miss Wright? (*Gesturing*) It's long here, and it's long here, and it's short here and —

KAREN. Come up to my room later and I'll see if I can fix it for you.

MRS. MORTAR. And hereafter we'll have no more haircutting.

KAREN. Helen, have you found your bracelet?

HELEN. No, I haven't, and I've looked everywhere.

KAREN. Have another look. It must be in your room somewhere.

(*Mary comes in right, with her flowers in a vase. Karen looks at the flowers in surprise.*)

MARY. Good afternoon, Miss Wright. (*Sits down, looks at Karen, who is staring hard at the flowers.*)

KAREN. Hello, Mary.

MRS. MORTAR (*fluttering around*). Peggy has been reading Portia for us.

(*Peggy sighs.*)

KAREN. Peggy doesn't like Portia?

MRS. MORTAR. I don't think she quite appreciates it, but—

KAREN (*patting Peggy on the head*). I don't think I do either. Where'd you get those flowers, Mary?

MRS. MORTAR. She picked them for me. (*Hurriedly*) It made her a little late to class, but she heard me say I loved flowers, and she went to get them for me. (*With a sigh*) The first wild flowers of the season.

KAREN. But not the very first, are they, Mary?

MARY. I don't know.

KAREN. Where did you get them?

MARY. Near Conway's cornfield, I think.

KAREN. It wasn't necessary to go so far. There was a bunch exactly like this in the garbage can this morning.

MRS. MORTAR (*after a second*). Oh, I can't believe it! What a nasty thing to do! (*To Mary*) And I suppose you have just as fine an excuse for being an hour late to breakfast this morning, and last week— (*To Karen*) I haven't wanted to tell you these things before, but—

KAREN (*hurriedly, as a bell rings off stage*). There's the bell.

LOIS (*walking toward door*). Ad, ab, ante, in, de, inter, con, post, præ— (*Looks up at Karen*) I *can't* seem to remember the rest.

KAREN. Præ, pro, sub, super. Don't worry, Lois. You'll come out all right. (*Lois smiles, exits. Mary attempts to make a quick exit*) Wait a minute, Mary. (*Reluctantly Mary turns back as the girls file out. Karen moves the small chairs, clearing the room as she talks*) Mary, I've had the feeling—and I don't think I'm wrong—that the girls here are happy; that they like Miss Dobie and me, that they like the school. Do you think that's true?

MARY. Miss Wright, I have to get my Latin book.

KAREN. I thought it was true until you came here a year ago. I don't think you're very happy here, and I'd like to find out why. (*Looks at Mary, waits for an answer, gets none, shakes her head*) Why, for example, do you find it necessary to lie to us so often?

MARY (*without looking up*). I'm not lying. I went out walking and I saw the flowers and they looked pretty and I didn't know it was so late.

KAREN (*impatiently*). Stop it, Mary! I'm not interested in hearing that foolish story again. I *know* you got the flowers out of the garbage can. What I do want to know is why you feel you have to lie out of it.

MARY. I *did* pick the flowers near Conway's. You never believe me. You believe everybody but me. It's always like that. Everything I say you fuss at me about. Everything I do is wrong.

KAREN. You know that isn't true. (*Goes to Mary, puts her arm around her, waits until the sobbing has stopped*) Look, Mary, look at me. (*Raises Mary's face with her hand*) Let's try to understand each other. If you feel that you *have* to take a walk, or that you just *can't* come to class, or that you'd like to go into the village by yourself, come and tell me — I'll try to understand. I don't say that I'll always agree that you should do exactly what you want to do, but I've had feelings like that, too — everybody has — and I won't be unreasonable about yours. But this way, this kind of lying you do, makes everything wrong.

MARY (*looking steadily at Karen*). I got the flowers near Conway's cornfield.

KAREN (*looks at Mary, sighs, moves back toward desk and stands there for a moment*). Well, there doesn't seem to be any other way with you; you'll have to be punished. Take your recreation periods alone for the next two weeks. No horseback riding and no hockey. Don't leave the school grounds for any reason whatsoever. Is that clear?

MARY (*carefully*). Saturday, too?

KAREN. Yes.

MARY. But you said I could go to the boat races.

KAREN. I'm sorry, but you can't go.

MARY. I'll tell my grandmother. I'll tell her how everybody treats me here and the way I get punished for every little thing I do. I'll tell her, I'll —

MRS. MORTAR. Why, I'd slap her hands!

KAREN (*turning back from door, ignoring Mrs. Mortar's speech. To Mary*). Go upstairs, Mary.

MARY. I don't feel well.

KAREN (*wearily*). Go upstairs now.

MARY. I've got a pain. I've had it all morning. It hurts right here. (*Pointing vaguely in the direction of her heart*) Really it does.

KAREN. Ask Miss Dobie to give you some hot water and bicarbonate of soda.

MARY. It's a bad pain. I've never had it before. My heart! It's my heart! It's stopping or something. I can't breathe. (*She takes a long breath and falls awkwardly to the floor.*)

KAREN (*sighs, shakes her head, kneels beside Mary. To Mrs. Mortar*). Ask Martha to phone Joe.

MRS. MORTAR (*going out*). Do you think — ? Heart trouble is very serious in a child.

(*Karen picks Mary up from the floor and carries her off right. After a moment Martha Dobie enters center. She is about the same age as Karen. She is a nervous, high-strung woman.*)

KAREN (*enters right*). Did you get Joe?

MARTHA (*nodding*). What happened to her? She was perfectly well a few hours ago.

KAREN. She probably still is. I told her she couldn't go to the boat races and she had a heart attack. (*Sits down at desk and begins to mark papers*) She's a problem, that kid. Her latest trick was kidding your aunt out of a sewing lesson with those faded flowers we threw out. Then she threatened to go to her grandmother with some tale about being mistreated.

MARTHA. And, please God, Grandma would believe her and take her away.

KAREN. Which would give the school a swell black eye. But we ought to do something.

MARTHA. How about having a talk with Mrs. Tilford?

KAREN (*smiling*). You want to do it? (*Martha shakes her head*) I hate to do it. She's been so nice to us. Anyway, it wouldn't do any good. She's too crazy about Mary to see her faults very clearly — and the kid knows it.

MARTHA. How about asking Joe to say something to her? She'd listen to him.

KAREN. That would be admitting that we can't do the job ourselves.

MARTHA. Well, we can't, and we might as well admit it. We've tried everything we can think of. She's had more attention than any other three kids put together. And we still haven't the faintest idea what goes on inside her head.

KAREN. She's a strange girl.

MARTHA. That's putting it mildly.

KAREN (*laughs*). We always talk about her as if she were a grown woman.

MARTHA. It's not so funny. There's something the matter with the kid. That's been true ever since the first day she came. She causes trouble here; she's bad for the other girls. I don't know what it is — it's a feeling I've got that it's wrong somewhere —

KAREN. All right, all right, we'll talk it over with Joe. Now what about our other pet nuisance?

MARTHA (*laughs*). My aunt the actress? What's she been up to now?

KAREN. Nothing unusual. Last night at dinner she was telling the girls about the time she lost her trunks in Butte, Montana, and how she gave her best performance of Rosalind during a hurricane. Today in the kitchen you could hear her on what Sir Henry said to her.

MARTHA. Wait until she does Hedda Gabler standing on one foot. Sir Henry taught her to do it that way. He said it was a test of great acting.

KAREN. You must have had a gay childhood.

MARTHA (*bitterly*). Oh, I did. I did, indeed. God, how I used to hate all that —

KAREN. Couldn't we get rid of her soon, Martha? I hate to make it hard on you, but she really ought not to be here.

MARTHA (*after a moment*). I know.

KAREN. We can scrape up enough money to send her away. Let's do it.

MARTHA (*goes to her, affectionately pats her head*). You've been very patient about it. I'm sorry and I'll talk to her today. It'll probably be a week or two before she can be ready to leave. Is that all right?

KAREN. Of course. (*Looks at her watch*) Did you get Joe himself on the phone?

MARTHA. He was already on his way. Isn't he always on his way over here?

KAREN (*laughs*). Well, I'm going to marry him, you know.

MARTHA (*looking at her*). You haven't talked of marriage for a long time.

KAREN. I've talked of it with Joe.

MARTHA. Then you *are* thinking about it — soon?

KAREN. Perhaps when the term is over. By that time we ought to be out of debt, and the school should be paying for itself.

MARTHA (*nervously playing with a book on the table*). Then we won't be taking our vacation together?

KAREN. Of course we will. The three of us.

MARTHA. I had been looking forward to someplace by the lake — just you and me — the way we used to at college.

KAREN (*cheerfully*). Well, now there will be three of us. That'll be fun, too.

MARTHA (*after a pause*). Why haven't you told me this before?

KAREN. I'm not telling you anything we haven't talked about often.

MARTHA. But you're talking about it as *soon* now.

KAREN. I'm glad to be able to. I've been in love with Joe a long time. (*Martha crosses to window and stands looking out, her back to Karen. Karen finishes marking papers and rises*) It's a big day for the school. Rosalie's finally put an "l" in could.

MARTHA (*not turning from window*). You really *are* going to leave, aren't you?

KAREN. I'm not going to leave, and you know it. Why do you say things like that? We agreed a long time ago that my marriage wasn't going to make any difference to the school.

MARTHA. But it will. You know it will. It can't help it.

KAREN. That's nonsense. Joe doesn't want me to give up here.

MARTHA (*turning from window*). It's been so damned hard building this thing up, slaving and going without things to make ends meet — think of having a winter coat without holes in the lining again! — and now when we're getting on our feet, you're all ready to let it go to hell.

KAREN. This is a silly argument, Martha. Let's quit it. You haven't listened to a word I've said. I'm not getting married tomorrow, and when I do, it's not going to interfere with my work here. You're making something out of nothing.

MARTHA. It's going to be hard going on alone afterward.

KAREN. For God's sake, do you expect me to give up my marriage?

MARTHA. I don't mean that, but it's so —

(*Door, center, opens and Doctor Joseph Cardin comes in. He is a large, pleasant-looking, carelessly dressed man of about thirty-five.*)

CARDIN. Hello, darling. Hi, Martha. What's the best news?

MARTHA. Hello, Joe.

KAREN. We tried to get you on the phone. Come in and look at your little cousin.

CARDIN. What's the matter with her now?

KAREN. You'd better come and see her. She says she has a pain in her heart. (*Goes out, right.*)

CARDIN (*stopping to light a cigarette*). Our little Mary pops up in every day's dispatches.

MARTHA (*impatiently*). Go and see her. Heart attacks are nothing to play with.

CARDIN (*looks at her*). Never played with one in my life. (*Exits right.*)

(*Martha walks around room and finally goes to stare out window. Mrs. Mortar enters right.*)

MRS. MORTAR. *I* was asked to leave the room. (*Martha pays no attention*) It seems that I'm not wanted in the room during the examination.

MARTHA (*over her shoulder*). What difference does it make?

MRS. MORTAR. What difference does it make? Why, it was a deliberate snub.

MARTHA. There's very little pleasure in watching a man use a stethoscope.

MRS. MORTAR. Isn't it natural that the child should have me with her? Isn't it natural that an older woman should be present? (*No answer*) Very well, if you are so thick-skinned that you don't resent these things —

MARTHA. What are you talking about? Why, in the name of heaven, should *you* be with her?

MRS. MORTAR. It — it's customary for an older woman to be present during an examination.

MARTHA (*laughs*). Tell that to Joe. Maybe he'll give you a job as duenna for his office.

MRS. MORTAR. It was I who saved Delia Lampert's life the time she had that heart attack in Buffalo. We almost lost her that time. Poor Delia! We went over to London together. She married Robert Laffonne. Not seven months later he left her and ran away with Eve Cloun, who was playing the Infant Phenomenon in Birmingham —

MARTHA. Console yourself. If you've seen one heart attack, you've seen them all.

MRS. MORTAR. So you don't resent your aunt being snubbed and humiliated?

MARTHA. Oh, Aunt Lily!

MRS. MORTAR. Karen is consistently rude to me, and you know it.

MARTHA. I know that she is very polite to you, and — what's more important — very patient.

MRS. MORTAR. Patient with me? *I,* who have worked my fingers to the bone!

MARTHA. Don't tell yourself that too often, Aunt Lily; you'll come to believe it.

MRS. MORTAR. I *know* it's true. Where could you have gotten a woman of my reputation to give these children voice lessons, elocution lessons? Patient with me! Here I've donated my services —

MARTHA. You are being paid.

MRS. MORTAR. That small thing! I used to earn twice that for one performance.

MARTHA. The gilded days. It was very extravagant of them to pay you so much. (*Suddenly tired of the whole thing*) You're not very happy here, are you, Aunt Lily?

MRS. MORTAR. Satisfied enough, I guess, for a poor relation.

MARTHA (*makes a motion of distaste*). But you don't like the school or the farm or —

MRS. MORTAR. I told you at the beginning you shouldn't have bought a place like this. Burying yourself on a farm! You'll regret it.

MARTHA. We like it here. (*After a moment*) Aunt Lily, you've talked about London for a long time. Would you like to go over?

MRS. MORTAR (*with a sigh*). It's been twenty years, and I shall never live to see it again.

MARTHA. Well, you can go any time you like. We can spare the money now, and it will do you a lot of good. You pick out the boat you want and I'll get the passage. (*She has been talking rapidly, anxious to end the whole thing*) Now that's all fixed. You'll have a grand time seeing all your old friends, and if you live sensibly I ought to be able to let you have enough to get along on. (*She begins to gather books, notebooks, and pencils.*)

MRS. MORTAR (*slowly*). So you want me to leave?

MARTHA. That's not the way to put it. You've wanted to go ever since I can remember.

MRS. MORTAR. You're trying to get rid of me.

MARTHA. That's it. We don't want you around when we dig up the buried treasure.

MRS. MORTAR. So? You're turning me out? At my age! Nice, grateful girl you are.

MARTHA. Oh, my God, how can anybody deal with you? You're going where you want to go, and we'll be better off alone. That suits everybody. You complain about the farm, you complain about the school, you complain about Karen, and now you have what you want and you're still looking for something to complain about.

MRS. MORTAR (*with dignity*). Please do not raise your voice.

MARTHA. You ought to be glad I don't do worse.

MRS. MORTAR. I absolutely refuse to be shipped off three thousand miles away. I'm not going to England. I shall go back to the stage. I'll write to my agents tomorrow, and as soon as they have something good for me —

MARTHA. The truth is I'd like you to leave soon. The three of us can't live together, and it doesn't make any difference whose fault it is.

MRS. MORTAR. You wish me to go tonight?

MARTHA. Don't act, Aunt Lily. Go as soon as you've found a place you like. I'll put the money in the bank for you tomorrow.

MRS. MORTAR. You think I'd take your money? I'd rather scrub floors first.

MARTHA. You'll change your mind.

MRS. MORTAR. I should have known by this time that the wise thing is to stay out of your way when *he's* in the house.

MARTHA. What are you talking about now?

MRS. MORTAR. Never mind. I should have known better. You always take your spite out on me.

MARTHA. Spite? (*Impatiently*) Oh, don't let's have any more of this today. I'm tired. I've been working since six o'clock this morning.

MRS. MORTAR. Any day that he's in the house is a bad day.

MARTHA. When *who* is in the house?

MRS. MORTAR. Don't think you're fooling me, young lady. I wasn't born yesterday.

MARTHA. Aunt Lily, the amount of disconnected unpleasantness that goes on in your head could keep a psychologist busy for years. Now go take your nap.

MRS. MORTAR. I know what I know. Every time that man comes into this house, you have a fit. It seems like you just can't stand the idea of them being together. God knows what you'll do when they get married. You're jealous of him, that's what it is.

MARTHA (*her voice is tense and the previous attitude of good-natured irritation is gone*). I'm very fond of Joe, and you know it.

MRS. MORTAR. You're fonder of Karen, and I know that. And it's unnatural, just as unnatural as it can be. You don't like their being together. You were always like that even as a child. If you had a little girl friend, you always got mad when she liked anybody else. Well, you'd better get a beau of your own now — a woman of your age.

MARTHA. The sooner you get out of here the better. You are making me sick and I won't stand for it any longer. I want you to leave —

(*At this point there is a sound outside the large doors center. Martha breaks off. After a moment she crosses to the door and opens it. Evelyn and Peggy are to be seen on the staircase. For a second she stands still as they stop and look at her. Then, afraid that her anger with her aunt will color anything she might say to the children, she crosses the room again and stands with her back to them.*)

MARTHA. What were you doing outside the door?

EVELYN (*hurriedly*). We were going upthtairth, Mith Dobie.

PEGGY. We came down to see how Mary was.

MARTHA. And you stopped long enough to see how we were. Did you deliberately listen?

PEGGY. We didn't mean to. We heard voices and we couldn't help —

MRS. MORTAR (*a social tone*). Eavesdropping is something nice young ladies just don't do.

MARTHA (*turning to face the children*). Go upstairs now. We'll talk about this later. (*Slowly shuts door as they begin to climb the stairs.*)

MRS. MORTAR. You mean to say you're not going to do anything about that? (*No answer. She laughs nastily*) That's the trouble with these new-fangled notions of discipline and —

MARTHA (*thoughtfully*). You know, it's really bad having you around children.

MRS. MORTAR. What exactly does that mean?

MARTHA. It means that I don't like them hearing the things

you say. Oh, I'll "do something about it," but the truth is that this is their home, and things shouldn't be said in it that they can't hear. When you're at your best, you're not for tender ears.

MRS. MORTAR. So now it's my fault, is it? Just as I said, whenever he's in the house you think you can take it out on me. You've got to have some way to let out steam and —

(Door opens, right, and Cardin comes in.)

MARTHA. How is Mary?

(Mrs. Mortar, head in air, gives Martha a malicious half-smile and exits center.)

MRS. MORTAR. Good day, Joseph.

CARDIN. What's the matter with the Duchess?

MARTHA. Just keeping her hand in, in case Sir Henry's watching her from above. What about Mary?

CARDIN. Nothing. Absolutely nothing.

MARTHA *(sighs)*. I thought so.

CARDIN. I could have managed a better faint than that when I was six years old.

MARTHA. Nothing the matter with her at all?

CARDIN *(laughs)*. No, ma'am, not a thing. Just a little something she thought up.

MARTHA. But it's such a silly thing to do. She knew we'd have you in. *(Sighs)* Maybe she's not so bright. Any idiots in your family, Joe? Any inbreeding?

CARDIN. Don't blame her on me. It's another side of the family. *(Laughs)* You can look at Aunt Amelia and tell: old New England stock, never married out of Boston, still thinks honor is honor and dinner's at eight. Yes, ma'am, we're a proud old breed.

MARTHA. The Jukes were an old family, too. Look, Joe, have you any idea what is the matter with Mary? I mean, has she always been like this?

CARDIN. She's always been a honey. Aunt Amelia's spoiling hasn't helped any, either.

MARTHA. We're reaching the end of our rope with her. This kind of thing —

CARDIN *(looking at her)*. Aren't you taking it too seriously?

MARTHA *(after a second)*. I guess I am. But you stay around kids long enough and you won't know what to take seriously, either. But I do think somebody ought to talk to Mrs. Tilford about her.

CARDIN. You wouldn't be meaning me now, would you, Miss Dobie?

MARTHA. Well, Karen and I were talking about it this afternoon and —

CARDIN. Listen, friend, I'm marrying Karen, but I'm not writing Mary Tilford in the contract. (*Martha moves slightly. Cardin takes her by the shoulders and turns her around to face him again. His face is grave, his voice gentle*) Forget Mary for a minute. You and I have got something to fight about. Every time anything's said about marrying — about Karen marrying me — you — I'm fond of you. I always thought you liked me. What is it? I know how fond you are of Karen, but our marriage oughtn't to make a great deal of difference —

MARTHA (*pushing his hands from her shoulders*). God damn you. I wish — (*She puts her face in her hands. Cardin watches her in silence, mechanically lighting a cigarette. When she takes her hands from her face, she holds them out to him. Contritely*) Joe, please, I'm sorry. I'm a fool, a nasty, bitter —

CARDIN (*takes her hands in one of his, patting them with his other hand*). Aw, shut up. (*He puts an arm around her, and she leans her head against his lapel. They are standing like that when Karen comes in, right.*)

MARTHA (*to Karen, as she wipes her eyes*). Your friend's got a nice shoulder to weep on.

KAREN. He's an admirable man in every way. Well, the angel child is now putting her clothes back on.

MARTHA. The angel child's influence is abroad even while she's unconscious. Her roommates were busy listening at the door while Aunt Lily and I were yelling at each other.

KAREN. We'll have to move those girls away from one another.

(*A bell rings from the rear of the house.*)

MARTHA. That's my class. I'll send Peggy and Evelyn down. You talk to them.

KAREN. All right. (*As Martha exits center, Karen goes toward door, right. As she passes Cardin she kisses him*) Mary!

(*Mary opens door, comes in, stands buttoning the neck of her dress.*)

CARDIN (*to Mary*). How's it feel to be back from the grave?

MARY. My heart hurts.

CARDIN (*laughing. To Karen*). Science has failed. Try a hairbrush.

MARY. It's *my* heart, and it hurts.

KAREN. Sit down.

MARY. I want to see my grandmother. I want to —

(*Evelyn and Peggy timidly enter center.*)

KAREN. Sit down, girls, I want to talk to you.

PEGGY. We're awfully sorry, really. We just didn't think and —

KAREN. I'm sorry too, Peggy. (*Thoughtfully*) You and Evelyn never used to do things like this. We'll have to separate you three.

EVELYN. Ah, Mith Wright, we've been together almotht a year.

KAREN. Peggy, you will move into Lois's room, and Lois will move in with Evelyn. Mary will go in with Rosalie.

MARY. Rosalie hates me.

KAREN. I can't imagine Rosalie hating anyone.

MARY (*starting to cry*). And it's all because I had a pain. If anybody else was sick they'd be put to bed and petted. You're always mean to me. I get blamed and punished for everything. (*To Cardin*) I do, Cousin Joe. All the time for everything.

(*Mary by now is crying violently and as Karen half moves toward her, Cardin, who has been frowning, picks Mary up and puts her down on the couch.*)

CARDIN. You've been unpleasant enough to Miss Wright. Lie here until you've stopped working yourself into a fit. (*Picks up his hat and bag, smiles at Karen*) I've got to go now. She's not going to hurt herself crying. The next time she faints, I'd wait until she got tired lying on the floor. (*Passing Mary, he pats her head. She jerks away from him.*)

KAREN. Wait a minute. I'll walk to the car with you. (*To girls*) Go up now and move your things. Tell Lois to get her stuff ready.

(*She and Cardin exit center. A second after the door is closed, Mary springs up and throws a cushion at the door.*)

EVELYN. Don't do that. She'll hear you.

MARY. Who cares if she does? (*Kicks table*) And she can hear that, too.

(*Small ornament falls off table and breaks on floor. Evelyn and Peggy gasp.*)

EVELYN (*frightened*). Now what are you going to do?

PEGGY (*stooping down in a vain effort to pick up the pieces*). You'll get the devil now. Dr. Cardin gave it to Miss Wright. I guess it was kind of a lover's gift. People get awfully angry about a lover's gift.

MARY. Oh, leave it alone. She'll never know we did it.

PEGGY. *We* didn't do it. You did it yourself.

MARY. And what will you do if I say *we* did do it? (*Laughs*) Never mind, I'll think of something else. The wind could've knocked it over.

EVELYN. Yeh. She'th going to believe that one.

MARY. Oh, stop worrying about it. I'll get out of it.

EVELYN. Did you really have a pain?

MARY. I fainted, didn't I?

PEGGY. I wish I could faint sometimes. I've never even worn glasses, like Rosalie.

MARY. A lot it'll get you to faint.

EVELYN. What did Mith Wright do to you when the clath left?

MARY. Told me I couldn't go to the boat races.

EVELYN. Whew!

PEGGY. But we'll remember everything that happens and we'll give you all the souvenirs and things.

MARY. I won't let you go if I can't go. But I'll find some way to go. What were *you* doing?

PEGGY. We came down to see what was happening to you, but the doors were closed and we could hear Miss Dobie and Mortar having an awful row. Then Miss Dobie opens the door and there we were.

MARY. And a lot of crawling and crying you both did too, I bet.

EVELYN. We were thort of thorry about lithening. I gueth it wathn't —

MARY. Ah, you're always sorry about everything. What were they saying?

PEGGY. What was who saying?

MARY. Dobie and Mortar, silly.

PEGGY (*evasively*). Just talking, I guess.

EVELYN. Fighting, you mean.

MARY. About what?

EVELYN. Well, they were talking about Mortar going away to England and —

PEGGY. You know, it really wasn't very nice to've listened, and I think it's worse to tell.

MARY. You do, do you? You just don't tell me and see what happens.

(*Peggy sighs.*)

EVELYN. Mortar got awful thore at that and thaid they juth wanted to get rid of her, and then they thtarted talking about Dr. Cardin.

MARY. What about him?

PEGGY. We'd better get started moving; Miss Wright will be back first thing we know.

MARY (*fiercely*). Shut up! Go on, Evelyn.

EVELYN. They're going to be married.

MARY. Everybody knows that.

PEGGY. But everybody doesn't know that Miss Dobie doesn't want them to get married. How do you like that?

(*The door opens and Rosalie Wells sticks her head in.*)

ROSALIE. I have a class soon. If you're going to move your things —

MARY. Close that door, you idiot. (*Rosalie closes door, stands near it*) What do you want?

ROSALIE. I'm trying to tell you. If you're going to move your things — not that I want you in with me — you'd better start right now. Miss Wright's coming in a minute.

MARY. Who cares if she is?

ROSALIE (*starts for door*). I'm just telling you for your own good.

PEGGY (*getting up*). We're coming.

MARY. No. Let Rosalie move our things.

ROSALIE. You crazy?

PEGGY (*nervously*). It's all right. Evelyn and I'll get your things. Come on, Evelyn.

MARY. Trying to get out of telling me, huh? Well, you won't get out of it that way. Sit down and stop being such a sissy. Rosalie, you go on up and move my things and don't say a word about our being down here.

ROSALIE. And who was your French maid yesterday, Mary Tilford?

MARY (*laughing*). You'll do for today. Now go on, Rosalie, and fix our things.

ROSALIE. You crazy?

MARY. And the next time we go into town, I'll let you wear my gold locket and buckle. You'll like that, won't you, Rosalie?

ROSALIE (*draws back, moves her hands nervously*). I don't know what you're talking about.

MARY. Oh, I'm not talking about anything in particular. You just run along now and remind me the next time to get my buckle and locket for you.

ROSALIE (*stares at her a moment*). All right, I'll do it this time, but just 'cause I got a good disposition. But don't think you're going to boss me around, Mary Tilford.

MARY (*smiling*). No, indeed. (*Rosalie starts for door*) And get the things done neatly, Rosalie. Don't muss my white linen bloomers —

(*The door slams as Mary laughs.*)

EVELYN. Now what do you think of that? What made her tho agreeable?

MARY. Oh, a little secret we got. Go on, now, what else did they say?

PEGGY. Well, Mortar said that Dobie was jealous of them, and that she was like that when she was a little girl, and that she'd better get herself a beau of her own because it was unnatural, and that she never wanted anybody to like Miss Wright, and that was unnatural. Boy! Did Miss Dobie get sore at that!

EVELYN. Then we didn't hear any more. Peggy dropped a book.

MARY. What'd she mean Dobie was jealous?

PEGGY. What's unnatural?

EVELYN. Un for not. Not natural.

PEGGY. It's funny, because everybody gets married.

MARY. A lot of people don't — they're too ugly.

PEGGY (*jumps up, claps her hand to her mouth*). Oh, my God! Rosalie'll find that copy of *Mademoiselle de Maupin*. She'll blab like the dickens.

MARY. Ah, she won't say a word.

EVELYN. Who getth the book when we move?

MARY. You can have it. That's what I was doing this morning — finishing it. There's one part in it —

PEGGY. What part?

(*Mary laughs.*)

EVELYN. Well, what wath it?

MARY. Wait until you read it.

PEGGY. It's a shame about being moved. I've got to go in with Helen, and she blows her nose all night. Lois told me.

MARY. It was a dirty trick making us move. She just wants to see how much fun she can take away from me. She hates me.

PEGGY. No, she doesn't, Mary. She treats you just like the rest of us — almost better.

MARY. That's right, stick up for your crush. Take her side against mine.

PEGGY. I didn't mean it that way.

EVELYN (*looks at her watch*). We'd better get upthtairth.

MARY. I'm not going.

PEGGY. Rosalie isn't so bad.

EVELYN. What you going to do about the vathe?

MARY. I don't care about Rosalie and I don't care about the vase. I'm not going to be here.

EVELYN *and* PEGGY (*together*). Not going to be here! What do you mean?

MARY (*calmly*). I'm going home.

PEGGY. Oh, Mary —

EVELYN. You can't do that.

MARY. Can't I? You just watch. (*Begins to walk around the room*) I'm not staying here. I'm going home and tell Grandma I'm not staying anymore. (*Smiles to herself*) I'll tell her I'm not happy. They're scared of Grandma — she helped 'em when they first started, you know — and when she tells 'em something, believe me, they'll sit up and listen. They can't get away with treating me like this, and they don't have to think they can.

PEGGY (*appalled*). You just going to walk out like that?

EVELYN. What you going to tell your grandmother?

MARY. Oh, who cares? I'll think of something to tell her. I can always do it better on the spur of the moment.

PEGGY. She'll send you right back.

MARY. You let me worry about that. Grandma's very fond of me, on account my father was her favorite son. I can manage *her* all right.

PEGGY. I don't think you ought to go, really, Mary. It's just going to make an awful lot of trouble.

EVELYN. What'th going to happen about the vathe?

MARY. Say I did it — it doesn't make a bit of difference anymore to me. Now listen, you two got to help. They won't miss me before dinner if you make Rosalie shut the door and keep it shut. Now, I'll go through the field to French's, and then I can get the bus to Homestead.

EVELYN. How you going to get to the thtreetcar?

MARY. Taxi, idiot.

PEGGY. How are you going to get out of here in the first place?

MARY. I'm going to walk out. You know where the front door is? Well, I'm going right out that front door.

EVELYN. Gee, I wouldn't have the nerve.

MARY. Of course you wouldn't. You'd let 'em do anything to you they want. Well, they can't do it to me. Who's got any money?

EVELYN. Not me. Not a thent.

MARY. I've got to have at least a dollar for the taxi and a dime for the bus.

EVELYN. And where you going to find it?

PEGGY. See? Why don't you just wait until your allowance comes Monday, and then you can go anyplace you want. Maybe by that time —

MARY. I'm going today. *Now.*

EVELYN. You can't *walk* to Lanthet.

MARY (*goes to Peggy*). You've got money. You've got two dollars and twenty-five cents.

PEGGY. I — I —

MARY. Go get it for me.

PEGGY. No! No! I won't get it for you.

EVELYN. You can't have *that* money, Mary —

MARY. Get it for me.

PEGGY (*her voice is scared*). I won't. I won't. Mamma doesn't send me much allowance — not half as much as the rest of you get — I saved this so long — you took it from me last time —

EVELYN. Ah, she wantth that bithycle tho bad.

PEGGY. I haven't gone to the movies, I haven't had any candy, I haven't had anything the rest of you get all the time. It took me so long to save that and I —

MARY. Go upstairs and get me the money.

PEGGY (*hysterically, backing away from her*). I won't. I won't. I won't.

(*Mary makes a sudden move for her, grabs her left arm, and jerks it back, hard and expertly. Peggy screams softly. Evelyn tries to take Mary's arm away. Without releasing her hold on Peggy, Mary slaps Evelyn's face. Evelyn begins to cry.*)

MARY. Just say when you've had enough.

PEGGY (*softly, stiflingly*). All — all right — I'll get it.

(*Mary nods her head as the curtain falls.*)

Curtain

Act Two

Scene 1.

SCENE: *Living room at Mrs. Tilford's. It is a formal room, without being cold or elegant. The furniture is old, but excellent. The exit to the hall is left; glass doors, right, lead to a dining room that cannot be seen.*

AT RISE: *Stage is empty. Voices are heard in the hall.*

AGATHA (*offstage*). What are *you* doing here? Well, come on in — don't stand there gaping at me. Have they given you a holiday or did you just decide you'd get a better dinner here? (*Agatha enters left, followed by Mary. Agatha is a sharp-faced maid, not young, with a querulous voice*) Can't you even say hello?

MARY. Hello, Agatha. You didn't give me a chance. Where's Grandma?

AGATHA. Why aren't you in school? Look at your face and clothes. Where have you been?

MARY. I got a little dirty coming home. I walked part of the way through the woods.

AGATHA. Why didn't you put on your middy blouse and your old brown coat?

MARY. Oh, stop asking me questions. Where's Grandma?

AGATHA. Where ought any clean person be at this time of day? She's taking a bath.

MARY. Is anybody coming for dinner?

AGATHA. She didn't say anything about you coming.

MARY. How could she, stupid? She didn't know.

AGATHA. Then what are you doing here?

MARY. Leave me alone. I don't feel well.

AGATHA. Why don't you feel well? Who ever heard of a person going for a walk in the woods when they didn't feel well?

MARY. Oh, leave me alone. I came home because I was sick.

AGATHA. You look all right.

MARY. But I don't feel all right. I can't even come home without everybody nagging at me.

AGATHA. Don't think you're fooling me, young lady. You might pull the wool over some people's eyes, but — I bet you've been up to something again. (*Stares suspiciously at Mary*) Well, you wait right here till I tell your grandmother. And if you feel so sick, you certainly won't want any dinner. A good dose of rhubarb and soda will fix you up. (*Exits left.*)

(*Mary makes a face in the direction Agatha has gone and stops sniffling. She looks nervously around the room, then goes to a low mirror and tries several experiments with her face in an attempt to make it look sick and haggard. Mrs. Tilford, followed by Agatha, enters left. Mrs. Tilford is a large, dignified woman in her sixties, with a pleasant, strong face.*)

AGATHA (*to Mrs. Tilford, as she follows her into the room*). Why didn't you put some cold water on your chest? Do you want to catch your death of cold at your age? Did you have to hurry so?

MRS. TILFORD. Mary, what are you doing home?

(*Mary rushes to her and buries her head in Mrs. Tilford's dress, crying. Mrs. Tilford pats her head, then puts an arm around her and leads her to a sofa.*)

MRS. TILFORD. Never mind, dear; now stop crying and tell me what is the matter.

MARY (*gradually stops crying, fondling Mrs. Tilford's hand*). It's so good to see you, Grandma. You didn't come to visit me all last week.

MRS. TILFORD. I was coming tomorrow.

MARY. I missed you so. (*Smiling up at Mrs. Tilford*) I was awful homesick.

MRS. TILFORD. I'm glad that's all it was. I was frightened when Agatha said you were not well.

AGATHA. Did I say that? I said she needed a good dose of rhubarb and soda. Most likely she only came home for Wednesday night fudge cake.

MRS. TILFORD. We all get homesick. But how did you get here? Did Miss Karen drive you over?

MARY. I — I walked most of the way, and then a lady gave me a ride and — (*Looks timidly at Mrs. Tilford.*)

AGATHA. Did she have to walk through the woods in her very best coat?

MRS. TILFORD. Mary! Do you mean you left without permission?

MARY (*nervously*). I ran away, Grandma. They didn't know —

MRS. TILFORD. That was a very bad thing to do, and they'll be worried. Agatha, phone Miss Wright and tell her Mary is here. John will drive her back before dinner.

MARY (*as Agatha starts toward telephone*). No, Grandma, don't do that. Please don't do that. Please let me stay.

MRS. TILFORD. But, darling, you can't leave school anytime you please.

MARY. Oh, please, Grandma, don't send me back right away. You don't know how they'll punish me.

MRS. TILFORD. I don't think they'll be that angry. Come, you're acting like a foolish little girl.

MARY (*hysterically, as she sees Agatha about to pick up the telephone*). Grandma! Please! I can't go back! I can't! They'll kill me! They will, Grandma! They'll kill me!

(*Mrs. Tilford and Agatha stare at Mary in amazement. She puts her head in Mrs. Tilford's lap and sobs.*)

MRS. TILFORD (*motioning with a hand for Agatha to leave the room*). Never mind phoning now, Agatha.

AGATHA. If you're going to let her —

(*Mrs. Tilford repeats the gesture. Agatha exits, right.*)

MRS. TILFORD. Stop crying, Mary.

MARY. It's so nice here, Grandma.

MRS. TILFORD. I'm glad you like being home with me, but at your age you can hardly — What made you say such a terrible thing about Miss Wright and Miss Dobie? You know they wouldn't hurt you.

MARY. Oh, but they would. They — I — (*Breaks off, looks around as if hunting for a clue*) I fainted today!

MRS. TILFORD. Fainted?

MARY. Yes, I did. My heart — I had a pain in my heart. I couldn't help having a pain in my heart, and when I fainted right in class, they called Cousin Joe and he said I didn't. He said it was maybe only that I ate my breakfast too fast and Miss Wright blamed me for it.

MRS. TILFORD (*relieved*). I'm sure if Joseph said it wasn't serious, it wasn't.

MARY. But I did have a pain in my heart — honest.

MRS. TILFORD. Have you still got it?

MARY. I guess I haven't got it much anymore, but I feel a little weak, and I was so scared of Miss Wright being so mean to me just because I was sick.

MRS. TILFORD. Scared of Karen? Nonsense. It's perfectly possible that you had a pain, but if you had really been sick your Cousin Joseph would certainly have known it. It's not nice to frighten people by pretending to be sick when you aren't.

MARY. I didn't *want* to be sick, but I'm always getting punished for everything.

MRS. TILFORD (*gently*). You mustn't imagine things like that, child, or you'll grow up to be a very unhappy woman. I'm not going to scold you anymore for coming home this time, though I suppose I should. Run along upstairs and wash your face and change your dress, and after dinner John will drive you back. Run along.

MARY (*happily*). I can stay for dinner?

MRS. TILFORD. Yes.

MARY. Maybe I could stay till the first of the week. Saturday's your birthday and I could be here with you.

MRS. TILFORD. We don't celebrate my birthday, dear. You'll have to go back to school after dinner.

MARY. But — (*She hesitates, then goes up to Mrs. Tilford and puts her arms around the older woman's neck. Softly*) How much do you love me?

MRS. TILFORD (*smiling*). As much as all the words in all the books in all the world.

MARY. Remember when I was little and you used to tell me that right before I went to sleep? And it was a rule nobody could say another single word after you finished? You used to say "Wor-rr-ld," and then I had to shut my eyes tight. I miss you an awful lot, Grandma.

MRS. TILFORD. And I miss you, but I'm afraid my Latin is too rusty — you'll learn it better in school.

MARY. But couldn't I stay out the rest of this term? After the summer maybe I won't mind it so much. I'll study hard, honest, and —

MRS. TILFORD. You're an earnest little coaxer, but it's out of the question. Back you go tonight. (*Gives Mary a playful slap*) Let's not have any more talk about it now, and let's have no more running away from school ever.

MARY (*slowly*). Then I really have to go back there tonight?

MRS. TILFORD. Of course.

MARY. You don't love me. You don't care whether they kill me or not.

MRS. TILFORD. Mary.

MARY. You don't! You don't! You don't care what happens to me.

MRS. TILFORD (*sternly*). But I *do* care that you're talking this way.

MARY. I'm sorry I said that, Grandma. I didn't mean to hurt your feelings. (*Puts her arms around Mrs. Tilford's neck*) Forgive me?

MRS. TILFORD. What made you talk like that?

MARY (*in a whisper*). I'm scared, Grandma, I'm scared. They'll do dreadful things to me.

MRS. TILFORD. Dreadful? Nonsense. They'll punish you for running away. You deserve to be punished.

MARY. It's not that. It's not anything I do. It never is. They — they just punish me anyhow, just like they got something against me. I'm afraid of them, Grandma.

MRS. TILFORD. That's ridiculous. What have they ever done to you that is so terrible?

MARY. A lot of things — all the time. Miss Wright says I can't go to the boat races and — (*Realizing the inadequacy of this reply, she breaks off, hesitates, and finally stammers*) It's — it's after what happened today.

MRS. TILFORD. You mean something else besides your naughtiness in pretending to faint and then running away?

MARY. I *did* faint. I didn't pretend. They just said that to make me feel bad. Anyway, it wasn't anything that I did.

MRS. TILFORD. What was it, then?

MARY. I can't tell you.

MRS. TILFORD. Why?

MARY (*sulkily*). Because you're just going to take their part.

MRS. TILFORD (*a little annoyed*). Very well. Now run upstairs and get ready for dinner.

MARY. It was — it was all about Miss Dobie and Mrs. Mortar. They were talking awful things and Peggy and Evelyn heard them and Miss Dobie found out, and then they made us move our rooms.

MRS. TILFORD. What has that to do with you? I don't understand a word you're saying.

MARY. They made us move our rooms. They said we couldn't be together anymore. They're afraid to have us near them, that's what it is, and they're taking it out on me. They're scared of you.

MRS. TILFORD. For a little girl you're imagining a lot of big things. Why should they be scared of me?

MARY. They're afraid you'll find out.

MRS. TILFORD. Find out what?

MARY (*vaguely*). Things.

MRS. TILFORD. Run along, Mary.

MARY (*slowly starting for door*). All right. But there're a lot of things. They have secrets or something, and they're afraid I'll find out and tell you.

MRS. TILFORD. There's not necessarily anything wrong with people having secrets.

MARY. But they've got funny ones. Peggy and Evelyn heard Mrs. Mortar telling Miss Dobie that she was jealous of Miss Wright marrying Cousin Joe.

MRS. TILFORD. You shouldn't repeat things like that.

MARY. But that's what she said, Grandma. She said it was unnatural for a girl to feel that way.

MRS. TILFORD. What?

MARY. I'm just telling you what she said. She said there was something funny about it, and that Miss Dobie had always been like that, even when she was a little girl, and that it was unnatural —

MRS. TILFORD. Stop using that silly word, Mary.

MARY (*vaguely realizing that she is on the right track, hurries on*). But that was the word *she* kept using, Grandma, and then they got mad and told Mrs. Mortar she'd have to get out.

MRS. TILFORD. That was probably not the reason at all.

MARY (*nodding vigorously*). I bet it was, because honestly, Miss Dobie does get cranky and mean every time Cousin Joe comes, and today I heard her say to him: "God damn you," and then she said she was just a jealous fool and —

MRS. TILFORD. You have picked up some fine words, haven't you, Mary?

MARY. That's just what she said, Grandma, and one time Miss Dobie was crying in Miss Wright's room, and Miss Wright was trying to stop her, and she said that all right, maybe she wouldn't get married right away if —

MRS. TILFORD. How do you know all this?

MARY. We couldn't help hearing because they — I mean Miss

Dobie — was talking awful loud, and their room is right next to ours.

MRS. TILFORD. Whose room?

MARY. Miss Wright's room, I mean, and you can just ask Peggy and Evelyn whether we didn't hear. Almost always Miss Dobie comes in after we go to bed and stays a long time. I guess that's why they want to get rid of us — of me — because we hear things. That's why they're making us move our room, and they punish me all the time for —

MRS. TILFORD. For eavesdropping, I should think. *(She has said this mechanically. With nothing definite in her mind, she is making an effort to conceal the fact that Mary's description of the life at school has worried her)* Well, now I think we've had enough gossip, don't you? Dinner's almost ready, and I can't eat with a girl who has such a dirty face.

MARY (*softly*). I've heard other things, too. I've heard other things. Plenty of other things, Grandma.

MRS. TILFORD. What things?

MARY. Bad things.

MRS. TILFORD. Well, what were they?

MARY. I can't tell you.

MRS. TILFORD. Mary, you're annoying me very much. If you have anything to say, then say it and stop acting silly.

MARY. I mean I can't say it out loud.

MRS. TILFORD. There couldn't possibly be anything so terrible that you couldn't say it out loud. Now either tell the truth or be still.

MARY. Well, a lot of things I don't understand. But it's awful, and sometimes they fight and then they make up, and Miss Dobie cries and Miss Wright gets mad, and then they make up again, and there are funny noises and we get scared.

MRS. TILFORD. Noises? I suppose you girls have a happy time imagining a murder.

MARY. And we've seen things, too. Funny things. (*Sees the impatience of her grandmother*) I'd tell you, but I got to whisper it.

MRS. TILFORD. Why must you whisper it?

MARY. I don't know. I just got to. (*Climbs on the sofa next to Mrs. Tilford and begins whispering. At first the whisper is slow and hesitant, but it gradually works up to fast, excited talking. In the middle of it Mrs. Tilford stops her.*)

MRS. TILFORD (*trembling*). Do you know what you're saying?

(Without answering, Mary goes back to the whispering until the older woman takes her by the shoulders and turns her around to stare in her face) Mary! *Are you telling me the truth?*

MARY. Honest, honest. You just ask Peggy and Evelyn and — *(After a moment Mrs. Tilford gets up and begins to pace about the room. She is no longer listening to Mary, who keeps up a running fire of conversation)* They know too. And maybe there're other kids who know, but we've always been frightened and so we didn't ask, and one night I was going to go and find out, but I got scared and we went to bed early so we wouldn't hear, but sometimes I couldn't help it, but we never talked about it much, because we thought they'd find out and — Oh, Grandma, don't make me go back to that awful place.

MRS. TILFORD *(abstractedly)*. What? *(Starts to move about again.)*

MARY. Don't make me go back to that place. I just couldn't stand it anymore. Really, Grandma, I'm so unhappy there, and if only I could stay out the rest of the term, why, then —

MRS. TILFORD *(makes irritated gesture)*. Be still a minute. *(After a moment)* You can stay here tonight.

MARY *(hugging Mrs. Tilford)*. You're the nicest, loveliest grandma in all the world. You — you're not mad at me?

MRS. TILFORD. I'm not mad at you. Now get ready for dinner. *(Mary kisses her and runs happily out left. Mrs. Tilford stands staring after her for a long moment. Then, very slowly, she puts on her eyeglasses and crosses to the phone. She dials a number)* Is Miss Wright — is Miss Wright in? *(Waits a second, hurriedly puts down the receiver)* Never mind, never mind. *(Dials another number)* Dr. Cardin, please. Mrs. Tilford. *(She remains absolutely motionless while she waits. When she does speak, her voice is low and tense)* Joseph? Joseph? Can you come to see me right away? Yes, I'm perfectly well. No, but it's important, Joseph, very important. I must see you right away. I — I can't tell you over the phone. Can't you come sooner? It's not about Mary's fainting — I said it's not about Mary, Joseph; in one way it's about Mary — *(Suddenly quiet)* But will the hospital take so long? Very well, Joseph, make it as soon as you can. *(Hangs up the receiver, sits for a moment undecided. Then, taking a breath, she dials another number)* Mrs. Munn, please. This is Mrs. Tilford. Miriam? This is Amelia Tilford. Could you come over right away? I want some advice — I want to tell you — Thank you.

Curtain

Scene 2.

SCENE: *The same as Scene 1. The curtain has been lowered to mark the passing of a few hours.*

AT RISE: *Mary is lying on the floor playing with a puzzle. Agatha appears lugging blankets and pillows across the room. Almost at the door, she stops and gives Mary an annoyed look.*

AGATHA. And see to it that she doesn't get my good quilt all dirty, and let her wear your green pajamas.

MARY. Who?

AGATHA. Who? Rosalie Wells is coming over to spend the night with you.

MARY. You mean she's going to sleep *here?*

AGATHA. You heard me.

MARY. What for?

AGATHA. Do I know all the crazy things that are happening around here? Mrs. Munn comes over and then they phone Mrs. Wells all the way to New York, three dollars and eighty-five cents and families starving, and Mrs. Wells wanted to know if Rosalie could stay here until tomorrow.

MARY (*relieved*). Oh. Couldn't Evelyn Munn come instead?

AGATHA. Sure. We'll have the whole town over to entertain you.

MARY. I won't let Rosalie Wells wear my new pajamas.

AGATHA (*exits as the front doorbell rings*). Don't tell me what you won't do. You'll act like a lady for once in your life. (*Offstage*) Come on in, Rosalie. Just go on in there and make yourself at home. Have you had your dinner?

ROSALIE (*offstage*). Good evening. Yes'm.

AGATHA (*offstage*). Hang up your pretty coat. Have you had your bath?

ROSALIE (*offstage*). Yes, ma'am. This morning.

AGATHA (*offstage*). Well, you better have another one.

(*She is climbing the stairs as Rosalie comes into the room. Mary, lying in front of the couch, is hidden from her. Gingerly Rosalie sits down on a chair.*)

MARY (*softly*). Whoooooo. (*Rosalie jumps*) Whoooooo. (*Rosalie, frightened, starts hurriedly for the door. Mary sits up, laughs*) You're a goose.

ROSALIE (*belligerently*). Oh, so it's you. Well, who likes to hear funny noises at night? You could have been a werewolf.

MARY. A werewolf sure wouldn't want you.

ROSALIE. You know everything, don't you? (*Mary laughs. Rosalie comes over, stands staring at puzzle*) Isn't it funny about school?

MARY. What's funny about it?

ROSALIE. Don't act like you can come home every night.

MARY. Maybe I can from now on. (*Rolls over on her back luxuriously*) Maybe I'm never going back.

ROSALIE. Am I going back? I don't want to stay home.

MARY. What'll you give to know?

ROSALIE. Nothing. I'll ask Mamma.

MARY. Will you give me a free T.L. if I tell you?

ROSALIE (*thinks for a moment*). All right. Lois Fisher told Helen that you were very smart.

MARY. That's an old one. I won't take it.

ROSALIE. You got to take it.

MARY. Nope.

ROSALIE (*laughs*). You don't know, anyway.

MARY. I know what I heard, and I know Grandma phoned your mother in New York. You're just going to spend the night here.

ROSALIE. But what's happened? Peggy and Helen and Evelyn and Lois went home tonight, too. Do you think somebody's got scarlet fever or something?

MARY. No.

ROSALIE. Do *you* know what it is? How'd you find out? (*No answer*) You're always pretending you know everything. You're just faking. (*Flounces away*) Never mind, don't bother telling me. I think curiosity is very unladylike, anyhow. I have no concern with your silly secrets.

MARY. Suppose I told you that I just may have said that you were in on it?

ROSALIE. In on what?

MARY. The secret. Suppose I told you that I *may have* said that you told me about it?

ROSALIE. Why, Mary Tilford! You can't do a thing like that. I didn't tell you about anything. (*Mary laughs*) Did you tell your grandmother such a thing?

MARY. Maybe.

ROSALIE. Did you?

MARY. Maybe.

ROSALIE. Well, I'm going right up to your grandmother and tell her I didn't tell you anything — whatever it is. You're just trying to get me into trouble and I'm not going to let you. (*Starts for door.*)

MARY. Wait a minute, I'll come with you. I want to tell her about Helen Burton's bracelet.

ROSALIE (*sits down suddenly*). What about it?

MARY. Just that you stole it.

ROSALIE. Shut up. I didn't do any such thing.

MARY. Yes, you did.

ROSALIE (*tearfully*). You made it up. You're always making things up.

MARY. You can't call me a fibber, Rosalie Wells. That's a kind of a dare and I won't take a dare. I guess I'll go tell Grandma, anyway. Then she can call the police and they'll come for you and you'll spend the rest of your life in one of those solitary prisons and you'll get older and older, and when you're very old and can't see anymore, they'll let you out maybe and your mother and father will be dead and you won't have anyplace to go and you'll beg on the streets —

ROSALIE. I didn't steal anything. I borrowed the bracelet and I was going to put it back as soon as I'd worn it to the movies. I never meant to keep it.

MARY. Nobody'll believe that, least of all the police. You're just a common, ordinary thief. Stop that bawling. You'll have the whole house down here in a minute.

ROSALIE. You won't tell? Say you won't tell.

MARY. Am I a fibber?

ROSALIE. No.

MARY. Then say: "I apologize on my hands and knees."

ROSALIE. I apologize on my hands and knees. Let's play with the puzzle.

MARY. Wait a minute. Say: "From now on, I, Rosalie Wells,

am the vassal of Mary Tilford and will do and say whatever she tells me under the solemn oath of a knight."

ROSALIE. I won't say that. That's the worst oath there is. (*Mary starts for the door*) Mary! Please don't —

MARY. Will you swear it?

ROSALIE (*sniffling*). But then you could tell me to do anything.

MARY. And you'd have to do it. Say it quick or I'll —

ROSALIE (*hurriedly*). From now on, I, Rosalie Wells, am the vassal of Mary Tilford and will do and say whatever she tells me under the solemn oath of a knight. (*She gasps, and sits up straight as Mrs. Tilford enters.*)

MARY. Don't forget that.

MRS. TILFORD. Good evening, Rosalie, you're looking very well.

ROSALIE. Good evening, Mrs. Tilford.

MARY. She's getting fatter every day.

MRS. TILFORD (*abstractedly*). Then it's very becoming. (*Doorbell rings*) That must be Joseph. Mary, take Rosalie into the library. Be sure you're both fast asleep by half past ten. (*Rosalie starts to exit right, sees Mary, stops and hesitates.*)

MARY. Go on, Rosalie. (*Waits until Rosalie reluctantly exits*) Grandma.

MRS. TILFORD. Yes?

MARY. Grandma, Cousin Joe'll say I've got to go back. He'll say I really wasn't —

(*Cardin enters and she runs from the room.*)

CARDIN. Hello, Amelia. (*Looks curiously at the fleeing Mary*) Mary home, eh?

MRS. TILFORD (*watching Mary as she leaves*). Hello, Joseph. Sit down. (*He sits down, looks at her curiously, waits for her to speak*) Whisky?

CARDIN. Please. How are you feeling? Headaches again?

MRS. TILFORD (*puts drink on table*). No.

CARDIN. Those are good powders. Bicarbonate of soda and water. Never hurt anybody yet.

MRS. TILFORD. Yes. How have you been, Joseph? (*Vaguely, sparring for time*) I haven't seen you the last few weeks. Agatha misses you for Sunday dinners.

CARDIN. I've been busy. We're getting the results from the mating season right about now.

MRS. TILFORD. Did I take you away from a patient?

CARDIN. No. I was at the hospital.

MRS. TILFORD. How's it getting on?

CARDIN. Just the same. No money, badly equipped, a lousy laboratory, everybody growling at everybody else — Amelia, you didn't bring me here to talk about the hospital. What's the matter with you?

MRS. TILFORD. I — I have something to tell you.

CARDIN. Well, out with it.

MRS. TILFORD. It's a very hard thing to say, Joseph.

CARDIN. Hard for you to say to *me?* (*No answer*) Don't be worried about Mary. I guessed that she ran home to tell you about her faint. It was caused by nothing but bad temper and was very clumsily managed, at that. Amelia, she's a terribly spoilt —

MRS. TILFORD. I heard about the faint. That's not what is worrying me.

CARDIN (*gently*). Are you in some trouble?

MRS. TILFORD. We all are in trouble. Bad trouble.

CARDIN. We? Me, you mean? Nothing's the matter with me.

MRS. TILFORD. When did you last see Karen?

CARDIN. Today. This afternoon.

MRS. TILFORD. Oh. Not since seven o'clock?

CARDIN. What's happened since seven o'clock?

MRS. TILFORD. Joseph, you've been engaged to Karen for a long time. Are your plans any more definite than they were a year ago?

CARDIN. You can get ready to buy the wedding present. We'll have the wedding here, if you don't mind. The smell of clean little girls and boiled linen would worry me.

MRS. TILFORD. Why has Karen decided so suddenly to make it definite?

CARDIN. She has not suddenly decided anything. The school is pretty well on its feet, and now that Mrs. Mortar is leaving —

MRS. TILFORD. I've heard about their putting Mrs. Mortar out.

CARDIN. Putting her out? Well, maybe. But a nice sum for a trip and a promise that a good niece will support you the rest of your life is an enviable way of being put out.

MRS. TILFORD (*slowly*). Don't you find it odd, Joseph, that they want so much to get rid of that silly, harmless woman?

CARDIN. I don't know what you're talking about, but it isn't odd at all. Lily Mortar is not a harmless woman, although God knows she's silly enough. She's a tiresome, spoilt old bitch. If you're forming a Mortar Welfare Society, you're wasting your time. (*Gets up, puts down his glass*) It's not like you to waste your time. Now, what's it that's really on your mind?

MRS. TILFORD. You must not marry Karen.

CARDIN (*shocked, he grins*). You're a very impertinent lady. Why must I — (*imitates her*) not marry Karen?

MRS. TILFORD. Because there's something wrong with Karen — something horrible.

(*The doorbell is heard to ring loud and long.*)

CARDIN. I cannot allow you to say things like that, Amelia.

MRS. TILFORD. I have good reason for saying it. (*Breaks off as she hears voices offstage*) Who is that?

KAREN (*offstage*). Mrs. Tilford, Agatha. Is she in?

AGATHA (*offstage*). Yes'm. Come on in.

MRS. TILFORD. I won't have her here.

CARDIN (*angrily*). What are you talking about?

MRS. TILFORD. I won't have her here.

CARDIN. Then you don't want me here either. (*Turns to face Karen and Martha*) Darling, what? —

KAREN (*stops when she sees him, puts her hand over her eyes*). Is it a joke, Joe?

MARTHA (*with great force to Mrs. Tilford*). We've come to find out what you are doing.

CARDIN (*kissing Karen*). What is it?

KAREN. It's crazy! It's crazy! What did she do it for?

CARDIN. What are you talking about? What do you mean?

MRS. TILFORD. You shouldn't have come here.

CARDIN. What is all this? What's happened?

KAREN. I tried to reach you. Hasn't she told you?

CARDIN. Nobody's told me anything. I haven't heard anything but wild talk. What is it, Karen? (*She starts to speak, then dumbly shakes her head*) What's happened, Martha?

MARTHA (*violently*). An insane asylum has been let loose. How do we know what's happened?

CARDIN. What was it?

KAREN. We didn't know what it was. Nobody would talk to us, nobody would tell us anything.

MARTHA. I'll tell you, I'll tell you. You see if you can make any sense out of it. At dinnertime Mrs. Munn's chauffeur said that Evelyn must be sent home right away. At half past seven Mrs. Burton arrived to tell us that she wanted Helen's things packed and that she'd wait outside because she didn't want to enter a place like ours. Five minutes later the Wells's butler came for Rosalie.

CARDIN. What was it?

MARTHA. It was a madhouse. People rushing in and out, the children being pushed into cars —

KAREN. Mrs. Rogers finally told us.

CARDIN. What? What?

KAREN. That — that Martha and I are — in love with each other. In love with each other. Mrs. Tilford told them.

CARDIN (*for a moment stands staring at her incredulously. Then he walks across the room, stares out of the window, and finally turns to Mrs. Tilford*). Did you tell them that?

MRS. TILFORD. Yes.

CARDIN. Are you sick?

MRS. TILFORD. You know I'm not sick.

CARDIN (*snapping the words out*). Then what did you do it for?

MRS. TILFORD (*slowly*). Because it's true.

KAREN (*incredulously*). You think it's true, then?

MARTHA. You fool! You damned, vicious —

KAREN. Do you realize what you're saying?

MRS. TILFORD. I realize it very well. And —

MARTHA. You realize nothing, nothing, nothing.

MRS. TILFORD. And that's why I don't think you should have come here. (*Quietly*) I shall not call you names, and I will not allow you to call me names. I can't trust myself to talk about it with you now or ever.

KAREN. What's she talking about, Joe? What's she mean? What is she trying to do to us? What is everybody doing to us?

MARTHA (*softly, as though to herself*). Pushed around. We're being pushed around by crazy people. (*Shakes herself slightly*) That's an awful thing. And we're standing here — (*Cardin puts his arm around Karen, walks with her to the window. They stand there together*) We're standing here taking it. (*Suddenly with violence*) Didn't you know we'd come here? Were we supposed to lie down and grin while you kicked us around with these lies?

MRS. TILFORD. This can't do any of us any good, Miss Dobie.

MARTHA (*scornfully imitating her*). "This can't do any of us any good." Listen, listen. Try to understand this: you're not playing with paper dolls. We're human beings, see? It's our lives you're fooling with. *Our* lives. That's serious business for us. Can you understand that?

MRS. TILFORD. I can understand that, and I regret it. But you've been playing with children's lives, and that's why I stopped you. (*More calmly*) I know how serious this is for you, how serious it is for all of us.

CARDIN (*bitterly*). I don't think you do know.

MRS. TILFORD. I wanted to avoid this meeting because it can't do any good. You came here to find out if I had made the charge. You've found out. Let's end it there. I'm sorry this had to be done to you, Joseph.

CARDIN. I don't like your sympathy.

MRS. TILFORD. Very well. There's nothing I mean to do, nothing I want to do. There's nothing anybody can do.

CARDIN (*carefully*). You have already done a terrible thing.

MRS. TILFORD. I have done what I had to do. What they are may be their own business. It becomes a great deal more than that when children are involved.

KAREN (*wildly*). It's not true. Not a word of it is true; can't you understand that?

MRS. TILFORD. There won't be any punishment for either of you. This — this thing is your own. Go away with it. I don't understand it and I don't want any part of it.

MARTHA (*slowly*). So you thought we would go away?

MRS. TILFORD. I think that's best for you.

MARTHA. There must be something we can do to you, and, whatever it is, we'll find it.

MRS. TILFORD. That will be very unwise.

KAREN. You are right to be afraid.

MRS. TILFORD. I am not afraid, Karen.

CARDIN. You *are* old — and you *are* irresponsible.

KAREN (*goes to Mrs. Tilford*). I don't want to have anything to do with your mess, do you hear me? It makes me feel dirty and sick to be forced to say this, but here it is; there isn't a single word of truth in anything you've said. We're standing here defending ourselves — and against what? Against a lie. A great, awful lie.

MRS. TILFORD. I'm sorry that I can't believe that.

KAREN. Damn you!

CARDIN. But you can believe this: they've worked eight long years to save enough money to buy that farm, to start that school. They did without everything that young people ought to have. You wouldn't know about that. That school meant things to them: self-respect, and bread and butter, and honest work. Do you know what it is to try so hard for anything? Well, now it's gone. (*Suddenly hits the side of the table with his hand*) What the hell did you do it for?

MRS. TILFORD (*softly*). It had to be done.

CARDIN. Righteousness is a great thing.

MRS. TILFORD (*gently*). I know how you must feel.

CARDIN. You don't know anything about how I feel. And you don't know how they feel, either.

MRS. TILFORD. I've loved you as much as I loved my own boys. I wouldn't have spared them; I couldn't spare you.

CARDIN (*fiercely*). I believe you.

MARTHA. What is there to do to you? What can we do to you? There must be something — something that makes you feel the way we do tonight. You don't want any part of this, you said. But you'll get a part. More than you bargained for. (*Suddenly*) Listen: are you willing to stand by everything you've said tonight?

MRS. TILFORD. Yes.

MARTHA. All right. That's fine. But don't get the idea we'll let you whisper this lie: you made it and you'll come out with it. Shriek it to your town of Lancet. We'll *make* you shriek it — and we'll make you do it in a courtroom. (*Quietly*) Tomorrow, Mrs. Tilford, you will have a libel suit on your hands.

MRS. TILFORD. That will be very unwise.

KAREN. Very unwise — for you.

MRS. TILFORD. It is you I am thinking of. I am frightened for you. It was wrong of you to brazen it out here tonight; it would be criminally foolish of you to brazen it out in public. That can bring you nothing but pain. You must not be punished any further.

MARTHA. You feel that you are too old to be punished. You believe we should spare you.

MRS. TILFORD. You know that is not what I meant.

CARDIN (*turns from the window*). So you took a child's word for it?

MARTHA (*looks at him*). I knew it, too.

KAREN. That is really where you got it? I can't believe — it couldn't be. Why, she's a child.

MARTHA. She's not a child any longer.

KAREN. Oh, my God, it all fits so well now. That girl has hated us for a long time. We never knew why, we never could find out. There didn't seem to be any reason —

MARTHA. There wasn't any reason. She hates everybody and everything.

KAREN. Your Mary's a strange girl, a bad girl. There's something very awful the matter with her.

MRS. TILFORD. I was waiting for you to say that, Miss Wright.

KAREN. I'm telling you the truth. We should have told it to you long ago. (*Stops, sighs*) It's no use.

MARTHA. Where is she? Bring her out here and let us hear what she has to say.

MRS. TILFORD. You cannot see her.

CARDIN. Where is she?

MRS. TILFORD. I won't have that, Joseph.

CARDIN. I'm going to talk to her.

MRS. TILFORD (*to Karen and Martha*). You came here demanding explanations. It was I who should have asked them from you. You attack me, you attack Mary. I've told you I didn't mean you any harm. I still don't. You claim that it isn't true; it may be natural that you should say that, but I *know* that it is true. No matter what you say, you know very well I wouldn't have acted until I was absolutely sure. All I wanted was to get those children away. That has been done. There won't be any talk about it or about you — I'll see to that. You have been in my house long enough. Get out.

KAREN (*gets up*). The wicked very young, and the wicked very old. Let's go home.

CARDIN. Sit down. (*To Mrs. Tilford*) When two people come here with their lives spread on the table for you to cut to pieces, then the only honest thing to do is to give them a chance to come out whole. Are you honest?

MRS. TILFORD. I've always thought so.

CARDIN. Then where is Mary? (*After a moment she moves her head to door, right. Quickly Cardin goes to the door and opens it*) Mary! Come here.

(*After a moment Mary appears, stands nervously near door. Her manner is shy and afraid.*)

MRS. TILFORD (*gently*). Sit down, dear, and don't be afraid.

MARTHA (*her lips barely moving*). Make her tell the truth.

CARDIN (*walking about in front of Mary*). Look, everybody lies all the time. Sometimes they have to, sometimes they don't. I've lied for a lot of different reasons, but there was seldom a time when, if I'd been given a second chance, I wouldn't have taken back the lie and told the truth. You're lucky if you ever get that chance. I'm telling you this because I'm about to ask you a question. Before you answer the question, I want to tell you that if you've l—, if you made a mistake, you must take this chance and say so. You won't be punished for it. Do you get all that?

MARY (*timidly*). Yes, Cousin Joe.

CARDIN (*grimly*). All right, let's get started. Were you telling your grandmother the truth this afternoon? The exact truth about Miss Wright and Miss Dobie?

MARY (*without hesitation*). Oh, yes.

(*Karen sighs deeply. Martha, her fists closed tight, turns her back to the child. Cardin smiles as he looks at Mary.*)

CARDIN. All right, Mary, that was your chance; you passed it up. (*Pulls up a chair, sits down in front of her*) Now let's find out things.

MRS. TILFORD. She's told you. Aren't you through?

CARDIN. Not by a long shot. You've started something and we'll finish it for you. Will you answer some more questions, Mary?

MARY. Yes, Cousin Joe.

MARTHA. Stop that sick, sweet tone.

(*Mrs. Tilford half rises; Cardin motions her back.*)

CARDIN. Why don't you like Miss Dobie and Miss Wright?

MARY. Oh, I do like them. They just don't like me. They never have liked me.

CARDIN. How do you know?

MARY. They're always picking on me. They're always punishing me for everything that happens. No matter what happens, it's always me.

CARDIN. Why do you think they do that?

MARY. Because — because they're — because they — (*Stops, turns*) Grandma, I —

CARDIN. All right, we'll skip that one. Did you get punished today?

MARY. Yes, and it was just because Peggy and Evelyn heard them and so they took it out on me.

KAREN. That's a lie.

CARDIN. Sssh. Heard what, Mary?

MARY. Mrs. Mortar told Miss Dobie that there was something funny about her. She said that she had a funny feeling about Miss Wright, and Mrs. Mortar said that was unnatural. That was why we got punished, just because —

KAREN. That was not the reason they got punished.

MRS. TILFORD (*to Martha*). Miss Dobie?

MARTHA. My aunt is a stupid woman. What she said was unpleasant; it was said to annoy me. It meant nothing more than that.

MARY. And, Cousin Joe, she said every time you came to the school Miss Dobie got jealous, and that she didn't want you to get married.

MARTHA (*to Cardin*). She said that, too. This — this child is taking little things, little family things, and making them have meanings that — (*Stops, suddenly regards Mary with a combination of disgust and interest*) Where did you learn so much in so little time?

CARDIN. What do you think Mrs. Mortar meant by all that, Mary?

MRS. TILFORD. Stop it, Joseph!

MARY. I don't know, but it was always kind of funny and she always said things like that and all the girls would talk about it when Miss Dobie went and visited Miss Wright late at night —

KAREN (*angrily*). And we go to the movies at night and sometimes we read at night and sometimes we drink tea at night. Those are guilty things, too, Mrs. Tilford.

MARY. And there are always funny sounds and we'd stay awake and listen because we couldn't help hearing and I'd get frightened because the sounds were like —

MARTHA. Be still!

KAREN (*with violence*). No, no. You don't want her still now. What else did you hear?

MARY. Grandma, I —

MRS. TILFORD (*bitterly to Cardin*). You are trying to make her name it.

CARDIN (*ignoring her, speaks to Mary*). Go on.

MARY. I don't know; there were just sounds.

CARDIN. But what did you think they were? Why did they frighten you?

MARY (*weakly*). I don't know.

CARDIN (*smiles at Mrs. Tilford*). She doesn't know.

MARY (*hastily*). I saw things, too. One night there was so much noise I thought somebody was sick or something and I looked through the keyhole and they were kissing and saying things and then I got scared because it was different sort of and I —

MARTHA (*her face distorted, turns to Mrs. Tilford*). That child — that child is sick.

KAREN. Ask her again how she could see us.

CARDIN. How could you see Miss Dobie and Miss Wright?

MARY. I — I —

MRS. TILFORD. Tell him what you whispered to me.

MARY. It was at night and I was leaning down by the keyhole.

KAREN. *There's no keyhole on my door.*

MRS. TILFORD. What?

KAREN. There — is — no — keyhole — on — my — door.

MARY (*quickly*). It wasn't her room, Grandma, it was the other room, I guess. It was *Miss Dobie's* room. I saw them through the keyhole in Miss Dobie's room.

CARDIN. How did you know anybody was in Miss Dobie's room?

MARY. I told you, I told you. Because we heard them. Everybody heard them —

MARTHA. I share a room with my aunt. It is on the first floor at the other end of the house. It is impossible to hear anything from there. (*To Cardin*) Tell her to come and see for herself.

MRS. TILFORD (*her voice shaken*). What is this, Mary? Why did you say you saw through a keyhole? *Can* you hear from your room? —

MARY (*starts to cry*). Everybody is yelling at me. I don't know what I'm saying with everybody mixing me all up. I did see it! I did see it!

MRS. TILFORD. *What* did you see? *Where* did you see it? I want the truth, now. The truth, whatever it is.

CARDIN (*gets up, moves his chair back*). We can go home. We are finished here. (*Looks around*) It's not a pleasant place to be.

MRS. TILFORD (*angrily*). Stop that crying, Mary. Stand up.

(*Mary gets up, crying hysterically. Mrs. Tilford stands directly in front of her.*)

MRS. TILFORD. *I want the truth.*

MARY. All — all right.

MRS. TILFORD. What is the truth?

MARY. It was Rosalie who saw them. I just said it was me so I wouldn't have to tattle on Rosalie.

CARDIN (*wearily*). Oh, my God!

MARY. It *was* Rosalie, Grandma, she told us all about it. She said she had read about it in a book and she knew. (*Desperately*). You ask Rosalie. You just ask Rosalie. She'll tell you. We used to talk about it all the time. That's the truth, that's the honest truth. She said it was when the door was open once and she told us all about it. I was just trying to save Rosalie, and everybody jumps on me.

MRS. TILFORD (*to Cardin*). Please wait a minute. (*Goes to library door*) Rosalie!

CARDIN. You're giving yourself an awful beating, Amelia, and you deserve whatever you get.

MRS. TILFORD (*stands waiting for Rosalie, passes her hand over her face*). I don't know. I don't know, anymore. Maybe it's what I do deserve. (*As Rosalie, frightened, appears at the door, making bows to everybody, she takes the child gently by the hand, brings her down center, talking nervously*) I'm sorry to keep you up so late, Rosalie. You must be tired. (*Speaks rapidly*) Mary says there's been a lot of talk in the school lately about Miss Wright and Miss Dobie. Is that true?

ROSALIE. I — I don't know what you mean.

MRS. TILFORD. That things have been said among you girls.

ROSALIE (*wide-eyed, frightened*). What things? I never — I — I —

KAREN (*gently*). Don't be frightened.

MRS. TILFORD. What was the talk about, Rosalie?

ROSALIE (*utterly bewildered*). I don't know what she means, Miss Wright.

KAREN. Rosalie, Mary has told her grandmother that certain things at school have been — er — puzzling you girls. You, particularly.

ROSALIE. History puzzles me. I guess I'm not very good at history, and Helen helps me sometimes, if that —

KAREN. No, that's not what she meant. She says that you told her that you saw certain — certain acts between Miss Dobie and myself. She says that once, when the door was open, you saw us kissing each other in a way that — (*Unable to bear the child's look, she turns her back*) women don't kiss one another.

ROSALIE. Oh, Miss Wright, I didn't, didn't, I didn't. I *never* said such a thing.

MRS. TILFORD (*grimly*). That's true, my dear?

ROSALIE. I never saw any such thing. Mary always makes things up about me and everybody else. (*Starts to weep in excitement*) I never said any such thing ever. Why I never even could have thought of —

MARY (*staring at her, speaks very slowly*). Yes, you did, Rosalie. You're just trying to get out of it. I remember just when you said it. I remember it, because it was the day Helen Burton's bracelet was —

ROSALIE (*stands fascinated and fearful, looking at Mary*). I never did. I — I — you're just —

MARY. It was the day Helen's bracelet was stolen, and nobody knew who did it, and Helen said that if her mother found out, she'd have the thief put in jail.

KAREN (*puzzled, as are the others, by the sudden change in Rosalie's manner*). There's nothing to cry about. You must help us by telling the truth. Why, what's the matter, Rosalie?

MARY. Grandma, there's something I've got to tell you that —

ROSALIE (*with a shrill cry*). Yes. Yes. I did see it. I told Mary. What Mary said was right. I said it. I said it —

(*Throws herself on the couch, weeping hysterically; Martha stands leaning against the door; Karen, Cardin, and Mrs. Tilford are staring at Rosalie; Mary slowly sits down as the curtain falls.*)

Curtain

Act Three

SCENE: *The same as Act One. Living room of the school.*

AT RISE: *The room has changed. It is not dirty, but it is dull and dark and uncared for. The windows are tightly shut, the curtains tightly drawn. Karen is sitting in a large chair, right center, feet flat on floor. Martha is lying on the couch, her face buried against the pillows, her back to Karen. It is a minute or two after the rise of the curtain before either speaks.*

MARTHA. It's cold in here.

KAREN. Yes.

MARTHA. What time is it?

KAREN. I don't know.

MARTHA. I was hoping it was time for my bath.

KAREN. Take it early today.

MARTHA (*laughs*). Oh, I couldn't do that. I look forward all day to that bath. It's my last touch with the full life. It makes me feel important to know that there's one thing ahead of me, one thing I've *got* to do. You ought to get yourself something like that. I tell you, at five o'clock every day you comb your hair. How's that? It's better for you, take my word. You wake up in the morning and you say to yourself, the day's not entirely empty, life is rich and full: at five o'clock I'll comb my hair.

(*They fall back into silence. A moment later the phone rings. Neither of them pays the slightest attention to it. But the ringing becomes too insistent. Karen rises, takes the receiver off, goes back to her chair and sits down.*)

KAREN. It's raining.

MARTHA. Hungry?

KAREN. No. You?

MARTHA. No, but I'd like to be hungry. Remember how much we used to eat at college?

KAREN. That was ten years ago.

MARTHA. Well, maybe we'll be hungry in another ten years. It's cheaper this way.

KAREN. What's the old thing about time being more nourishing than bread?

MARTHA. Maybe.

KAREN. Joe's late today. What time is it?

MARTHA (*turns again to lie on her side*). We've been sitting here for eight days asking each other the time. Haven't you heard? There isn't any time anymore.

KAREN. It's been days since we've been out of this house.

MARTHA. Well, we'll have to get off these chairs sooner or later. In a couple of months they'll need dusting.

KAREN. What'll we do when we get off?

MARTHA. God knows.

KAREN (*almost in a whisper*). It's awful.

MARTHA. Let's not talk about it. (*After a moment*) What about eggs for dinner?

KAREN. All right.

MARTHA. I'll make some potatoes with onions, the way you used to like them.

KAREN. It's a week ago Thursday. It never seemed real until the last day. It seems real enough now, all right. Let's go out.

MARTHA (*turns over, stares at her*). Where to?

KAREN. We'll take a walk.

MARTHA. Where'll we walk?

KAREN. Why shouldn't we take a walk? We won't see anybody, and suppose we do, what of it? We'll just —

MARTHA (*slowly gets up*). Come on. We'll go through the park.

KAREN. They might see us. (*They stand looking at each other*) Let's not go. (*Martha goes back, lies down again*) We'll go tomorrow.

MARTHA (*laughs*). Stop kidding yourself.

KAREN. But Joe says we've got to go out. He says that all the people who don't think it's true will begin to wonder if we keep hiding this way.

MARTHA. If it makes you feel better to think there *are* such people, go ahead.

KAREN. He says we ought to go into town and go shopping and act as though —

MARTHA. Shopping? That's a sound idea. There aren't three stores in Lancet that would sell us anything. Hasn't he heard about the ladies' clubs and their meetings and their circulars and their visits and their —

KAREN (*softly*). Don't tell him.

MARTHA (*gently*). I won't. (*There are footsteps in the hall, and the sound of something being dragged*) There's our friend.

(*A grocery boy appears lugging a box. He brings it into the room, stands staring at them, giggles a little. Walks toward Karen, stops, examines her. She sits tense, looking away from him. Without taking his eyes from Karen, he speaks.*)

GROCERY BOY. I knocked on the kitchen door but nobody answered.

MARTHA. You said that yesterday. All right. Thanks. Good-bye.

KAREN (*unable any longer to stand the stare*). Make him stop it.

GROCERY BOY. Here are the things. (*Giggles, moves toward Martha, stands looking at her. Suddenly Martha thrusts her hand in the air.*)

MARTHA. I've got eight fingers, see? I'm a freak.

GROCERY BOY (*giggling*). There's a car comin' here. (*Starts backing out of door, still looking.*) Good-bye. (*Exits.*)

MARTHA. You still think we should go into town?

KAREN. I don't know. I don't know about anything anymore. (*After a moment*) Martha, Martha, Martha —

MARTHA (*gently*). What is it, Karen?

KAREN. What are we going to do? It's like that dark hour of the night when half awake you struggle through the black mess you've been dreaming. Then, suddenly, you wake up and you see your own bed or your own nightgown and you know you're back again in a solid world. But now it's all the nightmare; there is no solid world. Oh, Martha, *why* did it happen. *What* happened? What are we doing here like this?

MARTHA. Waiting.

KAREN. For what?

MARTHA. I don't know.

KAREN. We've got to get out of this place. I can't stand it anymore.

MARTHA. You'll be getting married soon. Everything will be all right then.

KAREN (*vaguely*). Yes.

MARTHA (*looks up at the tone*). What is it?

KAREN. Nothing.

MARTHA. There mustn't be anything wrong between you and Joe. Never.

KAREN (*without conviction*). Nothing's wrong. (*As footsteps are heard in the hall, her face lights up*) There's Joe now.

(*Mrs. Mortar, small suitcase in hand, stands in the doorway, her face pushed coyly forward.*)

MRS. MORTAR. And here I am. Hello, hello.

MARTHA (*she has turned over on her back and is staring at her aunt. She speaks to Karen*). The Duchess, isn't it? Returned at long last. (*Too jovially*) Come on in. We're delighted to see you. Are you tired from your journey? Is there something I can get you?

MRS. MORTAR (*surprised*). I'm very glad to see you both, and (*looks around*) I'm very glad to see the old place again. How is everything?

MARTHA. Everything's fine. We're splendid, thank you. You're just in time for tea.

MRS. MORTAR. You know, I should like some tea, if it isn't too much trouble.

MARTHA, No trouble at all. Some small sandwiches and a little brandy?

MRS. MORTAR (*puzzled*). Why, Martha.

MARTHA. Where the hell have you been?

MRS. MORTAR. Around, around. I had a most interesting time. Things —

MARTHA. Why didn't you answer my telegrams?

MRS. MORTAR. Things have changed in the theater — drastically changed, I might say.

MARTHA. *Why didn't you answer my telegrams?*

MRS. MORTAR. Oh, Martha, there's your temper again.

MARTHA. Answer me and don't bother about my temper.

MRS. MORTAR (*nervously*). I was moving around a great deal. (*Conversationally*) You know, I think it will throw a very revealing light on the state of the new theater when I tell you that the Lyceum in Rochester now has a toilet backstage.

MARTHA. To hell with the toilet in Rochester. Where were you?

MRS. MORTAR. Moving around, I tell you.

KAREN. What difference does it all make now?

MRS. MORTAR. Karen is quite right. Let bygones be bygones.

As I was saying, there's an effete something in the theater now, and that accounts for —

MARTHA. Why did you refuse to come back here and testify for us?

MRS. MORTAR. Why, Martha, I didn't refuse to come back at all. That's the wrong way to look at it. I was on a tour; that's a moral obligation, you know. Now don't let's talk about unpleasant things anymore. I'll go up and unpack a few things; tomorrow's plenty of time to get my trunk.

KAREN (*laughs*). Things have changed here, you know.

MARTHA. She doesn't know. She expected to walk right up to a comfortable fire and sit down and she very carefully waited until the whole thing was over. (*Leans forward, speaking to Mrs. Mortar*) Listen. Karen Wright and Martha Dobie brought a libel suit against a woman called Tilford because her grandchild had accused them of having what the judge called "sinful sexual knowledge of one another." (*Mrs. Mortar holds up her hand in protest, and Martha laughs*) Don't like that, do you? Well, a great part of the defense's case was based on remarks made by Lily Mortar, actress in the toilets of Rochester, against her niece, Martha. And a greater part of the defense's case rested on the telling fact that Mrs. Mortar would not appear in court to deny or explain those remarks. Mrs. Mortar had a moral obligation to the theater. As you probably read in the papers, we lost the case.

MRS. MORTAR. I didn't think of it that way, Martha. It couldn't have done any good for all of us to get mixed up in that unpleasant notoriety — (*Sees Martha's face. Hastily*) But now that you've explained it, why, I do see it your way, and I'm sorry I didn't come back. But now that I am here, I'm going to stand shoulder to shoulder with you. I know what you've gone through, but the body and heart *do* recover, you know. I'll be here working right along with you and we'll —

MARTHA. There's an eight o'clock train. Get on it.

MRS. MORTAR. Martha.

MARTHA. You've come back to pick the bones dry. There's nothing here for you.

MRS. MORTAR (*sniffling a little*). How can you talk to me like that?

MARTHA. Because I hate you. I've always hated you.

MRS. MORTAR (*gently*). God will punish you for that.

MARTHA. He's been doing all right.

MRS. MORTAR. When you wish to apologize, I will be temporarily in my room. (*Starts to exit, almost bumps into Cardin, steps back with dignity*) How do you do?

CARDIN (*laughs*). Look who's here. A little late, aren't you?

MRS. MORTAR. So it's you. Now, I call *that* loyal. A lot of men wouldn't still be here. They would have felt —

MARTHA. Get out of here.

KAREN (*opening door*). I'll call you when it's time for your train.

(*Mrs. Mortar looks at her, exits.*)

CARDIN. Now, what do you think brought her back?

KAREN. God knows.

MARTHA. I know. She was broke.

CARDIN (*pats Martha on the shoulder*). Don't let her worry you this time, Martha. We'll give her some money and get rid of her. (*Pulls Karen to him*) Been out today, darling?

KAREN. We started to go out.

CARDIN (*shakes his head*). Feel all right?

(*Karen leans over to kiss him. Almost imperceptibly he pulls back.*)

KAREN. Why did you do that?

MARTHA. Karen.

CARDIN. Do what?

KAREN. Draw back that way.

CARDIN (*laughs, kisses her*). If we sit around here much longer, we'll all be bats. I sold my place today to Foster.

KAREN. You did what?

CARDIN. We're getting married this week. Then we're going away — all three of us.

KAREN. You can't leave here. I won't have you do this for me. What about the hospital and —

CARDIN. Shut up, darling, it's all fixed. We're going to Vienna and we're going quick. Fischer wrote that I can have my old place back.

KAREN. No! No! I'm not going to let you.

CARDIN. It's already done. Fischer can't pay me much, but it'll be enough for the three of us. Plenty if we live cheap.

MARTHA. I couldn't go with you, Joe.

CARDIN. Nonsense, Martha, we're all going. We're going to have fun again.

KAREN (*slowly*). You don't want to go back to Vienna.

CARDIN. No.

KAREN. Then why?

CARDIN. Look: I don't want to go to Vienna; I'd rather have stayed here. But then you don't want to go to Vienna; you'd rather have stayed here. Well, to hell with that. We *can't* stay here, and Vienna offers enough to eat and sleep and drink beer on. Now don't object any more, please, darling. All right?

KAREN. All right.

MARTHA. I can't go. It's better for all of us if I don't.

CARDIN (*puts his arm around her*). Not now. You stay with us now. Later on, if you want it that way. All right?

MARTHA (*smiles*). All right.

CARDIN. Swell. I'll buy you good coffee cakes and take you both to Ischl for a honeymoon.

MARTHA (*picking up grocery box, she starts for door*). A big coffee cake with a lot of raisins. It would be nice to like something again. (*Exits.*)

CARDIN (*with a slightly forced heartiness*). I'll be going back with a pretty girl who belongs to me. I'll show you off all over the place — to Dr. Engelhardt, and the nurse at the desk, and to the fat gal in the cake shop, and to Fischer. (*Laughs*) The last time I saw him was at the railroad station. He took me back of the baggage car. (*With an imitation of an accent*) "Joseph," he said, "you'll be a good doctor; I would trust you to cut up my Minna. But you're not a great doctor, and you never will be. Go back where you were born and take care of your sick. Leave the fancy work to the others." I came home.

KAREN. You'll be coming home again someday.

CARDIN. Let's not talk about it. (*After a moment*) You'll need some clothes?

KAREN. A few. Oh, your Dr. Fischer was so right. This is where you belong.

CARDIN. I need an overcoat and a suit. You'll need a lot of things — heavy things. It's cold there now, much colder than you'd expect —

KAREN. I've done this to you. I've taken you away from everything you want.

CARDIN. But it's lovely in the mountains, and that's where we'll go for a month.

KAREN. They — *they've* done it. They've taken away every chance we had. Everything we wanted, everything we were going to be.

CARDIN. And we've got to stop talking like that. (*Takes her by the shoulder*) We've got a chance. But it's just one chance, and if we miss it we're done for. It means that we've got to start putting the whole business behind us now. *Now,* Karen. What you've done, you've done — and that's that.

KAREN. What *I've* done?

CARDIN (*impatiently*). What's been done to you.

KAREN. What did you mean? (*When there is no answer*) What did you mean when you said: "What you've done"?

CARDIN (*shouting*). Nothing. Nothing. (*Then very quietly*) Karen, there are a lot of people in this world who've had bad trouble in their lives. We're three of those people. We could sit around the rest of our lives and exist on that trouble, until in the end we had nothing else and we'd want nothing else. That's something I'm not coming to and I'm not going to let you come to.

KAREN. I know. I'm sorry. (*After a moment*) Joe, can we have a baby right away?

CARDIN (*vaguely*). Yes, I guess so. Although we won't have much money now.

KAREN. You used to want one right away. You always said that was the way you wanted it. There's some reason for your changing.

CARDIN. My God, we *can't* go on like this. Everything I say to you is made to mean something else. We don't talk like people anymore. Oh, let's get out of here as fast as we can.

KAREN (*as though she is finishing the sentence for him*). And every word will have a new meaning. You think we'll be able to run away from that? Woman, child, love, lawyer — no words that we can use in safety anymore. (*Laughs*) Sick, high-tragic people. That's what we'll be.

CARDIN (*gently*). No, we won't, darling. Love is casual — that's the way it should be. We must find that out all over again. We must learn again to live and love like other people.

KAREN. It won't work.

CARDIN. What?

KAREN. The two of us together.

CARDIN (*sharply*). Stop talking like that.

KAREN. It's true. (*Suddenly*). I want you to say it now.

CARDIN. I don't know what you're talking about.

KAREN. Yes, you do. We've both known for a long time. I knew surely the day we lost the case. I was watching your face in court. It was ashamed — and sad at being ashamed. Say it now, Joe. Ask it now.

CARDIN. I have nothing to ask. Nothing — (*Quickly*) All right. Is it — was it ever —

KAREN (*puts her hand over his mouth*). No. Martha and I have never touched each other. (*Pulls his head down on her shoulder*) That's all right, darling. I'm glad you asked. I'm not mad a bit, really.

CARDIN. I'm sorry, Karen, I'm sorry. I didn't mean to hurt you, I —

KAREN. I know. You wanted to wait until it was all over, you really never wanted to ask at all. You didn't know for sure; you thought there might be just a little truth in it all. (*With great feeling*) You've been good to me and loyal. You're a fine man. (*Afraid of tears, she pats him, walks away*) Now go and sit down, Joe. I have things to say. They're all mixed up and I must get them clear.

CARDIN. Don't let's talk any more. Let's forget and go ahead.

KAREN (*puzzled*). Go ahead?

CARDIN. Yes, Karen.

KAREN. You believe me, then?

CARDIN. Of course I believe you. I only had to hear you say it.

KAREN. No, no, no. That isn't the way things work. Maybe you believe me. I'd never know whether you did or not. You'd never know whether you did, either. We couldn't do it that way. Can't you see what would happen? We'd be hounded by it all our lives. I'd be frightened, always, and in the end my own fright would make me — would make me hate you. (*Sees slight movement he makes*) Yes, it would; I know it would. I'd hate you for what I thought I'd done to you. And I'd hate myself, too. It would grow and grow until we'd be ruined by it. (*Sees him about to speak*) Ah, Joe, you've seen all that yourself. You knew it first.

CARDIN (*softly*). I didn't mean it that way; I don't now.

KAREN (*smiles*). You're still trying to spare me, still trying to tell yourself that we might be all right again. But we won't be all right. Not ever, ever, ever. I don't know all the reasons why. Look, I'm standing here. I haven't changed. (*Holds out her hands*) My hands look just the same, my face is the same, even my dress is old. We're in a room we've been in so many times before; you're sitting where you always sit; it's nearly time for dinner. I'm like everybody else. I can have all the things that everybody has. I can have you and I can go to market, and we can go to the movies, and people will talk to me and — (*Suddenly notices the pain in his face*) Oh, I'm sorry. I mustn't talk like that. That couldn't be true anymore.

CARDIN. It could be, Karen. We'll make it be like that.

KAREN. No. That's only what we'd like to have had. It's what we can't have now. Go home, darling.

CARDIN (*with force*). Don't talk like that. No matter what it is, we can't leave each other. I can't leave you —

KAREN. Joe, Joe. Let's do it now and quick; it will be too hard later on.

CARDIN. No, no, no. We love each other. (*His voice breaks*) I'd give anything not to have asked questions, Karen.

KAREN. It had to be asked sooner or later — and answered. You're a good man — the best I'll ever know — and you've been better to me than — But it's no good now, for either of us; you can see that.

CARDIN. It can be. You say I helped you. Help me now; help me to be strong and good enough to — (*Goes toward her with his arms out*) Karen!

KAREN (*drawing back*). No, Joe! (*Then, as he stops*) Will you do something for me?

CARDIN. No. I won't —

KAREN. Will you — will you go away for two days — a day — and think this all over by yourself — away from me and love and pity? Will you? And then decide.

CARDIN (*after a long pause*). Yes, if you want, but it won't make any difference. We will —

KAREN. Don't say anything. Please go now. (*She sits down, smiles, closes her eyes. For a moment he stands looking at her, then slowly puts on his hat*) And all my heart goes with you.

CARDIN (*at door, leaving*). I'll be coming back. (*Exits, slowly, reluctantly, closing door.*)

KAREN (*a moment after he has gone*). No, you won't. Never, darling. (*Stays as she is until Martha enters right.*)

MARTHA (*goes to lamp, lights it*). It gets dark so early now. (*Sits down, stretches, laughs*) Cooking always makes me feel better. Well, I guess we'll have to give the Duchess some dinner. When the hawks descend, you've got to feed 'em. Where's Joe? (*No answer*) Where's Joe?

KAREN. Gone.

MARTHA. A patient? Will he be back in time for dinner?

KAREN. No.

MARTHA (*watching her*). We'll save dinner for him, then. Karen! What's the matter?

KAREN. He won't be back anymore.

MARTHA (*slowly and carefully*). You mean he won't be back anymore tonight.

KAREN. He won't be back at all.

MARTHA (*quickly, walks to Karen*). What happened? (*Karen shakes her head*) What happened, Karen?

KAREN. He thought that we had been lovers.

MARTHA (*tensely*). I don't believe you.

(*Wearily Karen turns her head away.*)

KAREN. All right.

MARTHA (*automatically*). I don't believe it. He's never said a word all these months, all during the trial — (*Suddenly grabs Karen by the shoulder, shakes her*) Didn't you tell him? For God's sake, didn't you tell him it wasn't true?

KAREN. Yes.

MARTHA. He didn't believe you?

KAREN. I guess he believed me.

MARTHA (*angrily*). Then what have you done?

KAREN. What had to be done.

MARTHA. It's all wrong. It's silly. He'll be back in a little while and you'll clear it all up — (*Realizes why that can't be, covers her mouth with her hand*) Oh, God, I wanted that for you so much.

KAREN. Don't. I feel sick to my stomach.

MARTHA (*goes to couch opposite Karen, puts her head in her arms*). What's happened to us? What's really happened to us?

KAREN. I don't know. I want to be sleepy. I want to go to sleep.

MARTHA. Go back to Joe. He's strong; he'll understand. It's too much for you this way.

KAREN (*irritably*). Stop talking about it. Let's pack and get out of here. Let's take the train in the morning.

MARTHA. The train to where?

KAREN. I don't know. Someplace; anyplace.

MARTHA. A job? Money?

KAREN. In a big place we could get something to do.

MARTHA. They'd know about us. We've been famous.

KAREN. A small town, then.

MARTHA. They'd know more about us.

KAREN (*as a child would say it*). Isn't there anywhere to go?

MARTHA. No. We're bad people. We'll sit. We'll be sitting the rest of our lives wondering what's happened to us. You think this scene is strange? Well, get used to it; we'll be here for a long time. (*Suddenly pinches Karen on the arm*) Let's pinch each other sometimes. We can tell whether we're still living.

KAREN (*shivers, listlessly gets up, starts making a fire in the fireplace*). But this isn't a new sin they tell us we've done. Other people aren't destroyed by it.

MARTHA. They are the people who believe in it, who want it, who've chosen it. We aren't like that. We don't love each other. (*Suddenly stops, crosses to fireplace, stands looking abstractedly at Karen. Speaks casually*) I don't love you. We've been very close to each other, of course. I've loved you like a friend, the way thousands of women feel about other women.

KAREN (*only half listening*). Yes.

MARTHA. Certainly that doesn't mean anything. There's nothing wrong about that. It's perfectly natural that I should be fond of you, that I should —

KAREN (*listlessly*). Why are you saying all this to me?

MARTHA. Because I love you.

KAREN (*vaguely*). Yes, of course.

MARTHA. I love you that way — maybe the way they said I loved you. I don't know. (*Waits, gets no answer, kneels down next to Karen*) Listen to me!

KAREN. What?

MARTHA. *I have loved you the way they said.*

KAREN. You're crazy.

MARTHA. There's always been something wrong. Always — as long as I can remember. But I never knew it until all this happened.

KAREN (*for the first time looks up*). Stop it!

MARTHA. You're afraid of hearing it; I'm more afraid than you.

KAREN (*puts her hands over her ears*). I won't listen to you.

MARTHA. Take your hands down. (*Leans over, pulls Karen's hands away*) You've got to know it. I can't keep it any longer. I've got to tell you how guilty I am.

KAREN (*deliberately*). You are guilty of nothing.

MARTHA. I've been telling myself that since the night we heard the child say it; I've been praying I could convince myself of it. I can't, I can't any longer. It's there. I don't know how, I don't know why. But I did love you. I do love you. I resented your marriage; maybe because I wanted you; maybe I wanted you all along; maybe I couldn't call it by a name; maybe it's been there ever since I first knew you —

KAREN (*tensely*). It's a lie. You're telling yourself a lie. We never thought of each other that way.

MARTHA (*bitterly*). No, of course *you* didn't. But who says I didn't? I never felt that way about anybody but you. I've never loved a man — (*Stops. Softly*) I never knew why before. Maybe it's that.

KAREN (*carefully*). You are tired and sick.

MARTHA (*as though she were talking to herself*). It's funny; it's all mixed up. There's something in you, and you don't know it and you don't do anything about it. Suddenly a child gets bored and lies — and there you are, seeing it for the first time. (*Closes her eyes*) I don't know. It all seems to come back to *me*. In some way I've ruined your life. I've ruined my own. I didn't even *know*. (*Smiles*) There's a big difference between us now, Karen. I feel all dirty and — (*Puts out her hand, touches Karen's head*) I can't stay with you anymore, darling.

KAREN (*in a shaken, uncertain tone*). All this isn't true. You've never said it; we'll forget it by tomorrow —

MARTHA. Tomorrow? Karen, we would have had to invent a new language, as children do, without words like tomorrow.

KAREN (*crying*). Go and lie down, Martha. You'll feel better.

(*Martha looks around the room, slowly, carefully. She is very quiet. Exits right, stands at door for a second looking at Karen, then slowly shuts the door behind her. Karen sits alone without moving. There is no sound in the house until, a few minutes after Martha's exit, a shot is heard. The sound of the shot should not be too loud or too strong. For a few seconds after the noise has died out, Karen does not move. Then, suddenly, she springs from the chair, crosses the room, pulls open door, right. Almost at the same moment footsteps are heard on the staircase.*)

MRS. MORTAR. What was that? Where is it? (*Enters door center, frightened, aimlessly moving about*) Karen! Martha! Where are you? I heard a shot. What was — (*Stops as she sees Karen reappear, right. Walks toward her, still talking. Stops when she sees Karen's face*) What — what is it? (*Karen moves her hands, shakes her head slightly, passes Mrs. Mortar, and goes toward window. Mrs. Mortar stares at her for a moment, rushes past her through door right. Left alone, Karen leans against the window. Mrs. Mortar reenters crying. After a minute*) What shall we do? What shall we do?

KAREN (*in a toneless voice*). Nothing.

MRS. MORTAR. We've got to get a doctor — right away. (*Goes to phone, nervously, fumblingly starts to dial.*)

KAREN (*without turning*). There isn't any use.

MRS. MORTAR. We've got to do something. Oh, it's awful. Poor Martha. I don't know what we can do — (*Puts phone down, collapses in chair, sobs quietly*) You think she's dea—

KAREN. Yes.

MRS. MORTAR. Poor, poor Martha. I can't realize it's true. Oh, how could she — she was so — I don't know what — (*Looks up, still crying, surprised*) I'm — I'm frightened.

KAREN. Don't cry.

MRS. MORTAR. I can't help it. How can I help it? (*Gradually the sobs cease, and she sits rocking herself*) I'll never forgive myself for the last words I said to her. But I was good to her, Karen, and you know God will excuse me for that once. I always tried to do everything I could. (*Suddenly*) Suicide's a sin. (*No answer. Timidly*) Shouldn't we call somebody to —

KAREN. In a little while.

MRS. MORTAR. She shouldn't have done it, she shouldn't have done it. It was because of all this awful business. She would have got a job and started all over again — she was just worried and sick and —

KAREN. That isn't the reason she did it.

MRS. MORTAR. What — why — ?

KAREN (*wearily*). What difference does it make now?

MRS. MORTAR (*reproachfully*). You're not crying.

KAREN. No.

MRS. MORTAR. What will happen to me? I haven't anything. Poor Martha —

KAREN. She was very good to you; she was good to us all.

MRS. MORTAR. Oh, I know she was, Karen, and I was good to her too. I did everything I could. I — I haven't any place to go. (*After a few seconds of silence*) I'm afraid. It seems so queer — in the next room. (*Shivers.*)

KAREN. Don't be afraid.

MRS. MORTAR. It's different for you. You're young.

(*The doorbell rings. Mrs. Mortar jumps. Karen doesn't move. It rings again.*)

MRS. MORTAR (*nervously*). Who is it? (*The bell rings again*) Shall I answer it? (*Karen shrugs*) I think we'd better. (*Exits through center doors. Returns in a minute followed by Agatha, who stands in the door*) It's a woman. (*No answer*) It's a woman to see you, Karen. (*Getting no answer, she turns to Agatha*) You can't come in now; we've had a — we've had trouble here.

AGATHA. Miss Karen, I've *got* to speak to you.

KAREN (*turns slowly, mechanically*). Agatha.

AGATHA (*goes to Karen*). Please, Miss Karen. We've tried so hard to get you. I been phoning here all the time. Trying to get you. Phoning and phoning. Please, please let her come in. Just for a minute, Miss Karen. Please —

MRS. MORTAR. Who wants to come in here?

AGATHA. Mrs. Tilford. (*Looks at Karen*) Don't you feel well? (*Karen shakes her head*) You ain't mad at *me?*

MRS. MORTAR. That woman can't come in here. She caused all —

KAREN. I'm not mad at you, Agatha.

AGATHA. Can I — can I get you something?

KAREN. No.

AGATHA. You poor child. You look like you got a pain. (*Hesitates, takes Karen's hands*) I only came cause she's so bad off. She's got to see you, Miss Karen, she's just got to. She's been sittin' outside in the car, hoping you'd come out. She can't get Dr. Joe. He — he won't talk to her anymore. I wouldn't a come — I always been on your side — but she's sick. If only you could see her, you'd let her come for just a minute.

KAREN. I couldn't do that, Agatha.

AGATHA. I don't blame you. But I had to tell you. She's old. It's going to kill her.

KAREN (*bitterly*). Kill her? Where is Mrs. Tilford?

AGATHA. Outside.

KAREN. All right.

AGATHA (*presses Karen's arm*). You always been a good girl. (*Hurriedly exits.*)

MRS. MORTAR. You going to allow that woman to come in here? With Martha lying there? How can you be so feelingless? (*She starts to cry*) I won't stay and see it. I won't have anything to do with it. I'll never let that woman — (*Rushes sobbing from the room.*)

(*A second after, Mrs. Tilford appears in the doorway. Her face, her walk, her voice have changed.*)

MRS. TILFORD. Karen, let me come in.

(*Without turning, Karen bows her head. Mrs. Tilford enters, stands staring at the floor.*)

KAREN. Why have you come here?

MRS. TILFORD. I had to come. (*Stretches out her hand to Karen, who does not turn. She drops her hand*) I know now; I know it wasn't true.

KAREN. What?

MRS. TILFORD (*carefully*). I know it wasn't true, Karen.

KAREN (*stares at her, shudders*). You know it wasn't true? I don't care what you know. It doesn't matter anymore. If that's what you had to say, you've said it. Go away.

MRS. TILFORD (*puts her hand to her throat*). I've *got* to tell you.

KAREN. I don't want to hear you.

MRS. TILFORD. Last Tuesday Mrs. Wells found a bracelet in Rosalie's room. The bracelet had been hidden for several months. We found out that Rosalie had taken the bracelet from another girl, and that Mary — (*Closes her eyes*) that Mary knew that and used it to force Rosalie into saying that she had seen you and Miss Dobie together. I — I've talked to Mary. I've found out. (*Karen suddenly begins to laugh, high and sharp*) Don't do that, Karen. I have only a little more to say. I've tried to say it to you for six days. I've talked to Judge Potter. He will make all arrangements.

There will be a public apology and an explanation. The damage suit will be paid to you in full and — and any more that you will be kind enough to take from me. I — I must see that you won't suffer anymore.

KAREN. We're not going to suffer anymore. Martha is dead. (*Mrs. Tilford gasps, shakes her head as though to shake off the truth, and covers her face. Karen watches her for a minute*) So you've come here to relieve your conscience? Well, I won't be your confessor. It's choking you, is it? (*Violently*) And you want to stop the choking, don't you? You've done a wrong and you have to right that wrong or you can't rest your head again. You want to be "just," don't you, and you wanted us to help you be just? You've come to the wrong place for help. You want to be a "good" woman again, don't you? (*Bitterly*) Oh, I know. You told us that night you had to do what you did. Now you "have" to do this. A public apology and money paid, and you can sleep again and eat again. That done and there'll be peace for you. You're old, and the old are callous. Ten, fifteen years left for you. But what of me? It's a whole life for me. A whole God-damned life. (*Suddenly quiet, points to door, right*) And what of her?

MRS. TILFORD (*she is crying*). You are still living.

KAREN. Yes. I guess so.

MRS. TILFORD (*with a tremendous effort to control herself*). I didn't come here to relieve myself. I swear to God I didn't. I came to try — to try anything. I knew there wasn't any relief for me, Karen, and that there never would be again. (*Tensely*) But what I am or why I came doesn't matter. The only thing that matters is you and — You, now.

KAREN. There's nothing for me.

MRS. TILFORD. Oh, let's try to make something for you. You're young and I — I can help you.

KAREN (*smiles*). You can help me?

MRS. TILFORD (*with great feeling*). Take whatever I can give you. Take it for yourself and use it for yourself. It won't bring me peace, if that's what's worrying you. (*Smiles*) Those ten or fifteen years you talk about! They will be bad years.

KAREN. I'm tired, Mrs. Tilford. You will have a hard time ahead, won't you?

MRS. TILFORD. Yes.

KAREN. Mary?

MRS. TILFORD. I don't know.

KAREN. You can send her away.

MRS. TILFORD. No. I could never do that. Whatever she does, it must be to me and no one else. She's — she's —

KAREN. Yes. Your very own, to live with the rest of your life. (*For a moment she watches Mrs. Tilford's face*) It's over for me now, but it will never end for you. She's harmed us both, but she's harmed you more, I guess. (*Sits down beside Mrs. Tilford*) I'm sorry.

MRS. TILFORD (*clings to her*). Then you'll try for yourself.

KAREN. All right.

MRS. TILFORD. You and Joe.

KAREN. No. We're not together anymore.

MRS. TILFORD (*looks up at her*). Did I do that, too?

KAREN. I don't think anyone did anything, anymore.

MRS. TILFORD (*makes a half-movement to rise*). I'll go to him right away.

KAREN. No, it's better now the way it is.

MRS. TILFORD. But he must know what I know, Karen. You must go back to him.

KAREN (*smiles*). No, not anymore.

MRS. TILFORD. You must, you must — (*Sees her face, hesitates*) Perhaps later, Karen?

KAREN. Perhaps.

MRS. TILFORD (*after a moment in which they both sit silent*). Come away from here now, Karen. (*Karen shakes her head*) You can't stay with — (*Moves her hand toward door, right.*)

KAREN. When she is buried, then I will go.

MRS. TILFORD. You'll be all right?

KAREN. I'll be all right, I suppose. Good-bye, now.

(*They both rise. Mrs. Tilford speaks, pleadingly.*)

MRS. TILFORD. You'll let me help you? You'll let me try?

KAREN. Yes, if it will make you feel better.

MRS. TILFORD (*with great feeling*). Oh, yes, oh, yes, Karen. (*Karen walks toward the window.*)

KAREN (*suddenly*). Is it nice out?

MRS. TILFORD. It's been cold. (*Karen opens the window slightly, sits on the ledge.*)

KAREN. It feels very good.

MRS. TILFORD. You'll write me sometime?

KAREN. If I ever have anything to say. Good-bye, now.
MRS. TILFORD. Good-bye, my dear.
(Karen smiles as Mrs. Tilford exits. She does not turn, but a minute later she raises her hand.)
KAREN. Good-bye.

Curtain

Days to Come

For Julia and Max Hellman

Days to Come was first produced at the Vanderbilt Theatre, New York City, on December 15, 1936, with the following cast:

(In the order of their appearance)

HANNAH	CLARE WOODBURY
LUCY	MURIEL GALLICK
CORA RODMAN	FRIEDA ALTMAN
HENRY ELLICOTT	NED WEVER
ANDREW RODMAN	WILLIAM HARRIGAN
JULIE RODMAN	FLORENCE ELDRIDGE
THOMAS FIRTH	JOSEPH SWEENEY
LEO WHALEN	BEN SMITH
SAM WILKIE	CHARLES DINGLE
MOSSIE DOWEL	JACK CARR
JOE EASTER	THOMAS FISHER

Produced and directed by
HERMAN SHUMLIN

Settings designed by
ALINE BERNSTEIN

Scenes

Act One

Living room of the Rodman house.
Late morning in October.

Act Two

Scene 1. The same. Four weeks later.
Scene 2. The same. Immediately following Scene 1.
Scene 3. Same as Act One.

Act Three

The same as Act One.
Seven-thirty the next morning.

Act One

Late morning in October.

SCENE: *The living room of the Rodman house in Callom, Ohio, two hundred miles from Cleveland. The room is deep and the left stage window-wall is curved into the room. All furniture gives the impression of being arranged for the entrance doors which are on the right center stage wall. On the backstage wall, on the extreme right, is a door leading into the library. On the curved left stage wall are two high windows. These windows open on a circular porch and are used as an entrance by people who know the house well. Between the windows, and well out on the stage, is a large drum table. There are chairs on each side of the table. Back from the table is an antique flat topped table desk. Left downstage is a high circular cabinet, unglassed, in which there are many small figures of animals. Near the cabinet is a couch. The room is beautiful, simple. But the objects in the cabinet are too neatly placed and the effect is rigid and bad.*

Left and right stage directions are the audience's left and right.

AT RISE: *A large vigorous woman is sitting on the floor in front of the window, comfortably arranging flowers in several bowls. (The bowls and the flowers are on the porch.) She has on a house dress, but is not in servant's uniform. Lucy, in uniform, is dusting. On a chair next to Hannah is a bowl of half-shelled peas.*

LUCY (*finishes dusting the animals*). That's enough for them today.

HANNAH (*hands her a bowl of flowers and laughs*). Did you get your wages this morning? (*No answer*) Huh?

LUCY (*reluctantly*). Yes.

HANNAH (*cheerfully*). Then hand it over.

LUCY. I was going to. But Hannah, I got to keep five dollars out of it because I owe somebody the five dollars.

HANNAH. Is the five-dollar somebody in this town?

LUCY. No.

HANNAH. Then don't pay 'em. The boys need it — (*Soberly*) and I got a hunch will need it more. (*As Lucy gives her the money from her apron pocket*) Thanks, Lucy. You're a nice kid. I'll tell them how it comes from you.

LUCY. But when's it going to be over? Seems funny, don't it?

HANNAH. I'm not laughing. (*She hands Lucy another bowl of flowers. Lucy takes it to a table near the couch and puts it very carefully in a certain spot*) I don't know when it's going to be over. But I guessed it was going to be. I haven't lived in this house twenty years for nothing. (*Hannah has been watching Lucy place the bowl. She laughs and makes a this-way gesture with her hands*) Uh-uh. Bring it over.

LUCY (*as if this joke had been played before*). What's the use? Miss Cora will only — (*Makes imitative gestures on the table*) move it right back here.

HANNAH. I know. I like to see her do it.

LUCY. But Aunt Lundee says that all they do is sit around talking and that a man should be at work and that Uncle Jim and the rest should go on back and stop this crazy strike and —

HANNAH. Since when does anybody listen to your Aunt Lundee?

LUCY. I don't know.

HANNAH (*cheerfully*). Lucy, there were people made to think and people made to listen. I ain't sure either you or Lundee were made to do either.

LUCY (*pointing to the vase*). Miss Cora's been downtown already this morning. So was Mrs. Rodman, and when I came out of the butcher store there was Miss Cora standing on one side of the street, looking at Mrs. Rodman in the funniest way, and she didn't call to her, she just stood watching and not saying anything —

HANNAH. And *you* just stood watching and not saying anything, too, huh?

LUCY (*hurt*). What's wrong with that now?

HANNAH. Nothing. (*Half-seriously, half-teasingly*) As long as you just watch and don't say anything.

(*Cora Rodman enters from the center doors. She is a thin, nervous-looking woman of about forty-two. She has a small clay Chinese horse in her hand. Hannah doesn't look up, but*

Lucy watches Cora as she crosses to the cabinet with the horse.)

CORA. I brought this down. I'll take the elephant up for my desk. It will make a nice change.

LUCY. Yes'm.

CORA (*to Hannah*). Did you make something sweet?

HANNAH (*to Cora*). Chocolate cake. All over.

CORA (*to Lucy, who has picked up carpet sweeper, rags, etc., and is exiting*). Well, don't cut me such a small piece. You didn't bring me enough butter on my tray this morning, and I had a roll left over.

LUCY. Yes'm. (*She exits.*)

CORA (*she crosses to flower bowl and, with the motions Lucy has imitated, moves it back to its particular spot*). Always seems to be something the matter with the breakfast tray. I read in the morning paper about a thirteen-year-old girl who had a baby in the county hospital. Why don't they watch those things?

HANNAH (*who has smiled maliciously as Cora moved the bowl*). Who's going to watch 'em?

CORA. It was a very dangerous Caesarian operation. Maybe that always happens when the mother is under age. What's the name of that man who boards with your sister?

HANNAH. Now you can go over and ask Doc Morris about the girl — and he can tell you, the way he did that time about cats, which you never gotten straight.

CORA. I asked you what is the name of that man.

HANNAH. I don't know which you mean. She's got five boarders regular.

CORA. He was walking up and down in front of the factory, the way they've been doing and wasting their time, and I said good morning and he didn't answer. I said it again and he walked to the other side. So I went right up and told him I didn't like rudeness —

HANNAH: That's Odave. He's only been here a year. Maybe that's not time enough to fall in love with the Rodman family. (*Thoughtfully*) You know, Miss Cora, they tell me that in places where there's a strike, the men forget sometimes to bow to the boss's sister.

CORA. There is never any need for rudeness.

HANNAH. She's getting a new boarder. Guess he's moved in by now. Leo Whalen.

CORA (*after a pause*). That's very wrong of your sister. And disloyal of you to let her. He's a bad character—

HANNAH. How do you know? You never spoke to him.

CORA. I know why he's here. That's enough. He's trying to make trouble and you know it. That's what he came here for—

HANNAH. Not my business. She's in the boardinghouse business and it's open to anybody who don't steal. (*Picks up bowl of peas and starts to exit*) Anyway, she likes him. Lots of people here like him. (*So casually that it has meaning*) Women, too, I guess.

(*She passes Henry Ellicott, who is entering. He has on a hat and overcoat. He is about forty, good-looking in a worldly kind of way.*)

ELLICOTT. Good morning. Did anyone call me, Cora?

CORA (*as he takes off his coat*). A woman called you about a month ago. I told you about that, although I don't see why she called you here.

ELLICOTT. You told me about that. Several times.

CORA. She hasn't called you since. I think I gave her to understand that you should conduct your affairs at your own house.

ELLICOTT. I'm not talking about women, Cora. I'm talking about my office.

CORA. *They* did *not* call.

HANNAH (*as Ellicott crosses to desk*). You be here for lunch? We got a good lunch.

CORA. Hannah, will you please allow *me* to invite Mr. Ellicott for lunch?

ELLICOTT. You, and you alone, may invite me to lunch.

CORA (*to Hannah*). *I* have invited Mr. Ellicott to lunch.

(*Hannah nods, pleased at the effect she has had on Cora, then exits.*)

ELLICOTT. You put your foot down very firmly on that important matter. Where is Julie? (*He is moving around the room.*)

CORA (*holds out a small box*). Don't move around so. Want one? They're pepsin drops with chocolate. Doctor Morris says they're good for me. I'm going to get a dog this week. I've ordered it. A male this time. Females are too difficult to take care of during, er, during. I was reading only this morning about a thirteen-year-old girl who had a baby. You travel around. Have you ever seen that before?

ELLICOTT. I haven't actually seen it. But they tell me that in warm countries —

CORA. In *warm* countries. But not in Cleveland. (*He goes to the window, and after a second she says softly*) Julie is out, Henry.

ELLICOTT. Where is she?

CORA (*as if she had been waiting for it*). I don't know. I don't spy on Julie.

ELLICOTT (*turns and looks at her*). You've such a pleasant way of saying things. (*Then he looks at his watch and goes to the telephone, dials a number*) This is Mr. Ellicott. Joe still there? (*To Cora*) Andrew around?

CORA. I suppose so. I shall have to move my room if he doesn't stop walking up and down in the library all night. I sleep badly enough anyway and if a pin drops it wakes me. I've always been like that —

ELLICOTT (*into phone*). Joe? I've been waiting for you to call. Everything all right? Good. (*Andrew Rodman comes in through the library doors. He has a pleasant, serious face. His motions are those of a man who is puzzled and tired. He crosses to the desk and looks at some papers, idly, as he listens to Ellicott on the phone*) Take them off a few at a time. Then drive Wilkie up to Mr. Rodman's. (*Gets up, to Andrew*) That's good. They'll be off the train about lunch-time. The train will come in on the siding. They won't be noticed much.

ANDREW. Are these high-jinks necessary? As long as they're coming, let them in at the station.

ELLICOTT. There's no sense walking into trouble.

ANDREW (*nods his head*). So you're admitting now that there might be trouble? That they might not see it the way — the way we do?

CORA. But why should there be any trouble? We can run the factory when we want to. It's ours. I don't understand why there should be any trouble —

ELLICOTT (*sharply*). I didn't say there'd be any trouble.

CORA (*placatingly to Andrew*). Now you see. Henry says there won't be a bit of trouble.

ELLICOTT (*smiles, obviously irritated*). Andrew, do we have to start this all over again now?

ANDREW. No. Don't pay any attention to me. We've made up our minds and that's that.

ELLICOTT. And a damn good thing! The loan's okay now. But Nelson says you couldn't've gotten a nickel in Cleveland if you hadn't made this decision. He had to swear to them that you wouldn't change your mind again.

CORA. See? As long as you have to spend the money anyway, you should have hired these new workers weeks ago. The way Henry and I told you to.

ANDREW. I didn't want to do it that way. I don't now.

CORA. No, of course you didn't. You thought kind talk and reason would do it. Well, it didn't work, did it? Papa would have known what to do. And without wasting time and money. Papa would have known —

(Her speech is interrupted by Julie Rodman, who comes in from the porch windows. She is a very attractive, slim, slightly tired-looking woman of about thirty-two. She is wearing a sweater and skirt, low shoes, a loose tweed coat, no hat. Her clothes are expensive and careless.)

JULIE (*slowly, as if she didn't expect the room to be full: as if thinking of something else*). Good morning.

CORA. The man was here about the tree planting. I told him that you always did that. Forgetting about things.

JULIE. I did forget. You could have told him about the planting.

CORA. You know my rules. Not to interfere.

JULIE. There are so many rules. It's hard to remember them all. It's funny to go walking now. The Carlsen kids were coming from school. (*Smiles*) They had a bad minute wondering whether to say hello to me. (*Andrew has moved on her speech as if he knew what she meant, and didn't like hearing it. She has gone to the decanters on the table*) Sherry? It's cold.

ELLICOTT. Your walks take you in all directions, don't they?

JULIE (*without answering, turns to Andrew, motions to sherry glass*). Andy? Do you good.

ANDREW. No, darling. (*As he gathers up papers*) I have work to do before lunch.

ELLICOTT. Wilkie should be here soon.

ANDREW (*slowly, at door*). I haven't forgotten.

JULIE (*gently*). You look so tired.

CORA. Certainly he looks tired. He's worn himself out for no reason. Papa would have settled this strike weeks ago —

ANDREW (*at door, smiles, speaks slowly*). Yes. I suppose so. Maybe Papa was a better man than I am.

CORA (*gets up, gently to Julie*). I will see about the trees. Before my headache gets worse. (*Julie begins to protest, but is interrupted by Cora's wheeling sharply on Ellicott as if she had just thought of something*) Incidentally, I hope you didn't touch my securities for this loan? You are my lawyer. You must protect me —

ELLICOTT (*smiles*). Certainly. Increased protection, increased fees.

CORA. I'm unmarried. It's different with me. I have no one to support me. It's different when you're not married —

ELLICOTT. Unfortunately, in the business world there is no reward for virginity. (*Sharply, quickly, as he sees the question coming again*) No. Andrew wouldn't let me take your securities. I don't know why —

CORA (*pleasantly now*). Because I'm his sister.

ELLICOTT. Really? Is that the reason? (*Annoyed at her sudden turn to good nature*) However, when it's cleaned up, you will pay your part of the expenses.

CORA. I don't understand that.

ELLICOTT. Then it's not because I haven't tried to explain it to you. You own as much of the factory as Andy does. As you share the profits, you must share the losses.

CORA. Why should I pay for Andrew's mistakes? If we'd been able to make him do this three weeks ago —

ELLICOTT. You will still be well this side of starvation. You can have two pieces of cake instead of your usual three.

CORA. I shall have to talk the losses business over with Andrew. I don't understand why — (*As if she had just heard him*) And I shall eat just as much as I please. Just as much as I please. (*She closes the door as Ellicott looks after her.*)

JULIE (*smiling, watching him*). Cora worries you too much.

ELLICOTT. And you, happily, very little. She seems to be watching you these days — (*As her face changes*) Or am I imagining it? Where have you been, Julie?

JULIE. Walking.

ELLICOTT. In town?

JULIE. I must be getting old. I don't like autumn anymore.

The river is full of leaves and it was too cold to walk very far.

ELLICOTT. Weren't you in town?

JULIE (*very deliberate*). The storm broke the big elm. The heavy branch is lying in the river. There's a big lizard on the branch that looks as if it grew there —

ELLICOTT. You were near the strike office. I saw you. I think Cora saw you, too.

JULIE (*annoyed*). Really? Were you both hiding?

ELLICOTT. That's the second time you've lied about being in town. Why?

JULIE. Maybe because I like to lie. Maybe it's because I'm tired of your questions.

ELLICOTT (*quietly*). I don't like your being tired. (*After a second*) I'm going down to White Sulphur when things are cleared up here. Are you coming?

JULIE. No.

ELLICOTT (*suddenly, sharply*). I want to know where we stand, Julie. It's time for me to know.

JULIE (*lightly, kindly*). We stand nowhere. We've always stood nowhere. I knew about you — and you knew about me. (*Quickly*) Staying for lunch?

ELLICOTT. Yes, I knew about you. And what I didn't know our friends told me. (*Carefully*) But I find, more to my surprise than to yours, that you mean something to me. I think you have for a long time.

JULIE. I don't think so. (*Kindly*) Look. It doesn't mean anything to me — and that's where I've got to quit.

ELLICOTT. "And that's where I've got to quit." There isn't a man living who doesn't know about the woman who allows herself anything, but who invents the one rule that will keep her this side of what she thinks is respectable. She'll lie, but not on Thursdays. She'll sleep with you, but not immediately after lunch. Usually it's funny. In your case, for me, it's not so funny. (*Angrily*) What the hell did you expect me to mean to you?

JULIE (*puts her hand on his arm*). What did I expect you to mean to me? I don't know. I haven't any excuse, really. I've hoped for a very long time that everybody or anybody would mean something. (*Smiles*) Things start as hopes and end up as habits. (*Earnestly*) Look. Don't let's talk about it.

You like civilized conversations about love too much, and I like them too little. One of the things that brings people like you and me together is the understanding that there won't be any talk about it at the end.

ELLICOTT. That's true. And it's too callous for me.

JULIE (*violently*). And for me, too. That's why I don't like it. I'm ashamed of its callousness — and I don't want any more of it. I don't mean to hurt you. (*She gets up, smiles, takes off her coat*) I asked you if you were staying for lunch.

ELLICOTT (*after a second, watching her*). Yes, I'm staying. If you ever saw what you wanted, Julie, would you know it?

JULIE (*quickly, unconsciously, very seriously, as if to herself*). Yes. I knew it. I knew about it quick.

ELLICOTT (*suddenly wheels about and takes her arm, tightly*). That's foolish what you're saying. Too foolish to believe. (*Tensely*) And what's more important, it's dangerous. Don't start anything, Julie —

JULIE (*softly*). I don't know what you are talking about.

(*They stand for a second as they are. He does not release her arm until the window-doors open and Thomas Firth, followed by Leo Whalen, appears on the porch. Then he quickly releases her arm and moves away. Firth taps on the window-wood. He is a big, lean, middle-aged American workingman. He is obviously nervous and excited. Whalen is attractive in a simple, clean, undistinguished way. All his movements from this moment until the end of the play show calmness, and are the movements of a man who knows he can take care of himself.*)

FIRTH. Mrs. Rodman.

JULIE. Oh. (*Then cordially*) Hello, Tom. (*To Whalen, her tone changed and nervous*) Hello, Mr. Whalen. Come in.

ELLICOTT (*to both*). Good morning.

FIRTH. I want to see Andrew. I came to see him.

JULIE (*surprised at the tenseness of his tone*). Yes. But come in, won't you? (*Abruptly Firth steps into the room, standing straight and rigid. Whalen moves in casually*) I thought you were leaving us, Mr. Whalen. I haven't seen you in town the last few days.

WHALEN. Leaving? Not for a while yet.

ELLICOTT (*to Firth*). Andrew's busy. Will I do?

FIRTH. No.

JULIE (*moves to the wall bell, presses it, speaks nervously to Whalen*). I thought — I thought perhaps you would come and have dinner with us one night —

WHALEN (*laughs*). The boss asks me for dinner. Well, that's very pleasant. It's never happened to me before. (*Looks at Firth*) But strange things happen in this town.

FIRTH. Mrs. Rodman, can I see Andrew now?

(*Lucy appears at the door.*)

JULIE. Tell Mr. Rodman that Tom Firth is here and wants to see him. (*Lucy disappears. To Whalen*) Why should that be so strange? We don't get many visitors here and because you and my husband happen to be, well, happen to think differently, is no reason we can't eat together.

WHALEN (*pleasantly*). In my business it's a good reason.

ELLICOTT. Julie. Whalen is in the business of hating. It pays well, I imagine.

WHALEN. Very well. All labor organizers are racketeers, Mr. Ellicott, as you and I both know from the papers. (*He has started to roll a cigarette. Quickly Julie offers him a box from the table*) But there's no hate *here*. The boss loves the workers, and the workers — (*To Firth*) the worker — loves the boss. In other towns I've heard that called something else.

FIRTH. Shut up.

(*There is a second's embarrassed silence. Whalen, however, is pleased.*)

JULIE (*to Whalen*). Old Mrs. Hicks tells me you like our river. That you walk there very often.

WHALEN. Yes. You've got a nice river. You've kept it clean.

JULIE (*to Whalen*). When I first moved here I used to fish in it. Do you like to fish?

WHALEN. Yes. Very much. (*To Firth*) Maybe Mr. Rodman doesn't want to see you.

FIRTH. You don't have to wait.

ELLICOTT (*to Whalen*). No. I'm sure you're busy —

WHALEN. I'll wait. (*To Julie*) If it's all right.

JULIE (*smiles warmly, quickly*). It's very all right.

FIRTH (*to Whalen*). You're staying to watch. I don't need you to watch me. You and nobody is going to make me act blind. You and nobody is going to make me hate a man who's been my friend.

WHALEN (*to Firth*). I don't give a damn who you hate and

who you love. I'm trying to see that that Christian heart of yours doesn't do too much harm.

(*On Whalen's words, Firth moves toward him angrily, and then turns and stands rigidly as Andrew comes into the room.*)

ANDREW (*slowly*). Hello, Tom. (*Less friendly*) Hello, Mr. Whalen.

FIRTH. Andrew, I went out on strike with the rest. That was my duty. But I stood by you in a lot of ways.

WHALEN (*unpleasantly*). He did. I can vouch for it.

FIRTH. We've all been trying to see it from both our sides and we've been friends about it —

WHALEN. Ask your question.

FIRTH. He says that a trainload of strikebreakers came through Callom Junction this morning. And I said I didn't believe it. I said you didn't know no more about things like that than we did, and that I knew you —

ANDREW. Tom, I wanted to talk to you this afternoon.

ELLICOTT. Which would still be wisest. This afternoon.

FIRTH. I'm here. I don't want to wait. Talk to me now. (*After a second's silence, speaks to Whalen over his shoulder*) Read him that fool thing.

WHALEN (*takes a telegram from his pocket, reads it in a pleasant, unconcerned way*). "Wilkie on way probably fifty sixty of the boys including Gans Easter Malloy which gives you rough idea stop Easter just out of jail with toothache so watch your heart and anything else." That's from a friend of mine in Cleveland. He's a wit.

FIRTH. I don't know about these people he's talking about. And neither do you. That's why I know it's got to be wrong. (*Watches Andrew, gets no answer, then slowly, firmly*) Andrew. It's got to be wrong.

ANDREW. Tom, I've tried to explain. I tried from the first day you came to me. (*Touches a paper on the desk, looks at it*) The figures are here. They're as much yours to see as they are mine.

FIRTH. I don't have to see 'em again.

ANDREW. You don't. But I have to see them again and again and again. We've got to sell the brushes we make.

WHALEN. Some places make what they can sell.

ANDREW (*sharply*). Yes. They make them cheaper than we do — (*Slowly*) and they make them cheaper because they cost less. You know that Partee cut salaries two years ago —

FIRTH. I know that. I told you to cut us a little. That we'd take a little for you. And I told you to make three, four model brushes, not eighteen —

ANDREW. I can't, against the others.

WHALEN. Then make them the way they make them.

ANDREW. You mean cheaper brushes? Ask Tom what he thinks of that.

FIRTH. We make the best brush in America.

ANDREW (*to Firth*). You tell me a way out, I'll take it. Seven years ago we were making a lot of money. (*Touches the paper*) I can't stay in business losing it this way. We'd be out in another year.

WHALEN. You haven't been answering his question, Mr. Rodman.

ANDREW. I'm doing my best to answer him. (*After a second*) I knew the cuts had to come. I tried hard to keep them off as long as I could. I thought you'd see that the only way you could stay working and I could stay working was if we took the bad times together. I couldn't do anything else.

FIRTH. And I know we can't live on forty-cent piecework. I told you it was too big a cut. And I told you they wouldn't take it.

ANDREW. Do you think I want to cut you that way? It's just for a little while —

FIRTH. And who's going to pay our bills for the little while?

ANDREW (*shakes his head*). I know. I don't blame you. But you mustn't blame us, either.

FIRTH (*quickly*). Who's us?

ANDREW. Me, I mean. That's the story. I wish I'd known what else to do.

(*Slowly Whalen rises, smiling. Firth turns and looks at him, looks around the room, and then crosses quickly to Andrew as if he didn't believe the answer had been made.*)

FIRTH. All right. We knew all that. That's what I been saying to myself, and I ain't got the answer for either of us. (*Hits the table*) But that's something between us to settle. We ain't foreigners. Our people came here with your people, and worked along with them and helped them, too. In 'twelve when they came and tried to make a union, we threw 'em out. There ain't never been any trouble here, Andrew —

ELLICOTT (*to Andrew*). It's late.

FIRTH. I ain't believing that you're bringing foreigners —

ANDREW (*slowly*). You've been out three weeks. The place had to start running again.

FIRTH (*slowly*). You mean you're giving away our jobs. You mean other people are taking our work — (*Breaks off sharply and stands staring at Andrew, shaking his head.*)

WHALEN. Sad to grow up, isn't it? (*To Firth*) Well, come on. Cry at home. You've wasted enough time now. The world is a bad place and you're a big boy.

ELLICOTT (*to Firth*). You could have talked this over with me. It may be all right for you to walk out, but it is also all right for Andrew to keep his own machines going his own way.

FIRTH (*shouting*). And this was his way of keeping 'em going, eh? I could've known you had a hand in it.

ELLICOTT (*sharply*). He's got to start making brushes again. If you've made up your mind not to make them, then somebody else has to.

WHALEN. No? You're kidding. (*To Andrew*) Who sold you the idea Wilkie's boys can run machines? (*Makes the motion of pointing a pistol*) That's the kind they meant. That's the kind you'll get run — and they do that fine. (*To Firth*) And be sure you're there to make speeches about the boat your grandfather came over on, and God is love, and your heart's breaking. Turn the other cheek, and crawl back. It hurts less that way, I guess.

FIRTH (*slowly*). I told the boys we'd be settling it like friends. I was wrong. (*To Whalen*) I won't be turning the other cheek. I won't be crawling back. Nobody else will either. (*Without turning to look at Andrew, he moves quickly to the window and out.*)

ELLICOTT (*slowly, to Whalen*). We don't want trouble here. We're sorry that you do want it. But I suppose that's your job.

WHALEN. Sometimes it is. Sometimes it isn't. But what you and I want won't make much difference. When the guns start popping and the skulls start cracking, they won't be thinking about us.

ANDREW (*angrily*). There won't be any guns here — on either side.

ELLICOTT. Unless you have them.

WHALEN. I? No, sir. I'm scared to death of them. (*To Andrew, moving toward the window*) I hope you're right, Mr. Rodman.

(*As Whalen moves toward the window the front doorbell starts to ring, steadily, loudly. They have all turned, startled by it. Hannah, calm, quiet, appears in the door.*)

JULIE. What is it, Hannah?

HANNAH. Lucy's watching my oven so the things don't burn.

ANDREW (*looking at her*). Then you answer it, Hannah.

HANNAH. No, Mr. Andrew. If what I heard is right, that's one bell I ain't going to answer. I can't help what other people do, but I don't have to help 'em out.

JULIE. Hannah —

HANNAH. And Lucy can't answer because she's watching my oven so the things don't burn. (*Ellicott, quickly, angrily, moves past Hannah and out into the hall. To Whalen*) Like boarding at my sister's?

WHALEN. Sure. It's a good place. (*Smiles at her*) I'm no boarder, I'm charity.

HANNAH. She can afford it. (*She exits.*)

(*Whalen, in the first quick motion he has made, moves to Andrew's desk, leans over it, speaks tensely, hurriedly.*)

WHALEN. Rodman. It's hard to believe, but I'm believing it. You don't know (*He points toward center doors*) about things like this. I do. This is a nice town. I hate to see it hurt. (*Then quietly*) Give them their sixty-cent hour. Give them their union. They'll be back to work in ten minutes.

ANDREW. They can have any union they want. But I can't pay the salaries. I want to — and I can't. I don't know what you've seen in the past. But there won't be any trouble here. I won't let there be. I hope you won't either.

(*Ellicott, followed by Samuel Wilkie, comes in from the hall. Wilkie is of medium height, heavy. He looks like any husky businessman. Directly behind him are Mossie Dowel and Joe Easter. Mossie is fat and pleasant-looking. Easter is thin, nervous, tough. Mossie and Easter stand stiffly at the door.*)

WILKIE. Mr. Rodman. I'm Samuel Wilkie. (*He bows to Julie*) How do you do?

ELLICOTT (*as Wilkie looks at Whalen*). This is Mr. Whalen. You'll meet, I think.

WHALEN (*pleasantly*). I've heard of Mr. Wilkie.

WILKIE. Seems I've heard of you, too. (*To the others*) We're in the same line, you might say.

WHALEN. You knew my friend Cliff Taylor?

WILKIE. I knew who he was.

WHALEN (*conversationally to the others*). Taylor was an organizer. He had his throat cut last year in Gainesville.

WILKIE. They tell me he was a nice guy.

WHALEN. Yeah. And they tell me a side-burn guy did it. He worked for you, I think, and he played with knives a lot.

WILKIE (*thoughtfully*). No. I don't think he worked for me. But you can't tell. Lot of people come in and out of the office. Were you in Gainesville?

WHALEN (*laughs*). No. (*Touches his throat*) Fortunately, I was in Akron.

WILKIE. Now we're talking. That's the job I wanted. That's money for you. But they pieced it out in New York. You been here long?

WHALEN. About two weeks. I haven't done much. How many men you got?

WILKIE. Fifty-two, three. (*Whalen says* "um") Yes. That's what I say. I been trying to tell these gentlemen that it isn't enough. Better to spend it now than later. (*Hastily, as he sees Ellicott's face*) But they're paying, and they should know.

ANDREW. The men with you are good brush makers?

WILKIE (*puzzled, turns to look at Whalen, who is smiling*). Good? Well, we'll hope so.

WHALEN (*laughs*). They are also skilled motormen, miners, car loaders, longshoremen — and anything you like. They're the best.

WILKIE (*laughs*). Now that's the kind of recommendation we want. (*To Whalen*) How many men you signed? What kind?

ANDREW. What I need, and what I ordered, were brush workers.

WILKIE (*looks at him*). We'll see how it works out.

WHALEN. Hundred and ninety-two men and not bad for a new union. Decent and — (*Looks at Wilkie*) peaceful, the right way.

WILKIE (*heartily*). And that's the way we like it.

WHALEN (*laughs*). Yes. That's the way we like it.

ELLICOTT. If you gentlemen are finished with your conference, perhaps, Wilkie —

WHALEN. Certainly. I talk too much. (*Moves toward windows, and as he passes Julie*) And if I promise not to talk at all, may I still walk by your river?

JULIE (*smiles*). Yes. But I hope you will talk. I like to listen.

(*As he exits, he collides with Cora, who is coming in from the porch.*)

WHALEN. Oh. Sorry.

JULIE. This is Mr. Whalen, Cora. (*Cora looks up at him, then lowers her eyes, says "Hum," and marches past him into the room. Whalen looks at her, amazed, then grins and runs off the porch. Julie speaks to Cora*) Don't do that in my house again.

CORA. What? What did you say to me?

JULIE. I said you were not to do that in my house again.

LUCY (*at door*). Lunch is ready, Mrs. Rodman.

ELLICOTT (*looks at Julie*). You're very upset, aren't you?

CORA. How dare you talk to me that way —

JULIE (*to Andrew, touching his arm*). I'm sorry, Andy.

ANDREW. There's nothing to be sorry for, darling.

CORA (*to Julie*). So it's *your* house now? My father built it, but it's your house now.

JULIE. Please. I'm sorry.

CORA. You've thought that all these years. It's very strange that you waited to tell me until now, about *that* man —

ANDREW (*sharply*). Stop that silly shouting.

JULIE. I don't want lunch, Andy. Go in without me.

(*She pats his arm and exits quickly through library door. Cora sits down and begins to sniffle. Andrew and Ellicott stare after Julie.*)

WILKIE (*after a moment*). Um.

ELLICOTT (*turns*). It's late. You'd better have lunch here, Wilkie. It'll save time.

ANDREW (*has turned and is looking at Mossie and Joe*). Who are these gentlemen, Mr. Wilkie?

WILKIE. Mr. Easter, Mr. Dowell. I'll be staying at the hotel. They'll be here with you. (*To Ellicott*) Thank you. Can I wash up?

ANDREW. Staying here? Why should they be staying here? (*To Cora, who is sniffling and arranging the figures in the cabinet*) Please stop that, Cora.

WILKIE. They're here to take good care of you and your family, Mr. Rodman. You won't have anything to worry about.

ANDREW (*carefully*). I don't understand what you are talking about. Neither I nor my family need any taking care of.

WILKIE. I hope not. I believe not. But I don't like taking chances with people who pay my bills.

ANDREW (*to Ellicott*). What kind of nonsense is this?

CORA. It's not nonsense. It's not nonsense. I'm paying my share of this and it's my house, too, and if Julie is going to have people like that around — (*Motions toward window*) in and out of the house, we will all need protection. She treats that man like —

ELLICOTT (*sharply*). Cora.

CORA. I insist on my rights. If you don't care what happens to me, then *I* must care —

ANDREW (*wearily, to Wilkie*). My sister needs protection. It makes no difference. (*Starts slowly for the door.*)

LUCY (*back at door*). Lunch is getting cold.

ANDREW (*at door, over his shoulder to Ellicott*). I don't want lunch. Go ahead.

ELLICOTT (*stares after him for a moment. Then to Cora*). We're a small party. Let's go in now. You can take up the hysterics again after lunch. (*Cora rises, sweeps past him, exits.*)

ELLICOTT (*as he starts out, to Wilkie*). Miss Rodman is a nervous lady.

WILKIE. They're all nervous, aren't they?

(*Without answering, Ellicott exits.*)

MOSSIE. It's like a society picture, what they were doing. (*Touches his throat*) They talk so high (*Watches Wilkie who is standing in the middle of the room*) You look like you're puzzling something, boss. What's a brush worker? (*He cracks his knuckles.*)

WILKIE (*laughs*). I don't know. Somebody who makes a brush, I guess.

EASTER (*suddenly, as Mossie cracks knuckles again*). For Christ's sake quit that. You're getting me crazy.

WILKIE (*turns*). Sit down. Both of you. Try to act like you've been in a house with a bathroom before. (*Looks at Easter*) I don't want to have to worry about your nerves this time. (*He exits.*)

MOSSIE (*sits down near cabinet*). I couldn't follow what they were saying. They talk fast, don't they? (*Easter has wandered over to desk. Idly he looks at papers on it, examines a few things on it*) They were mad. I got that. But it don't sound bad when you talk high. (*He cracks his knuckles.*)

EASTER. I liked it for myself in Cleveland. Fifty of us. What kind of piker job is this? That Wilkie goes crazy when he smells a dollar. Always has.

MOSSIE. I don't get what he's doing. The boys sit in the factory and we sit here, huh? What's that for?

EASTER. Something he made up. We're going to get a lot extra sitting here.

MOSSIE (*cheerfully*). Well, we're eating on him. (*Mossie cracks his knuckles.*)

EASTER. Just keep that up for a few days, hear me? I can feed myself. I told him that.

MOSSIE (*laughs*). Yeah. But it tastes better when somebody else buys it.

EASTER. There might be streetcar trouble on the coast next month. I found out. I told him about it. So would he stay and wait and play for big stuff? No. He's got to take this, 'cause they let him smell a dollar bill first.

MOSSIE (*thoughtfully*). Well, he ain't working for us. He don't care about us. Jesus Christ. Passing up streetcar work. He made enough money in New Orleans to keep him for a year.

EASTER. So did you.

MOSSIE. And so did you. I got some of mine yet. I took a little insurance for my mother. That's what you should've done. Instead of that sucker diamond Phil walked you in to —

EASTER (*irritated*). You said that before. (*Looks at his watch*) What do we do? Cook our food in here?

MOSSIE. They couldn't invite us to eat inside. We're out here protecting her. (*Cracks his knuckles. During his next speech Easter has idly started to play with a cigarette lighter on the desk. After the second light, it stops working. He picks up a paper-knife and begins fixing it. Mossie looks down at his hand, smiles*) That's a good one. Protecting her. But there ain't even an inch anymore to protect. But the other one looks good. You can't tell about people like this. They say, in the papers, talking fine, what they wouldn't do, and then they sneak off and take a shot in bed at the first thing that comes along — (*He has cracked his knuckles again. Quickly, Easter throws the paper-knife at him. Mossie ducks, the knife misses him and knocks over a vase on a small table.*

Slowly, Mossie adjusts his chair, shakes his head, stares at the vase) Starting it again, huh? When you get time, Joe, you ought to take a rest cure. Ain't natural to be so nervous. (*Shakes his head, looking at the vase*) You certainly ain't neat with other people's things.

Curtain

Act Two

Scene 1.

SCENE: *Same as Act One. Four weeks later.*

AT RISE: *Mossie Dowel is seated and Joe Easter is standing at the table between the windows. They are playing poker. Wilkie, in hat and overcoat, is sitting on the arm of a chair, looking idly out of the window. The radio is playing softly. For a few seconds after the rise of the curtain there are no sounds but the shuffling of cards, the sound of money on the table, the radio.*

EASTER (*after a second, sharply*). All right. All right. Show 'em. Stop flirting with 'em.

(*Mossie puts his hand down, smiles, rakes in the center money. Easter puts down his cards, crosses to radio, angrily snaps it off.*)

MOSSIE. Funny. Losers never like music. It's good luck for me, to the contrary. (*To Wilkie*) It's after nine. Must be something big keeping you out of bed.

EASTER. It's got to be money to keep him out of those woolen nightgowns.

WILKIE. It's payday, or it should be. That always gives me insomnia. (*They have started to play again*) Ellicott been here?

EASTER. Nope.

MOSSIE. He's coming. Always is. Looking for Mrs. Rodman with the legs.

EASTER (*to Wilkie, pointing upstairs*). You think Rodman knows about 'em?

WILKIE (*unpleasantly*). What do you know?

MOSSIE. What does he know? He's guessing. He sees it everywhere. It comes from watching the flies go to it on cell doors.

WILKIE (*sharply, to Easter*). I'd get the shakedown out of my head, if I were you.

EASTER. You think I'm crazy? (*Mossie cracks his knuckles*) Deal 'em. And stop that cracking. (*He wins a small hand and begins to shuffle the cards. Maliciously, casually to Wilkie*) So things ain't going so good, huh?

MOSSIE (*cheerfully*). It's nice and easy here. I like a rest job once in a while.

WILKIE. Another few weeks like this and you'll get a long rest.

MOSSIE. It ain't our fault, Sam.

EASTER. When you got nothing to do, we can't do it for you.

MOSSIE. Finger tried a fight. Eddie tried a fight. I even had Sig chase the old guy Firth's girl around. (*Puzzled*) Any guy'd protect his thirteen-year-old kid.

EASTER. Three sevens.

MOSSIE. But nobody'll fight. No matter what you do, they don't fight. Must be some kind of new religion, maybe. (*Turns up his hand, cracks his knuckles*) Three nines.

EASTER (*through his teeth*). They *are* running pretty easy the last two days, huh? (*To Wilkie*) I'm crazy for this place. Losing to him and following that dame around.

WILKIE. Just keep on doing it.

(*Ellicott appears at the center doors. He looks around the room, then after a second.*)

ELLICOTT. Good evening. I hear you were looking for me today. You're active on payday, aren't you?

WILKIE. Yes, sir. (*Pointing to desk*) The account's over there.

ELLICOTT (*as he passes Mossie and Joe*). I'm glad to see that nothing has disturbed your game, gentlemen. (*Picks up the sheet*) Yes. It's a very full account. Well, you're right to get it while you can. I'm not so sure how many more paydays there are going to be. You do nothing and your bills get bigger.

WILKIE. That's the way it seems to have worked out.

ELLICOTT. The Cincinnati *Herald* is crying its eyes out tonight over model town being overrun with toughs. None of that helps any. (*Looking at Mossie and Joe*) Do you think they could have meant these gentlemen and the other friends you brought with you?

WILKIE. I read the papers. (*Looks speculatively at Mossie and Joe*) They don't look like anything Oscar Wilde would have wanted, do they? (*Gets up*) Well, I know I haven't done too much, and I like it less than you. We're in hunting country. You didn't tell me that.

ELLICOTT. What?

WILKIE. The people around here hunt. In the season, I mean. That right?

ELLICOTT. What's that got to do with it?

WILKIE. It's got a lot to do with it. Every man for five miles owns a gun. Flintlocks, maybe, but clean. But they won't use 'em on me. They won't use 'em at all. You know why? Because somebody in Cleveland made a mistake and sent down a smart organizer. He won't let 'em use 'em. There hasn't even been a nose bleed for me to stop. I can't work with nothing.

ELLICOTT. We didn't bargain to cut the plan out for you. That's your business, and you've done a bad job of it.

WILKIE. Now, now. It's not all my fault. Even if there had been something to do, I couldn't have done it. Because I'm working for a man who doesn't want me to do anything. I'm working for a man who doesn't want me to work for him. That's a bad set-up, Mr. Ellicott.

ELLICOTT (*starting to exit, slowly*). You'd better come up and see Mr. Rodman. As a lawyer I have found that for my client's own good, it is often wise not to ask his permission on little details.

(*Wilkie has turned to stare at him as he reaches the door and passes Cora, who is entering.*)

CORA (*to Ellicott*). Don't you ever stay in your own house anymore? There are people who can never stay quietly at home and read a book. (*He exits without answering her*) Good evening. Rain. Rain. Rain. Are there several types of detectives, Mr. Wilkie?

WILKIE. Only one kind, Miss Rodman. Lousy.

CORA. I mean, very funny things are happening here. Things are missing from the pantry — (*Coquettishly*) Or is that too unimportant work for you?

WILKIE. Not at all. I don't seem to be doing much else.

CORA (*goes to cabinet*). On Thursday, I was taking my weekly supply list. Just as a matter of routine. Mrs. Rodman was out —

WILKIE. Mrs. Rodman is out a good deal, isn't she?

CORA. Yes, Mrs. Rodman always manages to go off by herself. Well, when I looked in the closet I was amazed to find that at least eight or ten dollars' worth of canned goods —

WILKIE (*rises, politely*). Mr. Dowel is a specialist at just such detection. He's at your service, Miss Rodman. I'll be down later and we can lay our trap. (*He exits.*)

MOSSIE (*giggles*). Sure. Who, me? Sure.

CORA. I like to see a nice little card game. Do you know that nightclub singer who got killed in the paper this morning?

MOSSIE. No ma'am.

EASTER (*motioning to the cards*). Beat the straight.

MOSSIE. Easy. (*He rakes in the money as Easter stares at him.*)

CORA (*to Easter*). My. You were beaten. Are you playing for money?

(*Hannah enters with a tray of drinks which she puts on the other side of the room. Cora watches her as she empties ashtrays into a saucer.*)

HANNAH (*slamming ashtray on table, pointing to the floor*). Ain't it *more* trouble to lean over the ashtrays to get the ashes on the rug?

MOSSIE. My Ma used to say ashes were good for rugs.

HANNAH. Your Ma never saw a rug.

CORA. Hannah. We were just talking about the things that were stolen from the pantry.

HANNAH. Were you now? Anybody in jail?

CORA. It's ridiculous that you shouldn't know where they've disappeared to —

HANNAH (*has picked up Joe's cigarette which is lying on the table, and carefully placed the lighted end nearer the wood*). Put it like this. It'll burn the table faster.

CORA. Hannah! You haven't been listening to a word I've said — (*Andrew enters from the rear library door. Goes to desk*) Henry and Mr. Wilkie are upstairs. Henry's been here three times today. In, out. In, out.

ANDREW (*as Easter has noisily slammed down his cards*). Would you play in the other room, please?

MOSSIE (*softly, not paying any attention and not moving*). Yes, sir.

CORA (*as Hannah goes to the door*). Andrew. It's time for you to know that groceries have been missing from the kitchen. Regularly. Hannah refuses to tell me who's been doing it and I can't allow it to go on. I have asked Mr. Wilkie to take a hand.

HANNAH (*turning*). Have you? (*Laughs. The noise of the game, the words, the raking in of the money has become sharp once more.*)

ANDREW. *Get out of this room.* (*Mossie and Easter turn, surprised. Then slowly, without hurry, they gather up their things and move out.*)

CORA (*after a second*). Andrew. I was telling you that —

HANNAH (*crossing to him quickly*). Miss Cora was telling you that food's been missing. It has. I've been taking it. I wish I could've taken more. (*Motions with her hand toward windows*) People need it. Do what you want about it, Mr. Andrew.

ANDREW (*slowly, staring at her*). I don't want to do anything about it, Hannah.

(*Hannah exits. She passes Julie, in hat and coat, entering. For a fraction, Julie draws back when she sees the room is not empty.*)

CORA. Sometimes I think you're crazy. And sometimes I think you are doing things just to humiliate me.

ANDREW. It's raining, darling.

JULIE. I know. But I'd like a walk anyway.

CORA. I say one thing. You say another. Telling her it's all right to steal. What *right* have you to humiliate me in front of servants?

JULIE (*gently*). Cora, do stop nagging at Andy —

CORA. Nagging at him. Nagging at him. He's gone crazy —

ANDREW. I like my wife. Could I ever, anymore, be alone with her? For just a few minutes? And then you can start with me all over again.

CORA (*at door*). Certainly you can be alone. I daresay you have a great many things to ask.

JULIE. She has one of her bad headaches. She's upset. (*Andrew smiles, shakes his head. She looks around the room*) How messy this room looks.

ANDREW (*comes up to her as he speaks*). Our friends have been using it as a club. I don't blame you for wanting to go out. (*Leans down, kisses her hair*) But not tonight, Julie. It's cold and it's raining, and —

JULIE (*slowly*). I want to go.

ANDREW (*moves away from her to chair*). And I'm lonely.

JULIE (*turns, looks at him, puzzled*). You? Lonely?

ANDREW (*smiles*). Yes. I. Lonely. I always thought loneliness meant alone, without people. It means something else.

JULIE (*softly*). That's a late discovery. You're lucky.

ANDREW (*laughs*). Why do people always think it's lucky to find out the simple things long after one should have known them?

JULIE. Because each year you can put off knowing about them gives you one more year of peace.

ANDREW. I don't think so. Unless you can put it off forever. (*Smiles*) I think that's what I was trying to do. But I'm at a bad age to start looking at the world, to start looking at myself. (*Very simply*) It confuses me, Julie. I am mixed up.

JULIE. I know. I've guessed. But I'm no one to help. I'm more mixed up than you.

ANDREW. I've walked up and down this room so much for so many nights, that I'm sick of it and sick of myself. I try to tell myself that I can think things straight, and every night I start the same way — by taking stock of this house. Bums walking in and out, followed by Henry, as undisturbed and as anxious to get down to White Sulphur as always; Hannah, trying to make me into the villain she wants me to be. And Cora. Taking up one unpleasant sentence where she left off the last. (*Softly*) And you. I've missed you.

JULIE. Missed me?

ANDREW (*looks at her, laughs*). You're embarrassed. Strange. We've lived together so long it seems almost indecent to talk about ourselves. We used to talk about ourselves. Remember?

JULIE. Yes. When we were young. We belonged to the time when talk was part of the marriage ceremony. Such cynical, smooth talk, about marriage and life and freedom. Not you. Me, I mean.

ANDREW. I suppose. I remember I used to be a little puzzled by it. But that's what we were then. (*Affectionately*) You always hate yesterday, don't you, Julie?

JULIE. Yes. (*She moves again to window and then turns back suddenly*) Andy. We haven't talked about it much. I knew you didn't want to. But the strike, these people here — it's wrong for you. I know it's wrong for you. Settle it now. It doesn't make any difference who wins —

ANDREW (*sharply*). I don't care who wins. If it were that simple, it would be fine. But it isn't that simple. I can't fit the pieces together. That's what is happening to me. I suddenly don't know where my place in the whole thing is. Don't tell me that's one of the things I was lucky to worry about late. That doesn't do any good. I've only loved two things in my whole life: you and this town. Papa never loved it. He just wanted to be boss and get to Carlsbad for the season. But my grandfather loved it. I think the way I do. Remember how I never wanted to go to Europe or to anyplace else — even when you went? This was my home, these were my people, I didn't want much else. (*With feeling*) But that's been changed. I don't know how. And I don't know where I stand anymore.

JULIE. Try to set it right again.

ANDREW. I wish I knew how. I worked well because I worked one way, without thinking about any other. They worked one way, without thinking about any other. How do I set that right again? Don't you see? It would be like us. If anything ever happened to us we could come together again and pretend it had never happened. But what good would that be if it had really happened, and we couldn't be the same anymore? (*Laughs suddenly*) Well, I'm not the strong man Papa was, and Cora will be down in a minute to remind me of it.

JULIE (*after a second*). Andy. Look at me. You've talked because you wanted help. You wanted me to help you, about yourself. I can't do that. I need help myself. It's a mean thing I'm saying: that I can't stay and listen, because I want to talk myself. I want help, too.

ANDREW (*after a second he nods, smiles*). Where are you going, Julie? Down by the river in the rain?

JULIE. I don't know. Probably the river. I always do. (*Then suddenly, softly*) And perhaps not.

ANDREW (*rises*). Good night, darling.

JULIE. Good night, Andy.

(*He watches her leave, stands looking after her as Mossie opens the library door.*)

MOSSIE. Mr. Ellicott says he's waiting for you. (*Andrew, his eyes on the window, pays no attention to Mossie, who, after a minute*) Mr. Ellicott's waiting.

(*Andrew slowly, without looking at Mossie, exits. Mossie comes into the room, idly, pushes the door shut with his foot as he turns on the radio. The radio is playing something banal and loud. Then he sits down — the corner near the cabinet has no light on it — comfortably leans back to listen to the music. After a second, Easter comes slowly in from the library door. He has a pack of cards in his hand and is playing with them. He crosses to the large table and lays out six or seven of them, face-down on the table.*)

MOSSIE. Funny how a lot of rich people don't like noise. (*No answer*) What you doing, Joe?

EASTER (*through his teeth*). Playing solitaire. (*As he leans very close to look at the backs of the cards*) A new way. (*As Mossie cracks his knuckles*) You doing it worse today. *Stop it.*

MOSSIE (*looks at cabinet*). Screwy. The way she plays with these things. And the other one. Walking up and down, up and down. Tim says she's had him crazy trying to follow her. Bet she's doing it tonight, in the rain. She just went out.

EASTER (*looks up*). Your fingernails need cutting, Mossie.

MOSSIE (*looks at him, laughs*). You buying me a manicure?

EASTER. That'd be better than having you wear them down making marks on the back of these cards — and it wouldn't cost me as much.

MOSSIE. You're nuts.

EASTER (*straightens up*). Put the sixty-five bucks you won over here on the table, Mossie.

MOSSIE. *You* got the cards out of *that* drawer. My God, Joe, you don't mean to tell me you think people like this would fool around with wrong cards — Jesus, Joe, I been telling you you'd better take a rest cure. You're getting too nervous about nothing. You're seeing things. Rodman fixing the cards — (*Laughs, then quietly*) Was it Rodman's dice you made that killing with at Phil's? Joe, you're getting good and batty.

EASTER. The cards are scratched. Put that money on the table.

MOSSIE (*slowly, as he cracks his knuckles, turns toward the radio*). You don't want to come over here and get the dough, Joe, and I don't blame you. So stay over there and quiet yourself. Sit down and whittle yourself some straight dice.

EASTER (*slowly*). For the last time. Put the money on the table.

MOSSIE (*quietly*) No.

(*As he turns back to the radio, Easter, pressing the spring of his knife, lets it fly through the air. Mossie screams softly, pushes with his feet from the ground as he topples from the chair. He falls noisily to the floor. For a second Easter stands watching him, listening to the two soft groans. The groans cease and Easter suddenly begins to move. His movements are quick but aimless, as if he didn't know what to do first. He turns out the lamp nearest him, shuts the library door, and moves to center doors. As he starts to turn the key, the door is violently pushed open by Wilkie. Easter steps back, frightened.*)

WILKIE. What's it? (*Easter looks out in the hall for a second, then quickly closes the door, nods his head toward Mossie and the chair. Wilkie crosses quickly, leans down, looks at Mossie. Then quickly, he moves toward Easter, grabs the lapel of his coat with one hand as he hits him in the face with the other*) You tough guy. You God-damned tough guy.

EASTER (*hoarsely*). I couldn't help it, Sam — he had his gun out.

WILKIE. Yeah, out in his pocket. Okay, the hell with you. (*Lets go his lapels and shoves him.*)

EASTER. Sam. Give me some money. Please. Sam. Please.

WILKIE. I'll give you money — to get your hair waved for the chair.

EASTER. I'm telling you, I'm telling you. What could I do? He tried the gun. I'm telling you — (*Hysterically, as he watches Wilkie move toward telephone*) Sam. Sam. What are you doing —

WILKIE. I'm trying to think which cop would like to have you most. (*Turning on him violently*) This whole damn job wasn't lousy enough. You got to make it better. That boy scout upstairs you got to spell words in front of is going to like this in his house. I can sit in the office now and knit for a year — until they forget you worked for me. (*Picks up telephone*) Well, I'll take you in myself and make a pretty speech about how I didn't know your record, and the only dope who'll believe that is some guy milking a cow, and I'd never have worked for him anyway. You tough guy.

EASTER. No. No. Sam. No —

WILKIE (*as he starts to dial*). You son of a bitch. I can't get a nose bleed where I want it, but you've got to start carving — (*His last words have become slower, as if he were thinking. Then he looks up at Easter, and slowly puts the receiver back on the hook. Stands at the table, staring at it, as Easter watches him. After a long silence*) This way you'd hang during the warm weather. My way might keep you alive for the winter — maybe. (*Comes over and stands in front of Easter*) Take that knife out of him. Take him out and dump him. (*Carefully*) Dump him in the right place — with no fancy work. Do you hear me? (*Easter nods quickly, and as he starts to move, Wilkie jerks him back*) Remember, I don't promise you anything. If it goes wrong, you slob, it goes wrong for you. I'll turn you in myself — and with plenty of story to keep me in the clear. Do you understand me? (*Waits, gets no answer*) Do you understand me?

EASTER (*very quietly*). Yes.

Curtain

Scene 2.

The time is immediately following Scene 1.

SCENE: *A bare, clean office-room, the empty side of a store. The office is in an alley. The entrance is left stage. There is a desk, a few chairs, a filing cabinet, a typewriter, a mimeographing machine, an electric stove.*

AT RISE: *Whalen is sitting at the desk chair, leaning over to hammer on a box. Firth is sitting by the window, staring idly out into the alley. Neither of them speaks for a minute after the curtain rises. Then Firth gets slowly to his feet and goes to the chair on which his hat and raincoat are lying.*

FIRTH. Well. Want to come to my house for a bowl of something hot?

WHALEN (*shakes his head, points to a cardboard container on his desk*). Odave treated me to a pint of whisky. It tastes like he made it on the picket line.

FIRTH. Bad for your stomach.

WHALEN. Don't worry about my stomach. (*Waves toward the window*) Worry about the stomachs out there.

FIRTH. I been worrying enough.

WHALEN. How much we got?

FIRTH. Hannah brought down canned stuff and Richmondville sent over a pig. It ain't enough. I don't say anybody's starving, but it's tough to watch kids not get enough.

WHALEN. Yep.

FIRTH. Funny. All the boys had a little something. But we

were talking last night how you work all your life to save it, then it runs out fast. Funny.

WHALEN. Very funny.

FIRTH (*suddenly, as if he had been thinking of it all along*). I couldn't tell her what they meant. I was so ashamed for the kid. (*Violently*) I'll kill 'em if they ever go near my girl again. I'll kill 'em —

WHALEN. That's just what they want you to do. You boys were hot stuff Thursday. You couldn't take a little pushing around. You got to push back. So what? So it winds up Wilkie gets half his boys sworn in as deputy sheriffs. They're law and order now and you're un-American.

FIRTH. There's some things you can't take. Nobody can. Nobody.

WHALEN. Speak for yourself. There's not much I can't take, if I have to. (*Slowly*) You gave me your word that you wouldn't fight again, and that you'd keep the boys from fighting.

FIRTH. And I've kept my word. But it gets too much —

WHALEN (*wearily*). We've been over all this before. The longer you're quiet the sooner you'll win. Wilkie's been in this business for a long time. They've all got one gag — to make you fight. And no matter what *they* do to start it, you'll be surprised to read in the paper, and to hear from the police, that *you* started it. (*Slowly, with force*) And once they start a real fight here, you're lost.

FIRTH. You don't believe we can take care of ourselves, do you? You don't —

WHALEN. No. I don't believe it. There are men in your spot who know what it's about and who can take what's coming. I believe in *their* fighting, but not *you*. Your idea of fighting is not to hit below the waist — (*Laughs*) Now be good. And don't let your kid or anybody else go out alone.

FIRTH (*shakes his head, passes his hand over his face wearily, and begins to put on his coat*). Hannah says Andrew don't like things much. Might be a good sign. He's an easygoing man. I don't believe he'd have ever got us into this if it hadn't been for the others.

WHALEN (*smiles*). That's the stuff. That kind of talk will do you a lot of good.

FIRTH (*sighs*). I don't know how much longer we can hold out here, when kids aren't getting enough. (*As he turns he looks at Whalen, who is paying no attention to him*) I wouldn't be the one to know. What do you think?

WHALEN. I told you what I thought. Wilkie wants a fight, and as long as we're not giving him one we're sitting not bad. Now go on home. And if they cut your grandmother in half, don't lift a hand. Wait'll they cut her in slices and then maybe, but I don't promise, I'll let you take a sock at one of 'em.

FIRTH. That ain't what I meant. That ain't telling me how much longer we can feed. You ain't never told me.

WHALEN (*irritated*). And I'm never going to. That may be part of my job, too, but it's not for me. You pick your own minute. You'll get no speeches from me about the beauty of starving for what you think. I don't mind so much doing it for myself, but I don't do it for other people.

(*After a second Firth sighs, moves toward the door.*)

FIRTH (*softly*). I could bring you back something hot.

WHALEN (*affectionately*). Good night, Tom.

(*He exits. Whalen watches him, smiling. Then with a few loud hammerings, he finishes with the box and gets up, carrying it to the other side of the room. He goes to a basin, washes his hands, dabs at his face, lights a cigarette, pours himself a drink. He stands smoking as the door opens and Julie Rodman comes slowly in. She stands away from the door, waiting for him to speak.*)

WHALEN (*turns, looks at her, then after a moment's silence, says loudly, as if he is talking for somebody outside*). Please close the door, Mrs. Rodman — unless there is somebody with you.

JULIE (*closing the door, without turning*). There is nobody with me. (*She stands waiting for him to speak*) I — I — Can't I come in?

WHALEN (*slowly, pleasantly*). I'm guessing. But I want to save you time. You can go back and tell them that I don't want any bribes — the gag is too stale.

JULIE (*crosses to him. Intensely*). No. No. Really, no. I haven't come for any reason — I mean, any reason except my own. Really, really, Mr. Whalen —

WHALEN (*picks up two cheap glasses from the windowsill*). You look cold. Like a drink? (*She nods, shy, embarrassed, watching him*) It's filthy, but it's a drink. (*He hands her a glass, sits down at desk, smiles, pours himself a drink*) Don't listen to the doctors. Cheap whisky is good for you. Why did you come, Mrs. Rodman?

JULIE. I — er — I — It won't sound like the truth. I wanted to talk to you. Just talk to you. Not about anything. I just wanted to talk to you.

WHALEN (*after a pause*). Well. That sounds too pleasant. Don't you know that you're not supposed to feel friendly enough for a visit and — (*Slowly*) and that I'm not supposed to let you make the visit?

JULIE (*rises, softly*). Yes, I suppose I knew it. I'm sorry. I just wanted to talk to you.

WHALEN (*kindly*). What did you want to say?

JULIE. I don't know. Although I've thought about it a lot. (*Turns to him and smiles*) You don't remember, but I do. The first evening you came here, you talked to me.

WHALEN. I do remember. I didn't know who you were.

JULIE. I've walked past your alley often. Tonight I didn't think. I just came in. (*Quickly*) Haven't you ever wanted to talk to somebody you thought knew more about things than you did, and you just hoped the talk would start, and — (*Smiles*) there wouldn't be any questions about why you came?

WHALEN (*pours himself another drink*). Yes. Once. When I was in college. I thought that Lafayette — (*Bows*) Lafayette, of all people — was a fake and I wanted to know about it. But the professor was eating his dinner, and he thought Lafayette was fine. It never seems to work out very well.

JULIE (*without snobbishness*). College?

WHALEN (*laughs*). Yes, ma'am. No, it's not as good as it sounds. I only went to college for seven months. That cost four hundred dollars. (*Bows*) Almost half of what my father could earn in a year. The old story.

JULIE. I went to college, too. But it cost more than that.

WHALEN. My mother found happiness in crowing over our half-starved neighbors. My mother hated what she was and what she came from. None of that love of beauty stuff in my mother. I was to become a priest.

JULIE. I'd have guessed that.

WHALEN (*smiles*). You would have been wrong. When that failed, she just wanted me to get rich enough to hate what I was and what I came from. I fooled her. I hated her instead. I kind of liked my father, and that four hundred bucks would have been plenty of carfare for him. He had rheumatism bad and the places where they could pay a gardener were in the suburbs and he had to walk most of the way. He'd come home at night and it would hurt him to take his pants off and he'd sit in a chair and hold them out from his legs so the goods couldn't touch the skin. He was nice. (*Stops, leans over to look at her, then slowly*) What is your reason for coming here?

JULIE (*puts up her hand, softly*). In a minute. In a minute. What did you do then?

WHALEN. Nothing. I hoboed. Once in a while I'd work. But not when I could help it. Then one day, or one month, or one year, I began to get worried. I couldn't understand about things, and it scared hell out of me. (*Laughs, pours himself out a drink, pours her one*) When you don't feel yourself anything, I mean any part of anything, that's when you get scared. I was that way for a long time.

JULIE (*softly*). My husband said he felt that.

WHALEN. Well, it took me a long time. I had listened too much to what was wrong with the world from every louse from New Orleans to Seattle. I was sick of it all. (*Smiles at her*) I'm not bright, but I'm stubborn. I've been working ever since.

JULIE. For poor people? You love them.

WHALEN (*laughs*). Love them? Do you think you can love the smell that comes from dirty skin, or the scum on dishes, or the holes in the floor with the bugs coming through — (*Sharply*) Or the meanness and the cowardice that comes with poverty? I hate the poor, Mrs. Rodman. But I love what they could be. Do you hate the poor, Mrs. Rodman?

JULIE. No.

WHALEN. Not even hate? You've never thought that much about them?

JULIE (*simply*). I've never seen many poor people.

WHALEN. I imagine one of the ladies' charities would be delighted to let you peep over the fence. It would not be unpleasant, since the poor *they* will show you will lick your boots — in gratitude for nothing. Or rather for the gift of seeing a handsome, clean lady who can eat three meals every day.

JULIE (*angrily*). That's not what I am. I never wanted to see a selected world: I never knew how to see any other. I think that is one of the reasons I wanted to talk to you.

WHALEN (*laughs*). I'm not a teacher, Mrs. Rodman. And I believe that if one wants to see the world, one knows where to find it. It's all about you. They tell me you've been married here a long time and that they don't know you very well.

JULIE. No, they don't. They're a hard people with strangers — as you've probably found out.

WHALEN (*smiles*). Yes.

JULIE. But it's really my fault. I've been busy. Busy, like you, finding out. I was finding out about myself. That took all my time.

WHALEN. What were you finding out?

JULIE. I don't know. When I was young, I guess I was looking for something I could do. Then for something I could be. (*Smiles*) Finally, just for something to want, or to think, or to believe in. I always wanted somebody to show me the way.

WHALEN. Certainly. That's what we all want. It's easy. Were you lucky?

JULIE. No.

WHALEN (*looks at his watch, begins to put papers away in desk*). Then you should try for yourself. That works sometimes.

JULIE. No. I decided a long time ago that there were people who had to learn from other people. I'm one of them. (*Gets up, slowly*) That's why I wanted to talk to you.

WHALEN (*looks up at her, laughs, shakes his head*). Is that why you came?

JULIE (*slowly*). Yes. And I'd like to stay.

WHALEN (*slowly, puzzled*). To stay?

JULIE. Sounds crazy, doesn't it? It isn't crazy for me. I know the things you're going to say about a silly, rich woman. But I've thought about it, and I know it isn't that. I have no right to come here and talk to you like this —

WHALEN. What are you talking about, Mrs. Rodman?

JULIE (*angrily*). I've told you. I've told you. (*Then softly, quietly*) I want to stay, I want to stay here. I mean, I —

WHALEN (*there is a second's silence. Then he moves to her quickly, takes her roughly by the arm*). All right. Now go back and tell Wilkie this isn't a new one either. (*She draws her face away from him, sharply*) Don't look so hurt. What am I supposed to think?

JULIE. I've told you the truth. I don't care what you think. (*He looks at her, drops her arm, moves back to desk.*)

WHALEN. Who have you told this nonsense to?

JULIE (*carefully*). I haven't told this — this nonsense to anybody.

WHALEN. What the hell do you think I am?

JULIE. I know what a fool I've sounded. But it's been the truth. I've never in my life talked that way before. (*To herself*) I should have known that when I did, I wouldn't be believed.

WHALEN. And if I do believe you, then you are a silly rich woman who doesn't know what to do with her life and who sees the solution for it in the first man she meets who doesn't stutter: sick of your own world, aren't you, and you think I know another? What do you think mine is? A new game to be learned in an evening and played for a week? I don't like that kind of playing, Mrs. Rodman.

JULIE (*after a second, slowly, carefully*). Maybe what you've said is true. Maybe it isn't. But I'm not playing — and you don't think I am.

WHALEN (*stares at her, as if he were thinking of something else*). You could blow me out of here with this. (*Carefully*) Please. Don't mention your — don't mention your coming here.

JULIE (*softly*). I won't. (*She begins to move toward the door*).

WHALEN. I'd like to say something kind. But I'm worrying about my job. (*Smiles*) I'm tired and I've got a lot of work to do.

JULIE (*without turning*). Do you think I'm pretty?

WHALEN (*as he starts to speak, there is the noise of a car outside, and he stops to listen. When he hears nothing more, he smiles*). No. Better than pretty. (*Looks at her, nods*) Yes, that I feel. Sure. I feel a lot of that. You'd be fun. If you ever feel like it, and I'm not working, you bring your maids, and your trunks, and your cars, and —

JULIE. No.

WHALEN (*laughs*). All right. And now, good night.

(*As she walks toward the door, the noise of a car, the grinding of gears, becomes very sharp and close. She stops, and he looks quickly toward the door and window. Then, as if he is wondering whether the noise means anything to her, he looks at her. Quickly, he moves toward the door, jerks it open, runs out, as she draws back into the room. A minute later he returns, stands staring as if unconscious that she was there.*)

JULIE. What is it?

WHALEN (*slowly*). Your friends have been playing tricks.

JULIE. What do you mean?

WHALEN. I mean that the dead body of that fat thug who was living in your house has just been planted in the alley.

JULIE. Dead? He's dead? I don't understand —

WHALEN. You heard the car. He was put there to get somebody in trouble. (*Stops, thinks*) Yep. (*Moves quickly to the telephone. Into phone*) Corley? Run next door and get me Tom Firth. Quick. (*Puts phone down. Crosses back to her*) Go out the other end of the alley, Mrs. Rodman. Please don't let anybody see you.

JULIE. But you —

WHALEN (*quickly, firmly*). Good night. (*She turns, stares at him, hesitates, and begins to run out of the door. He watches her, shuts the door, moves quickly back to the telephone*) Tom. One of Wilkie's boys is outside in the alley, dead. They planted him there. I don't know. For me or you or anybody else. Listen to me. I'm going to be in jail in a few minutes. (*Sharply*) Stay where you are and don't worry about me. I don't know what he's going to start, but I know he's going to start something. Stop worrying about me, and listen. (*Very carefully*) No matter what he starts, let him alone. *Don't fight with him.* (*Loudly*) Do you hear me? Let him do what he wants and don't fight with him. (*Pleasantly*) Just get ready to do nothing. That'll take all the guts you've got. No. I'll be all right. Good night. (*He hangs up, sits quietly for a second, then gets up and takes his hat and coat from the floor behind the desk, puts them on, sits down again, turns his chair to face the door, lights a cigarette. A second later there is a loud knocking on the door. He smiles, starts to rise, as the curtain falls.*)

Curtain

Scene 3.

SCENE: *Same as Act One.*

AT RISE: *The living room of the Rodman house. Some of the lamps have been turned off, as if to keep attention off the room.*

Wilkie has moved a large chair to face the center doors. A second after the curtain rises, there is the noise of someone descending the hall stairs. Wilkie lights a cigarette, slowly, and leans forward.

WILKIE. Mr. Ellicott.

ELLICOTT (*coming into the room, putting on his overcoat*). I thought you'd gone home long ago. (*Slowly*) What are you doing here, Wilkie?

WILKIE (*gets up, nodding his head toward card table*). My man Dowel was found knifed, dead, down near strike headquarters.

ELLICOTT. Oh. (*After a second, puzzled*) But he was here —

WILKIE (*watching him*). He went out.

ELLICOTT (*carefully*). You think they killed him?

WILKIE (*looks at him, amused, laughs*). I think so.

ELLICOTT. Why?

WILKIE. Whalen was there. Any of the others could have been there, too.

ELLICOTT (*carefully*). They got into a fight and killed him —

WILKIE (*smiles*). Maybe. Or maybe they thought he was snooping around and jumped him.

ELLICOTT. Well?

WILKIE. Well. That gives us a job of law enforcement to do. The boys we had sworn in as deputy sheriffs last week will have to go to work for justice.

ELLICOTT. What do you intend to do?

WILKIE. Find the guy who put the knife in Mossie, and find the guys he did it for.

ELLICOTT. And where does that lead?

WILKIE. Well, we'll hope it leads somewhere. (*Casually*) Is this Judge Alcott a good enough friend of yours that I can count on his not getting up out of bed to issue any court orders that could get in my way?

ELLICOTT (*slowly*). Yes.

WILKIE. And could you ask your marshal to go home and go to bed?

ELLICOTT (*carefully*). Rodman isn't going to stand for your making any trouble here, Wilkie.

WILKIE. I'm not going to make any and I'm going to leave it to you to tell him what's happened and to make him see it right.

ELLICOTT. I'll talk to him. (*Starts for door, stops, turns back to look at Wilkie*) You needn't wait. I should think you'd be needed downtown.

WILKIE. My boys know what to do. I'm waiting for Mrs. Rodman.

ELLICOTT. Why are you waiting for Mrs. Rodman?

WILKIE. Your guess should be pretty good.

ELLICOTT (*after a second*). Where's Whalen?

WILKIE. In jail, I hope.

ELLICOTT. You think he —

WILKIE. I don't know. I'm only thinking for a little while. It don't hurt to have him in jail while I'm thinking. That —

(*The window-doors open and Julie comes quickly in. She looks as if she has been running. She starts for the door, ignores Wilkie, speaks to Ellicott.*)

JULIE. Where's Andy?

WILKIE. Mrs. Rodman. (*Sharply, as she does not turn*) Mrs. Rodman. (*Crosses in front of her*) I think Mr. Rodman's gone to bed. But I've been waiting for you. I thought you'd like to talk to me first.

JULIE. Yes. I'd like to talk to you. (*To Ellicott*) Do you know what's happened? (*He nods*) Do you know that he had that man's body put in the alley —

ELLICOTT (*sharply*). Julie. Those are dangerous guesses.

JULIE. They're not guesses. I was there.

ELLICOTT. I knew where you were. Your adventures finally carried you to an unpleasant place at an unpleasant hour. I —

WILKIE. I'd like to talk to Mrs. Rodman. (*Looks toward the hall*) Will you — ?

ELLICOTT (*exiting*). Yes.

JULIE (*furiously*). How dare you think you can do a thing like this in Mr. Rodman's name?

WILKIE. Mr. Ellicott was right. You are making dangerous guesses.

JULIE. I am making no guesses. I was there to see and hear.

WILKIE. So you're going to tell your husband where you were?

JULIE (*staring at him*). Of course. (*She starts again for door.*)

WILKIE. I thought you would. That's why I waited. You're a fine lady, and I'm frightened of fine ladies. They usually land the men they know in cemeteries. (*As she opens the door*) And that's where you're getting ready to land Leo Whalen. (*She takes her hand off the door, stands without turning*) You're throwing a monkey wrench, Mrs. Rodman, and it's going to hit both Whalen and Mr. Rodman.

JULIE (*softly, without turning*). What did you mean about — about Whalen?

WILKIE. I meant several things. Now you tell me that you're going upstairs to tell your husband that Whalen couldn't have had anything to do with Mossie, because you were with him?

JULIE. Yes.

WILKIE. And that's too bad. Right this minute Whalen's probably playing checkers — (*Smiles*) somewhere. But your way, he won't be for long.

JULIE. I don't know what you're talking about.

WILKIE. Then it's because you haven't thought about it. (*Pleasantly*) You see, Mrs. Rodman, *your husband* might believe you, *I* might believe you, but the police might not. It sounds foolish, since you and I know better, but they might think that — that Mossie caught you together and Whalen killed him for it. That's my guess, and I've been in the business a long time. And even if my guess is wrong — he'll be through anyway. When the strikers find out he's been carrying on with the boss's wife —

JULIE. He was not carrying on —

WILKIE. It's going to look like a sellout, and if he gets out all in one piece he's lucky.

(*Cora opens the library door and comes in. She has on a warm woolen robe.*)

CORA (*crossing to bell, ringing it*). My milk and fruit aren't upstairs. We can't help it if he got killed. Whatever we do now isn't going to do him any good. Henry just told me. He puts everything so badly, that it came as a shock. (*Hannah appears carrying milk and a small plate of fruit*) Yes. You forgot it, didn't you?

HANNAH (*looking at Wilkie, curiously*). I didn't think you'd starve. (*Watches Cora drink the milk*) Funny how you drink it just like you need it — (*To Julie*) Do you want something, Mrs. Rodman?

JULIE (*softly, without looking up*). No, thank you, Hannah.

(*Andrew and Ellicott enter from the center doors. Andrew comes directly into the room, Ellicott stands at the door. Julie gets up as if she were going to turn to Andrew, then slowly turns away again.*)

ANDREW (*to Wilkie*). I'm sorry about Dowel, Wilkie. But I won't pretend that I am not more sorry that murder happened in this town. We're not a tough people here, and we're not used to it.

WILKIE. Somebody was tough enough.

ANDREW. Yes. That's true, and that shocks me most. But that means that I pushed them into it, and that I'm responsible for it. I know these people here.

CORA. Do you know that they won't come around to murder us, too?

ANDREW (*to Wilkie*). This murder is for the police. Not for you and me. Your bill will be paid for the week, of course. Wilkie, I want you and your people out of here tonight.

JULIE (*turns quickly*). Yes. Yes. That's right for you, Andy —

ELLICOTT. I told you upstairs that the decision wasn't entirely up to you.

ANDREW. But my part *is* up to me. (*To Wilkie*) I know I've been a hard man to work for. I didn't want you here, and I was right. We can't undo what's been done. But we can stop any further trouble.

WILKIE (*quietly*). I want to find out who did it, Mr. Rodman.

ANDREW. I understand. The police will do that for you.

WILKIE (*pleasantly*). I don't think you do understand. I'm not talking about Mossie. I'm not crying about that. That was his job. He got paid for it. But somebody's been killed and that somebody worked for me. If I'm going to stay in business I can't let people get the idea they can slice up my folks. And I won't. I can't make you let me keep this job. But I can't leave tonight. I'm the police here, Mr. Rodman, and if I wasn't worrying about finishing a job I was hired for, I'd have to think of that.

ANDREW (*with force*). *I won't have any more trouble.*

WILKIE. That's just what I'm trying to avoid for you. I want the guns and the knives and the bricks cleaned out, and no more murders. That's what you want too, isn't it? When the guns get put away in a nice, safe spot, you and your boys can talk things over. But before I leave here, they're going to be put away. (*Gets up, looks at his watch*) That's the way it'll have to be, Mr. Rodman. No reason why things shouldn't be swell and peaceful. All I want is the guns, and if they don't intend to use 'em, they should be glad to give 'em up.

CORA. That's right. That's the nice way to do it —

ANDREW (*furiously*). No. That's not what I want done. No —

HANNAH. You can't let him do that. They can't walk in a house and take anything. Maybe the government can take things, but you — (*Motioning to the others in the room*) you can't take them. Why, you let him go near one of their houses and they'll think you're crazy. You ain't got any rights they haven't got. They could come in here and take from you —

ELLICOTT. Andrew. We want this thing finished. It's gone on for weeks now. We've got to get it over soon —

JULIE (*to Ellicott*). Andy's right. There's been trouble enough.

CORA (*to Andrew*). I don't know why you're so worried about *them*. You should protect us —

JULIE (*to Cora*). What are you talking about? How can you talk that way about people you went to school with, people you've known all your life —

ANDREW (*to Ellicott*). I won't have any more trouble.

ELLICOTT. He's told you there won't be any trouble —

(*As he speaks, there is the sudden, distant sound of firing. They all turn slowly to stare at the window. Wilkie puts his watch back into his pocket, moves toward his overcoat. The firing starts again, this time four or five shots in rapid succession.*)

WILKIE (*shakes his head*). That's too bad. Too bad. (*Starts for door*) Rest easy, Miss Cora, the law will protect you.

(*He exits as they stand stiff and silent. Hannah begins to run from the room. The others do not move until Cora rises, brushes off her robe, starts for the door.*)

CORA. It is too bad. Well, all this excitement has made me very nervous. (*As she gets to door*) Mr. Wilkie knows more about these things than we do.

Curtain

Act Three

SCENE: *The same as Act One. Seven-thirty the next morning.*

AT RISE: *Julie is sitting in a chair, wrapped in a coat. Several of the lamps are still lit, although the dull early light of a rainy morning is beginning to come through. The room is as it was at the end of the second act, but it has the mussed, unaired look of a morning-after living room. A few seconds after the rise of the curtain, Andrew, in an overcoat, opens the center doors. He comes in slowly, tired. Automatically, he puts the bunch of door keys back into his pocket.*

JULIE (*without looking up*). It stopped a little while ago. Thank God. (*She shudders, looks up at him*) Are you all right, Andy?

ANDREW (*slowly*). Remember the last time we went riding early in the morning? Well, when we came to the high point on Tucker's Road, I thought that I didn't like to ride much anymore. When you don't know anything about poetry, you know how you feel sometimes when you see things? That's the way I always felt about the high point, because I could look down on the town and that made me happy. It always looks so scrubbed and clean and I thought the way I used to, when I was a kid: that I could stop in any house and have a good breakfast and they'd be glad to see me. It doesn't look so pretty this morning. And they wouldn't be glad to have me for breakfast. (*Turns away, then quickly*) Yes, I'm all right. The partnership of Ellicott and Wilkie locked me in the office. They were busy and I'd only have been a nuisance.

JULIE (*again*). It stopped a while ago. Why did it stop? Did you stop it?

ANDREW (*bitterly*). No. Not me. I didn't stop it. (*Slowly*) People got hurt. I guess that's why it stopped.

JULIE (*gets up, starts to turn out lamps*). I've been using guns all my life — (*Turns*) Who got hurt?

ANDREW. But the guns sound different when they're not for

fun, don't they? I don't know who got hurt. There was some fuss around Corley's house and — (*Softly*) around Firth's.

JULIE (*carefully*). Was Whalen — was Leo Whalen — was he hurt?

ANDREW. He's in jail.

JULIE. In jail? What for? Wilkie told me —

ANDREW (*wearily*). I don't know. Something about that fat man. They think he got into a fight with him and — (*Sits down suddenly*) My God, I'm tired.

JULIE. He can't — I can't — (*She stands watching him, then turns away as if she had changed her mind.*)

ANDREW. I tried to get down to Firth's, but they wouldn't let me.

JULIE. Maybe it was just a fight. Maybe no one was hurt.

ANDREW. Maybe. Maybe.

JULIE (*suddenly, violently*). Why didn't you stop it? Why did you let it go on like this? They talked you into it. Why did you let them?

ANDREW (*smiles*). You make me sound like a child. And you're right.

JULIE. You didn't want any of this. Why did you ever have to start it? Then why didn't you stop it?

ANDREW. There are a lot of reasons. The reason I tell myself is that I couldn't stop anything. I owe money. A lot of money. I've been borrowing it for a long time. I've borrowed on the factory and on this house and on how many brushes I thought I could make in five years —

JULIE. Oh. (*Carefully*) From Henry?

ANDREW. From banks, from dealers — Mostly from Henry.

JULIE. But why did you borrow it? We didn't need it —

ANDREW. Oh, I got pushed and pushed until — until I couldn't help myself. (*Looks up at her, smiles*) If I were another kind of man, I guess I wouldn't have let that make any difference.

JULIE. I didn't know any of that. (*After a second*) There are a lot of things we don't know about each other.

ANDREW. I suppose so, darling. That's the way with most marriages, I guess.

JULIE. Andy. He can't stay in jail. He had nothing to do with that man. I was with him last night when it happened. With Whalen.

ANDREW (*there is a pause. Then he slowly raises his head to look at her, speaks quietly, carefully*). Then you shouldn't let him stay in jail, Julie. That's not right. Why are you acting so strange? Why didn't you say so and get him out? There's nothing to be ashamed of — (*She looks at him, nods, starts for windows*) Julie! (*She turns*) Never mind. I'll do it. (*He rises as she watches him go to telephone. Into phone*) Operator, call Judge Alcott's house. (*To Julie*) Didn't you know he'd been arrested?

JULIE. No. I'd been told —

ANDREW (*through her last words, into phone*). Jim? This is Andrew Rodman. I want you to let Leo Whalen out of jail immediately. We — er — I know where he was last night. I'll be down later and explain. (*Sharply*) Jim. I don't give a damn what anybody said. Let him out. (*Wearily*) Yes. Yes. Thanks. No. Everything's all right.

JULIE. Thank you, Andy.

ANDREW. What are you thanking me for? It's not important. You don't have to thank me.

JULIE (*quietly*). We've been dealing with people shrewder than we are.

ANDREW. Yes, I suppose so. I suppose that's it.

(*He passes his hand over his eyes. She makes a half motion toward him, changes her mind, turns away. A second later, Firth appears in the center doors. He is dirty, bruised and tired-looking. In his hand is a gun. It is hanging at his side, as if he had forgotten it. Through all his speeches, through his exit, he holds the gun, unconscious that he has it. He stands in the doorway as they both look up.*)

FIRTH (*aimlessly*). The front door's open. The rain's coming in. I don't know what to do with you, Andrew.

JULIE (*in a whisper*). What is it, Tom? What is it?

(*Andrew is standing by the desk, staring at Firth.*)

FIRTH. When you can't have a kid, that's bad. It makes a man feel funny, like he can't do anything, and not the way it should be. Specially a big man. You feel like you can't do what you're here for. (*Directly to Andrew*) Remember once when you were at that college and you came home for Christmas and you came to a meal and after Miriam went up, I told you about it. I cried. Remember? They hit her here. (*Puts his hand on the back of his head*) They said she threw a brick. A little kid threw a brick. They broke something.

ANDREW (*horror in his voice*). Where's Morris? Where is he?

FIRTH (*shakes his head as if he were drunk*). It's worse, I guess, when it's an adopted kid. You like it better that way. It makes up for the other thing and you like it better — (*Quietly*) Doc Morris? He's down there. Talking. Telling me what broke. Telling me why it happened. Talking and talking. Talking won't make her live again.

JULIE (*in a whisper*). Oh my God.

ANDREW. They killed her. (*He nods slowly, puts his hand to his mouth, comes to Firth, takes him by the arm, then lets him go suddenly.*)

FIRTH. I don't know what to do. I beat everybody up for a while like crazy, telling myself what I was going to do to you. (*Violently, shaking his finger at Andrew*) But I know you. I know you. It's better to tell you. It'll do worse for you. (*Suddenly, quietly*) I can't touch you, Andrew. I'm too tired. (*He sits down, as if he couldn't stand any longer. Then, as if it were an old familiar position between them, Andrew sits opposite him. For a second, neither of them speaks. To Julie, without looking up*) Once she saw you coming home from school and she told me you were pretty and I told her that you weren't half as pretty as her, and not an ounce as pretty as she'd grow to be. She laughed and got red and said she wasn't pretty and that I just liked her — How can I go home? How can I live? How can I sit and eat with Miriam when only yesterday the kid sat between us —

JULIE (*to Andrew*). Do something for him.

ANDREW (*looks up at her in surprise*). What is there to do?

FIRTH. There's nothing to do. And I wouldn't let you do it. I've known you all your life. All my life I worked for your father, or for you. I liked you more — more than anybody except my own, I guess. (*Puzzled*) I guess you can't know anybody. You must have been bad all along.

ANDREW. I must have been.

JULIE. Tom, Andrew didn't know. He didn't know anything bad would happen —

FIRTH. That does a lot of good. (*Slowly*) If my kid had — had died any other way, you'd been the first I'd come to. I guess I never knew you. I don't understand that.

ANDREW. I don't understand it, either.

FIRTH. Well, I can't fight anymore. I wouldn't know how. We ain't used to things like last night. Lundee got his hand shot off — (*Andrew gets up and turns away sharply*) they burnt

Carlsen's house all to pieces. We always used to play penny-ante there. We had to drag Berthe out, she was half crazy. She got burnt a little. (*On the next speech, Whalen appears in the open center doors. Easter has him by the arm. All three people see him, and all three stare at him. Firth's voice becomes defiant, and the next speech is meant for Whalen, but is said directly to Andrew*) I don't know, but I guess I can speak for most of 'em. We can't fight you when you fight like this. It's our town more'n it's yours. Our folks came and built it. We can't watch it go like this. (*Gets up, wearily, quietly*) You call off your dogs. Keep 'em away from us, so there won't be no more killing. Get 'em out of here. I guess we'll go back to work.

EASTER. I picked him up trying to shove in the front door. There wouldn't been any door in a minute. He's in jail.

ANDREW (*to Easter*). Get out of here.

EASTER. Oh. (*Looks at him and exits.*)

WHALEN (*comes into the room*). Somebody got soft and let me out of jail. (*To Firth*) They told me where you were. I could have guessed.

FIRTH. They killed my kid.

WHALEN. I got all the news.

FIRTH. I feel bad. I can't fight anymore.

WHALEN. I heard you.

FIRTH (*angrily*). It wasn't your kid.

WHALEN (*angrily*). Didn't I tell you not to fight?

FIRTH (*quietly*). You were right.

WHALEN (*looks at Firth and then at Rodman*). You both look the same kind of surprised. What are you surprised at? What the hell did you think Wilkie was after — (*To Andrew*) Or do you still believe he came down to make brushes for you?

ANDREW (*slowly*). No.

WHALEN (*to Firth*). He wanted you to fight. He's been trying to make you fight for weeks. So as soon as he gets me out of the way for a couple of hours, you give him the fight he's been waiting for.

FIRTH. I couldn't do anything. When they come in talking and shoving, you don't think. Then they hit my kid — (*As if he hadn't said it before*) My girl's dead.

WHALEN (*shouting*). She's dead. You wanted to fight — till the time came. Well, here's your time. If they killed my kid, I wouldn't come crawling back to any lousy job —

JULIE. There's been enough trouble. Don't let's make any more.

FIRTH. I don't want any more. We ain't used to this. We're tired. We don't care so much who wins, like you —

WHALEN (*quietly*). You *will* care. More than I do. For me, you're only one of a thousand fights. But you've only got one fight. This one.

FIRTH. There's no use arguing. I'm trying to tell you why and what and you don't understand. (*Gets up, wearily.*)

WHALEN. Your why and what aren't any good to me.

FIRTH. I can't seem to say what I'm getting at. We didn't know about the things you know about. Everybody's got to see for themselves, I guess.

WHALEN. You haven't seen anything. They didn't scratch the surface here.

FIRTH (*nods his head*). Yeah? Well, maybe you were right, when you said that all the time. I guess I'm worse than anybody, because of my kid. We'll go on back, make the best of it. (*Turns, quietly*) And maybe if the time comes again — I don't like him now. He killed my kid. They don't like him, either. We won't forget.

ANDREW (*with force, to Whalen*). That's the truth. He's telling you the truth. They won't forget.

WHALEN (*to Firth*). He didn't kill your kid. Don't start that, or you'll get the wrong answer again. He hasn't much to do with it. He's got to go his way, and you've got to go yours. And they're not the same way.

FIRTH (*softly*). We used to be good friends.

WHALEN. I know. And you're as good as he is. It says so in the book. Until the time comes. Don't let 'em tell you that because your grandfather voted for Jefferson, you're any different from some Polack in Pittsburgh whose grandfather couldn't write his name.

FIRTH. Well, maybe we'll try again someday.

WHALEN (*smiles, as if he were pleased*). I hope so. And the guy they send in my place, you give him a better chance.

FIRTH (*starts for door*). You coming? They'd like to see you.

WHALEN (*shakes his head*). No. I'm going to be busy for a while.

ANDREW (*softly*). Tom, would you let me do anything for you and Miriam and the others?

FIRTH (*puzzled*). What? Stay away from downtown, Andrew. For a while. (*Firth speaks to Whalen*) Well, if it comes again, I hope they'll be sending you.

WHALEN (*simply, sincerely*). I hope so, too. (*Firth exits. No one speaks for a second*) Well, it's time for me to see whether your pink-cheeked policeman is holding me for murder or because I've got two legs. He's having a tough time deciding. (*He has started for door.*)

JULIE (*quickly*). Wait. You don't have to go back there. They won't hold you —

ANDREW (*who is still looking at the door, as if he were thinking of Firth*). I've spoken to Judge Alcott. There's no need for you to go back. Everything will be straightened out.

WHALEN. Straightened out, Mr. Rodman?

JULIE (*after a second, softly*). I've told my husband that I was in your office last night when it happened.

WHALEN (*has turned to look at Andrew, and then back to Julie*). Is that what you are going to say?

JULIE. Yes. I wanted to before. But — but I was told that you weren't in any trouble, and that I'd be doing you harm.

WHALEN. You were told right. Please. Don't do that. They've got nothing on me, and they know it. A few days of nuisance, maybe, and that's all. That's my job.

JULIE (*looking at him*). Why don't you want any help from us? From me?

WHALEN. It's not my job to take help from the boss, or — the boss's wife. I can't take chances on anybody thinking I do.

(*Wilkie comes in through center doors.*)

WILKIE. Good morning. (*To Andrew*) Glad to see you here. We were worried about you. (*To Whalen*) Good morning.

WHALEN. Had a good breakfast?

WILKIE. Pretty good. I'm like the English, I eat big in the mornings.

WHALEN. I thought so. You look like you've been licking the cream.

WILKIE. You need some breakfast?

WHALEN (*laughs*). No, thank you. I'm eating on the county. With the marshal.

WILKIE (*looking toward Julie, then back to Whalen*). That. Oh. That's yokel stuff. They got nothing to hold you on.

WHALEN. They held me long enough to make it easy for you.

WILKIE. My break this time. Maybe yours the next.

(*Ellicott appears in the hall. Comes in, throws his coat and hat on a chair.*)

ELLICOTT. Good morning.

WHALEN (*to Wilkie*). Your Spick outside looks like a knife thrower to me. What do you think?

WILKIE. I don't know. Maybe so. You can't keep track of everybody. I don't like to see a man get buried without finding who did it — If you know anything —

WHALEN (*laughs*). I don't know anything. Some other time. (*Crosses to Julie and says kindly, with meaning*) Don't worry about last night. There's no honor involved in any of it. And if there was it wouldn't be practical to remember it. (*Holds out his hand to her*) Good-bye, Mrs. Rodman.

JULIE (*touches his hand*). Good-bye.

WHALEN (*to Andrew*). Good-bye.

ANDREW. Good-bye.

(*Whalen exits.*)

ELLICOTT (*to Julie*). You look tired. (*No answer. He looks at his watch*) Almost eight o'clock. I haven't been up this early in a long time.

WILKIE. Does you good sometimes.

JULIE (*to Andrew*). What are they talking about?

ANDREW (*slowly*). I don't know.

JULIE (*to Ellicott*). Did you have a good time? Was it more exciting than being at the club? Is it fun to see a killing?

ELLICOTT (*sharply*). Stop it. (*After a second*) We've been fighting your husband's battles for him.

ANDREW. Yes. That's quite true. The delicate prince in his ivory tower — (*Carefully*) was carefully protected from the dust and din of battle. You are noble warriors and you've done a noble night's work. (*Sharply to Ellicott*) I'll see to it that when the history is written, it will be mentioned that you were fighting for yourself, too.

ELLICOTT. I knew nothing about the child until Morris told me.

WILKIE. I knew you were going to feel this way, Mr. Rodman. But nobody wanted any trouble. Sometimes these things can't be helped. I understand it's going to be settled now and I'm glad for you, and glad for me. I don't like to take money for losing, and for a while —

ANDREW. Send us your bill. We'll mail you a check.

WILKIE. Yes, sir. (*Goes to him, puts out his hand*) Thank you, Mr. Rodman —

ANDREW (*ignores the hand*). That's all. Good-bye.

WILKIE (*looks down at his hand, laughs*). Well, that's your business. But I want to tell you, I've worked for a lot of men, some of them deacons of the church who were breaking strikes for the good of America, but I never worked for a man before who believed I could come in, run his factory, and break his strike without walking on anybody's toes. You actually believed that. I come in to break strikes. That's my business. It's *not* a tearoom business. You ought to have known that.

ELLICOTT. Does this speech go on your bill?

WILKIE. No. I'm giving it free of charge. But the next time I have to waste weeks acting like it was a tea party, the next time I have to nurse along a blind man — (*Laughs carefully*) a blind man who calls the turns when they're over — I'm going to charge extra. (*Picks up his hat as he passes Ellicott*) There'll be expense items on my bill.

ELLICOTT. You'll get your check.

WILKIE. Good morning.

(*There is a long silence. Ellicott lights a cigarette, looks at Julie, moves uncomfortably about the room.*)

ELLICOTT. Well, Andy — (*No answer*) What's the matter with you?

ANDREW. I'm over here thinking how I don't like being a murderer. You are fortunate. You don't seem to mind so much.

ELLICOTT (*angrily*). I knew nothing about the child. But I did know there had to be trouble. (*Carefully*) And I'm not willing to act the saint about it now.

ANDREW. That's wise for you. I hope the trouble last night won't keep you from White Sulphur.

ELLICOTT. It won't. I'm going tonight.

ANDREW. I wish you a happy journey, and I hope that your dreams are free.

ELLICOTT (*angrily*). If it makes you feel better to enjoy your conscience, go ahead. There was a lot of truth in what that bum just said.

ANDREW. Yes. There was. But did he know that *you* were also his employer? You own so much of me now — (*Julie has turned to look at them as Andrew breaks off. Andrew sees her, and speaks as if he had been thinking of her all along*) Why were you with Whalen last night?

JULIE. You don't want to hear about it now, Andy.

(*Andrew begins to speak as Lucy comes into the room, carrying a small table with breakfast on it. She is followed by Cora, in a bathrobe.*)

CORA. The noise that's been going on here this morning. (*Puts up a commanding hand*) Now. Please. Please. Don't tell me about last night. I've heard all about it. Lucy had it from Morris' nurse. It's awful. Simply awful. (*Leans over, smells the chocolate pot. Then to Lucy*) Did Hannah make this chocolate? Take it back.

LUCY. No, ma'am. I made it. Hannah's out.

CORA. Out? At this time of the morning? (*To everybody as Lucy exits*) What do you think of that? Out at this time of the morning.

ELLICOTT. Do you have to have your breakfast here? In this room?

CORA (*as she starts to eat*). Mind your business. I've had it here for thirty years. I shall continue —

ANDREW (*who has been staring at Julie, paying no attention to Cora*). Julie! Why were you in Whalen's office?

JULIE (*desperately*). Andy, I don't want to — Don't let's talk about it now.

ANDREW. Julie. Answer me.

JULIE. I liked him. I wanted to know him. And more than that.

(*Andrew rises from his chair, and then, slowly, sits down again. Cora puts down her spoon suddenly.*)

ELLICOTT. My God, you're a foolish woman.

JULIE. It was what I wanted.

CORA (*looking around the room, in a daze*). Is she crazy?

ELLICOTT. But he didn't want you?

JULIE. No.

ANDREW. Leave her alone.

CORA. Look at you. So you're just finding out about your wife, are you? Then you're the only one who is. She's been doing this for years.

ELLICOTT. Cora. Cora —

CORA. Now she's decided to tell you, finally. (*With great scorn*) "Leave her alone" you tell him. How can he leave her alone? All that's his business, too.

ELLICOTT (*furiously*). Cora, I tell you —

JULIE (*quietly*). Let her say it. She's wanted to for a long time.

CORA. Yes. I could have told you about them a long time ago. She's just as much Henry's business as she is yours. Just as much. You fool. You fool. All these years —

ANDREW (*he has been staring at her, then as if he were speaking to an insane person*). Control yourself. Get away from my desk. Go back to your breakfast.

ELLICOTT (*after a long silence, while Cora paces around restlessly*). Well, it's a nasty story, Andy. Your best friend and —

CORA. And his wife.

ANDREW (*looks up at Ellicott, smiles*). In what strange ways you think of things. Did you read somewhere that it was wicked to sleep with your best friend's wife? Was it a vulgar book you read it in? Or does the fact that it was *my* wife make it more sinful, and therefore more pleasant?

CORA (*to Julie*). I knew what you were doing to my brother. I knew every bit of it.

JULIE (*comes toward Andrew*). I wasn't doing anything to you. Not the way she means. (*She sits down, opposite him*) Andy. I wasn't in love with you when I married you. That was what I did to you. The rest had only to do with me. I didn't want to get married. I didn't want to live here. I wanted to make something for myself, something that would be right for me. I told you all that when we were young. You thought marriage would be all that for me. But it wasn't. (*Gets up*) And when I found it wasn't, I took the wrong way. But I thought someday I might find somebody who —

ELLICOTT. You thought you found Whalen, didn't you?

JULIE (*to Andrew*). Yes. I was going to tell you that, Andy. But the rest — the rest was just me and just exactly as shabby as she's made it sound. (*Leans across the desk, suddenly*) Darling, I'm not in love with you. But I love you. More than anybody I've ever known.

ANDREW (*softly*). Julie. Julie. (*Motioning toward Cora and Ellicott*) Don't listen to what they say. I know what you mean. You have done nothing to me.

CORA. Done nothing to you. She's broken you, that's what she's done. She's why you owe money — (*Julie has turned and is staring at her*) to Henry and to everybody else. She's why —

ELLICOTT (*violently*). Is that your business, too?

CORA. No, thank you. It's not my money he's lost. But you needn't think I didn't know. I knew where it was going. The year her family lost their money and how her mother had to have the best doctors and how her brother had to go to Paris to study, and how she always had to have trips and clothes, and a year in Europe — (*With scorn*) to make her happy. Thousands and thousands he had to borrow for it —

JULIE. I didn't know that. I swear I didn't. We always had so much. Why didn't you tell me?

ANDREW. It wasn't your business. It isn't now. I wanted it that way. Isn't it strange? The three of us — (*Pointing to Cora and Ellicott*) have known each other since we were born. My sister — (*Bows*) my best friend — my best friend. We grew up in this town knowing all about each other. Henry and I, for example, know that Cora, all her life —

CORA. Be still.

ANDREW. All her life has been, well, slightly ill. Then Cora and I know all about Henry, the rich and worldly Henry, and all the very legal manipulating he does with his money and with his life. They, on the other hand, Cora and Henry know all about me. They've always thought me a soft, weak man and they've always had contempt for me. Hannah shares the secrets of all of us. That's why Cora can't get rid of her, isn't it, Cora? Ten years ago you married me and came here, and so you were one of us, too. Our married life always had an audience — my sister and my best friend and my cook. All the things we knew about each other, all the things that accumulate through a lifetime, or through ten years, sat quietly, waiting for us, while we lived politely and tried, like most people, to push them out of sight. Polite and blind, we lived.

JULIE (*softly*). And then early one morning, it all blew up.

ANDREW. It blew up last night. All the things we know, were there to know a long time ago. We were doing our best to live happily. Well, there's no need for being polite anymore. You were my wife. (*To Ellicott*) You and I and Cora made me a murderer. (*To Cora*) You hate me and I hated you from the day I was old enough to think about you. You hate my wife and you have always hated her. (*To Ellicott*) Since we were old enough to play together, you've never had anything but toleration for me — and I've never had anything but contempt for you. That's a lot of hate, isn't it? It was all there before. (*Pleasantly*) It can be said now.

ELLICOTT (*after a moment's silence*). I'm sorry all this had to come now, Andy. That's straight. (*Motioning toward Cora*) And I'm sorry it had to come from Cora.

CORA (*calmly*). I think both of you are drunk.

ELLICOTT (*to Julie*). Do you want me to stay?

JULIE. What? Oh no. (*He looks at her for a second and then exits quickly. After his exit, nobody speaks. Then after a second, Julie says softly*) What do you want me to do, Andy?

ANDREW (*puzzled*) What do you mean?

JULIE. Do you want me to go away? Do you want a divorce?

ANDREW (*sadly, reproachfully*). Oh, Julie. Even you haven't understood. I'm not sitting here in tears for you or me. A year ago, a month ago, what you told me about you, about us, would have broken my heart. But not now. Because last night I lost the place and the land where I was born. I can't go downtown, he said. It isn't safe. It isn't safe for *me* to go into that town. You see what I mean. I lost what I thought I was. I lost Firth his child. (*Suddenly, violently*) Murder is worse than lost love. Murder is worse than a broken heart.

JULIE. Yes.

ANDREW. In a little while I'll think about us. About how I lost you, and how I never had you, and how much I loved you. But now it seems almost right that it should be this way and that you should have told me this morning. It was right that it should have come. I don't know what you should do, Julie. Go to White Sulphur, if you like.

JULIE. That would be what I deserved.

ANDREW. That's foolish. You don't deserve anything. Go anywhere you like. Or nowhere. Whatever is left here is as much yours as it is mine. *That's* your punishment — if you're looking for it. For the rest of your life, my wife, for all the days to come — (*Laughs*) You can have half of all this. Half of me. I'm sorry for you. (*He has motioned with his arm around the room, toward Cora. Suddenly his face is dead and heavy, and he sits down in the desk chair.*)

(*Julie exits.*)

CORA (*after a long silence, she pours herself some chocolate*). Things went entirely too far. It comes from everybody getting too excited. Now, you go get some sleep and nothing will seem as bad when you wake up. (*No answer. She takes a bite of toast*) People said a lot of things they didn't mean, Andy. A lot of things they didn't mean. I'm sure of that.

Curtain

The Little Foxes

For Arthur Kober and Louis Kronenberger

"Take us the foxes, the little foxes,
that spoil the vines; for our vines have tender grapes."
— *Song of Solomon*

The Little Foxes was first produced at the National Theatre, New York City, on February 15, 1939, with the following cast:

(In the order of their appearance)

ADDIE	ABBIE MITCHELL
CAL	JOHN MARRIOTT
BIRDIE HUBBARD	PATRICIA COLLINGE
OSCAR HUBBARD	CARL BENTON REID
LEO HUBBARD	DAN DURYEA
REGINA GIDDENS	TALLULAH BANKHEAD
WILLIAM MARSHALL	LEE BAKER
BENJAMIN HUBBARD	CHARLES DINGLE
ALEXANDRA GIDDENS	FLORENCE WILLIAMS
HORACE GIDDENS	FRANK CONROY

Produced and staged by
HERMAN SHUMLIN

Settings designed by
HOWARD BAY

Costumes designed by
ALINE BERNSTEIN

Scenes

The scene of the play is the living room of the Giddens house, in a small town in the South.

Act One

The Spring of 1900, evening.

Act Two

A week later, early morning.

Act Three

Two weeks later, late afternoon.

There has been no attempt to write Southern dialect. It is to be understood that the accents are Southern.

Act One

SCENE: *The living room of the Giddens home, in a small town in the deep South, the spring of 1900. Upstage is a staircase leading to the second story. Upstage, right, are double doors to the dining room. When these doors are open we see a section of the dining room and the furniture. Upstage, left, is an entrance hall with a coatrack and umbrella stand. There are large lace-curtained windows on the left wall. The room is lit by a center gas chandelier and painted china oil lamps on the tables. Against the wall is a large piano. Downstage, right, are a high couch, a large table, several chairs. Against the left back wall are a table and several chairs. Near the window there are a smaller couch and tables. The room is good-looking, the furniture expensive; but it reflects no particular taste. Everything is of the best and that is all.*

AT RISE: *Addie, a tall, nice-looking Negro woman of about fifty-five, is closing the windows. From behind the closed dining-room doors there is the sound of voices. After a second, Cal, a middle-aged Negro, comes in from the entrance hall carrying a tray with glasses and a bottle of port. Addie crosses, takes the tray from him, puts it on table, begins to arrange it.*

ADDIE (*pointing to the bottle*). You gone stark out of your head?

CAL. No, smart lady, I ain't. Miss Regina told me to get out that bottle. (*Points to bottle*) That very bottle for the mighty honored guest. When Miss Regina changes orders like that you can bet your dime she got her reason.

ADDIE (*points to dining room*). Go on. You'll be needed.

CAL. Miss Zan she had two helpings frozen fruit cream and she tell that honored guest, she tell him that you make the best frozen fruit cream in all the South.

ADDIE. Did she? Well, see that Belle saves a little for her. She like it right before she go to bed. Save a few little cakes, too, she like —

(*The dining-room doors are opened and closed again by Birdie*

Hubbard. Birdie is a woman of about forty, with a pretty, well-bred, faded face. Her movements are usually nervous and timid, but now, as she comes running into the room, she is gay and excited. Cal turns to Birdie.)

BIRDIE. Oh, Cal. I want you to get one of the kitchen boys to run home for me. He's to look in my desk drawer and — (*To Addie*) My, Addie. What a good supper! Just as good as good can be.

ADDIE. You look pretty this evening, Miss Birdie, and young.

BIRDIE (*laughing*). Me, young? (*Turns back to Cal*) Maybe you better find Simon and tell him to do it himself. He's to look in my desk, the left drawer, and bring my music album right away. Mr. Marshall is very anxious to see it because of his father and the opera in Chicago. (*To Addie*) Mr. Marshall is such a polite man with his manners and very educated and cultured and I've told him all about how my mama and papa used to go to Europe for the music — (*Laughs*) Imagine going all the way to Europe just to listen to music. Wouldn't that be nice, Addie? Just to sit there and listen and — (*Turns*) *Left* drawer, Cal. Tell him that twice because he forgets. And tell him not to let any of the things drop out of the album and to bring it right in here when he comes back.

(*The dining-room doors are opened and quickly closed by Oscar Hubbard. He is a man in his late forties.*)

CAL. Simon he won't get it right. But I'll tell him.

BIRDIE. Left drawer, Cal, and tell him to bring the blue book and —

OSCAR (*sharply*). Birdie.

BIRDIE (*turning nervously*). Oh, Oscar. I was just sending Simon for my music album.

OSCAR (*to Cal*). Never mind about the album. Miss Birdie has changed her mind.

BIRDIE. But, really, Oscar. Really I promised Mr. Marshall. I — (*Cal exits.*)

OSCAR. Why do you leave the dinner table and go running about like a child?

BIRDIE. But, Oscar, Mr. Marshall said most specially he *wanted* to see my album. I told him about the time Mama met Wagner, and Mrs. Wagner gave her the signed program and the big picture. Mr. Marshall wants to see that. Very, very much. We had such a nice talk and —

OSCAR. You have been chattering to him like a magpie. You haven't let him be for a second. I can't think he came South to be bored with you.

BIRDIE (*quickly, hurt*). He wasn't bored. I don't believe he was bored. He's a very educated, cultured gentleman. (*Her voice rises*) I just don't believe it. You always talk like that when I'm having a nice time.

OSCAR (*turning to her, sharply*). You have had too much wine. Get yourself in hand now.

BIRDIE (*drawing back, about to cry, shrilly*). What am I doing? I am not doing anything. What am I doing?

OSCAR (*taking a step to her*). I said get yourself in hand. Stop acting like a fool.

BIRDIE. I don't believe he was bored. I just don't believe it. Some people like music and like to talk about it. That's all I was doing.

(*Leo Hubbard comes hurrying through the dining-room door. He is a young man of twenty, with a weak kind of good looks.*)

LEO. Mama! Papa! They are coming in now.

OSCAR (*softly*). Sit down, Birdie. Sit down now. (*Birdie sits down, bows her head as if to hide her face.*)

(*The dining-room doors are opened by Cal. We see people beginning to rise from the table. Regina Giddens comes in with William Marshall. Regina is a handsome woman of forty. Marshall is forty-five, pleasant-looking, self-possessed. Behind them comes Alexandra Giddens, a pretty, rather delicate-looking girl of seventeen. She is followed by Benjamin Hubbard, fifty-five, with a large jovial face and the light graceful movements that one often finds in large men.*)

REGINA. Mr. Marshall, I think you're trying to console me. Chicago may be the noisiest, dirtiest city in the world but I should still prefer it to the sound of our horses and the smell of our azaleas. I should like crowds of people, and theaters, and lovely women — *Very* lovely women, Mr. Marshall?

MARSHALL. In Chicago? Oh, I suppose so. But I can tell you this: I've never dined there with *three* such lovely ladies.

(*Addie begins to pass the port.*)

BEN. Our Southern women are well favored.

LEO (*laughs*). But one must go to Mobile for the ladies, sir. Very elegant worldly ladies, too.

BEN (*looks at him*). Worldly, eh? *Worldly,* did you say?

OSCAR (*hastily, to Leo*). Your Uncle Ben means that worldliness is not a mark of beauty in any woman.

LEO (*quickly*). Of course, Uncle Ben. I didn't mean —

MARSHALL. Your port is excellent, Mrs. Giddens.

REGINA. Thank you, Mr. Marshall. We had been saving that bottle, hoping we could open it just for you.

ALEXANDRA (*as Addie comes to her with the tray*). Oh. May I *really,* Addie?

ADDIE. Better ask Mama.

ALEXANDRA. May I, Mama?

REGINA (*nods, smiles*). In Mr. Marshall's honor.

ALEXANDRA. Mr. Marshall, this will be the first taste of port I've ever had.

MARSHALL. No one ever had their first taste of a better port. (*He lifts his glass in a toast; she lifts hers; they both drink*) Well, I suppose it is all true, Mrs. Giddens.

REGINA. What is true?

MARSHALL. That you Southerners occupy a unique position in America. You live better than the rest of us, you eat better, you drink better. I wonder you find time, or want to find time, to do business.

BEN. A great many Southerners don't.

MARSHALL. Do all of you live here together?

REGINA. Here with me? (*Laughs*) Oh, no. My brother Ben lives next door. My brother Oscar and his family live in the next square.

BEN. But we are a very close family. We've always wanted it that way.

MARSHALL. That is very pleasant. Keeping your family together to share each other's lives. My family moves around too much. My children seem never to come home. Away at school in the winter; in the summer, Europe with their mother —

REGINA (*eagerly*). Oh, yes. Even down here we read about Mrs. Marshall in the society pages.

MARSHALL. I dare say. She moves about a great deal. And all of you are part of the same business? Hubbard Sons?

BEN (*motions to Oscar*). Oscar and me. (*Motions to Regina*) My sister's good husband is a banker.

MARSHALL (*looks at Regina, surprised*). Oh.

REGINA. I am so sorry that my husband isn't here to meet you.

He's been very ill. He is at Johns Hopkins. But he will be home soon. We think he is getting better now.

LEO. I work for Uncle Horace. (*Regina looks at him*) I mean I work for Uncle Horace at his bank. I keep an eye on things while he's away.

REGINA (*smiles*). Really, Leo?

BEN (*looks at Leo, then to Marshall*). Modesty in the young is as excellent as it is rare.

OSCAR (*to Leo*). Your uncle means that a young man should speak more modestly.

LEO (*hastily, taking a step to Ben*). Oh, I didn't mean, sir —

MARSHALL. Oh, Mrs. Hubbard. Where's that Wagner autograph you promised to let me see? My train will be leaving soon and —

BIRDIE. The autograph? Oh. Well. Really, Mr. Marshall, I didn't mean to chatter so about it. Really I — (*Nervously, looking at Oscar*) You must excuse me. I didn't get it because, well, because I had — I — I had a little headache and —

OSCAR. My wife is a miserable victim of headaches.

REGINA (*quickly*). Mr. Marshall said at supper that he would like you to play for him, Alexandra.

ALEXANDRA (*who has been looking at Birdie*). It's not I who play well, sir. It's my aunt. She plays just wonderfully. She's my teacher. (*Rises. Eagerly*) May we play a duet? May we, Mama?

BIRDIE. Thank you, dear. But I have my headache now. I —

OSCAR (*sharply*). Don't be stubborn, Birdie. Mr. Marshall wants you to play.

MARSHALL. Indeed I do. If your headache isn't —

BIRDIE (*hesitates, then gets up, pleased*). But I'd like to, sir. Very much. (*She and Alexandra go to the piano.*)

MARSHALL. It's very remarkable how you Southern aristocrats have kept together. Kept together and kept what belonged to you.

BEN. You misunderstand, sir. Southern aristocrats have *not* kept together and have *not* kept what belonged to them.

MARSHALL (*laughs, indicates room*). You don't call this keeping what belongs to you?

BEN. But we are not aristocrats. (*Points to Birdie at the piano*) Our brother's wife is the only one of us who belongs to the Southern aristocracy.

(*Birdie looks toward Ben.*)

MARSHALL (*smiles*). My information is that you people have been here, and solidly here, for a long time.

OSCAR. And so we have. Since our great-grandfather.

BEN. Who was *not* an aristocrat, like Birdie's.

MARSHALL. You make great distinctions.

BEN. Oh, they have been made for us. And maybe they are important distinctions. Now you take Birdie's family. When my great-grandfather came here they were the highest-tone plantation owners in this state.

LEO (*steps to Marshall. Proudly*). My mother's grandfather was *governor* of the state before the war.

OSCAR. They owned the plantation Lionnet. You may have heard of it, sir?

MARSHALL (*laughs*). No, I've never heard of anything but brick houses on a lake, and cotton mills.

BEN. Lionnet in its day was the best cotton land in the South. It still brings us in a fair crop. Ah, they were great days for those people — even when I can remember. They had the best of everything. (*Birdie turns to them*) Cloth from Paris, trips to Europe, horses you can't raise anymore, niggers to lift their fingers —

BIRDIE. We were good to our people. Everybody knew that. We were better to them than —

REGINA (*quickly*). Why, Birdie. You aren't playing.

BEN. But when the war comes these fine gentlemen ride off and leave the cotton, *and* the women, to rot.

BIRDIE. My father was killed in the war. He was a fine soldier, Mr. Marshall. A fine man.

REGINA. Oh, certainly, Birdie. A famous soldier.

BEN (*to Birdie*). But that isn't the tale I am telling Mr. Marshall. (*To Marshall*) Well, sir, the war ends. Lionnet is almost ruined, and the sons finish ruining it. And there were thousands like them. Why? Because the Southern aristocrat can adapt himself to nothing. Too high-tone to try.

MARSHALL. Sometimes it is difficult to learn new ways. (*Birdie and Alexandra begin to play. Marshall leans forward, listening.*)

BEN. Perhaps, perhaps. (*He sees that Marshall is listening to the music. Irritated, he turns to Birdie and Alexandra at the piano, then back to Marshall*) You're right, Mr. Marshall. It is difficult to learn new ways. But maybe that's why it's profitable. *Our* grandfather and *our* father learned the new ways and learned how to make them pay. (*Smiles*) *They* were in trade. Hubbard Sons, Merchandise. Others, Birdie's family, for example, looked down on them. (*Settles back in chair*) To make a long story short, Lionnet now belongs to *us.* (*Birdie stops playing*) Twenty years ago we took over their land, their cotton, and their daughter. (*Birdie rises and stands stiffly by the piano. Marshall, who has been watching her, rises.*)

MARSHALL. May I bring you a glass of port, Mrs. Hubbard?

BIRDIE (*softly*). No, thank you, sir. You are most polite.

REGINA (*sharply, to Ben*). You are boring Mr. Marshall with these ancient family tales.

BEN. I hope not. I hope not. I am trying to make an important point — (*Bows to Marshall*) for our future business partner.

OSCAR (*to Marshall*). My brother always says that it's folks like us who have struggled and fought to bring to our land some of the prosperity of your land.

BEN. Some people call that patriotism.

REGINA (*laughs gaily*). I hope you don't find my brothers too obvious, Mr. Marshall. I'm afraid they mean that this is the time for the ladies to leave the gentlemen to talk business.

MARSHALL (*hastily*). Not at all. We settled everything this afternoon. (*He looks at his watch*) I have only a few minutes before I must leave for the train. (*Smiles at her*) And I insist they be spent with you.

REGINA. *And* with another glass of port.

MARSHALL. Thank you.

BEN. My sister is right. (*To Marshall*) I am a plain man and I am trying to say a plain thing. A man ain't only in business for what he can get out of it. It's got to give him something here. (*Puts hand to his breast*) That's every bit as true for the nigger picking cotton for a silver quarter, as it is for you and me. (*Regina gives Marshall a glass of port*) If it don't give him something here, then he don't pick the cotton right. Money isn't all. Not by three shots.

MARSHALL. Really? Well, I always thought it was a great deal.

REGINA. And so did I, Mr. Marshall.

MARSHALL (*pleasantly, but with meaning*). Now you don't have to convince me that you are the right people for the deal. I wouldn't be here if you hadn't convinced me six months ago. You want the mill here, and I want it here. It isn't my business to find out why you want it.

BEN. To bring the machine to the cotton, and not the cotton to the machine.

MARSHALL (*amused*). You have a turn for neat phrases, Hubbard. Well, however grand your reasons are, mine are simple: I want to make money and I believe I'll make it on you. (*As Ben starts to speak, he smiles*) Mind you, I have no objections to more high-minded reasons. They are mighty valuable in business. It's fine to have partners who so closely follow the teachings of Christ. (*Gets up*) And now I must leave for my train.

REGINA. I'm sorry you won't stay over with us, Mr. Marshall, but you'll come again. Anytime you like.

BEN (*motions to Leo, indicating the bottle*). Fill them up, boy, fill them up. (*Leo moves around filling the glasses as Ben speaks*) Down here, sir, we have a strange custom. We drink the *last* drink for a toast. That's to prove that the Southerner is always still on his feet for the last drink. (*Picks up his glass*) It was Henry Frick, your Mr. Henry Frick, who said, "Railroads are the Rembrandts of investments." Well, *I* say, "Southern cotton mills *will be* the Rembrandts of investment." So I give you the firm of Hubbard Sons and Marshall, Cotton Mills, and to it a long and prosperous life. (*They all pick up their glasses. Marshall looks at them, amused. Then he, too, lifts his glass, smiles.*)

OSCAR. The children will drive you to the depot. Leo! Alexandra! You will drive Mr. Marshall down.

LEO (*eagerly, looks at Ben who nods*). Yes, sir. (*To Marshall*) Not often Uncle Ben lets *me* drive the horses. And a beautiful pair they are. (*Starts for hall*) Come on, Zan.

ALEXANDRA. May I drive tonight, Uncle Ben, please? I'd like to and —

BEN (*shakes his head, laughs*). In your evening clothes? Oh, no, my dear.

ALEXANDRA. But Leo always — (*Stops, exits quickly.*)

REGINA. I don't like to say good-bye to you, Mr. Marshall.

MARSHALL. Then we won't say good-bye. You have promised that you would come and let me show you Chicago. Do I have to make you promise again?

REGINA (*looks at him as he presses her hand*). I promise again.

MARSHALL (*moves to Birdie*). Good-bye, Mrs. Hubbard.

BIRDIE. Good-bye, sir.

MARSHALL (*as he passes Regina*) Remember.

REGINA. I will.

(*Marshall exits, followed by Ben and Oscar. For a second Regina and Birdie stand looking after them. Then Regina throws up her arms, laughs happily.*)

REGINA. And there, Birdie, goes the man who has opened the door to our future.

BIRDIE (*surprised at the unaccustomed friendliness*). What?

REGINA. *Our future.* Yours and mine, Ben's and Oscar's, the children — (*Looks at Birdie's puzzled face, laughs*) Our future! (*Gaily*) You were charming at supper, Birdie. Mr. Marshall certainly thought so.

BIRDIE (*pleased*). Why, Regina! Do you think he did?

REGINA. Can't you tell when you're being admired?

BIRDIE. Oscar said I bored Mr. Marshall. But he admired *you.* He told me so.

REGINA. What did he say?

BIRDIE. He said to me, "I hope your sister-in-law will come to Chicago. Chicago will be at her feet." He said the ladies would bow to your manners and the gentlemen to your looks.

REGINA. Did he? He seems a lonely man. Imagine being lonely with all that money. I don't think he likes his wife.

BIRDIE. Not like his wife? What a thing to say.

REGINA. She's away a great deal. He said that several times. And once he made fun of her being so social and high-tone. But that fits in all right. (*Sits back, stretches*) Her being social, I mean. She can introduce me. It won't take long with an introduction from her.

BIRDIE (*bewildered*). Introduce you? In Chicago? You mean you really might go? Oh, Regina, you can't leave here. What about Horace?

REGINA. Don't look so scared about everything, Birdie. I'm going to live in Chicago. I've always wanted to. And now there'll be plenty of money to go with.

BIRDIE. But Horace won't be able to move around. You know what the doctor wrote.

REGINA. There'll be millions, Birdie, millions. You know what I've always said when people told me we were rich? I said I think you should either be a nigger or a millionaire. In between, like us, what for? (*Laughs*) But I'm not going away tomorrow, Birdie. There's plenty of time to worry about Horace when he comes home. If he ever decides to come home.

BIRDIE. Will we be going to Chicago? I mean, Oscar and Leo and me?

REGINA. You? I shouldn't think so. (*Laughs*) Well, we must remember tonight. It's a very important night and we mustn't forget it. We shall plan all the things we'd like to have and then we'll really have them. Make a wish, Birdie, any wish. It's bound to come true now. (*Ben and Oscar enter.*)

BIRDIE (*laughs*). Well. Well, I don't know. Maybe. (*Regina turns to look at Ben*) Well, I guess I'd know right off what I wanted. (*Oscar stands by the upper window, waves to the departing carriage.*)

REGINA (*looks up at Ben, smiles. He smiles back at her*). Well, you did it.

BEN. Looks like it might be we did.

REGINA (*springs up*). Looks like it! Don't pretend. You're like a cat who's been licking the cream. (*Crosses to wine bottle*) Now we must all have a drink to celebrate.

OSCAR. The children, Alexandra and Leo, make a very handsome couple, Regina. Marshall remarked himself what fine young folks they were. How well they looked together!

REGINA (*sharply*). Yes. You said that before, Oscar.

BEN. Yes, sir. It's beginning to look as if the deal's all set. I may not be a subtle man — but — (*Turns to them. After a second*) Now somebody ask me how I know the deal is set.

OSCAR. What do you mean, Ben?

BEN. You remember I told him that down here we drink the *last* drink for a toast?

OSCAR (*thoughtfully*). Yes. I never heard that before.

BEN. Nobody's ever heard it before. God forgives those who invent what they need. I already had his signature. But we've all done business with men whose word over a glass is better than a bond. Anyway it don't hurt to have both.

OSCAR (*turns to Regina*). You understand what Ben means?

REGINA. Yes, Oscar. I understand. I understood immediately.

BEN (*looks at her admiringly*). Did you, Regina? Well, when he lifted his glass to drink, I closed my eyes and saw the bricks going into place.

REGINA. And *I* saw a lot more than that.

BEN. Slowly, slowly. As yet we have only our hopes.

REGINA. Birdie and I have just been planning what we want. I know what I want. What will you want, Ben?

BEN. Caution. Don't count the chickens. (*Leans back, laughs*) Well, God would allow us a little daydreaming. Good for the soul when you've worked hard enough to deserve it. (*Pauses*) I think I'll have a stable. For a long time I've had my good eyes on Carter's in Savannah. A rich man's pleasure, the sport of kings, why not the sport of Hubbards? Why not?

REGINA (*smiles*). Why not? What will you have, Oscar?

OSCAR. I don't know. (*Thoughtfully*) The pleasure of seeing the bricks grow will be enough for me.

BEN. Oh, of course. Our greatest pleasure will be to see the bricks grow. But we are all entitled to a little side indulgence.

OSCAR. Yes, I suppose so. Well, then, I think we might take a few trips here and there, eh, Birdie?

BIRDIE (*surprised at being consulted*). Yes, Oscar. I'd like that.

OSCAR. We might even make a regular trip to Jekyll Island. I've heard the Cornelly place is for sale. We might think about buying it. Make a nice change. Do you good, Birdie, a change of climate. Fine shooting on Jekyll, the best.

BIRDIE. I'd like —

OSCAR (*indulgently*). What would you like?

BIRDIE. Two things. Two things I'd like most.

REGINA. Two! I should like a thousand. You are modest, Birdie.

BIRDIE (*warmly, delighted with the unexpected interest*). I should like to have Lionnet back. I know you own it now, but I'd like to see it fixed up again, the way Mama and Papa had it. Every year it used to get a nice coat of paint — Papa was very particular about the paint — and the lawn was so smooth all the way down to the river, with the trims of zinnias and red-feather plush. And the figs and blue little plums and the scuppernongs — (*Smiles. Turns to Regina*) The organ is still there and it wouldn't cost much to fix. We could have parties for Zan, the way Mama used to have for me.

BEN. That's a pretty picture, Birdie. Might be a most pleasant way to live. (*Dismissing Birdie*) What do you want, Regina?

BIRDIE (*very happily, not noticing that they are no longer listening to her*). I could have a cutting garden. Just where Mama's used to be. Oh, I do think we could be happier there. Papa used to say that *nobody* had ever lost their temper at Lionnet, and *nobody* ever would. Papa would never let anybody be nasty-spoken or mean. No, sir. He just didn't like it.

BEN. What do you want, Regina?

REGINA. I'm going to Chicago. And when I'm settled there and know the right people and the right things to buy — because I certainly don't now — I shall go to Paris and buy them. (*Laughs*) I'm going to leave you and Oscar to count the bricks.

BIRDIE. Oscar. Please let me have Lionnet back.

OSCAR (*to Regina*). You are serious about moving to Chicago?

BEN. She is going to see the great world and leave us in the little one. Well, we'll come and visit you and meet all the great and be proud you are our sister.

REGINA (*gaily*). Certainly. And you won't even have to learn to be subtle, Ben. Stay as you are. You will be rich and the rich don't have to be subtle.

OSCAR. But what about Alexandra? She's seventeen. Old enough to be thinking about marrying.

BIRDIE. And, Oscar, I have one more wish. Just one more wish.

OSCAR (*turns*). What is it, Birdie? What are you saying?

BIRDIE. I want you to stop shooting. I mean, so much. I don't like to see animals and birds killed just for the killing. You only throw them away —

BEN (*to Regina*). It'll take a great deal of money to live as you're planning, Regina.

REGINA. Certainly. But there'll be plenty of money. You have estimated the profits very high.

BEN. I have —

BIRDIE (*Oscar is looking at her furiously*). And you never let anybody else shoot, and the niggers need it so much to keep from starving. It's wicked to shoot food just because you like to shoot, when poor people need it so —

BEN (*laughs*). I have estimated the profits very high — for myself.

REGINA. What did you say?

BIRDIE. I've always wanted to speak about it, Oscar.

OSCAR (*slowly, carefully*). What are you chattering about?

BIRDIE (*nervously*). I was talking about Lionnet and — and about your shooting —

OSCAR. You are exciting yourself.

REGINA (*to Ben*). I didn't hear you. There was so much talking.

OSCAR (*to Birdie*). You have been acting very childish, very excited, all evening.

BIRDIE. Regina asked me what I'd like.

REGINA. What did you say, Ben?

BIRDIE. Now that we'll be so rich everybody was saying what they would like, so *I* said what *I* would like, too.

BEN. I said — (*He is interrupted by Oscar.*)

OSCAR (*to Birdie*). Very well. We've all heard you. That's enough now.

BEN. I am waiting. (*They stop*) I am waiting for you to finish. You and Birdie. Four conversations are three too many. (*Birdie slowly sits down. Ben smiles, to Regina*) I said that I had, and I do, estimate the profits very high — for myself, and Oscar, of course.

REGINA. And what does that mean? (*Ben shrugs, looks toward Oscar.*)

OSCAR (*looks at Ben, clears throat*). Well, Regina, it's like this. For forty-nine percent Marshall will put up four hundred thousand dollars. For fifty-one percent — (*Smiles archly*) a controlling interest, mind you — we will put up two hundred and twenty-five thousand dollars besides offering him certain benefits that our (*looks at Ben*) local position allows us to manage. Ben means that two hundred and twenty-five thousand dollars is a lot of money.

REGINA. I know the terms and I know it's a lot of money.

BEN (*nodding*). It is.

OSCAR. Ben means that we are ready with our two-thirds of the money. Your third, Horace's I mean, doesn't seem to be ready. (*Raises his hand as Regina starts to speak*) Ben has written to Horace, I have written, and you have written. He answers. But he never mentions this business. Yet we have explained to him in great detail, and told him the urgency. Still he never mentions it. Ben has been very patient, Regina. Naturally, you are our sister and we want you to benefit from anything we do.

REGINA. And in addition to your concern for me, you do not want control to go out of the family. (*To Ben*) That right, Ben?

BEN. That's cynical. (*Smiles*) Cynicism is an unpleasant way of saying the truth.

OSCAR. No need to be cynical. We'd have no trouble raising the third share, the share that you want to take.

REGINA. I am sure you could get the third share, the share you were saving for me. But that would give you a strange partner. And strange partners sometimes want a great deal. (*Smiles unpleasantly*) But perhaps it would be wise for you to find him.

OSCAR. Now, now. Nobody says we *want* to do that. We would like to have you in and you would like to come in.

REGINA. Yes. I certainly would.

BEN (*laughs, puts up his hand*). But we haven't heard from Horace.

REGINA. I've given my word that Horace will put up the money. That should be enough.

BEN. Oh, it was enough. I took your word. But I've got to have more than your word now. The contracts will be signed this week, and Marshall will want to see our money soon after. Regina, Horace has been in Baltimore for five months. I know that you've written him to come home, and that he hasn't come.

OSCAR. It's beginning to look as if he doesn't want to come home.

REGINA. Of course he wants to come home. You can't move around with heart trouble at any moment you choose. You know what doctors are like once they get their hands on a case like this —

OSCAR. They can't very well keep him from answering letters, can they? (*Regina turns to Ben*) They couldn't keep him from arranging for the money if he wanted to —

REGINA. Has it occurred to you that Horace is also a good businessman?

BEN. Certainly. He is a shrewd trader. Always has been. The bank is proof of that.

REGINA. Then, possibly, he may be keeping silent because he doesn't think he is getting enough for his money. Seventy-five thousand he has to put up. That's a lot of money, too.

OSCAR. Nonsense. He knows a good thing when he hears it. He knows that we can make *twice* the profit on cotton goods manufactured here than can be made in the North.

BEN. That isn't what Regina means. May I interpret you, Regina? (*To Oscar*) Regina is saying that Horace wants *more* than a third of our share.

OSCAR. But he's only putting up a third of the money. You put up a third and you get a third. What else could he expect?

REGINA. Well, *I* don't know. I don't know about these things. It would seem that if you put up a third you should only get a third. But then again, there's no law about it, is there? I should think that if you knew your money was very badly needed, well, you just might say, I want more, I want a bigger share. You boys have done that. I've heard you say so.

BEN (*after a pause, laughs*). So you believe he has deliberately held out? For a larger share? Well, I don't believe it. But I do believe that's what *you* want. Am I right, Regina?

REGINA. Oh, I shouldn't like to be too definite. But I could say that I wouldn't like to persuade Horace unless he did get a larger share. I must look after his interests. It seems only natural —

OSCAR. And where would the larger share come from?

REGINA. I don't know. That's not my business. (*Giggles*) But perhaps it could come off your share, Oscar. (*Regina and Ben laugh.*)

OSCAR (*rises and wheels on both of them as they laugh*). What kind of talk is this?

BEN. I haven't said a thing.

OSCAR (*to Regina*). *You* are talking very big tonight.

REGINA (*stops laughing*). Am I? Well, you should know me well enough to know that I wouldn't be asking for things I didn't think I could get.

OSCAR. Listen. I don't believe you can even get Horace to come home, much less get money from him or talk quite so big about what you want.

REGINA. Oh, I can get him home.

OSCAR. Then why haven't you?

REGINA. I thought I should fight his battles for him, before he came home. Horace is a very sick man. And even if *you* don't care how sick he is, I do.

BEN. Stop this foolish squabbling. How can you get him home?

REGINA. I will send Alexandra to Baltimore. She will ask him to come home. She will say that she wants him to come home, and that *I* want him to come home.

BIRDIE (*rises*). Well, of course she wants him here, but he's sick and maybe he's happy where he is.

REGINA (*ignores Birdie, to Ben*). You agree that he will come home if she asks him to, if she says that I miss him and want him —

BEN (*looks at her, smiles*). I admire you, Regina. And I agree. That's settled now and — (*Starts to rise.*)

REGINA (*quickly*). But before she brings him home, I want to know what he's going to get.

BEN. What do you want?

REGINA. Twice what you offered.

BEN. Well, you won't get it.

OSCAR (*to Regina*). I think you've gone crazy.

REGINA. I don't want to fight, Ben —

BEN. I don't either. You won't get it. There isn't any chance of that. (*Roguishly*) You're holding us up, and that's not pretty, Regina, not pretty. (*Holds up his hand as he sees she is about to speak*) But we need you, and I don't want to fight. Here's what I'll do: I'll give Horace forty percent, instead of the thirty-three and a third he really should get. I'll do that, provided he is home and his money is up within two weeks. How's that?

REGINA. All right.

OSCAR. I've asked before: where is this extra share coming from?

BEN (*pleasantly*). From you. From your share.

OSCAR (*furiously*). From me, is it? That's just fine and dandy. That's my reward. For thirty-five years I've worked my hands to the bone for you. For thirty-five years I've done all the things you didn't want to do. And this is what I —

BEN (*turns to look at Oscar. Oscar breaks off*). My, my. I am being attacked tonight on all sides. First by my sister, then by my brother. And I ain't a man who likes being attacked. I can't believe that God wants the strong to parade their strength, but I don't mind doing it if it's got to be done. You ought to take these things better, Oscar. I've made you money in the past. I'm going to make you more money now. You'll be a very rich man. What's the difference to any of us if a little more goes here, a little less goes there — it's all in the family. And it will stay in the family. I'll never marry. (*Addie enters, begins to gather the glasses from the table*) So my money will go to Alexandra and Leo. They may even marry someday and — (*Addie looks at Ben.*)

BIRDIE (*rising*). Marry — Zan and Leo —

OSCAR (*carefully*). That would make a great difference in my feelings. If they married.

BEN. Yes, that's what I mean. Of course it would make a difference.

OSCAR (*carefully*). Is that what *you* mean, Regina?

REGINA. Oh, it's too far away. We'll talk about it in a few years.

OSCAR. I want to talk about it now.

BEN (*nods*). Naturally.

REGINA. There's a lot of things to consider. They are first cousins, and —

OSCAR. That isn't unusual. Our grandmother and grandfather were first cousins.

REGINA (*giggles*). And look at us. (*Ben giggles.*)

OSCAR (*angrily*). You're both being very gay with my money.

BEN (*sighs*). These quarrels. I dislike them so. (*To Regina*) A marriage might be a very wise arrangement, for several reasons. And then, Oscar has given up something for you. You should try to manage something for him.

REGINA. I haven't said I was opposed to it. But Leo is a wild boy. There were those times when he took a little money from the bank and —

OSCAR. That's all past history —

REGINA. Oh, I know. And I know all young men are wild. I'm only mentioning it to show you that there are considerations —

BEN (*irritated because she does not understand that he is trying to keep Oscar quiet*). All right, so there are. But please assure Oscar that you will think about it very seriously.

REGINA (*smiles, nods*). Very well. I assure Oscar that I will think about it seriously.

OSCAR (*sharply*). That is not an answer.

REGINA (*rises*). My, you're in a bad humor and you shall put me in one. I have said all that I am willing to say now. After all, Horace has to give his consent, too.

OSCAR. Horace will do what you tell him to.

REGINA. Yes, I think he will.

OSCAR. And I have your word that you will try to —

REGINA (*patiently*). Yes, Oscar. You have my word that I will think about it. Now do leave me alone. (*There is the sound of the front door being closed.*)

BIRDIE. I — Alexandra is only seventeen. She —

LEO (*comes into the room*). Mr. Marshall got off safe and sound. Weren't those fine clothes he had? You can always spot clothes made in a good place. Looks like maybe they were done in England. Lots of men in the North send all the way to England for their stuff.

BEN (*to Leo*). Were you careful driving the horses?

LEO. Oh, yes, sir. I was. (*Alexandra has come in on Ben's question, hears the answer, looks angrily at Leo.*)

ALEXANDRA. It's a lovely night. You should have come, Aunt Birdie.

REGINA. Were you gracious to Mr. Marshall?

ALEXANDRA. I think so, Mama. I liked him.

REGINA. Good. And now I have great news for you. You are going to Baltimore in the morning to bring your father home.

ALEXANDRA (*gasps, then delighted*). Me? Papa said I should come? That must mean — (*Turns to Addie*) Addie, he must be well. Think of it, he'll be back home again. We'll bring him home.

REGINA. You are going alone, Alexandra.

ADDIE (*Alexandra has turned in surprise*). Going alone? Going by herself? A child that age! Mr. Horace ain't going to like Zan traipsing up there by herself.

REGINA (*sharply*). Go upstairs and lay out Alexandra's things.

ADDIE. He'd expect me to be along —

REGINA. I'll be up in a few minutes to tell you what to pack. (*Addie slowly begins to climb the steps. To Alexandra*) I should think you'd like going alone. At your age it certainly would have delighted me. You're a strange girl, Alexandra. Addie has babied you so much.

ALEXANDRA. I only thought it would be more fun if Addie and I went together.

BIRDIE (*timidly*). Maybe I could go with her, Regina. I'd really like to.

REGINA. She is going alone. She is getting old enough to take some responsibilities.

OSCAR. She'd better learn now. She's almost old enough to get married. (*Jovially, to Leo, slapping him on shoulder*) Eh, son?

LEO. Huh?

OSCAR (*annoyed with Leo for not understanding*). Old enough to get married, you're thinking, eh?

LEO. Oh, yes, sir. (*Feebly*) Lots of girls get married at Zan's age. Look at Mary Prester and Johanna and —

REGINA. Well, she's not getting married tomorrow. But she is going to Baltimore tomorrow, so let's talk about that. (*To Alexandra*) You'll be glad to have Papa home again.

ALEXANDRA. I wanted to go before, Mama. You remember that. But you said *you* couldn't go, and that *I* couldn't go alone.

REGINA. I've changed my mind. (*Too casually*) You're to tell Papa how much you missed him, and that he must come home now — for your sake. Tell him that you *need* him home.

ALEXANDRA. Need him home? I don't understand.

REGINA. There is nothing for you to understand. You are simply to say what I have told you.

BIRDIE (*rises*). He may be too sick. She couldn't do that —

ALEXANDRA. Yes. He may be too sick to travel. I couldn't make him think he had to come home for me, if he is too sick to —

REGINA (*looks at her, sharply, challengingly*). You *couldn't* do what I tell you to do, Alexandra?

ALEXANDRA (*quietly*). No. I couldn't. If I thought it would hurt him.

REGINA (*after a second's silence, smiles pleasantly*). But you are doing this for Papa's own good. (*Takes Alexandra's hand*) You must let me be the judge of his condition. It's the best possible cure for him to come home and be taken care of here. He mustn't stay there any longer and listen to those alarmist doctors. You are doing this entirely for his sake. Tell your papa that I want him to come home, that I miss him very much.

ALEXANDRA (*slowly*). Yes, Mama.

REGINA (*to the others*). I must go and start getting Alexandra ready now. Why don't you all go home?

BEN (*rises*). I'll attend to the railroad ticket. One of the boys will bring it over. Good night, everybody. Have a nice trip, Alexandra. The food on the train is very good. The celery is so crisp. Have a good time and act like a little lady. (*Exits.*)

REGINA. Good night, Ben. Good night, Oscar — (*Playfully*) Don't be so glum, Oscar. It makes you look as if you had chronic indigestion.

BIRDIE. Good night, Regina.

REGINA. Good night, Birdie. (*Exits upstairs.*)

OSCAR (*starts for hall*). Come along.

LEO (*to Alexandra*). Imagine your not wanting to go! What a little fool you are. Wish it were me. What I could do in a place like Baltimore!

ALEXANDRA. Mind your business. I can guess the kind of things *you* could do.

LEO (*laughs*). Oh, no, you couldn't. (*He exits.*)

REGINA (*calling from the top of the stairs*). Come on, Alexandra.

BIRDIE (*quickly, softly*). Zan.

ALEXANDRA. I don't understand about my going. Aunt Birdie. (*Shrugs*) But anyway, Papa will be home again. (*Pats Birdie's arm*) Don't worry about me. I can take care of myself. Really I can.

BIRDIE (*shakes her head, softly*). That's not what I'm worried about. Zan —

ALEXANDRA (*comes close to her*). What's the matter?

BIRDIE. It's about Leo —

ALEXANDRA (*whispering*). He beat the horses. That's why we were late getting back. We had to wait until they cooled off. He always beats the horses as if —

BIRDIE (*whispering frantically, holding Alexandra's hands*). He's my son. My own son. But you are more to me — more to me than my own child. I love you more than anybody else —

ALEXANDRA. Don't worry about the horses. I'm sorry I told you.

BIRDIE (*her voice rising*). *I am not worrying about the horses.* I am worrying about *you.* You are *not* going to marry Leo. I am not going to let them do that to you —

ALEXANDRA. Marry? To Leo? (*Laughs*) I wouldn't marry, Aunt Birdie. I've never even thought about it —

BIRDIE. But they have thought about it. (*Wildly*) Zan, I couldn't stand to think about such a thing. You and — (*Oscar has come into the doorway on Alexandra's speech. He is standing quietly, listening.*)

ALEXANDRA (*laughs*). But I'm not going to marry. And I'm certainly not going to marry Leo.

BIRDIE. Don't you understand? They'll make you. They'll make you —

ALEXANDRA (*takes Birdie's hands, quietly, firmly*). That's foolish, Aunt Birdie. I'm grown now. Nobody can make me do anything.

BIRDIE. I just couldn't stand —

OSCAR (*sharply*). Birdie. (*Birdie looks up, draws quickly away from Alexandra. She stands rigid, frightened.*) Birdie, get your hat and coat.

ADDIE (*calls from upstairs*). Come on, baby. Your mama's waiting for you, and she ain't nobody to keep waiting.

ALEXANDRA. All right. (*Then softly, embracing Birdie*) Good night, Aunt Birdie. (*As she passes Oscar*) Good night, Uncle Oscar. (*Birdie begins to move slowly toward the door as Alexandra climbs the stairs. Alexandra is almost out of view when Birdie reaches Oscar in the doorway. As Birdie attempts to pass him, he slaps her hard, across the face. Birdie cries out, puts her hand to her face. On the cry, Alexandra turns, begins to run down the stairs*) Aunt Birdie! What happened? What happened? I —

BIRDIE (*softly, without turning*). Nothing, darling. Nothing happened. (*Anxious to keep Alexandra from coming close*) Now go to bed. (*Oscar exits*) Nothing happened. I only — I only twisted my ankle. (*She goes out. Alexandra stands on the stairs looking after her.*)

Curtain

Act Two

SCENE: *Same as Act One. A week later, morning.*

AT RISE: *The light comes from the open shutter of the right window; the other shutters are tightly closed. Addie is standing at the window, looking out. Near the dining-room doors are brooms, mops, rags, etc. After a second, Oscar comes into the entrance hall, looks in the room, shivers, decides not to take his hat and coat off, comes into the room. At the sound of the door, Addie turns.*

ADDIE (*without interest*). Oh, it's you, Mr. Oscar.

OSCAR. What is this? It's not night. What's the matter here? (*Shivers*) Fine thing at this time of the morning. Blinds all closed. (*Addie begins to open shutters*) Where's Miss Regina? It's cold in here.

ADDIE. Miss Regina ain't down yet.

OSCAR. She had any word?

ADDIE. No, sir.

OSCAR. Wouldn't you think a girl that age could get on a train at one place and have sense enough to get off at another?

ADDIE. Something must have happened. If Zan say she was coming last night, she's coming last night. Unless something happened. Sure fire disgrace to let a baby like that go all that way alone to bring home a sick man without —

OSCAR. You do a lot of judging around here, Addie, eh? Judging of your white folks, I mean.

REGINA (*speaking from the upstairs hall*). Who's downstairs, Addie? (*She appears in a dressing gown, peers down from the landing. Addie picks up broom, dustpan and brush and exits*) Oh, it's you, Oscar. What are you doing here so early? I haven't been down yet. I'm not finished dressing.

OSCAR (*speaking up to her*). You had any word from them?

REGINA. No.

OSCAR. Then something certainly has happened. People don't

just say they are arriving on Thursday night, and they haven't come by Friday morning.

REGINA. Oh, nothing has happened. Alexandra just hasn't got sense enough to send a message.

OSCAR. If nothing's happened, then why aren't they here?

REGINA. You asked me that ten times last night. My, you do fret so, Oscar. Anything might have happened. They may have missed connections in Atlanta, the train may have been delayed — oh, a hundred things could have kept them.

OSCAR. Where's Ben?

REGINA (*as she disappears upstairs*). Where should he be? At home, probably. Really, Oscar, I don't tuck him in his bed and I don't take him out of it. Have some coffee and don't worry so much.

OSCAR. Have some coffee? There isn't any coffee. (*Looks at his watch, shakes his head. After a second Cal enters with a large silver tray, coffee urn, small cups, newspaper*) Oh, there you are. Is everything in this fancy house always late?

CAL (*looks at him, surprised*). You ain't out shooting this morning, Mr. Oscar?

OSCAR. First day I missed since I had my head cold. First day I missed in eight years.

CAL. Yes, sir. I bet you. Simon he say you had a mighty good day yesterday morning. That's what Simon say. (*Brings Oscar coffee and newspaper.*)

OSCAR. Pretty good, pretty good.

CAL (*laughs, slyly*). Bet you got enough bobwhite and squirrel to give every nigger in town a Jesus-party. Most of 'em ain't had no meat since the cotton picking was over. Bet they'd give anything for a little piece of that meat —

OSCAR (*turns his head to look at Cal*). Cal, if I catch a nigger in this town going shooting, you know what's going to happen. (*Leo enters.*)

CAL (*hastily*). Yes, sir, Mr. Oscar. It was Simon who told me and — Morning, Mr. Leo. You gentlemen having your breakfast with us here?

LEO. The boys in the bank don't know a thing. They haven't had any message. (*Cal waits for an answer, gets none, shrugs, exits.*)

OSCAR (*peers at Leo*). What you doing here, son?

LEO. You told me to find out if the boys at the bank had any message from Uncle Horace or Zan —

OSCAR. I told you if they had a message to bring it here. I told you that if they didn't have a message to stay at the bank and do your work.

LEO. Oh, I guess I misunderstood.

OSCAR. You didn't misunderstand. You just were looking for any excuse to take an hour off. (*Leo pours a cup of coffee*) You got to stop that kind of thing. You got to start settling down. You going to be a married man one of these days.

LEO. Yes, sir.

OSCAR. You also got to stop with that woman in Mobile. (*As Leo is about to speak*) You're young and I haven't got no objections to outside women. That is, I haven't got no objections so long as they don't interfere with serious things. Outside women are all right in their place, but *now* isn't their place. You got to realize that.

LEO (*nods*). Yes, sir. I'll tell her. She'll act all right about it.

OSCAR. Also, you got to start working harder at the bank. You got to convince your Uncle Horace you going to make a fit husband for Alexandra.

LEO. What do you think has happened to them? Supposed to be here last night — (*Laughs*) Bet you Uncle Ben's mighty worried. Seventy-five thousand dollars worried.

OSCAR (*smiles happily*). Ought to be worried. Damn well ought to be. First he don't answer the letters, then he don't come home — (*Giggles.*)

LEO. What will happen if Uncle Horace don't come home or don't —

OSCAR. Or don't put up the money? Oh, we'll get it from outside. Easy enough.

LEO (*surprised*). But *you* don't want outsiders.

OSCAR. What do I care who gets my share? I been shaved already. Serve Ben right if he had to give away some of his.

LEO. Damn shame what they did to you.

OSCAR (*looking up the stairs*). Don't talk so loud. Don't you worry. When I die, you'll have as much as the rest. You might have yours *and* Alexandra's. I'm not so easily licked.

LEO. I wasn't thinking of myself, Papa —

OSCAR. Well, you should be, you should be. It's every man's duty to think of himself.

LEO. You think Uncle Horace don't want to go in on this?

OSCAR (*giggles*). That's my hunch. He hasn't showed any signs of loving it yet.

LEO (*laughs*). But he hasn't listened to Aunt Regina yet, either. Oh, he'll go along. It's too good a thing. Why wouldn't he want to? He's got plenty and plenty to invest with. He don't even have to sell anything. Eighty-eight thousand worth of Union Pacific bonds sitting right in his safe deposit box. All he's got to do is open the box.

OSCAR (*after a pause. Looks at his watch*). Mighty late breakfast in this fancy house. Yes, he's had those bonds for fifteen years. Bought them when they were low and just locked them up.

LEO. Yeah. Just has to open the box and take them out. That's all. Easy as easy can be. (*Laughs*) The things in that box! There's all those bonds, looking mighty fine. (*Oscar slowly puts down his newspaper and turns to Leo*) Then right next to them is a baby shoe of Zan's and a cheap old cameo on a string, and, *and* — nobody'd believe this — a piece of an old violin. Not even a whole violin. Just a piece of an old thing, a piece of a violin.

OSCAR (*very softly, as if he were trying to control his voice*). A piece of a violin! What do you think of that!

LEO. Yes, sirree. A lot of other crazy things, too. A poem, I guess it is, signed with his mother's name, and two old schoolbooks with notes and — (*Leo catches Oscar's look. His voice trails off. He turns his head away.*)

OSCAR (*very softly*). How do you know what's in the box, son?

LEO (*draws back, frightened, realizing what he has said*). Oh, well. Well, er. Well, one of the boys, sir. It was one of the boys at the bank. He took old Manders' keys. It was Joe Horns. He just up and took Manders' keys and, and — well, took the box out. (*Quickly*) Then they all asked me if I wanted to see, too. So I looked a little, I guess, but then I made them close up the box quick and I told them never —

OSCAR (*looks at him*). Joe Horns, you say? He opened it?

LEO. Yes, sir, yes, he did. My word of honor. (*Very nervous now*) I suppose that don't excuse *me* for looking — (*Looking at Oscar*) but I did make him close it up and put the keys back in Manders' drawer —

OSCAR (*leans forward, very softly*). Tell me the truth, Leo. I am not going to be angry with you. Did you open the box yourself?

LEO. *No, sir, I didn't.* I told you I didn't. No, I —

OSCAR (*irritated, patient*). I am *not* going to be angry with you.

(*Watching Leo carefully*) Sometimes a young fellow deserves credit for looking round him to see what's going on. Sometimes that's a good sign in a fellow your age. Many great men have made their fortune with their eyes. Did you open the box?

LEO (*very puzzled*). No. I —

OSCAR (*moves to Leo*). Did you open the box? It may have been — well, it may have been a good thing if you had.

LEO (*after a long pause*). I opened it.

OSCAR (*quickly*). Is that the truth? (*Leo nods*) Does anybody else know that you opened it? Come, Leo, don't be afraid of speaking the truth to me.

LEO. No. Nobody knew. Nobody was in the bank when I did it. But —

OSCAR. Did your Uncle Horace ever know you opened it?

LEO (*shakes his head*). He only looks in it once every six months when he cuts the coupons, and sometimes Manders even does that for him. Uncle Horace don't even have the keys. Manders keeps them for him. Imagine not looking at all that. You can bet if I had the bonds, I'd watch 'em like —

OSCAR. If you had them. *If* you had them. Then you could have a share in the mill, you and me. A fine, big share, too. (*Pauses, shrugs*) Well, a man can't be shot for wanting to see his son get on in the world, can he, boy?

LEO (*looks up, begins to understand*). No, he can't. Natural enough. (*Laughs*) But I haven't got the bonds and Uncle Horace has. And now he can just sit back and wait to be a millionaire.

OSCAR (*innocently*). You think your Uncle Horace likes you well enough to lend you the bonds if he decides not to use them himself?

LEO. Papa, it must be that you haven't had your breakfast! (*Laughs loudly*) Lend me the bonds! My God —

OSCAR (*disappointed*). No, I suppose not. Just a fancy of mine. A loan for three months, maybe four, easy enough for us to pay it back then. Anyway, this is only April — (*Slowly counting the months on his fingers*) and if he doesn't look at them until Autumn he wouldn't even miss them out of the box.

LEO. That's it. He wouldn't even miss them. Ah, well —

OSCAR. No, sir. Wouldn't even miss them. How could he miss them if he never looks at them? (*Sighs as Leo stares at him*)

Well, here we are sitting around waiting for him to come home and invest his money in something he hasn't lifted his hand to get. But I can't help thinking he's acting strange. You laugh when I say he could lend you the bonds if he's not going to use them himself. But would it hurt him?

LEO (*slowly looking at Oscar*). No. No, it wouldn't.

OSCAR. People ought to help other people. But that's not always the way it happens. (*Ben enters, hangs his coat and hat in hall. Very carefully*) And so sometimes you got to think of yourself. (*As Leo stares at him, Ben appears in the doorway*) Morning, Ben.

BEN (*coming in, carrying his newspaper*). Fine sunny morning. Any news from the runaways?

REGINA (*on the staircase*). There's no news or you would have heard it. Quite a convention so early in the morning, aren't you all? (*Goes to coffee urn.*)

OSCAR. You rising mighty late these days. Is that the way they do things in Chicago society?

BEN (*looking at his paper*). Old Carter died up in Senateville. Eighty-one is a good time for us all, eh? What do you think has really happened to Horace, Regina?

REGINA. Nothing.

BEN. You don't think maybe he never started from Baltimore and never intends to start?

REGINA (*irritated*). Of course they've started. Didn't I have a letter from Alexandra? What is so strange about people arriving late? He has that cousin in Savannah he's so fond of. He may have stopped to see him. They'll be along today sometime, very flattered that you and Oscar are so worried about them.

BEN. I'm a natural worrier. Especially when I am getting ready to close a business deal and one of my partners remains silent *and* invisible.

REGINA (*laughs*). Oh, is that it? I thought you were worried about Horace's health.

OSCAR. Oh, that too. Who could help but worry? I'm worried. This is the first day I haven't been shooting since my head cold.

REGINA (*starts toward dining room*). Then you haven't had your breakfast. Come along. (*Oscar and Leo follow her.*)

BEN. Regina. (*She turns at dining-room door*) That cousin of

Horace's has been dead for years and, in any case, the train does not go through Savannah.

REGINA (*laughs, continues into dining room, seats herself*). Did he die? You're always remembering about people dying. (*Ben rises*) Now I intend to eat my breakfast in peace, and read my newspaper.

BEN (*goes toward dining room as he talks*). This is second breakfast for me. My first was bad. Celia ain't the cook she used to be. Too old to have taste anymore. If she hadn't belonged to Mama, I'd send her off to the country.

(*Oscar and Leo start to eat. Ben seats himself.*)

LEO. Uncle Horace will have some tales to tell, I bet. Baltimore is a lively town.

REGINA (*to Cal*). The grits isn't hot enough. Take it back.

CAL. Oh, yes'm. (*Calling into the kitchen as he exits*) Grits didn't hold the heat. Grits didn't hold the heat.

LEO. When I was at school three of the boys and myself took a train once and went over to Baltimore. It was so big we thought we were in Europe. I was just a kid then —

REGINA. I find it very pleasant (*Addie enters*) to have breakfast alone. I hate chattering before I've had something hot. (*Cal closes the dining-room doors*) Do be still, Leo.

(*Addie comes into the room, begins gathering up the cups, carries them to the large tray. Outside there are the sounds of voices. Quickly Addie runs into the hall. A few seconds later she appears again in the doorway, her arm around the shoulders of Horace Giddens, supporting him. Horace is a tall man of about forty-five. He has been good looking, but now his face is tired and ill. He walks stiffly, as if it were an enormous effort, and carefully, as if he were unsure of his balance. Addie takes off his overcoat and hangs it on the hall tree. She then helps him to a chair.*)

HORACE. How are you, Addie? How have you been?

ADDIE. I'm all right, Mr. Horace. I've just been worried about you.

(*Alexandra enters. She is flushed and excited, her hat awry, her face dirty. Her arms are full of packages, but she comes quickly to Addie.*)

ALEXANDRA. Don't tell me how worried you were. We couldn't help it and there was no way to send a message.

ADDIE (*begins to take packages from Alexandra*). Yes, sir, I was mighty worried.

ALEXANDRA. We had to stop in Mobile overnight. Papa didn't feel well. The trip was too much for him, and I made him stop and rest — (*As Addie takes the last package*) No, don't take that. That's Father's medicine. I'll hold it. It mustn't break. Now, about the stuff outside. Papa must have his wheelchair. I'll get that and the valises —

ADDIE (*very happy, holding Alexandra's arms*). Since when you got to carry your own valises? Since when I ain't old enough to hold a bottle of medicine? (*Horace coughs*) You feel all right, Mr. Horace?

HORACE (*nods*). Glad to be sitting down.

ALEXANDRA (*opening package of medicine*). He doesn't feel all right. He just says that. The trip was very hard on him, and now he must go right to bed.

ADDIE (*looking at him carefully*). Them fancy doctors, they give you help?

HORACE. They did their best.

ALEXANDRA (*has become conscious of the voices in the dining room*). I bet Mama was worried. I better tell her we're here now. (*She starts for door.*)

HORACE. Zan. (*She stops*) Not for a minute, dear.

ALEXANDRA. Oh, Papa, you feel bad again. I knew you did. Do you want your medicine?

HORACE. No, I don't feel that way. I'm just tired, darling. Let me rest a little.

ADDIE. They're all in there eating breakfast.

ALEXANDRA. Oh, are they all here? Why do they *always* have to be here? I was hoping Papa wouldn't have to see anybody, that it would be nice for him and quiet.

ADDIE. Then let your papa rest for a minute.

HORACE. Addie, I bet your coffee's as good as ever. They don't have such good coffee up North. Is it as good, Addie? (*Addie starts for coffee urn.*)

ALEXANDRA. No. Dr. Reeves said not much coffee. Just now and then. I'm the nurse now, Addie.

ADDIE. You'd be a better one if you didn't look so dirty. Now go take a bath. Change your linens, get out a fresh dress, give your hair a good brushing — go on —

ALEXANDRA. Will you be all right, Papa?

ADDIE. Go on.

ALEXANDRA (*on stairs, talks as she goes up*). The pills Papa must take once every four hours. And the bottle only when

— only if he feels very bad. Now don't move until I come back and don't talk much and remember about his medicine, Addie — (*As she disappears*) How's Aunt Birdie? Is she here?

ADDIE. It ain't right for you to have coffee? It will hurt you?

HORACE (*slowly*). Nothing can make much difference now. Get me a cup, Addie. (*She crosses to urn, pours a cup*) Funny. They can't make coffee up North. (*Addie brings him a cup*) They don't like red pepper, either. (*He takes the cup and gulps it greedily*) God, that's good. You remember how I used to drink it? Ten, twelve cups a day. So strong it had to stain the cup. (*Then slowly*) Addie, before I see anybody else, I want to know why Zan came to fetch me home. She's tried to tell me, but she doesn't seem to know herself.

ADDIE. I don't know. All I know is big things are going on. Everybody going to be high-tone rich. Big rich. You too. All because smoke's going to start out of a building that ain't even up yet.

HORACE. I've heard about it.

ADDIE. And, er — (*Hesitates, steps to him*) And — well, Zan, maybe she going to marry Mr. Leo in a little while.

HORACE (*looks at her, then very slowly*). What are you talking about?

ADDIE. That's right. That's the talk, God help us.

HORACE (*angrily*). *What's* the talk?

ADDIE. I'm telling you. There's going to be a wedding —

HORACE (*after a second, quietly*). Go and tell them I'm home.

ADDIE (*hesitates*). Now you ain't to get excited. You're to be in your bed —

HORACE. Go on, Addie. Go and say I'm back. (*Addie opens dining-room doors. He rises with difficulty, stands stiff, as if he were in pain, facing the dining room.*)

ADDIE. Miss Regina. They're home. They got here —

REGINA. Horace! (*Regina quickly, rises, runs into the room. Warmly*) Horace! You've finally arrived. (*As she kisses him, the others come forward, all talking together.*)

BEN (*in doorway, carrying a napkin*). Well, sir, you had us all mighty worried. (*He steps forward. They shake hands. Addie exits.*)

OSCAR. You're a sight for sore eyes.

HORACE. Hello, Ben.

(*Leo enters, eating a biscuit.*)

OSCAR. And how you feel? Tip-top, I bet, because that's the way you're looking.

HORACE (*irritated with Oscar's lie*). Hello, Oscar. Hello, Leo, how are you?

LEO (*shaking hands*). I'm fine, sir. But a lot better now that you're back.

REGINA. Now sit down. What did happen to you and where's Alexandra? I am so excited about seeing you that I almost forgot about her.

HORACE. I didn't feel good, a little weak, I guess, and we stopped overnight to rest. Zan's upstairs washing off the train dirt.

REGINA. Oh, I am so sorry the trip was hard on you. I didn't think that —

HORACE. Well, it's just as if I had never been away. All of you here —

BEN. Waiting to welcome you home.

(*Birdie bursts in. She is wearing a flannel kimono and her face is flushed and excited.*)

BIRDIE (*runs to him, kisses him*). Horace!

HORACE (*warmly pressing her arm*). I was just wondering where you were, Birdie.

BIRDIE (*excited*). Oh, I would have been here. I didn't know you were back until Simon said he saw the buggy. (*She draws back to look at him. Her face sobers*) Oh, you don't look well, Horace. No, you don't.

REGINA (*laughs*). Birdie, what a thing to say —

HORACE. Oscar thinks I look very well.

OSCAR (*annoyed. Turns on Leo*). Don't stand there holding that biscuit in your hand.

LEO. Oh, well. I'll just finish my breakfast, Uncle Horace and then I'll give you all the news about the bank — (*He exits into the dining room.*)

OSCAR. And what is that costume you have on?

BIRDIE (*looking at Horace*). Now that you're home, you'll feel better. Plenty of good rest and we'll take such fine care of you. (*Stops*) But where is Zan? I missed her so much.

OSCAR. I asked you what is that strange costume you're parading around in?

BIRDIE (*nervously, backing toward stairs*). Me? Oh! It's my wrapper. I was so excited about Horace I just rushed out of the house —

OSCAR. Did you come across the square dressed that way? My dear Birdie, I —

HORACE (*to Regina, wearily*). Yes, it's just like old times.

REGINA (*quickly to Oscar*). Now, no fights. This is a holiday.

BIRDIE (*runs quickly up the stairs*). Zan! Zannie!

OSCAR. Birdie! (*She stops.*)

BIRDIE. Oh. Tell Zan I'll be back in a little while. (*Whispers*) Sorry, Oscar. (*Exits.*)

REGINA (*to Oscar and Ben*). Why don't you go finish your breakfast and let Horace rest for a minute?

BEN (*crossing to dining room with Oscar*). Never leave a meal unfinished. There are too many poor people who need the food. Mighty glad to see you home, Horace. Fine to have you back. Fine to have you back.

OSCAR (*to Leo as Ben closes dining-room doors*). Your mother has gone crazy. Runing around the streets like a woman —

(*The moment Regina and Horace are alone, they become awkward and self-conscious.*)

REGINA (*laughs awkwardly*). Well. Here we are. It's been a long time. (*Horace smiles*) Five months. You know, Horace, I wanted to come and be with you in the hospital, but I didn't know where my duty was. Here, or with you. But you know how much I *wanted* to come.

HORACE. That's kind of you, Regina. There was no need to come.

REGINA. Oh, but there was. Five months lying there all by yourself, no kinfolks, no friends. Don't try to tell me you didn't have a bad time of it.

HORACE. I didn't have a bad time. (*As she shakes her head, he becomes insistent*) No, I didn't, Regina. Oh, at first when I — when I heard the news about myself — but after I got used to that, I liked it there.

REGINA. You *liked* it? Isn't that strange. You liked it so well you didn't want to come home?

HORACE. That's not the way to put it. (*Then, kindly, as he sees her turn her head away*) But there I was and I got kind of used to it, kind of to like lying there and thinking. I never had much time to think before. And time's become valuable to me.

REGINA. It sounds almost like a holiday.

HORACE (*laughs*). It was, sort of. The first holiday I've had since I was a little kid.

REGINA. And here I was thinking you were in pain and —

HORACE (*quietly*). I was in pain.

REGINA. And instead you were having a holiday! A holiday of thinking. Couldn't you have done that here?

HORACE. I wanted to do it before I came here. I was thinking about us.

REGINA. About us? About you and me? Thinking about you and me after all these years. You shall tell me everything you thought — someday.

HORACE (*there is silence for a minute*). Regina. (*She turns to him*) Why did you send Zan to Baltimore?

REGINA. Why? Because I wanted you home. You can't make anything suspicious out of that, can you?

HORACE. I didn't mean to make anything suspicious about it. (*Hesitantly, taking her hand*) Zan said you wanted me to come home. I was so pleased at that and touched. It made me feel good.

REGINA (*taking away her hand*). Touched that I should want you home?

HORACE. I'm saying all the wrong things as usual. Let's try to get along better. There isn't so much more time. Regina, what's all this crazy talk I've been hearing about Zan and Leo? Zan and Leo marrying?

REGINA (*turning to him, sharply*). Who gossips so much around here?

HORACE (*shocked*). Regina!

REGINA (*anxious to quiet him*). It's some foolishness that Oscar thought up. I'll explain later. I have no intention of allowing any such arrangement. It was simply a way of keeping Oscar quiet in all this business I've been writing you about —

HORACE (*carefully*). What has Zan to do with any business of Oscar's? Whatever it is, you had better put it out of Oscar's head immediately. You know what I think of Leo.

REGINA. But there's no need to talk about it now.

HORACE. There is no need to talk about it ever. Not as long as I live. (*Horace stops, slowly turns to look at her*) As long as I live. I've been in a hospital for five months. Yet since I've been here you have not once asked me about — about my health. (*Then gently*) Well, I suppose they've written you. I can't live very long.

REGINA. I've never understood why people have to talk about this kind of thing.

HORACE (*there is a silence. Then he looks up at her, his face cold*). You misunderstand. I don't intend to gossip about my sickness. I thought it was only fair to tell you. I was not asking for your sympathy.

REGINA (*sharply, turns to him*). What do the doctors think caused your bad heart?

HORACE. What do you mean?

REGINA. They didn't think it possible, did they, that your fancy women may have —

HORACE (*smiles unpleasantly*). Caused my heart to be bad? I don't think that's the best scientific theory. You don't catch heart trouble in bed.

REGINA (*angrily*). I thought you might catch a bad conscience — in bed, as you say.

HORACE. I didn't tell them about my bad conscience. Or about my fancy women. Nor did I tell them that my wife has not wanted me in bed with her for — (*Sharply*) How long is it, Regina? Ten years? Did you bring me home for this, to make me feel guilty again? That means you want something. But you'll not make me feel guilty anymore. My "thinking" has made a difference.

REGINA. I see that it has. (*She looks toward dining-room door. Then comes to him, her manner warm and friendly*) It's foolish for us to fight this way. I didn't mean to be unpleasant. I was stupid.

HORACE (*wearily*). God knows I didn't either. I came home wanting so much not to fight, and then all of a sudden there we were.

REGINA (*hastily*). It's all my fault. I didn't ask about — about your illness because I didn't want to remind you of it. Anyway, I never believe doctors when they talk about — (*Brightly*) when they talk like that.

HORACE. I understand. Well, we'll try our best with each other. (*He rises.*)

REGINA (*quickly*). I'll try. Honestly, I will. Horace, Horace, I know you're tired but, but — couldn't you stay down here a few minutes longer? I want Ben to tell you something.

HORACE. Tomorrow.

REGINA. I'd like to now. It's very important to me. It's very important to all of us. (*Gaily, as she moves toward dining room*) Important to your beloved daughter. She'll be a very great heiress —

HORACE. Will she? That's nice.

REGINA (*opens doors*). Ben, are you finished breakfast?

HORACE. Is this the mill business I've had so many letters about?

REGINA (*to Ben*). Horace would like to talk to you now.

HORACE. Horace would not like to talk to you now. I am very tired, Regina —

REGINA (*comes to him*). Please. You've said we'll try our best with each other. I'll try. Really, I will. Please do this for me now. You will see what I've done while you've been away. How I watched your interests. (*Laughs gaily*) And I've done very well too. But things can't be delayed any longer. Everything must be settled this week — (*Horace sits down. Ben enters. Oscar has stayed in the dining room, his head turned to watch them. Leo is pretending to read the newspaper*) Now you must tell Horace all about it. Only be quick because he is very tired and must go to bed. (*Horace is looking at her. His face hardens as she speaks*) But I think your news will be better for him than all the medicine in the world.

BEN (*looking at Horace*). It could wait. Horace may not feel like talking today.

REGINA. What an old faker you are! You know it can't wait. You know it must be finished this week. You've been just as anxious for Horace to get here as I've been.

BEN (*very jovial*). I suppose I have been. And why not? Horace has done Hubbard Sons many a good turn. Why shouldn't I be anxious to help him now?

REGINA (*laughs*). Help him! Help him when you need him, that's what you mean.

BEN. What a woman you married, Horace. (*Laughs awkwardly when Horace does not answer*) Well, then I'll make it quick. You know what I've been telling you for years. How I've always said that every one of us little Southern businessmen had great things — (*Extends his arm*) — right beyond our fingertips. It's been my dream: my dream to make those fingers grow longer. I'm a lucky man, Horace, a lucky man. To dream and to live to get what you've dreamed of. That's *my* idea of a lucky man. For thirty years I've cried bring the cotton mills to the cotton. (*Horace opens the medicine bot-*

tle) Well finally I got up nerve to go to Marshall Company in Chicago.

HORACE. I know all this. (*He takes the medicine. Regina rises, steps to him.*)

BEN. Can I get you something?

HORACE. Some water, please.

REGINA (*turns quickly*). Oh, I'm sorry. (*Brings him a glass of water. He drinks as they wait in silence*) You feel all right now?

HORACE. Yes. You wrote me. I know all that.

(*Oscar enters from dining room.*)

REGINA (*triumphantly*). But you don't know that in the last few days Ben has agreed to give us — you, I mean — a much larger share.

HORACE. Really? That's very generous of him.

BEN (*laughs*). It wasn't so generous of me. It was smart of Regina.

REGINA (*as if she were signaling Horace*). I explained to Ben that perhaps you hadn't answered his letters because you didn't think he was offering you enough, and that the time was getting short and you could guess how much he needed you —

HORACE (*smiles at her, nods*). And I could guess that he wants to keep control in the family.

REGINA (*triumphantly*). Exactly. So I did a little bargaining for you and convinced my brothers they weren't the only Hubbards who had a business sense.

HORACE. Did you have to convince them of that? How little people know about each other! (*laughs*) But you'll know better about Regina next time, eh, Ben? (*Ben, Regina, Horace laugh together. Oscar's face is angry*) Now let's see. We're getting a bigger share. (*Looking at Oscar*) Who's getting less?

BEN. Oscar.

HORACE. Well, Oscar, you've grown very unselfish. What's happened to you?

(*Leo enters from dining room.*)

BEN (*quickly*). Oscar doesn't mind. Not worth fighting about now, eh, Oscar?

OSCAR (*angrily*). I'll get mine in the end. You can be sure of that. I've got my son's future to think about.

HORACE (*sharply*). Leo? Oh, I see. (*Puts his head back, laughs.*

Regina looks at him nervously) I am beginning to see. Everybody will get theirs.

BEN. I knew you'd see it. Seventy-five thousand, and that seventy-five thousand will make you a million.

REGINA. It will, Horace, it will.

HORACE. I believe you. (*After a second*) Now I can understand Oscar's self-sacrifice, but what did you have to promise Marshall Company besides the money you're putting up?

BEN. They wouldn't take promises. They wanted guarantees.

HORACE. Of what?

BEN. Water power. Free and plenty of it.

HORACE. You got them that, of course.

BEN. Cheap. You'd think the Governor of a great state would make his price a little higher. From pride, you know. (*Horace smiles. Ben smiles*) Cheap wages. "What do you mean by cheap wages?" I say to Marshall. "Less than Massachusetts," he says to me, "and that averages eight a week." "Eight a week! By God," I tell him, *"I'd* work for eight a week myself." Why, there ain't a mountain white or a town nigger but wouldn't give his right arm for three silver dollars every week, eh, Horace?

HORACE. Sure. And they'll take less than that when you get around to playing them off against each other. You can save a little money that way, Ben. And make them hate each other just a little more than they do now.

REGINA. What's all this about?

BEN (*laughs*). There'll be no trouble from anybody, white or black. Marshall said that to me. "What about strikes? That's all we've had in Massachusetts for the last three years." I say to him, "What's a strike? I never heard of one. Come South, Marshall. We got good folks and we don't stand for any fancy fooling."

HORACE. You're right. (*Slowly*) Well, it looks like you made a good deal for yourselves, and for Marshall, too. Your father used to say he made the thousands and you boys would make the millions. I think he was right. (*Rises.*)

REGINA (*as they look at Horace. She laughs nervously*). Millions for *us,* too.

HORACE. Us? You and me? I don't think so. We've got enough money, Regina. We'll just sit by and watch the boys grow rich. (*They watch Horace as he begins to move toward the staircase. He passes Leo, looks at him for a second*) How's everything at the bank, Leo?

LEO. Fine, sir. Everything is fine.

HORACE. How are all the ladies in Mobile? (*Horace turns to Regina, sharply*) Whatever made you think I'd let Zan marry —

REGINA. Do you mean that you are turning this down? Is it possible that's what you mean?

BEN. No, that's not what he means. Turning down a fortune. Horace is tired. He'd rather talk about it tomorrow —

REGINA. We can't keep putting it off this way. Oscar must be in Chicago by the end of the week with the money and contracts.

OSCAR (*giggles, pleased*). Yes, sir. Got to be there end of the week. No sense going without the money.

REGINA (*tensely*). I've waited long enough for your answer. I'm not going to wait any longer.

HORACE (*very deliberately*). I'm very tired now, Regina.

BEN (*quickly*). Now, Horace probably has his reasons. Things he'd like explained. Tomorrow will do. I can —

REGINA (*turns to Ben, sharply*). I want to know his reasons now!

HORACE (*as he climbs the steps*). I don't know them all myself. Let's leave it at that.

REGINA. We shall not leave it at that! We have waited for you here like children. Waited for you to come home.

HORACE. So that you could invest my money. So that is why you wanted me home? Well, I had hoped — (*Quietly*) If you are disappointed, Regina, I'm sorry. But I must do what I think best. We'll talk about it another day.

REGINA. We'll talk about it now. Just you and me.

HORACE (*looks down at her. His voice is tense*). Please, Regina, it's been a hard trip. I don't feel well. Please leave me alone now.

REGINA (*quietly*). I want to talk to you, Horace. (*He looks at her for a minute, then moves on, out of sight. She begins to climb the stairs.*)

BEN (*softly. Regina turns to him as he speaks*). Sometimes it is better to wait for the sun to rise again. (*She does not answer*) And sometimes, as our mother used to tell you, (*Regina continues up stairs*) it's unwise for a good-looking woman to frown. (*Ben rises, moves toward stairs*) Softness and a smile do more to the heart of men — (*She disappears. Ben stands looking up the stairs. There is a long silence. Then Oscar giggles.*)

OSCAR. Let us hope she'll change his mind. Let us hope. (*After a second Ben crosses to table, picks up his newspaper. Oscar looks at Ben. The silence makes Leo uncomfortable.*)

LEO. The paper says twenty-seven cases of yellow fever in New Orleans. Guess the floodwaters caused it. (*Nobody pays attention*) Thought they were building the levees high enough. Like the niggers always say: a man born of woman can't build nothing high enough for the Mississippi. (*Gets no answer. Gives an embarrassed laugh.*)

(*Upstairs there is the sound of voices. The voices are not loud, but Ben, Oscar, Leo become conscious of them. Leo crosses to landing, looks up, listens.*)

OSCAR (*pointing up*). Now just suppose she don't change his mind? Just suppose he keeps on refusing?

BEN (*without conviction*). He's tired. It was a mistake to talk to him today. He's a sick man, but he isn't a crazy one.

OSCAR. But just suppose he is crazy. What then?

BEN (*puts down his paper, peers at Oscar*). Then we'll go outside for the money. There's plenty who would give it.

OSCAR. And plenty who will want a lot for what they give. The ones who are rich enough to give will be smart enough to want. That means we'd be working for them, don't it, Ben?

BEN. You don't have to tell me the things I told you six months ago.

OSCAR. Oh, you're right not to worry. She'll change his mind. She always has. (*There is a silence. Suddenly Regina's voice becomes louder and sharper. All of them begin to listen now. Slowly Ben rises, goes to listen by the staircase. Oscar, watching him, smiles. As they listen Regina's voice becomes very loud. Horace's voice is no longer heard*) Maybe. But I don't believe it. I never did believe he was going in with us.

BEN (*turning on him*). What the hell do you expect me to do?

OSCAR (*mildly*). Nothing. You done your almighty best. Nobody could blame you if the whole thing just dripped away right through our fingers. You can't do a thing. But there may be something I could do for us. (*Oscar rises*) Or, I might better say, Leo could do for us. (*Ben turns, looks at Oscar. Leo is staring at Oscar*) Ain't that true, son? Ain't it true you might be able to help your own kinfolks?

LEO (*nervously taking a step to him*). Papa, I —

BEN (*slowly*). How would he help us, Oscar?

OSCAR. Leo's got a friend. Leo's friend owns eighty-eight thousand dollars in Union Pacific bonds. (*Ben turns to look at Leo*) Leo's friend don't look at the bonds much — not for five or six months at a time.

BEN (*after a pause*). Union Pacific. Uh, huh. Let me understand. Leo's friend would — would lend him these bonds and he —

OSCAR (*nods*). Would be kind enough to lend them to us.

BEN. Leo.

LEO (*excited, comes to him*). Yes, sir?

BEN. When would your friend be wanting the bonds back?

LEO (*very nervous*). I don't know. I — well, I —

OSCAR (*sharply. Steps to him*). You told me he won't look at them until Autumn —

LEO. Oh, that's right. But I — not till Autumn. Uncle Horace never —

BEN (*sharply*). Be still.

OSCAR (*smiles at Leo*). Your uncle doesn't wish to know your friend's name.

LEO (*starts to laugh*). That's a good one. Not know his name —

OSCAR. Shut up, Leo! (*Leo turns away*) He won't look at them again until September. That gives us five months. Leo will return the bonds in three months. And we'll have no trouble raising the money once the mills are going up. Will Marshall accept bonds?

(*Ben stops to listen to the voices from above. The voices are now very angry and very loud.*)

BEN (*smiling*). Why not? Why not? (*Laughs*) Good. We are lucky. We'll take the loan from Leo's friend — I think he will make a safer partner than our sister. (*Nods toward stairs. Turns to Leo*) How soon can you get them?

LEO. Today. Right now. They're in the safe-deposit box and —

BEN (*sharply*). I don't want to know where they are.

OSCAR (*laughs*). We will keep it secret from you. (*Pats Ben's arm.*)

BEN. Good. Draw a check for our part. You can take the night train for Chicago. Well, Oscar (*Holds out his hand*), good luck to us.

OSCAR. Leo will be taken care of?

LEO. I'm entitled to Uncle Horace's share. I'd enjoy being a partner —

BEN (*wheels on him*). You would? You can go to hell, you little — (*Starts toward Leo.*)

OSCAR (*nervously*). Now, now. He didn't mean that. I only want to be sure he'll get something out of all this.

BEN. Of course. We'll take care of him. We won't have any trouble about that. I'll see you at the store.

OSCAR (*nods*). That's settled then. Come on, son. (*Starts for door.*)

LEO (*puts out his hand*). I was only going to say what a great day this was for me and —

BEN. Go on.

(*Leo turns, follows Oscar out. Again the voices upstairs can be heard. Regina's voice is high and furious. Ben looks up, smiles, winces at the noise.*)

ALEXANDRA (*upstairs*). Mama — Mama — don't . . . (*The noise of running footsteps is heard and Alexandra comes running down the steps, speaking as she comes*) Uncle Ben! Uncle Ben! Please go up. Please make Mama stop. Uncle Ben, he's sick, he's so sick. How can Mama talk to him like that — please, make her stop. She'll—

BEN. Alexandra, you have a tender heart.

ALEXANDRA (*crying*). Go on up, Uncle Ben, please —

(*Suddenly the voices stop. A second later there is the sound of a door being slammed.*)

BEN. Now you see. Everything is over. Don't worry. (*He starts for the door*) Alexandra, I want you to tell your mother how sorry I am that I had to leave. And don't worry so, my dear. Married folk frequently raise their voices, unfortunately. (*He starts to put on his hat and coat as Regina appears on the stairs.*)

ALEXANDRA (*furiously*). How can you treat Papa like this? He's sick. He's very sick. Don't you know that? I won't let you.

REGINA. Mind your business, Alexandra. (*To Ben. Her voice is cold and calm*) How much longer can you wait for the money?

BEN (*putting on his coat*). He has refused? My, that's too bad.

REGINA. He will change his mind. I'll find a way to make him. What's the longest you can wait now?

BEN. I could wait until next week. But I can't wait until next week. (*He giggles, pleased*) I could but I can't. Could and can't. Well, I must go now. I'm very late —

REGINA (*coming downstairs toward him*). You're not going. I want to talk to you.

BEN. I was about to give Alexandra a message for you. I wanted to tell you that Oscar is going to Chicago tonight, so we can't be here for our usual Friday supper.

REGINA (*tensely*). Oscar is going to Chi — (*Softly*) What do you mean?

BEN. Just that. Everything is settled. He's going on to deliver to Marshall —

REGINA (*taking a step to him*). I demand to know what — You are lying. You are trying to scare me. *You haven't got the money*. How could you have it? You can't have — (*Ben laughs*) You will wait until I —

(*Horace comes into view on the landing.*)

BEN. You are getting out of hand. Since when do I take orders from you?

REGINA. Wait, you — (*Ben stops*) How *can* he go to Chicago? Did a ghost arrive with the money? (*Ben starts for the hall*) I don't believe you. Come back here. (*Regina starts after him*) Come back here, you — (*The door slams. She stops in the doorway, staring, her fists clenched. After a pause she turns slowly.*)

HORACE (*very quietly*). It's a great day when you and Ben cross swords. I've been waiting for it for years.

ALEXANDRA. Papa, Papa, please go back! You will —

HORACE. And so they don't need you, and so you will not have your millions, after all.

REGINA (*turns slowly*). You hate to see anybody live now, don't you? You hate to think that I'm going to be alive and have what I want.

HORACE. I should have known you'd think that was the reason.

REGINA. Because you're going to die and you know you're going to die.

ALEXANDRA (*shrilly*). Mama! Don't — Don't listen, Papa. Just don't listen. Go away —

HORACE. Not to keep you from getting what you want. Not even partly that. I'm sick of you, sick of this house, sick of my life here. I'm sick of your brothers and their dirty tricks to make a dime. Why should I give you the money? (*Very angrily*) To pound the bones of this town to make dividends for you to spend? You wreck the town, you and your brothers, *you* wreck the town and live on it. Not me. Maybe it's easy for the dying to be honest. But it's not my fault I'm dying. I'll do no more harm now. I've done enough. I'll die my own way. And I'll do it without making the world any worse. I leave that to you.

REGINA (*looks up at him*). I hope you die. I hope you die soon. (*Smiles*) I'll be waiting for you to die.

ALEXANDRA (*shrieking*). Papa! Don't — Don't listen — Don't —

(*Horace turns slowly and starts upstairs.*)

Curtain

Act Three

SCENE: *Same as Act One. Two weeks later. It is late afternoon and it is raining.*

AT RISE: *Horace is sitting near the window in a wheelchair. On the table next to him is a safe-deposit box, and a small bottle of medicine. Birdie and Alexandra are playing the piano. On a chair is a large sewing basket.*

BIRDIE (*counting for Alexandra*). One and two and three and four. One and two and three and four. (*Nods — turns to Horace*) We once played together, Horace. Remember?

HORACE (*has been looking out of the window*). What, Birdie?

BIRDIE. We played together. You and me.

ALEXANDRA. *Papa* used to play?

BIRDIE. Indeed he did. (*Addie appears at the door in a large kitchen apron*) He played the fiddle and very well, too.

ALEXANDRA (*turns to smile at Horace*). I never knew —

ADDIE. Where's your mama?

ALEXANDRA. Gone to Miss Safronia's to fit her dresses.

(*Addie nods, starts to exit.*)

HORACE. Addie. Tell Cal to get on his things. I want him to go on an errand.

(*Addie nods, exits. Horace moves nervously in his chair, looks out of the window.*)

ALEXANDRA (*who has been watching him*). It's too bad it's been raining all day, Papa. But you can go out in the yard tomorrow. Don't be restless.

HORACE. I'm not restless, darling.

BIRDIE. I remember so well the time we played together, your papa and me. It was the first time Oscar brought me here to supper. I had never seen all the Hubbards together before, and you know what a ninny I am and how shy. (*Turns to look at Horace*) You said you could play the fiddle and you'd be much obliged if I'd play with you. *I* was obliged to *you*, all right, all right. (*Laughs when he does not answer her*) Horace, you haven't heard a word I've said.

HORACE. Birdie, when did Oscar get back from Chicago?

BIRDIE. Yesterday. Hasn't he been here yet?

ALEXANDRA (*stops playing*). No. Neither has Uncle Ben since — since that day.

BIRDIE. Oh, I didn't know it was *that* bad. Oscar never tells me anything —

HORACE. The Hubbards have had their great quarrel. I knew it would come someday. (*Laughs*) It came.

ALEXANDRA. It came. It certainly came all right.

BIRDIE (*amazed*). But Oscar was in such a good humor when he got home, I didn't —

HORACE. Yes, I can understand that.

(ADDIE *enters carrying a large tray with glasses, a carafe of elderberry wine and a plate of cookies, which she puts on the table.*)

ALEXANDRA. Addie! A party! What for?

ADDIE. Nothing for. I had the fresh butter, so I made the cakes, and a little elderberry does the stomach good in the rain.

BIRDIE. Isn't this nice! A party just for us. Let's play party music, Zan.

(*Alexandra begins to play a gay piece.*)

ADDIE (*to Horace, wheeling his chair to center*). Come over here, Mr. Horace, and don't be thinking so much. A glass of elderberry will do more good.

(*Alexandra reaches for a cake. Birdie pours herself a glass of wine.*)

ALEXANDRA. Good cakes, Addie. It's nice here. Just us. Be nice if it could always be this way.

BIRDIE (*nods happily*). Quiet and restful.

ADDIE. Well, it won't be that way long. Little while now, even sitting here, you'll hear the red bricks going into place. The next day the smoke'll be pushing out the chimneys and by church time that Sunday every human born of woman will be living on chicken. That's how Mr. Ben's been telling the story.

HORACE. They believe it that way?

ADDIE. Believe it? They use to believing what Mr. Ben orders. There ain't been so much talk around here since Sherman's army didn't come near.

HORACE (*softly*). They are fools.

ADDIE (*nods, sits down with the sewing basket*). You ain't born in the South unless you're a fool.

BIRDIE (*has drunk another glass of wine*). But we didn't play together after that night. Oscar said he didn't like me to play on the piano. (*Turns to Alexandra*) You know what he said that night?

ALEXANDRA. Who?

BIRDIE. Oscar. He said that music made him nervous. He said he just sat and waited for the next note. (*Alexandra laughs*) He wasn't poking fun. He meant it. Ah, well — (*She finishes her glass, shakes her head. Horace looks at her, smiles*) Your papa don't like to admit it, but he's been mighty kind to me all these years. (*Running her hand along his sleeve*) Often he'd step in when somebody said something and once — (*She stops, turns away, her face still*) Once he stopped Oscar from — (*She stops, turns. Quickly*) I'm sorry I said that. Why, here I am so happy and yet I think about bad things. (*Laughs nervously*) That's not right, now, is it? (*She pours a drink. Cal appears in the door. He has on an old coat and is carrying a torn umbrella.*)

ALEXANDRA. Have a cake, Cal.

CAL (*comes in, takes a cake*). You want me, Mr. Horace?

HORACE. What time is it, Cal?

CAL. 'Bout ten minutes before it's five.

HORACE. All right. Now you walk yourself down to the bank.

CAL. It'll be closed. Nobody'll be there but Mr. Manders, Mr. Joe Horns, Mr. Leo —

HORACE. Go in the back way. They'll be at the table, going over the day's business. (*Points to the deposit box*) See that box?

CAL (*nods*). Yes, sir.

HORACE. You tell Mr. Manders that Mr. Horace says he's much obliged to him for bringing the box, it arrived all right.

CAL (*bewildered*). He know you got the box. He bring it himself Wednesday. I opened the door to him and he say, "Hello, Cal, coming on to summer weather."

HORACE. You say just what I tell you. Understand?

(*Birdie pours another drink, stands at table.*)

CAL. No, sir. I ain't going to say I understand. I'm going down and tell a man he give you something he already know he give you, and you say "understand."

HORACE. Now, Cal.

CAL. Yes, sir. I just going to say you obliged for the box coming all right. I ain't going to understand it, but I'm going to say it.

HORACE. And tell him I want him to come over here after supper, and to bring Mr. Sol Fowler with him.

CAL (*nods*). He's to come after supper and bring Mr. Sol Fowler, your attorney-at-law, with him.

HORACE. That's right. Just walk right in the back room and say your piece. (*Slowly*) In front of everybody.

CAL. Yes, sir. (*Mumbles to himself as he exits.*)

ALEXANDRA (*who has been watching Horace*). Is anything the matter, Papa?

HORACE. Oh, no. Nothing.

ADDIE. Miss Birdie, that elderberry going to give you a headache spell.

BIRDIE (*beginning to be drunk. Gaily*). Oh, I don't think so. I don't think it will.

ALEXANDRA (*as Horace puts his hand to his throat*). Do you want your medicine, Papa?

HORACE. No, no. I'm all right, darling.

BIRDIE. Mama used to give me elderberry wine when I was a little girl. For hiccoughs. (*Laughs*) You know, I don't think people get hiccoughs anymore. Isn't that funny? (*Birdie laughs. Horace and Alexandra smile*) I used to get hiccoughs just when I shouldn't have.

ADDIE (*nods*). And nobody gets growing pains no more. That is funny. Just as if there was some style in what you get. One year an ailment's stylish and the next year it ain't.

BIRDIE. I remember. It was my first big party, at Lionnet I mean, and I was so excited, and there I was with hiccoughs and Mama laughing. (*Softly. Looking at carafe*) Mama always laughed. (*Picks up carafe*) A big party, a lovely dress from Mr. Worth in Paris, France, and hiccoughs. (*Pours drink*) My brother pounding me on the back and Mama with the elderberry bottle, laughing at me. Everybody was on their way to come, and I was such a ninny, hiccoughing away. (*Drinks*) You know, that was the first day I ever saw Oscar Hubbard. The Ballongs were selling their horses and he was going there to buy. He passed and lifted his hat — we could see him from the window — and my brother, to tease Mama, said maybe we should have invited the Hubbards to the party. He said Mama didn't like them because they kept a store, and he said that was old-fashioned of her. (*Her face lights up*) And then, and *then,* I saw Mama angry for the first time in my life. She said that wasn't the reason. She said she was old-fashioned, but not that way. She said she was old-fashioned enough not to like people who killed animals they couldn't use, and who made their money charging awful interest to ignorant niggers and cheating them on what they bought. She was very angry, Mama was. I had never seen her face like that. And then suddenly she laughed and said, "Look, I've frightened Birdie out of the hiccoughs." (*Her head drops. Then softly*) And so she had. They were all gone. (*Moves to sofa, sits.*)

ADDIE. Yeah, they got mighty well-off cheating niggers. Well, there are people who eat the earth and eat all the people on it like in the Bible with the locusts. And other people who stand around and watch them eat it. (*Softly*) Sometimes I think it ain't right to stand and watch them do it.

BIRDIE (*thoughtfully*). Like I say, if we could only go back to Lionnet. Everybody'd be better there. They'd be good and kind. I like people to be kind. (*Pours drink*) Don't you, Horace; don't you like people to be kind?

HORACE. Yes, Birdie.

BIRDIE (*very drunk now*). Yes, that was the first day I ever saw Oscar. Who would have thought — You all want to know something? Well, I don't like Leo. My very own son, and I don't like him. (*Laughs, gaily*) My, I guess I even like Oscar more.

ALEXANDRA. Why did you marry Uncle Oscar?

ADDIE. That's no question for you to be asking.

HORACE (*sharply*). Why not? She's heard enough around here to ask anything.

BIRDIE. I don't know. I thought I liked him. He was kind to me and I thought it was because he liked me too. But that wasn't the reason — (*Wheels on Alexandra*) Ask why *he* married *me*. I can tell you that: he's told it to me often enough.

ADDIE. Miss Birdie, don't —

BIRDIE (*speaking very rapidly*). My family was good and the cotton on Lionnet's fields was better. Ben Hubbard wanted the cotton and Oscar Hubbard married it for him. He was kind to me, then. He used to smile at me. He hasn't smiled at me since. Everybody knew that's what he married me for. (*Addie rises*) Everybody but me. Stupid, stupid me.

ALEXANDRA (*to Horace, softly*). I see. (*Hesitates*) Papa, I mean — when you feel better couldn't we go away? I mean, by ourselves. Couldn't we find a way to go?

HORACE. Yes, I know what you mean. We'll try to find a way. I promise you, darling.

ADDIE (*moves to Birdie*). Rest a bit, Miss Birdie. You get talking like this you'll get a headache and —

BIRDIE (*sharply*). I've never had a headache in my life. (*Begins to cry*) You know it as well as I do. (*Turns to Alexandra*) I never had a headache, Zan. That's a lie they tell for me. I drink. All by myself, in my own room, by myself, I drink. Then, when they want to hide it, they say, "Birdie's got a headache again" —

ALEXANDRA (*comes to her*). Aunt Birdie.

BIRDIE. Even you won't like me now. You won't like me anymore.

ALEXANDRA. I love you. I'll always love you.

BIRDIE (*angrily*). Well, don't. Don't love me. Because in twenty years you'll just be like me. They'll do all the same things to you. (*Begins to laugh*) You know what? In twenty-two years I haven't had a whole day of happiness. Oh, a little, like today with you all. But never a single, whole day. I say to myself, if only I had one more *whole* day, then — (*The laugh stops*) And that's the way you'll be. And you'll trail after them, just like me, hoping they won't be so mean that day or say something to make you feel so bad — only you'll be worse off because you haven't got my Mama to remember — (*Turns away, her head drops. She stands quietly, swaying a little, holding to the sofa*).

ALEXANDRA (*to Birdie*). I guess we were all trying to make a happy day. You know, we sit around and try to pretend nothing's happened. We try to pretend we are not here. We make believe we are just by ourselves, someplace else, and it doesn't seem to work. (*Kisses Birdie's hand*) Come now, Aunt Birdie, I'll walk you home. You and me. (*She takes Birdie's arm. They move slowly out.*)

BIRDIE (*softly as they exit*). You and me.

ADDIE (*after a minute*). Well. First time I ever heard Miss Birdie say a word. Maybe it's good for her. I'm just sorry

Zan had to hear it. (*Horace moves his head as if he were uncomfortable*) You feel bad, don't you? (*He shrugs.*)

HORACE. So you didn't want Zan to hear? It would be nice to let her stay innocent, like Birdie at her age. Let her listen now. Let her see everything. How else is she going to know that she's got to get away? I'm trying to show her that. I'm trying, but I've only got a little time left. She can even hate me when I'm dead, if she'll only learn to hate and fear this.

ADDIE. Mr. Horace —

HORACE. Pretty soon there'll be nobody to help her but you.

ADDIE. What can I do?

HORACE. Take her away.

ADDIE. How can I do that? Do you think they'd let me just go away with her?

HORACE. I'll fix it so they can't stop you when you're ready to go. You'll go, Addie?

ADDIE (*after a second, softly*). Yes, sir. I promise. (*He touches her arm, nods.*)

HORACE (*quietly*). I'm going to have Sol Fowler make me a new will. They'll make trouble, but you make Zan stand firm and Fowler'll do the rest. Addie, I'd like to leave you something for yourself. I always wanted to.

ADDIE (*laughs*). Don't you do that, Mr. Horace. A nigger woman in a white man's will! I'd never get it nohow.

HORACE. I know. But upstairs in the armoire drawer there's thirty-seven hundred-dollar bills. It's money left from my trip. It's in an envelope with your name. It's for you.

ADDIE. It's mighty kind and good of you. I don't know what to say for thanks —

CAL (*appears in doorway*). I'm back. (*No answer*) I'm back.

ADDIE. So we see.

HORACE. Well?

CAL. Nothing. I just went down and spoke my piece. Just like you told me. I say, "Mr. Horace he thank you mightily for the safe box arriving in good shape and he say you come right after supper to his house and bring Mr. Attorney-at-law Sol Fowler with you." Then I wipe my hands on my coat. Every time I ever told a lie in my whole life, I wipe my hands right after. Well, while I'm wiping my hands, Mr. Leo jump up and say to me, "What box? What you talking about?"

HORACE (*smiles*). Did he?

CAL. And Mr. Leo say he got to leave a little early cause he got something to do. And then Mr. Manders say Mr. Leo should sit right down and finish up his work and stop acting like somebody made him Mr. President. So he sit down. Now, just like I told you, Mr. Manders was mighty surprised with the message because he knows right well he brought the box — (*Points to box, sighs*) But he took it all right. Some men take everything easy and some do not.

HORACE (*laughs*). Mr. Leo was telling the truth; he *has* got something to do. I hope Manders don't keep him too long. (*Outside there is the sound of voices. Cal exits. Addie crosses quickly to Horace, begins to wheel his chair toward the stairs*) No. Leave me where I am.

ADDIE. But that's Miss Regina coming back.

HORACE (*nods, looking at door*). Go away, Addie.

ADDIE (*hesitates*). Mr. Horace. Don't talk no more today. You don't feel well and it won't do no good —

HORACE (*as he hears footsteps in the hall*). Go on. (*She looks at him for a second, then picks up her sewing from table and exits as Regina comes in from hall. Horace's chair is now so placed that he is in front of the table with the medicine. Regina stands in the hall, shakes umbrella, stands it in the corner, takes off her cloak and throws it over the banister. She stares at Horace.*)

REGINA (*as she takes off her gloves*). We had agreed that you were to stay in your part of this house and I in mine. This room is *my* part of the house. Please don't come down here again.

HORACE. I won't.

REGINA (*crosses toward bell cord*). I'll get Cal to take you upstairs.

HORACE. Before you do I want to tell you that after all, we have invested our money in Hubbard Sons and Marshall, Cotton Manufacturers.

REGINA (*stops, turns, stares at him*). What are you talking about? You haven't seen Ben — When did you change your mind?

HORACE. I didn't change my mind. *I* didn't invest the money. (*Smiles*) It was invested for me.

REGINA (*angrily*). What — ?

HORACE. I had eighty-eight thousand dollars' worth of Union Pacific bonds in that safe-deposit box. They are not there now. Go and look. (*As she stares at him, he points to the box*) Go and look, Regina. (*She crosses quickly to the box, opens it*) Those bonds are as negotiable as money.

REGINA (*turns back to him*). What kind of joke are you playing now? Is this for my benefit?

HORACE. I don't look in that box very often, but three days ago, on Wednesday it was, because I had made a decision —

REGINA. I want to know what you are talking about.

HORACE. Don't interrupt me again. Because I had made a decision, I sent for the box. The bonds were gone. Eighty-eight thousand dollars gone. (*He smiles at her.*)

REGINA (*after a moment's silence, quietly*). Do you think I'm crazy enough to believe what you're saying?

HORACE. Believe anything you like.

REGINA (*slowly*). Where did they go to?

HORACE. They are in Chicago. With Mr. Marshall, I should guess.

REGINA. What did they do? Walk to Chicago? Have you really gone crazy?

HORACE. Leo took the bonds.

REGINA (*turns sharply, then speaks softly, without conviction*). I don't believe it.

HORACE. I wasn't there but I can guess what happened. This fine gentleman, with whom you were bargaining your daughter, took the keys and opened the box. You remember that the day of the fight Oscar went to Chicago? Well, he went with my bonds that his son Leo had stolen for him. (*Pleasantly*) And for Ben.

REGINA (*slowly, nods*). When did you find out the bonds were gone?

HORACE. Wednesday night.

REGINA. I thought that's what you said. Why have you waited three days to do anything? (*Suddenly laughs*) This *will* make a fine story.

HORACE (*nods*). Couldn't it?

REGINA. A fine story to hold over their heads. How could they be such fools?

HORACE. But I'm not going to hold it over their heads.

REGINA (*the laugh stops*). What?

HORACE (*turns his chair to face her*). I'm going to let them keep the bonds — as a loan from you. An eighty-eight-thousand-dollar loan; they should be grateful to you. They will be, I think.

REGINA (*slowly, smiles*). I see. You are punishing me. But I won't let you punish me. If you won't do anything, I will. Now. (*She starts for door.*)

HORACE. You won't do anything. Because you can't. (*Regina stops*) It won't do you any good to make trouble because I shall simply say that I lent them the bonds.

REGINA (*slowly*). You would do that?

HORACE. Yes. For once in your life I am tying your hands. There is nothing for you to do. (*There is silence. Then she sits down.*)

REGINA. I see. You are going to lend them the bonds and let them keep all the profit they make on them, and there is nothing I can do about it. Is that right?

HORACE. Yes.

REGINA (*softly*). Why did you say that I was making this gift?

HORACE. I was coming to that. I am going to make a new will, Regina, leaving you eighty-eight thousand dollars in Union Pacific bonds. The rest will go to Zan. It's true that your brothers have borrowed your share for a little while. After my death I advise you to talk to Ben and Oscar. They won't admit anything and Ben, I think, will be smart enough to see that he's safe. Because I knew about the theft and said nothing. Nor will I say anything as long as I live. Is that clear to you?

REGINA (*nods, softly, without looking at him*). You will not say anything as long as you live.

HORACE. That's right. And by that time they will probably have replaced your bonds, and then they'll belong to you and nobody but us will ever know what happened. They'll be around any minute to see what I am going to do. I took good care to see that word reached Leo. They'll be mighty relieved to know I'm going to do nothing and Ben will think it all a capital joke on you. And that will be the end of that. There's nothing you can do to them, nothing you can do to me.

REGINA. You hate me very much.

HORACE. No.

REGINA. Oh, I think you do. (*Puts her head back, sighs*) Well, we haven't been very good together. Anyway, I don't hate you either. I have only contempt for you. I've always had.

HORACE. From the very first?

REGINA. I think so.

HORACE. I was in love with *you*. But why did *you* marry *me?*

REGINA. I was lonely when I was young.

HORACE. *You* were lonely?

REGINA. Not the way people usually mean. Lonely for all the things I wasn't going to get. Everybody in this house was so busy and there was so little place for what I wanted. I wanted the world. Then, and then — (*Smiles*) Papa died and left the money to Ben and Oscar.

HORACE. And you married me?

REGINA. Yes, I thought — But I was wrong. You were a small-town clerk then. You haven't changed.

HORACE (*nods*). And that wasn't what you wanted.

REGINA. No. No, it wasn't what I wanted. (*Pleasantly*) It took me a little while to find out I had made a mistake. As for you — I don't know. It was almost as if I couldn't stand the kind of man you were — (*Smiles, softly*) I used to lie there at night, praying you wouldn't come near —

HORACE. Really? It was as bad as that?

REGINA. Remember when I went to Doctor Sloan and I told you he said there was something the matter with me and that you shouldn't touch me anymore?

HORACE. I remember.

REGINA. But you believed it. I couldn't understand that. I couldn't understand that anybody could be such a soft fool. That was when I began to despise you.

HORACE (*puts his hand to his throat, looks at the bottle of medicine on table*). Why didn't you leave me?

REGINA. I told you I married you for something. It turned out it was only for this. (*Carefully*) This wasn't what I wanted, but it was something. I never thought about it much, but if I had I'd have known that you would die before I would. But I couldn't have known that you would get heart trouble so early and so bad. I'm lucky, Horace. I've always been lucky. (*Horace turns slowly to the medicine*) I'll be lucky again. (*Horace looks at her. Then he puts his hand to his throat. Because he cannot reach the bottle he moves the chair closer. He reaches for the medicine, takes out the cork, picks up the spoon. The bottle slips and smashes on the table. He draws in his breath, gasps.*)

HORACE. Please. Tell Addie — The other bottle is upstairs.

(*Regina has not moved. She does not move now. He stares at her. Then, suddenly as if he understood, he raises his voice. It is a panic-stricken whisper, too small to be heard outside the room*) Addie! Addie! Come — (*Stops as he hears the softness of his voice. He makes a sudden, furious spring from the chair to the stairs, taking the first few steps as if he were a desperate runner. Then he slips, gasps, grasps the rail, makes a great effort to reach the landing. When he reaches the landing, he is on his knees. His knees give way, he falls on the landing, out of view. Regina has not turned during his climb up the stairs. Now she waits a second. Then she goes below the landing, speaks up.*)

REGINA. Horace. Horace. (*When there is no answer, she turns, calls*) Addie! Cal! Come in here. (*She starts up the steps. Addie and Cal appear. Both run toward the stairs*) He's had an attack. Come up here. (*They run up the steps quickly.*)

CAL. My God. Mr. Horace —

(*They cannot be seen now.*)

REGINA (*her voice comes from the head of the stairs*). Be still, Cal. Bring him in here.

(*Before the footsteps and the voices have completely died away, Alexandra appears in the hall door, in her raincloak and hood. She comes into the room, begins to unfasten the cloak, suddenly looks around, sees the empty wheelchair, stares, begins to move swiftly as if to look in the dining room. At the same moment Addie runs down the stairs. Alexandra turns and stares up at Addie.*)

ALEXANDRA. Addie! What?

ADDIE (*takes Alexandra by the shoulders*). I'm going for the doctor. Go upstairs. (*Alexandra looks at her, then quickly breaks away and runs up the steps. Addie exits. The stage is empty for a minute. Then the front doorbell begins to ring. When there is no answer, it rings again. A second later Leo appears in the hall, talking as he comes in.*)

LEO (*very nervous*). Hello. (*Irritably*) Never saw any use ringing a bell when a door was open. If you are going to ring a bell, then somebody should answer it. (*Gets in the room, looks around, puzzled, listens, hears no sound*) Aunt Regina. (*He moves around restlessly*) Addie. (*Waits*) Where the hell — (*Crosses to the bell cord, rings it impatiently, waits, gets no answer, calls*) Cal! Cal! (*Cal appears on the stair landing.*)

CAL (*his voice is soft, shaken*). Mr. Leo. Miss Regina says you stop that screaming noise.

LEO (*angrily*). Where is everybody?

CAL. Mr. Horace he got an attack. He's bad. Miss Regina says you stop that noise.

LEO. Uncle Horace — What — What happened? (*Cal starts down the stairs, shakes his head, begins to move swiftly off. Leo looks around wildly*) But when — You seen Mr. Oscar or Mr. Ben? (*Cal shakes his head. Moves on. Leo grabs him by the arm*) Answer me, will you?

CAL. No, I ain't seen 'em. I ain't got time to answer you. I got to get things. (*Cal runs off.*)

LEO. But what's the matter with him? When did this happen — (*Calling after Cal*) You'd think Papa'd be someplace where you could find him. I been chasing him all afternoon.

(*Oscar and Ben come quickly into the room.*)

LEO. Papa, I've been looking all over town for you and Uncle Ben —

BEN. Where is he?

OSCAR. Addie just told us it was a sudden attack, and —

BEN (*to Leo*). Where is he? When did it happen?

LEO. Upstairs. Will you listen to me, please? I been looking for you for —

OSCAR (*to Ben*). You think we should go up? (*Ben, looking up the steps, shakes his head.*)

BEN. I don't know. I don't know.

OSCAR. But he was all right —

LEO (*yelling*). *Will you listen to me?*

OSCAR. What is the matter with you?

LEO. I been trying to tell you. I been trying to find you for an hour —

OSCAR. Tell me what?

LEO. Uncle Horace knows about the bonds. He knows about them. He's had the box since Wednesday —

BEN (*sharply*). Stop shouting! What the hell are you talking about?

LEO (*furiously*). I'm telling you he knows about the bonds. Ain't that clear enough —

BEN (*grabbing Leo's arm*). You God-damn fool! Stop screaming! Now what happened? Talk quietly.

LEO. You heard me. Uncle Horace knows about the bonds. He's known since Wednesday.

BEN (*after a second*). How do you know that?

LEO. Because Cal comes down to Manders and says the box came okay and —

OSCAR (*trembling*). That might not mean a thing —

LEO (*angrily*). No? It might not, huh? Then he says Manders should come here tonight and bring Sol Fowler with him. I guess that don't mean a thing either.

OSCAR (*to Ben*). Ben — What — Do you think he's seen the —

BEN (*motions to the box*). There's the box. (*Both Oscar and Leo turn sharply. Leo makes a leap to the box*) You ass. Put it down. What are you going to do with it, eat it?

LEO. I'm going to —

BEN (*furiously*). Put it down. Don't touch it again. Now sit down and shut up for a minute.

OSCAR. Since Wednesday. (*To Leo*) You said he had it since Wednesday. Why didn't he say something — (*To Ben*) I don't understand —

LEO (*taking a step*). I can put it back. I can put it back before anybody knows.

BEN (*who is standing at the table, softly*). He's had it since Wednesday. Yet he hasn't said a word to us.

OSCAR. *Why? Why?*

LEO. What's the difference why? He was getting ready to say plenty. He was going to say it to Fowler tonight —

OSCAR (*angrily*). Be still. (*Turns to Ben, looks at him, waits.*)

BEN (*after a minute*). I don't believe that.

LEO (*wildly*). *You* don't believe it? What do I care what *you* believe? I do the dirty work and then —

BEN (*turning his head to Leo*). I'm remembering that. I'm remembering that, Leo.

OSCAR. What do you mean?

LEO. You —

BEN (*to Oscar*). If you don't shut that little fool up, I'll show you what I mean. For some reason he knows, but he don't say a word.

OSCAR. Maybe he didn't know that *we* —

BEN (*quickly*). That *Leo* — He's no fool. Does Manders know the bonds are missing?

LEO. How could I tell? I was half crazy. I don't think so. Because Manders seemed kind of puzzled and —

OSCAR. But we got to find out — (*He breaks off as Cal comes into the room carrying a kettle of hot water.*)

BEN. How is he, Cal?

CAL. I don't know, Mr. Ben. He was bad. (*Going toward stairs.*)

OSCAR. But when did it happen?

CAL (*shrugs*). He wasn't feeling bad early. (*Addie comes in quickly from the hall*) Then there he is next thing on the landing, fallen over, his eyes tight —

ADDIE (*to Cal*). Dr. Sloan's over at the Ballongs. Hitch the buggy and go get him. (*She takes the kettle and cloths from him, pushes him, runs up the stairs*) Go on. (*She disappears. Cal exits.*)

BEN. Never seen Sloan anywhere when you need him.

OSCAR (*softly*). Sounds bad.

LEO. He would have told *her* about it. Aunt Regina. He would have told his own wife —

BEN (*turning to Leo*). Yes, he might have told her. But they weren't on such pretty terms and maybe he didn't. Maybe he didn't. (*Goes quickly to Leo*) Now listen to me. If she doesn't know, it may work out all right. If she does know, you're to say he lent you the bonds.

LEO. Lent them to me! Who's going to believe that?

BEN. Nobody.

OSCAR (*to Leo*). Don't you understand? It can't do no harm to say it —

LEO. Why should I say he lent them to me? Why not to you? (*Carefully*) Why not to Uncle Ben?

BEN (*smiles*). Just because he didn't lend them to me. Remember that.

LEO. But all he has to do is say he didn't lend them to me —

BEN (*furiously*). But for some reason, he doesn't seem to be talking, does he?

(*There are footsteps above. They all stand looking at the stairs. Regina begins to come slowly down.*)

BEN. What happened?

REGINA. He's had a bad attack.

OSCAR. Too bad. I'm sorry we weren't here when — when Horace needed us.

BEN. When *you* needed us.

REGINA (*looks at him*). Yes.

BEN. How is he? Can we — can we go up?

REGINA (*shakes her head*). He's not conscious.

OSCAR (*pacing around*). It's that — it's that bad? Wouldn't you think Sloan could be found quickly, just once, just once?

REGINA. I don't think there is much for him to do.

BEN. Oh, don't talk like that. He's come through attacks before. He will now.

(*Regina sits down. After a second she speaks softly.*)

REGINA. Well. We haven't seen each other since the day of our fight.

BEN (*tenderly*). That was nothing. Why, you and Oscar and I used to fight when we were kids.

OSCAR (*hurriedly*). Don't you think we should grow up? Is there anything we can do for Horace —

BEN. You don't feel well. Ah —

REGINA (*without looking at them*). No, I don't. (*Slight pause*) Horace told me about the bonds this afternoon. (*There is an immediate shocked silence.*)

LEO. The bonds. What do you mean? What bonds? What —

BEN (*looks at him furiously. Then to Regina*). The Union Pacific bonds? *Horace's* Union Pacific bonds?

REGINA. Yes.

OSCAR (*steps to her, very nervously*). Well. Well what — what about them? What — what could he say?

REGINA. He said that Leo had stolen the bonds and given them to you.

OSCAR (*aghast, very loudly*). That's ridiculous, Regina, absolutely —

LEO. I don't know what you're talking about. What would I — Why —

REGINA (*wearily to Ben*). Isn't it enough that he stole them? Do I have to listen to this in the bargain?

OSCAR. You are talking —

LEO. I didn't steal anything. I don't know why —

REGINA (*to Ben*). Would you ask them to stop that, please? (*There is silence. Ben glowers at Oscar and Leo.*)

BEN. Aren't we starting at the wrong end, Regina? What did Horace tell you?

REGINA (*smiles at him*). He told me that Leo had stolen the bonds.

LEO. I didn't steal —

REGINA. Please. Let me finish. Then he told me that he was going to pretend that he had lent them to you (*Leo turns sharply to Regina, then looks at Oscar, then looks back at Regina*) as a present from me — to my brothers. He said there was nothing I could do about it. He said the rest of his money would go to Alexandra. That is all. (*There is a silence, Oscar coughs, Leo smiles slyly.*)

LEO (*taking a step to her*). I told you he had lent them — I could have told you —

REGINA (*ignores him, smiles sadly at Ben*). So I'm very badly off, you see. Horace said there was nothing I could do about it as long as he was alive to say he had lent you the bonds.

BEN. You shouldn't feel that way. It can all be explained, all be adjusted. It isn't as bad —

REGINA. So you, at least, are willing to admit the bonds were stolen?

BEN (*Oscar laughs nervously*). I admit no such thing. It's possible that Horace made up that part of the story to tease you — (*Looks at her*) Or perhaps to punish you. Punish you.

REGINA (*sadly*). It's not a pleasant story. I feel bad, Ben, naturally. I hadn't thought —

BEN. Now you shall have the bonds safely back. That was the understanding, wasn't it, Oscar?

OSCAR. Yes.

REGINA. I'm glad to know that. (*Smiles*) Ah, I had greater hopes —

BEN. Don't talk that way. That's foolish. (*Looks at his watch*) I think we ought to drive out for Sloan ourselves. If we can't find him we'll go over to Senateville for Doctor Morris. And don't think I'm dismissing this other business. I'm not. We'll have it all out on a more appropriate day.

REGINA. I don't think you had better go yet. I think you had better stay and sit down.

BEN. We'll be back with Sloan.

REGINA. Cal has gone for him. I don't want you to go.

BEN. Now don't worry and —

REGINA. You will come back in this room and sit down. I have something more to say.

BEN (*turns, comes toward her*). Since when do I take orders from you?

REGINA (*smiles*). You don't — yet. (*Sharply*) Come back, Oscar. You too, Leo.

OSCAR (*sure of himself, laughs*). My dear Regina —

BEN (*softly, pats her hand*). Horace has already clipped your wings and very wittily. Do I have to clip them, too? (*Smiles at her*) You'd get farther with a smile, Regina. I'm a soft man for a woman's smile.

REGINA. I'm smiling, Ben. I'm smiling because you are quite safe while Horace lives. But I don't think Horace will live. And if he doesn't live I shall want seventy-five percent in exchange for the bonds.

BEN (*steps back, whistles, laughs*). Greedy! What a greedy girl you are! You want so much of everything.

REGINA. Yes. And if I don't get what I want I am going to put all three of you in jail.

OSCAR (*furiously*). You're mighty crazy. Having just admitted —

BEN. And on what evidence would you put Oscar and Leo in jail?

REGINA (*laughs, gaily*). Oscar, listen to him. He's getting ready to swear that it was you and Leo! What do you say to that? (*Oscar turns furiously toward Ben*) Oh, don't be angry, Oscar. I'm going to see that he goes in with you.

BEN. Try anything you like, Regina. (*Sharply*) And now we can stop all this and say good-bye to you. (*Alexandra comes slowly down the steps*) It's his money and he's obviously willing to let us borrow it. (*More pleasantly*) Learn to make threats when you can carry them through. For how many years have I told you a good-looking woman gets more by being soft and appealing? Mama used to tell you that. (*Looks at his watch*) Where the hell is Sloan? (*To Oscar*) Take the buggy and — (*As Ben turns to Oscar, he sees Alexandra. She walks stiffly. She goes slowly to the lower window, her head bent. They all turn to look at her.*)

OSCAR (*after a second, moving toward her*). What? Alexandra — (*She does not answer. After a second, Addie comes slowly down the stairs, moving as if she were very tired. At foot of steps, she looks at Alexandra, then turns and slowly crosses to door and exits. Regina rises. Ben looks nervously at Alexandra, at Regina.*)

OSCAR (*as Addie passes him, irritably to Alexandra*). Well, what is — (*Turns into room — sees Addie at foot of steps*) — what's? (*Ben puts up a hand, shakes his head*) My God, I didn't know — who *could* have known — I didn't know he was that sick. Well, well — I — (*Regina stands quietly, her back to them.*)

BEN (*softly, sincerely*). Seems like yesterday when he first came here.

OSCAR. Yes, that's true. (*Turns to Ben*) The whole town loved him and respected him.

ALEXANDRA (*turns*). Did you love him, Uncle Oscar?

OSCAR. Certainly, I — What a strange thing to ask! I —

ALEXANDRA. Did you love him, Uncle Ben?

BEN (*simply*). Alexandra, I —

ALEXANDRA (*starts to laugh very loudly*). And you, Mama, did you love him, too?

REGINA. I know what you feel, Alexandra, but please try to control yourself.

ALEXANDRA. I'm trying, Mama. I'm trying very hard.

BEN. Grief makes some people laugh and some people cry. It's better to cry, Alexandra.

ALEXANDRA (*the laugh has stopped. She moves toward Regina*). What was Papa doing on the staircase?

(*Ben turns to look at Alexandra.*)

REGINA. Please go and lie down, my dear. We all need time to get over shocks like this. (*Alexandra does not move. Regina's voice becomes softer, more insistent*) Please go, Alexandra.

ALEXANDRA. No, Mama. I'll wait. I've got to talk to you.

REGINA. Later. Go and rest now.

ALEXANDRA (*quietly*). I'll wait, Mama. I've plenty of time.

REGINA (*hesitates, stares, makes a half shrug, turns back to Ben*). As I was saying. Tomorrow morning I am going up to Judge Simmes. I shall tell him about Leo.

BEN (*motioning toward Alexandra*). Not in front of the child, Regina. I —

REGINA (*turns to him. Sharply*). I didn't ask her to stay. Tomorrow morning I go to Judge Simmes —

OSCAR. And what proof? What proof of all this —

REGINA (*turns sharply*). None. I won't need any. The bonds are missing and they are with Marshall. That will be enough. If it isn't, I'll add what's necessary.

BEN. I'm sure of that.

REGINA (*turns to Ben*). You can be quite sure.

OSCAR. We'll deny —

REGINA. Deny your heads off. You couldn't find a jury that wouldn't weep for a woman whose brothers steal from her. And you couldn't find twelve men in this state you haven't cheated and who hate you for it.

OSCAR. What kind of talk is this? You couldn't do anything like that! We're your own brothers. (*Points upstairs*) How can you talk that way when upstairs not five minutes ago —

REGINA. Where was I? (*Smiles at Ben*) Well, they'll convict you.

But I won't care much if they don't. Because by that time you'll be ruined. I shall also tell my story to Mr. Marshall, who likes me, I think, and who will not want to be involved in your scandal. A respectable firm like Marshall and Company. The deal would be off in an hour. (*Turns to them angrily*) And you know it. Now I don't want to hear any more from any of you. *You'll do no more bargaining in this house.* I'll take my seventy-five percent and we'll forget the story forever. That's one way of doing it, and the way I prefer. You know me well enough to know that I don't mind taking the other way.

BEN (*after a second, slowly*). None of us has ever known you well enough, Regina.

REGINA. You're getting old, Ben. Your tricks aren't as smart as they used to be. (*There is no answer. She waits, then smiles*) All right. I take it that's settled and I get what I asked for.

OSCAR (*furiously to Ben*). Are you going to let her do this —

BEN (*turns to look at him, slowly*). You have a suggestion?

REGINA (*puts her arms above her head, stretches, laughs*). No, he hasn't. All right. Now, Leo, I have forgotten that you ever saw the bonds. (*Archly, to Ben and Oscar*) And as long as you boys both behave yourselves, I've forgotten that we ever even talked about them. You can draw up the necessary papers tomorrow. (*Ben laughs. Leo stares at him, starts for door. Exits. Oscar moves toward door angrily. Regina looks at Ben, nods, laughs with him. For a second, Oscar stands in the door, looking back at them. Then he exits.*)

REGINA. You're a good loser, Ben. I like that.

BEN (*picks up his coat, turns to her*). Well, I say to myself, what's the good? You and I aren't like Oscar. We're not sour people. I think that comes from a good digestion. Then, too, one loses today and wins tomorrow. I say to myself, years of planning and I get what I want. Then I don't get it. But I'm not discouraged. The century's turning, the world is open. Open for people like you and me. Ready for us, waiting for us. After all this is just the beginning. There are hundreds of Hubbards sitting in rooms like this throughout the country. All their names aren't Hubbard, but they are all Hubbards and they will own this country someday. We'll get along.

REGINA (*smiles*). I think so.

BEN. Then, too, I say to myself, things may change. (*Looks at*

Alexandra) I agree with Alexandra. What is a man in a wheelchair doing on a staircase? I ask myself that.

REGINA (*looks up at him*). And what do you answer?

BEN. I have no answer. But maybe someday I will. Maybe never, but maybe someday. (*Smiles. Pats her arm*) When I do, I'll let you know. (*Goes toward hall.*)

REGINA. When you do, write me. I will be in Chicago. (*Gaily*) Ah, Ben, if Papa had only left me his money.

BEN. I'll see you tomorrow.

REGINA. Oh, yes. Certainly. You'll be sort of working for me now.

BEN (*as he passes Alexandra*). Alexandra, you're turning out to be a right interesting girl. Well, good night all. (*He exits.*)

REGINA (*sits quietly for a second, stretches*). What do you want to talk to me about, Alexandra?

ALEXANDRA (*slowly*). I've changed my mind. I don't want to talk.

REGINA. You're acting very strange. Not like yourself. You've had a bad shock today. I know that. And you loved Papa, but you must have expected this to come someday. You knew how sick he was.

ALEXANDRA. I knew. We all knew.

REGINA. It will be good for you to get away from here. Good for me, too. Time heals most wounds, Alexandra. You're young, you shall have all the things I wanted. I'll make the world for you the way I wanted it to be for me. (*Uncomfortably*) Don't sit there staring. You've been around Birdie so much you're getting just like her.

ALEXANDRA (*nods*). Funny. That's what Aunt Birdie said today.

REGINA. Be good for you to get away from all this.

(*Addie enters.*)

ADDIE. Cal is back, Miss Regina. He says Dr. Sloan will be coming in a few minutes.

REGINA. We'll leave in a few weeks. A few weeks! That means two or three Saturdays, two or three Sundays. (*Sighs*) Well, I'm very tired. I shall go to bed. I don't want any supper. Put the lights out and lock up. (*Addie moves to the piano lamp, turns it out*) You go to your room, Alexandra. Addie will bring you something hot. You look very tired. (*Rises. To Addie*) Call me when Dr. Sloan gets here. I don't want to see anybody else. I don't want any condolence calls tonight. The whole town will be over.

ALEXANDRA. Mama, I'm not coming with you. I'm not going to Chicago.

REGINA (*turns to her*). You're very upset, Alexandra.

ALEXANDRA. I mean what I say. With all my heart.

REGINA. We'll talk about it tomorrow. The morning will make a difference.

ALEXANDRA. It won't make any difference. And there isn't anything to talk about. I am going away from you. Because I want to. Because I know Papa would want me to.

REGINA (*careful, polite*). You *know* your papa wanted you to go away from me?

ALEXANDRA. Yes.

REGINA (*softly*). And if I say no?

ALEXANDRA. Say it Mama, say it. And see what happens.

REGINA (*softly, after a pause*). And if I make you stay?

ALEXANDRA. That would be foolish. It wouldn't work in the end.

REGINA. You're very serious about it, aren't you? (*Crosses to stairs*) Well, you'll change your mind in a few days.

ALEXANDRA. No.

REGINA (*going up the steps*). Alexandra, I've come to the end of my rope. Somewhere there has to be what I want, too. Life goes too fast. Do what you want; think what you want; go where you want. I'd like to keep you with me, but I won't make you stay. Too many people used to make me do too many things. No, I won't make you stay.

ALEXANDRA. You couldn't, Mama, because I want to leave here. As I've never wanted anything in my life before. Because now I understand what Papa was trying to tell me. All in one day: Addie said there were people who ate the earth and other people who stood around and watched them do it. And just now Uncle Ben said the same thing. Really, he said the same thing. (*Tensely*) Well, tell him for me, Mama, I'm not going to stand around and watch you do it. I'll be fighting as hard as he'll be fighting (*Rises*) someplace else.

REGINA. Well, you have spirit, after all. I used to think you were all sugar water. We don't have to be bad friends. I don't want us to be bad friends, Alexandra. (*Starts, stops, turns to Alexandra*) Would you like to come and talk to me, Alexandra? Would you — would you like to sleep in my room tonight?

ALEXANDRA (*takes a step toward the stairs*). Are you afraid, Mama? (*Regina does not answer. She moves up the stairs and out of sight. Addie, smiling, begins to put out the lamps.*)

Curtain

Watch on the Rhine

For Herman Shumlin

Watch on the Rhine was first produced at the Martin Beck Theatre, New York City, on April 1, 1941, with the following cast:

(In the order of their appearance)

ANISE	EDA HEINEMANN
JOSEPH	FRANK WILSON
FANNY FARRELLY	LUCILE WATSON
DAVID FARRELLY	JOHN LODGE
MARTHE DE BRANCOVIS	HELEN TRENHOLME
TECK DE BRANCOVIS	GEORGE COULOURIS
SARA MÜLLER	MADY CHRISTIANS
JOSHUA MÜLLER	PETER FERNANDEZ
BODO MÜLLER	ERIC ROBERTS
BABETTE MÜLLER	ANNE BLYTH
KURT MÜLLER	PAUL LUKAS

Produced and staged by
HERMAN SHUMLIN

Setting designed by
JO MIELZINER

Costumes designed by
HELENE PONS

Scenes

The scene of the play is the living room of the Farrelly country house, about twenty miles from Washington. The time is late spring, 1940.

Act One

Early on a Wednesday morning.

Act Two

Ten days later.

Act Three

A half hour later.

Act One

SCENE: *The living room of the Farrelly house, about twenty miles from Washington, D.C., on a warm spring morning.*

Center stage are large French doors leading to an elevated open terrace. On the terrace are chairs, tables, a large table for dining. Some of this furniture we can see; most of it is on the left side of the terrace, beyond our sight. Left stage is an arched entrance, leading to an oval reception hall. We can see the main staircase as it goes off to the back of the hall. Right stage is a door leading to a library. The Farrelly house was built in the early nineteenth century. It has space, simplicity, style. The living room is large. Upstage right is a piano; downstage left, a couch; downstage right, a couch and chairs; upstage a few smaller chairs. Four or five generations have furnished this room and they have all been people of taste. There are no styles, no periods; the room has never been refurnished. Each careless aristocrat has thrown into the room what he or she liked as a child, what he or she brought home when grown up. Therefore the furniture is of many periods: the desk is English, the couch is Victorian, some of the pictures are modern, some of the ornaments French. The room has too many things in it: vases, clocks, miniatures, boxes, china animals. On the right wall is a large portrait of a big, kind-faced man in an evening suit of 1900. On another wall is a large, very ugly landscape. The room is crowded. But it is cool and clean and its fabrics and woods are in soft colors.

AT RISE: *Anise, a thin Frenchwoman of about sixty, in a dark housekeeper's dress, is standing at a table sorting mail. She takes the mail from a small basket, holds each letter to the light, reads each postal card, then places them in piles. On the terrace, Joseph, a tall, middle-aged Negro butler, wheels a breakfast wagon. As he appears, Fanny Farrelly comes in from the hall. She is a handsome woman of about sixty-three. She has on a fancy, good-looking dressing gown.*

Left and right are the audience's left and right.

FANNY (*stops to watch Anise. Sees Joseph moving about on terrace. Calls*). Joseph! (*To Anise*) Morning.

ANISE (*continues examining mail*). Good morning, Madame.

JOSEPH (*comes to terrace door*). Yes'm?

FANNY. Everybody down?

JOSEPH. No'm. Nobody. I'll get your tea. (*He returns to breakfast wagon on terrace.*)

FANNY. Mr. David isn't down yet? But he knows he is to meet the train.

JOSEPH (*comes in from the terrace with the cup of tea*). He's got plenty of time, Miss Fanny. The train ain't in till noon.

FANNY. Breakfast is at nine o'clock in this house and will be until the day after I die. Ring the bell.

JOSEPH. It ain't nine yet, Miss Fanny. It's eight-thirty.

FANNY. Put the clocks up to nine and ring the bell.

JOSEPH. Mr. David told me not to ring it anymore. He says it's got too mean a ring, that bell. It disturbs folks.

FANNY. That's what it was put there for. What's the matter with disturbing people?

JOSEPH. Yes'm.

FANNY. You slept well, Anise. You were asleep before I could dismantle myself.

ANISE. I woke several times during the night.

FANNY. Did you? Then you were careful not to stop snoring. We must finally get around to moving you further away. (*Anise hands her three or four letters. Fanny opens a letter, begins to read it. After a minute*) What time is it?

ANISE. It is about eight-thirty. Joseph just told you.

FANNY. I didn't hear him. I'm nervous. Naturally. My mail looks dull. (*Reading the letter*) Jenny always tells you a piece of gossip three times, as if it grew fresher with the telling. Did you put flowers in their rooms?

ANISE. Certainly.

FANNY. David ought to get to the station by eleven-thirty.

ANISE (*patiently*). The train does not draw in until ten minutes past noon.

FANNY. But it might come in early. It's been known.

ANISE. Never. Not in the Union Station in Washington, the District of Columbia.

FANNY (*irritably*). But it might. It might. Don't argue with me about everything. What time is it?

ANISE. It's now twenty-seven minutes before nine. It will be impossible to continue telling you the time every three minutes from now until Miss Sara arrives. I think you are having a nervous breakdown. Compose yourself.

FANNY. It's been twenty years. Any mother would be nervous. If your daughter were coming home and you hadn't seen her, and a husband, *and* grandchildren —

ANISE. I do not say that it is wrong to be nervous. I, too, am nervous. I say only that you are.

FANNY. Very well. I heard you. *I* say that I am. (*She goes back to reading her letter*) Jenny's still in California. She's lost her lavallière again. Birdie Chase's daughter is still faire l'amouring with that actor. Tawdry, Jenny says it is. An actor. Fashions in sin change. In my day, it was Englishmen. I don't understand infidelity. If you love a man, then why? If you don't love him, then why stay with him? (*Without turning, she points over her head to Joshua Farrelly's portrait*) Thank God, I was in love. I thought about Joshua last night. Three grandchildren. He would have liked that. I hope I will. (*Points to other letters*) Anything in anybody else's mail?

ANISE. Advertisements for Mr. David and legal things. For our Count and Countess, there is nothing but what seems an invitation to a lower-class embassy tea and letters asking for bills to get paid.

FANNY. That's every morning. (*Thoughtfully*) In the six weeks the Balkan nobility have been with us, they seem to have run up a great many bills.

ANISE. Yes. *I* told you that. Then there was a night letter for Mr. David.

(*A very loud, very unpleasant bell begins to ring.*)

FANNY (*through the noise*). Really? From whom?

ANISE. From her. I took it on the telephone, and —

(*Bell drowns out her voice.*)

FANNY. Who is "her"? (*Bell becomes very loud*) Go tell him to stop that noise —

ANISE (*goes toward terrace, calling*). Joseph! Stop that bell. Miss Fanny says to stop it.

JOSEPH (*calls*). Miss Fanny said to start it.

FANNY (*shouts out to him*). I didn't tell you to hang yourself with it.

JOSEPH (*appears on terrace*). Your breakfast is ready. (*Disappears.*)

FANNY (*to Anise*). Who is "her"?

ANISE. That Carter woman from Lansing, Michigan.

FANNY. Oh, my. Is she back in Washington again? What did the telegram say?

ANISE. It said the long sickness of her dear Papa had terminated in full recovery. She was returning, and would Mr. David come for dinner a week from Thursday? "Love," it said, "to you and your charming mother." (*To Fanny*) That's you. I think Miss Carter from Lansing, Michigan, was unwise in attending the illness of her Papa.

FANNY. I hope so. Why?

ANISE (*shrugs*). There is much winking of the eyes going on between our Countess and Mr. David.

FANNY (*eagerly*). I know that. Anything new happen?

ANISE (*too innocently*). Happen? I don't know what you mean.

FANNY. You know damn well what I mean.

ANISE. *That?* Oh, no, I don't think that.

JOSEPH (*appears in the door*). The sausage cakes is shrinking.

FANNY (*rises. To Anise*). I want everybody down here immediately. Is the car ready? (*Anise nods*) Did you order a good dinner? (*Shrieks*) David! Oh.

(*David Farrelly, a pleasant-looking man of thirty-nine, comes in from the entrance hall, almost bumps into Fanny.*)

DAVID. Good morning, everybody.

ANISE (*to Fanny*). Everything is excellent. You have been asking the same questions for a week. You have made the kitchen very nervous.

DAVID (*to Joseph*). Why did you ring that air-raid alarm again?

JOSEPH. Ain't me, Mr. David. I don't like noise. Miss Fanny told me.

FANNY. Good morning, David.

DAVID (*to Joseph*). Tell Fred to leave the car. I'll drive to the station.

JOSEPH (*nods*). Yes, sir. (*Exits.*)

DAVID (*to Fanny, half amused, half annoyed, as he begins to read his mail*). Mama, I think we'll fix up the old chicken house for you as a playroom. We'll hang the room with bells and you can go into your second childhood in the proper privacy.

FANNY. I find it very interesting. You sleep soundly, you rise at your usual hour — although your sister, whom you haven't seen in years, is waiting at the station —

DAVID. She is not waiting at the station. (*Laughs*) The train does not come in until ten minutes past twelve.

FANNY (*airily*). It's almost that now.

ANISE (*turns to look at her*). Really, Miss Fanny, contain yourself. It is twenty minutes before nine.

DAVID. And I have *not* slept soundly. And I've been up since six o'clock.

FANNY. The Balkans aren't down yet. Where are they?

DAVID. I don't know.

ANISE. There's nothing in your mail, Mr. David. Only the usual advertisements.

DAVID. That is all that is ever likely to come — here.

ANISE (*haughtily, as she starts toward hall*). I cannot, of course, speak for Miss Fanny. *I* have never opened a letter in my life.

DAVID. I know. You don't have to. For you they fly open.

FANNY (*giggles*). It's true. You're a snooper, Anise. I rather admire it. It shows an interest in life. (*Anise exits. Fanny looks up at Joshua's portrait*) You know, I've been lying awake most of the night wondering what Papa would have thought about Sara. He'd have been very pleased, wouldn't he? I always find myself wondering what Joshua would have felt.

DAVID. Yes. But maybe it would be just as well if you didn't expect me to be wondering about it, too. I wasn't married to him, Mama. He was just my father.

FANNY. My. You got up on the wrong side of the bed. (*She points to the mail which he is still opening*) The bills are for our noble guests. Interesting, how many there are every morning. How much longer are they going to be with us?

DAVID (*without looking at her*). I don't know.

FANNY. It's been six weeks. Now that Sara and her family are coming, even this house might be a little crowded — (*He looks up at her*) Yes. I know I invited them. I felt sorry for Marthe, and Teck rather amused me. He plays good cribbage, and he tells good jokes. But that's not enough for a lifetime guest. If you've been urging her to stay, I wish you'd stop it. They haven't any money; all right, lend them some —

DAVID. I have been urging them to stay?

FANNY. I'm not so old I don't recognize flirting when I see it.

(*Marthe de Brancovis, an attractive woman of thirty-one or thirty-two, enters.*)

MARTHE. Good morning, Fanny. Morning, David.

FANNY. Good morning, Marthe.

DAVID (*warmly*). Good morning.

MARTHE. Fanny, darling, couldn't you persuade yourself to let me have a tray in bed and some cotton for my ears?

DAVID. Certainly not. My father ate breakfast at nine, and whatever my father did —

FANNY (*carefully, to David*). There was a night letter for you from that Carter woman in Lansing, Michigan. She is returning and you are to come to dinner next Thursday. (*As she exits on terrace*) C-A-R-T-E-R. Lansing, Michigan.

DAVID (*laughs as Fanny exits*). Do you understand my mother?

MARTHE. Sometimes.

DAVID. Miss Carter was done for your benefit.

MARTHE (*smiles*). That means she has guessed that I would be jealous. And she has guessed right.

DAVID. Jealous?

MARTHE. I know I've no right to be, but I am. And Fanny knows it.

DAVID (*carelessly*). Don't pay any attention to Mama. She has a sure instinct for the women I like, and she begins to hammer away early. Marthe — (*Goes to decanter on side-table*) I'm going to have a drink. I haven't had a drink before breakfast since the day I took my bar examination. (*Pours himself a drink, gulps it down*) What's it going to be like to stand on a station platform and see your sister after all these years? I'm afraid, I guess.

MARTHE. Why?

DAVID. I don't know. Afraid she won't like me — (*Shrugs*) We were very fond of each other, but it's been a long time.

MARTHE. I remember Sara. Mama brought me one day when your father was stationed in Paris. I was about six and Sara about fifteen and you were —

DAVID. You were a pretty little girl.

MARTHE. Do you really remember me? You never told me before.

FANNY (*yelling from the terrace*). David! Come to breakfast.

DAVID. You know, I've never met Sara's husband. Mama did. I think the first day Sara met him, in Munich. Mama didn't like the marriage much in those days — and Sara didn't care, and Mama didn't like Sara not caring. Mama cut up about it, bad.

MARTHE. Why?

DAVID. Probably because they didn't let her arrange it. Why does Mama ever act badly? She doesn't remember ten minutes later.

MARTHE. Wasn't Mr. Müller poor?

DAVID. Oh, Mama wouldn't have minded that. If they'd only come home and let her fix their lives for them — (*Smiles*) But Sara didn't want it that way.

MARTHE. You'll have a house full of refugees — us and —

DAVID. Are you and Teck refugees? I'm not sure I know what you're refugees from.

MARTHE. From Europe.

DAVID. From what Europe?

MARTHE (*smiles, shrugs*). I don't know. I don't know myself, really. Just Europe. (*Quickly, comes to him*) Sara will like you. I like you. That doesn't make sense, does it?

(*On her speech, Teck de Brancovis appears in the hall. He is a good-looking man of about forty-five. She stops quickly.*)

TECK (*to Marthe and David*). Good morning.

(*The bell gives an enormous ring.*)

DAVID (*goes to terrace*). Good morning, Teck. For years I've been thinking they were coming for Mama with a net. I'm giving up hope. I may try catching her myself. (*Disappears, calling*) Mama! Stop that noise.

TECK (*goes to table, picks up his mail*). Many mistaken people, Marthe, seem to have given you many charge accounts.

MARTHE. The Countess de Brancovis. That still does it. It would be nice to be able to pay bills again —

TECK. Do not act as if I refused to pay them. I did not sleep well last night. I was worried. We have eighty-seven dollars in American Express checks. (*Pleasantly, looking at her*) That's all we have, Marthe.

MARTHE (*shrugs*). Maybe something will turn up. It's due.

TECK (*carefully*). David? (*Then, as she turns to look at him*) The other relatives will arrive this morning?

MARTHE. Yes.

TECK (*points to porch*). I think Madame Fanny and Mr. David may grow weary of accents and charity guests. Or is the husband of the sister a rich one?

MARTHE. No. He's poor. He had to leave Germany in '33.

TECK. A Jew?

MARTHE. No. I don't think so.

TECK. Why did he have to leave Germany?

MARTHE (*still reading*). Oh, I don't know, Teck. He's an anti-Nazi.

TECK. A political?

MARTHE. No, I don't think so. He was an engineer. I don't know. I don't know much about him.

TECK. Did you sleep well?

MARTHE. Yes. Why not?

TECK. Money does not worry you?

MARTHE. It worries me very much. But I just lie still now and hope. I'm glad to be here. (*Shrugs*) Maybe something good will happen. We've come to the end of a road. That's been true for a long time. Things will have to go one way or the other. Maybe they'll go well, for a change.

TECK. I have not come to the end of any road.

MARTHE (*looks at him*). No? I admire you.

TECK. I'm going into Washington tonight. Phili has a poker game every Wednesday evening. He has arranged for me to join it.

MARTHE (*after a pause*). Have you been seeing Phili?

TECK. Once or twice. Why not? Phili and I are old friends. He may be useful. I do not want to stay in this country forever.

MARTHE. You can't leave them alone. Your favorite dream, isn't it, Teck? That they will let you play with them again? I don't think they will, and I don't think you should be seeing Phili, or that you should be seen at the Embassy.

TECK (*smiles*). You have political convictions now?

MARTHE. I don't know what I have. I've never liked Nazis, as you know, and you should have had enough of them. They seem to have had enough of you, God knows. It would be just as well to admit they are smarter than you are and let them alone.

TECK (*after a minute*). That is interesting.

MARTHE. What is interesting?

TECK. I think you are trying to say something to me. What is it?

MARTHE. That you ought not to be at the Embassy, and that it's insane to play cards in a game with Von Seitz with eighty-seven dollars in your pocket. I don't think he'd like your not being able to pay up. Suppose you lose?

TECK. I shall try not to lose.

MARTHE. But if you do lose and can't pay, it will be all over Washington in an hour. (*Points to terrace*) They'll find out about it, and we'll be out of here when they do.

TECK. I think I want to be out of here. I find that I do not like the picture of you and our host.

MARTHE (*carefully*). There is no picture, as you put it, to like or dislike.

TECK. Not yet? I am glad to hear that. (*Comes toward her slowly*) Marthe, you understand that I am not really a fool? You understand that it is unwise to calculate me that way?

MARTHE (*as if it were an effort*). Yes, I understand that. And I understand that I am getting tired. Just plain tired. The whole thing's too much for me. I've always meant to ask you, since you played on so many sides, why we didn't come out any better. I've always wanted to ask you what happened. (*Sharply*) I'm tired, see? And I just want to sit down. Just to sit down in a chair and stay.

TECK (*carefully*). Here?

MARTHE. Anyplace —

TECK. You have thus arranged it with David?

MARTHE. I've arranged nothing.

TECK. But you are trying, eh? (*He comes close to her*) I think not. I would not like that. Do not make any arrangements, Marthe. I may not allow you to carry them through. Come to breakfast now. (*He passes her, disappears on the terrace. She stands still and thoughtful. Then she, too, moves to the terrace, disappears. Joseph appears on the terrace, carrying a tray toward the unseen breakfast table. The stage is empty. After a minute, there are sounds of footsteps in the hall. Sara Müller appears in the doorway, comes toward the middle of the room as if expecting to find somebody, stops, looks around, begins to smile. Behind her in the doorway, are three children; behind them, Kurt Müller. They stand waiting, watching Sara. Sara is forty-one or forty-two, a good-looking woman, with a well-bred, serious face. She is very badly dressed: her dress is too long, her shoes were bought a long time ago and have no relation to the dress, and the belt of her dress has become untied and is hanging down. As she looks around the room, her face is gay and surprised.*

Smiling, without turning, absently, she motions to the children and Kurt. Slowly, the children come in. Bodo Müller, a boy of nine, comes first. He is carrying coats. Behind him, carrying two cheap valises, is Joshua Müller, a boy of fourteen. Behind him is Babette Müller, a pretty little girl of twelve. They are dressed for a much colder climate. They come forward, look at their mother, stand waiting. Behind them is Kurt Müller, a large, powerful, German-looking man of about forty-seven. He is carrying a shabby valise and a briefcase. He stands watching Sara. Joshua puts down the valises, goes to his father, takes the valise from Kurt, puts it neatly near the rest, and puts the briefcase near Kurt. Babette goes to Sara, takes a package from her, places it near the valises. Then she turns to Bodo, takes the coats he is carrying, puts them neatly on top of the valises. After a second, Kurt sits down. As he does so, we see that his movements are slow and careful, as if they are made with effort.)

BABETTE (*points to a couch near which they are standing. She has a slight accent*). Is it allowed?

KURT (*smiles. He has an accent*). Yes. It is allowed. (*Babette and Bodo sit stiffly on the couch.*)

JOSHUA (*nervously. He has a slight accent*). But we did not sound the bell —

SARA (*idly, as she wanders around the room, her face excited*). The door isn't locked. It never was. Never since I can remember.

BODO (*softly, puzzled*). The entrance of the home is never locked. So.

KURT. You find it curious to believe there are people who live and do not need to watch, eh, Bodo?

BODO. Yes, Papa.

KURT. You and I.

JOSHUA (*smiles*). It is strange. But it must be good, I think.

KURT. Yes.

SARA. Sit back. Be comfortable. I — I wonder where Mama and David — (*Delighted, sees portrait of Joshua Farrelly, points to it*) And that was my Papa. That was the famous Joshua Farrelly. (*They all look up at it. She wanders around the room*) My goodness, isn't it a fine room? I'd almost forgotten — (*Picks up a picture from the table*) And this was my grandmother. (*Very nervously*) Shall I go and say we're here? They'd be having breakfast, I think. Always on the side terrace in nice weather. I don't know. Maybe — (*Picks up another picture*) "To Joshua and Fanny Farrelly. With admiration. Alfonso, May 7, 1910." I had an ermine boa and a pink coat. I was angry because it was too warm in Madrid to wear it.

BODO. Alfons von Spanien? Der hat immer Bilder von sich verschenkt. Ein schlechtes Zeichen für einen Mann.

JOSHUA. Mama told you it is good manners to speak the language of the country you visit. Therefore, speak in English.

BODO. I said he seemed always to give his photograph. I said that is a bad flag on a man. Grow fat on the poor people and give pictures of the face. (*Joshua sits down.*)

SARA. I remember a big party and cakes and a glass of champagne for me. I was ten, I guess — (*Suddenly laughs*) That was when Mama said the first time a king got shot at, he was a romantic, but the fifth time he was a comedian. And when my father gave his lecture in Madrid, he repeated it — right in Madrid. It was a great scandal. You know, Alfonso was always getting shot at or bombed.

BODO (*shrugs*). Certainement.

JOSHUA. Certainement? As-tu perdu la tête?

BABETTE. Speak in English, please.

KURT. You are a terrorist, Bodo?

BODO (*slowly*). No.

JOSHUA. Then since when has it become *natural* to shoot upon people?

BODO. Do not give me lessons. It is neither right nor natural to shoot upon people. I know that.

SARA (*looks at Babette, thoughtfully*). An ermine boa. A boa is a scarf. I should like to have one for you, Babbie. Once, in Prague, I saw a pretty one. I wanted to buy it for you. But we had to pay our rent. (*Laughs*) But I almost bought it.

BABETTE. Thank you. Tie your sash, Mama.

SARA (*thoughtfully*). Almost twenty years.

BODO. You were born here, Mama?

SARA. Upstairs. And I lived here until I went to live with your father. (*Looks out beyond terrace*) Your Uncle David and I used to have a garden, behind the terrace. I wonder if it's still there. I like a garden. I've always hoped we'd have a house someday and settle down — (*Stops, nervously, turns to stare at Kurt, who is looking at her*) I am talking so foolish. Sentimental. At my age. Gardens and ermine boas. I haven't wanted anything —

KURT (*comes toward her, takes her hand*). Sara. Stop it. This is a fine room. A fine place to be. Everything is so pleasant and full of comfort. This will be a good piano on which to play again. And it is all so clean. I like that. Now, you shall not be a baby. You must enjoy your house, and not be afraid that you hurt me with it. Yes?

BABETTE. Papa, tie Mama's sash, please.

SARA (*shyly smiles at him as he leans down to tie the belt*). Yes, of course. It's strange, that's all. We've never been in a place like this together —

KURT. That does not mean, and should not mean, that we do not remember how to enjoy what comes our way. We are on a holiday.

JOSHUA. A holiday? But for how long? And what plans afterward?

KURT. We will have plans when the hour arrives to make them. (*Anise appears from the hall. She starts into the room, stops, bewildered. The Müllers have not seen her. Then, as Sara turns, Anise speaks. As she speaks, the children rise.*)

ANISE. What? What?

SARA (*softly*). Anise. It's me. It's Sara.

ANISE (*coming forward slowly*). What? (*Then as she approaches Sara, she begins to run toward her*) Miss Sara! Miss Sara! (*They reach each other, both laugh happily. Sara kisses Anise*) I would have known you. Yes, I would. I would have known — (*Excited, bewildered, nervous, she looks toward Kurt*) How do you do, sir? How do you do? (*Turns toward the children*) How do you do?

JOSHUA. Thank you, Miss Anise. We are in good health.

SARA (*very happily*). You look the same. I think you look the same. Just the way I've always remembered. (*To the others*) This is the Anise I have told you about.

ANISE. But how — Did you just come in? What a way to come home! And after all the plans we've made! But you were to come on the twelve o'clock train, and Mr. David was to meet you —

BABETTE. The twelve o'clock train was most expensive. We could not have come with that train. We liked the train we came on.

ANISE (*very nervously, very rattled*). But Madame Fanny will have a fit. I will call her — She will not be able to contain herself. She —

SARA (*softly*). I wanted a few minutes. I'm nervous about coming home, I guess.

BODO (*conversationally*). You are French, Madame Anise?

ANISE. Yes, I am from the Bas Rhin. (*She looks past Sara, and bobs her head idiotically at Kurt*) Sara's husband. That is nice. That is nice.

BODO. Yes. Your accent is from the North. That is fine country. We were in hiding there once. (*Babette quickly pokes him.*)

ANISE. Hiding? You — (*Turns nervously to Kurt*) But here we stand and talk. You have not had your breakfast, sir!

BABETTE (*eagerly*). It would be nice to have breakfast.

ANISE. Yes, of course — I will go and order it.

SARA (*to the children*). What would you like for breakfast?

BABETTE (*surprised*). What would we like? Why, Mama! If an egg is not too rare or too expensive —

ANISE (*amazed*). Rare? Why — Oh, I — I must call Miss Fanny now. It is of a necessity. (*Excited, rushing toward terrace, calling*) Miss Fanny. Miss Fanny. (*Back to Sara*) Have you forgotten your Mama's nature? Miss Fanny! What a way to come home! After twenty years and nobody at the station —

FANNY'S VOICE. Don't yell at me. What is the matter with you?

ANISE (*excitedly, as Fanny draws near*). She's here. They're here. Miss Sara. She's here, I tell you. (*Fanny comes up to her, stares at her, then looks slowly around until she sees Sara.*)

SARA (*softly*). Hello, Mama.

FANNY (*after a long pause, softly, coming toward her*). Sara. Sara, darling. You're here. You're really here. (*She reaches her, takes her arms, stares at her, smiles*) Welcome. Welcome. Welcome to your house. (*Slowly*) You're not young, Sara.

SARA. No, Mama. I'm forty-one.

FANNY (*softly*). Forty-one. Of course. (*Presses her arms again*) Oh, Sara, I'm — (*Then quickly*) You look more like Papa now. That's good. The years have helped you. (*Turns to look at Kurt*) Welcome to this house, sir.

KURT (*warmly*). Thank you, Madame.

FANNY (*turns to look at Sara again, pats her arm. Nods, turns again to stare at Kurt. She is nervous and chatty*). You are a good-looking man, for a German. I didn't remember you that way. I like a good-looking man. I always have.

KURT (*smiles*). I like a good-looking woman. I always have.

BODO (*to Sara*). Ist das Grossmama?

FANNY (*looks down*). Yes. I am your grandmother. Also, I speak German, so do not talk about me. I speak languages very well. But there is no longer anybody to speak with. Anise has half forgotten her French, which was always bad; and I have nobody with whom to speak my Italian or German or — Sara, it's very good to have you home. I'm chattering away, I —

JOSHUA. Now you have us, Madame. We speak ignorantly, but much, in German, French, Italian, Spanish —

KURT. And boastfully in English.

BODO. There is never a need for boasting. If we are to fight for the good of all men, it is to be accepted that we must be among the most advanced.

ANISE. My God.

FANNY (*to Sara*). Are these *children?*

SARA (*laughs*). These are my children, Mama. This, Babette. (*Babette bows*) This, Joshua. (*Joshua bows*) This is Bodo. (*Bodo bows.*)

FANNY. Joshua was named for Papa. You wrote me. (*Indicates picture of Joshua Farrelly*) You bear a great name, young man.

JOSHUA (*smiles, indicates his father*). My name is Müller.

FANNY (*looks at him, laughs*). Yes. You look a little like your grandfather. (*To Babette*) And so do you. You are a nice-looking girl. (*To Bodo*) You look like nobody.

BODO. I am not beautiful.

FANNY (*laughs*). Well, Sara, well. Three children. You have done well. (*To Kurt*) You, too, sir, of course. Are you quite recovered? Sara wrote that you fought in Spain and —

BODO. Did Mama write that Papa was a great hero? He was brave, he was calm, he was expert, he was resourceful, he was —

KURT (*laughs*). My unprejudiced biographer.

SARA. Where is David? Has he changed much? Does he . . .

FANNY (*to Anise*). Don't stand there. Go and get him right away. Go get David. (*Anise exits*) He's out having breakfast with the titled folk. Do you remember Marthe Randolph? I mean, do you remember Hortie Randolph, her mother, who was my friend? Can you follow what I'm saying? I'm not speaking well today.

SARA. Of course I remember Marthe and Hortie. You and she used to scream at each other.

FANNY. Well, Marthe, her daughter, married Teck de Brancovis. *Count* de Brancovis. He was fancy when she married him. Not so fancy now, I suspect. Although still chic and tired. You know what I mean, the way they are in Europe. Well, they're here.

SARA. What's David like now? I —

FANNY. Like? Like? I don't know. He's a lawyer. You know that. Papa's firm. He's never married. You know that, too —

SARA. Why hasn't he married?

FANNY. Really, I don't know. I don't think he likes his own taste. Which is discriminating of him. He's had a lot of girls, of course, one more ignorant than the other — (*Goes toward terrace, begins to scream*) And where is he? David! David!

ANISE'S VOICE. He's coming, Miss Fanny. He's coming. Contain yourself. He was down at the garage gettting ready to leave —

FANNY. I don't care where he is. Tell him to come — David! (*Suddenly points to picture of Joshua*) That's my Joshua. Handsome, eh? We were very much in love. Hard to believe of people nowadays, isn't it?

SARA. Kurt and I love each other.

FANNY. Oh. You do? I daresay. But there are ways and ways of loving.

SARA. How dare you, Mama —

KURT (*laughs*). Ladies, ladies.

SARA (*giggles*). Why, I almost got mad then. You know, I don't think I've been mad since I last saw you.

BODO. My! You and Mama must not get angry. Anger is protest. And so you must direction it to the proper channels and then harness it for the good of other men. That is correct, Papa?

FANNY (*peers down at him*). If you grow up to talk like that, and stay as ugly as you are, you are going to have one of those successful careers on the lecture platform. (*Joshua and Babette laugh.*)

JOSHUA (*to Bodo*). Ah. It is a great pleasure to hear Grandma talk with you.

BODO (*to Fanny, tenderly*). We will not like each other. (*Kurt has wandered to the piano. Standing, he touches the keys in the first bars of a Mozart Rondo.*)

FANNY. You are wrong. I think we are rather alike; if that is so, we will certainly admire each other. (*David comes running in from the entrance hall. At the door he stops, stares at Sara.*)

DAVID. Sara. Darling —

SARA (*wheels, goes running toward him. She moves into his arms. He leans down, kisses her with great affection*). David. David.

DAVID (*softly*). It's been a long, long time. I got to thinking it would never happen. (*He kisses her hair.*)

SARA. David, I'm excited. Isn't it strange? To be here, to see each other — But I am forgetting. This is my husband. These are my children. Babette, Joshua, Bodo. (*They all three advance, stand in line to shake hands.*)

BODO (*shaking hand*). How do you do, Uncle David?

DAVID. How do you do, Bodo? (*David shakes hands with Joshua*) Boys can shake hands. But so pretty a girl must be kissed. (*He kisses Babette. She smiles, pleased, and crosses to the side of Sara.*)

BABETTE. Thank you. Fix your hair, Mama. (*Sara shoves back a falling hairpin.*)

DAVID (*crossing to Kurt*). I'm happy to meet you, sir, and to have you here.

KURT. Thank you. Sara has told me so much from you. You have a devoted sister.

DAVID. Have I? Still? That's mighty good to hear. (*Anise comes in from the library.*)

ANISE. Your breakfast is coming. Shall I wash the children, Miss Sara?

JOSHUA (*amazed*). Wash us? Do people wash each other?

SARA. No, but the washing is a good idea. Go along now, and hurry. (*All three start for the hall*) And then we'll all have a fine, big breakfast again. (*The children exit.*)

FANNY. Again? Don't they usually have a good breakfast?

KURT (*smiles*). No, Madame. Only sometimes.

SARA. Oh, we do all right, usually. (*Very happily, very gaily*) Ah, it's good to be here. (*Puts her arm in David's*) We were kids. Now we're all grown up! I've got children, you're a lawyer, and a fine one, I bet —

FANNY. The name of Farrelly on the door didn't, of course, hurt David's career.

DAVID (*smiles*). Sara, you might as well know Mama thinks of me only as a monument to Papa and a not very well-made monument at that. I am not the man Papa was.

SARA (*to Fanny*). How do you know he's not?

FANNY (*carefully*). I beg your pardon. That is the second time you have spoken disrespectfully of your father. (*Sara and David laugh. Fanny turns to Kurt*) I hope you will like me.

KURT. I hope so.

SARA (*to David*). Now I want to hear about you — (*Looks at him, laughs*) I'm awfully nervous about seeing you. Are you, about me?

DAVID. Yes. I certainly am.

SARA. I'm like an idiot. I want to see everything right away. The lake, and my old room — and I want to talk and ask questions . . .

KURT (*laughs*). More slow, Sara. It is most difficult to have twenty years in a few minutes.

SARA. Yes, I know, but — Oh, well. Kurt's right. We'll say it all slowly. It's just nice being back. Haven't I fine children?

DAVID. Very fine. You're lucky. I wish I had them.

FANNY. How could you have them? All the women you like are too draughty, if you know what I mean. I'm sure that girl from Lansing, Michigan, is sterile. Which is as God in his wisdom would have it.

SARA. Oh. So you have a girl?

DAVID. I have no girl. This amuses Mama.

FANNY. He's very attractive to some women. (*To Kurt*) Both my children are attractive, whatever else they're not. Don't you think so? (*Points to David*) He's flirting with our Countess now, Sara. You will see for yourself.

DAVID (*sharply*). You are making nervous jokes this morning, Mama. And they're not very good ones.

FANNY (*gaily*). I tell the truth. If it turns out to be a joke, all the better.

SARA. Ah, Mama hasn't changed. And that's good, too.

FANNY. Don't mind me, Sara. I, too, am nervous about seeing you. (*To Kurt*) You are still an engineer?

KURT. Yes.

FANNY. Do you remember the day we met in München? The day Sara brought you to lunch? I thought Sara would have a miserable life with you. I was wrong. (*To David*) You see? I always admit when I'm wrong.

DAVID. You are a noble woman in all things, at all times.

FANNY. Oh, you're mad at me. (*To Kurt*) I hope you'll like it here. I've made some plans. The new wing will be for you and Sara. The old chicken house we'll fix up for the children. A nice, new bathroom, and we'll put in their own kitchen, and Anise will move in with them —

SARA. That's kind of you, Mama. But — but — we won't make any plans for a while — (*Very quietly*) A good, long vacation; God knows Kurt needs it —

FANNY. A vacation? You'll be staying here, of course. You don't have to worry about work — engineers can always get jobs, David says, and he's already begun to inquire —

KURT. I have not worked as an engineer since many years, Madame.

DAVID. Haven't you? I thought — Didn't you work for Dornier?

KURT. Yes. Before '33.

FANNY. But you have worked in other places. A great many other places, I should say. Every letter of Sara's seemed to have a new postmark.

KURT. We move most often.

DAVID. You gave up engineering?

KURT. I gave it up? (*Shrugs*) One could say it that way.

FANNY. What do you do?

SARA. Mama, we —

KURT. It is difficult to explain.

DAVID. No need to explain.

FANNY. No, I — I'm trying to find out something. (*To Kurt*) May I ask it, sir?

KURT. Let me help you, Madame. You wish to know whether not being an engineer buys breakfasts for my family. It does not. I have no wish to make a mystery of what I have been doing; it is only that it is awkward to place neatly. (*Smiles, motions with his hand*) It sounds so big: it is so small. I am an Anti-Fascist. And that does not pay well.

FANNY. Do you mind questions?

SARA. Yes.

KURT (*sharply*). Sara. (*To Fanny*) Perhaps I shall not answer them. But I shall try.

FANNY. Are you a radical?

KURT. You would have to tell me what that word means to you, Madame.

FANNY (*after a slight pause*). That is just. We all have private definitions. We all are Anti-Fascists, for example —

SARA. Yes. But Kurt works at it.

FANNY. What kind of work?

KURT. Any kind. Anywhere.

FANNY (*sharply*). I will stop asking questions.

SARA (*very sharply*) That would be sensible, Mama.

DAVID. Darling, don't be angry. We've been worried about you, naturally. We knew so little, except that you were having a bad time.

SARA. I didn't have a bad time. We never —

KURT. Do not lie for me, Sara.

SARA. I'm not lying. I didn't have a bad time, the way they mean. I —

FANNY (*slowly*). You had a bad time just trying to live, didn't you? That's obvious, Sara, and foolish to pretend it isn't. Why wouldn't you take money from us? What kind of nonsense —

SARA. We've lived the way we wanted to live. I don't know the language of rooms like this anymore. And I don't want to learn it again.

KURT. Do not bristle about it.

SARA. I'm not bristling. (*To Fanny*) I married because I fell in love. You can understand that.

FANNY. Yes.

SARA. For almost twelve years, Kurt went to work every morning and came home every night, and we lived modestly, and happily — (*Sharply*) As happily as people could in a starved Germany that was going to pieces —

KURT. Sara, please. You are angry. I do not like it that way. I will try to find a way to tell you with quickness. Yes. (*Sara turns, looks at him, starts to speak, stops*) I was born in a town called Fürth. (*Smiles*) There is a holiday in my town. We call it Kirchweih. It was a gay holiday with games and music and a hot white sausage to eat with the wine. I grow up, I move away — to school, to work — but always I come back for Kirchweih. It is for me, the great day of the year. (*slowly*) But after the war, that day begins to change. The sausage is made from bad stuff, the peasants come in without shoes, the children are sick — It is bad for my people, those years, but always I have hope. In the festival of August, 1931, more than a year before the storm, I give up that hope. On that day, I see twenty-seven men murdered in a Nazi street fight. I cannot stay by now and watch. My time has come to move. I remember Luther, "Here I stand. I can do nothing else. God help me. Amen."

SARA. It doesn't pay well to fight for what we believe in. But I wanted it the way Kurt wanted it. (*Shrugs*) They don't like us in Europe; I guess they never did. So Kurt brought us home. You've always said you wanted us. If you don't, I will understand.

DAVID. Darling, of course we want you —

FANNY (*rises*). I am old. And made of dry cork. And bad-mannered. Please forgive me.

SARA (*goes quickly to Fanny*). Mama. We're all acting like fools. I'm glad to be home. That's all I know. So damned glad.

DAVID. And we're damned glad to have you. Let's walk to the lake. We've made it bigger and planted the island with blackberries — (*She smiles and goes to him. Together they move out the hall entrance.*)

FANNY (*after a silence*). They've always liked each other. We're going to have Zwetschgen-Knoedeln for dinner. In honor of you. You like them?

KURT. Indeed.

MARTHE (*coming in from the terrace. Stops in the doorway*). Oh, I'm sorry, Fanny. We were waiting. I didn't want to interrupt the family reunion. I —

FANNY. This is my son-in-law, Herr Müller. The Countess de Brancovis.

KURT AND MARTHE (*together*). How do you do?

MARTHE. And how is Sara, Herr Müller? I haven't seen her since I was a little girl. She probably doesn't remember me at all. (*Teck comes in from the hall. She turns*) This is my husband, Herr Müller.

KURT. How do you do?

TECK. How do you do, sir? (*Kurt bows. They shake hands*) Would it be impertinent for one European to make welcome another?

KURT (*smiles*). I do not think so. It would be friendly.

BODO (*appears at the hall door*). Papa — (*Sees Teck and Marthe, bows*) Oh, good morning. Miss Anise says you are the Count and Countess. Once before we met a Count and Countess. They had a small room bordering on ours in Copenhagen. They were more older than you, and more poor. We shared with them our newspaper.

MARTHE (*laughs*). It wasn't us, but it might have been. What's your name?

BODO. My name is Bodo. It's a strange name. No? (*To Kurt*) Papa, this is the house of great wonders. Each has his bed, each has his bathroom. The arrangement of it, that is splendorous.

FANNY (*laughs*). You are a fancy talker, Bodo.

KURT. Oh, yes. In many languages.

BODO (*to Fanny*). Please to correct me when I am wrong. Papa, the plumbing is such as you have never seen. Each implement is placed on the floor, and all are simultaneous in the same room. You will therefore see that being placed most solidly on the floor allows of no rodents or crawlers, and is most sanitary. (*To the others*) Papa will be most interested. He likes to know how each thing of everything is put together. And he is so fond of being clean —

KURT (*laughs. To Fanny*). I am a hero to my children. It bores everybody but me.

TECK. It is most interesting, Herr Müller. I thought I had a good ear for the accents of your country. But yours is most difficult to place. It is Bayrisch? Or is it —

BODO. That's because Papa has worked in so many —

KURT (*quickly*). German accents are the most difficult to identify. I, myself, when I try, am usually incorrect. Yours would be Roumanian?

MARTHE (*laughs*). My God, is it that bad?

KURT (*smiles*). I am showing off. I know the Count de Brancovis is Roumanian.

TECK (*heartily*). So? We have met before? I thought so, but I cannot remember —

KURT. No, sir. We have not met before. I read your name in the newspapers.

TECK (*to Kurt*). Strange. I was sure I had met you. I was in the Paris Legation for many years, and I thought perhaps —

KURT. Oh, no. If it is possible to believe, I am the exile who is not famous. (*To Fanny*) I have been thinking with pleasure, Madame Fanny, of breakfast on your porch. (*He points to the picture of Joshua Farrelly*) Your husband once wrote: "I am getting older now and Europe seems far away. Fanny and I will have an early breakfast on the porch and then I shall drive the boys into Washington." And then he goes on: "Henry Adams tells me he has been reading Karl Marx. I shall have to tell him my father made me read Marx many years ago and that, since he proposes to impress me, will spoil Henry's Sunday."

FANNY (*laughs, delighted. Takes Kurt's arm*). And so it did. I am pleased with you. I shall come and serve your food myself. I had forgotten Joshua ever wrote it. (*They start out of the terrace doors together, followed by Bodo.*)

KURT (*as they disappear*). I try to impress you. I learned it last night. (*Fanny laughs. They disappear.*)

TECK (*smiles*). He is a clever man. A quotation from Joshua Farrelly is a sure road to Fanny's heart. Where did you say Herr Müller was from?

MARTHE. Germany.

TECK. I know that. (*Goes to a valise. He leans over, stares at it, looks at the labels, pushes the lock. The lock opens; he closes it. Then he turns and, as he speaks, picks up the briefcase*) What part of Germany?

MARTHE. I don't know. And I never knew you were an expert on accents.

TECK. I never knew it either. Are you driving into Washington with David this morning?

MARTHE. I was going to. But he may not be going to the office, now that Sara's here. I was to have lunch with Sally Tyne. (*Teck puts down the briefcase*) What are you doing?

TECK. Wondering why luggage is unlocked and a shabby briefcase is carefully locked.

MARTHE. You're very curious about Mr. Müller.

TECK. Yes. And I do not know why. Something far away . . . I am curious about a daughter of the Farrellys' who marries a German who has bullet scars on his face and broken bones in his hands.

MARTHE (*sharply*). Has he? There are many of them now, I guess.

TECK. So there are. But this one is in this house. (*He goes to the bell cord, pulls it. She watches him nervously.*)

MARTHE. Is it — is he any business of yours?

TECK. What is my business? Anything might be my business now.

MARTHE. Yes — unfortunately. You might inquire from your friend Von Seitz. They always know their nationals.

TECK (*pleasantly, ignoring the sharpness with which she has *spoken*). Oh, yes, I will do that, of course. But I do not like to ask questions without knowing the value of the answers.

MARTHE. Teck. This man is a German Sara married years ago. I remember Mama talking about it. He was nothing then and he isn't now. They've had a tough enough time already without —

TECK. Have you been sleeping with David?

MARTHE (*stops, stares at him, then simply*). No. I have not been. And that hasn't been your business for a good many years now.

TECK. You like him?

MARTHE. What's this for, Teck?

TECK. Answer me, please.

MARTHE. I —

TECK. Yes? Answer me.

MARTHE. I do like him.

TECK. What does he feel about you?

MARTHE. I don't know.

TECK. But you are trying to find out. You have made plans with him?

MARTHE. Of course not. I —

TECK. But you will try to make him have plans. I have recognized it. Well, we have been together a long — (*Joseph enters. Teck stops*) Joseph, Miss Fanny wishes you to take the baggage upstairs.

JOSEPH. Yes, sir. I was going to. (*He begins to pick up the baggage. Marthe has turned sharply and is staring at Teck. Then she rises, watches Joseph pick up the baggage, turns again to look at Teck.*)

TECK. It is perhaps best that we had this talk.

MARTHE (*waits for Joseph to move off. He exits, carrying the valises*). Why did you do that? Why did you tell Joseph that Fanny wanted him to take the baggage upstairs.

TECK. Obviously it is more comfortable to look at baggage behind closed doors.

MARTHE (*very sharply*). What kind of silliness is this now? Leave these people alone — (*As he starts to exit*) I won't let you —

TECK. What? (*As he moves again, she comes after him.*)

MARTHE. I said I won't let you. You are not to do —

TECK. How many times have you seen me angry? Run along

now and have lunch with something you call Sally Tyne. But do not make plans with David. You will not be able to carry them out. You will go with me, when I am ready to go. (*His last words are spoken as he goes through the door, and as the curtain falls.*)

Curtain

Act Two

SCENE: *The same as Act One, about ten days later. During the act it will begin to grow dark; but the evening is warm and the terrace doors are open.*

AT RISE: *Sara is sitting on the couch, crocheting. Fanny and Teck are sitting at a small table playing cribbage. Bodo is sitting near them, at a large table, working on a heating pad. The cord is torn from the bag, the bag is ripped open. Anise sits next to him, anxiously watching him. Outside on the terrace, Joshua is going through baseball motions, coached by Joseph. From time to time they move out of sight, reappear, move off again.*

FANNY (*playing a card*). One.

BODO (*after a minute, to Teck*). The arrangement of this heating pad grows more complex.

TECK (*smiles, moves on the cribbage board*). And the more wires you remove, the more complex it will grow.

BODO (*points to bag*). Man has learned to make man comfortable. Yet all cannot have the comforts. (*To Anise*) How much did this cost you?

ANISE. It cost me ten dollars. And you have made a ruin of it.

BODO. That is not yet completely true. (*To Fanny*) Did I not install for you a twenty-five-cent button-push for your radio?

TECK (*playing a card*). Two and two. (*Moves pegs on the cribbage board.*)

FANNY. Yes, you're quite an installer.

BODO (*to Teck*). As I was wishing to tell you, Count de Brancovis, comfort and plenty exist. Yet all cannot have them. Why?

TECK. I do not know. It has worried many men. Why?

BODO (*takes a deep breath, raises his finger as if about to lecture*). Why? (*Considers a moment, then deflates himself*) I am not as yet sure.

ANISE. I thought not.

FANNY (*turns to look at Joshua and Joseph on the terrace*). Would you mind doing that dancing someplace else?

JOSEPH (*looking in*). That ain't dancing. I'm teaching Josh baseball.

FANNY. Then maybe he'd teach you how to clean the silver.

JOSEPH. I'm a good silver-cleaner, Miss Fanny.

FANNY. But you're getting out of practice.

JOSEPH (*after a moment's thought*). Yes'm. I see what you trying to say. (*He exits.*)

FANNY (*playing a card*). Three.

JOSHUA. It is my fault. I'm crazy about baseball.

BODO. Baseball players are among the exploited people in this country. I read about it.

FANNY. You never should have learned to read.

BODO. Their exploited condition is foundationed on the fact that —

JOSHUA (*bored*). All right, all right.

SARA. Founded, Bodo, not foundation.

JOSHUA. He does it always. He likes long words. In all languages.

TECK. How many languages do you children speak?

BODO. Oh, we do not really know any very well, except German and English. We speak bad French and —

SARA. And bad Danish and bad Czech.

TECK. You seem to have stayed close to the borders of Germany. Did Herr Müller have hopes, as so many did, that National Socialism would be overthrown on every tomorrow?

SARA. We have not given up that hope. Have you, Count de Brancovis?

TECK. I never had it.

JOSHUA (*pleasantly*). Then it must be most difficult for you to sleep.

TECK. I beg your pardon?

SARA. Schweig doch, Joshua!

FANNY (*to Teck*). Sara told Joshua to shut up. (*Playing a card*) Twelve.

TECK. I have offended you, Mrs. Müller. I am sorry.

SARA (*pleasantly*). No, sir, you haven't offended me. I just don't like polite political conversations.

TECK. All of us, in Europe, had too many of them.

SARA. Yes. Too much talk. By this time all of us know where we are and what we have to do. It's an indulgence to sit in a room and discuss your beliefs as if they were the afternoon's golf game.

FANNY. You know, Sara, I find it very pleasant that Kurt, considering his history, doesn't make platform speeches. He hasn't tried to convince anybody of anything.

SARA. Why should he, Mama? You are quite old enough to have your own convictions — or Papa's.

FANNY (*turns to look at her*). I am proud to have Papa's convictions.

SARA. Of course. But it might be well to have a few new ones, now and then.

FANNY (*peers over at her*). Are you criticizing me?

SARA (*smiles*). Certainly not.

BABETTE (*comes running in from the right entrance door. She has on an apron and she is carrying a plate. She goes to Fanny*). Eat it while it's hot, Grandma.

(*Fanny peers down, takes the fork, begins to eat. Anise and Bodo both rise, move to Fanny, inspect the plate.*)

FANNY (*to them*). Go away.

ANISE. It is a potato pancake.

FANNY. And the first good one I've eaten in many, many years. I love a good potato pancake.

BODO. I likewise.

BABETTE. I am making a great number for dinner. Move away, Bodo.

TECK (*playing a card*). Fifteen and two.

ANISE (*who has followed Bodo back to the table, leans over to look at the heating pad*). You've ruined it! I shall sue you.

JOSHUA. I told you not to let him touch it.

SARA (*laughs*). I remember you were always saying that, Anise — that you were going to sue. That's very French. I was sick once in Paris, and Babbie stayed up for a whole night and day and finished a dress I was making for a woman in the Rue Jacob. I told her to tell the woman she'd done it — I thought perhaps the woman would give her a candy or something — and anyway, I was very proud of her work. But no. The woman admitted the dress was well done, but said she was going to sue because I hadn't done it myself. Fancy that.

FANNY (*slowly*). You sewed for a living?

SARA. Not a very good one. But Babbie and I made a little something now and then. Didn't we, darling?

FANNY (*sharply*). Really, Sara, were these — these things necessary? Why couldn't you have written?

SARA (*laughs*). You've asked me that a hundred times in the last week.

JOSHUA (*gently*). I think it is only that Grandma feels sorry for us. Grandma has not seen much of the world.

FANNY. Don't you start giving me lectures, Joshua. I'm fond of you. And of you, Babbie. (*To Anise*) Are there two desserts for dinner? And are they sweet?

ANISE. Yes.

FANNY. (*turns to Bodo*). I wish I were fond of you.

BODO. You are. (*Happily*) You are very fond of me.

FANNY (*playing a card*). Twenty-five.

BABETTE (*holds up a piece of lace*). This is for you, Grandma. I'm making a bed jacket. It is nice lace. Papa brought it to me from Spain and I mean for you to have it.

FANNY. Thank you, darling. A sequence and three. A pair and five. (*To Teck, as they finish the cribbage game*) There. That's two dollars off. I owe you eight-fifty.

TECK. Let us carry it until tomorrow. You shall give it to me as a going-away token.

FANNY (*too pleased*). You're going away?

TECK (*laughs*). Ah, Madame Fanny. Do not sound *that* happy.

FANNY. Did I? When are you going?

TECK. In a few days, I think. (*Turns to look at Sara*) We're too many refugees, eh, Mrs. Müller?

SARA (*pleasantly*). Perhaps.

TECK. Will you be leaving, also?

SARA. I beg your pardon?

TECK. I thought perhaps you, too, would be moving on. Herr Müller does not give me the feeling of a man who settles down. Men who have done his work, seldom leave it. Not for a quiet country house.

(*All three children look up.*)

SARA (*very quietly*). What work do you think my husband has done, Count de Brancovis?

TECK. Engineering?

SARA (*slowly*). Yes. Engineering.

FANNY (*very deliberately to Teck*). I don't know what you're saying. They shall certainly not be leaving — ever. Is that understood, Sara?

SARA. Well, Mama —

FANNY. There are no wells about it. You've come home to see me die and you will wait until I'm ready.

SARA (*laughs*). Really, Mama, that isn't the reason I came home.

FANNY. It's a good enough reason. I shall do a fine death.

ANISE. I daresay.

FANNY. I shall take to my bed early and stay for years. In great pain.

ANISE. I am sure of it. You will duplicate the disgrace of the birth of Miss Sara.

SARA. Was I born in disgrace?

ANISE. It was not your fault. But it was disgusting. Three weeks before you were to come — all was excellent, of course, in so healthy a woman as Madame Fanny — a great dinner was given here and, most unexpectedly, attended by a beautiful lady from England.

FANNY. Do be still. You are dull and fanciful —

ANISE. Mr. Joshua made the great error of waltzing the beauty for two dances, Madame Fanny being unfitted for the waltz and under no circumstances being the most graceful of dancers.

FANNY (*her voice rising*). I danced magnificently.

ANISE. A minute did not elapse between the second of the waltzes and a scream from Madame Fanny. She was in labor. Two hundred people, and if we had left her alone, she would have remained in the ballroom —

FANNY. How you invent! How you invent!

ANISE. Do not call to me that I am a liar. For three weeks you are in the utmost agony —

FANNY. And so I was. I remember it to this day —

ANISE (*to Sara, angrily*). Not a pain. Not a single pain. She would lie up there in state, stealing candy from herself. Then, when your Papa would rest himself for a minute at the dinner or with a book, a scream would dismantle the house — it was revolting. (*Spitefully to Fanny*) And now the years have passed I may disclose to you that Mr. Joshua knew you were going through the play-acting —

FANNY (*rises*). He did not. You are a malicious —

ANISE. Once he said to me, "Anise, it is well that I love my wife. This is of a great strain and her uncle Freddie was not right in the head, neither."

FANNY (*screaming*). You will leave this house — You are a liar, a woman of —

SARA. Mama, sit down.

ANISE. I will certainly leave this house. I will —

SARA (*sharply*). Both of you. Sit down. And be still.

ANISE. She has intimated that I lie —

FANNY (*screaming*). Intimated! Is that what I was doing — (*Anise begins to leave the room*) All right. I beg your pardon. I apologize.

(*Anise turns.*)

SARA. Both of you. You are acting like children.

BODO. Really, Mama. You insult us.

ANISE. I accept your apology. Seat yourself.

(*They both sit down.*)

FANNY (*after a silence*). I am unloved.

BABETTE. I love you, Grandma.

FANNY. Do you, Babbie?

JOSHUA. And I.

FANNY (*nods, very pleased. To Bodo*). And you?

BODO. *I* loved you the primary second I saw you.

FANNY. You are a charlatan.

ANISE. As for me, I am fond of all the living creatures.

(*David and Kurt come in from the terrace. Both are in work clothes, their sleeves rolled up.*)

FANNY. Where have you been?

DAVID. Helping Mr. Chabeuf spray the fruit trees.

ANISE. Mr. Chabeuf says that Herr Müller has the makings of a good farmer. From a Frenchman that is a large thing to say.

KURT (*who has looked around the room, looked at Teck, strolled over to Bodo*). Mr. Chabeuf and I have an excellent time exchanging misinformation. My father was a farmer. I have a wide knowledge of farmer's misinformation.

FANNY. This is good farm land. Perhaps, in time —

DAVID (*laughs*). Mama would give you the place, Kurt, if you guaranteed that your great-grandchildren would die here.

KURT (*smiles*). I would like to so guarantee.

TECK. A farmer. That is very interesting. Abandon your ideals, Herr Müller?

KURT. Ideals? (*Carefully*) Sara, heisst das auf deutsch "Ideale"?

SARA. Yes.

KURT. Is that what I have? I do not like the word. It gives to me the picture of a small, pale man at a seaside resort. (*To Bodo*) What are you doing?

BODO. Preparing an elderly electric pad for Miss Anise. I am confused.

KURT (*wanders toward the piano*). So it seems.

BODO. Something has gone wrong with the principle on which I have been working. It is probably that I will ask your assistance.

KURT. Thank you. Whenever you are ready. (*Begins to pick out notes with one hand.*)

FANNY. We shall have a little concert tomorrow evening. In honor of Babbie's birthday. (*To Kurt*) Kurt, you and I will play "The Clock Symphony." Then Joshua and I will play the duet we've learned, and Babbie will sing. And I shall finish with a Chopin Nocturne.

DAVID (*laughs*). I thought you'd be the last on the program.

TECK. Where is Marthe?

FANNY. She'll be back soon. She went into town to do an errand for me. (*To David*) Did you buy presents for everybody?

DAVID. I did.

SARA (*smiles, to Babette*). We always did that here. If somebody had a birthday, we all got presents. Nice, isn't it?

DAVID (*to Anise*). I will buy you an electric pad. You will need it.

ANISE. Indeed.

FANNY. Did you buy me a good present?

DAVID. Pretty good. (*Pats Babette's head*) The best present goes to Babbie; it's *her* birthday.

FANNY. Jewelry?

DAVID. No, not jewelry.

FANNY. Oh. Not jewelry.

DAVID. Why?

FANNY (*too casually*). I just asked you.

TECK. It was a natural mistake, David. You see, Mrs. Mellie Sewell told your mother that she had seen you and Marthe in Barstow's. And your mother said you were probably buying her a present, or one for Babbie.

DAVID (*too sharply*). Yes.

TECK (*laughs*). Yes what?

DAVID. Just yes.

FANNIE (*too hurriedly*). Mellie gets everything wrong. She's very anxious to meet Marthe because she used to know Francie Cabot, her aunt. Marthe's aunt, I mean, not Mellie's.

SARA (*too hurriedly*). She really came to inspect Kurt and me. But I saw her first. (*She looks anxiously at David*) You were lucky to be out, David.

DAVID. Oh, she calls every Saturday afternoon, to bring Mama all the Washington gossip of the week. She gets it all wrong, you understand, but that doesn't make any difference to either Mama or her. Mama then augments it, wits it up, Papa used to say —

FANNY. Certainly. I sharpen it a little. Mellie has no sense of humor.

DAVID. So Mama sharpens it a little, and delivers it tomorrow afternoon to old lady Marcy down the road. Old lady Marcy hasn't heard a word in ten years, so she unsharpens it again, and changes the names. By Wednesday afternoon —

TECK (*smiles*). By Wednesday afternoon it will not be you who were in Barstow's, and it will be a large diamond pin with four sapphires delivered to a movie star.

DAVID (*turns, looks at him*). Exactly.

FANNY (*very nervously*). Francie Cabot, Marthe's aunt, you understand — (*To Kurt*) Did you ever know Paul von Seitz, a German?

KURT. I have heard of him.

FANNY (*very rapidly*). Certainly. He was your Ambassador to somewhere, I've forgotten. Well, Francie Cabot married him. I could have. Any American, not crippled, whose father had money — He was crazy about me. I was better-looking than Francie. Well, years later when he was your Ambassador — my father was, too, as you probably know — not your Ambassador, of course, ours — but I am talking about Von Seitz.

DAVID (*laughs to Kurt*). You can understand how it goes. Old lady Marcy is not entirely to blame.

FANNY. Somebody asked me if I didn't regret not marrying him. I said, "Madame, je le regrette tous les jours et j'en suis heureuse chaque soir." (*Fanny turns to David*) That means I regret it every day and am happy about it every night. You understand what I meant, by *night?* Styles in wit change so.

DAVID. I understood it, Mama.

BABETTE. It was most witty.

BODO. I do not know that I understood. You will explain to me, Grandma?

SARA. Later.

FANNY (*turns to look at Teck*). You remember the old Paul von Seitz?

TECK. He was stationed in Paris when I first was there.

FANNY. Of course. I always forget you were a diplomat.

TECK. It is just as well.

FANNY. There's something insane about a Roumanian diplomat. Pure insane. I knew another one, once. He wanted to marry me, too.

SARA (*laughs*). All of Europe.

FANNY. Not all. Some. Naturally. I was rich, I was witty, my family was of the best. I was handsome, unaffected —

DAVID. And noble and virtuous and kind and elegant and fashionable and simple — it's hard to remember everything you were. I've often thought it must have been boring for Papa to have owned such perfection.

FANNY (*shrieks*). Your father bored with me! Not for a second of our life —

DAVID (*laughs*). Oh God, when will I learn?

BODO. Do not shriek, Grandma. It is an unpleasant sound for the ear.

FANNY. Where was I? Oh, yes. What I started out to say was — (*She turns, speaks carefully to Teck*) Mellie Sewell told me, when you left the room, that she had heard from Louis Chandler's child's governess that you had won quite a bit of money in a poker game with Sam Chandler and some Germans at the Embassy. (*Kurt, who has been playing the piano, stops playing very abruptly. Teck turns to look at him*) *That's* how I thought of Von Seitz. His nephew Philip was in on the game.

DAVID (*looks at Teck*). It must have been a big game. Sam Chandler plays in big games.

TECK. Not big enough.

DAVID. Have you known Sam long?

TECK. For years. Every Embassy in Europe knew him.

DAVID (*sharply*). Sam and Nazis must make an unpleasant poker game.

(*Kurt begins to play a new melody.*)

TECK (*who has not looked away from Kurt*). I do not play poker to be amused.

DAVID. What's Sam selling now?

TECK. Bootleg munitions. He always has.

DAVID. You don't mind?

TECK. Mind? I have not thought about it.

FANNY. Well, you ought to think about it. Sam Chandler has always been a scoundrel. All the Chandlers are. They're cousins of mine.

TECK. Do you know the young Von Seitz, Herr Müller? He was your military attaché in Spain.

KURT. He was the German government attaché in Spain. I know his name, of course. He is a famous artillery expert. But the side on which I fought was not where he was stationed, Count de Brancovis.

ANISE (*Babette and Joshua begin to hum the song Kurt is playing. Sara begins to hum*). It is time for the bath and the change of clothes. I will give you five more minutes —

FANNY. What is the song?

TECK. It was a German soldiers' song. They sang it as they straggled back in '18. I remember hearing it in Berlin. Were you there then, Herr Müller?

KURT (*the playing and the humming continue*). I was not in Berlin.

TECK. But you were in the war, of course?

KURT. Yes. I was in the war.

FANNY. You didn't think then you'd live to see another war.

KURT. Many of us were afraid we would.

FANNY. What are the words?

SARA. The Germans in Spain, in Kurt's Brigade, wrote new words for the song.

KURT (*begins to sing*).

"Wir zieh'n Heim, wir zieh'n Heim,
Mancher kommt nicht mit,
Mancher ging verschütt,
Aber Freunde sind wir stets."

"We come home. We come home.
Some of us are gone, and some of us are lost, but we are friends:
Our blood is on the earth together.
Some day. Some day we shall meet again.
Farewell."

(*Stops singing*) At a quarter before six on the morning of November 7th, 1936, eighteen years later, five hundred Germans walked through the Madrid streets on their way to defend the Manzanares River. We felt good that morning.

You know how it is to be good when it is needed to be good? So we had need of new words to say that. I translate with awkwardness, you understand. (*Begins to sing.*)

"And so we have met again.
The blood did not have time to dry.
We lived to fight again.
This time we fight for people.
This time the bastards will keep their hands away.
Those who sell the blood of other men, this time,
They keep their hands away.
For us to stand.
For us to fight.
This time no farewell, no farewell."

(*Music dies out. There is silence for a minute*) We did fight but we did not win. It would have been a different world if we had.

SARA. Papa said so years ago. Do you remember, Mama? "For every man who lives without freedom, the rest of us must face the guilt."

FANNY. Yes. "We are liable in the conscience-balance for the tailor in Lodz, the black man in our South, the peasant in —" (*Turns to Teck. Unpleasantly*) Your country, perhaps.

ANISE. Come. Baths for everybody. (*To Bodo*) Gather the wires. You have wrecked my cure.

BODO. If you would allow me a few minutes more —

ANISE. Come along. I have been duped for long enough. Come Joshua. Babette. Baths.

JOSHUA (*starts out after Anise. Babette begins to gather up her sewing*). My tub is a glory. But I do not like it so prepared for me and so announced by Miss Anise. (*He exits.*)

BODO (*to Anise*). You are angry about this. I do not blame you with my heart or my head. I admit I have failed. But Papa will repair it, Anise. Will you not, Papa? In a few minutes —

TECK (*to Bodo*). Your father is an expert electrician?

BODO. Oh yes, sir.

TECK. And as good with radio —

(*Bodo nods.*)

KURT (*sharply*). Count de Brancovis. Make your questions to me, please. Not to my children.

(*The others look up, surprised.*)

TECK (*pleasantly*). Very well, Herr Müller.

ANISE (*as she exits*). Nobody can fix it. You have made a pudding of it.

BODO (*as he follows her*). Do not worry. In five minutes Papa will — (*As Bodo reaches the door he bumps into Marthe who is carrying large dress boxes*) Oh. Your pardon. Oh, hello. (*He disappears.*)

MARTHE (*gaily*). Hello. (*To Fanny*) I waited for them. I was afraid they wouldn't deliver this late in the day. (*To Sara*) Come on, Sara. I can't wait to see them.

SARA. What?

MARTHE. Dresses. From Fanny. A tan linen, and a dark green with wonderful buttons, a white net for Babbie, and a suit for you, and play dresses for Babbie, and a dinner dress in gray to wear for Babbie's birthday — gray should be good for you, Sara — all from Savitt's. We sneaked the measurements, Anise and I —

SARA. How nice of you, Mama. How very kind of you. And of you, Marthe, to take so much trouble — (*She leans down, kisses Fanny*) You're a sweet woman, Mama.

DAVID. That's the first time Mama's ever heard that word. (*He takes the boxes from Marthe, puts them near the staircase. Marthe smiles at him, touches his hand, as Teck watches them.*)

FANNY. I have a bottom sweetness, if you understand what I mean.

(*Babette goes over to stare at the boxes.*)

SARA. From Savitt's. Extravagant of you. They had such lovely clothes. I remember my coming-out dress — (*Goes to Kurt*) Do you remember the black suit with the braid, and the Milan hat? Not the *first* day we met, but the picnic day? (*He smiles up at her*) Well, they were from Savitt's. That was over twenty years ago — I've known you a long time. Me, in an evening dress. Now you'll have to take me into Washington. I want to show off. Next week, and we'll dance, maybe — (*Sees that he is not looking at her*) What's the matter, darling? (*No answer. Slowly he turns to look at her*) What's the matter, Kurt? (*Takes his arms, very unhappily*) What have I done? It isn't that dresses have ever mattered to me, it's just that —

KURT. Of course, they have mattered to you. As they should. I do not think of the dresses. (*Draws her to him*) How many years have I loved that face?

SARA (*very happy*). So?

KURT. So. (*He leans down, kisses her, as if it were important.*)

SARA (*pleased*). There are other people here.

MARTHE (*slowly*). And good for us to see.

TECK. Nostalgia?

MARTHE. No. Nostalgia is for something you have known.

(*Fanny coughs.*)

BABETTE. Grandma, is it allowed to look at my dresses?

FANNY. Of course, child. Run along.

BABETTE (*picks up the boxes, goes toward the hall entrance*). I love dresses, I have a great fondness for materials and colors. Thank you, Grandma. (*She runs out of the room.*)

JOSEPH (*appears in the doorway*). There is a long-distance operator with a long-distance call for Mr. Müller. She wants to talk with him on the long-distance phone.

KURT. Oh — Excuse me, please —

(*Kurt rises quickly. Sara turns sharply to look at him. Teck looks up. Kurt goes quickly out. Sara stands staring after him.*)

MARTHE (*laughs*). I feel the same way as Babbie. Come on, Sara. Let's try them on.

(*Sara does not turn.*)

TECK. You also have a new dress?

MARTHE. Yes. Fanny was kind to me, too.

TECK. You are a very generous woman, Madame Fanny. Did you also give her a sapphire bracelet from Barstow's?

FANNY. I beg your —

DAVID (*slowly*). No. I gave Marthe the bracelet. And I understand that it is not any business of yours.

(*Fanny rises. Sara turns.*)

FANNY. Really, David —

DAVID. Be still, Mama.

TECK (*after a second*). Did you tell him that, Marthe?

MARTHE. Yes.

TECK. I shall not forgive you for that. (*Looks at David*) It is a statement which no man likes to hear from another man. You understand that? (*Playfully*) That is the type of thing about which we used to play at duels in Europe.

DAVID. We are not so musical comedy here. And you are not in Europe.

TECK. Even if I were, I would not suggest any such action. I would have reasons for not wishing it.

DAVID. It would be well for you not to suggest *any* action. And the reason for *that* is you might get hurt.

TECK (*slowly*). That would not be my reason. (*To Marthe*) Your affair has gone far enough —

MARTHE (*sharply*). It is not an affair —

TECK. I do not care what it is. The time has come to leave here. Go upstairs and pack your things. (*She does not move*) Go on, Marthe.

MARTHE (*to David*). I am not going with him. I told you that.

DAVID. I don't want you to go with him.

FANNY (*carefully*). Really, David, aren't you interfering in all this —

DAVID. Yes, Mama. I am.

TECK (*to Marthe*). When you are speaking to me, please say what you have to say to me.

MARTHE (*comes to him*). You are trying to frighten me. But you are not going to frighten me anymore. I will say it to you: I am not going with you. I am never going with you again.

TECK (*softly*). If you do not fully mean what you say, or if you might change your mind, you are talking unwisely, Marthe.

MARTHE. I know that.

TECK. Shall we talk about it alone?

MARTHE. You can't make me go, can you, Teck?

TECK. No, I can't make you.

MARTHE. Then there's no sense talking about it.

TECK. Are you in love with him?

MARTHE. Yes.

FANNY (*sharply*). Marthe! What is all this?

MARTHE (*sharply*). I'll tell *you* about it in a minute.

DAVID. You don't have to explain anything to anybody.

TECK. Is he in love with you?

MARTHE. I don't think so. You won't believe it, because you can't believe anything that hasn't got tricks to it, but David hasn't much to do with this. I told you I would leave someday, and I remember where I said it — (*Slowly*) — and why I said it.

TECK. I also remember. But I do not believe you. I have not had much to offer you these last years. But if now we had some money and could go back —

MARTHE. No. I don't like you, Teck. I never have.

TECK. And I have always known it.

FANNY (*stiffly*). I think your lack of affections should be discussed with more privacy. Perhaps —

DAVID. Mama —

MARTHE. There is nothing to discuss. Strange. I've talked to myself about this scene for almost fifteen years. I knew a lot of things to say to you and I used to lie awake at night or walk along the street and say them. Now I don't want to. When you're sure, then what's the sense of saying it? "This is why and this is why and this —" But when you know you can do it, you don't have to say anything; you can just go. And I'm going. There is nothing you can do. I would like you to believe that now.

TECK. Very well, Marthe. I think I made a mistake. I should not have brought you here. I believe you now.

MARTHE (*after a pause, she looks at David*). I'll move into Washington, and —

DAVID. Yes. Later. But I'd like you to stay here for a while, with us, if you wouldn't mind.

SARA. It would be better for you, Marthe —

FANNY. It's very interesting that I am not being consulted about this. (*To Marthe*) I have nothing against you, Marthe. I am sorry for you, but I don't think —

MARTHE. Thank you, Sara, David. But I'd rather move now. (*Turns, comes toward Fanny*) But perhaps I have something against you. Do you remember my wedding?

FANNY. Yes.

MARTHE. Do you remember how pleased Mama was with herself? Brilliant Mama, handsome Mama — everybody thought so, didn't they? A seventeen-year-old daughter, marrying a pretty good title, about to secure herself in a world that Mama liked — she didn't ask me what I liked. And the one time I tried to tell her, she frightened me — (*Looks up*) Maybe I've always been frightened. All my life.

TECK. Of course.

MARTHE (*to Fanny, as if she had not heard Teck*). I remember Mama's face at the wedding — it was *her* wedding, really, not mine.

FANNY (*sharply*). You are very hard on your mother.

MARTHE. Nineteen hundred and twenty-five. No, I'm not hard on her. I only tell the truth. She wanted a life for me, I suppose. It just wasn't the life I wanted for myself. (*Sharply*) And that's what you have tried to do. With your children.

In another way. Only Sara got away. And that made you angry — until so many years went by that you forgot.

FANNY. I don't usually mind people saying anything they think, but I find that —

MARTHE. I don't care what you mind or don't mind. I'm in love with your son —

FANNY (*very sharply*). That's unfortunate —

MARTHE. And I'm sick of watching you try to make him into his father. I don't think you even know you do it and I don't think he knows it, either. And that's what's most dangerous about it.

FANNY (*angrily*). I don't know what you are talking about.

DAVID. I think you do. (*Smiles*) You shouldn't mind hearing the truth — and neither should I.

MARTHE (*to Fanny*). Look. That pretty world Mama got me into was a tough world, see? I'm used to trouble. So don't try to interfere with me, because I won't let you. (*She goes to David*) Let's just have a good time. (*He leans down, takes both her hands, kisses them. Then slowly, she turns away, starts to exit. To Teck*) You will also be going today?

TECK. Yes.

MARTHE. Then let us make sure we go in different directions, and do not meet again. Good-bye, Teck.

TECK. Good-bye, Marthe. You will not believe me, but I tried my best, and I am now most sorry to lose you.

MARTHE. Yes. I believe you. (*She moves out. There is silence for a minute.*)

FANNY. Well, a great many things have been said in the last few minutes.

DAVID (*crosses to bell cord. To Teck*). Joseph will pack for you.

TECK. Do not bother. I will ring for him when I am ready. (*Kurt comes in from the study door. Sara turns, stares at him. waits. He does not look at her*) It will not take me very long. (*He starts for the door, looking at Kurt.*)

SARA. What is it, Kurt?

KURT. It is nothing of importance, darling — (*He looks quickly at Teck, who is moving very slowly.*)

SARA. Don't tell me it's nothing. I know the way you look when —

KURT (*sharply*). I said it was of no importance. I must get to California for a few weeks. That is all.

SARA. I —

TECK (*turns*). It is in the afternoon newspaper, Herr Müller. (*Points to paper on table*) I was waiting to find the proper moment to call it to your attention. (*He moves toward the table, picks up the paper, turns it over, begins to read*) "Zurich, Switzerland: The Zurich papers today reprinted a despatch from the *Berliner Tageblatt* on the capture of Colonel Max Freidank. Freidank is said — (*Sara begins to move toward him*) — to be the chief of the Anti-Nazi Underground Movement. Colonel Freidank has long been an almost legendary figure. The son of the famous General Freidank, he was a World War officer and a distinguished physicist before the advent of Hitler."

SARA. Max —

KURT. Be still, Sara.

TECK. They told me of it at the Embassy last night. They also told me that with him they had taken a man who called himself Ebber, and a man who called himself Triste. They could not find a man called Gotter. (*He starts toward the door*) I shall be a lonely man without Marthe. I am also a very poor one. I should like to have ten thousand dollars before I go.

DAVID (*carefully*). You will make no loans in this house.

TECK. I was not speaking of a loan.

FANNY (*carefully*). God made you not only a scoundrel but a fool. That is a dangerous combination.

DAVID (*suddenly leaps toward Teck*). Damn you, you —

KURT (*pounds on the top of the piano, as David almost reaches Teck*). Leave him alone. (*Moves quickly to stop David*) Leave him alone! *David! Leave him alone!*

DAVID (*angrily to Kurt*). Keep out of it. (*Starts toward Teck*) I'm beginning to see what Marthe meant. Blackmailing with your wife — You —

KURT (*very sharply*). He is not speaking of his wife. Or you. He means me. (*Looks at Teck*) Is that correct?

TECK. Good. It was necessary for me to hear you say it. You understand that?

KURT. I understand it.

SARA. (*frightened, softly*). Kurt —

DAVID. What is all this about? What the hell are you talking about?

TECK. Be still. (*To Kurt*) At your convenience. Your hands are shaking, Herr Müller.

KURT (*quietly*). My hands were broken: they are bad when I have fear.

TECK. I am sorry. I can understand that. It is not pleasant. (*Motions toward Fanny and David*) Perhaps you would like a little time to — I will go and pack, and be ready to leave. We will all find that more comfortable, I think. You should get yourself a smaller gun, Herr Müller. That pistol you have been carrying is big and awkward.

KURT. You saw the pistol when you examined our bags.

TECK. You knew that?

KURT. Oh, yes. I have the careful eye, through many years of needing it. And then you have not the careful eye. The pistol was lying to the left of a paper package and when you leave, it is to the right of the package.

SARA. Kurt! Do you mean that —

KURT (*sharply*). Please, darling, do not do that.

TECK. It is a German Army Luger?

KURT. Yes.

TECK. You will have no need to use it. And, in any case, I am not afraid of it. You understand that?

KURT (*slowly*). I understand that you are not a man of fears. That is strange to me, because I am a man who has so many fears.

TECK (*laughs*). Are you? That is interesting. (*He exits.*)

DAVID (*softly*). What is this about?

KURT. He knows who I am and what I do and what I carry with me.

SARA (*carefully*). What about Max?

KURT. The telephone was from Mexico. Ilse received a cable. Early on the morning of Monday, they caught Ebber and Triste. An hour after they took Max in Berlin. (*She looks up at him, begins to shake her head. He presses her arm*) Yes. It is hard.

FANNY (*softly*). You said he knew who you were and what you carried with you. I don't understand.

KURT. I am going to tell you: I am an outlaw. I work with many others in an illegal organization. I have so worked for seven years. I am on what is called a desired list. But I did not know I was worth ten thousand dollars.

DAVID (*slowly*). And what do you carry with you?

KURT. Twenty-three thousand dollars. It has been gathered

from the pennies of the poor who do not like Fascism, and who believe in the work we do. I came here to bring Sara home and to get the money. I had hopes to rest here for a while, and then —

SARA (*slowly*). And I had hopes someone else would take it back and you would stay with us — (*Shakes her head, then*) Max is not dead?

KURT. No. The left side of his face is dead. (*Softly*) It was a good face.

SARA (*to Fanny and David, as if she were going to cry*). It was a very good face. He and Kurt — in the old days — (*To Kurt*) After so many years. If Max got caught, then nobody's got a chance. Nobody. (*She suddenly sits down.*)

DAVID (*points upstairs*). He wants to sell what he knows about you? Is that right?

KURT. Yes.

FANNY. Wasn't it careless of you to leave twenty-three thousand dollars lying around to be seen?

KURT. No, it was not careless of me. It is in a locked briefcase. I have thus carried money for many years. There seemed no safer place than Sara's home. It was careless of you to have in your house a man who opens baggage and blackmails.

DAVID. Yes. It was very careless.

FANNY. But you said you knew he'd seen it —

KURT. Yes. I knew it the first day we were here. What was I to do about it? He is not a man who steals. I knew that it would come some other way. I have been waiting to see what the way would be. That is all I could do.

DAVID (*to Kurt*). If he wants to sell to you, he must have another buyer. Who?

KURT. The Embassy. Von Seitz, I think.

DAVID. You mean he has told Von Seitz about you and —

KURT. No. I do not think he has told him anything. As yet. It would be foolish of him. He has probably only asked most guarded questions.

DAVID. But you're here. You're in this country. They can't do anything to you. They wouldn't be crazy enough to try it. Is your passport all right?

KURT. Not quite.

FANNY. Why not? Why isn't it?

KURT (*wearily, as if he were bored*). Because people like me are not given visas with such ease. And I was in a hurry to bring my wife and my children to safety. (*Sharply*) Madame Fanny, you must come to understand it is no longer the world you once knew.

DAVID. It doesn't matter. You're a political refugee. We don't turn back people like you. People who are in danger. You will give me your passport and tomorrow morning I'll see Barens. We'll tell him the truth — (*Points to the door*) Tell de Brancovis to go to hell. There's not a damn thing he or anybody else can do.

SARA (*looks up at Kurt, who is staring at her*). You don't understand, David.

DAVID. There's a great deal I don't understand. But there's nothing to worry about.

SARA. Not much to worry about as long as Kurt is in this house. But he's not going to —

KURT. The Count has made the guess that —

SARA. That you will go back to get Ebber and Triste and Max. Is that right, Kurt? Is that right?

KURT. Yes, darling, I will try. They were taken to Sonnenburg. Guards can be bribed — It has been done once before at Sonnenburg. We will try for it again. I must go back, Sara. I must start.

SARA. I guess I was trying to think it wouldn't come. But — (*To Fanny and David*) Kurt's got to go back. He's got to go home. He's got to buy them out. He'll do it, too. You'll see. (*She stops, breathes*) It's hard enough to get back. Very hard. But if they knew he was coming — They want Kurt bad. Almost as much as they wanted Max — And then there are hundreds of others, too — (*She gets up, comes to him. He holds her, puts his face in her hair. She stands holding him, trying to speak without crying*) Don't be scared, darling. You'll get back. You'll see. You've done it before — you'll do it again. Don't be scared. You'll get Max out all right. And then you'll do his work, won't you? That's good. That's fine. You'll do a good job, the way you've always done. (*She is crying very hard. To Fanny*) Kurt doesn't feel well. He was wounded and he gets tired — (*To Kurt*) You don't feel well, do you? Don't be scared, darling. Don't worry, you'll get home. Yes, you will.

Curtain

Act Three

SCENE: *The same. A half hour later.*

AT RISE: *Fanny is sitting in a chair. Kurt is at the piano, his head resting on one hand. He is playing softly with the other hand. Sara is sitting very quietly on the couch. David is pacing on the terrace.*

FANNY (*to David*). David, would you stop that pacing, please? (*David comes in*) And would you stop that one-hand piano playing? Either play, or get up.

(*Kurt gets up, crosses to the couch, sits. Sara looks at him, gets up, crosses to the decanters, begins to make a drink.*)

SARA (*to David*). A drink?

DAVID. What? Yes, please. (*To Kurt*) You intend to buy your friends out of jail.

KURT. I intend to try.

FANNY. It's all very strange to me. I thought things were so well run that bribery and —

KURT. What a magnificent work Fascists have done in convincing the world that they are men from legends.

DAVID. They have done very well for themselves — unfortunately.

KURT. But not by themselves. Does it make us all uncomfortable to remember that they came in on the shoulders of the most powerful men in the world? Of course. And so we would prefer to believe they are men from the planets. They are not. Let me reassure you. They are smart, and they are cruel. But given men who know what they fight for — (*Shrugs*) I will console you. A year ago last month, at three o'clock in the morning, Freidank and I, with two elderly pistols, raided the home of the Gestapo chief in Konstanz, got what we wanted, and the following morning Freidank was eating his breakfast three blocks away, and I was over the Swiss border.

FANNY (*slowly*). You are brave men.

KURT. *I* do not tell you the story to prove we are remarkable, but to prove they are not.

(*Sara brings him a drink. Gives one to David.*)

SARA (*softly*). Kurt loves Max.

KURT. Always since I came here I have a dream: that he will come into this room someday. How he would like it here, eh, Sara? He loves good food and wine, and you have books — (*Laughs happily*) He is fifty-nine years of age. And when he was fifty-seven, he carried me on his back, seven miles across the border. I had been hurt — That takes a man, does it not?

FANNY (*to Kurt*). You look like a sick man to me.

KURT. No. I'm only tired. I do not like to wait. It will go. It is the waiting that is always most bad for me.

DAVID (*points upstairs*). Damn him! He's doing it deliberately.

KURT. It is then the corruption begins. Only then I think why must our side fight always with naked hands. All is against us but ourselves.

SARA. You will not think that when the time comes. It will go.

KURT. Of a certainty.

FANNY. But does it have to go on being your hands?

KURT. For each man, his own hands. He has to sleep with them.

DAVID (*uncomfortably, as if he did not like to say it*). That's right. I guess it's the way all of us should feel. But — but you have a family. Isn't there somebody else who hasn't a wife and children —

KURT. Each could have his own reason. Some have bullet holes, some have fear of the camps, some are sick, many are getting older. (*Shrugs*) Each could find a reason. And many find it. My children are not the only children in the world, even to me.

FANNY. That's noble of you, of course. But they are your children, nevertheless. And Sara, she —

SARA. Mama —

KURT. One means always in English to insult with that word noble?

FANNY. Of course not, I —

KURT. It is not noble. It is the way I must live. Good or bad, it is what I am. (*Turns deliberately to look at Fanny*) And what I am is not what you wanted for your daughter, twenty years ago or now.

FANNY. You are misunderstanding me.

KURT (*smiles*). We each have our way. I do not convert you to mine.

DAVID. You are very certain of your way.

KURT (*smiles*). I seem so to you? Good.

(*Joseph appears in the hall doorway. He is carrying valises and overcoats.*)

JOSEPH. What'll I do with these, Miss Fanny?

FANNY. They're too large for eating, aren't they? What were you thinking of doing with them?

JOSEPH. I mean, it's Fred's day off.

DAVID. All right. You drive him into town.

JOSEPH. Then who's going to serve at dinner?

FANNY (*impatiently*). Belle can do it tonight.

JOSEPH. Belle's upstairs packing with Miss Marthe. My, there's quite a lot of departing, ain't there? You just better wait for your dinner till I get back from Washington.

FANNY (*shouting*). We are not cripples and we were eating dinner in this house before you arrived to show us how to use the knife and fork. (*Joseph laughs*) Go on. Put his things in the car.

JOSEPH. You told me the next time you screamed to remind you to ask my pardon.

FANNY. You call that screaming?

JOSEPH. Yes'm.

FANNY. Very well. I ask your pardon. Go on!

JOSEPH. Yes'm. (*Exits.*)

(*Teck appears in the door. He is carrying his hat and the briefcase we have seen in Act One. Sara, seeing the briefcase, looks startled, looks quickly at Kurt. Kurt watches Teck as he comes toward him. Teck throws his hat on a chair, comes to the table at which Kurt is sitting, puts the briefcase on the table. Kurt puts out his hand, puts it on the briefcase, leaves it there.*)

TECK (*smiles at the gesture*). Nothing has been touched, Herr Müller. I brought it from your room, for your convenience.

FANNY (*angrily*). Why didn't you steal it?

TECK. That would have been very foolish of me, Madame Fanny.

KURT. Very.

TECK. I hope I have not kept you waiting too long. I wanted to give you an opportunity to make any explanations —

DAVID (*angrily*). Does your price include listening to this tony conversation?

TECK (*turns to look at him*). My price will rise if I am interrupted by you. I will do my business with Herr Müller. I will take from you no interruptions, no exclamations, no lectures, no opinions of what I am or what I am doing.

KURT. You will not be interrupted.

TECK (*sits down at table with Kurt*). I have been curious about you, Herr Müller. Even before you came here. Because Fanny and David either knew very little about you, which was strange, or wouldn't talk about you, which was just as strange. Have you ever had come to you one of those insistent half-memories of some person or some place?

KURT. You had such a half-memory of me?

TECK. Not even a memory, but something. The curiosity of one European for another, perhaps.

KURT. A most sharp curiosity. You lost no time examining — (*Pats the case*) — this. You are an expert with locks?

TECK. Only when I wish to be.

FANNY (*angrily*). I would like you out of this house as quickly as —

TECK (*turns to her*). Madame Fanny, I have just asked Mr. David not to do that. I must now ask you. (*Leans forward to Kurt*) Herr Müller, I got one of the desired lists from Von Seitz, without, of course, revealing anything to him. As you probably know, they are quite easy to get. I simply told him that we refugees move in small circles and I might come across somebody on it. If, however, I have to listen to any more of this, I shall go immediately to him.

KURT (*to David and Fanny*). Please allow the Count to do this in his own way. It will be best.

TECK (*takes a sheet of paper from his pocket*). There are sixty-three names on this list. I read them carefully, I narrow the possibilities and under "G" I find Gotter. (*Begins to read*) "Age, forty to forty-five. About six feet. One hundred seventy pounds. Birthplace unknown to us. Original occupation unknown to us, although he seems to know Munich and Dresden. Schooling unknown to us. Family unknown to us. No known political connections. No known trade-union connections. Many descriptions, few of them in agreement and none of them of great reliability. Equally unreliable, though often asked for, were Paris, Copenhagen, Brussels police descriptions. Only points on which there is agreement: married to a foreign woman, either American or English; three children; has used name of Gotter, Thomas Bodmer, Karl Francis. Thought to have left Germany in 1933, and to have joined Max Freidank shortly after. Worked closely with Freidank, perhaps directly under his orders. Known to have crossed border in 1934 — February, May, June, October. Known to have again crossed border with Max Freidank in 1935 — August, twice in October, November, January —"

KURT. The report is unreliable. It would have been impossible for God to have crossed the border that often.

TECK (*laughs*). "In 1934, outlaw radio station announcing itself as Radio European, begins to be heard. Station was located in Düsseldorf: the house of a restaurant waiter was searched, and nothing was found. Radio heard during most of 1934 and 1935. In an attempt to locate it, two probable Communists killed in the toolhouse of a farm near Bonn. In three of the broadcasts, Gotter known to have crossed border immediately before and after. Radio again became active in early part of 1936. Active attempt made to locate Freidank. Gotter believed to have then appeared in Spain with Madrid Government army, in one of the German brigades, and to have been a brigade commander under previously used name of Bodmer. Known to have stayed in France the first months of 1938. Again crossed German border some time during week when Hitler's Hamburg radio speech interrupted and went off the air." (*Looks up*) That was a daring deed, Herr Müller. It caused a great scandal. I remember. It amused me.

KURT. Thank you.

TECK. "Early in 1939, informer in Konstanz reported Gotter's entry, carrying money which had been exchanged in Paris and Brussels. Following day, home of Konstanz Gestapo chief raided for spy list by two men —" (*Kurt turns to look at Fanny and David, smiles*) My God, Herr Müller, that job took two good men. Now I conclude a week ago that you are Gotter, Karl Francis —

KURT. Please. Do not describe me to myself again.

TECK. And that you will be traveling home — (*Points to brief-case*) — with this. But you seem in no hurry, and so I must wait. Last night when I hear that Freidank has been taken, I guess that you will now be leaving. I will tell you free of charge, Herr Müller, that they have got no information from Freidank or the others.

KURT. I was sure they would not. I know all three most well. They will take what punishment will be given them.

TECK (*softly*). There is a deep sickness in the German character, Herr Müller. A pain-love, a death-love —

DAVID (*very angrily*). Oh, for God's sake, spare us *your* moral judgments.

FANNY (*very sharply*). They are sickening. Get on!

KURT. Fanny and David are Americans and they do not understand our world — as yet. (*Turns to David and Fanny*) All Fascists are not of one mind, one stripe. There are those who give the orders, those who carry out the orders, those who watch the orders being carried out. Then there are those who are half in, half hoping to come in. They are made to do the dishes and clean the boots. Frequently they come in high places and wish now only to survive. They came late: some because they did not jump in time, some because they were stupid, some because they were shocked at the crudity of the *German* evil, and preferred their own evils, and some because they were fastidious men. For those last, we may well someday have pity. They are lost men, their spoils are small, their day is gone. (*To Teck*) Yes?

TECK (*slowly*). Yes. You have the understanding heart.

KURT (*smiles*). I will watch it.

TECK. We are both men in trouble, Herr Müller. The world, ungratefully, seems to like your kind even less than it does mine. Now. Let us do business. You will not get back if Von Seitz knows you are going.

KURT. You are wrong. Instead of crawling a hundred feet an hour in deep night, I will walk across the border with as little trouble as if I were a boy again on a summer walking trip. There are many men they would like to have. I would be allowed to walk directly to them — until they had all the names and all the addresses. (*Laughs, points his finger at Teck*) *Roumanians* would pick me up ahead of time. *Germans* would not.

TECK (*smiles*). Still the national pride?

KURT. Why not? For that which is good.

FANNY (*comes over, very angrily, to Teck*). I have not often in my life felt what I feel now. Whatever you are, and however you became it, the picture of a man selling the lives of other men —

TECK. Is very ugly, Madame Fanny. I do not do it without some shame, and therefore I must sink my shame in money. (*Puts his hand on the briefcase*) The money is here. For ten thousand, you go back to save your friends, nobody will know that you go, and I will give you my good wishes. (*Slowly, Kurt begins to shake his head. Teck waits, then carefully*) No?

KURT. This money is going home with me. It was not given to me to save my life, and I shall not so use it. It is to save the lives and further the work of more than I. It is important to me to carry on that work and to save the lives of three valuable men, and to do that with all speed. But — (*Sharply*) Count de Brancovis, the first morning we arrived in this house, my children wanted their breakfast. That is because the day before we had been able only to buy milk for them. If I would not touch this money for them, I would not touch it for you. (*Very sharply*) It goes back with me. The way it is. And if it does not get back, it is because I will not get back.

(*There is a long pause. Sara gets up, turns away.*)

TECK. Then I do not think you will get back. Herr Müller, you will not get back.

DAVID (*coming toward Kurt*). Is it true that if this swine talks, you and the others will be —

SARA (*very softly*). Caught and killed. Of course. If they're lucky enough to get killed quickly. (*Points to the table*) You should have seen his hands in 1935.

FANNY (*violently, to David*). We'll give him the money. For God's sake, give it to him and get him out of here.

DAVID (*to Sara*). Do you want Kurt to go back?

SARA. Yes. I do.

DAVID. All right. You're a good girl.

KURT. That is true. Brave and good, my Sara. She is everything. She is handsome and gay and — (*Puts his hand over his eyes. Sara turns away.*)

DAVID (*after a second, comes to stand near Teck*). If we give you the money, what is to keep you from selling to Von Seitz?

TECK. I do not like your thinking I would do that. But —

DAVID (*tensely*). I'm sick of what you'd like or wouldn't like.

And I'm sick of your talk. We'll get this over with now, without any more fancy talk from you. I can't take much more of you at any cost.

TECK (*smiles*). It is your anger which delays us. I was about to say that I understood your fear that I would go to Von Seitz, and I would suggest that you give me a small amount of cash now and a check dated a month from now. In a month, Herr Müller should be nearing home, and he can let you know. And if you should not honor the check because Herr Müller is already in Germany, Von Seitz will pay a little something for a reliable description. I will take my chance on that. You will now say that I could do that in any case — and that is the chance you will take.

DAVID (*looks at Kurt, who does not look up*). Is a month enough? For you to get back?

KURT (*shrugs*). What? I do not know.

DAVID (*to Teck*). How do you want the cash and how do you want the check?

TECK. Five thousand in a check. Five in cash.

DAVID. I haven't anywhere near that much cash in the house. Leave your address and I'll send it to you in the morning.

TECK (*laughs*). Address? I have no address, and I wish it now. Madame Fanny has cash in her sitting-room safe.

FANNY. Have you investigated that, too?

TECK (*laughs*). No. You once told me you always kept money in the house.

DAVID (*to Fanny*). How much have you got upstairs?

FANNY. I don't know. About four thousand.

TECK. Very well. That will do. Make the rest in the check.

DAVID. Get it, Mama, please. (*He starts toward the library door. Fanny starts for the hall exit.*)

FANNY. Years ago, I heard somebody say that being Roumanian was not a nationality but a profession. The years have brought no change.

KURT (*softly*). Being a Roumanian aristocrat is a profession.

(*Fanny exits. After her exit, there is silence. Kurt does not look up, Sara does not move.*)

TECK (*awkwardly*). The new world has left the room. I feel less discomfort with you. We are Europeans, born to trouble and understanding it.

KURT. My wife is not a European.

TECK. Almost. (*Points upstairs*) They are young. The world has gone well for most of them. For us — (*Smiles*) we are like peasants watching the big frost. Work, trouble, ruin — (*Shrugs*) But no need to call curses at the frost. There it is, it will be again, always — for us.

SARA (*gets up, moves to the window, looks out*). You mean my husband and I do not have angry words for you. What for? We know how many there are of you. They don't, yet. My mother and brother feel shocked that you are in their house. For us — we have seen you in so many houses.

TECK. I do not say you *want* to understand me, Mrs. Müller. I say only that you do.

SARA. You are not difficult to understand.

KURT (*slowly gets up, stands stiffly. Then he moves toward the decanter table*). A whiskey?

TECK. No, thank you. (*He turns his head to watch Kurt move. He turns back.*)

KURT. Sherry?

TECK (*nods*). Thank you, I will.

KURT (*as he pours*). You, too, wish to go back to Europe.

TECK. Yes.

KURT. But they do not much want you. Not since the Budapest oil deal of '31.

TECK. You seem as well informed about me as I am about you.

KURT. That must have been a conference of high comedy, that one. Everybody trying to guess whether Kessler was working for Fritz Thyssen, and what Thyssen *really* wanted — and whether this "National Socialism" was a smart blind of Thyssen's, and where was Wolff — I should like to have seen you and your friends. It is too bad: you guessed an inch off, eh?

TECK. More than an inch.

KURT. And Kessler has a memory? (*Playfully*) I do not think Von Seitz would pay you money for a description of a man who has a month to travel. But I think he would pay you in a visa and a cable to Kessler. I think you want a visa almost as much as you want money. Therefore, I conclude you will try for the money here, and the visa from Von Seitz. (*He comes toward the table carrying the sherry glass*) I cannot get anywhere near my friends in a month and you know it. (*He is about to place the glass on the table*) I have been bored with this talk of paying you money. Whatever made you think I would take such a chance? Or *any* chance? You are a gambler. But you should not gamble with your life. (*Teck has turned to stare at him, made a half motion as if to rise. As he does so, and on the words, "gamble with your life," Kurt drops the glass, hits Teck in the face. Struggling, Teck makes a violent effort to rise. Kurt throws himself on Teck, knocking him to the floor. As Teck falls to the floor, Kurt hits him on the side of the head. At the fourth blow, Teck does not move. Kurt rises, takes the gun from his pocket, begins to lift Teck from the floor. As he does, Joshua appears in the hall entrance. He is washed and ready for dinner. As he reaches the door, he stops, sees the scene, stands quietly as if he were waiting for orders. Kurt begins to balance Teck, to balance himself. To Joshua*) Hilf mir. (*Joshua comes quickly to Kurt*) Mach die Tür auf! (*Joshua runs toward the doors, opens them, stands waiting*) Bleib da! Mach die Tür zu! (*Kurt begins to move out through the terrace. When he is outside the doors, Joshua closes them quickly, stands looking at his mother.*)

JOSHUA. Do not worry. I will go up now. I will pack. In ten minutes all will be ready. I will say nothing. I will get the children ready — (*He starts quickly for the hall.*)

SARA (*softly*). We're not going this time, darling. There's no need to pack.

JOSHUA (*stares at her puzzled*). But Papa —

SARA. Go upstairs, Joshua. Take Babbie and Bodo in your room, and close the door. Stay there until I call you. (*Sara sits down*) There's nothing to be frightened of, darling. Papa is all right. (*Very softly*) Papa is going home.

JOSHUA. To Germany?

SARA. Yes.

JOSHUA. Oh. Alone?

SARA. Alone. Don't say anything to the children. He will tell them himself. (*As he hesitates*) I'm all right. Go upstairs now. (*He moves slowly out, she watches him, he disappears. For a minute she sits quietly. Then she gets up, moves to the terrace doors, stands with her hands pressed against them. Then she crosses, picks up the overturned chair, places it by the table, picks up the glass, puts it on the table. As if without knowing what she is doing, she wipes the table with her handkerchief.*)

(Fanny comes in from hall. After a second, David comes in from library. Stops, looks around room.)

DAVID. Where is he? Upstairs?

SARA. No. They went outside.

FANNY. Outside? They went outside. What are they doing, picking a bouquet together?

SARA *(without turning)*. They just went outside.

DAVID *(looks at her)*. What's the matter, Sara?

(Sara shakes her head. Goes to the desk, opens the telephone book, looks at a number, begins to dial the telephone.)

FANNY. Eleven hundred, fifteen hundred —

SARA *(into the telephone)*. Hello. What time is your next plane? Oh. To — South. To El Paso, or — Brownsville. Yes.

DAVID *(to Fanny)*. Is Joseph ready?

FANNY. I don't know.

SARA. To Brownsville? Yes. Yes. That's all right. At what time? Yes. No. The ticket will be picked up at the airport. *(David begins to cross to the bell cord. She looks up)* No. David. Don't call Joseph. *David! Please!* *(He draws back, stares at her. Looking at him, she goes on with the conversation)* Ritter. R-I-T-T-E-R. Samuel. Yes. Yes. *(She hangs up, walks away.)*

DAVID. Sara! What's happening? What is all this? *(She does not answer)* Where is Kurt? What — *(He starts for the terrace door.)*

SARA. David. *Don't go out.*

FANNY *(rises)*. Sara! What's happening —

SARA. For seven years now, day in, day out, men have crossed the German border. They are always in danger. They always may be going in to die. Did you ever see the face of a man who never knows if this day will be the last day? *(Softly)* Don't go out on the terrace, David. Leave Kurt alone.

FANNY. Sara! What is —

SARA. For them, it may be torture, and it may be death. Someday, when it's all over, maybe there'll be a few of them left to celebrate. There aren't many of Kurt's age left. He couldn't take a chance on them. They wouldn't have liked it. *(Suddenly, violently)* He'd have had a bad time trying to explain to them that because of this house and this nice town and my mother and my brother, he took chances with their work and with their lives. *(Quietly)* Sit down, Mama.

I think it's all over now. (*To David*) There's nothing you can do about it. It's the way it had to be.

DAVID. Sara —

FANNY. Do you mean what I think you — (*She sits down.*)

SARA (*she turns, looks out toward the doors. After a pause*). He's going away tonight and I don't think he's ever coming back anymore. Never, never, never. (*She looks down at her hands, as if she were very interested in them*) I don't like to be alone at night. I guess everybody in the world's got a time they don't like. Me, it's right before I go to sleep. And now it's going to be for always. (*She looks up as Kurt comes in from the terrace*) I've told them. There is an eight-thirty plane going as far south as Brownsville. I've made you a reservation. In the name of Ritter.

KURT (*stands looking at her*). Liebe Sara! (*Then he goes to the table at which Fanny is sitting. To Fanny*) It is hard for you, eh? (*He pats her hand*) I am sorry.

FANNY (*without knowing why, she takes her hand away*). Hard? I don't know. I — I don't — I don't know what I want to say.

KURT (*turns to David*). Before I come in, I stand and think. I say, I will make Fanny and David understand. I say, how can I? Does one understand a killing? No. To hell with it, I say. I do what must be done. What do you wish to make them understand, I ask myself. Wait. Stand here. Just stand here. What are you thinking? Say it to them just as it comes to you. And this is what came to me. When you kill in a war, it is not so lonely; and I remember a cousin I have not seen for many years; and a melody comes back and I begin to make it with my fingers; a staircase in a house in Bonn years ago; an old dog who used to live in our town; Sara in a hundred places — Shame on us. Thousands of years and we cannot yet make a world. Like a child I am. I have stopped a man's life. (*Points to the place on the couch where he had been sitting opposite Teck*) I sit here. I listen to him. You will not believe — but I pray that I will not have to touch him. Then I know I will have to. I know that if I do not, it is only that I pamper myself, and risk the lives of others. I want you from the room. I know what I must do. (*Loudly*) All right. Do I now pretend sorrow? Do I now pretend it is not I who act thus? No. I do it. I have done it. I will do it again. I have a great hate for the violent. They are the sick of the world. (*Softly*) Maybe I am sick now, too.

SARA. Stop that. It's late. You must go soon.

KURT (*he puts out his hands, she touches them*). I want to say good-bye now to my children. Then I am going to take your car — (*Motions with his head*) I will take him with me. After that, it is up to you. Two ways: You can let me go and keep silent. I believe I can hide him and the car. At the end of two days, if they have not been found, you will tell as much of the truth as is safe for you to say. Tell them the last time you saw us we were on our way to Washington. You did not worry at the absence, we might have rested there. Two crazy foreigners fight, one gets killed, you know nothing of the reason. I will have left the gun, there will be no doubt who did the killing. If you will give me those two days, I think I will be far enough away from here. If the car is found before then — (*Shrugs*) I will still try to move with speed. And all that will make you, for yourselves, part of a murder. For the world, I do not think you will be in bad trouble. (*He pauses*) There is another way. You can call your police. You can tell them the truth. I will not get home. (*To Sara*) I wish to see the children now. (*She goes out into the hall and up the stairs. There is silence.*)

FANNY. What are you thinking, David?

DAVID. I don't know. What are you thinking?

FANNY. Me? Oh, I was thinking about Joshua. I was thinking that a few months before he died, we were sitting out there. (*Points to terrace*) He said, "Fanny, the complete American is dying." I said what do you mean, although I knew what he meant, I always knew. "A complete man," he said, "is a man who wants to know. He wants to know how fast a bird can fly, how thick is the crust of the earth, what made Iago evil, how to plow a field. He knows there is no dignity to a mountain, if there is no dignity to man. You can't put that in a man, but when it's there, put your trust in him."

DAVID (*smiles at Fanny*). You're a smart woman sometimes. (*Sara enters with Joshua. To Kurt*) Don't worry about things here. I'll take care of it. You'll have your two days. And good luck to you.

FANNY. You go with my blessing, too. I like you. (*Bodo enters.*)

SARA. See? I come from good stock. (*Kurt begins to smile. Nods to David. Turns, smiles at Fanny.*)

FANNY. Do you like me?

KURT. I like you, Madame, very much.

FANNY. Would you be able to cash that check?

KURT (*laughs*). Oh, no.

FANNY. Then take the cash. I, too, would like to contribute to your work.

KURT. Thank you. (*He takes the money from the table, puts it in his pocket.*)

BODO (*to Kurt*). You like Grandma? I thought you would, with time. (*Babette enters. Joshua stands away from the others, looking at his father. Kurt turns to look at him.*)

JOSHUA. Alles in Ordnung?

KURT. Alles in Ordnung.

BODO. What? All is well? Why not? (*There is an awkward silence.*)

BABETTE (*as if she sensed it*). We are all clean for dinner. And I have on Grandma's dress to me —

FANNY (*very nervously*). Of course. And you look very pretty.

BODO (*looks around the room*). What is the matter? Everybody is acting like such a ninny. I got that word from Grandma.

KURT. Come here. (*Slowly Babette comes toward him, followed by Bodo. Joshua comes more slowly, to stand at the side of Kurt's chair*) We have said many good-byes to each other, eh? We must now say another. (*As they stare at him, he smiles, slowly, as if it were difficult*) This time, I leave you with good people to whom I believe you also will be good. (*Half playfully*) Would you allow me to give away my share in you, until I come back?

BABETTE (*slowly*). If you would like it.

KURT. Good. To your mother, her share. My share, to Fanny and David. It is all I have to give. (*Laughs*) There. I have made a will, eh? Now. I have something to say to you. It is important for me to say it.

JOSHUA (*softly*). You are talking to us as if we were children.

KURT. Am I, Joshua? I wish you were children. I wish I could say love your mother, do not eat too many sweets, clean your teeth — (*Draws Bodo to him*) I cannot say these things. You are not children. I took it all away from you.

BABETTE. We have had a most enjoyable life, Papa.

KURT (*smiles*). You are a gallant little liar. And I thank you for it. I have done something bad today —

FANNY (*shocked, sharply*). Kurt —

SARA. Don't, Mama. (*Bodo and Babette have looked at Fanny and Sara, puzzled. Then they have turned again to look at Kurt.*)

KURT. It is not to frighten you. In a few days, your mother will tell you.

BODO. You could not do a bad thing.

BABETTE. You could not.

KURT (*shakes his head*). Now let us get straight together. The four of us. Do you remember when we read *Les Misérables?* Do you remember that we talked about it afterward and Bodo got candy on Mama's bed?

BODO. I remember.

KURT. Well. He stole bread. The world is out of shape we said, when there are hungry men. And until it gets in shape, men will steal and lie and — (*Slowly*) and — kill. But for whatever reason it is done, and whoever does it — you understand me — it is all bad. I want you to remember that. Whoever does it, it is bad. (*Then gaily*) But perhaps you will live to see the day when it will not have to be. All over the world there are men who are fighting for that day. (*He picks Bodo up, rises*) Think of that. It will make you happy. In every town and every village and every mud hut in the world, there is a man who might fight to make a good world. And now good-bye. Wait for me. I shall try to come back for you. (*He moves toward the hall, followed by Babette, and more slowly, by Joshua*) Or you shall come to me. At Hamburg, the boat will come in. It will be a fine, safe land — I will be waiting on the dock. And there will be the three of you and Mama and Fanny and David. And I will have ordered an extra big dinner and we will show them what Germany can be like — (*He has put Bodo down. He leans down, presses his face in Babette's hair. Tenderly, as her mother has done earlier, she touches his hair.*

JOSHUA. Of course. Of course. But — but if you should find yourself delayed — (*Very slowly*) Then I will come to you. Mama.

SARA (*she has turned away*). I heard you, Joshua.

KURT (*he kisses Babette*). Gute Nacht, Liebling!

BABETTE. Gute Nacht, Papa. Mach's gut!

KURT (*leans to kiss Bodo*). Good night, baby.

BODO. Good night, Papa. Mach's gut! (*Babette runs up the steps. Slowly Bodo follows her.*)

KURT (*kisses Joshua*). Good night, son.

JOSHUA. Good night, Papa. Mach's gut! (*He begins to climb the steps. Kurt stands watching them, smiling. When they disappear, he turns to David.*)

KURT. Good-bye, and thank you.

DAVID. Good-bye, good luck.

KURT (*he moves to Fanny*). Good-bye. I have good children, eh?

FANNY. Yes, you have. (*Kurt kisses her hand.*)

KURT (*slowly, he turns toward Sara*). Men who wish to live have the best chance to live. I wish to live. I wish to live with you. (*She comes toward him.*)

SARA. For twenty years. It is as much for me today — (*Takes his arms*) Just once, and for all my life. (*He pulls her toward him*) Come back for me, darling. If you can. (*Takes brief-case from table and gives it to him.*)

KURT. I will try. (*He turns*) Good-bye, to you all. (*He exits. After a second, there is the sound of a car starting. They sit listening to it. Gradually the noise is no longer heard. A second later, Joshua appears.*)

JOSHUA. Mama — (*He is very tense*) Bodo cries. Babette looks very queer. I think you should come.

SARA (*gets up, slowly*). I'm coming.

JOSHUA (*to Fanny and David*). Bodo talks so fancy, we forget sometimes he is a baby. (*He waits for Sara to come up to him. When she reaches him, she takes his hand, goes up the steps, disappears. Fanny and David watch them.*)

FANNY (*after a minute*). Well, here we are. We are shaken out of the magnolias, eh?

DAVID. Yes. So we are.

FANNY. Tomorrow will be a hard day. But we'll have Babbie's birthday dinner. And we'll have music afterward. You can be the audience. I think you'd better go up to Marthe now. Be as careful as you can. She'd better stay here for a while. I daresay I can stand it. Well, I think I shall go and talk to Anise. I like Anise best when I don't feel well. (*She begins to move off.*)

DAVID. Mama. (*She turns*) We are going to be in for trouble. You understand that?

FANNY. I understand it very well. We will manage. I'm not put together with flour paste. And neither are you — I am happy to learn.

DAVID. Good night, Mama. (*As she moves out, the curtain falls.*)

Curtain

The Searching Wind

For Dorothy Parker

The Searching Wind was first produced at the Fulton Theatre, New York City, on April 12, 1944, with the following cast:

(*In the order of their appearance*)

MOSES TANEY	DUDLEY DIGGES
SAMUEL HAZEN	MONTGOMERY CLIFT
PONETTE	ALFRED HESSE
SOPHRONIA	MERCEDES GILBERT
EMILY HAZEN	CORNELIA OTIS SKINNER
ALEXANDER HAZEN	DENNIS KING
CATHERINE BOWMAN	BARBARA O'NEIL
ELDERLY ITALIAN WAITER	EDGAR ANDREWS
YOUNG ITALIAN WAITER	JOSEPH DE SANTIS
MANAGER OF THE GRAND HOTEL	WALTER KOHLER
EPPLER	WILLIAM F. SCHOELLER
EDWARD HALSEY	ERIC LATHAM
JAMES SEARS	EUGENE EARL
COUNT MAX VON STAMMER	ARNOLD KORFF

Soldiers, restaurant guests, waiters, people in the street

Produced and directed by
HERMAN SHUMLIN

Settings designed by
HOWARD BAY

Scenes

Act One

SCENE 1. The drawing room of the Hazen house, Washington, D.C., about seven-thirty of a Spring evening, 1944.
SCENE 2. A room in the Grand Hotel, Rome, October 1922.
SCENE 3. Same as Scene 1. About nine-thirty that evening.

Act Two

SCENE 1. A corner of a restaurant in Berlin, Autumn 1923.
SCENE 2. A room in the Hotel Meurice, Paris, September 1938.
SCENE 3. Same as Scene 1, Act One, later that evening.

Act One

Scene 1.

SCENE: *The drawing room of the Hazen house, a room of fine proportions with good furniture, good pictures, and good ornaments. Right stage is a large arch leading to an entrance hall; left stage are French doors which open on a terrace; right center stage is a door leading to a hall off which are the dining room and kitchen quarters. Downstage, left, are a chair and a table. A small couch is center stage. Upstage, right, is a piano; downstage, right, a large couch and a chair. Books and magazines are piled on the tables. The doors leading to the terrace are open; two chairs are on the terrace, a table between them. Throughout the play stage directions left and right are the audience's left and right.*

AT RISE: *Moses Taney, a man of about seventy, is sitting in a large chair. He is in dinner clothes and he is reading a newspaper. Corporal Samuel Hazen, a pleasant-looking young man of twenty, is sitting on the small couch, his right leg propped up on a chair. He, too, is reading a newspaper. Near the couch is a heavy cane.*

MOSES. What do you think of it, Sam?

SAM. I don't know, Grandpa. I don't read as fast as you do. I have to spell out the words.

MOSES (*smiles, nods*). I know. Must be hard to learn to read in only one year at Harvard. If your international mother and father hadn't taught you so many other languages — I don't believe in teaching Americans other languages. We never really learn them. Only the words in which to gossip, or eat, or be malicious. Hey, Sam, answer me.

SAM. Shut up, Grandpa, and let me read.

MOSES. Maybe it would be quicker if I read it to you. (*Begins to read*) "This is the first of a series of articles by former

Ambassador Alexander Hazen. Mr. Hazen has just returned from a tour of Africa and Southern Italy. Although Mr. Hazen has never before been willing to write his impressions of the current scene, this newspaper convinced him that although —" What in hell do they think "although" means? Nowadays people write English as if a rat were caught in the typewriter and they were trying to hit the keys which wouldn't disturb it.

SAM (*laughs*). All right, Grandpa. I'll read Father's article after you go to bed.

MOSES. Why do you have to read it twice? In three thousand words of diplomatic double-talk it says that sometimes democracies have to deal with people they don't approve and sometimes, in order to save something or other, you have to do something else or other. It's simple.

SAM (*laughs*). It's not simple to me.

MOSES. Why?

SAM (*uncomfortably*). Oh, I'm nobody to judge. What did I see of Italy? The people in a little town, a river, some hills, a hospital. Father is an important man, he saw important people. I —

MOSES. Does that make you incapable of thinking?

SAM. Now don't give me lecture six on thinking for myself. I'm trying. I'm slow at it. Children of famous fathers and famous grandfathers learn to walk late. I used to tell that to my friend Leck.

MOSES. Does your friend Leck think, or does he comes from a famous father?

SAM. He was a good thinker. His father was a baker in Jersey City and so was Leck. He's dead, Grandpa, and I told you that once before.

MOSES. Sorry, sorry, Sam. At my age you forget what's important and —

SAM. I liked Leck.

MOSES. — and remember what isn't. (*Points to the newspaper*) I can almost remember the words in which your father and I talked about this same Victor Emmanuel gentleman twenty-two years ago, the day Mussolini marched into Rome. (*Waves the paper*) I ran the paper then — (*As he speaks the hall door opens and a tall Frenchman of about forty-five comes in carrying a tray on which are bottles, glasses, soda. He is in butler's uniform but it does not look well on him.*

He slowly crosses the room, bows to Moses and Sam, goes out into the entrance hall.)

SAM. Where's he going with that?

MOSES. I've come to think it's best not to ask him. Tonight he seems headed for the garage.

SAM (*points to the paper*). Grandpa, why did you ever sell the paper? Everybody says it used to be so good, and now it's nothing when it's not downright bad.

MOSES. I didn't sell it. I never could have sold it. It was that way in my father's will. I leased it to them.

SAM (*after a second*). How could you let them make it into something like this? I'd always thought you sold it, needed the money or something —

MOSES. I don't read it often. I advise you not to.

SAM (*frowns*). Don't you care? How could you have given it up?

MOSES. It's a long story, son. Like all former thinkers, I'm writing a book. Or rather I keep a book. It's meant for you to read.

SAM. I'll have plenty of time to read it. I think they'll discharge me soon.

MOSES (*quickly, nervously*). Discharge you? Why should they do that? You told us Roberts said your leg —

SAM. I just think they will. I don't know what I'll do with myself after two years of the army.

MOSES. Go sit in the library and read. You smile, but that would be a serious thing to do and you're going to be a serious man. If I'm wrong and you're not serious, I'll give you the newspaper and you can spend the rest of your life acting important and misinforming folks. That would break my heart, Sam.

(Ponette reappears with the tray. He moves to the table near Sam, starts to put the tray on it, changes his mind, moves toward a very small table, puts down the tray, catches it as it totters. Then he moves toward the large table, puts the tray on it. Turns, sees that Moses and Sam are staring at him.)

PONETTE (*in a heavy French accent*). Pardon. You think that Madame Hazen tonight wishes here, or table terrace?

SAM. It doesn't matter. Put it anyplace.

(Ponette stares at the tray, decides to push it to other end of table. As he pushes it, a glass falls, doesn't break. He sighs, picks it up, shakes his head.)

PONETTE. In my country to drop and not to break is thought to be ill-luckness.

MOSES. In our country it is considered to be awkessism. Don't worry about it, Ponette.

(*Sophronia, a nice-looking Negro woman of about sixty, comes in from the open hall door. She is carrying a rag.*)

SOPHRONIA. What spilled tonight?

PONETTE. Not one meter drop.

(*Emily Hazen comes rapidly into the room. She is a handsome woman of about forty-three or four. She has on a dinner dress. She is frowning; she is nervous.*)

EMILY. Is anything wrong in the kitchen? There's been so much noise.

PONETTE. It is most difficult for woman like my wife to be cook. She was a lady at home, such as you, Madame —

SOPHRONIA (*sharply*). Yes. Remember, Mr. Taney, how every Southerner came from a family that had been ruined by the Civil War? Now there's never a refugee who wasn't rich.

EMILY (*quickly*). All right, Sophronia. (*To Ponette, as she runs toward the hall door*) Will you make martinis, please? (*He picks up a bottle of scotch*) With gin, please, gin. (*She moves out.*)

SAM. I've never seen Mother nervous before. What's the matter tonight?

PONETTE (*having poured the gin into the pitcher, hesitates*). With soda, Monsieur?

SAM (*laughs*). Try it that way. Might be interesting.

SOPHRONIA. Vermouth, vermouth. Six to one.

PONETTE (*delighted*). Ah, vermouth. Merci. (*Picks up bottle*) Le vermouth de France.

MOSES. You sound as if vermouth is a relative. (*Quickly crosses the room, takes the bottle from Ponette*) Thank you. But let me do it, please.

SOPHRONIA. It is all the fault of the United Front.

PONETTE (*as Moses and Sam laugh*). Ah, you gentlemen laugh. But it is not a joke. If it had not been for the radicals of France — (*Shrugs*) If it comes in your country, should God forbid, you will see the danger. Léon Blum — Like me, you will lose your store, your beautiful house, your —

MOSES. We have no store. (*Ponette exits.*)

SAM (*to Sophronia*). What's he talking about?

SOPHRONIA. He used to have a dry goods store in Toulouse.

MOSES. Some people don't think that's the best training for a butler.

SOPHRONIA (*points to the kitchen*). And his wife used to have a servant of her own, and lock the icebox every night and why don't we lock our iceboxes and if it hadn't been for those people who used to go on strikes the Germans would never have come into France and if it hadn't been for their crazy son-in-law who was a Socialist they would never have had to leave. (*She exits toward the hall door as Emily re-enters.*)

EMILY. Sophronia doesn't like our refugees.

MOSES. No old American stock likes foreigners. Narrow of us.

EMILY. Are you dining here?

MOSES. Yes.

EMILY. Oh. (*Hesitantly, nervously to Sam*) You told me this morning, Sam, you wanted dinner in your room.

SAM. I had to go out this afternoon, so I thought I'd stay up and eat downstairs tonight. I'm tired of bed.

EMILY. You had to go out? But the doctor told you not to get up for more than a few hours a day —

SAM (*quickly*). I'm all right, Mother. I didn't move around much.

EMILY. Please don't do it again, darling. Please do what the doctor tells you. Then in another month you'll be fine.

SAM. All right, Mother.

EMILY (*to Moses*). You said you were going to the Hapgoods for dinner.

MOSES. I changed my mind. I want to be with Sam.

EMILY (*hesitates*). You see, er — I — er — Catherine Bowman is coming. I haven't seen her in over twenty years and —

MOSES. And you don't want us here. Then we shall certainly stay.

EMILY. Father, why don't you take an apartment at the Shoreham and have tea with us on Sundays?

SAM (*laughs*). I wouldn't like that. I'd miss Grandpa.

MOSES (*pleased*). Would you, son? Well, I'm not going. Your mother always forgets this house belongs to me. And when I die, it will belong to you.

EMILY (*to Sam*). I wonder what's happened to your father? I heard him come home an hour ago. (*Turns to Moses, chattering*) So you're not leaving the house to me?

MOSES. You've got too much money as it is. You and Alex don't need a house. You'll always be busy ambassadoring in Europe, talking away in eight languages, in that diplomatic basic baby talk — (*To Emily*) Do stop moving about. You're not a fidgety woman and it doesn't become you. (*To Sam*) If *you* turn out to be a diplomat, I'll cut you out of my will.

(*As he speaks, Alexander Hazen, a good-looking man of about fifty, comes in from the hall. He is in dinner clothes. He smiles at Emily, crosses to Sam, pats him on the arm.*)

SAM. I'm not going to be a diplomat, but that won't be my reason. (*He looks up at Alex, smiles, presses Alex's arm.*)

MOSES. Don't be so sure. You come from a long line of men who've meddled in the affairs of this country. Your father's father, for example.

ALEX (*smiles*). My father didn't like you either. Sam, Sears told me he saw you going into the hospital this afternoon. I went over immediately, but nobody knew anything about it and Colonel Roberts wasn't there. What's the matter?

EMILY (*comes quickly to Sam*). Why didn't you tell me? What did you go to the hospital for?

SAM (*pleasantly*). I didn't go to the hospital. Sears was mistaken. (*He pats Emily's hand*) Nothing's the matter, Mother.

ALEX. How could Sears have been mistaken?

SAM (*firmly*). He was mistaken, Father. (*To Emily*) Can I have another? (*Both Emily and Alex look at him; then Emily takes his glass, moves toward the table.*)

ALEX (*points to the newspaper*). What did you think of my piece, Sam?

SAM (*uncomfortably*). You can't read in a room with Grandpa.

ALEX (*pleasantly*). That means you didn't like it.

SAM. There were some things I didn't understand. We didn't see Italy the same way —

ALEX. Then it must be that I saw it wrong. (*Smiles*) Funny. I remember my father telling me about France. I kept wanting to say, for God's sake, I fought there: you can't know about it the way I do.

EMILY (*moves toward the door*). Is that a taxi coming in? (*Shakes her head*) Alex —

ALEX. I had hoped we were dining alone. I've had a tough day. Who's coming?

EMILY. Cassie Bowman. (*Very quickly*) Have another cocktail, Father?

ALEX (*very slowly*). Why is Cassie coming here?

EMILY (*brightly, to Sam*). Cassie's never seen you or Sarah, which seems strange to me. Cassie and I grew up together, school and college and down the street, and your grandfather used to take us to Europe in the summer. Your father used to take us both to dances and —

ALEX. Why is Cassie coming?

EMILY (*too lightly*). Why not? You've seen her — when was the last time? — but I haven't in twenty, twenty-one years. Well, it seems it's her sabbatical — (*Cheerily, to Sam and Moses*) She's teaching girls the age we were when I last saw her. That makes me feel so old — (*To Alex*) She's visiting the Taylors. It seemed crazy, sort of, for Cassie to be in Washington and not to have her here —

ALEX. I saw her — (*Slowly*) last week.

EMILY (*quickly*). But *I* haven't seen her, Alex.

ALEX. You haven't wanted to. Neither has she. Why tonight?

SAM. Why didn't you see each other, if you were such good friends? A fight?

EMILY. No, no. No fight. I don't know why. Or maybe I —

MOSES. No martinis need that much stirring, Alex. Do stop it and pour. (*To Emily*) Couldn't you stop fidgeting? (*The front doorbell rings. Emily immediately turns toward the terrace doors, frowns, turns to face the hall. Alex moves toward the hall, stops*) This must be like the reconciliation of General Grant and General Lee.

(*Catherine Bowman comes in the door. She is a good-looking woman of about forty-four. She has on a simple dinner dress. Her movements are hesitant, cautious, as if she were unsure of herself. She stands for a minute staring at Emily, then looks at Alex, looks back at Emily.*)

CASSIE (*softly, to Emily*). I wanted to come in by the terrace. The way I used to when we were kids.

EMILY (*coming toward her, smiles*). I know. I turned that way, expecting you to come up the terrace steps. (*They kiss. There is an awkward pause, and then Cassie turns to Alex, who has come up to her.*)

CASSIE. Hello, Alex.

ALEX. Cassie.

CASSIE (*shakes hands with Moses. Warmly*). Hello, Mr. Taney. It's been a long time.

EMILY. Well. We've finally met again. (*To Moses, too brightly*) How do you think Cassie looks, Father, after all those years?

MOSES. Perhaps a little younger than you, if that's what you wanted not to hear.

EMILY (*To Cassie*). And this is my son, Sam. Our girl is away at school —

(*Sam, leaning on his cane, is moving toward Cassie.*)

CASSIE. I'm glad to know you. Your father has spoken of you so often. (*Points to the ribbon on Sam's chest*) Does he tell you how proud he is of that? Your father told me last night that your leg was getting better. I'm so glad to hear that.

(*Emily moves nervously. Alex turns away.*)

SAM (*smiles*). There's too much talk about my leg. You'd think it was the only leg that had been in a war.

EMILY. Do give us a cocktail, Alex. (*To Cassie, smiling*) Well. Well. That seems to be all I can say after all these years. (*As Alex comes to them with the pitcher, to Cassie*) Let's have several cocktails quick. They'll help. Don't go away, Alex. We'll swallow this one and you stand by for another. (*Cassie laughs, gulps her cocktail*) I'm not used to drinking much, are you?

CASSIE. No, but it might be a good idea tonight.

(*Emily motions for Alex to pour another. They both drink, both cough.*)

MOSES (*to Sam*). They're going to fall flat on each other's faces.

CASSIE. You used to say that, Mr. Taney.

MOSES (*bows*). Cassie, it takes a fine woman to remember what I used to say.

CASSIE. Or one who has missed you.

MOSES. You and I may fall in love.

SAM (*laughs*). Don't, Grandpa. You'd keep me awake nights telling me about it.

EMILY (*to Cassie*). I want to hear about you, Cassie. How's college and have you liked teaching?

CASSIE. Most of the time.

EMILY (*smiles, helplessly*). Oh, come on, Cassie. Help me.

CASSIE. Well. Not much about me. I'm head of the English department now. Everybody's got a specialty, so mine's poetry. The town still looks the same. Old lady Carter in the history department — remember her? — she died and I've got her house and I go down to New York whenever I can and oh, well, I don't know, I see the same people, I take long vacations when I can —

MOSES. Didn't you ever get married, Cassie?

CASSIE. No, sir, I didn't. I'm an old maid, I —

MOSES. How'd that happen? You're a good-looking woman —

CASSIE (*quickly, to Emily*). It's a small life, mine. Not like yours. It just goes on — (*Smiles, lamely*) I guess that's all.

EMILY. All right, then I'll get me over with. We've been abroad most of the time, as you know. I'm sorry I missed you that day in Paris. Well, after '39 Alex stayed on in London as a kind of Ambassador without a country, or maybe with too many countries, the governments-in-exile, I mean —

CASSIE (*looks toward Alex, uncomfortably*). I know, Em. I —

EMILY. I came back home last year and Sam went into the army, before that, I mean, and Alex stayed on for a while —

ALEX. Emily —

EMILY. Then Alex went to Italy as an observer — Sam and Alex were there at the same time, but they didn't see each other — and then Sam came back wounded and Alex got back last month. I'm not talking English.

ALEX (*carefully*). Em, I've been trying to tell you that Cas knows all that. You've forgotten I've seen her.

EMILY. Oh, you mean at dinner last week, last night. Well, I wanted to bring her up to date. (*Helplessly*) It's been so long — We have to start somewhere —

MOSES. Who are we sending over, Alex, to take care of those elderly clowns who call themselves governments-in-exile?

ALEX (*sharply*). I don't know. And they're not clowns.

MOSES. Not *all* of them. Only most. Ah, well, our time likes its old men to run the world. In our world we won't let the young run our affairs —

ALEX. Ready with your lecture on Charles James Fox, Moses?

MOSES (*as if he hadn't heard him*). We think of young men as fit only for battle and for death.

SAM. Two years ago, Grandpa, I'd have yawned or laughed at that. I won't do either now.

ALEX. Those men, old men, as you call them, are doing the best they can. And so are we.

MOSES. So you say in your article. But the fact remains that every old mummy is being preserved: the gentlemen from Poland, the gentlemen from Italy —

ALEX. Moses, we have to work with what there is to work with, and that doesn't mean you always like them or trust them.

CASSIE. Sometimes that's a dangerous game, Alex. And it seems to me I've heard you say those words before. (*Laughs*) I remember: you both, the same way, and Rome in 1922 — (*She breaks off suddenly and suddenly stops laughing. Emily rises quickly, moves to the bell cord, pulls it, stands quietly near the door.*)

MOSES. A very dangerous game. Mr. Wilson played it. It goes on the assumption that bad men are stupid and good men are smart, and all diplomats are both good *and* smart. Well, the last time, Mr. Clemenceau was both bad and smart. Why don't you people ever read a book?

EMILY. Is it like old times, Cassie? Father and Alex —

CASSIE. Yes. It's as if I'd never been away from here.

EMILY (*carefully*). You were saying it was like that day in Rome. That famous, famous day.

SAM. Famous for what?

ALEX (*quickly*). Mussolini took over the city that day.

EMILY (*looks at him, laughs*). Yes. (*Ponette appears in the hall door*) Isn't dinner ready, Ponette? It's late.

PONETTE. It has been ready for a half hour.

EMILY. It was thought best not to tell me?

PONETTE. I think perhaps I did come to tell you. Or perhaps I did not.

ALEX. Well, I think perhaps we can dine. (*Comes toward Cassie as if to take her in*) Cassie — (*As he reaches her he stops, looks at her, turns away, goes quickly toward hall door. Sam has risen and is moving toward the hall door. Moses and Cassie also move toward it.*)

MOSES (*to Cassie, suddenly, as if he had just remembered*). I remember that day in Rome. That was the time I duennaed you and Emily to Italy. And you and I and Sophronia came home alone and Emily stayed on to play the piano. That was the day I decided to retire and let the world go to hell without my help.

(*Alex has stopped to listen. Then quickly moves on, passes through the door.*)

SAM (*as he gets to the door, to Emily*). Were you and Father married then?

EMILY. No, darling. That was 1922. You weren't born until '24, and you're legitimate.

MOSES (*as he takes Sam's arm*). Certainly are. Everything was quite in order. (*They go out the door.*)

CASSIE (*smiles, nervously*). Why are we talking so much about the past? Are martinis for remembrance?

EMILY. It's natural to talk about it. We haven't seen each other for so long. It's natural we remember what used to be.

CASSIE. Is it natural? I have the feeling you wanted us to remember.

EMILY (*after a second, shrugs, softly*). Let it come as it will, Cas. Better for all of us if we're not frightened of it.

CASSIE (*turns*). Frightened of what? What do you mean, Em? Why did you ask me here, why did I come? It's too difficult for us to meet again. Why did you ask me, why did I come? —

EMILY. Because we wanted to see each other again.

CASSIE. I don't think that's the truth.

EMILY. I don't think so either. Come along to dinner, Cas. (*Cassie turns slowly toward the door. As she turns, she drops her evening bag. Both of them stare at it*) Remember the tennis match and how you broke your racket and then you dropped your mother's best cut-glass punch bowl? And at college, before exams, you always dropped everything? Whenever you were frightened or nervous you'd always drop things. (*Before Cassie can move, Emily stoops down to pick up the bag.*)

CASSIE (*takes the bag, looks steadily at Emily*). That's right, Em. Everybody does something when they get nervous: you speak more slowly. You always did. (*Smiles*) You're doing it now.

EMILY (*speaks very slowly, as if on purpose*). I know. Come along now.

(*As they go through the door, the curtain falls.*)

Curtain

Scene 2.

SCENE: *The living room of a suite in the Grand Hotel, Rome, October 1922. The furniture has been pushed from the center of the room to allow space for three large trunks. The trunks are open and partly packed. A couch and two chairs have been arranged near the large, center windows. A piano is in one corner of the room. Downstage, left, there is a door leading to a bedroom; upstage, right, there is a door leading to another bedroom; downstage, right, is a door leading to the hotel corridor. Near the left bedroom door is a table on which is a news ticker.*

AT RISE: *Sophronia, about forty years old, is in the upstage left corner, ironing underwear at a board. A few seconds after the curtain rises there is the sound of guns. Sophronia puts down her iron, goes to the window, opens it. As she opens the window, the gun sounds increase and then suddenly die away. The telephone rings.*

SOPHRONIA (*crosses to the phone*). Hello. Hello. Hello. Oh. No, Mr. Hazen. Like I told you. He hasn't been asleep at all, but I don't think he'll come to the phone. The girls are up, but they haven't come in for breakfast. No, sir, if anybody's frightened they haven't showed it to me. All right, I'll — (*Crosses to the bedroom door on left, knocks. There is no answer; she knocks again. Then she opens the door*) Mr. Taney, it's Alex Hazen on the phone again. (*No answer*) He says the Ambassador told him to tell you, you and the girls and me should come and stay in the Embassy until our boat leaves. Mr. Hazen says he'll come down in an Embassy car and take us —

MOSES' VOICE. Tell Alex to tell the Ambassador to go to hell.

SOPHRONIA. You better tell him that yourself.

MOSES' VOICE. Shut the door, Sophronia.

SOPHRONIA (*crosses to phone*). Mr. Taney says we'll stay here. (*Hangs up phone, goes back to ironing board. After a second there is a knock on the door that leads to the corridor. She looks up as the door opens and a table is wheeled in by an Elderly Waiter. He is followed by a Young Waiter, very thin, very stoop-shouldered. The Elderly Waiter wheels the table to the middle of the floor. The Young Waiter is carrying a large ovenish affair. The Elderly Waiter arranges chairs at the table, puts out the fruit, etc.*)

ELDERLY WAITER (*as he speaks there is again the booming of faraway guns, and what he says is not clearly heard*). Il direttore dice di preghare tutti gli ospite di non spaventarsi. (*The guns die off. Sophronia does not answer him. He turns to the Young Waiter*) Gli parlero io.

YOUNG WAITER (*with the accent of an Italian who has learned to speak English in London. He is a tired man and he speaks like one*). He says the manager will call on all guests to tell them not to be frightened by guns. Nobody, he says, need be frightened in the city of Rome, Italy.

SOPHRONIA. Good.

(*The Elderly Waiter looks at the Young Waiter. The Young Waiter shrugs, nods. The Elderly Waiter says "Resti," exits. There is a long pause.*)

YOUNG WAITER (*begins to cough. He tries hard to stifle it. He coughs hard, as if it hurts him. He looks at Sophronia, frightened. Then he backs up to the wall, as if to rest against it. Sophronia crosses to the table, picks up a glass of water, takes it to him. He hesitates, drinks, stops coughing. Quickly*). I did not cough near the table. I —

SOPHRONIA (*as he starts to cough again*). Sit down. (*She pushes a chair toward him. He sits down, looks up at her, smiles.*)

YOUNG WAITER (*after a moment*). You will not report I cough near the table?

SOPHRONIA. What's the matter with you?

YOUNG WAITER (*quickly*). From the cigarettes. (*Then shrugs*) My lungs are bad from the war. This is my second day here, in Grand Hotel, and if I am reported to be sick —

(*Sophronia has moved away from him toward the oven. She takes out a large thermos of coffee, opens the top, smells it, pours coffee into a cup.*)

SOPHRONIA (*brings him the cup*). Good for your cough.

YOUNG WAITER (*takes it eagerly*). You are kind.

(*The left bedroom door opens and Moses, in a dressing gown, comes in. Moses is about fifty years old.*)

YOUNG WAITER (*jumps to his feet, holds out the cup to Sophronia, backs away from the door*). I — your pardon. I —

MOSES (*goes to the ticker tape, picks it up*). What's the matter?

SOPHRONIA (*turns to the table to pour coffee for Moses*). He coughs because he got hurt in the war, and now he's scared to death you're going to get mad because he drinks a cup of coffee. They're all scared. I'm sick of it. You come to Europe next summer, you come without me.

MOSES. All right. All right. We're going home. (*Sophronia goes toward Moses' room; exits*) Sit down, Waiter, and finish your coffee.

(*The guns begin again. The noise is still far away, but there are more guns now and steadier firing.*)

MOSES (*reads from the ticker tape. Laughs unpleasantly*). The government is in control. King Victor Emmanuel returned this morning from bathing in the sea. The stories of Mussolini's armies are lies. He is not marching on the city. But everybody is to stay off the streets in case he is — (*Throws down the tape*) Those are government guns. They are not being answered. A child of six would conclude they are not being fired at anything, and won't be. The bastards are putting on a fake show and they won't even spend the money for a good one. (*Laughs*) Well, that means Signor Mussolini should be in the city in a few hours.

YOUNG WAITER (*takes dishes out of oven, brings them to Moses. Speaks cautiously*). I am told many foreigners here think it wise, sir.

MOSES. Yes, many foreigners. Are you a Fascist?

YOUNG WAITER. No, sir.

MOSES. You must feel out of place. Everybody else in the hotel is.

YOUNG WAITER (*smiles*). In every hotel. They live to please those who give orders.

MOSES. How many men do you think Mussolini's got? I've heard everything from sixty thousand to six hundred.

YOUNG WAITER. Not sixty thousand. My brother-in-law is one of them. He laughs and says the government garrison could stop them, but the garrison will not. He says the King and the Government are with the Fascisti now and want them to march in. What do you think, sir?

MOSES. Your brother-in-law is right. It's all finished now.

YOUNG WAITER. It has been finished for a long time.

MOSES. I've been awake all night. (*Motions toward the window*) Not with this. I knew most of this a year ago. But I should have known before that, and I did. But I didn't know I did. All night I've been trying to find out when I should have known.

YOUNG WAITER (*softly*). For me, for many Italians, it was there three years ago. Your President Wilson in the Piazza Venezia. The great man would speak to us, tell us what to do, tell us how to make a free country. Fifty thousand people came. Many of them walked all night. They carried their children — (*Looks at Moses, turns away*) I speak too much. (*Moses shakes his head*) But our King and our Government did not wish President Wilson to speak. They were afraid of us. All day they keep him inside the palace, meeting the great names who came to call. All day the people waited, until nighttime. Nighttime it was too late. I waited with the last. I did not know it then, but that night it was finished for me.

MOSES. Wilson is a man who likes fancy words and fancy names. That's one of the things I didn't know in time. I am sorry for that. I would have tried to save you some of this. (*There is a long silence.*)

YOUNG WAITER (*speaks timidly*). Shall I wait to serve, sir?

MOSES. No, thank you.

(*Young Waiter exits. The guns begin again. They are loud now and over them are the muffled sounds of distant shouting. The noises are sharp, mixed, and frightening. The left bedroom door opens and Emily, in a dressing gown, comes quickly in. She is twenty-two years old. She crosses to the window.*)

EMILY. Is it going to be bad, Father?

MOSES. It has been bad, it is bad, and it is going to be bad.

(*As he speaks, Cassie comes in. She is twenty-two years old. She has on a dressing gown. The noise of the guns begins to die away.*)

EMILY. It seems to me all we've ever known, since we grew up, are wars and revolutions.

MOSES. I'll tell them to stop it. I'll say that revolutions disturb you.

CASSIE (*laughs, pours herself a cup of coffee, takes it to the window*). They weren't very disturbed at Mrs. Hayworth's last night. Mrs. Hayworth has met Mussolini. She admires him. So did everybody there.

EMILY. Did you see Ann Hayworth and Jamie? Reeling around drunk and their mother didn't even notice. We looked like flowers from a Victorian garden. Flowers. Send flowers, Father, with apologies.

MOSES (*glares at her*). Did the guns interfere with Mrs. Hayworth's chamber music?

EMILY. No. Nobody seemed nervous. Signor Orlando was very disappointed you didn't come to dinner. He said he hadn't seen you since the Peace Conference but that he always read your articles. He said you were a great liberal, a great man.

MOSES. He's a son of a bitch.

EMILY (*laughs*). You were generally admired. A man called Perrone said he'd only come because he thought you might be there. He said he didn't think you understood the situation here. He said the Fascisti will mean a recovery for Italy —

MOSES. He's an impartial judge. He put up the money for Mussolini.

EMILY. He didn't mention that. He said the Fascist leaders were true idealists —

CASSIE. And would return to Rome the glory of Caesar —

MOSES. Is one allowed to spit at Mrs. Hayworth's table?

EMILY (*laughs*). You told me not to spit at dinner.

MOSES. I've changed my mind.

EMILY. Then it's just as well you weren't there. Alex didn't come, either, and Cassie came home early with a headache. I'll send flowers for you.

MOSES. You will not send flowers, you will not make an apology, and you will not go to the Hayworths' again.

(*He moves to his room as Sophronia comes from his room. She is carrying clothes. He goes into the room, closes the door. Sophronia puts the clothes on top of Moses' trunk, crosses to the right bedroom door.*)

SOPHRONIA. Did your laundry come back?

(*Emily has picked up the morning mail and is opening it. Cassie has taken a letter from the pile and is reading it.*)

EMILY. No, ma'am.

SOPHRONIA. I told you to phone for it. (*She goes into the bedroom.*)

EMILY. Now *there's* a good-humored pair to have on a vacation. I wish we could go back to Paris for a few weeks. (*Reading from the letter*) Sarah Sturgis is getting married. Well. She says she hopes we're home for the wedding.

CASSIE (*looks up from her letter*). Dr. Pierce says it's all right. The board of trustees has approved me. I can come back to college and teach. English department at fifteen hundred a year.

EMILY. I thought you were coming back to Washington and stay with us for a while until you decided what you really wanted to do.

CASSIE. Father can't afford anything anymore. I've got to have a job right away.

EMILY. Oh, what difference does the money make? Father's got plenty and in a few months I'll have all that Mother left me. Who wants to teach? Certainly not you. Come back and stay with us until you find something that's fun —

CASSIE. Thanks, Em. Really thanks. But I'm going to cable him today I'll take the job. It won't be bad — for a while, anyway.

EMILY (*looks at Cassie*). I don't understand why you didn't tell me.

CASSIE. I've known for a long time it would have to be. There was no need of talking about it until I had the job. (*Quickly*) What else does Sarah say?

EMILY. Oh. She says she told George that she'd had a beau before him, and he didn't seem to mind much, and she says that settles all the arguments — My entire memory of college is a discussion of whether you ought to have an affair before you marry and if you do, should you tell your husband? (*Laughs*) Baby talk. None of us would ever have had the nerve — except Sarah and then she had to get so drunk she couldn't remember a single interesting detail to tell us. Remember how daring we thought her?

CASSIE. I don't think I thought it daring. There's nothing daring about it.

EMILY. How do you know, Cas?

CASSIE (*arranging the drawers of her trunk. She hesitates and then speaks quickly*). I did have a headache last night. But that isn't why I left the Hayworths'. I met Alex.

EMILY (*after a second*). You mean you met him in the lobby downstairs or —

CASSIE. No. We had planned to meet.

EMILY (*slowly*). How strange. Why should you and Alex *plan* to meet?

CASSIE. Why not?

EMILY. What do you mean "why not"? We've grown up with Alex Hazen. We always saw him together. What — (*She gets up*) I understand. So it's not very daring. We've known each other all our lives. But sometimes I don't think we understand each other, Cas. I never thought you and Alex got along very well. You're so unlike. (*Quickly*) And then, of course, I suppose I'd always thought I might marry him someday —

CASSIE. I didn't know that. And I know he doesn't know it. You made it up this minute —

EMILY. I didn't say he knew it. I said that sometimes I thought that —

CASSIE (*slowly*). Then it was a fantasy, Emily. And as dangerous as most.

EMILY. Yes. What plans have you got? The two of you, I mean.

CASSIE. None. I —

EMILY (*comes to her*). Cassie, talk to me. Tell me things. Because otherwise we might get mixed up and —

CASSIE (*carefully*). We have nothing you would call plans. I suppose we said all the things people have always said to each other. (*Points to the window*) It's not a good time to talk about oneself. So much important happening to so many people —

EMILY: What high-falutin' talk, Cas. You sound like Father, only he means it. You know that no matter what happens, people go on talking about themselves, and always say they shouldn't because they think it sounds better that way. (*She turns, exits. Cassie stands looking after her as Sophronia comes into the room.*)

SOPHRONIA (*calling back to Emily*). Put the stuff that's for the trunks on the bed and the stuff that's for the valises — (*As Sophronia crosses toward the corridor door, a dressy, excited man opens the door. He looks like any manager of any fancy hotel.*)

MANAGER. Signori, Messieurs, Mesdames. Do not be uneasy. I have full assurance that the Grand Hotel will be protected. Please do not leave your beautiful apartments. All will be taken care of —

(*Alexander Hazen, twenty-seven years old, tries to push past him.*)

MANAGER (*turns to Alex*). Monsieur, no strangers are allowed in the hotel. You must not fly through the halls frightening the guests — (*Alex pushes him aside. Sophronia comes to the door. Manager speaks to her*) You cannot leave the apartment. My orders —

SOPHRONIA (*shoves him*). I need the laundry. Move.

ALEX (*to Manager*). I'm Hazen from the American Embassy. Close the door, please.

MANAGER. Oh. Then. The people from the newspapers downstairs, could you not take them away —

ALEX (*as the Manager closes the door*). It took me an hour to come six blocks. It's hell outside. The Ambassador wants all of you brought to the Embassy right away. We have assurances that no American will be touched, but with that crew outside, you can't tell. What's the matter?

CASSIE. Nothing.

ALEX. Where's Mr. Taney?

CASSIE. He won't go to the Embassy, and you know it.

ALEX. All right. But I want to talk to him about something else: the A.P., Reuters, Havas are downstairs. I want to ask him —

CASSIE (*points toward window*). What will happen?

ALEX. Second secretaries aren't told much. But I think they've decided to let Mussolini in. The government soldiers are really there to see that nobody stops him.

CASSIE (*sharply*). It's a dirty, dirty mess. What is the Ambassador going to do about it?

ALEX. Cassie, you asked me the same thing last night. What can he do? He's here to represent the United States and not to fight in civil wars. I can't seem to make you understand —

CASSIE. Perhaps because you don't understand it yourself.

ALEX. I don't think I do. But I know you don't, darling.

CASSIE. We're an ignorant generation. We see so much and know so little. Maybe because we think about ourselves so much. I just told Emily that, and she said I was faking. (*Turns to him*) She said that you and I never got along very well — (*As if to herself*) We don't really agree. And most of the time we don't know what we're disagreeing about.

ALEX. That's right. That's because you've decided I'm on something you call the other side.

CASSIE. A revolution is going on out there. But by this time next year it will be nothing more than dinner-table conversation. Things mean so little to us, to you —

ALEX. That's not true. I'm just not as sure as you are. I haven't had much time to think. A few years of college, then the army —

CASSIE. And three years of the Embassy. More than you know, you've come to think the way they think —

ALEX. For God's sake, Cassie, if you disapprove of me so much, why do you sleep with me? I don't believe people in love fight about things like this. They only use it as an excuse. It must be something else — (*Puts his arms around her*) Are you in love with me?

CASSIE (*softly*). I don't know. I think so. Are you, with me?

ALEX. Yes. Very much. Cassie, stay here. Stay in Rome with me. We'll find out here —

CASSIE (*very quickly, very nervously*). No, no. I can't. I want to go home and think about us. I couldn't stay here and see these people and lead this life. I'm mixed up about everything. I want to be alone and find out what I feel, what I want, what I want for you and me.

ALEX. All right, darling. I'll be coming back to Washington for Christmas. I know what I want. By then I want to know what you want.

CASSIE. Yes. Yes. In a few months maybe I'll make sense — (*Grips his arm*) I told Emily about us. And she was upset. She said — (*Tensely*) What's the difference what she said? This is a bad day. The guns outside seem to have come in here, and I don't want to think —

ALEX. All right, darling, all right. (*As he leans down to kiss her, Moses comes in from the bedroom.*)

MOSES. There must have been people who kissed through the French Revolution. I am in a bad humor; go down in the lobby and make love.

ALEX. We can't. It's filled with excited international ladies and gentlemen asking excited international questions. Also, the newspaper people waiting to see you — (*His last words are drowned out by loud shouting. Then there are three gun shots. As Cassie moves to the window, he shouts at her*) Get away from the window, Cas. I wish they'd get this over with. One way or —

MOSES (*as the shouting outside dies down*). They will. Like an operation. Just a few minutes more, and the patient will be an invalid for life. How's the Ambassador taking all this?

ALEX. I can't speak for the Ambassador.

(*Moses laughs as the door flies open and the Hotel Manager is propelled into the room. Behind him are two Fascist Soldiers.*)

MANAGER. Please control your fears. Please do not shout and cry out —

ALEX. You were here with that once before.

MANAGER. These two soldiers of Signor Mussolini are present only to certify the guests — Signor Taney, Signorina Bowman — (*The ticker tape begins to click.*)

MOSES. Shut up. (*Goes to the machine, reads from the tape*). A proclamation has been given to the press. King Victor

Emmanuel has asked Benito Mussolini to form a government. Proclamation to the people of Rome by the King of Italy reads: "My people, I wish to ask you—" (*Moses throws down the tape, looks at the two Soldiers. At the same minute, Emily opens her bedroom door.*)

MANAGER (*nervously, to Soldiers*). Sono degli Americani. Sono dei signori molto distinti.

MOSES (*softly*). Get yourself and these swine out of here.

MANAGER (*shrilly*). Signor, I must ask you —

SOLDIER. Casa dice?

MANAGER (*to Soldiers*). Dice lui — dice lui che partiránno stasera.

MOSES. I said no such thing. (*To Soldiers*) I said, Volevo voi altri porci via di quà.

(*The First Soldier moves quickly toward Moses. Alex moves up to the Soldier, pushes him back. The Second Soldier moves forward.*)

SOLDIER. Vecchio diavlo!

ALEX (*quickly*). American Embassy. There will be no trouble. L'ambasciata Americana. Non a sera nessun disturbo. Per piacere, andate via.

FIRST SOLDIER. Va bene. Andiamo.

(*The Soldier hesitates, then turns, motions to the Manager and to the Second Soldier. They go out and the Second Soldier slams the door. The Manager, shocked at the slamming, opens the door, looks in, smiles, says "Mi scusi," softly closes the door. Emily laughs.*)

EMILY. What was all that?

ALEX. That was your father. (*Crosses to Moses*) I came through the war without getting killed. I don't intend to get shot in a hotel room because you are a brave man.

MOSES (*laughs*). I will not show off again.

EMILY (*to Cassie*). Your stuff is ready to be packed now, Cassie.

ALEX. Mr. Taney, we heard that you were about to give out a statement. The newspaper people are waiting downstairs. You are a powerful man at home and your paper is a powerful paper. Any statement you give will be dangerous to the relations between our country and Italy. The Ambassador feels that we cannot take sides in an internal uprising —

MOSES (*sharply*). Stop that foolish talk. He long ago took sides. And so, I think, did you.

ALEX (*comes to Moses, softly*). You've been ragging me for

years, Mr. Taney. I don't usually mind it. I do today. (*Points to the window*) I can only speak for myself. I don't like this, and I don't like your thinking I do. But another few months of the kind of misery and starvation they've had, and there would have been a revolution. If Mussolini can put it down that doesn't make me like him, or the money behind him, or the people. But somebody had to do it, and you don't pick gentlemen to do the job. You were at the Peace Conference and you know that wasn't wild talk about Communism in Italy. (*Slowly, carefully*) And now I am going to tell you, Mr. Taney, that with all your liberal beliefs, I do not believe you want that. (*There is a pause.*)

MOSES. That's well said, and mostly true. But I didn't want this and I have fought hard, in my way, to stop it. I don't like to see people put down by gangsters who make a job of doing it for those who want it done. (*Very sharply*) Don't worry, and tell your boss not to worry. I'll give no interviews and write no pieces. I want no more of any of it. Anywhere. I'm through with the paper. (*Slowly, wearily, he goes toward his room*) I want to cry. And you should want to cry. You are young. This is a sad day, and you will pay for it. (*He goes into room.*)

EMILY (*after a minute*). Well.

ALEX (*uncomfortably*). He's making too much of it all. They're only exchanging one bad lot for another. But I admire your father, even when I don't agree with him or know what he's talking about. Ach. Nobody knows what they're talking about. Least of all me. (*Moves toward corridor door*) I'll see you later.

CASSIE (*goes toward bedroom door*). All right. (*Goes into her room, does not close the door.*)

ALEX. I'll be back in time to take you to the station.

EMILY. I've been thinking. I don't think I'll go. I want to go on with my music lessons. I've enjoyed them here — I don't want to go home yet. I think I'll stay here for a few months and —

ALEX. It's no time to be staying here. You can't stay alone, and Cassie wants to get back — Anyway, your father wouldn't like it —

EMILY (*smiles*). You forget that I don't have to ask anymore. I'm a great heiress. Anyway, he won't care. (*Gaily*) You could beau me around. We've known each other so long that there wouldn't be any gossip —

ALEX. I've got to get back. See you later. I think you better change your mind — (*Exits.*)

(*Emily stands looking after him. Then she begins to move about the room, idly, as if she were thinking. She goes to the piano, sits down, begins to play. As she plays, the guns start again, louder and closer than before. Cassie appears in the bedroom door carrying underwear and a box. She stands in the doorway looking at Emily.*)

EMILY. Why don't you stay in Rome, Cassie? Why are you leaving Alex now?

CASSIE. Do stop playing the piano. It doesn't go well with guns.

EMILY. Nothing goes well with guns. You haven't answered me. Be honest with me about what you feel —

CASSIE. I've been honest with you.

EMILY. I guess you don't want to talk to me. There were so many times, even when we were little girls, when that was true. Maybe it's best that you and I be away from each other for a while. I've decided not to sail with you and Father. I'm going to stay here. I'll ask Aunt Sophie to come. We'll take a house, I think, for a few months — (*Cassie drops the box that she is holding. Emily peers over the piano, sees that Cassie is staring at her*) What's the matter, Cassie? Why are you dropping things? That means you're nervous or hiding something. What is there to be nervous about or to hide?

(*As Cassie leans down to pick up the box, the curtain falls.*)

Curtain

Scene 3.

SCENE: *The drawing room of the Hazen house, about nine-thirty the same evening as Scene 1.*

AT RISE: *Sophronia is moving about the room emptying ash trays. On the center table is a silver tray with coffee, liqueurs, a brandy decanter, cups, etc. Ponette is sitting next to the table, watching Sophronia.*

PONETTE (*twists to look at the hall door, sighs, adjusts the cups on the tray*). Long dinner.

SOPHRONIA. Try to stay awake for a few minutes longer.

PONETTE. Two Chablis and two Haut Brion for five people is most extravagant. (*Leans forward, intimately*) I did not like the conversation at dinner. Much of it I did not understand, but much of it I did not like. For four bottles of wine people should be lighter, with jokes. Did you?

SOPHRONIA. Did I what?

PONETTE. The talk, the attitude, the tone.

SOPHRONIA (*sharply*). I wasn't listening.

PONETTE (*giggles*). That is not true. Mr. Taney asked you if it was not the twenty-eighth of October, that day in Rome, and you say no, it was the twenty-ninth. You could not answer if you did not listen. (*After a pause, bored*) Corporal Hazen does not eat much dinner. He looks bad today, sick.

SOPHRONIA. Sam wasn't hungry tonight. I'll make something for him later. He doesn't look sick at all.

PONETTE: He does not act well. John told me.

SOPHRONIA. Sam's getting along fine. Is John a doctor now?

PONETTE. John drive him today to the hospital. Corporal Hazen go in. A little time go by, the Corporal comes out, looks bad in the face, gets in the car, sits there. Ten, twenty minutes, maybe, John says he sits there, says nothing. Finally, John turns around and the Corporal says, "John, don't tell anybody we came to the hospital." (*Shrugs*) I am nobody, perhaps, so John tell me —

SOPHRONIA. Go out to the garage and tell John I want to see him in the kitchen right away.

PONETTE (*shakes his head*). Mrs. Hazen tells John she does not need car, so he goes to the movies. If it were me, I walk. The night is lovely, the moon is high.

SOPHRONIA. All right, poet. Take the coffee back to your wife and see if she can reheat it without blowing up the stove.

(*He sighs, rises, picks up the tray, starts for the hall door. As he reaches it, Emily and Cassie come slowly in.*)

PONETTE (*bows to Emily, points to tray*). I will return, Madame Hazen.

(*Emily stares at him as if she were thinking of something else.*)

SOPHRONIA (*turns to look at Emily and Cassie, as they seat themselves on the couch*). Nice to see you back, Miss Cassie.

CASSIE (*as if she'd been thinking of something else*). Oh. Thank you, Sophronia. It's good to see you again.

SOPHRONIA. How do you like Sam?

CASSIE. I like him. I can tell that you do, too.

SOPHRONIA (*as if she wanted to be reassured, to Emily*). He looks better, doesn't he, Miss Emily? Don't you think he does?

EMILY. Yes, I think he does.

(*Sophronia goes out the dining-hall door.*)

CASSIE (*after a second, looks at Emily, awkwardly*). I have a headache. Too much talk about the past, I guess. Or maybe too much wine. I'm not used to drinking.

EMILY. None of us. Shall I get you something for your headache?

CASSIE. No, no. Thank you, Em. I can't stay late. I must be going soon —

(*Moses, Alex, and Sam come in from the dining-hall door. They, too, come in slowly, as if they were thinking. All three turn to look at Cassie and Emily.*)

MOSES (*too brightly*). We decided to have our coffee in here with you. Filthy habit, leaving the men at the table. Arrange to stop it, Emily.

EMILY. I didn't start it, Father. You've been doing it ever since I can remember.

MOSES (*sits down*). That's true enough. I used to want it because two hours of your mother at dinner were long enough. Emily, you're old enough for me to tell you that I didn't like your mother.

EMILY. I always knew it, Father. Children don't miss things like that.

MOSES. I felt sorry when she died, but I said, to *myself,* of course, "Really, my dear, you didn't have to go that far to accommodate me. You could have moved across the street." It's a bad thing not to love the woman you live with. It tells on a man.

CASSIE. Tells on a woman, too, I should think.

MOSES. Comes out in ways you don't recognize. Now you take your father, Alex. Same thing with him. He didn't like your stepmother. So what did he do? He fell in love with the State Department and that's nothing to climb into bed with on a wintry night.

EMILY. Stop frowning, Sam. It's bad for the young.

SAM. I was thinking that you often know more about people in books than — than I've known about any of you, I guess. (*To Alex*) I didn't know you had been in Italy when Fascism first started. There you were on such a big day and it was so important how you figured out that day. Or maybe I think so because I was there and saw what it did — (*Lamely*) I can't seem to say what I mean.

ALEX. You mean that if people like me had seen it straight, maybe you wouldn't have had to be there twenty-two years later.

EMILY (*softly*). But most people don't see things straight on the day they happen. It takes years to understand —

SAM. If that were true then everybody would understand everything too late.

ALEX. There are men who see their own time as clearly as if it were history. But they're very rare, Sam. (*To Moses*) And before you speak, I want to say I don't think you're one of them.

MOSES (*laughs*). I don't think so either. Just because I understood things quicker than you did, didn't make me smart, if you know what I mean.

ALEX. I do.

SAM (*as if to himself*). I'd like to learn how to put things together, see them when they come —

EMILY. Maybe you will, darling. (*Sophronia reappears with the coffee tray, brandy, glasses*) Don't let us discourage you. Our generation made quite a mess. Come and have coffee on the terrace. Father, Sam. It's a lovely night.

MOSES. I don't like the terrace. I hate those damn chairs.

EMILY (*turns to look at him*). Come, Father, please.

MOSES (*sighs, moves toward the terrace*). What's the matter with you tonight?

(*As Sam begins to move toward the terrace, Sophronia comes to him.*)

SOPHRONIA. Go back to bed, Sam. You've been up too long. (*She is now very close to him. She speaks softly*) Why did you go to the hospital?

SAM (*puts his arm around her, very quickly*). If you don't stop fussing about me I may shoot you. (*He looks down at her, shakes his head. He puts his face against her hair, presses her arm, and moves to the terrace. Sophronia exits through the hall door. Emily comes out to the terrace.*)

MOSES (*squirming around in the chair*). You all right, Sam? Damn chairs. Emily, I'm getting too old —

EMILY (*laughs*). I'll buy you a box of that candy you like, Father, if you'll shut up for just five minutes. (*She puts her hand on Sam's arm, smiles at him.*)

(*Cassie crosses to Alex, who is standing near the piano.*)

ALEX (*softly*). Why did you come tonight, Cassie? And why didn't you tell me? (*As she looks nervously toward the terrace*) Don't worry. Emily has arranged this for us.

CASSIE (*softly*). Remember? A long time ago, I asked you if you were going to feel guilty. I told you then I didn't want it that way —

ALEX. And I told you then that it was between me and you, and me and Emily. I don't feel guilty, and you haven't answered me.

CASSIE. Emily called me at the Taylors'. Twice. I didn't know what to say —

ALEX (*frowns*). Simple to say you couldn't come, or didn't want to. What's the sense of sitting at a dinner table and talking about twenty-two years ago —

CASSIE (*sharply*). I didn't start that talk, Alex. And I didn't say anything that all of us didn't know.

ALEX. I don't understand what this is all about. I — Why did you tell Emily we had dinner together last night, when you meant last week?

CASSIE (*tensely*). I don't know. It was a slip. I didn't mean to say it. I don't like tonight any better than you do, and I don't like the way you're talking to me.

ALEX (*touches her hand*). I'm sorry, Cas. I —

EMILY (*comes in from the terrace*). It's warm and pleasant. Won't you come on the terrace, Cassie?

CASSIE. I must go now, Em.

EMILY. Why?

CASSIE. Because it's late. (*Looks at Emily, softly*) And because I think it was wrong for us to meet again, and because it's never a good idea to talk about the past. Let's remember by ourselves, Em, with the lights out. (*She moves toward the door. Emily moves with her.*)

EMILY. No. (*In front of Cassie*) No.

CASSIE (*after a second, quietly*). I want to go, Em.

EMILY. No.

ALEX (*comes to Emily*). What is it? What's —

EMILY. I don't want Cassie to leave. This has been coming for a good many years.

ALEX (*after a second, softly*). Whatever you want to know, Em, I'll tell you. It's between you and me, and we can do it alone.

EMILY (*softly*). I know what you would tell me. I've known for a long time. But there's a great deal that you don't know, and Cassie doesn't know, and I don't, either. It's time to find out.

(*Alex looks at her. Then, after a pause, he moves quickly to the terrace doors. As he moves, Sam gets up, stands in the door. As Alex reaches the doors and moves as if to close them, Sam puts his cane against the door.*)

SAM. If you and Mother would let me, I'd rather stay. I don't know what's happening, but I have a feeling it's got to do with me, too. Anyway, it's kind of an important night for me because — well, just because.

EMILY (*after a second*). You can stay, Sam.

CASSIE (*tensely*). Leave it alone, Em. Leave it alone. It's no good for people to sit in a room and talk about what they were, or what they wanted, or what they might have been —

EMILY (*softly*). Yes, it's hard. It scares me, too.

ALEX. What is it you want? What are you doing?

EMILY (*simply*). I don't know, Alex. But maybe we'll find out. (*Pleasantly*) Sit down, Cassie. Please.

Curtain

Act Two

Scene 1.

SCENE: *The corner of a restaurant in Berlin, the autumn of 1923. One table faces the audience and several other tables, in an offstage alcove, can be seen. Back of the table is a large window, partly opened, hung with heavy draperies.*

AT RISE: *Alex is sitting at the table, a cocktail in front of him. He is looking at a menu card. Standing next to the table is Eppler, a middle-aged German who owns the restaurant. He is holding a pad, waiting to take Alex's order.*

EPPLER (*after a second*). The Rostbraten? Mrs. Hazen liked it so much the last week we had it. Notice the price mounts. This morning I buy bread for one hundred and forty billion marks the loaf. You are lucky to have American money.

ALEX. I'm ashamed to use it with things as they are.

EPPLER (*laughs, looks around the restaurant*). There are not many such who are ashamed. In all my years I have not seen so many American dollars and English pounds. Here they buy a drink for more than a German can earn in a week. It is the fault of no one, but it causes bad feeling. You understand, Mr. Hazen. It is not wise to have tourists here now. You work in Berlin, you understand that.

ALEX. I understand, of course. But we can't keep them home. And your government seems to want them here.

EPPLER (*wearily*). Ach, I know. Bread for a hundred and forty billion marks. It is crazy — (*Through his speech there is the noise of a distant commotion. Now the noise comes nearer; it is the noise of a large mob, four or five blocks away, shouting and running. The words of the shouting are confused, but through them, at intervals, come "Juden. Judenstrasse. Juden." The Guests in the restaurant rush to the aisles; the Waiters pause and then move toward Eppler. Alex rises.*

Eppler moves toward the doors as five or six men come running past the window.)

EPPLER (*yells above the noise*). Die Türen zu. Die Türen zu.

ONE OF THE MEN IN THE STREET (*pauses, looks in the window, laughs, calls in*). Wir gehen auf die Juden los. Heraus mit denen die hier sind.

WAITER (*who is near Alex's table, shouting*). Schwein, Schwein.

ALEX (*grabs the Waiter*). Did I understand what he said? Did I? —

WAITER. He said they are going after the Jews. He said if we had any here we should bring them out. (*The Waiter moves hurriedly toward the windows, closes them, draws the curtains. There has been the noise of slamming doors, people talking loudly, Eppler screaming instructions. Now Eppler comes down the aisle toward Alex's table.*)

EPPLER (*shouting to be heard*). Meine Herren, bleiben Sie sitzen. Die Polizei versichert alles unter Kontroll zu haben. Und auserden, die Unordnungen sind nicht in diese Gegend. Bitte, bleiben Sie sitzen.

UNSEEN MAN. What was it? What was it?

Eppler (*shouting over other voices*). The Freikorps, a bread riot and they went to the Jewish section —

VOICE (*with an American accent*). What the hell is happening?

EPPLER (*screaming, nervous*). Please. Be seated. The doors have been closed. We cannot open them until the police tell us —

VOICE. We insist upon getting out of here. Open the doors —

EPPLER (*to Alex*). Please, Mr. Hazen. Please say for me —

ALEX (*turns to the restaurant*). I am Hazen of the American Embassy. Herr Eppler wishes me to tell you that there has been a disgraceful riot of hoodlums against the Jewish section. The police tell him that it is under control. In any case, it is not near here, but the doors must be kept closed until he is allowed to open them. Mr. Eppler asks you to go on with your lunch. There is nothing to be done now except by the police.

MAN. Disgraceful business. Yesterday —

WOMAN. How do we know they won't break in here? Why don't you get the police in here? —

EPPLER. Be calm. There is no danger here —

ALEX (*to Eppler*). Please see that the door is opened for Mrs. Hazen when she comes.

EPPLER. Ladies and gentlemen, I am most sorry. (*People who have been standing near Alex's table, move away. As they move away, Cassie is seen near the table, watching Alex*) I am most ashamed. Please resume your seats. (*He moves off. Cassie comes closer to the table.*)

CASSIE (*softly*). Hard to believe that we would live to see a pogrom in the year 1923.

ALEX. Yes. Very hard —

CASSIE (*as he recognizes her*). It scares me, Alex. It scares me.

ALEX (*gets up*). Cassie.

CASSIE. Hello, Alex.

ALEX (*nervous, bewildered*). You here in Berlin?

CASSIE (*smiles*). I seem to be.

ALEX. But you didn't phone us — Do sit down. Emily will be here any minute. Waiter, waiter. What will you drink, Cas? Will you have lunch with us? Are you with people? —

CASSIE (*quietly*). Easy, easy. You're nervous about seeing me.

ALEX. It's a surprise, that's all. I don't — What will you have to drink, Cas, what? —

CASSIE. Do be quiet, Alex. For just a minute.

ALEX (*nods, lowers his head*). When did you come over?

CASSIE. I've been in Paris for a month. I've been here for about a week. You've been here for seven months. You were changed from Rome, soon after the wedding. I know all about you.

ALEX (*nervously*). But you didn't call us when you got here —

CASSIE (*gently, touches his hand*). Look, Alex. You and I had a fight. It did bad things to me.

ALEX (*slowly*). It did bad things to me too.

CASSIE. I know. And I wanted to wait until I could see you, well, without feeling —

ALEX (*quickly*). Yes, I understand.

CASSIE. It's good to see you, Alex. I'd rather have had it someplace else, on a calmer day, without all that outside — I should be very unhappy here. Don't you mind?

ALEX. It's a horrible place to be. But my job is here. I don't think I ever could have believed in such misery and poverty. They're desperate people.

CASSIE (*who has been staring at him*). Are you — Are you glad to see me?

ALEX. I don't know, Cas.

CASSIE. Has it been a good marriage?

ALEX (*quickly*). Yes, it's been very good. And should you ask me questions like that? And should I be answering them?

CASSIE. Whose rules are those? I want to know about you.

ALEX. I want to know about you, too. (*Simply, warmly*) I do like seeing you, Cas.

CASSIE. And I like seeing you. We've been so close to each other for so many years. It's made me sad to do without you, not to know about you —

(*Emily, followed by a Young Man, comes swiftly up to the table. Emily immediately sits down, begins to speak. The Young Man stands waiting.*)

EMILY. Alex, Alex. The car had to cross the Judenstrasse. They were dragging a man through the streets. And they were beating an old lady on the head. We got out and tried to get through to help them, and the crowd began to scream at us and push us back. We were dirty Americans and should mind our business —

ALEX (*to the Young Man*). What is it, Halsey? Somebody's leading it — It isn't coming from nowhere —

EMILY (*softly*). Hello, Cas.

CASSIE. Hello, Emily.

HALSEY. The Freikorps people are in on it. I think its real leaders came from the Young People's League, just as they did last week. There's no question now it's tied up with the Bavarian trouble. The story around is that somebody from Thyssen put up the money for Ludendorff and for those clowns outside.

ALEX. That's hard to believe. He's a bad guy, but nobody's bad enough to put up the money for this —

CASSIE (*laughs*). Dear Alex. You haven't changed. Nobody's that bad, even when the proof is outside the door.

ALEX. I didn't say the proof wasn't outside the door. I said I didn't believe a man like Thyssen —

EMILY (*smiles*). It's like old times. You and Cassie.

ALEX (*suddenly turns, stares at Emily and Cassie*). Emily, you weren't surprised that Cassie was here.

EMILY. I forgot to be. It seemed so natural that the three of us should be together.

CASSIE. I don't think Emily and I could be surprised at seeing each other.

EMILY. No. And, of course, I did see you in here the other day. And you saw me.

ALEX. You saw each other the other day but you didn't speak?

HALSEY. Mr. Hazen, I've got the car outside. I'd better get back.

ALEX. I want to go to the police. We'll make a strong official protest. Put it on the grounds that many Americans are in Berlin —

CASSIE. Couldn't you put it on the grounds that it's a horror and a disgrace? Or would that be too simple?

ALEX (*smiles*). Have dinner with us tonight and I'll tell you about it. (*Leans down to kiss Emily*) Both of you stay here until I send Halsey back with the car. (*Eppler comes to the table.*)

EPPLER. The police are in control, Mr. Hazen. Everything is all right.

ALEX. Why the hell weren't they in control before anything happened? It's the second time in a week. It's beginning to look as if they don't want to be in control. All right, Halsey. (*Alex moves off. Halsey bows to Emily and Cassie, moves off.*)

EPPLER. How do you do, Mrs. Hazen. I will be back in a minute for your order. Excuse me. (*He moves away.*)

EMILY (*points to Eppler*). They all seem like figures in a dream. And a dream I don't understand. None of it. Berlin's an awful place. You always hated it. Even when we came as little girls.

CASSIE. Remember how the horn on the Kaiser's automobile used to play the horn call from *Siegfried* and how angry it always made your father? And once — we must have been about ten — you said you thought it was pretty and why didn't you have an automobile like that? I thought your father was going to kill you. How is he?

EMILY. He's fine. I haven't seen him for six or seven months. He came over for the wedding, of course, and — (*Stops*) Alex and I wrote you about the wedding. You never answered us.

CASSIE. I wrote to Alex.

EMILY (*after a second*). Yes? Why not to me?

CASSIE. Because I thought it was between Alex and me. Not for the three of us.

EMILY (*slowly*). What did Alex think?

CASSIE. I don't know. He wrote back he hoped we would all meet soon and that he thought you missed me.

EMILY. I do miss you.

CASSIE. Strange that Alex didn't tell you we had written to each other. Don't you talk about things like that?

EMILY. Things like what?

CASSIE. Like me.

EMILY (*softly*). You haven't been a problem, Cassie.

CASSIE (*laughs*). I feel dismissed. And I don't believe you.

EMILY. I know what's happening to you and me. We want to talk about ourselves, and we're frightened to. So we're ending up with the kind of talk that an hour from now neither of us will be sure we understood. So let's talk, or let's quit.

CASSIE. I said I didn't believe you.

EMILY (*quickly*). Cassie, I don't want to hurt you —

CASSIE (*sharply*). And I don't want you to patronize me by trying not to.

EMILY. I'm not doing that, Cassie.

CASSIE (*touches her hand*). All right, Em. I'm upset today and —

EMILY. I know. I am, too. This is a bad place to be. I'd like to go back home for a few months. I don't want to have the baby here.

CASSIE. When are you going to have the baby?

EMILY. March.

CASSIE. You always said you didn't think people should have babies so soon after they were married. That they should wait and find out if the marriage was going to work —

EMILY. This marriage has worked very well.

CASSIE. What did Alex tell you when he came back from seeing me? When he came back to Rome where you were waiting for him?

EMILY. I didn't make you and Alex fight. I didn't even know you'd had a fight for months after he came back to Rome. Then all he ever told me was that you disagreed with what he thought and what he was, and that you'd both decided to quit. What good is this, Cassie? It's all over now.

CASSIE. Is it, Em? Your best friend marries your beau and a year after it's as if it never happened. You've always done that, Em. You've always made things as simple as you wanted them to be.

EMILY. Your best friend married your beau. But only after you'd given him up, and Alex told me it was finished for him. You won't make me feel guilty about that now or ever. You and Alex would have been wrong for each other and you know it. Alex and I have a happy marriage and — Why are you in Berlin? Why are you here? (*Looks up, sees Cassie looking at her. Sharply*) Why are you in Berlin? Why are you here?

CASSIE. I worked hard at college last year and I wanted a vacation. (*Quickly*) No. I wanted to see you and Alex. I wanted to find out if we could be good friends. But all that was pretty fancy because I seemed to have been the only one who was disturbed. And now that's all right, I think, and we can —

EMILY. I don't believe it's all right now. Things are wrong between us. Cassie, let's not dine tonight. Let's not —

CASSIE (*softly*). Let's not see each other again. That's right. But it isn't easy to put away the people you've loved and been close to —

EMILY (*touches Cassie's hand*). It isn't easy for me, either. But it doesn't have to be for always. We'll forget after a while. You'll get married and have children and we'll rock on the porch of a summer hotel and watch our kids play together and laugh that it could ever have been any other way —

CASSIE (*very sharply*). Please. Please. Please stop talking that way.

EMILY (*stares at her, then after a second*). Good-bye, Cas. (*As she begins to rise, the curtain falls.*)

Curtain

Scene 2.

SCENE: *The living room of a large suite in the Hotel Meurice, Paris, 1938. It is a large room with the usual French hotel furniture. Upstage, right, is a door leading to a bedroom. Upstage, left, is a door leading to the hall of the apartment. Center stage, right, is a door leading into a small anteroom which is used as a waiting room for visitors. There is a large desk in one corner of the room.*

AT RISE: *James Sears, a thin, tired-looking man of fifty, is sitting at the desk. Near him is a typewriter. On the desk are many papers, long report sheets, a briefcase, a small file. As the curtain rises, Sears is clipping items from a newspaper. The phone rings.*

SEARS (*picks up the phone*). Hello. Could I take a message? This is James Sears, Ambassador Hazen's secretary. Hold on. Perhaps I can reach him now. (*He crosses to upstage right door, knocks, opens the door*) Mr. Hazen. It's the German Embassy again. Could you see the Count — (*He steps back as Alex comes into the room. It is 1938 and Alex is about forty-three*) — Count Max von Stammer who — (*Carefully*) — happens to be in Paris and would like to drop in?

ALEX. Yes, I know he "happens" to be here. All right. Make clear it's an informal call, I just "happen" to be in Paris, et cetera. (*As Sears turns to phone. Alex picks up a clip of papers.*)

SEARS. His Excellency will be glad to see Count von Stammer if he can be here within the next half hour. We're at the Hotel Meurice. You understand we are not receiving official visitors. The Ambassador is in Paris on a vacation. Yes, I will explain. Thank you. (*Hangs up, turns to Alex*) Count von Stammer will be making a "social" call. He, too, is only in Paris on a vacation, and —

ALEX. All right. You both got that nonsense on the record. (*Holds out the clippings*) Did Halsey get anything? Anything new here?

SEARS (*takes the clippings*). The children will be evacuated from Paris tomorrow; people who can afford it are leaving for the South of France, and the railroads are dangerously clogged; there are an estimated seventy-two anti-aircraft batteries around Paris, but Halsey says he doesn't believe it. Yesterday morning, Beneš telephoned London. There's the report, supposedly compiled by the Poles, with the figures on the Soviet Union war potential. The report says Russia is in no shape to fight Germany.

ALEX. That report is two months old. Why has it appeared again?

SEARS. I asked the same question and Halsey didn't know.

ALEX (*irritably*). God knows, we're not a nation of spies. Usually that pleases me. But this month it doesn't. Halsey never knows anything until the French and English have decided to give it to the Roumanians, and that's the last stop on the road to misinformation. Get Halsey. Get him on the phone for me — (*Sears picks up the phone*) Never mind. Never mind. I can't make sense out of any of it, and I'm trying to blame it on him.

SEARS. I've made you a calendar, sir — I don't think you'll need Halsey —

ALEX. Washington must think I'm dead. My report should have been sent five days ago — All right. Let's hear the calendar. Dates, at least, are facts.

SEARS (*takes a sheet of paper from the desk*). Two weeks ago Bonnet went to Geneva to see Litvinov. Halsey says it's true that Litvinov promised aid to Czechoslovakia and sent Bonnet to see if the Roumanians would consent to let the Russians cross the borders and go through. Three days later Bonnet, when he reported to the French Cabinet, said that Litvinov had *not* been that definite. Halsey is positive Bonnet was lying because —

ALEX. That's bright of Halsey; the one fact we have, maybe the one fact in all of Europe, is that Bonnet has never yet told the truth.

SEARS. Four days ago, Litvinov told the League of Nations that Russia will support France if she goes to the aid of Czechoslovakia, and strongly hinted she may do so even if France does not go to Czechoslovakia's aid —

ALEX. So once more out trots the supposed Polish report to discredit the quality of the Russian army. I understand. And so would a child of four.

SEARS. The rumor about the Munich meeting is still going the rounds. Halsey hasn't got anything new on it, but Halsey thinks —

ALEX. I don't want to hear what Halsey thinks. (*He lies down on the couch*) What's the matter with me, Jim? Am I just tired? I can't put the pieces together, or maybe I don't want to. I don't know. I can't believe in villainy. I can't. I always want to laugh when somebody else believes in it.

(*The door opens and Emily, in a tailored afternoon suit, comes in. It is 1938 and Emily is about thirty-seven.*)

EMILY. Have you seen the children, Jim?

SEARS (*nods, moves toward the door*). The last I saw of Sarah, Mademoiselle was dragging her to some art gallery. Sam and Mr. Taney went for a walk. (*He exits.*)

EMILY (*laughs*). We come to Paris every summer to meet the

children. Then Father arrives and that's the last we see of Sam.

ALEX. I'm used to that. He says he's educating Sam.

EMILY. You look tired, Alex. This hasn't been much of a vacation for you. Come along to the opera tonight. They're doing *Figaro* and you like it. (*Quickly*) Cassie Bowman is coming for tea. She's here this summer. I called her yesterday — (*Begins to speak as if she were embarrassed*) Of course, you had lunch with her last summer, and I think the summer before, wasn't it, but I haven't seen her since 1923, I suppose —

ALEX. I've seen her this trip. I saw her last week.

EMILY. I know. Maggie Taylor told me. I suppose you'd forgotten to tell me —

ALEX. She called here one evening. You were out somewhere, and we had a late dinner together.

EMILY (*pleasantly*). Yes. I'm sure you forgot to tell me —

ALEX. Oh, only half forgot, I suppose. I've never understood about you and Cassie. She's here every summer, usually when we are. I don't understand why you don't want to see each other — Or, for that matter, why it's important one way or the other.

EMILY (*slowly*). I don't know either. (*Then hesitantly*) But I think after all these years, I'd like to see her alone.

ALEX. Of course.

EMILY (*as she reaches the door*). Come and take a walk with me, Alex. I haven't really seen you for days. It's warm and pleasant out and we'll find a quiet street where nobody's selling papers or flying south or talking about war —

ALEX. Thank you, Em. I can't. I've got people coming.

(*As she exits, the door leading to the anteroom opens and Sears comes in.*)

SEARS. He's here. You want him in now? (*Alex nods, rises. Sears opens the door*) Count von Stammer. (*A very old man comes in from the anteroom.*)

VON STAMMER. The last time I saw you was at the Conference in Genoa in 1922. Your wife's father was with you. A remarkable man, Mr. Taney. Is he dead? How do you do?

ALEX. No, sir. He's very much alive. (*They shake hands*) He's here now. He comes to Europe every year to see our children.

VON STAMMER (*sits down near the desk. He is a calm man and he does not move during the scene*). I thought he died.

When you get my age you think everybody is dead. My apologies to Mr. Taney. Is he still, in politics, a great liberal?

ALEX. Mr. Taney retired many years ago.

VON STAMMER (*giggles*). All liberals retired with the Versailles Treaty. (*Leans down, strokes Alex's briefcase*) I like leather. I have never had for myself a briefcase. Next year I buy one. (*Pats it*) Expensive?

ALEX (*smiles*). I don't remember.

VON STAMMER. That is interesting: not to remember how much something costs. Now. The truth is, Your Excellency, I have made the journey from Berlin to see you. It was considered best to send such as me to see a man such as you. Otherwise, Von Ribbentrop would have come himself.

ALEX. I don't know Von Ribbentrop.

VON STAMMER. You should. An able man. It is the style to laugh at those who sold champagne, but that is not sensible.

ALEX. I don't find him laughed at. I am told he is a great social success here and in London.

VON STAMMER. Those people. They take up anybody.

ALEX (*carefully*). Yes. Homosexuals one year, Nazis the next.

VON STAMMER (*giggles*). And one year they combine both, eh? Well, now. I have come to influence you. The French and British and Russians and Poles will also send, eh? Ach, I have little faith in men influencing other men. Each of us goes the way he goes, and that way is decided early in a man's life. I have read a little Freud. (*Carefully, as if to a child*) Sigmund Freud, the Jewish Viennese psychiatric physician.

ALEX (*smiles*). I know his name. We have a few printing presses in America now. Count von Stammer, what have you come to influence me about, and why me?

VON STAMMER. I come to influence you about a war, and I come to *you* because you are about to send back a report to your government.

ALEX. Your Intelligence Department is remarkable. My report is not yet written, and there are none who know about it.

VON STAMMER. There was a long discussion of you and your report at a dinner party last night. By ten o'clock this morning, Mr. Kupczynski, the Polish Ambassador, having roused himself from his customary night of drinking, reported it to us. That meant the telephone was occupied, and so Monsieur

Melchior de Polignac, he is a friend of yours — or your wife's perhaps? — was kept waiting because he, too, wished to tell us.

ALEX (*after a second*). I have never met him. My wife knows him but — (*Looks at his watch, sharply*) Now, Count von Stammer, I am afraid —

VON STAMMER. Yes, yes. Everybody becomes bored with me in time. A great many men are bores when they grow old. Not so for me. I was always a bore.

ALEX. I remember my father spoke of you.

VON STAMMER (*laughs*). Now. So. Quickly. Hitler wishes the Sudetenland. He is convinced it belongs to the German Reich. The British and French will come to agree with him. With some reluctance, perhaps —

ALEX (*stares at him. After a pause*). I do not believe that. (*Points to the window*) The streets are filled with men being called up. People are being evacuated from Paris. Those are not the signs of people who wish —

VON STAMMER. I did not say *people* wished. I said the governments do not want a war, and they will not fight a war. The mobilization is to frighten the *people* out of a war. (*Sharply*) Your Excellency, I do not have to tell you that. You know it.

ALEX. Then, perhaps, you will tell me what I don't know.

VON STAMMER. What I have to say is most simple: we would like to know that your government will not bring pressure on England or France to make war with us.

ALEX. It is your country that is making the demands, it is your country that is trying to make war. Now, Count von Stammer, if you have come here to get assurances from me, your visit is wasted. I don't make the policy of my country. No one man makes it, thank God. And I am an unimportant man sending back an unimportant report.

VON STAMMER. No report is unimportant to my new bosses. (*Smiles, as Alex is about to speak*) Let us go back, Your Excellency. You have said that my country wishes to make war. That is a large generality. Let us put it this way: what war, with whom — and when? Not over the Sudetenland. Hitler has promised that if the Sudetenland is ceded, there will be no further attempt —

ALEX. What war, with whom — and when?

VON STAMMER. I speak unofficially, of course. But if we are

given the proper freedom and cooperation we might be prepared, in time, to turn East. East. To rid Europe of the menace of Russia. We realize you would wish such a promise to come from men more highly placed than I. So I have been instructed to suggest to you —

ALEX (*gets up*). I am an old-fashioned man. After all these years in Europe, my roots are still deep in America. Therefore, I don't like such promises or such deals, and I do not believe they will be considered by *any* other democracy. I resent the deals of war, and I don't like your coming here with them.

VON STAMMER (*puzzled, amused*). Well. Well. I have always admired Americans. If they eat dinner with a man, he must be honorable. If they ride with the Esterhazys in Hungary and the Potockis in Poland, they must be honorable men. How could men who dine out, or mount horses, be otherwise?

ALEX. I do not ride and I seldom dine out.

VON STAMMER (*rises*). Ambassador Hazen, encourage the English and French not to make war. They are now willing to give us —

ALEX. I know of nothing they are willing to give you. I know of no decision they have made. (*Rings the bell on the desk*) And now I hope you will excuse me. I have an appointment.

VON STAMMER. You know of no decision they have made? Is it possible? Well. By the end of this week a journey will be made and a conference will be held. And if there is no meddling from your side of the world, all will be settled. And if your side of the world does meddle, I would guess that — (*Shrugs*) Well — it will still be settled. (*Sears enters*) You look worried. Do not worry. Peace may come this year, but war will come another. Naturally, I speak this afternoon as if I thought it wise to be on the side of my country. But I do not always think that. And I do not much care. In two months I buy a house in Switzerland. And a briefcase. I have had a career of sorts, and I might like to write about it. I cannot be more foolish than the rest. (*He puts out his hand. They shake hands. The Count exits, Sears closes the door, exits.*)

ALEX (*picks up the phone*). Vaugirard 1209. Please. (*After a second*) This is Alex Hazen. Is Halsey there? Put him on. Halsey? Von Stammer was just here. He's hinting they've reached a decision. Has there been any news? All right. Call me. (*He hangs up. After a second, there is a knock on the hall door. Alex ignores it. A second later there is another knock. Irritably*) Come in, come in. (*Cassie comes in. Cassie is thirty-seven years old.*)

CASSIE (*stands looking at him*). You sound so irritable. I'll go away.

ALEX (*smiles*). I'm sorry, my dear. Come in. How are you?

CASSIE. You didn't phone to find out. But they were wonderful flowers, and I thank you for them.

ALEX. I wouldn't have been fun to be with. I've had a miserable week. I've got to send back a report and I —

CASSIE. Haven't you sent off that report? You mentioned it when we dined last week.

ALEX. No, I haven't sent it off. I've been stalling. I don't know what's the matter with me. I've never gone in for thinking about myself. Sometimes I've been right and when I was wrong I always thought, well, you've done your best; you can't sit around and cry about mistakes. Everybody makes them. But now —

CASSIE (*gently*). But now what?

ALEX. One minute I say to myself, what difference does it make what you write back? It'll be one of many reports coming in this week. But that's not true because I've got to do my best, even if it isn't important to anybody but me —

CASSIE. Then do your best.

ALEX (*wearily*). The truth is I don't know what's best.

CASSIE (*gently*). Back doing business at the old stand, Alex?

ALEX (*looks up at her*). A German just left here who remembered me at the Genoa Conference. When he said it, that time in Rome, and you and me, came back so sharply that I could have cried.

CASSIE (*after a second*). Why did Emily ask me here today?

ALEX. I don't know. I suppose she wants to see you again.

CASSIE. Does she know I saw you last week?

ALEX. Yes, I told her. But she knew it. Maggie Taylor had told her. I'm not sure how Maggie knew but — (*Looks at his watch*) Emily's late. I hope there wasn't trouble in the streets. She's never late.

CASSIE. Did she mind your seeing me?

ALEX. She knows I've seen you each summer. Why should she

mind? (*Shrugs*) You and she haven't wanted to see each other; you and I have.

CASSIE (*softly*). That simple? That simple for her, too?

ALEX. Isn't it simple? Is there anything wrong with it?

CASSIE. I must go now. Tell Em I couldn't wait.

ALEX. I'll be finished work tonight. How about lunch tomorrow? I'll drive you into the country —

CASSIE. I'm sorry. I can't.

ALEX. How about dinner? (*She shakes her head*) But I want to see you. It will be a whole year again —

CASSIE. I don't think I'll be coming next year. The world is cracking up, my dear; I don't think anybody will be coming.

ALEX (*catches her arm*). I want a day off. Spend it with me. I'll buy you flowers and —

CASSIE (*laughs*). No. I'm going to Fontainebleau for a week. Remember that little hotel we used to go to when we were kids? I still go back every year.

ALEX. Have you a beau, Cassie?

CASSIE (*after a second*). A half beau, I guess.

ALEX. Why haven't you ever gotten married?

CASSIE. Maybe I don't marry easy. Maybe — (*Stops suddenly*) Can I ask you? (*He nods*) Are you in love with Emily?

ALEX. I love Emily. Very much, I think. But I — (*Takes her arm*) Oh, Cassie, it's taken me fifteen years to say these words even to myself: I was only in love once.

CASSIE (*very softly*). Me, too.

ALEX (*turns, takes her arms*). Let me come down to the country to see you. Please, Cas.

CASSIE (*nervously*). I — er, I want to, Alex. The truth is, I've wanted to for a long time, I mean — But I don't want it to be wrong. I — I couldn't stand it if it worried you afterwards or you felt guilty, or Emily — Or I felt guilty —

ALEX. I don't feel guilty. Emily's been a good wife. And I've been a good husband, too. I think I'll go on being. This has nothing to do with Emily. This has to do with you and me. From a long, long time ago. It's a strange day for us to come together again. Strange for me to be thinking about myself and you when — (*He puts his arms around her*) Please, Cas. Let me come down.

CASSIE (*after a second, smiles*). All right, darling. It will make me happy. I hope it will make you happy, too. (*She touches his face, then moves away*) I'll go now. Tell Em I couldn't wait. And tell her I don't want to come again.

ALEX (*frowns*). Cas, I want no more talk of Emily. Yes? (*He leans down to kiss her*) Good-bye darling. I'll be down. (*She smiles, exits.*)

ALEX (*goes to the desk, sits down, picks up clippings. After a second, he puts his hand over his face, as if he were very tired. Then he goes back to the clippings, begins to read them. Suddenly he leans back, speaks sharply*). Jim, what is this? This clipping about Mrs. Hazen? What paper does it come from? Why don't you mark the papers? — It's a pretty item all right. Jim! Where are you? — (*Turns around, sees that Sears is not in the anteroom, slams the door. The hall door opens and Emily comes slowly in. She is carrying packages.*)

EMILY (*nervous and speaking rapidly*). I never saw so many cars in my life. Everybody is leaving Paris. They don't believe there's going to be a war, but they are leaving just in case.

ALEX. Cassie was here.

EMILY. I don't understand them. If we were at war and Washington or New York were in danger, I wouldn't leave. It's your country; you just don't pack up and go when there's trouble.

ALEX. I am glad to hear that.

EMILY. You're upset today, Alex.

ALEX (*picks up the clipping*). You've been seeing too much of the Renaults and Melchior de Polignac and the fashionable society trash who run with them. I don't like these gossip items of you with people like that. These are sharp times, Emily, and where one went to dinner a few years ago, one can't go any longer.

EMILY (*sits down*). I've been lonely, Alex. I see the people who come along. Sometimes I like them, sometimes I don't. They don't mean much to me one way or the other.

ALEX. Everybody thinks that about the people they see. And it's never true. I'm sorry you've been lonely, Em. I guess I have been, too. Cas was here.

EMILY (*very quickly*). Are you coming to the opera with us?

ALEX. No, I'm going to do the report. I've got to get to work now.

EMILY. Oh, I'm sorry you're not coming. I'd looked forward to it. But I am glad you're going to do the report. It's been worrying you so much. (*Slowly*) It's an important report. You're a sound man and you will be listened to. It comes down to peace or war now, doesn't it? Last night at dinner Toni said the Czechs were acting like fools. He said if Hitler got what he wanted now that would shut him up for good. And Baudouin said if there is war it means Russia in Europe and —

ALEX (*sharply*). That's what I meant. That kind of people and that kind of talk. Toni has been doing business with the Nazis for years and Baudouin's bank is tied up with the Japs.

EMILY. I have a lot of investments in his bank.

ALEX. That's bad news. I've never known about your money. (*Slowly*) Why are you telling me now, Em?

EMILY. You've made a point of not knowing about my money, and not touching it. I wonder if you were scared to find out we are rich; to find out we are the people we are.

ALEX. You've never talked about your money before. I don't know what you mean now. But if I thought you were trying to tell me that what I think or believe or will report should be influenced by it, I would be very angry, Em. Very angry with both of us.

EMILY. I don't mean to influence you with my money. I have it, I'm glad to have it, and it's never meant much to me. But I'm not willing to lie to myself about it, or where and how I was born, or the world I've lived in. But sometimes I think you pretend to yourself that you have no world that influences you — that you have no connections and no prejudices.

ALEX. I've always tried to push aside what I am, or where your money is, or how we live, and see what's best for my country. I've tried to do that. (*Sharply*) I'm going to keep on trying.

EMILY (*slowly*). Can you push aside your son?

ALEX. What's Sam got to do with this?

EMILY. If there is a war, he'll soon be old enough to fight in it. (*Tensely*) I don't want my son to die. I don't want you to have anything to do with his dying. I don't like Nazis any better than you do. But I don't want a war. I love Sam, and I want him to be happy, in a peaceful world.

ALEX (*very sharply*). I love Sam too. But I'll report what I think is the truth. And it will have nothing to do with my desire to keep Sam alive. I fought in a war and I wouldn't have wanted my father — (*Desperately*) What are we saying to each other? We've never had fights, we've never talked to each other this way.

EMILY (*softly*). You and I haven't been close to each other for a long time.

ALEX. I know. I've been lonely and so have you. This afternoon I suddenly knew it — Cassie was here, Em, and —

EMILY (*very quickly*). I know, Alex. You've told me that three times before. I saw her. I was in the lobby. I waited for her to leave. I didn't want to see her. It sounds crazy, but I was kind of afraid to come up —

ALEX. Afraid to see Cassie? You asked her here — (*Looks at her*) I never thought you were afraid of anything.

EMILY. I'm going to tell you about me — someday when we're very old and you're so deaf you can't hear me. I am afraid of a great many things. Including —

(*The anteroom door opens and Sears puts his head in.*)

SEARS (*tensely*). There's an announcement from London. On the radio. (*As Alex moves swiftly to the radio, Sears goes out, closes the door.*)

RADIO. The announcement has just been made that Prime Minister Chamberlain and Premier Daladier will fly to Munich tomorrow morning. There are already hints of Cabinet resignations. Although no official statement, other than the announcement of an hour ago, has been forthcoming, a high official source said a few minutes ago that —

ALEX (*snaps off the radio. After a second*). Well, there's your peace.

EMILY. Does that mean they will give him the Sudeten?

ALEX. Yes, of course.

EMILY. I'm sorry for that. I thought maybe they'd find another way — Oh, I don't know what I thought. (*Sharply*) Why did you call it *my* peace? I didn't want anybody to suffer —

ALEX. No, of course. Nobody wants anybody to suffer. Maybe even that decadent trash in the society columns don't want it.

EMILY (*coming to him, tensely, angrily*). If it makes you feel better to make fun of those people, then do it. But don't tell yourself that having contempt for them puts you on the opposite side. Why are you attacking me, and unjustly, I think?

ALEX. I suppose I am being unjust. I think I even know why.

EMILY. Oh.

ALEX. Em, maybe it is a good day to get things straight—

EMILY (*quickly*). I think we've talked enough, Alex. Sometimes putting things in words makes them too definite, before one really means them to be. You're having a hard time. (*Looks toward the window*) It's as if a machine were running us all down and we didn't know where to go or how to get away from it. (*After a second*) Shall I call Sears for you? (*He nods. She moves toward the anteroom door*) All right, Jim. The Ambassador's ready. I'll have them send up food for you and Jim. Good night, darling.

ALEX (*softly*). Good night, Em.

(*Emily exits. As she exits the anteroom door opens and Sears comes in. He goes to the typewriter, sits down, waits.*)

SEARS (*after a second*). Shall I take it straight on the machine?

ALEX. No. Yes. Take it any way you want. (*Lies down on the couch. After a second*) "By the time this reaches you the results of the Munich meeting will be known. But there is no doubt here that the Sudeten will be given to Germany in return for the promise that it will be the last of Hitler's demands. That I do not believe." (*Pause*) "I have been told by Count Max von Stammer that the agreement will probably carry a second promise: Hitler will talk of making war at some time in the future on the Soviet Union. That I do not believe, although it has long been a rumor here. It is my earnest recommendation—" (*Alex gets up, moves toward the typewriter*) "It is my belief—"

SEARS. "Earnest recommendation."

ALEX. What the hell has one man got to do with history? There's something crazy about sitting here and thinking that what I say makes any difference. What do I know? What does anybody know? What the hell could they do at home, anyway? "Earnest belief that we should protest against any further German aggressions or against any further concessions to them. But I am convinced that Mr. Chamberlain is working in the interests of peace and his actions must not be judged too sharply. If he can save his sons and our sons from war—" (*Stops suddenly*) Take out that last. "It is difficult to give you a picture of a muddled situation. On the side of peace there are many selfish and unpatriotic men willing to sacrifice the honor of their country for their own private and dishonorable reasons. Those who deplore the Munich meeting — and I am one of them — many see it as a complete capitulation and as the beginning of a world war. But I think that is a harsh and unwarranted judgment based on inadequate facts. If a generation can be kept from war, if we can spare our sons —" (*Looks up at Sears as if he were frightened. Then, violently*) All right. Code it and send it as a cable.

(*The door opens and Moses comes in. He is in dinner clothes, but without a tie.*)

ALEX. How many drinks does it take to get drunk? I haven't been drunk in twenty years — (*He looks up at Moses, annoyed, goes on speaking to Sears*) Finish it and let's go out and get drunk and forget about it for a few hours.

MOSES. Really? Drunk? I shall wait up to see you. Ah, I shouldn't interrupt the masterwork. So the news is all in? The boys are going to Munich. Well, I'll be glad to sail home and get back to my chair in the library. We may be crooks at home, but we aren't elegant about it. I can't stand elegant crooks. They talk too pious for me.

ALEX (*wearily*). Whatever I feel about them, or you feel about them, maybe they're acting for the best. It can't be easy to throw your country into a war.

MOSES. I feel sorry for people who are as tolerant as you.

ALEX (*gets up, moves toward his room. Slowly, angrily*). Thank you. I find I'm sorry for myself. (*Exits.*)

MOSES (*to Sears*). Mrs. Hazen is making me go to the opera. I need a tie. I hate the opera. There's something insane about people opening their mouths very wide. What's the Ambassador saying in his report, Jim?

SEARS. I'm a confidential secretary, Mr. Taney.

MOSES. Good for you.

(*Sears exits. Moses goes to the desk, picks up the report, stands reading it. After a second, Sears reappears carrying a black tie. He stares at Moses.*)

SEARS. For God's sake, Mr. Taney. That's official. Since when do people read other people's —

MOSES. Since when do people read other people's mail? Since always.

SEARS. I — I —

(*Moses takes the tie, waves Sears aside, moves to Alex's door.*)

MOSES (*calls in*). Difficult world, eh, Alex? So many men doing so many strange things. All we can do is compromise. Compromise and compromise. There's nothing like a good compromise to cost a few million men their lives. Well, I'm glad I retired. I don't like having anything to do with the death of other people. Sad world, eh, Alex?

(*The door slams. Moses smiles.*)

Curtain

Scene 3.

SCENE: *The drawing room of the Hazen house about an hour after Scene 3 of Act One.*

AT RISE: *Cassie is sitting on the couch. Emily is sitting near her. Alex is standing near the fireplace. Moses is sitting on the terrace, staring into the room. Sam is standing in the doorway.*

CASSIE (*after a long silence*). Well, Emily. Are we finished?

EMILY. Do you remember one summer Father took us to Fontainebleau and left us for a week with Sophronia? We rented bicycles—

(*Sam closes the terrace doors, disappears.*)

EMILY. And the first hour we had them, I fell down that steep hill and the rest of the week Sophronia made us play on the porch of the hotel so she could watch us—(*Turns to Cassie, slowly*) Why did you go back to *that* hotel the weekend that you and Alex first slept together?

ALEX. For God's sake, Emily. If you'd wanted to know about me and Cassie, I would have told you. Did we have to go through all the fumblings, all the mistakes of years, to find it out? I don't want to look back on what was wrong—

CASSIE (*with great force*). None of us. None of us. It hasn't been a pretty picture. (*To Emily*) And not of you, either.

EMILY. That's true. I haven't liked myself for a long time now. (*To Alex*) I knew about you and Cassie. I've known about you and Cassie for—

CASSIE. Then why did you do this? And why tonight?

EMILY. Tonight has been coming for a long time. When I found Cassie was in Washington I knew that I'd have to finish it. Always it's been the three of us, all our lives. We can't go on this way.

CASSIE (*softly*). That's right. That's right.

EMILY (*with great emotion*). Let's get it straight, Cassie. Do it now. Not only for me. Not only for Alex. For yourself. It's time to tell the truth. Please, Cassie. Please.

CASSIE. I know, I know. (*Softly*) In a minute, Em. (*After a second she slowly gets up, goes to Alex, stands next to him. Emily walks across the room as if to move away from them*) You know, when you don't think you're bad, then you have a hard time seeing you did things for a bad reason, and you fool yourself that way. It gets all mixed up and — maybe the hardest thing in the world is to see yourself straight. The truth is, I was haunted by Emily, all my life. You always said I talked too much about Emily and asked too many questions. I was angry when Emily married you — I felt it had been done against me. I had no plans then to do anything about it but — I wanted to take you away from Emily; there it is. It sounds as if I didn't care about you, but I did and I do. But I would never have done anything about you if I hadn't wanted, for so many years, to punish Emily — (*Puts her hands to her face*) That's a lie. I did know it. I — (*Alex takes her hand from her face, holds her hand*) This got in the way of everything: my work, other people. Well, I guess you pay for small purposes, and for bitterness. I can't say I'm sorry. I can say I got mixed up and couldn't help myself. (*Pauses, turns slowly to look at Emily*) I've always envied you, Emily. But if I learned about myself tonight, I also learned about you. And you, Alex. It's too bad that all these years I saw us wrong — (*With great feeling*) Oh, I don't want to see another generation of people like us who didn't know what they were doing or why they did it. You know something? We were frivolous people. All three of us, and all those like us — (*After a second*) Good-bye, my dear.

ALEX (*softly*). Good-bye, Cassie. (*He takes her hand. She smiles. Then she moves to Emily.*)

CASSIE. Somebody told me once that when something's been

wrong with you and it gets cured, you miss it very much, at first. I'm going to miss you, in a funny kind of way.

EMILY. Good-bye, Cas. (*She presses Cassie's arm. Cassie moves swiftly into the hall, disappears. After a second, Emily speaks affectionately*) You feel bad. I'm sorry.

ALEX. *You* feel bad and *I'm* sorry and what good does it do? (*Pauses*) Em, unless you want to, I'd like not to talk about it for a long time and then we can if —

EMILY. I don't ever want to talk about it. We'll just see how it works out.

(*Alex moves to the terrace doors, opens them. Sam is walking on the terrace.*)

ALEX (*after a pause*). The doctor told you not to walk much. Why are you doing it?

SAM (*as he comes into the room*) It feels good. (*Moving to hall*) Well, good night. I —

(*Moses comes into the room.*)

ALEX. Sam, don't pretend nothing's happened tonight. If you have anything to say, say it.

SAM. There was a lot I didn't understand tonight, and a lot that isn't any of my business. But there is — Never mind. Some other night.

EMILY. We've seen a good deal of you the last few months, and your father and I sense that things are worrying you, many things, some of them about us. We didn't want you here tonight; it was hard for us to take. But when you wanted to stay, I thought we owed it to you. You're not doing us a favor now by sparing us what you think.

SAM (*to Alex*). All right. That day before Munich, in your report, did you really — (*Haltingly*) — recommend appeasement?

ALEX. I didn't know that word then but that's what it came down to.

EMILY. I had a lot to do with it, Sam.

SAM. I know.

MOSES (*moves toward Sam*). Look here. There've been many times when I haven't agreed with your father. But you mustn't blame him too much. What he or anybody else recommended wouldn't have made any difference.

SAM (*to Moses*). History is made by the masses of people. One man, or ten men, don't start the earthquakes and don't stop them either. Only hero worshipers and ignorant historians think they do. You wrote me that in a letter once. You said it was what Tolstoi meant in *War and Peace.*

MOSES. And I hope you still agree with it.

SAM. I do, I do. But you've made it an excuse to just sit back and watch; nothing anybody can do makes any difference, so why do it?

ALEX. That isn't what Tolstoi meant. It's only what your grandfather wanted him to mean. At least I never kidded myself that way.

SAM (*turns to Moses, smiles*). I think you mixed me up quite a lot, Grandpa. (*Quickly, as Moses is about to speak*) But one fine thing you taught me: that I belong here. I never liked that school in France or the one in Switzerland. I didn't like being there.

EMILY. You should have told us.

SAM. I wouldn't have known how to say it. You know, I never felt at home anyplace until I got in the army. I never came across my kind of people until I met Leck and Davis. I guess I never could have belonged to your world nor to Grandpa's, either — I still don't know where I do belong. I guess that's what's been worrying me. But with only one leg you've got to start thinking faster — (*Gets up quickly, as if he were startled by what he'd said. Emily gets up; Alex moves toward Sam; Moses turns sharply. Sam looks around as if he were panic-stricken. Then he speaks quickly*) I have to go back to the hospital tomorrow night. They've decided it's something called traumatic sarcoma of the bone and they can't avoid the amputation any longer. I was going to tell you tomorrow.

(*Alex starts to move toward Sam, stops, puts his hand over his face.*)

EMILY (*very softly*). Sam, Sam.

MOSES (*after a long pause*). I guess I'll go to bed. (*As he moves toward Sam, he begins to cry*) I hope you won't laugh at me but I would have given my life if I could have saved you any — (*Without looking at Sam, he touches his arm. Sam smiles, presses Moses' arm*) Well, son. (*He moves slowly to the hall door, exits.*)

SAM (*softly*). I'm sorry I told you tonight —

ALEX (*with great feeling*). Don't be sorry for us.

EMILY (*with great feeling*). It's your leg. It's your trouble and nobody else will ever know anything about it. (*Very loudly*)

We'll be walking all right. But you won't — (*She puts her hands over her face.*)

SAM (*sharply*). All right, Mother. (*To Alex*) I was lucky. Out of nine men, four got killed. (*Nervously, looking at Emily, talking as if he wanted to make conversation*) Did you tour around that part of Italy, Father? They call the place Bloody Basin now because it's a sort of basin between two hills and so many guys got killed there that we called it Bloody Basin. (*Speaks chattily, as if for Emily*) I liked Leck, you know, the boy I've told you about who used to be a baker in Jersey City. We'd sit around and talk: why we were in the war, and what was going to happen afterwards, and all of us pretended we knew more than we did. But not Leck. He never pretended to anything because he really knew a lot. Sometimes they'd ask me about you, Father, and I'd tell them all the things you'd done. Then one day one of them handed me a clipping. His mother had sent it to him. I don't think I ever in my life was really ashamed before. After all the fine talk I'd done about my family — God in Heaven, it did something to me — (*Stops abruptly.*)

EMILY. What is it?

SAM. Never mind.

ALEX (*tensely*). Say it, say it.

SAM (*takes a newspaper clipping from his pocket*). Well, this kid wanted to make fun of me, I guess. It's from one of those women columnists. It's about a dinner party that she gave. Kind of international people were there, she says. A French novelist, and a milliner who used to be a White Russian, and a movie actress, and a banker from Holland — (*Slowly begins to read from the clipping*) "It was, if I say so myself, a brilliant gathering. The last to arrive was the handsome Mrs. Alexander Hazen. Her husband, Alex Hazen, used to be our Ambassador to —"

EMILY. Your father wasn't at the dinner.

ALEX. That doesn't matter. Go on, Sam.

SAM (*reads*). "I looked around the table and I thought, 'Europe isn't dead. These people will go home someday and once more make it the charming, gay, carefree place I knew so well.' " So the soldier who gave me the clipping says, "Glad to be sitting in mud here, Sam, if it helps to make a charming world for your folks — " And Leck tells him to shut up. But when we're alone, Leck says to me, "Sam, that banker the piece talked about, he used to deal with the Germans before it got too hot. He's a no good guy. And the rest of those people, they're all old tripe who just live in our country now and pretend they are on the right side. When the trouble came in their countries they sold out their people and beat it quick, and now they make believe they're all for everything good. My God, Sam," he said, "if you come from that you better get away from it fast, because they made the shit we're sitting in."

ALEX. Sometimes I was wrong because I didn't know any better. And sometimes I was wrong because I had reasons I didn't know about. But —

SAM (*as if he hadn't heard him*). Well, for a couple of days I thought about what Leck said and I was going to tell him something. But that afternoon we went down to Bloody Basin and he got blown to pieces and I got wounded. How do you say you like your country? I like this place. (*With great passion*) And I don't want any more fancy fooling around with it. I don't want any more of Father's mistakes, for any reason, good or bad, or yours, Mother, because I think they do it harm. I was ashamed of that clipping. But I didn't really know why. I found out tonight. I am ashamed of both of you, and that's the truth. I don't want to be ashamed that way again. I don't like losing my leg, I don't like losing it at all. I'm scared — but everybody's welcome to it as long as it means a little something and helps to bring us out someplace. All right. I've said enough. Let's have a drink.

(*As Emily moves toward the table, Alex moves toward Sam.*)

Curtain

Another Part of the Forest

Gregory Zilboorg

Another Part of the Forest was first produced at the Fulton Theatre, New York City, on November 20, 1946, with the following cast:

(In the order of their appearance)

REGINA HUBBARD	PATRICIA NEAL
JOHN BAGTRY	BARTLETT ROBINSON
LAVINIA HUBBARD	MILDRED DUNNOCK
CORALEE	BEATRICE THOMPSON
MARCUS HUBBARD	PERCY WARAM
BENJAMIN HUBBARD	LEO GENN
JACOB	STANLEY GREENE
OSCAR HUBBARD	SCOTT MC KAY
SIMON ISHAM	OWEN COLL
BIRDIE BAGTRY	MARGARET PHILLIPS
HAROLD PENNIMAN	PAUL FORD
GILBERT JUGGER	GENE O'DONNELL
LAURETTE SINCEE	JEAN HAGEN

Produced by
KERMIT BLOOMGARDEN

Directed by
MISS HELLMAN

Settings designed by
JO MIELZINER

Scenes

Act One

A Sunday morning in June, 1880, the Alabama town of Bowden, the side portico of the Hubbard house.

Act Two

The next evening, the living room of the Hubbard house.

Act Three

Early the next morning, the side portico of the Hubbard house.

Throughout the play, in the stage directions, left and right mean audience's left and right.

Act One

SCENE: *The side portico of the Hubbard house, a Sunday morning in the summer of 1880 in the Alabama town of Bowden. The portico leads into the living room by back center French doors. On the right side of the portico is an old wing of the house. An exterior staircase to this wing leads to an upper porch off which are the bedrooms of the house and behind the staircase are the back gardens and the kitchen quarters. Under the second-story porch is a door leading to the dining room of the house, and a back door leading to the kitchen. The other side of the portico leads to a lawn which faces the town's main street. The main part of the house, built in the 1850's is Southern Greek. It is not a great mansion but it is a good house built by a man of taste from whom Marcus Hubbard bought it after the Civil War. There is not much furniture on the portico: two chairs and a table at one end, one comfortable chair and a table at the other end. Twin heads of Aristotle are on high pedestals. There is something too austere, too pretended Greek about the portico, as if it followed one man's eccentric taste and was not designed to be comfortable for anyone else.*

AT RISE: *Regina Hubbard, a handsome girl of twenty, is standing looking down at John Bagtry. Regina has on a pretty negligee thrown over a nightgown. Her hair is pinned high, as if she had pinned it up in a hurry. John Bagtry is a man of thirty-six with a sad, worn face. He is dressed in shabby riding shirt and Confederate Cavalry pants.*

REGINA (*after a long silence*). Where were you going?

JOHN (*he has a soft, easy voice*). And what you doing awake so early?

REGINA. Watching for you. But you tried not to hear me when I called you. I called you three times before you turned.

JOHN. I didn't think this was the place or the hour for us to be meeting together. (*Looks around nervously*) We'll be waking your folks. You out here in your wrapper! That would make a pretty scandal, honey —

REGINA (*impatiently*). Nobody's awake. And I don't care. Why didn't you —

JOHN (*quickly, gaily*). Oh, your Mama's up all right. I saw her and your Coralee going into nigger church. I bowed to her —

REGINA (*softly*). Why didn't you meet me last night?

JOHN (*after a second*). I couldn't. And I didn't know how to send word.

REGINA. Why couldn't you? Plantation folks giving balls again? Or fancy dress parties?

JOHN (*smiles*). I haven't been to a party since I was sixteen years old, Regina. The Bacons gave the last ball I ever remember, to celebrate the opening of the war and say goodbye to us —

REGINA. You've told me about it. Why couldn't you come last night?

JOHN. I couldn't leave Aunt Clara and Cousin Birdie. They wanted to sit out and talk after supper, and I couldn't.

REGINA (*slowly*). They wanted to talk? And so they made you stay?

JOHN. No, they didn't *make* me. They're lonely, Regina, and I'm not with them much, since you and I —

REGINA. Why should you be with them? When I want to meet you, I go and do it.

JOHN. Things are different with us. Everything is bad. This summer is the worst, I guess, in all the years. They are lonely —

REGINA. It's not the first time you didn't come. And you think I shouldn't be angry, and take you back the next day. It would be better if you lied to me where you were. This way it's just insulting to me. Better if you lied.

JOHN. Lie? Why would I lie?

REGINA. Better if you said you were with another woman. But not meeting me because of those two mummies —

JOHN (*softly*). I like them, Regina. And they don't go around raising their voices in anger on an early Sunday day.

REGINA. I don't want you to tell me about the differences in your family and mine.

JOHN. I've never done that. Never.

REGINA. That's what you always mean when you say I'm screaming.

JOHN. I mean no such thing. I said only that I stayed with Aunt Clara and Cousin Birdie last night. And I'll do it again. (*Desperately*) Look, honey, I didn't mean not to come to meet you. But I've lived on them for fifteen years. They're good to me. They share with me the little they got, and I don't give back anything to them —

REGINA (*tensely*). I'm getting sick of them. They've got to know about you and me someday soon. I think I'm going to sashay right up on that sacred plantation grass and tell them the war's over, the old times are finished, and so are they. I'm going to tell them to stay out of my way —

JOHN (*sharply*). They've never mentioned you, Regina.

REGINA. That's good breeding: to know about something and not talk about it?

JOHN. I don't know about good breeding.

REGINA. They think they do. Your Cousin Birdie's never done more than say good morning in all these years — when she knows full well who I am and who Papa is. Knows full well he could buy and sell Lionnet on the same morning, its cotton and its women with it —

JOHN. I would not like to hear anybody talk that way again. No, I wouldn't.

REGINA (*pleadingly, softly*). I'm sorry, I'm sorry, I'm sorry. I give you my apology. I'm sorry, darling.

JOHN. We shouldn't be —

REGINA (*takes his arm*). I'm never going to be mean again, never going to talk mean — Look, honey, I was mad about last night because I wanted to tell you about my plan. I've been thinking about it for months, and I've got Papa almost ready for it. But I can't tell it to you tonight because Papa makes me read to him every Sunday. But late tomorrow night, after Papa's music — it's over early — please, darling, tomorrow night — tomorrow night — (*She clings to him.*)

JOHN. Regina, we mustn't. We mustn't anymore. It's not right for you, honey, we're a scandal now. I'm no good for you. I'm too old, I'm —

REGINA (*clinging to him, impatient*). Why do you say that? A man at thirty-six talking that way? It comes from hanging around this town and your kinfolk.

JOHN. I was only good once — in a war. Some men shouldn't

ever come home from a war. You know something? It's the only time I was happy.

REGINA (*wearily*). Oh, don't tell me that again. You and your damn war. Wasn't it silly to be happy when you knew you were going to lose?

JOHN. You think it silly. Of course you do. In this house you couldn't think anything else. (*She draws back*) And now *I'm* sorry. That was most rude. It's late, honey.

REGINA (*quickly*). You haven't even asked me about my plan.

JOHN. I have a plan, too. I have a letter from Cod Carter. He's in Brazil. He's fighting down there, he says —

(*Lavinia Hubbard and Coralee appear from around the portico, as if coming from street. John stares at them, draws back nervously. Regina watches him, amused. Lavinia Hubbard is a woman of about fifty-eight, stooped, thin, delicate-looking. She has a sweet, high voice and a distracted, nervous way of speaking. Coralee is a sturdy Negro woman of about forty-five. She is holding a parasol over Lavinia. John steps forward. Coralee folds parasol, stares at Regina's costume, exits under porch to kitchen.*)

LAVINIA (*as if this were an ordinary morning scene*). Morning, Captain Bagtry. Been for a nice little stroll?

JOHN (*quickly*). Morning, Mrs. Hubbard. No, ma'am. I was just riding by and glimpsed Miss Regina —

LAVINIA. That's nice. Coralee and I been to our church. The colored folks said a prayer for me and a little song. It's my birthday.

JOHN. Congratulations, ma'am. I sure give you my good wishes.

LAVINIA. Thank you, sir. And later I'm going back to the second service. And I know a secret: they're going to give me a cake. Ain't that lovely of them, and me undeserving? (*Looks at him*) I always go to the colored church. I ain't been to a white church in years. Most people don't like my doing it, I'm sure, but I got my good reasons —

REGINA. All right, Mama.

LAVINIA. There's got to be one little thing you do that you want to do, all by yourself you want to do it.

REGINA (*sharply*). All right, Mama.

LAVINIA (*hurries toward the doors of the living room*). Oh. Sorry. (*At the door of living room, looks back at John*) I remember you and your cousins the day you left town for war.

I blew you a kiss. Course we were living in our little house then and you didn't know. But I blew you all a kiss.

JOHN (*pleased*). I'm glad to know it, ma'am. It was a great day. A hot day — You know something, ma'am? It was my birthday, too, that day. I was sixteen, and my cousins not much older. My birthday. Isn't that a coincidence, ma'am?

REGINA. Why?

JOHN (*lamely*). Because it's your Mama's birthday today.

LAVINIA. And you know something else, Captain Bagtry? Tomorrow's my wedding anniversary day. Your birthday, my birthday, and a wedding anniversary day.

REGINA (*very sharply*). All right, Mama.

(*Marcus Hubbard opens the door of his bedroom and appears on the upper porch. He is a strong looking man of sixty-three, with a soft, deep voice. He speaks slowly, as if he placed value on the words.*)

MARCUS. Who's speaking on the porch?

(*At the sound of his voice Lavinia hurries into the house. John draws back into the living-room doors. Regina comes forward.*)

REGINA. I'm down here, Papa.

MARCUS. Morning, darling. Waiting for me?

REGINA. Er. Mama's just been to church.

MARCUS. Of course — where else would she go? Wait. Have your first coffee with me. (*He exits into his room.*)

REGINA (*amused at John's nervous movements, takes his arm*). I want you to meet Papa. Not now. But soon.

JOHN. I know your Papa. I'm in and out of your store —

REGINA. I want you to come *here*. I guess no Bagtry ever been inside our house. But would your Aunt Clara and your Cousin Birdie allow you to come, do you reckon?

JOHN. Allow me? I didn't think that was the way it was. I thought your Papa didn't want anybody here —

REGINA. He doesn't. But I'll find a way. Will you meet me tomorrow night, same place? Darling, darling, please. Please. (*She pulls him toward her. He hesitates for a second. Then he takes her in his arms, kisses her with great feeling. She smiles.*) Meet me?

JOHN (*softly*). I always do. No matter what I say or think, I always do.

(*He kisses her again. Then he runs off. She stands for a minute staring after him. Then, from the street side of the lawn, Benjamin Hubbard appears. He is followed by Jacob carrying a small valise and three boxes. Jacob is a tall, thin Negro of about thirty. Ben is thirty-five: a powerful, calm man with a quiet manner.*)

REGINA (*amused*). Morning, Ben. Have a good trip?

BEN. Was that Bagtry?

REGINA. He said that was his name.

BEN. What you doing having men on the porch, you in your wrapper?

REGINA (*gaily*). Isn't it a pretty wrapper? Came from Chicago.

BEN (*pointing to boxes*). And so did these, on the mail train. They got your name on 'em. Belong to you?

REGINA (*giggling*). Writing can't lie. Specially writing in ink.

MARCUS (*reappears on balcony, calls down*). Coffee ready for me, darling?

REGINA (*gaily, smiling at Ben*). Going in to brew it myself, honey.

(*She disappears into house. Marcus comes forward on the porch, sees Ben and Jake.*)

MARCUS (*stares at Jake*). Jake, take the boxes in. (*Jake starts in*) And put Mr. Benjamin's valise out of your hand. (*Jake hesitates, looks puzzled. Ben stares up at Marcus. Then Jake puts valise down, exits*) How was the world of fashion, Benjamin?

BEN. I was only in it for twenty-four hours.

MARCUS. Ah. That isn't long enough.

BEN. You ordered me back.

MARCUS. What for?

BEN. The pleasure of it, I think.

MARCUS (*giggles*). Certainly. But what did I call the pleasure?

BEN. You said the books needed checking, and I was to be back to do them today.

MARCUS. Books? I wouldn't let you touch the books in my library, Benjamin. Certainly you know that.

BEN (*annoyed*). Books for the store. *Store. Bookkeeping. Accounts.*

MARCUS. Oh. But why today?

BEN. I don't know, Papa. I'd like to have stayed in Mobile. I had some business —

MARCUS. But I brought you back on a Sunday to look at store books. Now why did I do that? I must have had some reason. I'll think of it later. (*He looks down, realizes Ben isn't going to answer*) What business did you have, Ben?

BEN. I wanted to invest two thousand dollars in Birmingham

Coal, Incorporated. It will bring fifty thousand someday. There's coal there, and they're sending down men from the North with money for it — But I couldn't raise it. And you wouldn't lend it to me.

MARCUS. That why you went? That foolish old scheme of yours? I had hoped you went to Mobile for a lady.

BEN. No, sir. I have no lady.

MARCUS. I believe you. But certainly you went to the concert last night?

BEN. No, I didn't. I told you: I was trying to borrow the two thousand you wouldn't let me have.

MARCUS. Well, you must hear a good concert before you die. (*Starts into his room*) Carry in your own valise, son. It is not seemly for a man to load his goods on other men, black or white.

(*Ben looks up, half annoyed, half amused. He picks up his valise, starts toward door as Coralee appears, carrying breakfast tray. Lavinia follows her. Ben watches them as Coralee puts tray on table. Lavinia, knowing that Marcus is on the balcony, but not knowing whether she should speak to him, helps Coralee by aimlessly fussing about with the tray.*)

LAVINIA (*to Ben*). Morning, son.

BEN. Morning, Mama.

LAVINIA. Pleasant trip?

BEN. No, unsuccessful.

LAVINIA. That's good, I'm sure. I mean — Morning, Marcus.

MARCUS. Coralee. I'll be right down. Lavinia, send everybody else to the dining room for breakfast.

(*He disappears. Lavinia spills coffee.*)

CORALEE (*quickly*). All right, Miss Viney. No harm. Go on in and have your breakfast before there's trouble.

(*Lavinia goes into living room as Marcus comes downstairs carrying a book. He goes immediately to table. Coralee pours coffee.*)

MARCUS. Who is down for breakfast?

CORALEE. I don't know.

LAVINIA (*reappears in living-room doorway*). Oh, Marcus, Colonel Isham is calling. Can he come out?

MARCUS. If he is capable of walking.

(*Colonel Isham, a man of sixty-five appears in the doorway.*)

MARCUS. Colonel Isham.

ISHAM. You will forgive this too early visit?

MARCUS. You're in town for church?

ISHAM. I've come to see you. I was asked to come to see you.

MARCUS. To talk about bad cotton?

ISHAM. No, sir. I don't mix with a man's Sunday breakfast, to talk about cotton. I come to talk about your son Oscar.

MARCUS. Then you will need coffee.

ISHAM. Thank you, no. Two nights ago —

MARCUS. People like you don't drink coffee with people like me?

ISHAM. I've had coffee. Now, Mr. Hubbard —

MARCUS. Then come again when you haven't had it.

(*There is a pause. Slowly Isham comes to the table. Marcus smiles, pours a cup of coffee, hands it to Isham, who takes it and sits down.*)

ISHAM. I have come here for your sake, Mr. Hubbard. There is dangerous feeling up in my town this morning —

MARCUS. Colonel, Sunday is my day of study. I don't wish to sound rude but please say quickly what you have come about.

ISHAM. Mr. Hubbard, I'm too old to frighten.

MARCUS. And I should be a daring man to try it. You, one of our great heroes. Commanding the first Alabama troops at —

ISHAM. I am not interested in talking to you about the War Between the States, or about your personal war on the people of this state — Now, please listen to me. Two nights ago Sam Taylor in Roseville was badly beaten up. Last night fourteen people identified the night riders as the Cross boys, from over the line, and your son Oscar.

MARCUS (*shouts into the house*). Benjamin! Rope Oscar and bring him out here immediately. I told you fifteen years ago you were damn fools to let Klansmen ride around, carrying guns —

ISHAM. Were you frightened of their riding on you? I came here to tell you to make your son quit. He can thank me he's not swinging from a rope this minute. You have good reason to know there's not a man in this county wouldn't like to swing up anybody called Hubbard. I stopped my friends last night but I may not be able to stop them again. Tell him what patriots do is our business. But he's got no right to be riding down on anybody —

(*Ben, followed by Oscar, appears in the dining-room doorway. Oscar, a thin young man of about twenty-eight, looks frightened, decides to be cute.*)

OSCAR. *Rope* me out. I can stand up, Papa. Never felt my Saturday night liquor that bad —

MARCUS (*to Oscar*). Colonel Isham has just saved you from a lynching party. Should I thank him?

OSCAR (*terrified*). Lynching! What did — Colonel Isham — I —

ISHAM. I don't want to speak with you.

MARCUS. Who does?

OSCAR. But what did I —

MARCUS. Do I have to tell you that if you ever put on those robes again, or take a gun to any man — (*Takes roll of bills from his pocket, throws it to Benjamin*) Count out five hundred dollars, Benjamin.

OSCAR (*very nervous*). You mean Taylor? I wasn't riding with the Klan boys. No, I wasn't. I was thinking about it, but —

BEN. No, he couldn't have been with them. He took me to the Mobile train, and the train was late, so we sat talking. He couldn't have got up to Roseville.

ISHAM. You say you're willing to swear to that, Mr. Benjamin? You sure you're willing to go against fourteen people identifying your brother —?

BEN. Oh, Oscar looks like anybody.

MARCUS (*smiles*). Give the money to Colonel Isham, Benjamin. Go away, Oscar. (*Oscar exits through dining-room door*) Please use the money for Taylor.

ISHAM. We'll take care of him, Hubbard. Good day, sir.

MARCUS. You won't take care of him, because you can't. Learn to be poor, Isham, it has more dignity. Tell Taylor there will be a check each month. Tell him that my other son, Benjamin, wishes to make amends. Ben has a most charitable nature.

(*Isham hesitates, decides, takes the money, looks at it.*)

ISHAM. There is no need for so much. A hundred would be more proper.

MARCUS. Good day, Colonel.

(*Isham starts to speak, changes his mind, exits left toward street. There is a pause. Ben looks at Marcus, drops the roll of money on Marcus's table.*)

BEN (*smiles*). You didn't like my story about Oscar?

MARCUS. Not much. Very loyal of you, however.

BEN. I like it.

MARCUS. Good. It's yours. Keep it. You must have one of your usual involved reasons for wanting it.

BEN. Five hundred dollars is a lot of money to a man who allows himself six dollars for a trip to Mobile.

MARCUS. Perhaps you're stingy.

BEN. You can't be much else on a salary of twenty dollars a week.

MARCUS. Is that all I pay you? Ah, well, you'll be better off when I — if and when I die. But I may not die; did I tell you, Benjamin?

(*Regina, Oscar and Lavinia appear from the living room. Regina hurries to Marcus.*)

REGINA. Forgive me, darling. I forgot your coffee.

(*Oscar is carrying a cup of coffee and a roll. Lavinia, who never sees anything, bumps into him. Oscar turns on her angrily.*)

OSCAR. Goodness' sake, Mama. Watch where you going.

REGINA. Oscar's in a bad humor this morning. Oscar's got one of those faces shows everything.

LAVINIA (*to everybody — nobody pays any attention*). I'm sorry. I'm sure I didn't mean to —

MARCUS. Oscar has good reason for being in a bad humor. He owes me five hundred dollars.

(*Oscar's hand begins to shake on the cup. He rattles the spoon and saucer.*)

BEN. For God's sake sit down and stop rattling that cup.

OSCAR. Papa, you can't mean that — Ben told you where I was. I wasn't even —

MARCUS (*to Regina*). You look charming. New?

REGINA. No. But I *did* buy a few new dresses.

MARCUS. A few? I saw the boxes coming in.

OSCAR. Seven dresses. Seven, I counted them.

REGINA. Can you count up to seven? And more coming next week, Papa.

MARCUS. What are you going to do with them, honey?

REGINA (*hesitates, then gaily*). Could we go for a walk?

BEN. You buying these clothes out of your allowance?

REGINA (*laughs*). Aren't you silly? How could I? There's a fur piece and a muff that cost three hundred dollars alone. They're charming, Papa, wait till you see them —

OSCAR (*delighted at the diversion in the conversation*). You really gone crazy? Nobody's ever worn furs in this climate since old lady Somers put that bear rug around her and jumped out the porch.

REGINA. I won't jump out the porch.

BEN. I will have to okay the bills, so would you tell me how much you've spent?

REGINA. I don't know. I didn't even ask.

OSCAR (*shrilly*). Didn't even ask? Didn't even ask? You gone real crazy, acting like Miss Vanderbilt, whatever her name is — rich people up North don't act that way. They watch their money, and their fathers' money.

REGINA. Oh, that's not true. Those people in Chicago, just the other day, gave their daughter a hundred-thousand-dollar check for a trousseau —

BEN. A trousseau? So that's what you're buying? I saw Horace Giddens in Mobile last evening, and he was mighty disappointed you haven't answered his letter about coming up for another visit here.

OSCAR. Hey, he wouldn't be bad for you, Regina —

BEN. He's in love with you. That was obvious when he was here. It's good society, that family, and rich. Solid, quiet rich.

OSCAR. And you'd get to like him. A lot of people get married not liking each other. Then, after marriage, they still don't like each other much, I guess —

BEN. Are you still drunk?

LAVINIA (*comes to life*). A wedding? That would be nice. I hope you make your plans right quick, Regina, because —

MARCUS (*slowly*). What is all this, Regina?

LAVINIA. I didn't say anything. I was twisting my handkerchief —

REGINA. It's nothing, Papa, nothing. You know Ben. You know he wants me to marry money for him. I'm not even thinking about Giddens.

BEN. Certainly I want you to marry money. More than that — (*She wheels around to stare at him*) You're twenty years old. You ought to be settled down. You been worrying us. (*Pleased at the nervousness Regina is showing*) Isn't that so, Mama? Hasn't Regina been worrying you?

LAVINIA. I really don't know, son. I really couldn't say.

OSCAR. Well, I could say she's been worrying me. Many's the time I thought of taking action. Sashaying around as open as —

REGINA (*to Oscar*). Oh, shut up. (*To Marcus*) Papa. You can't blame me if Ben thinks up one of his plans to annoy you, and Oscar chimes in like he always does. I bought the clothes because I — because I want to take a little trip. That's all, Papa.

MARCUS. A trip?

REGINA. All right. I'll send back the dresses. I don't know what all this talk's about. (*Comes to him*) Spoiling your Sunday. Come on, darling. Let's take our lunch and go on a picnic, just you and me. We haven't done that in a long time.

MARCUS. No, not for a long time. (*To Ben*) Something amuses you?

BEN. Yes. You and Regina.

MARCUS. The two of you have contrived to give me a bad morning. (*To Oscar*) And you have cost me five hundred dollars. How much you drawing at the store?

OSCAR (*nervous but determined*). I was going to talk to you about that, Papa. I'm drawing sixteen a week. It ain't enough, Papa, because, well, I'm getting on and I want a little life of my own. I was going to ask you if you couldn't sort of make a little advance against a little raise —

MARCUS. You'll get eleven a week hereafter. Five dollars will go to repay me for the five hundred.

OSCAR. My God, Papa. You can't — Eleven a week! My God, Papa — That wasn't what I meant. You misunderstood me 'cause I wasn't talking clear. I wanted a little *raise,* not a —

MARCUS (*to Ben*). Put aside your plans for your sister's future. Spend with profit your time today going over the store books. (*Amused*) You'll find we are short of cash. Call in some cotton loans or mortgages. (*Giggles*) Then go to church.

LAVINIA (*delighted*). Want to come with me, Benjamin? I'm going to my church, because they're saying a prayer for my birthday. (*To Marcus*) It's my birthday, Marcus.

MARCUS. Congratulations, Lavinia.

LAVINIA. Thank you. (*Comes to Marcus*) We were going to talk today. You promised, Marcus —

MARCUS. I promised to talk? Talk about what?

LAVINIA (*amazed, worried*). Talk about what? You know, Marcus. You promised last year, on my last birthday. You said you were too busy that day, but this year you said —

MARCUS. I'm still busy, my dear. Now you run and tell Belle to make us up a fine picnic basket. (*To Regina*) And a good bottle of wine. I'll get it myself.

LAVINIA. But, Marcus, I been waiting since last year —

MARCUS. Get the lunch now. (*She hesitates, looks frightened, goes toward kitchen door. To Regina*) I'll bring my Aristotle. You'll read in English, I'll follow you in Greek. Shall we walk or drive?

REGINA (*smiling*). Let's walk. You get the wine and your books. I'll change my clothes — (*He goes into house. She stops to look at Ben, smiles*) You never going to learn, Ben. Been living with Papa for thirty-five years, and never going to learn.

OSCAR. Regina, you got a few hundred dollars to lend me? Wouldn't take me long to pay it back —

BEN. Learn what, honey?

OSCAR. Papa's sure hard on me. It's unnatural. If a stranger came in he'd think Papa didn't like me, his own son.

REGINA (*to Oscar*). You want some money? If you had any sense, you'd know how to get it: just tell Papa Ben don't want you to have it. You'll get it. (*To Ben*) You ain't smart for a man who wants to get somewhere. You should have figured out long ago that Papa's going to do just whatever you tell him not to do, unless *I* tell him to do it. (*Pats his shoulder*) Goodness gracious, that's been working for the whole twenty years I been on earth.

BEN. You are right, and you're smart. You must give me a full lecture on Papa someday; tell me why he's so good to you, how you manage, and so on.

REGINA (*laughs*). I'm busy now, taking him on a picnic.

BEN. Oh, not now. Too hot for lectures. We'll wait for a winter night. Before the fire; you'll talk and I'll listen. And I'll think many things, like how you used to be a beauty but at fifty years your face got worn and sour. Papa'll still be living, and he'll interrupt us, the way he does even now: he'll call from upstairs to have you come and put him to bed. And you'll get up to go, wondering how the years went by — (*Sharply*) Because, as you say, he's most devoted to you, and he's going to keep you right here with him, all his long life.

REGINA. He's not going to keep me here. And don't you think he is. I'm going away. I'm going to Chicago — (*Ben gets up, stares at her. Oscar looks up. She catches herself*) Oh, well, I guess you'd have to know. But I wanted him to promise before you began any interfering — I'm going for a trip, and a nice long trip. So you're wrong, honey.

BEN (*slowly*). He's consented to the trip?

REGINA (*giggles*). No. But he will by the time the picnic's over.

OSCAR. Chicago? You sure got Mama's blood. Little while now, and you're going to be just as crazy as Mama.

REGINA (*to Ben*). And the trip's going to cost a lot of money. I got letters from hotels, and I know. But you'll be working hard in the store and sending it on to me —

BEN. You could come home occasionally and go on another picnic. (*Comes up to her*) This time I don't think so. Papa didn't just get mad about you and Horace Giddens. Papa got mad about you and any man, or any place that ain't near him. I wouldn't like to be in the house, for example, the day he ever hears about you and Bagtry — (*Sharply*) Or is Bagtry going to Chicago?

REGINA (*tensely, softly*). Be still, Ben.

OSCAR. And everybody sure is gossiping. Laurette even heard it up in Roseville. I said there's nothing between you. I wouldn't believe it. But if ever I thought there was I'd ride over to Lionnet, carrying a gun. I sure would —

REGINA. And the day you do I'll be right behind you. It'll be your last ride, darling.

OSCAR. All right, all right, I was joking. Everybody's talking so wild today —

REGINA (*turns back to Ben*). Look, Ben, don't start anything. I'll get you in trouble if you do.

BEN. I believe you.

REGINA. Wish me luck. I got a hard day's work ahead. (*She goes up steps to upper porch and into her room.*)

OSCAR (*yawns*). Where she going?

BEN. Why did you beat up Sam Taylor?

OSCAR (*after a second, sulkily*). He's a no-good carpetbagger.

BEN (*wearily*). All right. Let's try again. Why did you beat up Sam Taylor?

OSCAR. He tried to make evening appointments with Laurette. He tried it twice. I told him the first time, and I told her too.

BEN. Is Laurette the little whore you've been courting?

OSCAR (*slowly, tensely*). Take that back, Ben. Take back that word. (*Ben laughs. Oscar advances toward him*) I don't let any man —

BEN. Now listen to me, you clown. You put away your gun and keep it away. If those fools in your Klan want to beat up niggers and carpetbaggers, you let 'em do it alone. You are not going to make this county dangerous to me, or dangerous to the business. We had a hard enough time making them forget Papa made too much money out of the war, and I ain't ever been sure they forgot it.

OSCAR. Course they haven't forgot it. Every time anybody has two drinks, or you call up another loan, there's plenty of talk, and plenty of hints I don't understand. If I had been old enough to fight in the war, you just bet I'd been right there, and not like you, bought off. I'm a Southerner. And when I see an old carpetbagger or upstart nigger, why, I feel like taking revenge.

BEN. For what? Because Papa got rich on them? (*Very sharply*) Put away that gun, sonny, and keep it put away, you hear me?

OSCAR (*frightened*). All right, all right. I want to thank you. I forgot. For saying that I was talking to you on the train. Thanks, Ben.

BEN. I wasn't lying for you. I was trying to save five hundred dollars.

OSCAR. Oh. Guess I should have known. (*Sighs*) How'm I ever going to pay it back? I'm in a mess. I — Ben, help me, will you? I'm deeply and sincerely in love.

BEN. Go give yourself a cooling sponge bath.

OSCAR. I want to marry Laurette. I was going to ask Papa to advance me a little money, so we could ship on down to New Orleans. He's going to leave money when he dies, plenty of it. I just want a little of mine now, and I'll go away —

BEN. He won't leave much. Not at this rate. He's spent forty thousand on nothing in the last six months.

OSCAR. My God, forty thousand and us slaving away in the store! And that's the way it's always going to be. I'm telling you: I'm taking Laurette and I'm going. Laurette's a fine girl. Hasn't looked at another man for a year.

BEN. Well, she better take them up again if she's going away with you.

(*Jake appears from the living room.*)

JAKE. Mr. Ben, a lady who says she doesn't want to say her name, she would like to speak with you. She's in the front hall, waiting.

BEN. Who? Who is it?

JAKE. Miss Birdie Bagtry.

BEN (*after a minute*). Wants to see *me?* (*Jake nods vigorously*) Bring her out.

(*Jake exits.*)

OSCAR. Now what do you think of that? What's she want to come here for? To see *you?* (*Giggles*) What you been up to, boy?

BEN. Maybe she's come to look at you. Didn't you tell me she once gave you a glass of lemonade?

OSCAR. Did she?

BEN. I don't know. I only know that you told me so.

OSCAR. Then I guess it happened.

BEN. That doesn't necessarily follow.

OSCAR. Well, it was true. I was pushing a lame horse past Lionnet. I was lame myself from something or other —

BEN. Laurette Sincee?

OSCAR. I told you once, stop that. I am in love with Laurette, deeply and sincerely.

BEN. Better you'd stayed for the lemonade and fallen in love with Lionnet's cotton fields.

OSCAR. Oh, this girl's supposed to be silly. Melty-mush-silly. (*Smiles*) That's what Laurette calls people like that. Melty-mush-silly.

BEN. She's witty, Laurette, eh? (*Jake appears in the living-room door followed by a slight, pretty, faded-looking girl of twenty. Her clothes are seedy, her face is worn and frightened*) Good morning, ma'am.

OSCAR (*with charm*). Well, hello there, Miss Birdie!

BIRDIE (*bows*). Mr. Benjamin. And morning to you, Mr. Oscar. (*Nervously*) We haven't seen you in many a long day. You haven't been hunting lately?

OSCAR. Oh, my time's been taken up with so many things, haven't had much chance.

BIRDIE. I know, you gentlemen in business. Please, you all, forgive my coming to your house, particularly on this day of privacy. I'll just take a few minutes and —

OSCAR. Excuse me, Miss Birdie. Hope you'll come again. (*He starts toward room.*)

BEN. Wait inside, Oscar. (*Oscar turns to stare at him, then shrugs, disappears. To Birdie*) Please.

BIRDIE (*sits down*). Yes, sir. Thank you.

BEN. Can I get you coffee?

BIRDIE. No, sir. Thank you. You see, I only got a few minutes before Mama begins wondering. I'm sorry to worry you here, but I couldn't come to see you in the store, because then the whole town would know, wouldn't they? And my Mama and Cousin John would just about — (*Giggles nervously*) Isn't that so, Mr. Benjamin?

BEN. Isn't what so?

BIRDIE. About knowing. I must apologize for disturbing — Oh, I said that before. It's not good manners to take up all your time saying how sorry I am to take up all your time, now is it? Oh, and I'm doing that again, too. Mama says I say everything in a question. Oh.

BEN. What do you want to talk to me about, Miss Birdie?

BIRDIE. Yes. (*Rises. Desperately*) Mr. Benjamin, we're having a mighty bad time. It can't go on. It got so bad that last month Mama didn't want to do it, but she did it, and it was just awful for her.

BEN (*after a second, politely*). Did what?

BIRDIE. Went all the way to Natchez, just to keep from going to our kinfolk in Mobile. Course they're so poor now they couldn't have done anything anyway, but just to keep them from knowing she went all the way to Natchez.

BEN. Really?

BIRDIE. Yes, sir, all the way by herself. But they said they just couldn't. They said they'd like to, for Papa's dead sake and Grandpapa's, but they just couldn't. Mama said she didn't want it for anybody's sake, not like that, not for those reasons — well, you know Mama, Mr. Benjamin.

BEN. No, I don't.

BIRDIE. Oh. Well, I don't blame her, although . . . No, when everything else is gone, Mama says you at least got pride left. She did it to save me, Mr. Benjamin, the trip, I mean. I was such a ninny, being born when I did, and growing up in the wrong time. I'm much younger than my brothers. I mean I am younger, if they were living. But it didn't do any good.

BEN. I beg your pardon?

BIRDIE. The trip to Natchez. It didn't do any good.

BEN. What kind of good didn't it do? (*She looks puzzled*) Why did your Mama make the trip?

BIRDIE. To borrow money on the cotton. Or on the land — (*Softly*) — or even to sell the pictures, or the silver. But they said they couldn't: that everybody was raising cotton that nobody else wanted. I don't understand that. I thought people always wanted cotton.

BEN. They will again in fifty years.

BIRDIE (*after a pause*). Oh. Fifty years. (*Smiles*) Well, I guess we can't wait that long. The truth is, we can't pay or support our people, Mr. Benjamin, we can't — Well, it's just killing my Mama. And my Cousin John, he wants to go away.

BEN. Where does he want to go?

BIRDIE. Away from here. (*Tense, frightened*) Forgive me. Would you, I mean your father and you, would you lend money on our cotton, or land, or —

BEN. Your Cousin John, does he want to go to New York or Chicago, perhaps? Has he spoken of going to Chicago?

BIRDIE. Oh dear, no. There's no war going on in Chicago.

BEN. I beg your pardon?

BIRDIE. A war. He wants to go back to war. Mama says she can even understand that. She says there isn't any life for our boys anymore.

BEN. I see. Where will Captain Bagtry find a war?

BIRDIE. There's something going on in Brazil, John says. He looked it up in the paper, and he's got a map.

BEN. Brazil. Is there a nice war going on in Brazil?

BIRDIE. Yes. I think so. (*Eagerly*) You see, that was one of the things Mama was going to do with the money. Pay all our people and give John the carfare. He can earn a lot in Brazil, he can be a general. (*Pauses, breathes*) Now about the loan, Mr. Benjamin —

BEN. You will inherit Lionnet?

BIRDIE. Me? Er. Yes. You mean if Mama were to — You mustn't believe those old stories. Mama's not so sick that a little good care and — (*Very embarrassed*) I'm sorry.

BEN. You don't want your Mama to know you've come here?

BIRDIE. Oh, no, no. She'd never forgive me, rather die —

BEN (*laughs*). To think you had come to us.

BIRDIE. I didn't mean that. I didn't —

BEN. You have not offended me, ma'am. I only ask because as I understand it you don't own Lionnet, your Mama does. But you don't want her to know about the loan. And so who would sign for it?

BIRDIE (*stares at him*). I would. Oh. You mean you can't sign for what you don't own. Oh. I see. I hadn't thought of that.

Oh. That's how much of a ninny I am. Forgive me for bothering you. I shouldn't have. I'm sorry I just ruined your Sunday morning. Good day, sir.

BEN (*goes to dining-room door*). Oscar, Oscar, I know you want to walk Miss Bagtry home.

BIRDIE. Oh, no. Thank you. I —

OSCAR (*calling, offstage*). I have an appointment. I'm late.

BIRDIE (*embarrassed*). Please, sir —

BEN (*to Birdie*). How much of a loan were you thinking about?

BIRDIE. Five thousand dollars. It would take that much to pay our people and buy seed and pay debts and — But I guess I was as foolish about that as —

BEN. You know, of course, that all loans from our company are made by my father. I only work for him. Yours is good cotton and good land. But you don't own it. That makes it hard. It's very unusual, but perhaps I could think of some way to accommodate you. A promise from you, in a letter —

BIRDIE (*delighted*). Oh. Oh. Of course, I'd make the promise.

BEN. Why don't you talk to my father yourself? I'll tell him what it's all about, and you come back this afternoon —

BIRDIE (*backing away*). Oh, no. I couldn't say all that today again. I just couldn't — (*Softly*) That's silly. Of course I could. What time will I come?

BEN. I have a pleasanter idea. Come tomorrow evening. Once a month my father has a music evening with musicians from Mobile to play on the violin, and flatter him. He's always in a good humor after his music. Come in then, Miss Birdie, and please invite Captain Bagtry to escort you.

BIRDIE. You really think there's any chance? Your Papa would — And my Mama wouldn't ever have to find out?

BEN. I will do my best for you before you come.

BIRDIE (*after a second, with determination*). Thank you very much. I will be most pleased to come. Imagine having a concert right in your own house! I just love music. (*Oscar appears in the door, stares angrily at Ben*) Thank you for your courtesy in offering to walk me back, Mr. Oscar. And thank you, Mr. Benjamin. (*Birdie smiles happily, moves quickly off.*)

OSCAR (*comes close to Ben, in an angry whisper*). What the hell's the matter with you? Bossing me around, ruining my day?

BEN (*softly*). Be nice to the girl. You hear me?

OSCAR. I'm taking her home. That's enough. Damned little ninny.

BEN. I was thinking of trying to do you a favor. I was thinking if something works right for me, I'd lend you the five hundred to pay Papa back.

OSCAR. Squee, Ben! If you only could. What would you be doing it for?

BEN. Because I want you to be nice to this girl. Flatter her, talk nice. She's kind of pretty.

OSCAR. Pretty? I can't stand 'em like that.

BEN. I know. Virtue in woman offends you. Now go on. Be charming. Five-hundred-possible-dollars' charming.

OSCAR. All right.

(*He runs off. After a minute Marcus, carrying three books and a bottle of wine, appears on the porch.*)

MARCUS (*reading*). "The customary branches of education number four. Reading and writing." You know *those,* Benjamin, I think. "Gymnastic exercise —" (*Marcus laughs*) "and music." Aristotle. *You* don't know any music, Benjamin.

BEN. I've been too busy, Papa.

MARCUS. At what?

BEN. Working my life away for you. Doing a lot of dirty jobs. And then watching you have a wild time throwing the money around. But when I ask you to lend me a little . . .

MARCUS. You're a free man, Benjamin. A free man. You don't like what I do, you don't stay with me. (*Holding up the book*) I do wish you would read a little Aristotle, take your mind off money.

(*Regina comes down the steps, in a new dress, carrying a parasol and a steamer rug.*)

BEN (*looks at her*). Oh. Before I forget. I invited Miss Birdie Bagtry and her cousin to come here tomorrow night.

MARCUS. To come here? What do you mean?

BEN. I thought you'd like having the quality folk here. Come here to beg a favor of you.

MARCUS (*stares at him, giggles*). You teasing me?

BEN. No. The girl just left here. She wants us to lend money on the cotton. Her Mama didn't know, and mustn't know. But Miss Birdie doesn't own the place —

MARCUS. Then what kind of nonsense is that?

BEN. Maybe it's not nonsense. Take a note from her. If she dies before her mother —

MARCUS. Who said anything about dying? You're very concerned with people dying, aren't you?

BEN (*laughs*). You hate that word. Her mother could get out of it legally, maybe, but I don't think she would. Anyway, the old lady is sick, and it's worth a chance. Make it a short loan, call it in a few years. They've wrecked the place and the money won't do 'em much good. I think the time would come when you'd own the plantation for almost nothing — (*Looks at Regina*) A loan would make them happy and make us money. Make the Bagtrys grateful to us —

REGINA (*softly*). Course I don't know anything about business, Papa, but could I say something, please? I've been kind of lonely here with nobody nice having much to do with us. I'd sort of like to know people of my own age, a girl my own age, I mean —

MARCUS (*to Ben*). How much does she want?

BEN. Ten thousand.

MARCUS. On Lionnet? Ten thousand is cheap. She's a fool.

BEN. Yes, I think she's a fool.

MARCUS (*giggles*). Well, the one thing I never doubted was your making a good business deal. Kind of cute of you to think of their coming here to get it, too. Bagtrys in this house, begging. Might be amusing for an hour.

REGINA (*quickly*). Can't invite 'em for an hour, Papa. And we've got to be nice to them. Otherwise I just wouldn't want to see him come unless we'd be awful nice and polite.

MARCUS. They'll think we're nice and polite for ten thousand.

REGINA (*laughs, in a high good humor*). I guess. But you be pleasant to them —

MARCUS. Why, Regina? Why are you so anxious?

REGINA. Papa, I told you. I been a little lonesome. No people my age ever coming here — I do think people like that sort of want to forgive you, and be nice to us —

MARCUS (*sharply*). Forgive me?

REGINA (*turns away, little-girl tearful*). I'm mighty sorry. What have I done? Just said I'd like to have a few people to listen to your old music. Is that so awful to want?

MARCUS (*quickly*). Come on, darling. (*Shouts*) Lavinia, *where* is the basket? Lavinia! Coralee! (*To Regina*) Come on now, honey. It's been a long time since you been willing to spend a Sunday with me. If I was sharp, I'm sorry. Don't you worry. I'll be charming to the visiting gentry.

BEN. Miss Birdie got a fear of asking you for the loan and of her cousin, John, knowing about it. Might be better if you just gave your consent, Papa, and didn't make her tell the story all over again. I can do the details.

(*Lavinia appears with a basket. Marcus takes it from her, peers in it.*)

MARCUS (to *Regina*). That's mighty nice-looking. We'll have a good lunch. (*To Ben*) I don't want to hear the woes of Lionnet and Mistress Birdie. Most certainly you will do the details. Be kind of pleasant owning Lionnet. It's a beautiful house. Very light in motive, very well conceived —

LAVINIA. You going now, Marcus? Marcus! You promised you'd talk to me. Today —

MARCUS. I'm talking to you, Lavinia.

LAVINIA. Last year this morning, you promised me it would be today —

MARCUS (*gently*). I'm going out now, Lavinia.

LAVINIA. I've fixed you a mighty nice lunch, Marcus, the way you like it. I boiled up some crabs right fast, and —

MARCUS. I'm sure. Thank you. (*He starts to move off.*)

LAVINIA (*comes running to him*). Please, Marcus, I won't take up five minutes. Or when you come back? When you come back, Marcus?

MARCUS. Another day, my dear.

LAVINIA. It can't be another day, Marcus. It was to be on my birthday, this year. When you sat right in that chair, and I brought my Bible and you swore —

MARCUS. Another day.

LAVINIA. It ought to be today. If you swear to a day, it's got to be that day — (*Very frightened*) Tomorrow then. Tomorrow wouldn't hurt so much, because tomorrow is just after today — I've *got* to go this week, because I had a letter from the Reverend —

REGINA. Oh, Mama. Are you talking that way again?

LAVINIA (*wildly*). Tomorrow, Marcus? Tomorrow, tomorrow.

MARCUS (*to Ben*). Ben, get Coralee.

LAVINIA. Tomorrow — (*Ben exits. She grabs Marcus's arm*) Promise me tomorrow, Marcus. Promise me. I'll go get my Bible and you promise me —

MARCUS. Stop that nonsense. Get hold of yourself. I've had enough of that! I want no more.

LAVINIA (*crying*). I'm not making any trouble. You know that, Marcus. Just promise me tomorrow.

MARCUS. Stop it! I've had enough. Try to act like you're not crazy. Get your self in hand. (*He exits.*)

REGINA (*as Coralee appears*). Never mind, Mama. Maybe you'll be coming away with me. Would you like that? There are lots of churches in Chicago —

CORALEE. All right, Miss Regina. Don't tease her now.

REGINA (*gaily, as she goes off*). I'm not teasing.

(*After a pause, Lavinia sits down.*)

LAVINIA. You ready?

CORALEE (*as if this had happened a thousand times before*). All right.

LAVINIA. He didn't say any of those things. He said he would speak with me sure thing — (*Her voice rises*) No man breaks a Bible promise, and you can't tell me they do. You know I got my correspondence with the Reverend. He wants me to come and I got my mission and my carfare. In his last letter, the Reverend said if I was coming I should come, or should write him and say I couldn't ever come. "Couldn't ever come —" Why did he write that?

CORALEE. I don't know.

LAVINIA. Your people are my people. I got to do a little humble service. I lived in sin these thirty-seven years, Coralee. (*Rocks herself*) Such sin I couldn't even tell you.

CORALEE. You told me.

LAVINIA. Now I got to finish with the sin. Now I got to do my mission. And I'll be — I'll do it nice, you know I will. I'll gather the little black children round, and I'll teach them good things. I'll teach them how to read and write, and sing the music notes and —

CORALEE (*wearily*). Oh, Miss Viney. Maybe it's just as well. Maybe they'd be scared of a white teacher coming among them.

LAVINIA (*after a pause*). Scared of me?

CORALEE (*wearily*). No, ma'am. You're right.

LAVINIA. Course they could have many a better teacher. I know mighty little, but I'm going to try to remember better. (*Quietly*) And the first thing I'm going to remember is to speak to Marcus tomorrow. Tomorrow. (*Turns pleadingly to Coralee*) I was silly to speak today. And I did it wrong. Anyway, he didn't say I *couldn't* go, he just said — (*Stops suddenly*) My goodness, it's such a little thing to want. Just to go back where you were born and help little colored children grow up knowing how to read books and — You'll be proud of me. I'll remember things to teach them. You remember things when you're happy. And I'm going to be happy. You get to be fifty-nine, you don't be happy then, well, you got to find it. I'm going to be a very happy, happy, happy, happy — I'm going, Coralee. (*She suddenly stops, looks down in her lap.*)

CORALEE. Nice and cool in your room. Want to lie down? (*Lavinia doesn't answer*) Want to play a little on the piano? Nobody's inside. (*No answer. She waits, then gently*) All right, if you don't want to. I tell you what. Come on in the kitchen and rest yourself with us.

(*Lavinia gets up, follows Coralee as she moves off.*)

Curtain

Act Two

SCENE: *The living room of the Hubbard house. This is the room we have seen from the French doors of the first act, and now we are looking at the room as if we were standing in the French doors of the portico. A large bay window is center stage, leading to a porch that faces the first-act portico. Right stage is a door leading to the dining room. Left stage is an open arch leading to the entrance hall and main staircase. The furniture is from the previous owner but Marcus has cleared the room of the ornaments and the ornamented. Right stage is a round table and three chairs. Left stage is a sofa and chair. Right, upstage, is a desk. Left, upstage, is a piano. Right, upstage, is a long table. Center of the room, before the columns of the porch, are a table and chairs. The room is simpler, more severe, than many rooms of the 1880's. A Greek vase, glass-enclosed, stands on a pedestal; a Greek statue sits on the table; Greek battle scenes are hung on the walls.*

AT RISE: *Ben and Oscar are sitting at table, stage right. They each have a glass of port and the port decanter is in front of them. Marcus, Penniman and Jugger are standing at a music stand, looking down at a music score. Penniman is a tall, fattish man. Jugger looks like everybody. Penniman looks up from the score, hums, drains his glass, looks at the empty glass, and crosses to Ben and Oscar. Marcus is intent on the score.*

PENNIMAN (*meaning the score*). Very interesting. Harmonically fresh, eh, Mr. Benjamin?

BEN. I know nothing of music.

JUGGER. People always sound so proud when they announce they know nothing of music.

PENNIMAN (*quickly, as Oscar fills his glass*). A fine port, and a mighty good supper. I always look forward to our evening here. I tell my wife Mrs. Hubbard is a rare housekeeper.

BEN. You like good port, Mr. Penniman?

PENNIMAN. Yes, sir, and don't trust the man who don't.

(*Oscar goes off into gales of laughter. This pleases Penniman and he claps Oscar on the shoulder. Marcus looks up, annoyed, taps bow on music stand. Penniman and Oscar stop laughing, Penniman winks at Oscar, carries his glass back to music stand. Jake comes from the hall entrance carrying two chairs, a lamp, and passes through to porch. Lavinia hurries in from the dining room. Her hair is mussy, her dress spotted. She looks around the room, smiles at everybody. When nobody notices her, she crosses to Marcus, leans over to examine the score, nods at what she reads.*)

LAVINIA. Oh, it's nice, Marcus. Just as nice as anybody could have. It's going to be a cold collation. Is that all right?

MARCUS (*who is in a good humor*). Yes, certainly. What's that?

LAVINIA. A cold collation? That's what you call food when you have guests. A cold collation.

PENNIMAN (*looks toward the dining room, delighted*). More food? After that fine supper —

LAVINIA. This is a special night. Guests. Isn't that pleasant? My, we haven't had guests — I don't think I remember the last time we had guests —

MARCUS. All right, Lavinia.

LAVINIA. There'll be a dish of crabs, of course. And a dish of crawfish boiled in white wine, the way Belle does. And a chicken salad, and a fine strong ham we've been saving. (*Stops*) Oh. I'm worrying you gentlemen —

PENNIMAN (*lifting his glass*). Worrying us? You, the honor of Rose County, and the redeemer of this family.

(*Jugger and Marcus look up sharply. Ben laughs. Marcus reaches over and takes Penniman's glass, carries it to table.*)

MARCUS. I am awaiting your opinion.

PENNIMAN (*who has the quick dignity of a man who has had too much port*). The judgment of music, like the inspiration for it, must come slow and measured, if it comes with truth.

OSCAR (*to Ben*). Talks like a Christmas tree, don't he?

LAVINIA. It's your third composition, isn't it, Marcus? Oh, I'm sure it's nice.

MARCUS. How would you know, Lavinia?

LAVINIA (*hurt*). I can read notes, Marcus. Why, I taught you how to read music. Don't you remember, Marcus? (*She goes toward Ben and Oscar*) I did. Yes, I did.

BEN (*amused*). Of course you did.

PENNIMAN (*hurriedly*). I would say this: It is done as the

Greeks might have imposed the violin upon the lute. (*Hums*) Right here. Close to Buxtehude — (*Inspiration*) Or, the Netherland Contrapuntalists. Excellent.

(*Oscar pours himself another port, Lavinia has wandered to the piano, mumbling to herself.*)

MARCUS (*very pleased, to* PENNIMAN). You like it?

PENNIMAN. I like it very much. And if you would allow us, I would like to introduce it in Mobile during the season. Play it first at the school, say, then, *possibly* —

MARCUS. That would make me very happy. And what do you think of it, Mr. Jugger?

JUGGER (*slowly*). Penniman speaks for me. He always does.

PENNIMAN (*quickly*). Come. We'll try it for you. I am most anxious to hear it. (*Points to Marcus's violin*) I daresay you know the solo part you have written for yourself?

MARCUS. Well, I — yes. I had hoped you would want to try it tonight. I — (*Jugger picks up his violin, starts for portico. Marcus turns to him*) Mr. Jugger. Would *you* like to try it now?

JUGGER (*turns, looks at Marcus, seems about to say something, changes his mind*). I would like to try.

PENNIMAN. But where *is* my cello? Goodness God —

JUGGER (*at door of portico*). It's out here. When will you learn that it's hard to mislay a cello? (*Penniman giggles, trips out to porch.*)

LAVINIA (*suddenly plays a few notes on the piano*). See? I told you, Marcus. *That's* it. I told you I could read music just as good as I used to —

MARCUS. Is there something disturbing you this evening, Lavinia?

(*Regina enters from the hall. She is dressed up, very handsome. They all turn to stare at her. She smiles, goes to Marcus.*)

MARCUS. You're a beautiful girl.

OSCAR. Looks like the decorated pig at the county fair.

REGINA (*wheels around for Marcus*). It's my Chicago dress. *One* of my Chicago dresses. (*Regina notices Lavinia*) Oh, Mama, it's late. Do go and get dressed.

LAVINIA. I'm dressed, Regina.

REGINA. You can't look like that. Put on a nice silk —

LAVINIA. I only have what I have —

REGINA. Put on your nice dress, Mama. It will do for tonight.

We must order you new things. You can't go to Chicago looking like a tired old country lady —

LAVINIA (*wheels around*). *Chicago?* I'm not going to Chicago. Where I'm going I don't need clothes or things of the world. I'm going to the poor, and it wouldn't be proper to parade in silk — Marcus! You tell Regina where I'm going. *Tell her where I'm going*. You tell her right now. You —

REGINA. All right, Mama. Now don't you fret. Go upstairs and get dressed up for the high-toned guests. (*She leads Lavinia to the hall*) Don't you worry now. Go on up, honey. Coralee's waiting for you. (*She comes back into room. To Marcus*) Whew! I'm sorry. I should have known. I hope she isn't going to act queer the rest of the evening. Well, don't let's worry. (*Gaily*) I'll see to everything. I'd better have a look in the kitchen, and more chairs — Let's have the very good champagne, Papa?

PENNIMAN (*from portico*). Mr. Hubbard —

MARCUS (*takes keys from his pocket, throws them to Ben*). Wine as good as Regina's dress. And count the bottles used. I don't want to find that Oscar has sold them again.

BEN (*to Regina*). So your picnic was successful? When do you leave for Chicago?

REGINA (*gaily*). In ten days, two weeks. Going to miss me?

BEN. Yes. Very much.

REGINA. (*calls into dining room as she exits*) Two more chairs, Jake —

OSCAR. Now just tell me how I'm going to get word to Laurette that I can't meet her till later tonight, just somebody tell me that.

MARCUS (*to Ben*). I told you to get the wine.

(*Ben looks at him, exits through dining-room door. Marcus goes to piano, looks through scores. Oscar moves nervously toward Marcus.*)

OSCAR (*desperately*). Papa, I'm in trouble. You see, I had an appointment with a lady from out of town, Roseville, I mean.

MARCUS. What were they doing?

OSCAR. Who?

MARCUS. Regina and Ben when they were standing together — (*Breaks off, turns away.*)

OSCAR. Oh, you know Ben. Always up to something. Yesterday,

trying to marry off Regina, tonight trying to press me on the Bagtry girl.

MARCUS. Oh, come. Ben's not a fool. You and a Bagtry is a comic idea.

OSCAR. I know, but Ben's figured they're so hard up for money they might even have me. It all fits in with this mortgage you're giving them, or something. He's got his eye on the cotton — (*Giggles*) And Ben's eye goes in a lot of directions, mostly around corners. It's true, Papa. He made me take the girl home yesterday —

MARCUS. The mortgage, and then the girl and you. Interesting man, Benjamin.

OSCAR (*pleadingly*). Papa, like I say. I've got a friend who's waiting for me right now. I want you to meet her. You see, I'm deeply and sincerely in love. Deeply and sincerely. She's a fine girl. But *Ben* cries her down. *Ben* don't want me to be happy.

MARCUS. Isn't that too bad. Your own brother. It's a shame.

OSCAR. Course she's of the lower classes, and that doesn't fit in with Ben's plans for us to marry money for him. But the lower classes don't matter to me; I always say it's not how people were born but what they are —

MARCUS. You always say that, eh? Well, some people are democrats by choice, and some by necessity. You, by necessity.

OSCAR. Could I go fetch her here — tonight? Could I, Papa?

MARCUS. What is this, a night at the circus?

OSCAR (*a last chance*). I think it would just about finish Mr. Ben to have a member of the lower classes, sort of, mixing with the gentry, here. I thought it would sort of, sort of amuse you, and well, you could meet her at the same time. Be a good joke on Ben, sort of —

MARCUS. Is this Laurette that, that little, er — little thing from Roseville you been steaming about?

OSCAR. She's not, Papa. Oh, maybe she was a little wild before I met her, but — She was left an orphan and she didn't know what else to do, starving and cold, friendless.

MARCUS. Oh God, shut up. (*Then laughs*) All right, go and get her, if you like. Er. Does she come dressed? I wouldn't like her here, er, unrobed.

OSCAR (*happy*). Aw, she's a fine woman, Papa, don't talk like that. And she loves music. She wants to learn just about everything — She admires you, Papa —

MARCUS. For what?

OSCAR. Well, just about, well, just for everything, I guess — (*Marcus makes a dismissive gesture, goes on porch as Regina comes into room. Oscar sees Regina, smiles*) I'll be back in a few minutes. Going across the square to get Laurette, bring her here.

REGINA (*starts toward him, as Ben comes in carrying champagne bottles*). Here? That girl — What's the matter with you? You're doing nothing of the kind. Come back here. You can't bring that —

OSCAR. Can't I? Well, just ask Papa. *He* wants her to meet my folks.

REGINA. Ben, stop him. He can't bring her here tonight — Stop him! (*But Oscar has disappeared*) Get him, Ben!

BEN. What am I supposed to do, shoot him? I'm too old to run down streets after men in love.

REGINA. He *can't* bring her here. You know what John will think. I saw him this afternoon: I had to beg him to come tonight. He doesn't know why Birdie wants him to come, but — Ben, he'll think we meant to do it, planned to insult them —

BEN. Yes, I'm sure he will.

(*The music on the porch begins.*)

REGINA. What's the matter with Papa? Why did he let Oscar —

BEN. *You're* going to learn someday about Papa. It's not as easy as you think, Regina. (*They stand looking toward the porch, listening to the music*) He gave those clowns five thousand last month for something they call their music school. Now that they are playing his composition he should be good for another five thousand —

REGINA (*softly, amazed*). Did he? Really? (*Shakes her head*) Well, anyway, he's promised me plenty for —

BEN. To marry Bagtry? Enough to support you the rest of your life, you and your husband? I'm taking a vacation the day he finds out about your marriage plans.

REGINA (*angrily, nervous*). I don't know what you're talking about. Marry — What are you saying — ? I — (*Turns to him*) Leave me alone, Ben. Leave me alone. Stop making trouble. If you dare say *anything* to Papa about John, I'll —

BEN (*sharply*). Don't threaten me. I'm sick of threats.

REGINA. You'll be much sicker of them if you — (*Then, softly*) Ben, don't. I'm in love with John.

BEN (*softly*). But he's not in love with you.

(*Lavinia comes into room, followed by Coralee who is pulling at her, trying to button her dress. Regina turns away from Ben.*)

LAVINIA. Don't bother with the lower buttons. (*Timidly*) Am I proper now, daughter? (*Regina doesn't answer her. Lavinia points out to porch, meaning the music*) You know, I've made myself cheer up. I know you were just teasing about Chicago, Regina, and I know full well I've never been good about teasing. What do people do now, curtsy or shake hands? I guess it's just about the first guests we had since the suspicion on your Papa.

REGINA. Please don't talk about any of that tonight. Don't talk at all about the war, or anything that happened. Please remember, Mama. Do you hear?

CORALEE (*quickly*). She won't. You all have been teasing her, and she's tired.

(*Jake comes in from the dining room carrying a tray of glasses and a punch bowl.*)

LAVINIA. Could I try the nice punch, Coralee?

CORALEE. You certainly can. (*Jake exits. Ben starts to the table. As if such courtesy were unusual, Coralee stares at him*) Thank you, Mr. Ben.

(CORALEE *exits. Ben pours three glasses of punch.*)

LAVINIA. Regina, when you don't frown you look like my Grandmama — (*As Ben brings her a glass of punch, and moves on to Regina*) — the one who taught me to read and write. And 'twas mighty unusual, a lady to know how to read and write, up in the piney woods.

BEN (*laughs*). Now, that's a safer subject, Mama. Tell the Bagtrys about our kinfolk in the piney woods. (*He lifts his glass to Regina*) To you, honey.

REGINA. And to you, *honey*.

(*On the porch the music comes to an end. Regina who has not, of course, been paying any attention, starts to applaud. She turns to Lavinia, indicates Marcus on porch.*)

LAVINIA. But I didn't hear it. I wasn't paying any attention.

(*Marcus comes into room.*)

REGINA. It's brilliant of you, Papa.

MARCUS. I'm glad you liked it. Come along. We're about to start — (*Laughs*) — the better-known classics.

BEN. Won't you wait for our guests?

MARCUS. Certainly not, I resent their thinking they can stroll in late on my music.

REGINA. You're right, darling. *We'll* come out.

(*Marcus goes to porch. Regina follows. Ben follows her. Lavinia puts down her glass, follows Ben. Regina and Ben sit down, Lavinia sits down. The musicians tune up. Marcus, Penniman, and Jugger begin to play a divertimento by Leopold Mozart, a trio for violin, viola, and cello. Then the hall door opens and closes. On the porch, Regina and Ben both turn, turn back again. After a second, Oscar appears in the living room pulling Laurette Sincee. Laurette is about twenty, pig-face cute, too fashionably dressed. She stands in the door, admiring the room.*)

LAURETTE. Squee!

OSCAR (*proud and excited*). Not bad, eh? (*Looks toward portico*) We got to talk soft.

LAURETTE. This *is* nice. You born here, Oskie?

OSCAR. No. Like I told you. Right after the war Papa bought — (*Giggles*) or something — this house from old man Reed. Like it?

LAURETTE. Squee. Who wouldn't?

OSCAR. Well, maybe, someday —

LAURETTE. Ah, go on, Oskie. Go on.

OSCAR. You just wait and see.

LAURETTE (*points to portico*). What's that?

OSCAR. What?

LAURETTE. The noise?

OSCAR. That's music, honey.

LAURETTE. Oh.

OSCAR. When you speak to Papa, tell him how much you like music. Tell him how fine he plays.

LAURETTE. What's he playing?

OSCAR. The violin.

LAURETTE. Ain't that a coincidence? I had a beau who said he played the violin. A Frenchman, much older than me. Had to leave his very own country.

OSCAR (*winces*). I don't like to hear about him, Laurette, him or any other men. I am deeply and sincerely in love with you.

LAURETTE (*pleasantly, but without much interest*). Are you really, Oskie?

OSCAR. Laurette, I'm going to ask Papa for a loan. Then we'll go on down to New Orleans. Would you, Laurette —

LAURETTE. You've asked me the same question for the last year, twenty times. But you never yet asked your Papa for the loan.

OSCAR. I've been waiting for the right opportunity. I want you to be my *wife,* honey. I am deeply and —

LAURETTE. We can't eat on deeply and sincerely.

OSCAR. No, I know. But this is the big night, don't you see? (*Happily*) I never thought he'd let you come here. And he's in a good humor about something. Now, darling, be very very — well, er. I tell you: you speak with him about what *he* likes. Tell him how much you think of music, not new music, mind you, but — and tell him how you stay awake reading.

LAURETTE. I've always been a reader. But I can't talk about it. What's there to say?

OSCAR. And he's fond of Mozart. Talk about Mozart.

LAURETTE. I can't do that.

OSCAR. Well, just try to please him. So much depends on it. We could have our own little place in New Orleans —

LAURETTE. What kind of place?

OSCAR. I'd find a job. You bet I would, and with you behind me to encourage and love me, with you to fight for, I'd forge ahead.

LAURETTE (*looks at him, puzzled*). Oh. Well, I'd certainly like to go to New Orleans. I know a girl there. She has an embroidery shop on Royal Street. I'm good at embroidery. It's what I always wanted to do. Did I ever tell you that? Always wanted to do embroidery.

OSCAR. Did you?

LAURETTE. Yep. (*Laughs — an old joke*) Instead of fancy whoring. I wanted to do fancy embroidery.

OSCAR (*loudly, in a hurt cry*). Don't, Laurette, don't talk that way! (*Ben and Regina, on the porch, look into room. Reginia coughs loudly*) We better go out now.

LAURETTE. Why did your Papa let me come tonight?

OSCAR. Don't let him worry you, honey. Just take it nice and easy. Pretend nobody knows anything about you, pretend you're just as good as them —

LAURETTE. *Pretend?* Pretend I'm as good as anybody called Hubbard? Why, my Pa died at Vicksburg. He didn't stay home bleeding the whole state of Alabama with money tricks, and suspected of worse. You think I been worried for that reason?

OSCAR (*desperately*). No, no. I — For God's sake don't talk like that —

LAURETTE. You may be the rich of this county, but everybody knows how. Why, the Frenchman, I used to sleep with, and his sister, the Countess. What you mean, boy, your folks — ?

OSCAR. I didn't mean anything bad. Haven't I just said I wanted to *marry* you? I think you're better than anybody.

LAURETTE. I'm not better than anybody, but I'm as good as piney wood crooks.

OSCAR (*puts his hand over her mouth, looks toward porch*). Stop, *please*. We've got to go outside. *Please* —

LAURETTE (*good-natured again*). Sometimes you bring out the worst in my nature, Oskie, and make me talk foolish. Squee, it's the truth — I am a little twitchy about coming here and meeting your folks. I ain't been in a place like this before. . . . (*Pats him*) All right, I'll be very good and nice. I would like to go to New Orleans.

(*Oscar takes her in his arms. The front bell rings, but they don't hear it.*)

OSCAR. Course you would, with me. You love me, honey? (*He leans down to kiss her.*) Tell me you love me.

LAURETTE. Now, Oskie, you know this ain't the place or the time for mush —

(*Ben rises at the sound of the bell. As Ben comes from the porch, Jake brings in the Bagtrys. As they enter, Oscar is kissing Laurette, she is giggling, trying to push him away. The Bagtrys stop in the doorway as they see the scene. Ben comes to meet them, crosses stage. As he passes Oscar and Laurette, he shoves Oscar.*)

BEN. Excuse me. (*As Laurette jumps away, Regina comes in from porch, tapping Lavinia on the arm as she comes. Ben speaks to Birdie*) My apologies.

(*Birdie smiles nervously. John stares at Laurette.*)

OSCAR. We were just, I was, we were —

REGINA (*sharply*). All right. (*Goes quickly to Birdie*) I am happy to have you here, Miss Birdie.

(*Birdie curtsies, puts out her hand, smiles warmly. Lavinia enters room.*)

JOHN (*bows to Regina, Ben, Oscar, then speaks to Laurette*). Hello, Laurette.

LAURETTE. Hello, John.

JOHN (*turns to Birdie*). Birdie, this is Miss Sincee.

LAURETTE. Finely, thank you.

(*Birdie bows.*)

LAVINIA (*hears Laurette speak and so hurries to her*). An honor to have you here, Miss Birdie —

REGINA (*sharply*). *This* is Miss Birdie, Mama.

LAVINIA. Oh. Sorry. I —

(*Oscar bumps into Lavinia, who is coming toward Birdie.*)

BIRDIE. I'm sorry we're late. I just couldn't seem to get dressed —

REGINA. Do come out now for the music.

(*They move out together. Lavinia speaks to Birdie.*)

LAVINIA. Come, ma'am. And you, Miss — (*Brightly, to Birdie*) Is the other lady your sister?

LAURETTE (*annoyed, shoves Oscar*). What's the matter with you?

OSCAR. Oh. Mama, this is Miss Laurette Sincee. She's a visitor in town.

LAVINIA. Who's she visiting?

BEN. Us.

(*Ben reaches the porch door, stands aside to let Lavinia pass him. She looks puzzled, passes on to porch. Laurette, Oscar, Regina, John, are now seated on the porch. Lavinia sits near them. Birdie and Ben stand for a minute listening to the music.*)

BIRDIE. Nice. To have a special night, just to play music — I've heard your father is a very cultured gentleman. Have you been able, did he, speak of the matter that I —

BEN. Yes. We will make the loan.

BIRDIE (*turns radiant — softly*). Oh, what fine news! You can't imagine how worried I've been. I am very grateful to you, sir —

BEN. You don't have to be. It is a good loan for Hubbard Company, or my father wouldn't be taking it. We'll meet tomorrow, you and I, and work out the details.

BIRDIE. Oh, you won't have any trouble with me, Mr. Ben.

BEN. You wanted five thousand dollars, Miss Birdie. I have asked my father to lend you ten thousand.

BIRDIE (*puzzled*). Oh. Mr. Ben, I don't need —

BEN. You can take five now, but if you should happen to need more, it will be there for you.

BIRDIE. But I won't need ten thousand dollars. No, indeed I won't. It's very kind of you, but —

BEN. You will only get five. I will keep the rest waiting for you. That's the way these things are done — (*Smiles*) — sometimes.

BIRDIE. But it's bad enough to owe five thousand, not less ten —

BEN. *You will only owe five.* Now don't worry about it. Will you take my advice now about something else? Don't speak to my father about the loan. It is all arranged. And he's a man of such culture, as you say, that talk of money would disturb him on his music night.

BIRDIE. Oh, of course. After all, it's a party, and as worried and pushing as I am, I wouldn't ever have talked business with him at a party.

BEN (*smiles down at her*). Good breeding is very useful. Thank you, Miss Birdie.

BIRDIE (*gently*). No, sir. It is I who must thank you.

(*He bows, stands aside, indicates porch. She moves to it, sits down. Ben stands in the doorway. The music continues. After a minute we see Oscar trying to move back into the room. He leans over, bends down, moves rapidly into room, passes Ben. Laurette turns and Oscar beckons to her to come into room.*)

OSCAR. Papa going to play all night? (*Crosses to get a drink.*) Laurette's getting restless, sitting there.

BEN. She's not accustomed to a sitting position? Have another drink. I got a feeling you're going to need it.

LAURETTE (*enters the room from the porch*). Squee. I don't like this punch. It don't mean anything.

BEN. Can I put in a little brandy? I think that would make it mean more.

(*Marcus appears on the porch, walks up the aisle of chairs. He bows to Birdie and to John, comes into room. Oscar rushes to get him a drink of punch.*)

OSCAR. Papa, this is Miss Sincee.

MARCUS. How do you do?

LAURETTE. Finely, thank you. (*Marcus stares at her. She becomes very nervous.*) I love music, Mr. Hubbard. I had an uncle who played. *He* taught me to love music.

OSCAR. Did he play the violin, like Papa?

LAURETTE. Er. Er. No. He had a little drum.

OSCAR. He liked Mozart. You told me, remember?

LAURETTE. Yeah. Sure did.

(*Regina and Birdie, followed by John and Lavinia, come in from the porch.*)

MARCUS. Sincee's uncle played Mozart on a little drum. Have you ever heard of that, Miss Bagtry?

BIRDIE. Oh. Well, *I* haven't, but I'm sure there must be such an arrangement.

MARCUS. That's very kind of you, to be so sure. Do you play any instrument, Miss Bagtry?

BIRDIE. Yes, sir. Not well. The piano.

MARCUS. Then you would oblige me — (*She smiles, moves toward the piano, quickly*) — some other night, very soon.

BIRDIE (*flustered*). Yes. Yes, sir.

OSCAR. It's a coincidence, ain't it, that Laurette's Papa liked Mozart?

REGINA (*to Laurette*). I thought it was your uncle? Was your Papa the same as your uncle?

LAURETTE. What do you mean? Mon père was on one side of my family, and mon oncle on the other.

BEN (*fills her glass from the brandy decanter*). Your family were French?

LAURETTE. No. I learned that from a French gentleman who came from France. I don't know where he is now. I liked him.

BEN. Perhaps we could locate him for you.

LAURETTE. No. He married money. I never blamed him. I figured, well —

BIRDIE (*to Marcus — making conversation*). John's been to Europe, you know.

MARCUS. I didn't know.

BIRDIE. Yes, he was. Just a few months before the war. Paris, France; London, England; St. Petersburg, Russia; Florence, Italy; Lake Como, Switzerland — John kept a book. Pictures and notes and menus — if the war hadn't come, and my Papa had lived, I would have gone to Europe. It was planned for me to study watercolor.

MARCUS. Watercolor?

BIRDIE. Small watercolor. I like small watercolor.

MARCUS. Is that different from large watercolor?

LAURETTE (*belligerently*). She means she likes small watercolor. What's the matter with that?

BIRDIE (*smiles at her*). Yes. (*To Marcus*) You've been to Europe, Mr. Hubbard?

MARCUS. No, but I'm going. Might even settle down there. Yes, Regina?

REGINA (*looks at John*). Maybe someday, Papa. Chicago first.

MARCUS. Of course, we'll take our residence in Greece, but someplace gayer, for Regina, at first. Perhaps you'd advise us, Captain Bagtry?

JOHN. I'd like to, sir. But I have no memory of Europe.

MARCUS (*turns elaborately in his chair*). Something unpleasant took it from your mind?

JOHN. No, sir. I just don't remember. It's as if I had never been there.

MARCUS. Amazing to forget Europe. Does anything stay in your memory?

JOHN. The war.

REGINA. Only the war?

LAVINIA (*to John, motherly*). Well, I just bet. That's natural: you rode off so young.

JOHN (*turns to her*). Yes, ma'am. I can't remember the years before, and the years after have just passed like a wasted day. But the morning I rode off, and for three years, three months, and eight days after, well, I guess I remember every soldier, every gun, every meal, even every dream I had at night —

(*Ben is pouring Laurette another drink. Oscar is trying to keep her from having it. She pushes Oscar's hand.*)

LAURETTE. I wouldn't ever name a boy Oscar. It's silly.

REGINA. Well?

(*Marcus and Ben laugh. The others look embarrassed. Oscar makes an angry move, decides not to speak.*)

LAVINIA. I can't remember why we chose the name. Can you, Marcus?

MARCUS. Your father's name was Oscar.

LAVINIA (*worried*). Oh, goodness, yes.

BIRDIE (*embarrassed, speaks quickly*). John's just wonderful about the war, Mr. Hubbard. Just as good as having a history book. He was everywhere: Vicksburg, Chattanooga, Atlanta.

MARCUS. What now seems to you the most important of your battles, Captain Bagtry?

JOHN. I don't know. But there's no need for us to talk about the war, sir.

MARCUS. Oh, I'm interested. I know more of the Greek wars than I do of our own.

LAURETTE. Bet you anything there's a good reason for that. There's a good reason for everything in this vale of tears.

(*Marcus turns to stare at her.*)

BIRDIE. John, Mr. Hubbard says he's interested. Bet he'd like to hear about Vicksburg, just the way you always tell it to Mamma and me.

(*Jake appears at the door.*)

JAKE. Supper's laid out, waiting.

MARCUS (*to John*). People remember what made them happy, and you were happy in the war.

JOHN. Yes, sir. I was happy. I thought we would win.

MARCUS. I never did. Never, from the first foolish talk to the last foolish day. (*John turns away*) I have disturbed you. I'm most sorry.

BIRDIE. Oh, John doesn't mind. He means — well, you see, it's hard for us to understand anybody who thought we'd lose —

JOHN (*sharply*). It's still hard for a soldier to understand.

BIRDIE (*quickly*). John means once a soldier, always a soldier. He wants to go to Brazil right now. Of course you know, Mr. Hubbard, the radical people down there are trying to abolish slavery, and ruin the country. John wants to fight for his ideals.

MARCUS. Why don't you choose the other side? Every man needs to win once in his life.

JOHN. I don't like that way of saying it. I don't fight for slavery, I fight for a way of life.

MARCUS. Supper, Captain. (*Turns, calls to the porch*) Put away the music, gentlemen, and have a little more to eat. (*Turns to Regina*) What is disturbing you, Regina?

(*Lavinia, Birdie, Oscar, and Laurette exit to dining room.*)

REGINA. Nothing.

(*Ben exits.*)

MARCUS (*looks at John*). You disapprove of me, Captain?

JOHN. I am in your house, sir, and you forced me into this kind of talk.

(*Penniman and Jugger come through the room, go into the dining room.*)

MARCUS. Well, I disapprove of you. Your people deserved to lose their war and their world. It was a backward world, getting in the way of history. Appalling that you still don't realize it.

REGINA (*angrily*). Papa, I didn't ask John here to listen to you lecture and be nasty and insulting.

MARCUS. *You* asked him here? You asked *John?* (*Sharply*) Come in to supper, Regina.

REGINA. When I'm ready, Papa. (*Marcus looks at her, hesitates for a second, then goes into dining room. There is a pause. She goes to John*) I am so sorry.

JOHN. Why should you be sorry? It's the way you feel, too.

REGINA (*impatiently*). All that damn war nonsense — Don't worry about Papa. I'll take care of him. You didn't give me a chance to tell you about Chicago —

JOHN. You didn't give me a chance to tell you about Brazil.

REGINA. Will you stop that silly joke —

JOHN. It may not be a joke. Birdie has a plan. She won't tell me about it. Anyway, she says there's going to be money to run Lionnet and enough for me to borrow a little. I'll go on down to Brazil right away. Cod Carter says there's no trick in getting a commission with good pay. The planters there are looking for Confederate officers. I want to be with fighting men again. I'm lonely for them.

REGINA. Now you stop frightening me. I'm going to Chicago, and a month later you're coming and we'll get married. When Papa finds out he'll have a fit. Then we'll come on home for a while, and I'll talk him out of his fit —

JOHN (*gently*). Now you're joking. Don't talk silly, honey.

REGINA. You don't want to come with me? You don't want to marry me?

JOHN (*after a second*). You don't ask that seriously.

REGINA. Answer me, please.

JOHN. No. I don't. I never said I did. (*Comes to her*) I don't want to talk this way, but I don't want to lie, either. Honey, I like you so much, but — I shouldn't have let us get like this. You're not in love with me. I'm no good for you —

REGINA. I am in love with you. I've never loved before, and I won't love again.

JOHN. My darling child, everybody thinks that, the first time.

You're a lonely girl and I'm the first man you've liked. You can have anybody you want —

REGINA. John. Come away with me. We'll be alone. And after a while, if you still don't want me, then — (*Softly*) I've never pleaded for anything in my life before. I might hold it against you.

JOHN. Oh, Regina, don't speak of pleading. You go away. By the time you come back, you'll be in love with somebody else, and I'll be gone.

REGINA (*stares at him*). Where did you say Miss Birdie was getting this money, this money for you to travel with?

JOHN. I don't know where: she won't tell me. But she says we'll have five thousand dollars this week.

REGINA. Five thousand?

JOHN (*nods*). I'd guess she's arranged something about the Gilbert Stuart or the West. We haven't anything but the portraits —

REGINA. Is that what you'd guess? Well, I'd guess different. So she's planning to get you away from me?

JOHN. Nobody's *planning* anything. Oh, look, honey. This isn't any good. We'll go home now —

REGINA (*quickly, looking toward dining room*). Papa's coming. Please go in to supper now. It will be bad for me if you make any fuss or left now — We'll talk tomorrow. I love you. Go in to supper.

(*Marcus appears in the dining-room door.*)

JOHN (*who has his back to the door*). I'm sorry, honey, if — (*He turns, moves across room, passes Marcus in the doorway, disappears into the dining room.*)

(*Marcus stares at Regina; she does not look at him.*)

MARCUS. Who is sillier, who is more dead, the captain or his cousin? You have a reason for not joining us at supper?

REGINA. I wanted to talk to — to Captain Bagtry.

MARCUS. Can he talk of anything but war?

REGINA. Have you agreed to make Ben's loan on Lionnet?

MARCUS. Ben's loan? Of course I'll make it. It is good for me, and bad for them. Got nothing to do with Ben.

REGINA. No? Have you asked yourself why Ben wants it so much?

MARCUS. I am not interested in Ben's motives. As long as they benefit me, he is welcome to them.

REGINA. How much money did he say Miss Birdie had asked for?

MARCUS. Ten thousand. (*Regina smiles*) Why does this interest you?

REGINA. Don't make the loan, Papa. I don't like the girl. I think she's come here tonight to make fun of us. She's snubbing all of us, laughing up her sleeve. Why should you pay her to do it?

MARCUS. That's not true and I don't think you think it is. You're lying to me about something. That hurts me. Tell me why you were talking to that man, why he called you honey —

REGINA (*carefully*). Ben is sometimes smarter than you are, and you are so sure he isn't, that you get careless about him. Bagtry doesn't know about *your* loan on Lionnet, but the girl told him she was getting five thousand dollars this week. *Five thousand dollars, not ten.* I'd like to bet the extra five is meant for Ben to keep. (*Carefully*) You're getting older, Papa, and maybe you're getting tired and don't think as fast. I guess that happens to everybody. You'll have to start watching Ben even more —

MARCUS (*sharply*). All right, Regina.

(*Penniman and Jugger come in from the dining room. They stand awkwardly, not knowing what to do. Regina goes into dining room.*)

PENNIMAN (*hesitates*). Shall we — would you like us to continue the music?

MARCUS. As soon as you have finished overeating.

(*Penniman coughs, embarrassed. Jugger starts forward angrily, then stops, follows Penniman out to the porch. Lavinia comes in from the dining room.*)

LAVINIA. I think that Miss Laurette has a touch of heart trouble. I asked the poor child what she was doing for it. She said she was trying to see if good, strong drinks would help. I've never heard that, although Ben says it's a good cure. She's a nice little thing.

(*Laurette, followed by Oscar, comes into the room. She is steady, but the liquor has blinded her a little, and she bumps into things. Oscar follows her, very nervous, staring at Marcus. Laurette finds herself near the piano. She strikes a note. Pleased, she presses her right hand on the keyboard. Delighted, she presses both hands. Oscar jumps toward her.*)

LAURETTE. Hello . . . I never had opportunities . . . (*Oscar grabs both her hands, she pulls them away, pounds again, grins, indicates Marcus*) Your Papa likes music.

MARCUS (*to Oscar*). Is there any effective way of stopping that?

(*Laurette throws off Oscar's hands, moves to Marcus.*)

LAURETTE. Oskie says he wants to marry little old Laurette.

MARCUS. Does little old Laurette think that fortunate?

LAURETTE (*laughs — puts her hand through his arm*). Sometimes yes, sometimes no. We're going on down to New Orleans.

(*Ben and Birdie come in from the dining room.*)

MARCUS (*takes Laurette's hand from his arm*). I have a nervous dislike of being touched.

LAURETTE. Oh, sure. Me, too. Can't stand people pressing me unless I know about it, I mean. (*Glares at Oscar*) Don't you ever press me, Oskie, unless I know about it.

MARCUS. That reminds me. I'm told you work for a living. That is good: Oscar is not a rich man.

LAURETTE. Rich? How could he be, on that stinking slave salary you pay him? That's why you're sure to repent and help us, Oskie says. When you die you're going to leave it to him anyway, so why not now, Oskie says.

MARCUS (*softly*). Oscar is a liar. Always has been. (*Birdie moves toward porch*) And he steals a little. Nothing much, not enough to be respectable. But you know all that, of course.

LAVINIA. Oh, Marcus. (*To Birdie*) My husband makes little jokes. All the time —

OSCAR. It's not true. It's just not true —

MARCUS (*to Birdie*). Miss Bagtry, don't you find that people always think you're joking when you speak the truth in a soft voice?

BIRDIE (*very embarrassed*). No, sir. I —

MARCUS (*to Laurette*). If you want him, Miss Laurette, do have him.

OSCAR (*with dignity*). Come on, Laurette. I'll settle this later.

(*Marcus laughs.*)

LAURETTE. Well, I'll just about say you will. A Papa talking about his son! No animal would talk about their own son that way. I heard tales about you ever since I was born, but —

OSCAR (*frantic*). Come on, Laurette.

LAURETTE. You old bastard.

LAVINIA (*To Laurette*). Dear child —

LAURETTE. Everybody in this country knows how you got rich, bringing in salt and making poor, dying people give up everything for it. Right in the middle of the war, men dying for you, and you making their kinfolk give you all their goods and money — and I heard how they suspected you of worse, and you only just got out of a hanging rope. (*Points to Oscar*) Why, the first night he slept with me, I didn't even want to speak to him because of you and your doings. My uncle used to tell me about —

BEN. Go on, Oscar. Get out.

(*John and Regina come in from dining room.*)

MARCUS (*to Oscar*). Take that girl out of here. Then come back.

(*Oscar stares at him, starts to speak, changes his mind. Then he hurries to Laurette, takes her arm, moves her out. John crosses to Birdie.*)

LAVINIA (*in an odd tone*). Why, Marcus. The girl only told the truth. Salt is just a word, it's in the Bible quite a lot. And that other matter, why, death, is also just a word. And —

MARCUS. You grow daring, Lavinia. (*Moves toward her*) Now stop that prattling or go to your room —

BEN (*moves in front of him*). We have guests.

JOHN (*takes Birdie's arm*). Good night and thank you, Mrs. Hubbard. (*To others*) Good night.

MARCUS. You came to beg a favor, and you stayed to be amused. Good night.

BIRDIE (*scared*). Mr. Hubbard, please . . .

JOHN. Came to ask a favor? From you? Who in this county would be so dishonored? If you were not an old man, Mr. Hubbard, I —

MARCUS. There is never so great a hero as the man who fought on a losing side.

BIRDIE (*to John, desperate*). Stop it, John. Go outside. Wait for me in the carriage.

JOHN. I don't want you here.

BIRDIE. I want to stay for a few minutes. Please go outside. *Please. Please.*

(*He stares at her, then he turns, moves quickly out of the room. Marcus is watching Regina. Regina looks at Marcus, then turns and moves quickly after John. Marcus wheels around as if to stop Regina.*)

BIRDIE. Mr. Hubbard, I am sorry. John is upset. You know that his twin brother was killed that night in the massacre, and any mention of it —

MARCUS (*sharply*). What night do you speak of, Miss Birdie, and what massacre?

BIRDIE (*desperately*). Oh, I don't know. I — I'm just so sorry it has been unpleasant. I was hoping we could all be nice friends. Your family and mine —

MARCUS. Your mother hasn't bowed to me in the forty years I've lived in this town. Does she wish to be my nice friend now?

BIRDIE (*desperate*). Mama is old-fashioned. I'll speak to her and after a bit — (*Pauses, looks down*) Oh. I've said the wrong thing again. I don't know how to — (*Turns to him, simply*) I guess I just better say it simple, the way it comes to me. I didn't only come tonight for the loan. I *wanted* to come. I was frightened, of course, but, well, it was a big holiday for me, and I tried to get all dressed up in Mama's old things, and that was why we were late because I haven't had a new dress, since — and I've never had a party dress since I was four years old, and I had to get the dress without Mama's knowing why or where we were going, and I had to sew —

MARCUS. I have bad news for you: I have decided not to make the loan.

(*Birdie draws back, turns to Ben, starts to speak, puts her hands to her face.*)

BEN (*slowly*). Why? Why? You said yourself —

BIRDIE. Oh, please, Mr. Hubbard. Please. I went around all day telling our people they would be paid and — I'll give more, whatever you want —

MARCUS. That is unjust of you. I am not bargaining.

BEN (*to Marcus*). I want to know why you have changed your mind.

MARCUS. I will tell you, in time. (*To Birdie*) I am sorry to disappoint you. Please come another night, without a motive, just for the music.

BIRDIE. Yes, I had a motive. Why shouldn't I have? It was why I was asked here — Oh, I mustn't talk proud. I have no right to. Look, Mr. Hubbard, I'll do anything. I'm sure you like good pictures: we have a Stuart and a West, and a little silver left. Couldn't I give — couldn't I bring them to you —

MARCUS (*gently*). Miss Birdie, Miss Birdie, please spare us both.

BIRDIE. I was going to use the first money to buy molasses and sugar. All that land and cotton and we're starving. It sounds crazy, to need even molasses —

MARCUS. Everybody with cotton is starving.

BIRDIE (*angrily*). That isn't what I mean. I mean starving. (*She looks up at him, her voice changes, sighs*) I should have known I couldn't do anything right. I'm sorry to have told you such things about us. You lose your manners when you're poor. (*Goes to Lavinia*) Thank you, ma'am.

LAVINIA (*smiles gently, takes her hand*). Good night, child. You ride over and see me, or come down by the river and we'll read together.

BIRDIE (*smiles, crosses to Ben*). Thank you, Mr. Ben. I know you acted as my good friend.

MARCUS (*laughs*). Good night.

(*She nods, runs out.*)

LAVINIA (*after a second*). Goodness, Marcus. Couldn't you have helped — it's pig mean, being poor. Takes away your dignity.

MARCUS. That's correct, Lavinia. And a good reason for staying rich.

PENNIMAN'S VOICE. We're waiting for you, Mr. Hubbard.

MARCUS. That will be all for tonight.

(*Regina appears from the hall.*)

REGINA (*to Marcus*). You have insulted them and made enemies of them.

MARCUS. Why are you so disturbed about the Bagtrys? (*Ben laughs*) You are amused?

BEN. Yes. I am amused.

MARCUS. (*Penniman and Jugger appear carrying their instruments. Marcus turns to them*). The Mozart was carelessly performed. The carriage is waiting to take you to the station. Good night.

JUGGER. "Carelessly performed." What do you know about music? Nothing, and we're just here to pretend you do. Glad to make a little money once a month — (*Angrily*) I won't do it any more, do you hear me?

MARCUS. Good night.

(*Jugger moves quickly out. Penniman comes forward, nervously.*)

PENNIMAN. He didn't mean — Gil is tired — Why, we're just

as happy to come here — (*No answer. Desperately*) Well, see you next month, sir. Just as usual. Huh?

(*When Marcus doesn't answer, Penniman sighs, exits as Oscar appears from porch.*)

OSCAR (*rushes toward Ben*). Trying to ruin my life, are you? Pouring liquor down her. Come on outside and fight it out like a man. I'll beat you up for it, the way you deserve —

LAVINIA (*as if she had come out of a doze*). Oh, goodness! The blood of brothers. (*To Ben*) You in trouble, Ben? (*Sees Oscar*) Oh, *you're* in trouble, Oscar.

OSCAR. Come on —

BEN. Oh, shut up.

(*Marcus laughs.*)

OSCAR (*turns on Marcus*). You laugh. I told you he had his eye on Birdie and Lionnet, and me getting it for him. So I fool him by bringing Laurette here. And then *he* fools *you:* gets Laurette drunk, and you get mad. That's just what he wanted you to do. And you did it for him. I think the joke's kind of on you.

REGINA. You must have told the truth once before in your life, Oscar, but I can't remember it.

MARCUS (*to Ben*). You're full of tricks these days. Did you get the girl drunk?

BEN. Just as good for Oscar to marry a silly girl who owns cotton, as a silly girl who doesn't even own the mattress on which she —

(*Oscar springs toward Ben, grabs his shoulder.*)

MARCUS (*to Oscar*). Will you stop running about and pulling at people? Go outside and shoot a passing nigger if your blood is throwing clots into your head.

OSCAR. I'm going to kill Ben if he doesn't stop —

MARCUS. Are you denying the girl makes use of a mattress, do you expect to go through life killing every man who knows she does?

OSCAR (*screaming*). Papa, stop it! I am deeply and sincerely in love.

MARCUS. In one minute I shall put you out of the room. (*Looks at Ben*) So that was the way it was supposed to work? Or better than that: the Bagtry girl was to borrow ten thousand from me and you were to keep five of it, and take your chances on her being a fool, and nobody finding out.

BEN. I understand now. (*To Regina*) Bagtry told *you*. Yes? (*Regina nods, smiles, sits down.*)

MARCUS. Your tricks are getting nasty and they bore me. I don't like to be bored: I've told you that before.

BEN (*shrugs*). I want something for myself. I shouldn't think you were the man to blame me for that.

MARCUS. I wouldn't, if you weren't a failure at getting it. I'm tired of your games, do you hear me? You're a clerk in my store and that you'll remain. You won't get the chance to try anything like this again. But in case you anger me once more, there won't be the job in the store, and you won't be here. Is that clear?

BEN. Very clear.

OSCAR (*who has been thinking*). Papa, you couldn't condemn a woman for a past that society forced upon her; a woman of inner purity made to lead a life of outward shame?

MARCUS (*softly*). At nine years old I was carrying water for two bits a week. I took the first dollar I ever had and went to the paying library to buy a card. When I was twelve I was working out in the fields, and that same year I taught myself Latin and French. At fourteen I was driving mules all day and most of the night, and that was the year I learned my Greek, read my classics, taught myself — Think what I must have wanted for sons. And then think what I got. One trickster, one illiterate. If you want to go away with this girl, who's detaining you?

OSCAR (*eagerly*). Your permission, sir.

MARCUS. Talk sense. Do you mean money?

OSCAR. Just a loan. Then we'd ship on down to New Orleans —

MARCUS. How much?

OSCAR. Could invest in a little business Laurette knows about — (*Regina laughs loudly*) Ten thousand could start me off fine, Papa —

MARCUS. There will be a thousand dollars for you, in an envelope, on that table by six in the morning. Get on the early train. Send a Christmas card each year to an aging man who now wishes you to go upstairs.

OSCAR (*starts to protest, changes his mind*). Well, thank you. Seems kind of strange to be saying good-bye after twenty-five years —

REGINA (*gaily*). Oh, don't think of it that way. We'll be coming to see you someday. You'll have ten children, and five of the thin ones may be yours.

LAVINIA. Good-bye, son. I'm sorry if — I'm sorry.

OSCAR. I'll write you, Mama. (*To Ben*) You've bullied me since the day I was born. But before I leave — (*Fiercely*) — you're going to do what I tell you. You're going to be on the station platform tomorrow morning. You're going to be there to apologize to Laurette.

MARCUS. Goodness, what a thousand dollars won't do!

OSCAR. And if you're not ready on time — (*Takes a pistol from his pocket*) — I'll get you out of bed with this. And then you won't apologize to her standing up, but on your knees —

MARCUS (*violently*). Put that gun away. How dare you, in this house —

BEN (*smiles*). You've always been frightened of guns, Papa. Ever since that night.

LAVINIA. That's true, ever since that night.

MARCUS. *Put that gun away. And get upstairs. Immediately.*

OSCAR (*to Ben*). See you at the station. (*He crosses room, exits.*)

BEN (*after a second*). No need to be so nervous. I could have taken the gun away from him.

LAVINIA. And they had hot tar and clubs and ropes that night —

MARCUS. *Stop your crazy talk, Lavinia.*

LAVINIA (*softly*). I don't like that word, Marcus. No, I don't. I think you use it just to hurt my feelings.

BEN. He's upset, Mama. Old fears come back, strong.

MARCUS (*slowly, to Ben*). You're wearing me thin.

REGINA (*yawns*). Oh, don't you and Ben start again. (*She pats Ben on the arm*) You know Papa always wins. But maybe you'll have your time someday. Try to get along, both of you. After Mama and I leave you'll be here alone together.

MARCUS. I don't know, darling. I'm going to miss you. I think I may join you.

REGINA (*turns, hesitantly*). Join me? But —

BEN. That would spoil the plan.

MARCUS (*to Regina*). I'll let you and Lavinia go ahead. Then I'll come and get you and we'll take a turn in New York. And then Regina and I will go on to Europe and you'll come back here, Lavinia.

LAVINIA. Oh, Marcus, you just can't have been listening to me.

I been telling you since yesterday, and for years before *that* —

MARCUS (*to Regina*). You want me to come, darling?

REGINA (*nervously*). Of course. When were you thinking of coming, Papa? Soon or —

BEN (*to Regina — laughs*). I'm dying to see you get out of this one, honey.

MARCUS (*to Ben*). What are you talking about?

BEN. I'm going to be sorry to miss the sight of your face in Chicago when Regina produces the secret bridegroom. (*Marcus wheels to stare at Regina*) Oh, you know about it. You guessed tonight. Captain Bagtry. I don't think he wants to marry her. I don't think he even wants to sleep with her anymore. But he's a weak man and — (*Marcus is advancing toward him*) That won't do any good. I'm going to finish. Yesterday, if you remember, Regina wanted you to make the loan to the girl. Tonight, when she found out John Bagtry wanted to use a little of the money to leave here, and her, she talked you out of it.

REGINA. *Ben, be still.* Ben — (*Goes swiftly to Marcus*) Don't listen, Papa. I have seen John, I told you that. I like him, yes. But don't you see what Ben is doing? He wanted to marry me off to money, he's angry —

BEN (*to Marcus*). I'm telling the truth. The whole town's known it for a year.

LAVINIA. Don't, Benjamin, don't! Marcus, you look so bad —

BEN. You do look bad. Go up to him, Regina, put your arms around him. Tell him you've never really loved anybody else, and never will. Lie to him, just for tonight. Tell him you'll never get in bed with anybody ever again —

(*Marcus slaps Ben across the face.*)

LAVINIA (*desperately*). God help us! Marcus! Ben!

BEN (*softly*). I won't forget that. As long as I live.

MARCUS. Lock your door tonight, and be out of here before I am down in the morning. Wherever you decide to go, be sure it's far away.

BEN. I spent twenty years lying and cheating to help make you rich. I was trying to outwait you, Papa, but I guess I couldn't do it. (*He exits.*)

LAVINIA. Twenty years, he said. Then it would be my fault, my sin, too — (*She starts for hall door, calling*) Benjamin!

I want to talk to you, son. You're my firstborn, going away —

(*She disappears. There is a long pause. Marcus sits down.*)

MARCUS. How could you let him touch you? When did it happen? How could you — *Answer me.*

REGINA (*wearily*). Are they questions that can be answered?

MARCUS. A foolish man, an empty man from an idiot world. A man who wants nothing but war, any war, just a war. A man who believes in nothing, and never will. A man in space —

REGINA (*softly, comes to him*). All right, Papa. That's all true, and I know it. And I'm in love with him, and I want to marry him. (*He puts his hands over his face*) Now don't take on so. It just won't do. You let me go away, as we planned. I'll get married. After a while we'll come home and we'll live right here —

MARCUS. *Are you crazy?* Do you think I'd stay in this house with you and —

REGINA. Otherwise, I'll go away. I say I will, and you know I will. I'm not frightened to go. But if I go that way I won't ever see you again. And you don't want that: I don't think you could stand that. My way, we can be together. You'll get used to it, and John won't worry us. There'll always be you and me — (*Puts her hand on his shoulder*) You must have known I'd marry someday, Papa. Why, I've never seen you cry before. It'll just be like going for a little visit, and before you know it I'll be home again, and it will all be over. You know? Maybe next year, or the year after, you and I'll make that trip to Greece, just the two of us. (*Smiles*) Now it's all settled. Kiss me good night, darling. (*She kisses him, he does not move. Then she moves toward door as Lavinia comes in.*)

LAVINIA. Ben won't let me talk to him. He'd feel better if he talked, if he spoke out — I'm his Mama and I got to take my responsibility for what —

REGINA. Mama, I think we'll be leaving for Chicago sooner than we thought. We'll start getting ready tomorrow morning. Good night. (*She exits.*)

LAVINIA (*after a minute*). Did you forget to tell her that I can't go with her? Didn't you tell them all where I'm going? I think you better do that, Marcus —

MARCUS (*very tired*). I don't feel well. Please stop jabbering, Lavinia.

LAVINIA. You tell Regina tomorrow. You tell her how you promised me. (*Desperately*) Marcus. It's all I've lived for. And it can't wait now. I'm getting old, and I've got to go and do my work.

MARCUS (*wearily*). It isn't easy to live with you, Lavinia. It really isn't. Leave me alone.

LAVINIA. I know. We weren't ever meant to be together. You see, being here gives me — well, I won't use bad words, but it's always made me feel like I sinned. And God wants you to make good your sins before you die. That's why I got to go now.

MARCUS. I've stood enough of that. Please don't ever speak of it again.

LAVINIA. Ever speak of it? But you swore to me over and over again.

MARCUS. Did you ever think I meant that nonsense?

LAVINIA. But I'm going!

MARCUS. You're never going. Dr. Seckles knows how strange you've been, the whole town knows you're crazy. Now I don't want to listen to any more of that talk ever. I try to leave you alone, try to leave me alone. If you worry me any more with it, I'll have to talk to the doctor and ask him to send you away. (*Softly — crying*) Please go to bed now, and don't walk around all night again.

LAVINIA (*stares at him*). Coralee. . . . Coralee! He never ever meant me to go. He says I can't go. Coralee — (*She starts to move slowly, then she begins to run*) Coralee, are you in bed —

Curtain

Act Three

SCENE: *Same as Act One, early the next morning.*

AT RISE: *Lavinia is moving about in the living room.*

LAVINIA (*singing*).

Got one life, got to hold it bold
Got one life, got to hold it bold
Lord, my year has come.

(*She comes on the porch. She is carrying a small Bible.*)

Got one life, got to hold it bold
Got one life, got to hold it bold
Lord, my year has come.

(*Ben, carrying a valise, comes from the living room. Lavinia gets up.*)

LAVINIA. All night I been waiting. You wouldn't let your Mama talk to you.

BEN. I put all my stuff in the ironing room. I'll send for it when I find a place.

LAVINIA. Take me with you, son. As far as Altaloosa. There I'll get off, and there I'll stay. Benjamin, he couldn't bring me back, or send me, or do, or do. He couldn't, if you'd protect me for a while and —

BEN. I, protect you? Didn't you hear him last night? Don't you know about me?

LAVINIA. I don't know. I heard so much. I get mixed. I know you're bad off now. (*She reaches up as if to touch his face*) You're my firstborn, so it must be my fault some way.

BEN. Do you like me, Mama?

LAVINIA (*after a second*). Well. You've grown away from — I loved you, Benjamin.

BEN. Once upon a time.

LAVINIA. Take me with you. Take me where I can do my little good. The colored people are forgiving people. And they'll help me. You know, I should have gone after that night, but I stayed for you children. I didn't know then that none of you would ever need a Mama. Well, I'm going now. *I tell you I'm going* (*Her voice rises*) I spoke with God this night, in prayer. He said I should go no matter. Strait are the gates, He said. Narrow is the way, Lavinia, He said —

BEN. Mama! You're talking loud. (*Turns to her*) Go to bed now. You've had no sleep. I'm late. (*Starts to move.*)

LAVINIA. Take me, Benjamin!

BEN. Now go in to Coralee before you get yourself in bad shape and trouble.

LAVINIA. You've got to take me. Last night he said he'd never ever meant me to go. Last night he said if ever, then he'd have Dr. Seckles, have him, have him — (*Turns, her fist clenched*) Take me away from here. For ten years he swore, for ten years he swore a lie to me. I told God about that last night, and God's message said, "Go, Lavinia, even if you have to tell the awful truth. If there is no other way, tell the truth." I think, now, I should have told the truth that night. But you don't always know how to do things when they're happening. It's not easy to send your own husband into a hanging rope.

BEN (*turns*). What do you mean?

LAVINIA. All night long I been thinking I should go right up those steps and tell him what I know. Then he'd have to let me leave or — (*Puts her hands to her face*) I've always been afraid of him, because once or twice —

BEN. Of course. But you're not afraid of me.

LAVINIA. Oh, I been afraid of you, too. I spent a life afraid. And you know that's funny, Benjamin, because way down deep I'm a woman wasn't made to be afraid. What are most people afraid of? Well, like your Papa, they're afraid to die. But I'm not afraid to die because my colored friends going to be right there to pray me in.

BEN. Mama, what were you talking about? Telling the truth, a hanging rope —

LAVINIA. And if you're not afraid of dying then you're not afraid of anything. (*Sniffs the air*) The river's rising. I can tell by the azalea smell.

BEN. For God's sake, Mama, try to remember what you were saying, if you were saying anything.

LAVINIA. I was saying a lot. I could walk up those steps and tell him I could still send him into a hanging rope unless he lets me go. I could say I saw him that night, and I'll just go and tell everybody I did see him —

BEN. *What night?*

LAVINIA. The night of the massacre, of course.

BEN (*sharply*). Where did you see him, how —

LAVINIA. You being sharp with me now. And I never been sharp with you. Never —

BEN (*carefully*). Mama. Now listen to me. It's late and there isn't much time. I'm in trouble, bad trouble, and you're in bad trouble. Tell me fast what you're talking about. Maybe I can get us both out of trouble. Maybe. But only if you tell me now. *Now.* And tell me quick and straight. You can go away and I —

LAVINIA. I saw him, like I told you, the night of the massacre, on the well-house roof.

BEN. All right. I understand what you mean. All right. But there's a lot I don't know or understand.

LAVINIA. One time last night, I thought of getting his envelope of money, bringing it out here, tearing it up, and watching his face when he saw it at breakfast time. But it's not nice to see people grovel on the ground for money —

BEN. The envelope of money?

LAVINIA. I could get it, tear it up.

BEN (*carefully*). Why not? Get it now and just tear it up.

LAVINIA. And I thought too about giving it to the poor. But it's evil money and not worthy of the poor.

BEN. No, the poor don't want evil money. That's not the way.

LAVINIA. No, but you can see how I have been tempted when I thought what the money could do for my little school. I want my colored children to have many things.

BEN (*desperately*). You can have everything for them if —

LAVINIA. Oh, nobody should have everything. All I want is a nice school place, warm in winter, and a piano, and books and a good meal every day, hot and fattening.

BEN (*comes to her, stands in front of her*). Get up, Mama. Come here. He'll be awake soon. (*Lavinia rises, he takes her by the arms*) Papa will be awake soon.

LAVINIA (*nods*). First part of the war I was so ill I thought it was brave of your Papa to run the blockade, even though I knew he was dealing with the enemy to do it. People were dying for salt and I thought it was good to bring it to them. I didn't know he was getting eight dollars a bag for it, Benjamin, a little bag, Imagine taking money for other people's misery.

BEN (*softly*). Yes, I know all that, Mama. Everybody does now.

LAVINIA. But I can't tell what you know, Benjamin. You were away in New Orleans in school and it's hard for me to put in place what you know and — (*Ben moves impatiently*) So — well, there was the camp where our boys were being mobilized. It was up the river, across the swamp fork, back behind the old river fields.

BEN. Yes, I know where it was. And I know that Union troops crossed the river and killed the twenty-seven boys who were training there. And I know that Papa was on one of his salt-running trips that day and that every man in the county figured Union troops couldn't have found the camp unless they were led through to it, and I know they figured Papa was the man who did the leading.

LAVINIA. He didn't lead them to the camp. Not on purpose. No, Benjamin, I am sure of that.

BEN. I agree with you. It wouldn't have paid him enough, and he doesn't like danger. So he didn't do it. And he proved to them he wasn't here so he couldn't have done it. So now where are we?

LAVINIA. They were murder mad the night they found the poor dead boys. They came with hot tar and guns to find your Papa.

BEN. But they didn't find him.

LAVINIA. But I found him. (*She opens the Bible, holds it up, peers at it. Ben comes toward her*) At four-thirty o'clock Coralee and I saw him and heard him, on the well-house roof. We knew he kept money and papers there, and so we guessed right away where to look, and there he was.

BEN (*looks at her, softly*). And there he was.

LAVINIA. So you see I hadn't told a lie, Benjamin. He wasn't ever in the *house*. But maybe half a lie is worse than a real lie.

BEN (*quickly*). Yes, yes. Now how did he get away, and how did he prove to them —

LAVINIA. Coralee and I sat on the wet ground, watching him. Oh, it was a terrible thing for me. It was a wet night and Coralee caught cold. I had to nurse her for days afterward, with —

BEN (*looks up at balcony*). *Mama!* It's got to be quick now.

Shall I tell you why? I've got to go unless — Now tell me how did he get away, and how did he prove to them that all the time he had been down Mobile road?

LAVINIA (*opens her Bible*). Twenty minutes to six he climbed down from the roof, unlocked the well-house door, got some money from the envelope, and went on down through the back pines. Coralee and I ran back to the house, shivering and frightened. I didn't know what was going to happen, so we locked all the doors and all the windows and Coralee coughed, and sneezed, and ran a fever.

BEN (*angrily*). I don't give a damn about Coralee's health.

LAVINIA (*gently*). That's the trouble with you, Benjamin. You don't ever care about other folks.

(*There is the sound of a door closing inside the house.*)

BEN (*quietly*). *There is not much time left now. Try, Mama, try hard.* Tell me how he managed.

LAVINIA (*looks down at the Bible*). Well, three days later, no, two days later, the morning of April 5, 1864, at exactly ten-five —

BEN (*sharply*). What are you reading?

LAVINIA. He rode back into town, coming up Mobile road. They were waiting for him and they roped him and searched him. But he had two passes proving he had ridden through Confederate lines the day before the massacre, and didn't leave till after it. The passes were signed by — (*Looks at Bible*) — Captain Virgil E. McMullen of the 5th Tennessee from Memphis. They were stamped passes, they were good passes, and they had to let him go. But he had no money when he came home. So Coralee and I just knew he paid Captain Virgil E. McMullen to write those passes. (*Looks down at book*) Virgil E. McMullen, Captain in the 5th Tennessee —

BEN (*points to Bible*). It's written down there?

LAVINIA. Coralee and I were half wild with what was the right thing to do and the wrong. So we wrote it all down here in my Bible and we each put our hand on the Book and swore to it.

BEN. Give me the Bible, Mama —

LAVINIA. I think there's one in your room, at least there used to be —

BEN. Oh, Mama. For God's sake. I need it. It's the only proof we've got, and even then he'll —

LAVINIA. You don't need half this proof. That's the trouble

with your kind of thinking, Benjamin. My, I could just walk down the street, tell the story to the first people I met. They'd believe me, and they'd believe Coralee. We're religious women and everybody knows it. (*Smiles*) And then they'd want to believe us, nothing would give them so much pleasure as, as, as, well, calling on your Papa. I think people always believe what they want to believe, don't you? I don't think I'd have any trouble, if you stood behind me, and gave me courage to do the right talking.

BEN (*laughs*). I'll be behind you. But I'd like the Bible behind me. Come, Mama, give it to me now. I need it for us. (*Slowly she hands the Bible to him*) All right. Now I'd like to have that envelope.

LAVINIA. But what has the money got to do with — I don't understand why the envelope — I'm trying hard to understand everything, but I can't see what it has —

BEN. I can't either. So let's put it this way: it would make me feel better to have it. There's nothing makes you feel better at this hour of the morning than an envelope of money.

LAVINIA. Oh. Well. (*Points into living room*) It's in the small upper left-hand drawer of your Papa's desk. But I don't know where he keeps the key.

BEN (*laughs*). We won't need the key. (*Takes her hand, takes her under balcony*) Now call Papa. I'll be back in a minute.

LAVINIA. Oh, I couldn't do that. I never have —

BEN (*softly*). You're going to do a lot of things you've never done before. Now I want you to do what I tell you, and trust me from now on, will you?

LAVINIA. I'm going to do what you tell me.

BEN (*goes into living room*). All right. Now go ahead.

(*Jake appears. He is carrying a mop and a pail.*)

JAKE. You all up specially early, or me, am I late?

LAVINIA (*calling*). Marcus. Marcus. (*To Jake*) What do you think of that, Jake?

JAKE (*takes a nervous step toward her — softly*). I don't think well of it. Please, Miss Viney, don't be doing —

LAVINIA. Marcus! Marcus! I want — we want to speak to you. (*To Jake*) Hear what I did? Everything's different — Marcus!

(*Marcus appears on the porch. He has been dressing; he is now in shirtsleeves. He peers down at Lavinia.*)

MARCUS. Are you shouting at me? What's the matter with you, Lavinia? Benjamin has gone?

LAVINIA (*looks into living room*). No, Marcus. He hasn't gone. He's inside knocking off the locks on your desk. My, he's doing it with a pistol. The other end of the pistol, I mean. (*During her speech, we hear three rapid, powerful blows. Marcus grips the rail of the porch. Ben comes onto the porch, the pistol in one hand, a large envelope in the other. He looks up at Marcus. There is a long pause.*)

MARCUS. Put the gun on the table. Bring me that envelope.

LAVINIA. Same old envelope. Like I said, I used to dream about tearing up that money. You could do it, Benjamin, right now. Make you feel better and cleaner, too.

BEN. I feel fine. (*To Marcus*) I like you better up there. So stay there. (*Ben turns to Jake, takes another envelope from his pocket, puts in money from first envelope*) Take this over to Lionnet. Ask for Miss Birdie Bagtry and talk to nobody else. Give her this and ask her to forget about last night. Go on, be quick —

MARCUS (*to Jake*). Come back here! (*To Ben*) How dare you touch —

BEN. Well, come and get it from me. (*Turns again to Jake*) And tell her I wish Captain Bagtry good luck. And stop at the wharf and buy two tickets on the sugar boat.

LAVINIA. Thank you, son. (*There is a long pause. She is puzzled by it*) Well. Why doesn't somebody say something?

BEN. We're thinking.

MARCUS. Yes. Shall I tell you what I'm thinking? That I'm going to be sorry for the scandal of a son in jail.

BEN. What would you put me in jail for?

MARCUS. For stealing forty thousand dollars.

BEN (*looking at the envelope, smiles*). That much? I haven't had time to count it. I always said there wasn't a Southerner, born before the war, who ever had sense enough to trust a bank. Now do you want to know what *I'm* thinking?

MARCUS. Yes, I'm puzzled. This isn't like you. In the years to come, when I do think about you, I would like to know why you walked yourself into a jail cell.

BEN. In the years to come, when you think about me, do it this way. (*Sharply*) You had been buying salt from the Union garrison across the river. On the morning of April second you rode over to get it. Early evening of April third you started back with it —

MARCUS. Are you writing a book about me? I would not have chosen you as my recorder.

BEN. You were followed back — which is exactly what Union officers had been waiting for — at eleven o'clock that night —

LAVINIA. Marcus didn't *mean* to lead them back. I explained that to you, Benjamin —

MARCUS (*sharply*). *You* explained it to him?

BEN. Eleven o'clock that night twenty-seven boys in the swamp camp were killed. The news reached here, and you, about an hour later.

LAVINIA. More than that. About two hours later. Or maybe more, Benjamin.

BEN. And the town, guessing right, and hating you anyway, began to look for you. They didn't find you. Because you were on the well-house roof.

LAVINIA. Yes, you were, Marcus, that's just where you were. I saw you.

MARCUS (*softly*). I don't know why I'm standing here listening to this foolishness, and I won't be for long. Bring me the envelope, and you will still have plenty of time to catch the train. You come up here, Lavinia —

BEN. I'll tell you why you're standing there: you are very, very, very — as Mama would say — afraid.

MARCUS (*carefully*). What should I be afraid of, Benjamin? A bungler who leaves broken locks on a desk to prove he's stolen, and gives away money to make sure I have further proof? Or a crazy woman, who dreams she saw something sixteen years ago?

LAVINIA. Marcus, I must ask you to stop using that awful word and —

MARCUS. And I must ask you to get used to it because within an hour you'll be where they use no other word —

BEN (*as Lavinia makes frightened motion*). Mama, stop it. (*To Marcus*) And you stop interrupting me. Mama saw you on the well-house roof. Coralee saw you. They saw you take money from an envelope —

LAVINIA. The same one. My, it wore well, didn't it?

BEN. To buy the passes that saved you from a hanging. You bought them from —

MARCUS (*tensely*). Get out of here. I —

BEN. From a Captain Virgil E. McMullen. Now I'd figure it

this way: by the grace of Captain McMullen you got sixteen free years. So if they swing you tonight, tell yourself sixteen years is a long time, and lynching is as good a way to die as any other.

LAVINIA. Benjamin, don't talk like that, don't, son —

MARCUS (*in a different voice*). Walk yourself down to the sheriff's office now. I'll catch up with you. If you're fool enough to believe some invention of your mother's, understand that nobody else will believe it. The whole town knows your mother's been crazy for years, and Dr. Seckles will testify to it —

BEN. Let's put it this way: they think Mama is an eccentric, and that you made her that way. And they know Seckles is a drunken crook. They know Mama is a good woman, they respect her. They'll take her word because, as she told me a little while ago, people believe what they want to believe.

MARCUS (*carefully*). Lavinia, you're a religious woman, and religious people don't lie, of course. But I know you are subject to dreams. Now, I wonder why and when you had this one. Remember, will you, that you were ill right after the incident of which you speak so incorrectly, and remember please that we took you — (*Sharply, to Ben*) — not to that drunken Seckles, but to Dr. Hammanond in Mobile. He told me then that you were — (*Lavinia draws back*) And he is still living to remember it, if you can't.

LAVINIA (*worried, rattled*). I was ill after that night. Who wouldn't have been? It had nothing to do with, with my nerves. It was taking part in sin, your sin, that upset me, and not knowing the right and wrong of what to do —

MARCUS. She didn't tell you about that illness, did she? You think they'd believe her against Hammanond's word that she was a very sick woman at the time she speaks about? (*Very sharply*) Now stop this damned nonsense and get out of here or —

BEN. Go change your dress, Mama. Get ready for a walk.

LAVINIA. But you told Jake — you said I could go on the sugar boat.

BEN. You will still catch the boat. And if you have to stay over a few hours more, I figure you can wear the same costume to a lynching as you can on a boat. We'll walk around first to old Isham, whose youngest son got killed that night. John Bagtry will remember that his twin brother also died that night. And Mrs. Mercer's oldest son and the two Sylvan boys and — We won't have to go any further because they'll be glad to fetch their kinfolk and, on their way, all the people who got nothing else to do tonight, or all the people who owe you on cotton or cane or land. Be the biggest, happiest lynching in the history of Roseville County. Go change your clothes —

MARCUS (*softly, carefully*). Lavinia. I —

LAVINIA. A lynching? *I don't believe in lynching.* If you lynch a white man, it can lead right into lynching a black man. No human being's got a right to take a life, in the sight of God.

MARCUS (*to Ben*). You're losing your witness. Only you would think your mother would go through with this, only you would trust her —

BEN. She won't have to do much. I'm taking her Bible along. (*Opens the book*) On this page, that night, she wrote it all down. The names, the dates, the hours. Then she and Coralee swore to it. Everybody will like the picture of the two innocents and a Bible, and if they don't, sixteen-year-old ink will be much nicer proof than your Mobile doctor. (*Softly*) Anyway, you won't have time to get him here. Want to finish now?

LAVINIA (*who has been thinking*). I never told you I was going to have anything to do with a lynching. No, I didn't.

MARCUS. Of course you wouldn't. Of course you wouldn't. Not of your husband —

LAVINIA. Not of my husband, not of anybody.

BEN. Mama, go upstairs and let me finish this —

LAVINIA. I only said I was going to tell the truth to everybody. And that I'm going to do. (*To Marcus*) But if there's any nasty talk of lynching —

BEN (*to Marcus*). I'll come tomorrow morning and cut you down from the tree, and bury you with respect. How did the Greeks bury fathers who were murdered? Tell me, and I'll see to it.

LAVINIA. Benjamin, don't talk that way —

MARCUS. You gave him the right to talk that way. You did, Lavinia, and I don't understand anything that's been happening. Do you mean that you actually wrote a lie in your Bible, you who —

LAVINIA (*angry*). Don't you talk like that. Nobody can say

there's a lie in my Bible — You take that back. You take it back right away. I don't tell lies, and then I don't swear to them, and I don't swear on my Bible to a false thing and neither does Coralee. You just apologize to me and then you apologize to Coralee, that's what you do —

MARCUS (*quickly*). No, no. I don't mean you knew it was a lie. Of course not, Lavinia. But let me see it, and then tell me —

BEN. Tell him to come down and look at it. I'll put it here, under the gun.

LAVINIA. I'm not going to have any Bibles in my school. That surprise you all? It's the only book in the world but it's just for grown people, after you know it don't mean what it says. You take Abraham: he sends in his wife, Sarah, to Pharaoh, and he lets Pharaoh think Sarah is his sister. And then Pharaoh, he, he, he. Well, he does, with Sarah. And afterward Abraham gets mad at Pharaoh because of Sarah, even though he's played that trick on Pharaoh. Now if you didn't understand, a little child could get mighty mixed up —

MARCUS. You want to go to your school, don't you, Lavinia?

LAVINIA. Or about Jesus. The poor are always with you. Why, I wouldn't have colored people believe a thing like that: that's what's the matter now. You have to be full grown before you know what Jesus meant.

BEN. Go upstairs now and start packing. You're going to be on the sugar boat.

LAVINIA. Am I? Isn't that wonderful —

MARCUS. Lavinia. (*She turns toward him*) It would be wrong of me to say ours had been a good marriage. But a marriage it was. And you took vows in church, sacred vows. If you sent me to trouble, you would be breaking your sacred vows —

BEN. Oh, shut up, Papa.

LAVINIA. I don't want trouble, for anybody. I've only wanted to go away —

MARCUS (*slowly, as he comes down from balcony*). I was wrong in keeping you.

BEN (*laughs*). Yes. That's true.

MARCUS. It was wrong, I can see it now, to have denied you your great mission. I should have let you go, helped you build your little schoolhouse in Altaloosa.

BEN. I built it about ten minutes ago.

LAVINIA. What? Oh, about the marriage vows, Marcus. I had a

message last night, and it said it was right for me to go now and do my work.

MARCUS. Yes. Yes, you'll want a lot of things for your colored pupils.

LAVINIA. That's absolutely true. I want to send for a teacher — I'm getting old and I'm ignorant — I want to make a higher learning.

MARCUS. Lavinia. I'll get her for you.

LAVINIA. Thank you. But it will all cost so much. Altaloosa's a mighty poor little village and everybody needs help there —

MARCUS. Would ten thousand be enough?

LAVINIA (*firmly*). It would be enough. I'd make it enough. Then, of course, I forget about Coralee coming with me. And Coralee supports a mighty lot of kinfolk right here in town. She got a crippled little cousin, her old Mama can't take washing anymore —

MARCUS. Oh, that's too bad. What could I do for them?

LAVINIA. Maybe two hundred dollars would take Coralee's mind from worrying.

MARCUS. I should think so. They'll be the richest family in the South. But, of course, your friends should have the best.

LAVINIA. You're being mighty nice to me, Marcus. I wish it had always been that way.

MARCUS. It started out that way, remember? I suppose little things happened, as they do with so many people —

LAVINIA. No, I don't really think it started out well. No, I can't say I do.

MARCUS. Oh, come now. You're forgetting. All kind of pleasant things. Remember in the little house? The piano? I saved and bought it for you and —

LAVINIA. Bought it for me? I always thought you bought it for yourself.

MARCUS. But perhaps you never understood why I did anything, perhaps you were a little unforgiving with me.

BEN (*to Marcus*). Aren't you getting ashamed of yourself?

MARCUS. For what? For trying to recall to Lavinia's mind that we were married with sacred vows, that together we had children, that she swore in a church to love, to honor —

LAVINIA (*thoughtfully*). I did swear. That's true, I —

BEN (*quickly*). Mama, please go upstairs. Please let me finish here. You won't get on the boat any other way —

MARCUS. Indeed you will, Lavinia. And there's no need to take the boat. I'll drive you up. We can stay overnight in Mobile, look at the churches, have a nice dinner, continue on in the morning —

LAVINIA. How did you guess? I always dreamed of returning that way. Driving in, nice and slow, seeing everybody on the road, saying hello to people I knew as a little girl, stopping at the river church — church . . . Now, what else did I think about last night?

MARCUS. Now bring me the envelope and the Bible, and we'll start immediately —

(*She puts her hand on the Bible, as if to pick it up.*)

BEN (*quickly takes her hand*). Do I really have to explain it to you? Do I really have to tell you that unless you go through with it, he's got to take you to the hospital? You don't really think that he's going to leave you free in Altaloosa with what you know, to tell anybody — Why do you think he took you to Dr. Hammanond in the first place? Because he thought you might have seen him, and because it wouldn't hurt to have a doctor say that you were —

MARCUS. That's a lie. Lavinia —

LAVINIA (*softly*). I don't ever want to hear such things again, or one person do or say such to another. Would you really have told me you would drive me to Mobile and then you would have taken me —

MARCUS. *Of course not.* If you listen to that scoundrel — You're my wife, aren't you? I also took vows. I also stood up and swore. Would I break a solemn vow —

LAVINIA (*appalled*). Oh, now, I don't believe what you're saying. One lie, two lies, that's for all of us: but to pile lie upon lie and sin upon sin, and in the sight of God —

BEN (*sharply*). Write it to him, Mama. Or you'll miss your boat.

LAVINIA. Oh, yes. Oh, I wouldn't want to do that. (*She picks up the Bible, exits.*)

MARCUS. You're a very ugly man.

BEN. Are you ready now?

MARCUS. For what?

BEN. To write a piece of paper, saying you sell me the store for a dollar.

MARCUS (*pauses*). All right. Bring me that envelope. I'll sell you the store for a dollar. Now I have had enough and that will be all.

BEN. You'll write another little slip of paper telling Shannon in Mobile to turn over to me immediately all stocks and bonds, your safe-deposit box, all liens, all mortgages, *all* assets of Marcus Hubbard, Incorporated.

MARCUS. I will certainly do no such thing. I will leave you your proper share of things in my will, or perhaps increase it, if you behave —

BEN (*angrily*). You're making fun of me again. A will? That you could change tomorrow? You've made fun of me for enough years. It's dangerous now. One more joke. So stop it now. Stop it.

MARCUS. I would like to give you a little advice — you're so new at this kind of thing. If you get greedy and take everything there's bound to be suspicion. And you shouldn't want that. Take the store, take half of everything else, half of what's in the envelope. Give me the rest. I'll go on living as I always have, and tell everybody that because you're my oldest son, I wanted you to have —

BEN. You'll tell nobody anything, because you can't, and you'll stop bargaining. You're giving me everything you've got. Is that clear? If I don't have to waste any more time with you, I'll give you enough to live on, here or wherever you want to go. But if I have to talk to you any longer, you won't get that. I mean what I'm saying, and you know I do. And it's the last time I'll say it. (*There is no answer. He smiles*) All right. Now start writing things down. When you finish, bring them to me. You're waiting for something?

MARCUS (*softly, as he goes up the porch steps*). To tell you the truth, I am trying to think of some way out.

BEN. Don't waste your time, or put yourself in further danger, or tempt me longer. Ever since you started your peculiar way of treating me, many years ago, I have had ugly dreams. Go in and start writing now. You a lucky man: you'll die in bed.

MARCUS. You will give me enough for a clean bed?

BEN. Yes, of course.

MARCUS. Well, I daresay one could make some small bargains with you still. But I don't like small bargains. You win or you lose —

BEN. And I don't like small talk. (*Marcus turns, goes into his room. Ben waits for a second, then crosses to kitchen door, calls in*) Breakfast here, please. (*As Jake comes from street side of porch*) Yes? Did you find Miss Birdie?

JAKE. Yes, sir. She was mighty happy and said to thank you.

BEN. Did you get the tickets?

JAKE. Sure. Boat's loading now.

BEN (*sits down at Marcus's table*). Take them up to Miss Lavinia, get the carriage ready. Get me coffee first.

(*The sound of knocking is heard from the hall of the second floor.*)

OSCAR'S VOICE (*with the knocking*). Papa! Papa! It's me. Hey, Papa. Please. Open your door. (*After a second Oscar runs in from the living room, runs up the porch steps, calls into Marcus's room*) Papa. I'm all ready. (*Pounds on Marcus's door.*)

BEN (*looking up at Oscar*). Traveling clothes? You look nice.

OSCAR. What you doing there? I told you to get on down to the station to make your apologies. I ain't changed my mind. (*Looks down, sees the gun on the table*) What's my pistol doing out?

BEN. Waiting for you.

OSCAR. You just put it back where you found it — (*Then as if he remembered*) Papa. Please. Let me in. *Please.* Papa, I can't find it. Papa — (*Regina appears on the balcony. She is arranging her hair. She has on a riding skirt and shirt*) Regina, go in and tell him, will you? *Please, Regina.* Laurette's waiting for me to fetch her up —

REGINA (*looks down at Ben on the porch. Looks at Oscar*). Oh, God. I slept late, hoping you'd both be gone. What's the matter with you, Oscar, what are you carrying on about?

(*Jake appears with coffee tray, brings cup to Ben, puts tray down, and exits.*)

OSCAR (*desperately*). The thousand dollars on the table. But it's *not* on the table. You heard him promise last night —

REGINA. Go look again. Papa certainly wouldn't stop your going.

OSCAR. I tell you it's not there. I been over the whole house. I crawled around under the table —

BEN. Come on down and crawl some more.

REGINA (*softly*). You're in Papa's chair, Ben, eating breakfast at Papa's table, on Papa's porch.

OSCAR (*very puzzled*). I'm telling you that Ben is a crazy Mama's crazy son.

BEN (*looks up at Regina*). Come on down and have breakfast with me, darling. I'm lonely for you.

REGINA. Papa told you to be out of here.

BEN. Come on down, honey.

REGINA. No, I'm going out before the horse-whipping starts.

BEN. Going to look for a man who needs a little persuading?

REGINA. That's right.

OSCAR. Regina. Help me. It's *not* there. (*Screaming*) Papa! *Papa!*

REGINA (*disappears into her room*). Oh, stop that screaming.

OSCAR. Papa, I got to go. The money's not there. Papa, answer me —

MARCUS (*comes out from his room*). You looking for me, son? Speak up.

OSCAR. It's getting late. The money. You forgot to leave it. (*When he gets no answer, his voice changes to a sudden shriek*) It just ain't there.

MARCUS. A voice injured at your age is possibly never recovered. The money isn't there, Oscar, because I didn't put it there. (*To Ben*) Would you like to give him a little — some — explanation, or will I, or —

BEN (*shakes his head*). I'm eating.

(*Oscar stares down at Ben, stares at Marcus.*)

MARCUS (*to Oscar*). An unhappy event interfered. I am thus unable to finance your first happy months in your rose-covered brothel. I assure you I am sorry, for many reasons, none of them having anything to do with you.

OSCAR. What the hell does all that mean? That you're *not* giving me the money to leave here —

BEN. It means that. And it means that Papa has found a new way of postponing for a few minutes an unpleasant writing job. Go back in, Papa.

(*Oscar stares at Marcus, stares down at Ben. Then he suddenly runs down the steps, off the porch, going toward the street. Ben smiles, Marcus smiles.*)

MARCUS. Where would you like me to have breakfast? A tray in my room, this side of the porch, the dining room or —

BEN. Anyplace you like. My house is your house.

MARCUS. I eat a large breakfast, as you know. Should that continue?

BEN. Certainly.

MARCUS. Thank you, Benjamin.

(*He reenters his room as Regina comes on the porch. She hears his last sentence, stares at Marcus. She comes down the steps, goes to the table, pours herself coffee, takes a biscuit, looks curiously at Ben and sits down.*)

REGINA. What's the matter with Papa?

BEN. He's changed. You think it's age?

REGINA. Why aren't you getting on the train?

BEN. I'm going to build a new house. I never liked this house; it wasn't meant for people like us. Too delicate, too fancy. Papa's idea of postwar swell.

REGINA (*stares at him*). I want to know why you aren't leaving this morning?

BEN. I can't tell you why. My lips are sealed in honor.

REGINA. Before there's any more trouble you better go quiet down Mama. She's *packing*. She says she's going to her destiny. You know what that always means. And I'm sick of fights —

BEN. But that's where she is going.

REGINA (*bewildered*). Papa said she could go?

BEN. No . . . I said so.

REGINA. And who have you become?

BEN. A man who thinks you have handled yourself very badly. It's a shame about you, Regina: beautiful, warm outside, and smart. That should have made a brilliant life. Instead, at twenty, you have to start picking up the pieces, and start mighty fast now.

REGINA (*gets up, laughs*). I like the pieces, and I'm off to pick them up.

BEN. To try to persuade the Captain by the deed of darkness to a future legal bed? So early in the morning?

REGINA (*pleasantly, as she passes him*). I'm sure something very interesting has happened here. But whatever it is, don't talk that way to me.

BEN. Can I talk this way? You're not going to Chicago. And for a very simple reason. Papa has no money at all — now. No money for you to travel with, or to marry with, or even to go on here with.

REGINA (*stands staring at him. Then, quietly*). *What are you talking about? What's happened?* What's he done with his money —

BEN. Given it to me.

REGINA. Do you take that new drug I've been reading about? What would make you think he had given it to you?

BEN. You mean what were his reasons? Oh, I don't know. I'm

the eldest son: isn't that the way with royalty? Maybe he could find me a Greek title — Go up and talk to him. I think he's been waiting.

(*Slowly she starts for the staircase. Then the speed of her movements increases, and by the time she is near the door of Marcus's room she is running. She goes into the room. Ben picks up his newspaper. There is low talking from Marcus's room. Ben looks up, smiles. After a moment, Regina comes slowly out of Marcus's room. She crosses porch, starts downstairs.*)

REGINA (*slowly*). He says there's nothing he can tell me. He's crying. What does all that mean?

BEN. It means there is nothing he can tell you, and that he's crying. Don't you feel sorry for him?

REGINA. Why can't he tell me? I'll make him —

BEN. He can't tell you, and I won't tell you. Just take my word: you're, er, you're not well off, shall we say?

REGINA (*tensely*). What have you been doing to Papa or —

BEN. A great deal. Whatever you think of me, honey, you know I'm not given to this kind of joke. So take it this way: what is in your room, is yours. Nothing else. And save your time on the talk. No Chicago, honey. No nothing.

REGINA. You can't stop my going, and you're not going to stop it —

BEN. Certainly not. You go ahead, your own way. Ride over to your soldier. Stand close and talk soft: he'll marry you. But do it quickly: he was angry last night and I think he wants to get away from you as fast as he can. Catch him quick. Marry him this morning. Then come back here to pack your nice Chicago clothes, and sell your pearls.

REGINA. Do you think I'm going to take your word for what's happening, or believe I can't talk Papa out of whatever you've done to him —

BEN. Believe me, you can't. Not because your charms have failed, but because there's nothing to talk him out of. Money from the pearls will be plenty. People in love should be poor.

REGINA. Ben, tell me what storm happened here this morning. Tell me so that I can — can find out what I think or —

BEN. Or if you don't want to go to the war in Brazil, stay here and starve with them at Lionnet. I'd love to see you in the house with those three ninnies, dying on the vine. Either way, he'd leave you soon enough and you'd find out there's never anybody nastier than a weak man. Hurry — Or have a cup of coffee.

REGINA (*softly*). I'll find out what's happened, and —

BEN. No you won't.

REGINA. And the day I do, I'll pay you back with carnival trimmings.

BEN. I won't blame you. But in the meantime, learn to lose. And don't stand here all day losing, because it's my house now, and I don't like loser's talk.

REGINA. You've ruined everything I wanted, you've —

BEN. Now, look here. Write *him* a poem, will you? I've ruined nothing. You're not in love; I don't think anybody in this family can love. You're not a fool; stop talking like one. The sooner you do, the sooner I'll help you.

REGINA. You heard me say I'd pay you back for this.

BEN. All right.

(*Marcus opens his door, comes out on the porch, comes down the steps. Regina turns to look at him. Marcus comes to Ben, hands him two pieces of paper. Ben takes them, reads them. Marcus puts his hand out to take the newspaper. Ben smiles, shakes his head, Marcus quickly takes his hand away.*)

REGINA (*desperately, to Marcus*). You still won't tell me? You're willing to see —

MARCUS (*softly*). Regina, honey, I can't, I —

(*Oscar, dejected and rumpled, appears.*)

REGINA (*to Oscar*). Do you know what's happened here? Did you have anything to do with it?

OSCAR. What?

(*Regina turns away from him. Oscar sits down, puts his head in his hands.*)

REGINA (*after a minute*). Well, what's the matter with you then? Ben Hubbard trouble?

OSCAR. She wouldn't wait. She wouldn't even wait for a few days until Papa could give me the money again.

BEN. Again?

OSCAR. That's how much she cared for me. Wouldn't even wait. Said she was going on to New Orleans, anyway. That she'd had enough — My God, I talked and begged. I even tried to carry her off the train.

MARCUS. Oh, how unfortunate.

BEN. I think it's charming. How did you do it, Oscar?

OSCAR (*to nobody*). You know what she did? She spat in my face and screamed in front of everybody that she was glad I wasn't coming, if I didn't have the money, what the hell did she need me for?

REGINA. Spat in your face! How could she do a thing like that?

MARCUS. How does one spit in your face?

BEN. Why, I imagine the way one spits in anybody's face.

REGINA. But it's special in a railroad station. How did she do it, Oscar? You can't just up and spit —

OSCAR (*spits out on the porch*). Just like that. The way you wouldn't do with a dog. And all the while yelling I was to let her alone, with everybody staring and laughing — (*Marcus, Regina, and Ben laugh. Oscar rises*) So. So, making fun of me, huh?

REGINA. Now really, Oskie, can you blame us? You in a railroad station trying to carry off a spitting — girl? You'd laugh yourself, if you didn't always have indigestion.

OSCAR (*carefully*). Your love didn't laugh. Your love, looking like a statue of Robert E. Lee. Dressed up and with his old medals all over him. (*Regina rises. Marcus rises*) So you didn't know he was going on the train, huh? I thought not. So you're no better off than me, are you, with all your laughing. Sneaked out on you, did he?

REGINA (*to Ben*). So you arranged that, too, so that I couldn't —

BEN. All right. That's enough. I'm sick of love. Both of you follow the trash you've set your hearts on or be still about it from now on. I don't want any more of this.

OSCAR. *You* don't want any more. What the —

BEN (*to Regina*). You, early-maturing flower, can go anyplace you want and find what it's like to be without Papa's money. (*To Oscar*) And you, lover, can follow your spitting heart and get yourself a wharf job loading bananas. Or you can stay, keep your job, settle down. I got a girl picked out for you — make yourself useful.

OSCAR (*completely bewildered, turns to Marcus*). What's he talking about, Papa? Since when —

BEN. It's not necessary to explain it to you. (*To Regina*) Now, honey, about you. You're a scandal in this town. Papa's the only person didn't know you've been sleeping with the warrior.

MARCUS. Benjamin —

BEN (*laughs*). Papa, and Horace Giddens in Mobile. How soon he'll find out about it, I don't know. Before he does, we're taking you up to see him. You'll get engaged to him by next week, or sooner, and you'll get married in the first church we bump into. Giddens isn't bad off, and if you're lucky it'll be years before he hears about you and the Brazilian general. I don't say it's a brilliant future, but I don't say it's bad.

MARCUS (*softly*). You don't have to marry a man, Regina, just because — We can go away, you and I —

OSCAR (*goes toward kitchen door*). I certainly don't know what's happened here. I certainly don't. I'm hungry. (*Calls in*) Where's breakfast, you all?

REGINA (*sharply*). Order breakfast for me, too, selfish.

BEN (*laughs*). That's my good girl. (*Picks up the newspaper*) Nothing for anybody to be so unhappy about. You both going to do all right. I got ideas. You'll go to Chicago someday, get everything you want — Then —

REGINA (*softly*). When I'm too old to want it.

MARCUS. Regina, you didn't hear me. We could go away, you and I — I could start again just as I started once before.

REGINA. When you did — whatever Ben made you do, did you realize what you were doing to me? Did you care?

MARCUS. I cared very much.

REGINA. And what good did that do?

OSCAR. Sure must have been an earthquake here since last night. You go to bed and Papa's one kind of man, and you wake up —

BEN (*reading newspaper*). They got that ad in again, Oscar. Dr. Melgoyd's "All Cure." Two bits, now, on special sale, for gentlemen only. Sluggish blood, cure for a wild manhood, nothing to be ashamed of, it says —

REGINA. He's still got the last bottle.

(*Jake appears with a large tray. He has on his hat and coat.*)

OSCAR (*annoyed*). I never bought that rot. Don't believe in it. Somebody gave it to me.

REGINA (*laughing*). That was tactless, wasn't it?

BEN. Big goings on all over the country. Railroads going across, oil, coal. I been telling you, Papa, for ten years. Things are opening up.

OSCAR (*who has started to eat*). That don't mean they're opening up in the South.

BEN. But they are. That's what nobody down here sees or

understands. Now you take you, Papa. You were smart in your day and figured out what fools you lived among. But ever since the war you been too busy getting cultured, or getting Southern. A few more years and you'd have been just like the rest of them.

MARCUS (*to Jake*). Bring my breakfast, Jake.

JAKE. Belle will have to do it, Mr. Marcus. Last breakfast I can bring. I got the carriage waiting to take Miss Viney. (*He exits.*)

BEN. But now we'll do a little quiet investing, nothing big, because I don't believe in going outside your class about anything —

OSCAR (*his mouth full*). Think we've got a chance to be big rich, Ben?

BEN. I think so. All of us. I'm going to make some for you and Regina and —

(*Lavinia appears in the living-room door. She is carrying a purse and the Bible. Coralee is standing behind her.*)

LAVINIA. Well, I'm off on my appointed path. I brought you each a little something. (*Goes to Regina*) This is my pin. (*Regina gets up, Lavinia kisses her*) Smile, honey, you're such a pretty girl. (*Goes to Oscar*) Here's my prayer book, Oscar. I had it since I was five years old. (*Oscar kisses her. She goes to Ben*) I want you to have my Papa's watch, Benjamin.

BEN. Thank you, Mama. (*He kisses her, she pats his arm.*)

LAVINIA (*goes to Marcus*). I didn't have anything left, Marcus, except my wedding ring.

MARCUS (*gets up, smiles*). That's kind, Lavinia.

LAVINIA. Well, I guess that's all.

BEN. Mama, could I have your Bible instead of Grandpa's watch? (*Marcus laughs*) It would make me happier, and I think —

MARCUS. Or perhaps you'd give it to me. I can't tell you how happy it would make me, Lavinia.

LAVINIA. Oh, I wouldn't like to give it up. This Bible's been in my Papa's family for a long time. I always keep it next to me, you all know that. But when I die, I'll leave it to you all. Coralee, you hear that? If I die before you, you bring it right back here.

CORALEE. Come on, Miss Viney.

LAVINIA. I'll be hearing from you, Benjamin?

BEN. You will, Mama. Every month. On time.

LAVINIA. Thank you, son. Thank you in the name of my colored children.

CORALEE. Miss Viney, it's late.

LAVINIA. Well. (*Wistfully*) Don't be seeing me off, any of you. Coralee and I'll be just fine. I'll be thinking of you, and I'll be praying for you, all of you. Everybody needs somebody to pray for them, and I'm going to pray for you all. (*Turns to Marcus*) I hope you feel better, Marcus. We got old, you and me, and — Well, I guess I just mean it's been a long time. Good-bye.

MARCUS. Good-bye, Lavinia.

(*Lavinia and Coralee exit. Marcus goes to sit by Regina.*)

MARCUS (*softly*). Pour me a cup of coffee, darling.

(*Regina looks at him, gets up, crosses to table, pours coffee, brings it to him. Marcus pulls forward the chair next to him. Regina ignores the movement, crosses to chair near Ben, sits down.*)

Curtain

Montserrat

ADAPTED FROM THE FRENCH PLAY
BY EMMANUEL ROBLÈS

Montserrat was first produced at the Fulton Theatre, New York City, on October 29, 1949, with the following cast:

(In the order of their appearance)

ZAVALA	RICHARD MALEK
ANTONANZAS	NEHEMIAH PERSOFF
SOLDIER	STEFAN GIERASCH
MONTSERRAT	WILLIAM REDFIELD
MORALES	GREGORY MORTON
IZQUIERDO	EMLYN WILLIAMS
FATHER CORONIL	FRANCIS COMPTON
SALAS INA	REINHOLD SCHUNZEL
LUHAN	WILLIAM HANSEN
MATILDE	VIVIAN NATHAN
JUAN SALCEDO ALVAREZ	JOHN ABBOTT
FELISA	JULIE HARRIS
RICARDO	GEORGE BARTENIEFF
MONK	EDWARD GROAG
MONK	KURT KASZNAR
SOLDIER	ROBERT CRAWLEY
LIEUTENANT	STEPHEN LAWRENCE

Produced by
KERMIT BLOOMGARDEN and GILBERT MILLER

Directed by
MISS HELLMAN

Setting designed by
HOWARD BAY

Costumes designed by
IRENE SHARAFF

Scene

The outer room of the General's Palace during the Spanish Occupation of Valencia, Venezuela. The year is 1812. The action of the play is continuous.

Act One

SCENE: *The outer room of the General's Palace during the Spanish Occupation of the city of Valencia in Venezuela, the year 1812.*

It is a simple room opening off the courtyard and opening into the main quarters of the palace. Right stage are steps leading to the doors of the courtyard. There are three grill windows in these large doors. On the upper left wall is a heavy, ornate door leading into His Excellency's quarters. Left stage is a table and two chairs; against the back walls are long benches; upper right stage is a chair and stool. On the right corner wall, near the doors, is a crucifix. On the upper left stage wall is a hanging cabinet for fruit, wine, glasses. Along the bench wall is a gun rack: hooks for coats, boots, flags of Spain, etc.

AT RISE: *Zavala and Antonanzas are seated at the table playing chess. A bottle of wine and a plate of biscuits are on the table. Offstage His Excellency is playing the piano. There are occasional street noises coming from the courtyard: carriage wheels over cobblestones, hawkers in the square and, suddenly, the loud sound of a street singer.*

Left and right mean audience's left and right.

ZAVALA (*pushes aside the chessboard*). I do not say you are the most ignorant chess player in the world. I say only that you might be. Why do you wish to play?

ANTONANZAS. I am no game player.

ZAVALA. What are you?

ANTONANZAS (*sharply*). A soldier. (*Pours himself a drink.*)

ZAVALA. You owe me another bottle. By the way, do you bottle it yourself?

ANTONANZAS. I beg your pardon. I pay in the best.

ZAVALA. Please stop begging my pardon. (*A Soldier enters from His Excellency's door, crosses to the windows, closes them.*)

ANTONANZAS (*to Soldier*). What are you doing? It is stifling in here. (*He moves toward windows, as if to open them.*)

SOLDIER. His Excellency is having his music.

ZAVALA (*laughs*). Yes, of course. His Excellency is having his music. (*Soldier exits. Antonanzas strides around, then decides to open windows*) No. You do the same thing every day. When will you learn not to cross a soldier of seventy-seven whose campaign has not taken its proper course, whose remaining tooth is worrying him, and who is no longer sure whether he is playing the pianoforte in Valencia, in the Americas, or at home in Valencia, Spain? And toward afternoon, no longer cares.

ANTONANZAS. I used to like a pleasant song, but I want to tell you something: I have learned to hate music. (*Points to door*) I have learned it here.

ZAVALA. That's treason.

ANTONANZAS. I beg your pardon?

ZAVALA. That phrase comes from your month in London?

ANTONANZAS. That is no word for an officer to be using here —

ZAVALA. What word? London?

ANTONANZAS. Treason. *That* word. You know very well what I mean.

ZAVALA. I have never thought about you, and thus could never have thought you a traitor. You're a soldier; you don't know anything or believe anything. Therefore what would you betray?

ANTONANZAS. That's a dangerous word now. And you know it is. We must watch and guard what we say here. (*Comes back to the table, begins to set up a new chess game*) I wonder if they found Bolivar. I wish Izquierdo had taken me with him.

ZAVALA. If Izquierdo didn't find Bolivar today, you will have your fill of war again tomorrow. That will be gay. You like war. One advances oneself during a war, eh?

ANTONANZAS. I like it better than sitting here. I am not made for sitting. Never was —

ZAVALA (*they begin to play chess*). More comfortable crawling? (*Points to His Excellency's door*) Closer to his boots?

ANTONANZAS. Man was never made to stand on two feet. My uncle always says that. Always. Ever since I can remember.

ZAVALA. It is always wittier to say something always.

ANTONANZAS. One can take the joke several ways: perhaps once upon a time man did not stand upright —

ZAVALA. Ah. Your uncle is a man of advanced ideas. I wouldn't have thought that.

ANTONANZAS. Or another way: that man was made to lie down. With a woman, of course. That's what my uncle says the joke could mean. Two interpretations —

ZAVALA. Your uncle is fascinating. You must tell me about him — but not today.

ANTONANZAS. I haven't had a woman since we took Siquisique. That was the place I saved nine girls. (*Points to His Excellency's door*) Against his orders to wipe out the town.

ZAVALA. So you have told me. You're certain you managed nine? It was five a few months ago.

ANTONANZAS. It was nine. (*Confidentially, points to door*) Tell me something. I don't think he has any use for women. Is that age, as one might expect at seventy-seven? At what age does it happen to a man?

ZAVALA. How old are you?

ANTONANZAS. Twenty-five.

ZAVALA (*thinks*). In about six months.

ANTONANZAS. I don't believe that. You're joking. (*Laughs*) Anyway, they are ugly here and crude. Although there was a girl when I first came — sixteen, sad, quiet. She wept when we made love.

ZAVALA. With pleasure?

ANTONANZAS. I don't ask questions —

ZAVALA. Or in horror?

ANTONANZAS. Who?

ZAVALA. Never mind.

ANTONANZAS. Zavala, you don't intend to have a career in the army?

ZAVALA. God, no.

ANTONANZAS. That is why I can come to you for advice. You have no jealousy of my career —

ZAVALA. You can be sure of that.

ANTONANZAS. I didn't sleep last night. I was thinking.

ZAVALA. You are certain?

ANTONANZAS. We are an occupation army. A professional army. Izquierdo and the rest. Is it, therefore, the place to advance oneself? Doesn't a man like Izquierdo resent me, my birth —

ZAVALA. The place of your birth, or the *fact* of your birth?

ANTONANZAS. You know what I mean.

ZAVALA. I do indeed. Shall I tell you something: do not try so hard, do not work away — it tires people.

ANTONANZAS. I am sick of this place: why don't we finish here and go home?

ZAVALA. Why don't we?

ANTONANZAS. I haven't seen Spain in two years. Zavala, do you believe it is wise for a man to stay too long away from his own country, his own culture —

ZAVALA. Wait for night to come again. In your dreams you'll find other small boys with whom to debate such questions.

ANTONANZAS (*annoyed*). If you're so wise and old, then tell me since when did it take a Spanish army this time to clean up a pocket rebellion of half-breeds? Since when? Am I to grow old here —

ZAVALA. You will never grow old, you will not even grow older. (*Montserrat comes in from the courtyard door. Zavala turns to look at Montserrat*) No duets today?

MONTSERRAT. No.

ZAVALA. His Excellency didn't ask you to join him?

MONTSERRAT. I haven't seen him. I have been to the cathedral.

ANTONANZAS. You pray too much. I don't trust a man who prays more than is necessary. Strange that you were not invited for your usual duet. Are you losing favor?

MONTSERRAT. I hope so. I have not thought about it.

ANTONANZAS (*sharply*). It's time you began to think about many things.

MONTSERRAT. I will try. (*To Zavala*) Have they come back?

ZAVALA. No.

MONTSERRAT (*too quickly*). How many men did Izquierdo take with him?

ZAVALA (*sharply*). Twenty. (*To Antonanzas, pointing to chessboard*) Move.

MONTSERRAT (*to Antonanzas*). And time for *you* to think. A small amount of thinking would keep you from moving the bishop.

ZAVALA. He's quite right. *Don't move it.* (*Antonanzas thinks for a minute, moves the bishop*) But we told you not to move it.

ANTONANZAS. I want to move it.

ZAVALA. And *that* is the history of Spain. Play by yourself, little one. (*Pushes the board toward Montserrat. Antonanzas gets up. Montserrat takes his place at the chessboard.*)

ANTONANZAS. They should have been back an hour ago.

ZAVALA (*looks at Montserrat, points to door*). I am going to ask for a three-day leave. I don't want to be here when Izquierdo applies himself to punishing Bolivar. It will be — (*To Montserrat*) Want to join me?

ANTONANZAS. Why did you say she wept? I have been thinking about it.

ZAVALA. What are you talking about?

ANTONANZAS. The girl I had, the one who wept? Did you insult me?

ZAVALA. I tried. Don't women always weep in your bed?

ANTONANZAS. No.

ZAVALA. But they must do something. Do they laugh?

ANTONANZAS. All women act different. (*Sharply*) What did you say? You asked if women laughed at me? I must demand that you retract that immediately. I must demand —

ZAVALA (*begins to sing loudly*).

> For God, for King, for Spain I fight.
> For God, for King, for Spain.
> Some day our wars will end, my love.
> So save for me our night.
> For God, for King, for Spain I fight —

SOLDIER (*appears at His Excellency's door*). Pardon, Captain . . . I only repeat words from His Excellency. He says Captain Zavala is most patriotic: tell him to stop it.

ZAVALA. Certainly. (*Soldier exits*) Are there any new vices? I need one. (*Noises are heard from the street. Antonanzas runs to the window.*)

ANTONANZAS. Nothing. The usual afternoon fight in the square between two local pigs. (*Shouts to the guard in the courtyard*) Send somebody out to stop that. The noise in this damn place. They'll change the song tonight when they see Bolivar's head on a pole, with his body —

MONTSERRAT. Be still!

ANTONANZAS. The death of your enemy offends you? That will be news for Izquierdo.

MONTSERRAT. You offend me. Have you ever thought that this is the happiest time of your life? What again can equal in pleasure a massacre? Even your family aren't going to allow you to slaughter peasants for excitement. Your mother is possibly gentle, possibly, and your father would think it bad business.

ANTONANZAS (*violently*). Get up!

MONTSERRAT. And how can you ever have a wife? You can't rape the same woman twice.

ANTONANZAS. Get up, I tell you —

MONTSERRAT. Go away. Go outside and kill a child. (*Antonanzas makes a sharp movement across the table. Montserrat catches his arms, throws him back. Zavala catches Antonanzas and holds him.*)

ZAVALA. Now, now. You can't fight with every man. You've already lost three teeth. Allow the rest to decay.

ANTONANZAS (*struggling*). I demand that you ask him out for tomorrow morning — *I demand it.*

MONTSERRAT. And I accept. (*Smiles*) Tomorrow morning.

ZAVALA. Does that quiet you? I don't enjoy holding you. Has your honor been satisfied?

ANTONANZAS. If Montserrat leaves the room immediately.

ZAVALA. He is not going to leave the room. Sit down. (*Puts Antonanzas in a chair*) He said your mother was doubtless gentle. Didn't you hear? That was nice, wasn't it? Shall I tell you a secret? (*Loudly*) You are an exceeding bore. Now be still. (*Antonanzas goes to cabinet, takes a bunch of grapes*) Play with your thumbs or eat your fruit. (*Zavala goes back to table, sighs, sits down at chessboard. To Montserrat*) You are not playing well today.

MONTSERRAT. What time did Izquierdo leave here? Why has he taken so long?

ZAVALA. He left at noon. (*Quickly, points to book*) If I can't find any other, is reading a vice?

MONTSERRAT. It is considered so here.

ANTONANZAS (*to Montserrat*). A great many matters are considered here. We are not such fools as we look.

MONTSERRAT. Nature seldom takes an expected path. You don't look like a fool.

ANTONANZAS. I want no compliments from you. (*Zavala laughs*) Why are you laughing?

ZAVALA. It is my new vice.

ANTONANZAS (*pointing to book*). What heresy is it today?

MONTSERRAT. Worse than yesterday's Voltaire.

ANTONANZAS. Just make certain you don't bring Byron in here again.

MONTSERRAT. I am surprised you don't approve of him. He has a title.

ANTONANZAS. You can buy anything in England.

ZAVALA (*who has been looking at the book*). This is unwise.

MONTSERRAT. Shall I give it to you?

ZAVALA (*sharply*). I have no desire to hang for the reading of a book.

ANTONANZAS (*to Zavala*). Who is Rodalso?

ZAVALA. He was our teacher at Salamanca. I thought him a great man once. But he was very old and I was very young.

MONTSERRAT (*smiles*). You grew old too early. You are older now than he.

ANTONANZAS. Is he the Rodalso brought before the Inquisition? I remember my father told me of his writing —

MONTSERRAT. Can your father read writing?

ANTONANZAS (*to Montserrat*). How dare you bring that man's book in here?

MONTSERRAT (*sharply*). I dare because I like what I read. (*Smiles*) Like this: "Now Spain is a country of the dark and the sad. The days of light have gone from us: we have only half light, half knowledge, half Christianity. There is no man in Church or University to light the candle; or if he be, and if he dare, he is killed and the candle flickers out. Back, back we go to the purge, the angelic water, the rejection of natural science, the refusal to honor human life. When will Spaniards understand that ignorance is cruelty and cruelty is death? Not to others, as he now interprets it, but to himself: the murderer is his own executioner. Far away and lonely, I tell myself that Spain is not at home." (*There is noise of hoofbeats in the courtyard.*)

ZAVALA (*to Montserrat, softly*). Put the book away.

MONTSERRAT. It is of no importance today. The time for reading is over. (*Morales comes down the steps. Montserrat gets up, moves to a corner.*)

MORALES. Get ready. The Colonel is angry as you have never seen him angry.

ANTONANZAS. What happened? What's the matter?

ZAVALA. You did not find Bolivar.

MORALES. We did not find Bolivar. We found nothing but a mud hut village and one stinking Indian.

ZAVALA (*softly*). So it happened again? (*Father Coronil enters from His Excellency's door.*)

ANTONANZAS. I told you. A man who drinks as much wine as Izquierdo should learn not to boast at dinner. It's the second time and it's a disgrace. (*Izquierdo enters from the courtyard door.*)

IZQUIERDO (*to Morales*). Have you been inside?

MORALES (*nervous*). No. He's playing the piano. I —

IZQUIERDO (*to Morales*). You are a good friend. Saving the bad news for me to report, eh?

ANTONANZAS. But what happened? By God, it's the *second* time —

IZQUIERDO (*to Antonanzas*). Since when do I owe you an explanation? (*He goes to His Excellency's door, tries to open it, finds it barred. Calling in*) Your Excellency. Have the door opened, please. I have bad news. Will you postpone your music until this evening? It is important I see you immediately — (*He gets no answer. He turns to Father Coronil*) Father, when will his senile Excellency complete the afternoon music? When can I see him?

FATHER CORONIL. I have no knowledge of his intentions, his senility, or his music. He does not come to me for any of them. Where is your prisoner?

ANTONANZAS (*as Izquierdo laughs*). I cannot see what there is to laugh about —

IZQUIERDO (*turns to Antonanzas*). Make yourself useful. Ride down to Cardenas and say if this time Bolivar gets by him on the Puebla road I will hang every Spanish soldier who survives the raid, men and officers. (*Antonanzas hesitates, then goes out.*)

FATHER CORONIL. This is a scandal. I advise you to take all measures possible. You cannot continue to lose this man.

IZQUIERDO. Father, take care of the matters spiritual — we are in deep need of your services. Allow me matters temporal.

FATHER CORONIL. You have not done well with matters temporal.

IZQUIERDO. No. I have not. (*The music stops. Izquierdo turns to Montserrat*) Why have you waited here? To give yourself the pleasure of my defeat?

MONTSERRAT. No.

IZQUIERDO. You are well acquainted with His Excellency's musical nonsense. Do you think I can go in now? Does anything follow the allegretto?

MONTSERRAT. Nothing follows.

IZQUIERDO (*to Zavala and Morales*). Come along. (*They hesitate*) You will be needed — to share my disgrace. (*Sharply*)

Gentlemen. Come along. (*They exit through His Excellency's door.*)

FATHER CORONIL. This time there will be grave trouble. Here and at home — (*He comes to Montserrat, takes the book from his hand*) As there should be. Every time Bolivar escapes he makes himself a greater hero and the Spanish army greater fools. I have twice asked that you put this book away, and with it the thoughts of the man.

MONTSERRAT. The man was your friend, you told me so.

FATHER CORONIL. The man changed. He was a pious man and then he was a dangerous man.

MONTSERRAT. He is a pious man today, the most pious I have ever known.

FATHER CORONIL. How do you know that?

MONTSERRAT. I write to him each week. He writes to me each month.

FATHER CORONIL (*tensely*). Do you realize what one such discovered letter could do to you? You are on a dangerous road, my son. If His Excellency understood half of what you say each night at dinner —

MONTSERRAT. There is no fear of that.

FATHER CORONIL. It is time for you to leave for Cadiz. It is dangerous here for you, dangerous for us. Our cause is just, and you deny it. I no longer have time to argue it with you. A boat for home will leave next week. Have you heard me?

MONTSERRAT. Father, I ask you once again: how can you bear what is happening here? What have these people done to deserve such punishment? They fight for themselves, as we fought at home —

FATHER CORONIL. We have spoken of this before. Many times. I want you to promise me that you will be on the boat —

MONTSERRAT. What will be left of them, and of us? (*Points to His Excellency's door*) This is the time for pity. Father, go to him — try to tell him it is our duty now to stop this.

FATHER CORONIL. Is it our duty to have pity for dangerous men who refuse to confess the Glory of God?

MONTSERRAT. They have not refused God. They have refused to accept the glory of our army. I wanted to understand — I came to you a year ago for help. I have asked you over and over again — does the prestige of God demand slaughterhouses? Father, you don't see what is happening: ride out with us — the stink of burning bodies will change your mind.

FATHER CORONIL. I do not condone such acts of violence. You know that I have many times condemned them —

MONTSERRAT. You have condemned the form. I am asking you to condemn the whole — we must get out of this land, Father, and stay out —

FATHER CORONIL. Have you lost your mind?

MONTSERRAT. I don't know.

FATHER CORONIL. Who are you to set yourself up against your church and your country —

MONTSERRAT. I don't know. That's the truth: I don't know. There is only one thing of which I am certain — we have come a long way from Christianity. I must find my way back.

FATHER CORONIL. *Your* way back? A personal religion? That is coming a long way, and a dangerous way. (*Slowly*) Go home. Go back to your people. Make yourself a normal life. A few years will change your troubles.

MONTSERRAT. Does time quiet every man, Father?

FATHER CORONIL. It calms the blood, puts the pieces of life in order, brings serenity and finds the duty. Yes, for most men. You will see. You will look back on this and smile.

MONTSERRAT (*smiles*). A dark girl, sweet children, a few winter balls, the house and lands of one's father. As the years pass the books lighter in weight and in thought — and then no books. Another dark girl or two, good horses, good wine and perhaps a gentleman's war in another land to occupy dull winters. And, as you say, a smile for the remembrance of all this; a smile for what you were, or could have been.

FATHER CORONIL. That is not all of life and you know it. Come to me in ten years and we will speak of this again. You have been a good student. Go on with your books. In the meantime, you will go home. (*Starts toward the door*) Isn't His Excellency a relative to your family?

MONTSERRAT. Not by blood. He was my grandmother's lover.

FATHER CORONIL. I have no need of the details of country life.

MONTSERRAT. Yes, they are complex. If you need higher connections to arrange my boat passage — which will be more difficult than you think — my mother had the same non-blood relationship to the royal house and my father serviced at least two cousins of the Queen and two aunts.

FATHER CORONIL. Captain Montserrat, I do not wish the gossip of your family.

MONTSERRAT (*smiles*). I only wished to say that I am a child of disorder. Such children often turn another way.

FATHER CORONIL. Then turn toward God.

MONTSERRAT (*with great feeling*). I am trying, Father, I am trying. (*Izquierdo, followed by Morales and Zavala, comes in.*)

IZQUIERDO (*to Father Coronil*). His Excellency is resting. It was difficult to make him understand that Bolivar had escaped. It was even more difficult to make him understand that Bolivar could not have escaped without being warned. "Who could have warned him," His Excellency kept asking, "who is it?"

FATHER CORONIL. What happened this morning?

IZQUIERDO. Nothing happened. When we arrived at the farm Bolivar was gone. One Indian was left in the house. He gave us a description of the man who came to Bolivar last night. (*To Montserrat*) Riding back I asked myself many questions — questions I should have asked a long time ago. But it has been fashionable among us not to take seriously our South American troubles. For the first time I asked myself is Bolivar a revolutionary, a reformer, a libertarian? Which word is correct for us to use?

MONTSERRAT. Whichever word consoles you most.

IZQUIERDO. I mean this: will he stay to fight or do we chase a fop who will next turn up in London with his memoirs? (*Sharply*) Which is it?

MONTSERRAT. He will stay to fight.

IZQUIERDO. Yes. (*To Morales*) Order two more patrols on the Curaçao road. Before you do that, go outside and bring six people from the square.

MORALES. Six people? What six people?

IZQUIERDO. Any six. Move. (*Morales exits.*)

FATHER CORONIL (*to Montserrat*). What is this conversation between you? What do you know of Bolivar and —

IZQUIERDO. Our stable guard reported that at ten last night an officer asked for a horse. The officer's face was covered but his voice was clear. The guard hesitated —

MONTSERRAT. Yes, he did. He said, "It is very dark, sir. You should wait for the moon."

IZQUIERDO. Yes. In any case, within five minutes of the officer's arrival at the farm, Bolivar was lifted to a black mare —

MONTSERRAT. And tied to the saddle because he was too sick to hold.

IZQUIERDO. Yes. Just so. Lifted tenderly up by the officer, and tied tenderly down. Our Indian informer said the visitor had a gentleman's face — and a Spanish uniform. (*After a minute of silence, to Montserrat*) Where can I find Bolivar? (*Montserrat shakes his head*) If I put you to torture what would happen? I'm in a hurry. Will torture do it?

MONTSERRAT (*carefully*). I don't know.

IZQUIERDO. The suggestion made His Excellency nervous: it seems he has some past connection with your family.

MONTSERRAT. He said: "Torture will make a scandal. His mother is a charming woman; I knew her as a child — Shoot him quickly — he died fighting the enemy."

IZQUIERDO (*smiles*). He said nothing of your mother. He mumbled of your grandmother.

MONTSERRAT. So he remembers her? (*Then softly*) I would like to go to the cathedral.

IZQUIERDO. I want Bolivar. I want Bolivar and I intend to make you give him to me.

MONTSERRAT. I hope that I will not give him to you. (*There is silence*) May I go to the cathedral now?

IZQUIERDO. When the time comes we will call Father Coronil to you.

MONTSERRAT (*turns, looks at Father Coronil, gently*). But I — I want to speak with Father Madaraga. I want him with me. He is waiting. (*When there is no answer*) Will you call him to me?

IZQUIERDO (*sharply*). Did you think it would be as easy as that? Has that been your problem? How to die as in a book? (*A Soldier pushes Luhan and Salas Ina through the courtyard door. Morales follows them. Both Luhan and Salas Ina draw against the wall*) Come down, please.

SALAS INA. Gentlemen officers. I have been arrested. Not arrested, because that would be ridiculous, but . . . well, I've been brought here.

IZQUIERDO. Come down, please. (*Hesitantly, they come down the steps.*)

LUHAN. Yes, sir. But I was only going through the square —

SALAS INA. Will our errand . . . Will our purpose . . . Will we be here long?

IZQUIERDO. I don't know. I hope not. You have an appointment?

SALAS INA. Well, er. I'm expected.

IZQUIERDO. By whom?

SALAS INA. At my house. My wife.

IZQUIERDO. She'll wait for you, don't you think? You can't always be with her. Wear you out at your age. Why did you marry so late in life?

SALAS INA (*feeling better*). How sharp you are, sir. I had sense enough to wait for just what I wanted.

IZQUIERDO. Who are you and what's your name?

SALAS INA. Salas Ina, the merchant in the Royal Square. I have attended you.

IZQUIERDO. Oh yes. You sell textiles and linens. Big business. You are rich?

SALAS INA. Er, I live in a little comfort by our modest standards. Not of course like you gentlemen in the motherland —

IZQUIERDO. I have been told about your wife. She is admired in church each Sunday. I haven't seen her because I rarely go to the cathedral, alas. But my younger officers report she is very handsome. Is she?

SALAS INA (*shyly*). Yes.

IZQUIERDO. How long have you been married?

SALAS INA. Fourteen and one-half months.

IZQUIERDO. And you love your wife very much?

SALAS INA. Yes.

IZQUIERDO. Would you put it this way: do you love her more than life? More than your life?

SALAS INA. I have never put it that way, sir. That isn't usual.

IZQUIERDO. Well, put it now.

SALAS INA. Yes, sir. I do. (*Montserrat has moved to His Excellency's door.*)

IZQUIERDO (*to Montserrat*). The door will not open for you.

MONTSERRAT. Send for me when you're ready.

IZQUIERDO. I am ready for you now. Stay here. (*Sharply*) You don't understand? You will. (*Turns back to Salas Ina*) You love your wife more than your life. Good. That's the way I would love a woman, if I had ever loved a woman. That is the way love should be. Now. How would you rate your fortune? You own the big store on the Square — what else?

SALAS INA. I have. Er. I have one, two.

IZQUIERDO (*laughs*). One, two what?

SALAS INA. Houses. But I have many relatives. As you know, this is a country of poverty. I always say all the poor in the world are related to me except those who are related to my wife. And there are the town charities and our cathedral —

IZQUIERDO. Yes. I'm sure you are charitable. You look it. Have you cattle and how many?

SALAS INA. Twelve hundred head. Or sixteen hundred. I —

IZQUIERDO. You are rich. Great store, fine cattle, handsome wife. You are indeed a lucky man. Answer me.

SALAS INA (*timidly*). Yes.

IZQUIERDO. Not like that. Say I'm a lucky man. (*Points to Montserrat*) Say it to that young gentleman.

SALAS INA (*softly, puzzled, frightened, to Montserrat*). I am a lucky man, sir.

IZQUIERDO. Think of that, Montserrat. Here is the happy man. Happiness came to him late and so he knows its value and wants to hold it close. Life is sweet — (*To Luhan*) But that's not the way it is for you. What's your name?

LUHAN. Arnaldo Luhan, a carpenter, a wood carver. (*To Zavala*) That gentleman knows me.

ZAVALA. I have bought from him. His carving is very fine.

IZQUIERDO (*to Zavala*). I didn't know you were a collector.

ZAVALA (*nods toward door*). His Excellency.

LUHAN (*to Zavala*). You will remember I fashioned the posts for the bedstead, and the small table. They were said to be —

IZQUIERDO (*to Zavala*). I have never seen the stuff. Where is it?

ZAVALA. His Excellency sold it to the Valencia Museum. At a high profit.

IZQUIERDO. Why did they want it?

ZAVALA. Because they sold it to the Seville Museum for a higher profit. You have missed a great deal in this country, Izquierdo.

IZQUIERDO (*laughs*). Indeed.

LUHAN. You see, sir? I have been of some small service. I even had a message from His Excellency saying that someday he would come himself and praise my work — Perhaps, sir, if *you* would come yourself I could make you a gift of — perhaps something to suit your taste, er — (*Morales enters, pushing four people ahead of him. They are Matilde, Salcedo, Felisa, Ricardo. Matilde pushes past the rest.*)

MATILDE (*to everybody, timidly*). I know nothing about these other people, I have never seen them before, but I've done nothing. I don't know why I've been brought here —

SALCEDO. Would you gentlemen explain immediately what this is all about?

MATILDE (*goes immediately to Father Coronil*). Father, I came out to make my marketing and buy my bread. I left my two children alone. They must be fed — I am in a hurry — Could you — I have two children. One is ten months old, and Juano is two. They are sleeping now, I hope, but — they will wake and —

SALCEDO. Officer, what do you want with me? What is this about? Certainly I have done nothing. I was strolling along the street. You can easily establish the truth of what I — (*During his speech Morales has been whispering to Izquierdo.*)

MONTSERRAT (*softly*). Why are these people here? *What are you doing?*

SALCEDO. Who has accused me, and of what? I have never seen any of you —

IZQUIERDO. But I am told we have seen you. You are Juan Salcedo, eh?

SALCEDO. Yes, Colonel. Juan Salcedo Alvarez. I came from Cadiz with the acting company from the Royal Theatre.

IZQUIERDO. We saw you play a special performance on board ship.

SALCEDO. Yes, of course. We played "Ascascio" that night. It's a powerful work for a modern play. You agree? (*To Montserrat, courtly*) You saw the play, sir?

MONTSERRAT (*softly*). No.

IZQUIERDO. Captain Montserrat has been occupied with — with more modern ideas. Philosophical and political. The traditional Spanish theatre does not interest him: it does not concern itself with egalité, the rights of man — Or it hasn't been allowed to.

SALCEDO. Colonel, it is a matter of how you use the phrase — the rights of man. In the French sense, of course *not*. But in the play you saw, the character of Ascascio himself is certainly based on a large philosophic concept, on a most serious and profound, if you understand me, deeply Spanish, most exalted, large, noble in motive, filled with charity, very — (*Lamely*) *You* liked the play?

IZQUIERDO (*laughs*). Overacted, in places, too much talk, far too long. I don't think myself a judge of art, even bad art. But it was a pleasant evening. You were Ascascius, Ascasium?

SALCEDO. Ascasci*o*.

IZQUIERDO. Oh. Well, you did the death scene very well.

SALCEDO. But I was not at my best that night. I find the drinking water of this country most upsetting. And then upon arrival here my costumes were found to be incomplete.

MONTSERRAT (*slowly, carefully*). Why are these people here? To talk about a shabby play —

SALCEDO (*gently*). Ah, sir, a shabby play? In the theatre it pains us to hear those who haven't seen our work, condemn it. (*To Izquierdo*) You were speaking of Ascascio's death, the first act scene, or the scene at the scaffold?

IZQUIERDO. I must have been dozing for the first death. I speak of the scene when you turn toward your executioners, refuse to hate them, speak only of forgiveness.

SALCEDO (*pleased*). Yes, yes. Exactly. The true death scene, as we call it. You understand Ascascio was struggling to die in purity. He wished to be worthy of Jesus. (*At a loss, turns to Father Coronil*) Isn't that so, Father? To be worthy one must die in love and forgiveness.

FATHER CORONIL. I do not know your profession.

IZQUIERDO. It is a remarkable profession. By day yourself, by night somebody else. You die when the candles are lit and you are reborn in time for bread and sausage. You are Ascascio, or Don Juan, or Sigismond, and yet you go to bed yourself.

FATHER CORONIL (*sharply to Izquierdo*). Who are these people and why are they here?

SALCEDO. Well, Colonel, I have often said to myself which side of me is me, which hand acts for me, which thought comes from where — I myself, the English Henry, or the young poet in the drama *I* have recently composed?

IZQUIERDO. Well, this afternoon you will have an opportunity to find yourself. If you play yourself well, you will be remembered here and your fame possibly sung at home. They will say of you — he was best when he played himself. Of this I am sure because I have seen men in battle. Faced with danger we are ourselves, to our surprise.

FATHER CORONIL. What nonsense are you talking? What are you doing with these people?

SALCEDO. I don't understand. I —

SALAS INA (*comes toward Father Coronil. Matilde and Salcedo also move forward*). Father, I was going home when suddenly the soldiers surrounded me — I did nothing. I swear to you. Nothing, nothing —

IZQUIERDO (*he speaks to the group*). I know you have done nothing. I know you are innocent. That is why you're here. You are guilty of nothing but innocence. Father Coronil might tell you that you can be accused of only one crime — having been born.

FATHER CORONIL. *Stop this.* Explain yourself.

IZQUIERDO (*to the group, pointing to Montserrat*). This man has hidden Bolivar. I want Bolivar and he knows where I can find him. I want you to persuade him to tell me.

(*There is a pause. Then . . . As One Voice*)

SALAS INA. What? How can we —

MATILDE. What's it to do with me —

LUHAN. I never saw him before —

SALCEDO. I don't know this man —

MONTSERRAT (*coming to Izquierdo*). *What have they to do with me or Bolivar?*

IZQUIERDO. It is now five o'clock. You will be alone with Captain Montserrat for no more than an hour.

MATILDE (*in a shrill voice*). An hour! I cannot stay here for an *hour. I must go now.*

IZQUIERDO. If he consents to tell you where Bolivar is hiding, you will go free with the thanks of His Excellency and a piece of preserved orange, a box of which His Excellency has just received. (*Very sharply*) If in an hour he has not told you where Bolivar is hiding, you will be killed. All six of you will be shot. (*There is a long silence.*)

SALCEDO. What did you say?

SALAS INA. What did he say?

MONTSERRAT (*comes to Izquierdo. Softly, unbelieving, points to His Excellency's door*). *Does he know what you are doing?*

IZQUIERDO. Yes.

MONTSERRAT. For God's sake. Kill *me.* Any way you want — in torture, for treason. I will confess it is treason — *Any way you want.*

IZQUIERDO. I am not interested in the methods of your death. You are of no importance. *I want Bolivar.* You will have your choice — *your* choice — the lives of six innocent people against the life of a man who is leading a revolution against your country.

SALCEDO. You are making jokes, sir —

MONTSERRAT (*softly*). I don't believe even you would —

IZQUIERDO (*sharply*). Believe me. But — (*To the six*) I think you are safe. This gentleman hates all violence. Take heart and do your best. (*As Montserrat starts to door*) *He has said he will not see you.*

MONTSERRAT (*to Zavala*). Go to His Excellency. Beg him to see me — *Please.*

ZAVALA (*gently, shakes his head*). I did ask him. He approved of this. It amused him. (*Softly to Montserrat*) Tell him about Bolivar. Nothing else will do. (*Turns, exits.*)

MONTSERRAT (*turns to Father Coronil*). Father, for God's sake, you will stop him from this. Let these people go. (*Desperately*) Father, help. *Go to him, help.*

FATHER CORONIL. I came here with the army as a priest. *I have nothing to do with the military.* You are a traitor and I did not know that. (*He moves toward door.*)

MONTSERRAT. Then treat *me* as a traitor. But these are innocent people —

FATHER CORONIL. Yes, remember they are innocent. And so speak out and save them. (*Father Coronil exits.*)

MATILDE. I must go home now. In thirty minutes I'll be back. (*As Matilde runs toward the stairs, Salas Ina moves with her.*)

SALAS INA. Yes. That is wise. We can go home and then come back — in an hour I'll be back.

IZQUIERDO (*his voice stops them*). You are not going to leave this room.

LUHAN (*slowly*). I don't know what to do. I can't understand. What is anything of this to us —

SALCEDO. *I* understand, but I don't believe. No Spanish gentleman, no officer, could consider, could — What are we? Puppets for you?

IZQUIERDO. Yes, that is what you are.

LUHAN. Like this woman says. Couldn't we go to tell our people we'll be late? To try to arrange a little? I can't disappear from my home — I have five children. Poor people can't leave where they are.

IZQUIERDO (*to Montserrat*). That is the truth. Your heart that weeps for all the poor must certainly weep for six. (*To group*) It is an important hour to you: use it well. Don't waste it running about, babbling that you don't understand. Good luck to you. (*Izquierdo starts toward door.*)

MATILDE (*screams*). Officer —

(*Izquierdo goes out. There is a long silence. One by one they turn to stare at Montserrat. Then Luhan and Matilde start toward him, as if to speak. Before they reach Montserrat, Salas Ina beckons them. They move to a corner, whisper. Felisa does not join them, but she watches them. Ricardo is not quite of them, but listens to them. Salas Ina and Salcedo are chosen as spokesmen. They separate themselves from the group, go toward Montserrat.*)

SALAS INA (*as if he is making a business deal*). Now look here, sir. We'd like to get this over quickly. You name what you want, anything honorable, and I myself will undertake and guarantee —

SALCEDO. Don't speak that way. This gentleman is a gentleman. (*To Montserrat*) Let us state immediately that we do not understand what is at issue. (*Matilde runs forward to Montserrat.*)

MATILDE (*timidly, pointing to door*). Could you call him back, sir —

SALAS INA. I don't believe the whole thing. Right now I think I'm crazy. You must explain this. (*No answer*) Speak up.

MONTSERRAT. It has been explained. There is nothing more I can tell you.

LUHAN. Nothing you can tell us? You who got us here?

MATILDE (*meaning Izquierdo*). He's trying to frighten us. That's all —

SALAS INA (*wildly*). He's succeeded.

LUHAN. I tell you even these bastards, even Spaniards, couldn't do — couldn't do a thing like he said.

SALCEDO. How dare you speak of Spaniards in that fashion? Make your apologies.

LUHAN (*furiously*). What are you talking about?

SALCEDO. You have insulted the honor —

RICARDO (*sharply*). Actor! It's not the day to play the clown.

SALCEDO (*angry*). And who are you, boy?

RICARDO (*to Montserrat*). Is he Colonel Izquierdo? (*Montserrat nods*) The massacre of Guarda? That one?

MONTSERRAT. Yes.

SALAS INA (*appalled*). Is he? The thousand prisoners —

RICARDO (*softly*). *That* one.

SALCEDO. I was not in this country when the supposed massacre happened. But the figures most certainly grow. I was told yesterday it was only four hundred prisoners —

RICARDO. We'll take six hundred off for you. Does that quiet you?

LUHAN (*angry*). It was a thousand. Our good priest went at night to help the dying. (*Furiously to Salcedo*) *It was a thousand.*

SALCEDO. I am sorry. These atrocity stories do not convince me. Down through history one reads of these matters and one never believes them.

SALAS INA. Oh, shut up. Let's get on. (*Pause*) Let's get on.

LUHAN. Well, get on.

SALAS INA. Are you married?

LUHAN (*to Salas Ina*). And what color is her hair? Are *you* crazy? What has this to do with us?

SALAS INA (*frantic*). I'm speaking as quick as I can. Don't get so nervous. Now see here — Er. Where is your wife —

LUHAN. What's this about his wife? You are wife-crazy, you old hog.

SALCEDO. Please. Have manners — (*Goes to Montserrat. Motions Salas Ina away*) Now, sir, let's get it finished. Let's come to the matter. Is it true that you helped Bolivar escape?

MONTSERRAT. Yes, it is true.

SALCEDO (*to the others, bewildered, horrified*). I didn't understand *that.* I must have missed — I didn't think he was a traitor to the King. To the King. I can't have anything to do with such a man — (*Marches toward courtyard door. Sees the guard at door, draws back frightened.*)

SALAS INA. I don't care what he has been a traitor to. I don't care what he is for or against. All I know, he is dangerous to us. (*Furiously to Montserrat*) I demand to know your intentions immediately.

MATILDE (*softly to Montserrat*). We just want to leave here, sir. Now would you go and tell that officer what he wants to know, and then we can go home. Please, sir — (*Montserrat looks at her, starts to speak, changes his mind.*)

SALAS INA. Look. He can't speak. Speak! Speak!

SALCEDO. Don't shout so. Now. (*Puts up his hand as Salas Ina starts to speak*) Let us go about things decently. Let's get at the root of the problem. Where were you born?

SALAS INA (*when Montserrat does not look up*). An idiot. Doesn't even know where he was born.

SALCEDO. Let me conduct the examination. Please.

MONTSERRAT (*tired, gently*). What do you want to know? What good will it do you? I was born in Madrid —

SALAS INA. In a cave? On a mule? Men are born different ways and it is of importance to know how —

SALCEDO. That *I* didn't have to ask. His family is well known. Great estates —

LUHAN. If you knew, why did you ask?

SALCEDO (*rattled*). I didn't know *exactly* where he was born.

MONTSERRAT (*sharply*). On the twentieth of June, in a large room, at nine in the morning. What difference does it make to you the little I am? I have no history.

SALAS INA. Are you married? Are you married?

SALCEDO. Why do you keep asking that?

SALAS INA. Because it is important to know if he has a heart within him. I did not have a proper heart until I married — (*Suddenly*) He is not married. I can see it.

LUHAN. And he has no children. And gives nothing for anybody's children.

MATILDE. It isn't always true that a man who has children loves children. Many men should never have children. *I* know that. I could tell you —

SALAS INA (*to Matilde*). All right. All right. (*To Montserrat*) You're not married. Are you in love? Do you like women? Is there somebody in this town —

LUHAN. You trade in everything, don't you? Do you think you can buy off your life with a whore? Keep us from dying with a bolt of linen?

SALCEDO. Don't talk so foolish. I have no intention of dying.

RICARDO. You don't believe in the atrocities of the Spanish army, so you can't believe in any of this. Then what are you so frightened about?

SALCEDO. Are you a member of a university? (*Ricardo laughs unpleasantly*) Then do not make use of logic. (*To Montserrat*) Now this is enough of this farcical talk. Jails, death — I have done nothing and I am Spanish. I had been to see my friend Roig. I will enjoy his face when I tell him of this nightmare. I who played before the Queen in 1807, I who was the first to recognize the injustice of the Goya portrait. *There,* by the way, is a man who should be dealt with as a traitor — the Queen is handsome. He made her look like a *vulture.*

LUHAN. Oh, shut up.

SALCEDO. I was engaged by the Royal Theatre of Madrid until the French invasion. I have had the greatest loyalty to His Majesty. Do you know what I refused to do? I refused to play before the French.

LUHAN. *Shut up.*

SALCEDO. But Juan Mantalbo Serena did not hesitate. How can a man with a smallpox face — sixty-one years old — play Orestes? It's not that I have anything against smallpox. God spare us from it — Well, Serena is still playing Orestes, and I am ordered out here for the Colonial troops. But I am going home soon, and the score between us is not yet finished —

LUHAN (*furiously*). Shall I tell the story of my life? I was born to my mother who was a woman. I ate some bread, I married my wife, I drank a little water — *Time is passing.*

MATILDE. Yes, yes. It's late. I still don't understand what is being said.

LUHAN. What is there to understand? Either he gives up Bolivar, or we are killed. I have five children.

MATILDE. I know, I know. But my children are little. Your wife will give them their dinner, but who will give mine —

LUHAN. And where is my wife to get dinner? I work, I carve all day, most of the night. I make good things, I know it. (*To Montserrat*) And what happens to them? You steal them. You steal everything. How long can it go on? You steal from us, you live from us, and you kill us if we try for another piece of bread.

MONTSERRAT. Then save the man who can lead you out of it.

LUHAN. I don't know what you're talking about. I'm saying things are no good. But I'm not saying this crazy revolution and that crazy man should do it for me — To hell with all that. Are you going to feed my family after I die? Is it you who will do it?

MONTSERRAT (*desperately*). What can I say to you? To any of you?

SALAS INA. You have nothing to say to us. (*Points to door*) Say it to him.

LUHAN. You know what His Excellency paid me for my work? Enough to eat for three days. I am no fool. I know what profit he made — Three days' food and any water I could get from licking his boots. Goddamn him. All of you! (*Sits down. There is a silence. He takes out knife and begins playing with it. After a second, holds it up to Montserrat*) I could do good work on his throat and yours.

MATILDE. Ssh. Ssh. (*There is a long silence.*)

SALAS INA (*to Montserrat*). Say something.

MONTSERRAT. What can I say?

SALAS INA (*comes to him. Softly*). You sit there. You're probably crazy. I asked you: have the doctors told you? *Are you crazy?*

LUHAN. Does a crazy man know he's crazy? You're a fool.

SALAS INA (*threateningly, to Luhan*). You're growing above yourself. You understand it would be easy to remove you and your fancy junk from the south corner of the square? Just a word from me to the police and you'd be out of Valencia —

LUHAN. You won't remove me so fast. You old hog. Buying a wife. Did you know the whole town heard the tears of the girl on your wedding night —

SALAS INA. That's a lie, you stinking half-breed —

LUHAN (*moves toward Salas Ina*). Did you ever hear the names of the men who beat up her father for allowing — (*Salas Ina moves toward him.*)

MATILDE. No, no. I'm sure the wedding was very nice. (*Very loud*) *Please, please, we must get out of here.* (*She goes to Montserrat*) Sir. It is late. I must go home. Could you tell me what you are doing? I don't come from this town. I don't know much of what happens — What do you want?

MONTSERRAT. I want to save Bolivar.

SALCEDO. Treason, treason.

MATILDE (*holds up her hand to silence Salcedo*). But why does he mean so much to you, sir? Some people think he is a good man, that he wants better things for us. But he won't get them, sir. Nobody will.

LUHAN. He is a high-born Creole. An adventurer enjoying himself with our blood. I have seen them before. (*To Montserrat*) A gentleman, like you. All of you are bad luck to us —

FELISA. Captain Montserrat, tell them why. Make them understand.

MONTSERRAT (*looks up at her, as if he sees her for the first time*). I don't know how.

FELISA. Tell them.

MONTSERRAT (*to others*). You have one last chance. That chance is Bolivar.

SALAS INA. Last chance for what?

MONTSERRAT (*with force*). To breathe in peace, to think, to speak, to eat, to feed your people — To live like men — *I* shouldn't have to tell *you*. Liberty.

SALAS INA (*softly*). Ah. Ah. We are lost. We are lost. They begin to talk of liberty they should be locked up. Now I know we are lost. He is a "good" man, a man who saves people — You are known as a friend of the people, eh?

MONTSERRAT. I am known as nothing. I am of no importance.

LUHAN. Ah. Now we will have *that* sickening talk: you are a saint, your life does not matter, you are humble, a hundred years and they will do your face in bronze. You will sacrifice yourself — Aah.

SALAS INA (*tensely*). Listen. Leave us alone. Just go home and leave us alone. Go play for liberty and such with your own kind. Easy to grow up fattened on sweet milk, bored with life. We never had anything. *Leave us alone.*

LUHAN. What's death to people like you? Five doctors and a funeral feast. You don't know anything about death. We know more about it than we do about life —

SALCEDO. Please allow me to speak for myself. I come from rather a different background. (*Ricardo laughs loudly. Salcedo turns on him angrily.*)

SALAS INA. Liberty. The liberty to kill six people for the life of one man?

MONTSERRAT. It is *not* the life of one man. I do not care about his life, he does not care about his *life*.

LUHAN. How do you know he doesn't? Because he told you so over meat and wine?

MONTSERRAT. Yes. Because he told me so. And because I've watched him for a year, listened to him, believed in him. He is a true man. (*Shouts*) *And I will not betray him.* (*There is a long silence. When he speaks again, he speaks quietly*) What happens here is the future of your people, not mine. In the name of God, there must come an end to what has been done to you. (*Softly*) I know, I know. I have no right to stand against you, but I didn't know last night this would happen, and Bolivar didn't know it.

LUHAN (*puts up his hand as Salas Ina is about to speak*). Do you know where Bolivar is hiding?

MONTSERRAT. Yes.

LUHAN. You want us to say that we will die to save Bolivar?

MONTSERRAT. Not to save *him*. But —

LUHAN. Yes, yes. Don't bother to say all that again.

SALAS INA (*suddenly*). So that's what you're doing? If we say we are willing to die for this nonsense you talk, then you will feel fine before God, your conscience will be clear, and we will all walk out before the guns holding hands, making you a joyful hero —

LUHAN. Muttering of the glory of man. If that is what you are dreaming, then give it up. We will not die to save anything. (*Very sharply*) Go in there now. Tell him where Bolivar is hiding. Tell them we don't give a Goddamn whether they catch him today or tomorrow —

SALAS INA. Tell them they can hang him in my store. I'll give it to them free.

SALCEDO. Tell them I'm a Royalist. A Royalist.

LUHAN. You asked us to die. We said no thank you, that's all you need to know. Go inside.

SALAS INA. Go ahead. Go ahead. We've told you. (*Montserrat does not move*) Aren't you going? *Go. Go* —

MATILDE. Don't scream at him. He will go. You'll see. He will do right — (*Montserrat sits down. Luhan lunges for him. Matilde pushes him back*) Ssh. Ssh. He is thinking. (*They begin to move about. Ricardo turns to stare at Felisa. Salcedo bumps into Salas Ina, and is shoved aside. Luhan moves back and forth in front of Montserrat. Matilde goes to window, shakes her head*) How long have we been here? The sun's getting darker. What time is it? It's going to storm. They'll be frightened — (*She picks up her package, goes toward the door, speaks absently*) I'll be back. I'll do the feeding, and I'll come back — (*She runs up the steps, pushes open the door. The guard at the door throws her back. It is done with such force that she tumbles down the steps. Salas Ina, Salcedo and Luhan start shouting at her. Ricardo moves up the steps as if to attack the guard. Felisa sits down beside Matilde, takes her hand, wipes Matilde's forehead.*)

LUHAN. Cry all you want. (*Gently, to Ricardo, who is laughing too loudly*) All right, child. All right.

MONTSERRAT. You are animals to him — To all of them. (*Points to other door*) Did you think otherwise? How much more can you stand, how much more can you take: put an end to it.

LUHAN (*quietly*). We don't need you to recite what has been done to us. Six little people can put an end to it, eh?

MONTSERRAT. You are not six people. There are thousands and thousands ready to fight —

SALAS INA. Ach, people here fight on any side. I could take you down the square and show you men, native men, who will fight with him, against him —

MONTSERRAT. There is one man who will bring all of you together.

RICARDO. Captain Montserrat, our partisans were defeated at San Mateo. We don't know where they've gone, how many are left, or what there is to fight with now.

MONTSERRAT. Bolivar knows where they are. And I know what they will fight with.

LUHAN. Bare hands and knives. That's all there's ever been to fight with, and all there ever will be. It's crazy to fight like that. There'll be another time, some other way —

SALAS INA (*furiously*). Of course. Some other way. Bolivar tells them to die, and after they're dead, he can go home to his fine house. You tell them to fight with their hands. Certainly. They're not your hands.

MONTSERRAT. They have guns.

RICARDO. Ten, twenty for five hundred men? Where would we get guns?

MONTSERRAT. From me. I have brought them each night for a month.

SALAS INA. You — you are dangerous.

FELISA (*running forward*). You are not to tell about the guns. You are not to tell.

SALAS INA (*as he goes to the door*). Yes. I will tell them about this. They will see how I feel.

SALCEDO (*to Montserrat*). You are a traitor. I will see the Colonel about this immediately.

LUHAN (*takes out his knife, motions to door*). Get away from there.

SALAS INA. What side are you on? I am trying to help us. You want to die?

LUHAN. No.

SALAS INA (*moves back*). Then why? Why?

LUHAN. I don't know why. Move away. (*Pushes Salcedo*) Move away.

SALCEDO (*pushes Luhan, wipes his coat*). Don't touch me! You dirty half-breed!

LUHAN (*smiles as he watches Salcedo brush his coat*). When I was nine years old a Spaniard said the same thing to me and then he wiped himself, the way you just did. I decided to kill him, and I spent three months planning how to do it. It was the only happy time of my childhood. But I didn't kill him because I was too frightened. (*Grabs Salcedo*) I always thought to myself, it ruined my life. If I had killed him, I'd have been another man. But there's nothing to be frightened of now — (*Ricardo grabs Luhan, pushes him away from Salcedo.*)

SALAS INA (*to Luhan*). You are special, you are different? Who hasn't wanted to kill a Spaniard? (*Screaming to Montserrat*) My wife is in a panic by now. She will be furious with me. One year of happiness in my whole life. I worked, I worked — I'm not young. Let me live a little.

SALCEDO (*coming to Montserrat*). Ask God to show you the way. Listen to His voice. He will show you our suffering and our despair.

LUHAN. Actor, you make me sick.

SALCEDO. Open your heart now and let God speak to you of the crime you do to us.

MONTSERRAT. I have done that. Every night for a year. I think I have heard His voice. (*With quiet exaltation*) He said, "It is nothing to give one's life if millions can be saved by so doing." He led me to the truth. I know He wants equality for men, the beast laid to rest — I know that for myself. I couldn't know then that your lives would be — (*Very softly*) God forgive me. God help me.

SALAS INA. He's delirious. What did you start that for?

SALCEDO (*softly*). He's insane. He needs to be bled.

LUHAN (*furious*). It is not the hand of God which strikes me down. It is your hand.

SALAS INA. Who are you to think God has picked you to make such a choice as this?

MONTSERRAT. I did not say that —

SALCEDO. Then stop pretending you have a divine injunction to kill us. You cannot fool us with that talk. It is *your* choice.

God hates murder — God does not wish to see six innocent people killed for the life of one man.

MONTSERRAT. If that one man can save millions of people — And if there is no other who can do it?

LUHAN (*furiously*). There's always another man, and another day. It will come when it comes. Some will die, and some will starve and some will be killed. That's the way it is, and that's the way it's going to be until, until — some other day.

MONTSERRAT. As long as we don't die, as long as it waits past our lives?

LUHAN. Yes. That's it. Let them fight when I am in the grave and my children on top of me. Then I'll send up the worms to help you with your dreams. Good luck — a long time from now.

MATILDE (*desperately, crying*). Please, sir. Please. Think of some way for me. I can't leave my children this way. They will die if I die. Nobody comes to my room, nobody knows me in this town. I have nothing in my life but my children. I can't leave them —

MONTSERRAT. I didn't know it would be like this. I would have run away last night. I would have killed myself.

SALAS INA. You should have killed yourself. We would never have been here, we would never have heard your name — It was your duty to kill yourself. (*The fury suddenly goes out of his voice. He stops talking and moves to Salcedo, motioning Luhan as he goes. The three of them begin to whisper. Ricardo sits near Montserrat.*)

RICARDO. How long have you believed this way?

MONTSERRAT. I don't know. As soon as I came here. And even then, it took me time. A year —

RICARDO. One year? I've known for eleven years.

MONTSERRAT. Have you?

RICARDO. Will your mother be lonely without you?

MONTSERRAT. No.

RICARDO. My mother will be lonely. My father died in the first insurrections, eleven years ago. Bolivar would know my name. My two brothers died fighting with him. My mother asked me to wait until the birthday after this. Then I was going, too. I wanted to fight. (*Hesitates*) But —

MONTSERRAT. Say what you want to say.

RICARDO. I asked how long you had believed. Because often

people who have just learned yesterday are sometimes too brave for our good.

MONTSERRAT. You think I am doing that?

RICARDO. Perhaps. I don't know. We are flesh and blood. Bolivar is sick and defeated. (*As Montserrat starts to speak*) Yes, we were defeated. Again and again. Always, it seems to me. Sometimes I've asked myself if he is really the man — (*He looks up at the whispering negotiations which are going on among Salas Ina, Luhan and Salcedo. Then he turns back to Montserrat*) Anyway, he's wounded. The chances are they've found him by now, or will tonight. Or maybe he'll take the road to Curaçao, and who could blame him? I am not afraid to die, if it serves a purpose. (*Tensely*) But we have only your word that it means anything. And you're not sure what you are doing, or what the end will be. (*Gets up, sharply*) My brother said it once. And he said it about Bolivar. He said, "He is a gentleman rider. He won't last a hard pull in the mountains."

MONTSERRAT. But he has lasted.

RICARDO (*slowly*). Yes, he has.

MONTSERRAT. No matter about Bolivar. Ask yourself this — is there anybody else? For years you've been fighting on one little hill, in one little village — And there isn't much time left. (*Points to door*) Because they are angry now, and frightened. What has been here is nothing to what will come. (*Violently*) All right. I will do what you tell me. *Tell me what to do.*

(*Ricardo starts to speak. Before he can speak Salas Ina comes forward.*)

SALAS INA. Now, now. No excitement. We will tell you what to do. We have the solution. But we must act quickly. (*Pushes Ricardo aside*) You will agree with our plan. You are an honorable man. I will guarantee to pay the price.

SALCEDO (*quickly*). Ssh. Let me speak to the Captain —

SALAS INA. I wasn't bribing him.

LUHAN. Talk less about money. (*To Salcedo*) Go ahead. Get it over.

SALAS INA. Nothing to get over. He'll understand and agree in a second. Er —

SALCEDO (*moves to Montserrat. Starts to speak, draws back*). Er. We have the solution. Er. You do not betray Bolivar, and we go out of here at liberty. Er.

LUHAN. Oh, say it. Don't carve it up. Say it.

SALCEDO. Er. (*He sighs, starts to speak, then he leans over Montserrat and whispers to him. Montserrat does not speak.*)

SALAS INA. Well? Well? (*Angry*) You talk of what you would do to save us, how you didn't know all this, what you would sacrifice, how your own life doesn't matter —

FELISA. Such a death is forbidden to him.

SALAS INA (*wildly*). And the slaughter of six innocent people is also forbidden to him. God is not going to stand on such ceremony. You shut up. God will bless him for it. I say God will welcome —

LUHAN. All right, all right. Stop that talk. (*To Montserrat*) *Do it or don't do it.*

MATILDE (*softly*). I don't clearly understand what these gentlemen — (*Shyly*) But it might be a way out, sir.

FELISA (*laughs unpleasantly*). You don't understand anything, do you? (*Montserrat rises, looks at Salas Ina and Salcedo. Then he nods to Luhan and holds out his hand for the knife.*)

FELISA (*violently*). It is useless. It will do no good. It — (*Izquierdo comes out of door. He is followed by Morales. All six people turn sharply to watch him as he takes the knife from Luhan's hand and gives it to Morales.*)

SALAS INA (*frantic*). We were — we were watching the time. We still have ten minutes. We —

IZQUIERDO (*to Felisa*). Were you here before? I didn't see. You're a pretty girl. (*To others*) Now which was it to be: were you to kill Captain Montserrat for me or was he to kill himself?

SALCEDO. No, no. We —

SALAS INA. Please, Colonel. We were making good progress for you —

SALCEDO. How did you know what we were saying? I don't understand —

IZQUIERDO. Tell me, is it necessary to be certified an idiot before going on the stage?

SALAS INA. *Please, Colonel —*

IZQUIERDO (*points to Montserrat*). He was telling you the truth. His suicide would have got you nothing but — So have no regrets. (*Sharply*) I said exactly what I meant: you will die unless he tells me where Bolivar is hiding. So don't waste your time on any other plan.

SALCEDO (*in a panic*). But you said an hour. Give us a few more minutes with him — he was beginning to agree —

IZQUIERDO. To cut his throat? (*To Morales, motioning toward courtyard*) Tell them to get ready. (*To Felisa*) Come and speak with me. (*Felisa moves slowly to him. He takes her hands*) Are you Spanish?

FELISA. My father was Spanish.

IZQUIERDO. What part of Spain did he come from?

FELISA. He didn't stop long enough to tell my mother.

IZQUIERDO (*smiles*). Are you as docile as your mother?

FELISA. When it doesn't matter to me.

IZQUIERDO (*laughs*). You have nice hair, a nice face. Would you spend a few days with me? (*She doesn't answer*) Tell me.

FELISA. What does it matter what I say? You will do what you wish.

IZQUIERDO (*gets up, goes toward window*). I wish to see you live. I like you.

SALAS INA (*shocked*). Look here, sir. It's not our fault if we're not girls. Is that fair to us? If you save one, you must save all. (*Furious, to Felisa*) Look at her. She won't even try to save us. Why don't you say that if he lets all your friends go free, then — (*Frantic*) Tell him you are honored. Tell him — Tell him. What is she doing? Tell him. Tell him.

IZQUIERDO (*calls outside*). Hurry up. Be ready quickly. (*As he moves past Salas Ina*) It's unpleasant in here.

Curtain

Act Two

AT RISE: *Salcedo is moving about. Salas Ina approaches Izquierdo, starts to speak, closes his mouth, circles Izquierdo. Luhan is sitting on the stool; he is crying. Ricardo is sitting near him, next to Matilde. Montserrat is sitting on the wall bench. Izquierdo is sitting near Felisa.*

IZQUIERDO (*To Felisa*). If I sent you home now, would you come back tonight?

FELISA. In chains.

IZQUIERDO (*smiles*). No. You would have to come back on your own. I do not enjoy the ravage and the rape or the woman against her will. Running around a room does not excite me.

FELISA (*smiles*). You want everything: you want love.

IZQUIERDO (*smiles*). Yes.

FELISA. Murder at five o'clock, love at eight. I would not come back.

SALAS INA. What is she saying? The fool! Look here, sir — you don't need her. Any woman in town would be honored. Any woman — (*He draws back as Izquierdo stares at him.*)

IZQUIERDO. I think we'll be rid of you first. I can't believe Captain Montserrat would give up Bolivar for you. I know I would not.

SALAS INA. Me. Why? Me. No. Me? What — (*Morales and guard come in from the courtyard. He stares at them and in panic begins to beat his fists against his head*) No, no, no. It's not happening. No, no, no.

IZQUIERDO (*to Montserrat*). You're not only costing these people their lives, you're costing them the little self-respect even this jibber should have. Look at him. This is the stuff with which Bolivar will fight?

SALAS INA. Bolivar. I hate such a man. I would fight such a man. He is more my enemy than he is yours. If he were here I would tear him with burning pincers —

IZQUIERDO. Yes, if we held him down for you.

SALAS INA. You would see. I would show you how much I love our King. I always speak of his noble character, his high aims —

IZQUIERDO. Then it is just as well you will never meet him.

SALAS INA. What? Go and ask people how I have spoken. Everybody knows me. Everybody knows I have contributed to the charity of *your* wounded. Go and ask in the square —

IZQUIERDO. Tomorrow.

SALAS INA. In my store I have not alone a painting of King Charles, but also of Ferdinand because I look forward to that blessed day when he will be restored — *Two* pictures hang there —

IZQUIERDO. You find them that attractive? (*Points to Montserrat*) Come. I don't think you are moving the Captain. And bear in mind, all of you, you must convince *him*. He doesn't admire the Spanish Royal Family. Try tacking in another direction.

SALAS INA. Oh. Er. I've tried — I — never said everything here was right. Certainly not. It's true Spain has no right to treat her colonies like slaves. I've always been a modern man, in my way. Many times I've said things *must* be corrected —

IZQUIERDO (*laughs*). Now we will have to shoot you as a liberal.

SALAS INA (*frantic*). You misunderstand me. I only said there are two sides to every question. I myself am a Royalist —

MONTSERRAT (*angrily to Izquierdo*). For God's sake, leave him alone.

IZQUIERDO (*to Montserrat*). This disturbs you? Good.

SALAS INA (*to Izquierdo*). Can't I talk with you? You are a patriot, a true soldier, a man from the gentlemen nobility — Er. I am rich — (*Leans over Izquierdo, softly*) Couldn't we, sensible men, couldn't an arrangement —

IZQUIERDO. Move away from me, please.

SALAS INA. I can give you — (*Izquierdo gives him a shove. Salas Ina topples backward. Montserrat comes toward him quickly, catches him. Salas Ina recovers himself and spits at Montserrat.*)

IZQUIERDO (*laughs*). The fate of all saviors and all martyrs. (*To Salas Ina*) In the meantime, stop that. Spitting does not usually melt the human heart. Please all of you keep in mind I am interested in how far you can move this gentleman to speak. Therefore, I do not wish him attacked by you.

SALAS INA. Yes, yes. I'm sorry. (*To Montserrat*) Forgive me, sir. Forgive me —

MONTSERRAT. Don't ask me to forgive you. (*To Izquierdo with great passion*) Put an end to this. Anything will be easier for him now.

IZQUIERDO. You think so? I don't. (*To Salas Ina*) Do you?

SALAS INA (*bewildered, shaking*). What? Do I what?

IZQUIERDO. Er. Would you rather die or degrade yourself a little further?

SALAS INA (*violently*). *I don't want to die.*

IZQUIERDO. Because of your wife? You love her. You told me.

SALAS INA (*in anguish*). Yes.

IZQUIERDO. More than life, you said.

SALAS INA. Yes.

IZQUIERDO. That's charming. Would you send your wife here tonight? Not for me, of course, but — (*Salas Ina turns away*) Come along. Will you send her here tonight? (*No answer, pounds on table*) Quickly. Answer me.

SALAS INA (*gasps*). Yes.

FELISA (*in a soft sound*). Aah.

IZQUIERDO (*turns to look at her, then to Salas Ina*). So you have been deceiving yourself? You believed up to now that your wife was worth more than your life. A street singer sang it that way, eh? Well, now you see your love for what it always was. Better to die in truth than to live in lies, they tell me. (*Crosses to Montserrat*) What do you say? His life is worth more than his honor and more than his love. Perhaps because he is like so many of us, he is most worth saving. What do you decide?

MONTSERRAT (*softly*). I ask him to forgive me, and to forgive you.

IZQUIERDO (*sighs, then turns back to Salas Ina*). He refuses you. (*Motions to Morales and Soldier. They come to Salas Ina.*)

SALAS INA (*in horror*). Colonel —

IZQUIERDO. And, of course, we must officially refuse your wife. (*Silent, gasping, Salas Ina throws himself at Izquierdo, but before he can reach him, the Soldier pulls him off, drags him along the floor. As they reach the steps, two Monks appear in the door. One stands in the door; the other comes down the steps, puts his arm around Salas Ina, and they go out. The drums begin to beat. As the drums increase the tempo, Montserrat moves toward Izquierdo.*)

MONTSERRAT. Izquierdo. Take me. Take *me* —

IZQUIERDO. I don't want you. I want Bolivar. (*Montserrat opens his mouth, stops, starts to speak, then moves slowly away. Izquierdo sighs, turns away. The drums increase, the volley is heard, a loud scream comes from the courtyard, and then the coup de grace. After a second's silence Izquierdo moves to Luhan*) All right. Get up. (*Morales comes in the door, waits near it.*)

LUHAN (*softly*). No.

IZQUIERDO. No?

LUHAN. I've done no crime. I have five children. I've done no crime.

IZQUIERDO. Most people die having done no crime. Death comes and is considered the will of God: we lie down and resign ourselves. Resign yourself.

LUHAN (*softly*). When you die the natural way, you feel bad and it's not so hard to get out. But I don't feel bad. I want to live out my life and die like other people.

IZQUIERDO. But this gentleman won't allow you to die like other people. I am sorry.

LUHAN (*with great force*). Keep the sorry. Just stop the killing.

IZQUIERDO. I can't do that. As much as you want your life, I want Bolivar.

LUHAN. You have already murdered one man. You've seen that this crazy fool won't talk — (*Gets up, violently*) I am good at what I do. I want to do what I do. I'm good. I want to live and see more, and make more with what I see — My work will get better. The last few years my carving is wonderful — (*Comes to Izquierdo*) Last year the Bishop of Merida came to Valencia. He's a great man of knowledge and culture —

IZQUIERDO. He dined here.

LUHAN. You think that's why he came, do you?

IZQUIERDO. No. I spent a week trying to find out why he came.

LUHAN. Ask me. He came to see me. What do you think of that?

IZQUIERDO. I think it must have been dull for you.

LUHAN (*softly*). You have no respect even for such a man?

IZQUIERDO. I hadn't thought about respect.

LUHAN. All that ride from the South — to see me. At night he came and said, "Luhan, the new cathedral will be finished in three, four years. Make the statues for it. Of all the artists on the continent I have come to you. We will pay you well." —

I said, "Thank you, but I don't take money for such an honor." He understood what I felt, like the great man he is and —

IZQUIERDO. I'm sure of it. Haven't you found people are understanding when it saves them money?

LUHAN (*as if he hadn't heard*). I am making the statues and people for all time will see them. Nobody will care how I was born. They will look at my work and have joy from it — (*To Izquierdo*) I want to finish that work. *I am going to finish it.*

IZQUIERDO. How many statues have you completed?

LUHAN. Two.

IZQUIERDO. I'll see they are delivered.

LUHAN (*wildly*). You won't. (*Points to His Excellency's door*) You will tell him and he will pay my wife a few coins and then he will send them to Spain for museum storekeepers to sell among themselves.

IZQUIERDO. They will be delivered to the Bishop. I promise you.

LUHAN. *I want to finish them.* And I want to take them myself and I want to put them in place and I want to hear the Bishop say, "They're good. They are like the best." And when I die I want to say to my sons, "*I* did the statues for the great Cathedral of Merida. Ask the Bishop if it is time to scratch in my name. If he says the time hasn't come yet, then wait until you die, and tell your sons to ask again. I want my name —

IZQUIERDO. You are a humble man. It makes me sick. Let's be finished now. Get up.

LUHAN (*softly*). No. I won't go.

IZQUIERDO (*points to Montserrat*). Speak to him.

LUHAN. No. He's crazy. Like all of them like him. He talks of many men, and the good for many men, and feels nothing for the life of one.

FELISA (*softly*). That isn't true.

IZQUIERDO (*turns to stare at her. Then to Morales*). Take him out. (*Morales pulls Luhan to his feet.*)

MONTSERRAT (*in a shout to Izquierdo*). For the sake of God stop this. Izquierdo, I beg you. I will do whatever you —

IZQUIERDO. Yes?

MONTSERRAT. Find another way. Do what you want with me. But —

IZQUIERDO (*to Morales*). Take him out. (*To Montserrat*) There is only one bargain you can make with me. No other. (*He waits. Montserrat wipes his face, and then slowly turns away. Izquierdo speaks to Luhan*) Try to die bravely. As we all must.

LUHAN (*the Monks come in the door, go to Luhan. Luhan turns to the Monk who has taken his arm, speaks quietly*). My mother is still alive. Father — tell her — (*They exit. There is silence in the room. Then the drums begin to beat. Montserrat moves quickly to the door. The beat of the drums increases. Montserrat turns back to Izquierdo as if to say something. Izquierdo waits, then picks up book from table.*)

IZQUIERDO (*reading*). "Remember, Spaniards, we must teach our people. Bring them to books and they will free themselves. There does exist the noble savage, we would not deny this, but only the thinking man has the full use of his soul, the full power of noble action —" (*To Montserrat*) *You* are the thinking man? (*Very sharply*) Are there many of you?

MONTSERRAT (*the tempo of the drums quickens; the coup de grace is heard during Montserrat's speech. Softly, as if to himself*). "Go about the land and teach. But before you do, make sure your strength will stand before the tragedies you will see, or the tests to which you will be strained. Take this blessing from an old man who believes in God and man." (*At the sound of the coup de grace, he covers his face.*)

IZQUIERDO. Did Bolivar find you, or you Bolivar? Why would he want a man who was bottled on *books?* If I were he I would be frightened of Spanish dreamers. Tell me, when such a man — (*Points to the book*) has such a dream, does he put a date upon it? Does he say tomorrow, or in five hundred years? Do *you* date your dream? Your local dream?

MONTSERRAT (*sharply*). Yes. I date it today. Tonight.

IZQUIERDO (*jumps up*). Does Bolivar date it tonight?

MONTSERRAT. Yes. Of course. Do you think I'm murdering these people —

IZQUIERDO. You mean I haven't much more time?

MONTSERRAT. No. No. I mean the patrols have probably found Bolivar by now. Let them go. If he isn't found, you can avenge yourself on me. (*Desperately*) Izquierdo, have pity —

IZQUIERDO. You're talking nonsense. *Don't waste time for me again.* (*Morales comes in from the courtyard. To Montserrat*) And are you ready for another?

MONTSERRAT. Wait for the patrols to come back —

IZQUIERDO. I am waiting for the answer: *where is Bolivar?* (*There is a pause*) I'm waiting. (*Pause*) Very well. (*During their conversation, Salcedo has been looking out of the window. He leaves the window and aimlessly sits on steps. Izquierdo watches him, points outside*) How did it go? Quietly? (*No answer*) You are offering yourself for the next in turn? Good of you.

SALCEDO (*sits up*). Sorry. I — What is it? (*Suddenly realizes what is meant*) I beg you.

IZQUIERDO. Turn your begging toward him. Use your art, now. You did very well as Ascascio. Now play for your own life.

SALCEDO (*weeping*). Don't take me. Don't kill me. Wait, wait —

IZQUIERDO (*hits the table, gets up, goes to Montserrat*). I've had bad luck. I should have known cowards wouldn't move you because they don't move me, either. (*Goes to Salcedo*) Did you hear what I said? You won't touch him your way. Stand up and play the hero for a few minutes. It's your only chance. Get up. Stand up. (*Salcedo gets to his feet*) Act like a man and perhaps he will wish to save the life of a man. Say one of those large things actors say when they're dying.

SALCEDO (*weeping*). Please leave me alone. Please — I'm just myself —

IZQUIERDO (*shoves him back*). Then say something that isn't you. Borrow another man. Play Ascascio for him and perhaps he'll think it's you. Try that noble speech.

SALCEDO. I can't remember — I can't — I —

IZQUIERDO. Try to remember. Come on.

SALCEDO (*then, after a pause*). "This night I will know the touch of thy wings. In twenty battles —"

IZQUIERDO. Speak up.

SALCEDO (*as a bad actor would do it*). "As for you, Castilians. As for you, Castilians, I do not hate you. The Savior commands that we forgive as He forgave."

IZQUIERDO. Play up.

SALCEDO. "I draw on God now for the strength to keep my soul in peace as I face the final minute. It will be a bitter battle to return love for torture, forgiveness for cruelty. But here is my day and now my hour. Almighty God, I need Your help. Look at me, read within me and show me the way."

IZQUIERDO (*applauds*). Dreadful.

SALCEDO (*he turns on Izquierdo*). You have made me call on God with a lie. Because that isn't me, and I do not return love for torture. I hate *you*. (*Goes to Izquierdo, with fury*) *I* am nothing, an unimportant man and you have made me say that I am noble. You are going to kill me. Isn't that enough? Did I have to play the fool for you? (*Softly, crying*) God forgive me for — lying words —

MONTSERRAT. For God's sake, Izquierdo —

IZQUIERDO. You thought men to be better than this, brave and fine? It shocks you to find they believe in nothing and are made of mess.

MONTSERRAT (*with great anger*). Save my story for a dull night at a barracks table. Don't concern yourself with me. Think of yourself and what you're doing — think of the day when *you'll* lie down to die remembering this — (*Turns away.*)

MATILDE (*loudly*). Everybody has forgotten my children. I stand here waiting —

SALCEDO. Be quiet. Stop screaming.

MATILDE. I say you have forgotten my children — (*Their voices are loud and wild as Father Coronil comes out of the door.*)

IZQUIERDO. Father, the noise awoke you?

FATHER CORONIL (*sharply*). His Excellency requested me in here.

SALCEDO. Father, Father. Help me. (*Pointing to Izquierdo*) He is going to kill me. Father, help us. *You don't know what is happening here.*

FATHER CORONIL (*gently*). I have nothing to do with what is happening here. (*Turns to Montserrat*) You have not confessed what you must confess. Then *you* are responsible for the torture of these people.

MATILDE. Make him speak. Father, tell him.

FATHER CORONIL (*to Montserrat*). Confess your sin. Take your punishment for it.

MONTSERRAT (*carefully, intensely*). I am a traitor here. Very well. There is punishment for a traitor, I knew that, and I accepted it. But this is outside punishment — For the sake of these people, Father, go in and beg His Excellency — Kill me for what I did. Not them for what they did not do.

FATHER CORONIL (*sharply*). I told you before: I have not and will not become involved in military affairs.

MONTSERRAT (*softly*). Aaaah.

FATHER CORONIL (*to Salcedo*). How can I help you, my son?

SALCEDO. Father, I am an innocent man.

FATHER CORONIL. Who of us is innocent?

SALCEDO. *I* am innocent.

FATHER CORONIL. Then you are the only man who is, and that you would not claim.

SALCEDO. I don't know what you mean. I am innocent of this. I have done nothing. *I want to live.*

FATHER CORONIL. When the bell tolls, under whatever circumstance, we must not regret life and the flesh, and false treasures. Jesus said, "Blessed are they which are persecuted for righteousness' sake for theirs is the Kingdom of Heaven."

SALCEDO (*softly, as if he is lost*). Father, I don't know what you are talking about. What has any of that to do with me? I am an artist, I lead a quiet life, I am a quiet man. All this is about Bolivar. I don't even know — I don't even know his Christian name. (*Suddenly*) My father is still alive. And my mother. I support them.

FATHER CORONIL. I am sure you have done your duties, and done them well.

SALCEDO. I planned to marry someday.

IZQUIERDO. So did I. But men who plan to marry someday never marry.

SALCEDO (*very angry*). I tell you I would have married. (*To Father Coronil*) I have done no good but I have done no harm.

FATHER CORONIL. I believe you.

SALCEDO. I say that in truth. (*He moves about. Then, as if to himself*) I have thought about dying. I remember one night a long time ago — I couldn't sleep. I thought that night, certainly you'll die, everybody dies. And now you'll think I'm crazy but I said to myself maybe you're the one person who won't ever die — (*Giggles*) That's what I thought that night.

IZQUIERDO. Did you?

SALCEDO. Another night I pictured myself an old man. Very, very old, walking into the sea on a bright day. And I had never seen the sea. Never until I came here. I mean I thought of it all long before I came here or saw the sea. But I've never thought of it since I came here, which was when I saw the sea.

IZQUIERDO. We all invent a death scene. You're no different. Only a soldier knows he won't have one.

FATHER CORONIL. You wish to understand? Why you are — why you are here, why you have this suffering? Will it comfort you to understand?

SALCEDO. I don't know. Maybe.

FATHER CORONIL. You believe that the King takes his authority from the All Powerful?

SALCEDO. Oh, yes.

FATHER CORONIL. If Bolivar is a rebel against the King, then it follows for us, for you and me, that he is a rebel against God. That is true?

MONTSERRAT. No. Nor does all the Church believe it. Tell him that there are three priests riding with Bolivar's men; *good* priests, fighting with their poor —

SALCEDO (*to Father Coronil, as if he hadn't heard Montserrat*). Yes, of course it's true.

FATHER CORONIL. Then is it not our duty, yours and mine, to defeat an enemy of God? Would that not lead us to make any sacrifice, no matter how?

SALCEDO. All I know is that I've done nothing. (*Looks at Father Coronil, points to Izquierdo*) I don't believe you should excuse such a man —

FATHER CORONIL. I have nothing to do with this man. But I have not spoken of men and their reasons. I have spoken of God.

SALCEDO (*violently*). It is a crime against God to torture people, to kill them — I've always been a good Christian, I've always believed. But I don't understand what you've said. I'm, I'm —

MONTSERRAT. Leave him his faith, Father. Give him back his faith.

SALCEDO (*desperately*). Father, you must defend us against the crime of this man.

FATHER CORONIL. I have no association with this man, now, before or ever.

IZQUIERDO (*wearily*). Let us put a stop to these discussions of who is in whose service. (*To Father Coronil*) His God has been a simple God of love and mercy. I can understand why he finds it hard to believe that such a God, at this minute, is in alliance with us.

FATHER CORONIL (*angrily*). An alliance with you?

IZQUIERDO (*amused*). Father, if it pleases you to think of me as the instrument carrying out the law of King and God, but outside the fold of either, use me thus. We all need some such figure to rise above. (*Sharply*) In the meantime, you should not have allowed yourself to be drawn into this discussion. My method is quicker and perhaps easier on everybody.

MONTSERRAT (*comes quickly to Father Coronil; desperately, slowly*). Father, what is true, who is guilty, what is the law, none of it matters. Let us forget all that. Go in to him. Plead with him. Tell him there has been punishment enough, revenge enough — (*Suddenly, in a new voice*) *I can't stand any more.*

IZQUIERDO. Good. Then give me Bolivar and we will finish.

MONTSERRAT (*to Father Coronil*). Father, I beg you.

IZQUIERDO. There is nothing Father Coronil can do. There is nothing His Excellency can do. I don't wish to kill this man. He is a Spaniard. He is loyal and stupid and devout and an artist. But I am in a hurry now. (*Sharply*) So if you want to save him save him quickly — (*Montserrat turns away. Izquierdo raises his hand to soldier at door*) I am as embarrassed as Pontius Pilate.

SALCEDO. Have pity on me. (*The two Monks appear at door.*)

IZQUIERDO (*to Salcedo*). There's no sense weeping and begging. The other two didn't know about acting. You do. Have a little dignity. Play a hero on your way out. (*Salcedo moves across the room, stumbles on the stairs. One of the Monks comes down the steps, puts his arm around Salcedo, whispers to him. Salcedo straightens up, goes out slowly, holding the hand of the Monk. They are followed by Father Coronil. The drums start up. Their tempo increases. Suddenly, Izquierdo grabs Montserrat, drags him to the window, holds him pinned to window*) No. No. Look back, look back. The wood carver over there. Little wonder we all want to die in bed, trusting those who will paint our faces and dress us fine. The merchant looks soggy and creased. Perhaps because he's old. Perhaps because his chest was crushed. (*The drums increase. Neither speaks. We hear the coup de grace. Izquierdo turns from window, comes into room, pours himself a drink of wine. Montserrat stands at the window as if praying, then turns away*) How do you console yourself? With the resurrection of Lazarus?

MONTSERRAT (*very sharply*). What has disturbed *you?* (*Points to the courtyard*) That he died in dignity?

IZQUIERDO (*wipes his face*). He died playing a part, poor fool — (*From behind His Excellency's door, we hear the piano. The music is light and pleasant.*)

MONTSERRAT. Then the more credit to him. It takes courage to pretend courage.

IZQUIERDO. Yes, I think so. It is impressive to see a man go beyond himself.

MONTSERRAT (*very bitterly*). It impressed *you,* eh? (*Violently*) But let somebody else write his funeral piece some other day.

IZQUIERDO (*points to His Excellency's door*). Listen to him. That is eccentricity tailored carefully to hide — nothing. (*Turns to Felisa*) Do you dance?

FELISA. No.

IZQUIERDO. Why?

FELISA. There has been no time to learn.

IZQUIERDO. You will have time to learn. Shall I teach you?

FELISA. It is too late.

IZQUIERDO (*smiles*). Dear child. Have you ever been with a man?

FELISA. No.

IZQUIERDO. Shall I teach you?

FELISA (*softly*). It was not the way I dreamed of learning.

IZQUIERDO. I will teach you. Perhaps I would fall in love for a few days. Would you like that?

FELISA. It would not matter to me.

IZQUIERDO. I think it would. Some way. (*Then coldly*) What has mattered to you? What have you wanted?

FELISA. More to eat. (*Puts her hand on her dress*) Less filth. And the death of you and all like you.

IZQUIERDO (*there is a pause. Then Izquierdo smashes his glass against His Excellency's door, shouts through the grill windows*). Stop that Goddamn music. Go up to your rooms, and don't come down again. (*To Felisa*) The death of me and all like me? Are you sure?

FELISA. I am sure. (*The music trails off, ceases. There is a pause. Zavala comes in. He stares at Montserrat. Then he goes to Izquierdo*)

ZAVALA. His Excellency asks that you discontinue the drums.

IZQUIERDO (*laughs*). Tell him we cannot abolish so honored a military tradition. (*Softly*) Go back and put more sherry in his hot water.

ZAVALA. I have done that. Have you any other remedies for

what is going on in here? (*Very sharply*) Izquierdo, I think His Excellency would like you to put an end to this.

IZQUIERDO. You think he would, eh?

MONTSERRAT. Zavala, go in. Save these people — *Talk to him — Make him —*

ZAVALA (*angry*). What do you think of me? I've done everything I could —

IZQUIERDO. I want no interference from you and I will take none now from him. Go back in and say that. And if you come out again with any message about the drums, I will see to it that Morales takes a rest and *you* will conduct the executions.

ZAVALA (*carefully*). You will not be able to do that. Each of us reserves a space for what we will not do. You have come to that space in me.

MONTSERRAT (*comes to Zavala, holds him*). *Speak to him again. Tell him —*

ZAVALA. I have begged. I have. He's frightened — (*Points to Izquierdo*) of him. Don't you know that? And of Bolivar, when he remembers who he is. Today is not today for him, and here is not here. He is home, in a summer garden, and they are talking of Napoleon.

IZQUIERDO (*as Zavala exits. Izquierdo turns to Ricardo*). Well, son, speak up. Tell us how innocent you are, how your uncle will starve without you —

RICARDO. No.

IZQUIERDO (*to Montserrat*). So there is a variation. This one is young and about to be brave. Does that touch you?

MONTSERRAT. Izquierdo, this is a child. Pity him. *Let him go.*

IZQUIERDO (*slowly*). *You* pity him, you let him go. (*Quickly, as if he had an idea, to Ricardo*) Could you take hard punishment if you thought it would save your life, and the lives of these women? What do you say? It will be bad but I have a feeling he won't allow you to take too much — (*Looks at his watch, to Montserrat*) You'll go along with him.

MONTSERRAT (*shouts*). *No. No.* You must not touch him. No, Izquierdo. (*Izquierdo turns. Montserrat looks at him, nods.*)

IZQUIERDO. Now?

MONTSERRAT. Yes.

RICARDO. *Don't save me, sir. Don't save me.* (*He runs to Montserrat*) Tell me once more that you believe in Bolivar.

MONTSERRAT (*pauses, then*). I believe in Bolivar. I swear it.

IZQUIERDO (*looks at Ricardo*). Did Captain Montserrat tell you about the letter?

MONTSERRAT. I have told him the truth as I know the truth.

IZQUIERDO (*to Ricardo*). Did he tell you about the letter?

MONTSERRAT. The letter had no meaning —

IZQUIERDO. Tell him about it.

MONTSERRAT (*to Ricardo*). He thought the fight was lost. He asked for refuge —

RICARDO (*softly*). He was going to leave us?

MONTSERRAT. He did not send the letter —

IZQUIERDO. He will send another: they always do. (*To Ricardo*) You and your kind will fight and die, and the Creole will arrange to save himself. Rich gentlemen make untrustworthy revolutionaries because they have their past to remember in their future. (*Softly*) But I don't need to tell you that. How often have you heard it said, "He isn't one of us; don't trust him. He'll betray us like the rest. Wait for a leader, born from the people." *How often have you heard it?*

RICARDO (*slowly*). Always. Word for word. (*To Montserrat*) I had heard about the letter. But I didn't believe it.

MONTSERRAT (*goes to Ricardo*). There is no man without a time of defeat and an hour of turning back. Bolivar had his defeat, he had his time of mourning, and passed through it. They may catch him tonight and kill him. But he will not turn back again. I know that as surely as I know that I am willing to die for it.

IZQUIERDO (*to Ricardo*). We will catch him tonight. Your death will have been a waste. You're very young. You have forty or fifty years of life.

RICARDO. We don't live so long here. (*To Montserrat*) He will not write another letter?

MONTSERRAT (*slowly*). If you think he will, I will save you.

RICARDO. No. I am with him. I wish I could have been with him when — I wish I could have been buried with flags, and — (*Laughs*) That is the way I thought of it when I was young. (*Turns to Izquierdo, nods*) All right.

IZQUIERDO (*motions to soldiers*). Take him away. (*The Soldier comes into the room. The Monks wait in the doorway. Ricardo moves to the door. When he reaches the door he turns, looks back at Montserrat. He exits, followed by the Soldier and the Monks. The drums begin. Montserrat cries out*) I will let him go. I promise you.

MONTSERRAT (*in a gasp*). The Valencia road.

IZQUIERDO (*runs toward Montserrat*). What? *What do you mean —*

MONTSERRAT. The road back to Valencia.

IZQUIERDO (*with great speed*). The road back here? What are you talking about —

FELISA (*very loudly*). I am ready to be next. (*Izquierdo and Montserrat turn to stare at her. She points to courtyard, speaks to Montserrat*) So was he. Be still. Tell nothing, nothing. I am ready. (*Montserrat opens his mouth as if to speak, then turns away.*)

IZQUIERDO (*very angry, to Felisa*). Are you? Well, I'm not ready for you — (*He crosses toward Montserrat, kicks a stool. Felisa, as she moves away, falls over the stool. Izquierdo speaks to Montserrat quickly, urgently*) He is not ready, and you know it. It was the high moment of a child.

FELISA. Be still! Be still!

IZQUIERDO. He's out there now, slobbering for his mother. (*The drums have reached the coup de grace*) You talk to me of tricks and murder — (*The shots are heard. Izquierdo turns away. After a second, Morales comes in. Izquierdo points to Matilde. Matilde backs toward the wall*) How did the boy behave?

MORALES. Refused the blindfold, refused to face the wall. He said his prayers and viva something or other —

IZQUIERDO. Viva something or other. You fool. (*Sharply*) Don't *touch the boy's body.* (*Morales nods. Begins to go toward Matilde.*)

MATILDE (*shouting*). Go away. Go away. (*To Montserrat*) I beg you. They are locked in a room. I will come back and die for whatever you are talking about. But for the sake of God let me go and save them. I can unlock the door. I don't know anybody but I'll leave them on the street and somebody will — *Listen to me.* You have no children but you know what a child is like. You can't lock a door and let babies die. Such a thing is not your right and God will curse you for it. Let me go home first to save them — (*She turns to Izquierdo, softly, sweetly*) Before God, in solemn oath, I will come back. I will go without a word. Anything, any way, but let me try to save them. (*To Montserrat with great force, with anger*) You have murdered four people. *You cannot kill babies.*

(*Montserrat nods slowly, pats her arm. Felisa moves quickly toward him.*)

FELISA. I tell you, *be still.* It's too late. Four people have died. What will you make it — that they have died for nothing? Stay with what you believe. (*Furiously*) Yes. It's bad about her babies. But death is death, no better for one than another.

MATILDE (*wildly, moving about*). I beg for God's curse on all of you. Damned, damned — (*To Felisa*) You I hate most. You I hate most. It has just happened to me that you I hate most.

IZQUIERDO (*slowly, wearily to Montserrat*). If you talk now, I will promise you the lives of these women. *And* deportation for you *and* Bolivar. I'll hate you for the bargain, but we will settle that another day. I'll have the deportation order for you immediately. I swear it.

MATILDE (*who has been mumbling through Izquierdo's speech*). We should have been married in a church, my good mother said. She said that. She said I would be punished.

FELISA (*moves to Matilde*). I had no chance for children. You had a little of life, more than I had, and if it was hard it was something. *All right. My* mother will cry for me tonight — (*Suddenly, to Izquierdo, pointing to Matilde*) Please, let me go with her. Please let us go together. (*Izquierdo looks at her, nods. Then he motions to Morales. Felisa goes to Matilde*) Come. We'll pray for your children, and other children, and those to come. (*She takes Matilde by the hand. Matilde mumbles, looks around as if she didn't know where she was. Felisa passes Montserrat, leans down and kisses him*) It is over for you now. Good-bye. (*Felisa begins quickly to move out, dragging Matilde with her. The two Monks stand at the door, help Matilde up the steps. Felisa and Matilde exit, Morales follows them out. There is silence as the drums start. The drums increase. Suddenly Matilde shrieks: "Nooooo," and the shriek ends on a volley. There is a second volley.*)

IZQUIERDO (*turns, slowly*). How long have you been here? When were you sent here from Spain? A year ago?

MONTSERRAT. Yes.

IZQUIERDO. When did we meet?

MONTSERRAT. The night I came.

IZQUIERDO. What did you think of me that night?

MONTSERRAT (*speaks as if he were in a dream*). Another Spaniard.

IZQUIERDO. And you seemed to me to be made of soft cloth, badly woven, with the threads running out and the holes running in.

MONTSERRAT. And so I was.

IZQUIERDO. I had seen your kind before. They always plan to act but they never do. If you were the exception, and turned a little traitor, you might be valuable. A little traitor, with a little handling, talks first and then turns home. I told myself that, and then forgot about you. (*Montserrat takes off his coat, wipes his face, looks at his watch, puts it on table.*)

MONTSERRAT. You are ready for me now?

IZQUIERDO. I saw you every night with the soup and I forgot about you with the brandy. Tell me, was I wrong, or have you changed and I not noticed it? (*Sharply, points to courtyard door*) I was sure that as the merchant went through that door, you would confess. Did you care for their lives as you claimed, or did you pretend a broken heart?

MONTSERRAT. You give me too much credit. If it hadn't been for the girl — (*Violently*) What use is this talk? What I feel, what has happened to me? Do you want me to tell you there could be no other torture now, that I could not have stood another minute without that girl? (*Very angry*) What do you want? *To hell with you.* Stop the talk of what I am or was, and what you think. *Get finished.*

IZQUIERDO. There was a high plain above the town of Caballo. No trees, no rocks, no weeds. Only earth and wind. Bolivar's gallant soldiers dug a round grave from here — (*Points to his feet*) to here. (*Touches his chin*) They took me in a raid, a year before you came.

MONTSERRAT (*wearily*). I heard about you.

IZQUIERDO. *No, you didn't.* They buried me up to here (*Touches his chin*) and packed the earth tight. Then they counted out ten men and ten men and ten, and on. And each ten came to me and pissed in my face. That was twenty-five months ago: there hasn't been a night since that I haven't heard their laughter and felt my face to see if — That laughter fills the world for me. The rest I've almost forgotten: the four days and four nights, my head like a stone placed in an empty land. That is the story as you heard it . . . about a miracle survival — but nobody knows what they did to me. Only you. (*Violently*) I can't live unless they don't live.

MONTSERRAT (*softly*). All of them?

IZQUIERDO. All of them, and all those like them.

MONTSERRAT. Did you think you would get delicate care from people who have seen hot pitch poured on prisoners, strips of skin torn off with pincers, villages raped and burned — Didn't you know they would learn from us?

IZQUIERDO. Understand me, I have no moral objection to what they do. I have no such judgments. I leave them to you. I care only what was done to me. *After* that, I serve a King. But I am not fool enough to believe in him. If he dies tomorrow, no hopes of mine go with him. There will be another, and it will make no difference. But you have put your hope in one man. And when he dies tonight or betrays you next year — (*Pauses*) Have you thought of that?

MONTSERRAT. We agree, you and I. There is no one man, and therefore no only man. You take the best man you find. That is what I have done. If I am wrong, then —

IZQUIERDO. Then you have killed six people.

MONTSERRAT. Yes, I have.

IZQUIERDO. It has been worth it to you?

MONTSERRAT (*furiously*). Leave off. Get through with me.

IZQUIERDO. Where is Bolivar?

MONTSERRAT (*stares at him, laughs*). Are you going to offer me my life now? I don't want it.

IZQUIERDO. Where is Bolivar?

MONTSERRAT (*smiles*). The six are dead. What could make me talk now? I have had my torture. It is over.

IZQUIERDO. But you almost talked. Only the girl saved you. You almost talked.

MONTSERRAT. Yes. But I did not talk.

IZQUIERDO. You were lucky to have the girl. There are not many such. There will be no girl this time. (*Montserrat wheels around. Izquierdo speaks to soldier at door*) Find Captain Morales. Tell him to go down to the square and bring six people here immediately. (*Montserrat stares at him, turns, sits down. There is a pause.*)

IZQUIERDO. All right? Is Bolivar armed?

MONTSERRAT. Yes.

IZQUIERDO. How many men with him?

MONTSERRAT. Three.

IZQUIERDO. They have guns?

MONTSERRAT. Yes.

IZQUIERDO. The Puebla road?

MONTSERRAT. Yes.

IZQUIERDO. Describe the place to me, and the distance from here.

MONTSERRAT. About three hours.

IZQUIERDO. How will we mark it?

MONTSERRAT (*as if he were speaking by rote*). Five rocks. Turn in there.

IZQUIERDO. House or a cave?

MONTSERRAT (*suddenly nervous*). I don't know.

IZQUIERDO (*very sharply*). Why don't you know?

MONTSERRAT. Because —

IZQUIERDO. House or cave?

MONTSERRAT. Cave.

IZQUIERDO. How do I find the cave?

MONTSERRAT. Five rocks —

IZQUIERDO. Five rocks were at the road. What are you saying?

ZAVALA (*offstage*). Izquierdo.

IZQUIERDO (*to Montserrat*). What can you hope to save by lying now? (*Shakes him*) You'll have another six people —

MONTSERRAT (*desperately*). I can't tell you where he is. He is not in hiding. (*Zavala enters*) He never was.

IZQUIERDO. What are you talking about?

MONTSERRAT. He has no hiding place. (*Wheels to Zavala, pleadingly*) Zavala, what time is it?

ZAVALA. Six-thirty. *Izquierdo* —

MONTSERRAT (*turns back*). I promised I would give him as long as I could. He said, "Try to give us until seven o'clock." (*Laughs*) Now either you've taken him, or he's joined his people.

IZQUIERDO. Where could he join? He couldn't get through either road —

ZAVALA (*sharply*). *Listen to me.* He got through. (*Izquierdo wheels around*) He went through El Pao an hour ago.

MORALES (*comes running through the courtyard door*). He rode through El Pao — They're back. The patrols are back —

IZQUIERDO (*to Morales*). What are *you* saying? How did he get through? —

MORALES. Antonanzas caught up with him on the road. Three

men were killed. Antonanzas is wounded — (*Frightened, as Izquierdo wheels to him, points to door*) Antonanzas will tell you. He'll tell you — (*Points to Montserrat*) They want him. They've come back for him — (*There are shouts in the courtyard.*)

IZQUIERDO (*slowly, to Montserrat*). He took the road back here. Very daring. Did you advise it?

MONTSERRAT. Yes.

IZQUIERDO. So this time has been valuable to you?

MONTSERRAT (*softly*). To me?

IZQUIERDO. To those who will revenge you?

MONTSERRAT. There will be no revenge for me.

IZQUIERDO (*points to courtyard door*). *They* will want revenge.

MONTSERRAT (*softly*). God will help me.

IZQUIERDO (*wearily*). You will need His help.

MONTSERRAT (*as if he hadn't heard him, to Zavala*). Bolivar rode toward Tinaco?

ZAVALA. Yes.

MONTSERRAT (*smiles, as if to himself*). They are waiting for him at Tinaco. He is there by now. The church bells are ringing, there are flowers in the square, the people are shouting and singing — He'll sleep for a few hours — (*To Izquierdo*) They will meet tonight. Tonight a thousand men will ride into Tinaco. And tomorrow when the news is out, there'll be another thousand. They will come now, they will stay with him now. I wish I could have seen Tinaco — (*Fervently*) God keep them and bless them, now and forever. (*Antonanzas and two young officers burst into the room. Antonanzas has a bandaged left hand. He goes quickly to Montserrat, knocks him down, then he hits Montserrat in the face with his gun. One officer leans over him, pulls Montserrat's arm from the socket. Montserrat shrieks. The second officer rolls him to the back of the room, picks him up, smashes his face against the wall.*)

ZAVALA (*in a shout to Izquierdo*). *Kill him fast. Give them the order.*

IZQUIERDO (*after a second, to Antonanzas*). Take him out. And finish it.

ANTONANZAS (*very angry*). He'll be lucky if he's dead by tomorrow.

IZQUIERDO (*coldly*). Take him out. Shoot him *now*. (*Antonanzas hesitates for a second, starts to speak, looks at Izquierdo*)

Now. (*Antonanzas nods at the officers. They drag Montserrat out.*)

MONTSERRAT (*in a shriek*). God help — (*One of the Monks comes quickly in the door, hurries to the crucifix, kneels, begins to cry.*)

MONTSERRAT'S VOICE	THE MONK'S VOICE
God come to me. God help me. God help me.	— They know not what they do. God forgive them —

(*Then there are three shots. The Monk rises and exits. There is a long silence. Offstage, His Excellency begins to play the piano. Father Coronil comes slowly in from His Excellency's door.*)

FATHER CORONIL (*goes to Izquierdo*). His Excellency wishes to see you. (*No answer*) He is an old man. Go in to him.

IZQUIERDO. No.

FATHER CORONIL (*to Zavala*). A message must be sent home immediately. His Excellency wishes you to prepare it. (*Motions toward courtyard*) What did he say? At the end? Did he repent?

ZAVALA. No. (*Zavala starts toward the courtyard door as the curtain falls.*)

Curtain

The Autumn Garden

For Dash

The Autumn Garden was first produced at the Coronet Theatre, New York City, on March 7, 1951, with the following cast:

(In the order of their appearance)

ROSE GRIGGS	FLORENCE ELDRIDGE
MRS. MARY ELLIS	ETHEL GRIFFIES
GENERAL BENJAMIN GRIGGS	COLIN KEITH-JOHNSTON
EDWARD CROSSMAN	KENT SMITH
FREDERICK ELLIS	JAMES LIPTON
CARRIE ELLIS	MARGARET BARKER
SOPHIE TUCKERMAN	JOAN LORRING
LEON	MAXWELL GLANVILLE
CONSTANCE TUCKERMAN	CAROL GOODNER
NICHOLAS DENERY	FREDRIC MARCH
NINA DENERY	JANE WYATT
HILDA	LOIS HOLMES

Produced by
KERMIT BLOOMGARDEN

Directed by
HAROLD CLURMAN

Settings designed by
HOWARD BAY

Scenes

The time is September 1949. The place is the Tuckerman house in a summer resort on the Gulf of Mexico, about a hundred miles from New Orleans.

Act One

Monday night after dinner.

Act Two

Scene 1. The following Sunday morning.
Scene 2. That night.

Act Three

Early the next morning.

Act One

SCENE: *The living room of the Tuckerman house in a town on the Gulf of Mexico, a hundred miles from New Orleans. A September evening, 1949, after dinner. To the right of the living room is a side porch, separated from the room by a glass door. Upstage left is a door leading into the entrance hall of the house: through this door we can see the hall and staircase. On the porch are chairs and tables. The furniture of the living room is handsome but a little shabby. It is all inherited from another day. (Right and left are the audience's right and left.)*

ON STAGE AT RISE OF CURTAIN: GENERAL GRIGGS, *a good-looking man of fifty-three, is seated at one side of the room reading a newspaper. His wife —*

ROSE GRIGGS, *ex-pretty soft-looking and about forty-three, is seated at a table wearing an evening dress that is much too young for her. She is chatting across the room with —*

CARRIE ELLIS, *a distinguished-looking woman of about forty-five, who is sitting on a side chair, near her son, Frederick, and her mother-in-law —*

MRS. MARY ELLIS, *in her seventies, sprightly in manner and movement when she wishes to be, broken and senile when she wishes to be broken and senile. She has piled cushions on her chair so she can read a manuscript over the shoulder of her grandson —*

FREDERICK ELLIS, *a pleasant-looking young man of about twenty-five. Occasionally he makes a correction in the manuscript, looks up amused and annoyed at his grandmother. On the right porch —*

EDWARD CROSSMAN, *about forty-six, tired, worn-looking as if he is not in good health, is sitting alone, his back to those in the room. There is a minute of silence after the curtain goes up.*

ROSE (*gets up from her chair. She finds silence uncomfortable. She hums, sings: "We stroll the lane together"*). Now where is it? Everything's been so topsy-turvy all evening. If I can't have it immediately after dinner then I just about don't want it. At home you can bet it's right waiting for us when we leave the dining room, isn't it, Ben? Too bad it's Thursday. I'd almost rather go and see him than go to the party. (*To Mrs. Ellis*) I think it's what keeps you awake, Mrs. Ellis. I mean a little is good for your heart, the doctor told me always to have a little, but my goodness the amount you have every night.

MRS. ELLIS (*pleasantly*). Would you mind telling me what you're talking about, Mrs. Griggs? You said if it wasn't for the party you'd go and see *him,* but you thought *I* drank too much on a Thursday?

ROSE (*giggles*). Coffee. I mean you drink too much coffee.

MRS. ELLIS. Then it is coffee you wish to go and see?

ROSE. Now, now. You're teasing. You know very well I mean Robert Taylor in that thing.

MRS. ELLIS. Believe me, I did *not* know you meant Robert Taylor in that thing. You know, General Griggs, after seven summers I have come to the conclusion that your wife considers it vulgar to mention anything by name. There's nothing particularly genteel about pronouns, my dear. Coffee is coffee and not it, Robert Taylor is Robert Taylor and not him, I suppose, and a fool is a fool and not her.

ROSE. I know. It's a naughty habit. Ben has been telling me for years. (*She is close to Ben*) Do you like my dress, Ben?

GRIGGS. It's nice.

ROSE. Have I too much rouge? (*To others*) Know what she used to say? (*Quickly*) Ben's mother, I mean. She used to say it before she died. (*To Crossman*) Come and join us. (*To others*) She used to say that Southern women painted a triangle of rouge on their faces as if they were going out to square the hypotenuse. Ben came from Boston, and his mother was sometimes a little sharp about Southerners.

MRS. ELLIS. Who could have blamed her?

ROSE (*calling out to Crossman*). Know what she told me last winter when I met her at the Club?

CROSSMAN (*turns, smiles*). Ben's mother?

ROSE. No. Your sister, of course. She said we see more of you here on your summer vacation than she sees all year round in New Orleans. She says you're getting to be a regular old hermit. You have to watch that as you get older. You might get to like being alone — and that's dangerous.

MRS. ELLIS. I used to like being alone. When you get old, of course, then you don't anymore. But somewhere in the middle years, it's fine to be alone. A room of one's own isn't nearly enough. A house, or, best, an island of one's own. Don't you agree, General Griggs? Happiest year of my life was when my husband died. Every month was springtime and every day I seemed to be tipsy, as if my blood had turned a lovely *vin rosé*.

CARRIE. You're lyrical tonight, Mother.

MRS. ELLIS (*to Frederick*). Do you know I almost divorced your grandfather, Frederick? During the racing season in 1901.

FREDERICK (*looks up, laughs*). You don't feel it's a little late to talk about it?

(*The phone rings.*)

MRS. ELLIS. Thought you might like to write my biography — when you're finished with poetry.

(*As the phone rings again, Sophie comes into the hall to answer it.*)

SOPHIE (*into the phone*). No, sir. We do not take transient guests. No, never, sir. Only permanent guests. You might telephone to Mrs. Prescott in the village. Thank you, sir.

ROSE (*calls into hall*). Dear Sophie, where *is* coffee?

(*Sophie comes to the hall door. She is a plain-looking, shy girl of about seventeen. She has a hesitant, overpolite manner and speaks with a slight accent. She has on a party dress, covered by a kitchen apron.*)

SOPHIE. Aunt Constance is most sorry for the delay. We bring it immediately.

(*She disappears.*)

ROSE. Frederick, do you know I've been giving Sophie dancing lessons, or trying to? She's a charming child, your intended, but she's never going to be a dancer.

FREDERICK. Terrible expression, Mrs. Griggs: my intended. Sounds like my indentured. Did you tell Mrs. Griggs, Mother? I thought we agreed that since there were no definite plans as yet —

CARRIE (*a little uncomfortable*). It's natural that I should speak about my son's marriage, isn't it?

ROSE. Why, goodness, yes indeed it is. I'd have felt hurt —

GRIGGS. Don't you know that women have no honor, Frederick, when it comes to keeping secrets about marriage or cancer?

FREDERICK (*looks at his mother*). No, sir. I didn't know. I'm too young for my age.

MRS. ELLIS (*who has been busy reading the manuscript*). I know I'm too young to be reading Payson's book. Full of the most confused sex. I can't tell who is what. And all out of doors. Is that new, so much sex out of doors? Is it, General?

GRIGGS. I don't think it's a question of "new." I think it's a question of climate.

MRS. ELLIS (*points to book*). But aren't sexual relations the way they used to be: between *men and women?* It's so twitched about in Mr. Payson's book. You know, I think the whole country is changing.

GRIGGS. Has Payson written a good book, Fred?

FREDERICK. It's a wonderful book. I think he's going to be the most important young writer —

CARRIE. You said the first two books were wonderful, Frederick. And they didn't sell very well.

MRS. ELLIS. I don't know why they didn't — I always thought houses of prostitution had a big lending-library trade.

(*Frederick gets up, as if he were angry.*)

CARRIE. Will this new book sell, Frederick?

FREDERICK. I don't know, Mother.

CARRIE. I hope it sells. Any man is better off supporting himself.

FREDERICK. Mother, sometimes I think no people are quite so moral about money as those who clip coupons for a living.

MRS. ELLIS. And why not? Particularly your mother who is given the coupons already clipped by me who has the hardship of clipping them. That leaves her more time to grow moral.

CARRIE (*to General Griggs*). You mustn't look uncomfortable, General. You should know by this time that my mother-in-law enjoys discussing family matters in public. And the more uncomfortable you look, the longer she will continue.

GRIGGS. Do I look uncomfortable? I was thinking how hard it is to be young.

ROSE (*to Ben*). Won't you come to the party? (*To others*) Ben has never gone to the Carter party. I am sure they're just as insulted every year —

GRIGGS. I don't think so.

ROSE. But what will you do with yourself? Why don't you go to see Robert Taylor? It's that war picture where he does so well and you'll want to see if it's accurate.

GRIGGS. No. I don't want to see if it's accurate.

ROSE. Do you like my dress?

GRIGGS. It's nice.

MRS. ELLIS. You are a patient man. (*To Rose*) Do you know you've asked him that five times since rising from dinner?

ROSE. Well, I feel young and gay, and I'm going to a party. I wish the Denerys would come before we leave. I like meeting new people and they sound so interesting. I thought they were supposed to arrive in time for dinner. (*To Carrie*) Is he absolutely fascinating?

CARRIE. I don't know, Mrs. Griggs. I haven't seen him in twenty years or more.

ROSE (*calling to Crossman*). Is he fascinating, Mr. Crossman?

CROSSMAN. You're making it a little harder than usual. Is who fascinating?

ROSE. Nicholas Denery, of course.

CROSSMAN. Of course. I don't know.

ROSE. But, goodness. Didn't you all grow up together? I mean you and Constance and Mrs. Ellis and —

CROSSMAN. I don't remember any of us as fascinating. Do you, Carrie?

(*Carrie shakes her head, laughs. Sophie, carrying a tray with brandy and brandy glasses, comes into the room. She is followed by Leon, a young, colored butler, carrying coffee and coffee cups. Frederick rises and takes the tray from Sophie. She looks at him and smiles.*)

ROSE. Let's see your dress, Sophie. (*Sophie smiles shyly, begins to take off her apron as Leon pours coffee*) Oh. It's right nice. But you should wear tighter things, dear. (*Comes in back of her, begins to fool with her hair*) I'd like to try your hair again. (*Sophie moves to help Leon but is cornered by Rose*) Now you just sit down. How's this?

(*Crossman comes into the room.*)

CROSSMAN. Makes her look like everybody else. That's desirable, isn't it?

ROSE. What does Frederick think? We're out to please Frederick, after all, aren't we, dear?

FREDERICK (*turns to look*). I like Sophie her own way.

SOPHIE. I have no "way."

ROSE. But most European girls have such chic — (*General Griggs gets up, as if he were annoyed*) They have, Ben. You said it yourself when you came back from the Pacific, and I was jealous.

MRS. ELLIS. Pacific? I thought you fought in Europe.

GRIGGS. I did. Robert Taylor fought in the Pacific.

(*He wanders off to the porch.*)

ROSE (*holding Sophie's hair another way*). Or is *this* better?

FREDERICK (*smiles to Sophie*). Don't you mind being pulled about?

SOPHIE. No. Well. (*Gently pulls away*) I am grateful for the trouble that Mrs. Griggs — Thank you.

CROSSMAN. Sophie doesn't mind anything. All she has said all summer is thank you.

(*Through his speech the phone rings. Frederick starts for the phone. At the same time, Constance Tuckerman comes through the hall. She is a handsome woman of forty-three or forty-four. She is carrying two flower vases. She puts down one of the vases in order to answer the phone.*)

CONSTANCE. Yes. Just a minute. Frederick. Mr. Payson would like to speak to you. (*She picks up the other vase, comes into the door, as if she were in a hurry. Frederick immediately moves to the phone*) Sorry coffee was late. You all want more, just ring. And do, Carrie, explain to the Carters why I can't come to their party this year —

ROSE. Any news from them, Constance?

CONSTANCE (*carefully*). News from whom?

ROSE (*laughs*). Oh, come now. Stop pretending. When do the Denerys arrive?

CONSTANCE. Don't wait up for them, Rose. You'll see them at breakfast.

(*She turns, goes out and goes up the stairs.*)

ROSE. My, Constance is nervous. Well, I suppose I should be if I were seeing an old beau for the first time in — But I don't believe in old beaux. Beaux should be brand-new, or just friends, don't you think? (*Crossman starts out to porch, carrying his coffee and the brandy bottle. Rose points outside, meaning General Griggs and Crossman*) Now are you boys just going to sit here and share the bottle —

CROSSMAN. General Griggs is only being kind when he says he shares the bottle with me.

(*He goes off. Frederick comes in, starts to speak, changes his mind.*)

CARRIE (*carefully*). Was that Mr. Payson on the phone? Is he coming to the party?

FREDERICK. How many generations do you have to summer in this joint before you're invited to the Carters'?

MRS. ELLIS. Oh, that's not true. They're very liberal lately. (*Points to Rose*) After all, the last few years they've always included Mrs. Griggs. (*To Rose*) And nobody can be more *nouveau riche* than your family, can they? I mean your brother during the war and all that.

ROSE (*giggles*). My. Everybody is so jealous of Henry.

MRS. ELLIS. Well, of course we are. I wish we were *nouveau riche* again.

FREDERICK (*sharply*). All right, Grandma.

ROSE. Oh, I don't mind. I enjoy your grandmother.

FREDERICK (*to his mother*). I'm sorry I'm not going to be able to take you to the party. I hope you'll excuse me, Sophie. Mother. Grandma.

CARRIE (*carefully*). What has happened, Frederick?

FREDERICK. Payson had a wire from his publishers. They want the manuscript in the mail tomorrow morning. (*He goes to take the manuscript from the table*) So I'll have to proofread it with him tonight. It's a nasty job alone, almost impossible —

CARRIE (*slowly*). I don't understand.

ROSE. I must fix my face. As you get older your face needs arranging more often. (*She goes off.*)

CARRIE. We're ready to leave, Frederick.

FREDERICK. Mother, I'm not going to the party, I wasn't making a joke —

CARRIE. Oh. I hoped you were. You have no obligation to us, or Sophie? An appointment broken, because Payson summons you?

FREDERICK. I am sorry, Sophie. Maybe I can pick you up later. (*Haltingly*) I am sorry.

SOPHIE. I do not mind, really. It is better this way.

CARRIE. Why not? (*No answer*) Why don't you mind, Sophie?

SOPHIE (*smiles*). I do not like parties. I did not want to go. Now Frederick has some important business and must leave quickly —

CARRIE. Perhaps you are going to make *too* good a wife.

FREDERICK. Suppose you let me decide that, Mother. Good night. Have a good time. See you in the morning —

CARRIE. I want to talk to you, Frederick.

FREDERICK. When you use that tone of voice you need two hours. Let's make it in the morning, Mother.

(*Sophie has turned away, as if she wanted to be as far away as possible.*)

CARRIE. I ask you to break your appointment with Payson. As a favor to me.

FREDERICK. There's nothing important about my being at the party and it is important to him. He wants to consult me —

CARRIE. He is always consulting you. You talk like a public accountant or a landscape gardener. Why should he want to consult *you* about his work?

FREDERICK. Maybe because I try to write and maybe because he thinks I know a little. I realize that's hard for you to believe —

CARRIE. I didn't meant that.

FREDERICK. I think you did. Good night.

CARRIE. You have no sense of obligation to me. (*Looks around for Sophie who is trying to leave the room*) And none to Sophie. Who evidently won't speak for herself. Do stay here, Sophie, it's your business as well as mine — (*Sophie stands still*) I am getting tired of Mr. Payson, Frederick, and with good reason. When he came to stay with us in town last winter, I fully understood that he was a brilliant and gifted man and I was glad for you to have such a friend. But when he followed you down here this summer —

FREDERICK (*slowly*). He did not follow me down here and I wouldn't like you to put it that way again. He came here for the summer and —

CARRIE. There is just too much of Mr. Payson. Every day or every evening — How often do you take Sophie with you? (*Sharply*) How often have you seen Mr. Payson this summer, Sophie? (*There is no answer*) Please answer me.

FREDERICK. And please stop using that tone to Sophie. Say what you have to say to me.

CARRIE (*Turning to Mrs. Ellis, who has been watching them*). Mother —

MRS. ELLIS. I've been dozing. How many hours have passed?

CARRIE. You are always dozing when there is something unpleasant to face out with Frederick.

MRS. ELLIS. What better time? You all want to know something's been worrying me all day? Nobody in the South has tapeworm anymore. In my day that was all you ever heard. Tapeworm, tapeworm, tapeworm. (*Gets up*) Now kiss your mother good night, boy. Otherwise she'll be most unhappy. And say you forgive her.

FREDERICK. I have nothing to forgive her for, Grandma.

MRS. ELLIS. Of course not. But even when your mother starts out being right she talks and talks until she gets around to being wrong.

(*She exits. There is silence.*)

CARRIE (*softly*). I'm sorry if I spoke unfairly, or at the wrong time —

FREDERICK (*comes to her, smiling*). You didn't, you didn't. Now don't feel bad. Nothing's happened. And don't let Grandma tease you.

CARRIE. I know. You go ahead, dear. Try to join us later.

(*He kisses her. She smiles, pleased, and goes out. Frederick turns to Sophie.*)

FREDERICK. Sophie, Mother didn't mean to be sharp with you. But when she is, you mustn't let her. She's a little bossy from time to time, but no harm in it. You look so worried.

SOPHIE (*very puzzled*). Your mother is not angry now?

FREDERICK. Of course not. You mustn't take these things too seriously. Mother is like that.

SOPHIE (*smiles*). You know it is most difficult in another language. Everything in English sounds important. I get a headache from the strain of listening.

FREDERICK (*laughs*). Don't. It's not worth it. (*Looks at her, then slowly*) Mother is right: I have been rude and neglectful. But I haven't meant to be, Sophie.

SOPHIE. No, no. You have not been.

FREDERICK. And in two weeks Mother and I will be going off to Europe. I hope you don't mind about the European trip. It was all arranged long before you and I — (*Stares at her, smiles*) got engaged. (*Sophie smiles at him as if she were embarrassed, then she coughs and clears her throat*) We're an awkward pair. I like you, Sophie.

SOPHIE (*warmly*). I like you, Frederick.

FREDERICK. Sophie, I think we'll have to sit down soon and talk about ourselves. I don't think we even know how we got engaged. We haven't said much of anything —

SOPHIE. Sometimes it is better not to say things. There is time and things will come as they come.

FREDERICK. The day we got engaged, we tried to speak as honestly as we both knew how but we didn't say much —

SOPHIE. And I think we should not try so hard to talk. Sometimes it is wise to let things grow more roots before one blows them away with words — (*Shyly touches his hand*) It will come better if we give it time.

FREDERICK. We will give it time. And you'll make no decisions and set no dates until you are sure about what you think and feel.

SOPHIE. Oh, I have made the decision for myself. And I am pleased.

FREDERICK (*pleased*). And you are quite sure of your decision?

SOPHIE. You know, sometimes I have thought that with rich people — (*Very quickly*) with educated people, I mean, decisions are made only in order to speak about changing them. It happens often with Aunt Constance and with your mother, also, I think. And the others.

FREDERICK. *Yes.* (*Takes her hand*) We'll get along fine. I want you to know that I feel very lucky —

SOPHIE. Lucky? You will have to be patient with me. I am not a good success here.

FREDERICK. Now, you stop that. I don't want you a good success. And you're to stop thinking it. You're to stop a lot of things: letting Mother boss you about, letting Mrs. Griggs tell you what to wear, or pull your hair —

SOPHIE. Oh, I do not mind. Because I look so bad makes Mrs. Griggs think she looks so good.

FREDERICK (*smiles*). Good night, my dear.

SOPHIE. Good night.

(*He exits. Sophie begins to pick up the coffee cups, brandy glasses, etc. After a minute Rose Griggs comes down the steps carrying a summer coat. She comes in the room.*)

ROSE. Where are the Ellises?

SOPHIE. They went to the party, Mrs. Griggs.

ROSE. No! Without me? I *must* say that's very rude. They can't have done that, Sophie — (*She hurries to the hall, looks out. Then she comes back in, goes to the porch*) Ben. (*He looks up*) The Ellises left without me, Ben!

GRIGGS. Yes?

ROSE. You'll have to walk me over. I just won't go in, alone.

GRIGGS. It's across the street, Rose. Not a dangerous journey.

ROSE (*gently*). Ben. (*He rises, comes in*) You know, I think it's shocking. In front of other people. God knows what they know or guess this summer. (*Suddenly notices Sophie who is collecting cups*) Sophie. Don't wait here listening.

(*Sophie turns, surprised, but before she can speak . . .*)

GRIGGS (*sharply*). Rose!

ROSE (*to Sophie*). I am sorry, my dear. Please most earnestly I ask your pardon —

SOPHIE. Yes, ma'am.

ROSE (*tries to catch her at door*). I'm just a nervous old silly these days. Now say you forgive me —

(*Sophie disappears.*)

GRIGGS (*smiles, as if he has seen this before*). All right, Rose. You're charming.

ROSE. You won't even walk over with me, just to the door?

GRIGGS. Certainly I will.

ROSE. No, you don't have to. I just wanted to see if you would. Will you call for me, at twelve, say?

GRIGGS. No.

ROSE. Then will you meet me at twelve, at the tavern?

GRIGGS. No. What mischief is this, Rose?

ROSE. Is it mischief to want to talk with you?

GRIGGS. Again? Tonight? And every night and every day? The same things over and over? We're worn out, Rose, both of us. (*Kindly*) There is no more to say.

ROSE (*softly*). No more to say. Do people get divorces, after twenty-five years, by just saying they want them and that's all and walking off?

GRIGGS. I suppose some men do. But I haven't walked off and I have said all I know how to say.

ROSE. But you haven't really explained anything to me. You tell me that you want a divorce — And I ask why, why, why. We've been happy together.

GRIGGS. You don't believe that.

ROSE. When people get our age, well, the worst is over — and what else can one do? (*Exasperated*) I never really heard of such a thing. I'm just not taking you seriously and I do wish you'd stop talking about it. (*After a pause*) You've never given me a good reason. I ask you ten times a day if there's another woman. I could understand that. Of course you say no, naturally —

GRIGGS. There is no other woman.

ROSE (*giggles*). You know what I think? I think it's that little blonde at the drugstore, and the minute my back is turned —

GRIGGS. Please, Rose. Please stop that.

ROSE. Never at any time, during this divorce talk, have you mentioned them. You'd think we didn't have sons, and the awful effect on them. Did you write them today?

GRIGGS. I did not write them because you begged me not to.

ROSE. Oh, yes, I forgot. It will break their hearts.

GRIGGS. Their hearts won't be broken. They won't even bother to finish the letter.

ROSE (*softly, shocked*). You can't love them, to speak that way.

GRIGGS. I don't love them. I did love them but I don't now. They're hard men to love.

ROSE. Oh, I don't believe a word you say. You've always enjoyed shocking me. You've been a wonderful father and you're just as devoted to them as they are to you.

GRIGGS. They aren't devoted to me — when they think about me it is to find my name useful and when it isn't useful they disapprove of me.

ROSE (*moving to door*). Look, Ben. I just can't stay and talk all night. I'm late now. There's no use our saying the same things over and over again — (*He laughs*) If you won't come to the party what are you going to do?

GRIGGS. I am going down by the water, sit on a bench and study from a Chinese grammar.

ROSE. You'll be lonely.

GRIGGS. Yes, but not for parties.

ROSE. It's very hard to take seriously a man who spends the evening with a Chinese grammar. I'll never forget that winter with the Hebrew phonograph records. (*Pats his arm*) Now, good night, darling. And don't worry about me: I am going to try to have a good time. We'll talk about all this another day.

GRIGGS (*sharply*). No. No, we're not going to do that. You're turning it into a pleasure, Rose, something to chatter about on a dull winter night in the years to come. I've told you it isn't going to be that way. (*She is in the hall*) It isn't going to be that way. When you go back to town next week I'm not going with you.

(*He turns to see that she has gone.*)

ROSE'S VOICE (*from the hall*). Good night, darling.

GRIGGS (*he stands still for a minute. Then he turns, sees his book on the porch table. Goes out to the porch, realizes the doors have been open. To Crossman*). I guess we thought the doors were closed. I am sorry.

CROSSMAN. Don't be.

GRIGGS. There are so many things I want to do that I don't know which to do first. Have you ever thought about starting a new life?

CROSSMAN (*smiles*). I've often thought that if I started all over again, I'd go right back to where I started and start from there. Otherwise, it wouldn't prove anything.

GRIGGS. Where'd you start from?

CROSSMAN. Nowhere. That's the trouble.

GRIGGS. I started with mathematics. Seems strange now, but that's why I went to West Point — wonderful mathematics department. So I got myself two wars instead. I want to go somewhere now and study for a few years, or — (*Smiles*) Anyway, sit down by myself and think.

CROSSMAN. Europe?

GRIGGS. I don't think so. Europe seemed like a tourist joint the last time. With all the aimless, dead bitterness of tourist joints. I don't want sentimental journeys to old battlefields. I'll start tame enough: I've written my sister that I'd like to stay with her for a month or two.

CROSSMAN. Isn't that a sentimental journey?

GRIGGS. I suppose it is. I really want to see her because she looks like my mother. The last six months I've thought a lot about my mother. If I could just go back to her for a day. Crazy at my age —

CROSSMAN. I know. We all do at times. Age has nothing to do with it. It's when we're in trouble.

GRIGGS. I don't know why I want to say this but, well, don't think too badly of my wife.

CROSSMAN. Why should I think badly of anybody?

GRIGGS (*as he turns to go*). All professional soldiers marry Rose. It's in the Army Manual. She is as she always was. It is my fault, not hers.

CROSSMAN. Haven't you lived in the South long enough to know that nothing is ever anybody's fault?

(*General Griggs laughs, starts out as Constance comes down-*

stairs. Constance has on a different dress and is buttoning the belt as she comes into the room. General Griggs crosses the room and exits by the stage left windows. Constance looks around, finds the room is neat, goes out to the porch, talking as she goes.)

CONSTANCE. I *think* everything is ready. I've put Nick in Sophie's room — Sophie says she doesn't mind sleeping down here. Anyway it happens every summer. And I've given Mrs. Denery the yellow room. They wanted *two* rooms, Nick said on the phone.

CROSSMAN. Fashionable people don't sleep together, don't you know that? It's not sanitary.

CONSTANCE (*sits down*). I'm tired, Ned.

CROSSMAN. Have a brandy.

CONSTANCE. No. It would make me nervous.

CROSSMAN. Remarkable the things that make people nervous: coffee, brandy, relatives, running water, too much sun, too little sun. Never anything in themselves, eh, Constance?

CONSTANCE. They have a maid and a chauffeur. I'll have to put them in the boathouse. It's all so much work at the end of the season. Sophie's been cleaning all day, and I've been cooking — Why did I say they could come?

CROSSMAN (*smiles*). I wonder why.

CONSTANCE. Well, of course, I want to see Nick again. But I am nervous about meeting her. (*Points to his glass*) Do you think perhaps a sip?

CROSSMAN. Only drunkards borrow other people's drinks. Have one of your own.

(*Through her next speech he pours her a drink and hands it to her. When she finishes it, he will take back the glass and pour himself a drink.*)

CONSTANCE. I got out Mama's good, old linen sheets. I don't care how rich the Denerys are, or where they've been, they never could have had finer linen. And I've stuffed some crabs and there's white wine — Remember how Nick loved stuffed crabs?

CROSSMAN. No. I don't remember.

CONSTANCE. It was twenty-three years ago, the eighteenth of next month. I mean the night he decided to go to Paris to study. Not so many young men from New Orleans went to Paris in those days.

CROSSMAN. Just as many young men met rich young ladies on boats.

CONSTANCE (*sharply*). *He fell in love.* People can't be blamed for changing their hearts — it just happens. They've had a fine marriage, and *that's* given me happiness all these years.

CROSSMAN. How do you know they've had a "fine" marriage?

CONSTANCE (*smiles*). I know.

CROSSMAN. The rest of us don't know anything about any marriage — but you know all about one you've never seen. You're very wise, Constance. It must come from not thinking.

CONSTANCE. Is this dress all right?

CROSSMAN. You've changed your dress three times since dinner.

CONSTANCE. My dresses are all sort of — She'll think they're cheap. (*Smiles*) Well, and so they are. (*There is silence*) Have we changed much, Ned?

CROSSMAN. Yes, my dear. You've changed, I've changed. But you're still handsome, if that's what you mean.

CONSTANCE. Ned, you don't look so well this summer. (*He is pouring himself another brandy. She points to bottle*) I wanted to tell you — Don't you think —

CROSSMAN (*very pleasantly*). Don't I think you should mind your business? Yes, I do.

(*Sophie comes into living room carrying sheets, a quilt, a pillow, puts them down and moves to porch.*)

CONSTANCE. Isn't what happens to you my business?

SOPHIE. You look pretty, Aunt Constance.

CONSTANCE (*to Crossman*). Sophie made this dress for me. Last winter. What could the girls at school have thought? Sophie sitting sewing for an old country aunt when she could have been out dancing —

SOPHIE. I sew better than I dance.

CONSTANCE (*to Crossman*). Sophie's mother taught her to sew. You know that Ann-Marie is a modiste?

SOPHIE (*laughs*). Oh, she is not. She is what you call here a home seamstress, or sometimes a factory worker.

CONSTANCE. But she *designs*. She wrote me and you told me —

SOPHIE (*laughs*). Oh no. You did not understand. She does —

(*Outside the house there is the noise of a car coming to a stop. Constance turns towards the room, then steps back, moves around the table and suddenly runs into the house. Crossman turns to stare at her.*)

SOPHIE (*timidly, pointing out towards living room*). Should I —Should I stay, Mr. Ned? Why is Aunt Constance so nervous about the visit of this lady and gentleman?

CROSSMAN. Because she was once in love with Nicholas Denery, this gentleman.

SOPHIE. Oh. Such a long, long time to stay nervous. Great love in tender natures. And things of such kind. (*As he turns to stare at her*) It always happens that way with ladies. For them it is once and not again: it is their good breeding that makes it so.

CROSSMAN. What is the matter with you?

SOPHIE (*laughs*). I try very hard to sound nice. I try too hard, perhaps?

(*She begins to move into the room; then, as she hears voices, she runs out of the room, exits off porch.*)

NICK'S VOICE (*offstage*). Constance!

(*Nick appears in the hall and comes into the room. He is about forty-five, handsome, a little soft-looking and in a few years will be too heavy. He is followed by Nina Denery, who is a woman of about forty, good-looking, chic, tired and delicate. She stops and stands in the doorway.*)

NICK (*calling*). Constance!

(*Nick and Nina are followed by a maid, Hilda, who stands waiting in the hall. She is carrying a jewelry case, an overnight bag, two coats. Crossman starts to come forward, changes his mind, draws back.*)

HILDA. Shall I take the bags upstairs, madame?

NINA. We don't know where upstairs is.

NICK. Oh, I know where upstairs is. I know every foot of this house. (*Examining the room*) It was *the* great summer mansion and as kids we were here more than we were at home —(*Softly*) The great summer mansion! Did the house change, or me? (*To Nina in doorway*) Come on in.

NINA. Perhaps it would be pleasanter for you to see old friends without me. In any case, I am very tired —

NICK. Oh, now don't get tired. We've just come. What have you got to be tired about? Do you realize how often these days you're tired?

NINA. I realize it very well. And I know it bores you.

NICK. It *worries* me. (*By this time, Nick, wandering around the room, has reached the porch. Crossman turns and, realiz-

ing that he has been seen, now comes forward) Could you tell me where we could find Miss Tuckerman?

CROSSMAN. Hello, Nick. Good to see you.

NICK (*after a second*). My God, Willy. How many years, how many years? (*He puts his arm around Crossman, embraces him*) Nina, this may be my oldest and best friend in the world. Nina, tell Willy how often I've talked about him and what I said.

CROSSMAN (*who is shaking hands with Nina, amused*). Then I hope he told you that my name is Edward, not Willy.

NINA (*amused*). I hope so — but I am not sure.

NICK. Your mother always called you Willy. Don't you remember?

CROSSMAN (*goes out into the hall*). No. I thought it was my brother's name. (*Calls out, loudly*) Constance, Nick is here.

NICK (*coming to Crossman*). Tell me before I see her. What has happened here? I don't know anything.

CROSSMAN. There's very little to know. Old man Tuckerman surprised everybody by dying broke. Constance sold the New Orleans house and managed to hang on to this by turning it into what is called a summer guest house. That's about all, Nick.

NICK. Where is Mrs. Tuckerman? I was crazy about her, Nina, she had style.

CROSSMAN. I don't know where she is. She died shortly after Mr. Tuckerman — just to show him anybody could do it.

NICK (*laughs, pats Crossman*). Good to see you, boy. You know, if anybody had asked me, I would have said this room was as large as an eighteenth-century ballroom and as elegant. I think it shrank. All the fine things were sold?

CROSSMAN. The size hasn't changed. And nothing was sold.

NICK. Could I have been so wrong all these years? Seems so shabby now and —

NINA (*quickly*). I think it is a pleasant room.

NICK. Does Sam live here?

CROSSMAN. Sam died during the war. He went to Europe, oh, in the thirties, married there and never came back. You'll meet his daughter. Constance imported her five years ago.

NICK. Well, Sam was always the devoted brother until it came to being devoted. And Constance sacrificed her life for him.

CROSSMAN (*to Nina*). Nick is still a Southerner. With us every well-born lady sacrifices her life for something: a man, a house, sometimes a gardenia bush.

(Through Crossman's speech, Constance appears in the hall. As she moves into the room, she trips, recovers herself, smiles nervously and waits for Nick to come to her. He takes her face in his hands and kisses her. Then he stands back to look at her.)

NICK. This is a good hour of my life, Constance.

CONSTANCE *(softly)*. And of mine.

NICK *(holds her face)*. You've changed and you've changed well. Do you still have the portrait, Constance?

CONSTANCE *(smiles)*. *Still* have the portrait! It's the only important thing I have got — *(Then she remembers Nina, becomes confused, moves away from him and comes to Nina)* Forgive me, Mrs. Denery.

NINA *(puts out her hand, warmly)*. Hello.

CONSTANCE. I should have been here to make you as welcome as you truly are. I was reading when you arrived, reading a book, and I didn't hear the car.

(She sees Crossman is staring at her and she looks nervously away from him.)

NICK. I had expected you standing in the driveway with the sun on your face, in the kind of lovely pink thing you used to wear —

NINA. The sun is not usually out at night — even for you.

NICK *(to Constance)*. Instead, you are reading. As if you were waiting for the groceries to come.

CONSTANCE *(quickly)*. I wasn't reading. It was a silly lie. I was just pretending — *(Embarrassed)* Well, I'm even forgetting my manners. You must be hungry, Mrs. Denery, and I've got —

NICK *(laughs, takes her hands, pulls her to the couch)*. No, no. Stop your manners, girl. There's a great deal I want to know. Now. Is the portrait as good as I remember it? I want Nina to see it. Nina knows a great deal about painting. Sometimes I think she knows more than I.

CONSTANCE *(smiles to Nina, nods. Then to Nick)*. You know, Nick, I subscribe to the New York Sunday *Times*. Because of the art section. I wanted to follow your career.

NICK. You haven't often found me in the *Times*. I've only exhibited in Europe.

CONSTANCE *(relieved)*. Oh. That explains it. *(There is an awk-*

ward pause) I like pictures. I like Renoir best. The summer ladies in the gardens, so very, very pretty.

NICK. This is the same wonderful place — My God, we had happy summers here, all of us. We loved each other so very much. Remember, Ned?

CROSSMAN. I don't remember that much love.

NINA. I like you, Mr. Crossman.

NICK. Of course you like him. These are my oldest friends. I think as one grows older it is more and more necessary to reach out your hand for the sturdy old vines you knew when you were young and let them lead you back to the roots of things that matter. (*Nina coughs. Crossman moves away, smiling. Even Constance is overwhelmed*) Isn't that true, Ned? Now what have you been up to all these years?

CROSSMAN. I still work in the bank and come here for my vacation. That's about all.

NICK. I bumped into Louis Prescott in Paris a couple of years ago and he told me you and Constance had never married — (*Pats Constance's hand; Constance looks embarrassed*) Couldn't understand it. No wonder you drink too much, Ned.

CROSSMAN. Louis Prescott go all the way to Paris to tell you that?

NICK (*anxious*). Oh, look old boy. I didn't mean anything — I drink too much myself. I only want to know about you and have you know about me. I hope you didn't mind, Ned.

CROSSMAN. Not a bit. I want to know about you, too. Ever had syphilis, Nick? Kind of thing one has to know right off, if you understand me.

CONSTANCE (*very disturbed*). Ned, how can you speak that way?

NICK (*smiles*). You've grown edgy. I didn't remember you that way.

CROSSMAN (*pleasantly*). Oh, I don't think I've changed. See you in the morning.

NICK. Hope you'll take me around, show me all the old places —

CROSSMAN. Of course I will. Good night, Mrs. Denery.

(*He exits up staircase.*)

NICK. I'm sorry if I said anything —

CONSTANCE. You know, for years I've been meeting you and Mrs. Denery — in my mind, I mean — and I've played all kinds of roles. Sometimes I was the dignified friend, and sometimes I was a very, very old lady welcoming you to a gracious table. It was so important to me — our first meeting — (*Sadly*) And now when it happens —

NICK (*heartily*). Nonsense. My homecoming is just as it should be. It's as if I had gone away yesterday. We took up right where we left off: even Ned and I. Let us be as we were, my dear, with no years between us, and no pretending.

CONSTANCE (*delighted with him*). Thank you. (*Goes to Nina*) All these years I wanted to write you. I did write but I never sent the letters. It seemed so intrusive of me. I could see you getting the letter and just not knowing who I was.

NICK. I told Nina about you the first night I met her and through the years she has done quite a little teasing — You are too modest, Constance. Now are you going to let me do another portrait of you?

CONSTANCE (*laughs*). Another portrait? No, no, indeed. I want to remember myself as I was in the picture upstairs.

NICK. Go and get it for me. I want to look at it with you. (*She smiles, exits. There is silence*) You haven't been too warm or gracious, Nina.

NINA. What can I do when I don't know the plot?

NICK. What are you talking about?

NINA. You told me about Constance Tuckerman the first night we met? And about dear Willy or Ned, and I've done quite a little teasing about her all these years?

NICK. I did tell you about her immediately —

NINA. You mentioned her very casually, last week, and you said that you could hardly remember anything more about her than a rather silly —

NICK (*quickly*). Are you going to be bad-tempered for our whole visit here? For years I've looked forward to coming back —

NINA. So you came to do her portrait?

NICK. No, I didn't "come to do her portrait." I thought about it driving down here. If the one I did is as good as I remember, it would be wonderful for the show. The young girl, the woman at forty-five. She's aged. Have we changed that much? I don't think you've changed, darling.

NINA. I've changed a great deal. And I wouldn't want it pointed out to me in a portrait to be hung side by side with a picture of what I used to be. That isn't a nice reason for being here and if I had known it —

NICK. We have no "reason" for being here. I just wanted to come back. Nothing mysterious about it —

NINA. You're simply looking for a new place in which to exercise yourself. It has happened many, many times before. But it *always* happens when we return from Europe and spend a month in New York. It's been too important to you, for many years, that you cannot manage to charm my family. And so, when our visit is finished there, you inevitably look around for — Well, you know. You know what's been and the trouble.

NICK (*cheerfully*). I don't know what the hell you're talking about.

NINA. I'm tired of such troubles, Nick —

NICK. Do you know that these sharp moods of yours grow more sharp with time? Now I would like to have a happy visit here. But if something is disturbing you and you'd prefer not to stay, I'll arrange immediately —

NINA. I'd only prefer to go to bed. Sorry if I've been churly about your — homecoming. (*She starts out, meets Constance who comes in carrying portrait*) Will you excuse me, Constance? The long drive gave me a headache.

CONSTANCE. I am sorry. Will I bring you a tray upstairs?

NINA. No, thank you.

(*Constance moves as if to show her the way.*)

NICK. Come, I want to see the picture. Nina will find her way.

(*He takes the picture from Constance.*)

CONSTANCE. The yellow room on the left. Your maid is unpacking. I peeked in. What lovely clothes. Can I come and see them tomorrow?

NINA (*going up the stairs*). Yes, of course. Thank you and good night.

NICK (*who is looking at the picture*). I was nervous about seeing it. Damn good work for a boy eighteen.

CONSTANCE. You were twenty-two, Nick.

NICK. No, I wasn't. I —

CONSTANCE. You finished it the morning of your birthday. (*She points to windows*) And when you put down your brushes you said damn good work for a boy of twenty-two, and then you asked me to marry you. Don't you remember — (*She stops, embarrassed*) Why should you remember? And I don't want to talk that way.

NICK. Oh, nonsense. Talk any way you like. We were in love, very much in love, and why shouldn't we speak of it?

CONSTANCE (*hastily*). After I die, the picture will go to the Delgado Museum.

NICK (*laughs*). I want to borrow it first. I'm having a retrospective show this winter, in London. I've done a lot of fancy people in Europe, you know that, but I'll be more proud of this — And I want to do another portrait of you as you are now. (*Moves toward window, excited*) You standing there. As before. Wonderful idea; young girl, woman at — Be a sensation. Constance, it's fascinating how faces change, mold firm or loose, have lines that start in youth and —

CONSTANCE. Oh, Nick. I don't want to see myself now. I don't want to see all the changes. And I don't want other people to stand and talk about them. I don't want people to laugh at me or pity me. (*Hurt*) Oh, Nick.

NICK. I see. Well, it would have meant a lot to me. But that's that. I'll be off to bed now —

CONSTANCE (*coming after him*). But we haven't had a minute. And I have supper all ready for you —

NICK. Good night, my dear.

CONSTANCE (*slowly*). You think I'm being selfish and vain? I mean, am I the only woman who wouldn't like —

NICK. No, I think most women would feel the same way.

(*He starts out.*)

CONSTANCE. Do you prefer breakfast in bed? And what shall I make for your dinner? Pompano —

(*He is at the door as Carrie and Rose come into the hall. Carrie is holding Rose's arm.*)

CARRIE. Hello, Nick.

NICK (*takes her hands*). My God, Carrie. I didn't know you were here. How come? It's wonderful —

CARRIE. We come every summer.

NICK. You're handsome, Carrie. But you always were.

CARRIE (*smiles*). And you always remembered to say so. (*Rose coughs delicately*) This is Mrs. Griggs. (*To Constance*) Mrs. Griggs didn't feel well, so I brought her home. She became a little dizzy, dancing.

ROSE (*to Nick, who is shaking hands with her*). You're a famous gentleman in this town, sir, and I've been looking forward so to seeing you. We lead dull lives here, you know —

NICK (*laughs*). *You* don't look as if you do.

ROSE. Oh, thank you. But I don't look well tonight. I became suddenly a little ill —

CARRIE (*tartly*). Yes. Well, come along. If you still feel ill.

NICK. Can I help you, Mrs. Griggs?

ROSE (*delighted*). Oh, thank you. That would be nice. I haven't been well this summer —

(*Nick starts into hall.*)

CONSTANCE. Nick —

(*He pays no attention. Carrie moves quickly ahead of him, takes Rose's arm.*)

CARRIE. Come. Good night, Nick. I look forward to seeing you in the morning. Hope you're staying for a while.

NICK. I think we'll have to leave tomorrow.

ROSE. Oh, don't do that. Constance, if Ben comes in would you tell him I was taken ill?

(*Carrie impatiently pushes her ahead and up the steps.*)

NICK (*meaning Rose*). Pretty woman, or was. (*Looks at Constance*) What is it, Con?

CONSTANCE. How can you talk of leaving tomorrow? Don't be mad with me, Nick.

NICK. I don't get mad, darling.

CONSTANCE (*catches him as he exits*). Please, Nick, please let me change my mind. You are welcome to take this picture and I am flattered you wish to do another. But I'll have to pose early, before they're all down for breakfast —

NICK (*turns, casually*). Good. We'll start in the morning. Do you make a living out of this place, darling?

CONSTANCE. Not much of one. The last few years have been a little hard. I brought Sam's daughter from Europe — she and her mother went through the occupation and were very poor — and I've tried to send her to the best school and then she was to make her debut only now she wants to get married, I think, and —

NICK. The girl expected all that from you?

CONSTANCE. Oh, no. Her mother didn't want to come and Sophie didn't want to leave her mother. I finally had really to *demand* that Sam's daughter was not to grow up — Well, I just can't describe it. At thirteen she was working in a fish store or whatever you call it over there. I just *made* her come over —

NICK. Why didn't you ever marry Ned?

CONSTANCE. I can't answer such questions, Nick. Even for you.

NICK. Why not? I'd tell you about myself or Nina.

CONSTANCE. Oh, it's one thing to talk about lives that have been good and full and happy and quite another — Well, I don't know. We just never did marry.

NICK. Well, then, tomorrow morning. I'll do a good portrait of you because it's the face of a good woman —

(*He stops as Sophie comes into the hall.*)

CONSTANCE. Sophie. (*Sophie comes into the room*) This is Sam's daughter.

SOPHIE. How do you do, sir?

NICK. You follow in the great tradition of Tuckerman good looks.

SOPHIE. Er. Er.

CONSTANCE (*smiles*). Don't er, dear. Say thank you. (*Griggs enters from left porch*) Do come in. This is General Griggs. My very old friend, Nicholas Denery.

NICK. Are you General Benjamin Griggs? I've read about you in Raymond's book and Powell's.

GRIGGS (*as they shake hands*). I hear they disagree about me.

NICK. We almost met before this. When your boys marched into Paris. I was in France during the German occupation.

(*Sophie turns sharply.*)

GRIGGS. That must have been unpleasant for you.

NICK. Yes, it was. But in the end, one has to be just; the Germans were damn smart about the French. They acted like gentlemen.

GRIGGS (*pleasantly*). That's a side of them I didn't see. (*Looks at Sophie*) You didn't either, Sophie?

(*During his speech Hilda, the maid, appears in the doorway.*)

HILDA (*in German*). Excuse me, Mr. Denery. Mrs. Denery would like you to come for a minute before you retire. She has a little surprise gift she bought for you in New Orleans.

NICK (*in German*). No. Tell Mrs. Denery I will see her in the morning. Tell her to take a sleeping pill.

HILDA (*in German*). Thank you, sir.

CONSTANCE (*who hasn't understood the German but who is puzzled because Sophie is frowning and Griggs has turned away*). Can I — Does Nina want something?

NICK. No, no, she's fine. (*Sophie begins to put sheets on the couch. Nick turns to her*) That means one of us must have put you out of your room. I'm sorry and I thank you.

SOPHIE. Not at all, sir. It is nothing.

NICK. You're a sweet child and I look forward to knowing you. Good night. (*To Griggs*) Good night, sir. A great pleasure. (*Griggs bows. Nick kisses Constance*) Wonderful to be here, darling.

(*He goes out. Constance moves to help Sophie. There is silence for a minute while they arrange the bedclothes.*)

CONSTANCE. I suppose I shouldn't ask but what did the German maid want? Something from the kitchen or — (*No answer*) Sophie. (*No answer*) Sophie.

SOPHIE. Mrs. Denery wanted to say good night to Mr. Denery.

GRIGGS. Mrs. Denery had bought a little gift for him in New Orleans and wanted to give it to him.

CONSTANCE. After all these years. To have a little gift for him. Isn't that nice? (*She looks at Griggs and Sophie. She becomes conscious of something strained*) What did Nick say?

SOPHIE. He said she should take a sleeping pill and go to sleep.

CONSTANCE. Just like that?

SOPHIE. Down at the beach there is the frankfurter concession. I think I will get the sleeping-pill concession and grow very rich.

CONSTANCE. Why, Sophie. Are you disturbed about something, dear? (*Looks at her dress*) You didn't go to the party! I've been so busy, I didn't realize — Why, where's Fred and —

SOPHIE. I did not wish to go to the party, Aunt Constance. And Frederick had a most important appointment.

CONSTANCE. More important than being with you? Young people get engaged and act toward each other with such — I don't know. (*To Griggs*) In our day we made marriage more romantic and I must say I think we had more fun. If you can't have fine dreams now, then when can you have them? (*Pats Sophie*) Never mind. I guess the new way is more sensible. But I liked our way better. (*To Griggs*) Oh, what's the matter with me? I forgot. Rose came back from the party. She said she was ill. I mean, I think she just didn't feel well — Carrie is upstairs with her. (*He doesn't move*) I think Carrie probably wants to go back to the party and is waiting for you to come.

GRIGGS. Yes. Of course. Thank you. Good night.

(*He exits.*)

CONSTANCE (*she kisses Sophie*). You'll be comfortable? See you in the morning, dear.

(*She exits through the hall. Sophie finishes with the couch, goes out. After a second, Crossman comes down the stairs. He sticks his head in the door, sees nobody, crosses the room, goes out to the porch, takes the bottle of brandy and a glass, moves back into the room and crosses it as Sophie returns carrying pajamas and a robe.*)

CROSSMAN (*His voice and his manner are different now*). I needed another book and another bottle. Royalty gone to bed? Does anybody improve with age? Just tell me that, Sophie, and I'll have something to lie awake and think about.

SOPHIE. I do not know, Mr. Ned.

CROSSMAN. For God's sake, Sophie, have an opinion about *something*. Try it, and see what comes out.

SOPHIE (*laughs*). Some people improve with age, some do not.

CROSSMAN. Wonderful, Sophie, wonderful. Some improve with age, some do not. You're beginning to talk wise, cautious — the very highest form of American talk. (*Sharply*) You shouldn't even understand the need.

SOPHIE. But I do understand.

CROSSMAN. That's dangerous to admit, Sophie. You've been busy cultivating a pseudostupidity. Another five years and you won't be *pseudo*stupid.

SOPHIE. I will not mind. It will be easier. (*Carefully*) You notice me too much, Mr. Ned. Please do not feel sorry or notice me so much.

CROSSMAN. You came here a nice little girl who had seen a lot of war and trouble. You had spirit, in a quiet way, and you were gay, in a quiet way, which is the only way women should be gay since they are never really gay at all. They are earnest instead. But earnestness has nothing to do with seriousness. So. What the hell is this marriage business between you and Fred Ellis?

SOPHIE (*softly*). It is the marriage business between me and Fred Ellis.

CROSSMAN. But what's the matter with you? Haven't you got sense enough to know —

SOPHIE (*quickly*). I do the best I can. I do the best I can. And I thank you for worrying about me, but you are an educated man with ideas in English that I am not qualified to understand.

CROSSMAN. Listen to me, Sophie. Sometimes when I've had enough to drink — just exactly enough — I feel as if I were given to understand that which I may not understand again.

And sometimes then — but rarely — I have an urge to speak out. Fewer drinks, more drinks, and I'm less certain that I see the truth, or I get bored, and none of my opinions and none of the people and issues involved seem worth the trouble. Right now, I've had just enough: so listen to me, Sophie. I say turn yourself around, girl, and go home. Beat it quick.

SOPHIE. You take many words to say simple things. All of you. Go home, shall I? Just like that, you say it. Aunt Constance has used up all her money on me, wasted it, and for why and what? How can I go home?

CROSSMAN. If that's all it is I'll find you the money to go home.

SOPHIE (*wearily*). Oh, Mr. Ned. We owe money in our village, my mother and I. In my kind of Europe you can't live where you owe money. Go home. Did I ever want to come? I have no place here and I am lost and homesick. I like my mother, I — Every night I plan to go. But it is five years now and there is no plan and no chance to find one. Therefore I will do the best I can. (*Very sharply*) And I will not cry about it and I will not speak of it again.

CROSSMAN (*softly, as if he were moved*). The best you can?

SOPHIE. I think so. Maybe you've never tried to do that, Mr. Ned. Maybe none of you have tried.

CROSSMAN. Sophie, lonely people talking to each other can make each other lonelier. They should be careful because lonely people can't afford to cry. I'm sorry.

(*He exits through the hall, goes up the stairs as the curtain falls.*)

Curtain

Act Two

Scene 1.

SCENE: The same as *Act One. A week later, eight-thirty Sunday morning.*

AT RISE: *Constance is standing against the outside edge of the porch, leaning on the railing. Nick is standing in front of an easel. Constance has on a most unbecoming house dress and her hair is drawn back tight. She looks ten years older. In the living room, Sophie has finished folding her bedclothes and is hurrying around the room with a carpet sweeper. After a second, Leon appears from the direction of the dining room with a tray and dishes and moves out to the porch. He puts down the tray, moves the table, begins to place the dishes. Constance tries desperately to ask him if everything is all right in the kitchen. She does this by moving her lips and trying not to move her head. Leon sees her motions but doesn't understand what she is trying to say. The noise of the rattling dishes, and the carpet sweeper, becomes sharp.*

NICK. Constance, please ask them to stop that noise. (*Waves his hand to Leon and Sophie*) Go away, both of you.

CONSTANCE. They can't, Nick. I explain it to you every morning. We simply have to get ready for breakfast. Sophie, is everything all right in the kitchen?

SOPHIE. Yes, ma'am. Everything is fine.

NICK (*to Constance, sharply*). Please keep the pose.

CONSTANCE (*to Leon*). Tell Sadie not to cook the liver until everybody is downstairs, like she always does. Did she remember about the grits this Sunday? (*To Nick*) All right. I'm sorry. But really, I can't run a boardinghouse and pose for —

(*She sighs, settles back. Sophie picks up her bedclothes and exits through the hall. Leon finishes with the porch table and comes back into the living room as Mrs. Ellis comes down the steps.*)

MRS. ELLIS (*to Leon*). My breakfast ready?

LEON. No, ma'am. We'll ring the bell.

MRS. ELLIS. What's the matter with my breakfast?

LEON. Nothing the matter with it. It will be like always.

MRS. ELLIS. It gets later and later every day.

LEON. No, ma'am. That's just you. Want it in the dining room or on the porch?

MRS. ELLIS. Too damp on the porch. Whole house is damp. I haven't slept all summer, Leon.

LEON. Just as well not to sleep in summer.

MRS. ELLIS (*as Leon exits*). You're going to have to explain that to me sometime. (*She turns, goes toward porch, comes around in front of Constance*) Constance, he's made you look right mean and ten years older. Why have you done that, Nicholas?

(*Sophie comes back into living room with a large urn of coffee and small cups. She puts the tray on a table.*)

NICK (*to Mrs. Ellis*). Shoo, shoo. This is forbidden ground.

MRS. ELLIS (*calls*). Sophie, give me a cup. I have to stay awake for church. (*To Constance*) Ten years older. When you pay an artist to paint your portrait he makes you ten years younger. I had my portrait done when I was twenty-one, holding my first baby. And the baby looked older than I did. Was rather a scandal or like those people in Tennessee.

NICK. You know if you wouldn't interrupt me every morning, I think I'd fall in love with you.

MRS. ELLIS (*she goes toward Sophie to get her coffee*). I wouldn't like that. Even if I was the right age I wouldn't like it. You would never have been my dish of tea, and isn't that a silly way of saying it? (*To Sophie*) Sophie, will you come up to town (*Crossman comes down the steps and into the room*) and stay with me for a few weeks while Carrie and Frederick are in Europe?

SOPHIE. I would like that.

MRS. ELLIS. Ned, what shall I give Sophie for her wedding present? My pearls or my mother's diamonds?

CROSSMAN (*to Sophie*). The rich usually give something old and precious to their brides. Something that doesn't cost them new money. Same thing true in your country?

SOPHIE (*smiles*). I do not know the rich in my country.

MRS. ELLIS. He's quite right, Sophie. Not only something old but something so old that we're sick of it.

CROSSMAN. Why don't you give her a nice new check?

MRS. ELLIS. Only if I have to.

CONSTANCE (*on porch*). Nick, my neck is breaking —

NICK. All right. All finished for this morning.

(*Turns the picture around so that Constance cannot see it. Sophie brings two cups of coffee to the porch.*)

CONSTANCE (*collapsing in a chair*). Whew.

(*Takes the coffee from Sophie, pats her arm. Sophie takes the other cup to Nick.*)

NICK. You're the girl I want to paint. Change your mind and we'll start today. Why not, Sophie?

SOPHIE. I am not pretty, Mr. Nicholas.

NICK. You are better than pretty.

(*Crossman comes out to the porch. Sophie moves off.*)

CROSSMAN (*staring at Constance*). My God, you look awful, Constance. What did you get done up like that for? You're poor enough not to have to pretend you are poor.

NICK (*laughing*). Go way, Ned. You've got a hangover. I know I have.

(*Nina comes down the steps, comes into the room, says good morning to Mrs. Ellis. She pours herself a cup of coffee. She is close enough to the porch to hear what is said.*)

CONSTANCE. You know, I waited up until twelve o'clock for you both —

NICK. We were late. We had a good get-together last night. Like old times, wasn't it, Ned? (*To Constance*) If you have the normal vanity you'd be pleased at the amount of time we spent on you. Ned loosened up and talked —

CROSSMAN. I did? I thought that was you.

NICK (*laughs*). I knew you wouldn't remember what you'd said — Don't regret it: did you good to speak your heart out — for once.

CROSSMAN. My heart, eh?

NICK. In a jukebox song called Constance.

CONSTANCE. What? I don't understand.

CROSSMAN (*who has turned sharply, then decided to laugh*). Neither do I.

(*Leon appears in the hall with a bell and begins to ring it.*)

NINA. Good morning, Mr. Crossman.

CROSSMAN. Good morning, Mrs. Denery. I'm sorry you didn't join us last night — to hear me pour my heart out.

NINA. I'm never invited to the pouring of a heart.

CROSSMAN. I looked for you, but Nick said you had a headache.

NINA. Nick always says I have a headache when he doesn't want me to come along, or sees to it that I do have one.

MRS. ELLIS (*gets up*). All right, Leon. I'm ready. I haven't eaten since four this morning. (*Goes out. As she passes stairs, she shouts up*) Carrie! Frederick! I simply won't wait breakfast any longer.

(*Crossman follows her out.*)

CONSTANCE. Well, they seemed to have managed in the kitchen without me. I reckon I better change now. Where'd you get this dress, Nick?

NICK. Place on Dreyenen Street.

CONSTANCE. In a Negro store! You bought this dress in a Negro store! (*He laughs*) I don't mean that. I mean Ned's right. You must have wanted to make me look just about as awful as — for some reason I don't understand. Nick, what *are* you doing? And why won't you let me see the portrait?

NICK. Haven't you yet figured out that Ned is jealous?

CONSTANCE. Jealous of what?

NICK. He's in love with you, girl. As much as he was when we were kids. You're all he talked about last night. How lonely he's been, how much he's wanted you, how often he asked you to marry him —

CONSTANCE. I just don't believe you. Ned never talks about himself. I just don't believe he said such things —

NICK. You know damn well he loves you and you know he's rotting away for you. He said last night —

CONSTANCE. Nick, if he did talk, and it's most out of character, I don't think I should hear what he said in confidence just to you.

NICK. Oh, run along, honey. You're pleased as punch. When you're not pretending to be genteel.

CONSTANCE (*laughs*). Genteel? How awful of me. Mama used to say gentility was the opposite of breeding and — Did Ned say — er —

(*Nick laughs, she laughs, and exits. Nick begins to put away portrait and to fold easel as Nina puts down her coffee and comes out to the porch.*)

NICK (*kisses her*). Morning, darling. (*Nina sits down, watches him*) What's the matter?

NINA. Why have you done that? To Constance?

NICK. Done what? Tell her the truth?

NINA. How could you know it to be the truth? I don't believe Crossman talked to you —

NICK. Look, it makes her happy — and if I can get a little sense into her head it will make him happy. I don't have to have an affidavit to know what's going on in the human heart.

(*He kisses her.*)

NINA (*laughs*). Oh, you are enjoying yourself here. I've seldom seen it this hog-wild. You're on a rampage of good will. Makes me nervous for even the trees outside. But there's something impertinent about warning a fig tree. How should I do it?

NICK. First tell me how to understand what you're talking about.

NINA. Are we staying much longer, Nick?

NICK. A few more days. The house officially closes this week, Constance says. The Ellises go tomorrow and the Griggses on Tuesday, I think. Just till I finish.

NINA. Finish what?

NICK (*carefully*). The portrait, Nina.

(*Rose Griggs comes down the stairs, carrying a small overnight case. She is done up in a too fussy hat and a too fussy dress. She looks in the room, puts the case down, comes hurrying out to the porch.*)

ROSE. Oh, good morning. Sorry to interrupt. You look so handsome together. (*Makes a gesture to Nick meaning "Could you come here?"*) Nick —

NICK. Come on out.

ROSE. I'd rather. Could you —

NICK. Come and join us.

ROSE (*Hesitantly*). Well, I wanted to tell *you* but I don't want to worry Nina. You see — I called him last night. Just like you advised. And I'm driving right over now. He's the executor of my trust fund, you know. He's very wise: I've got gilt-edged securities.

NICK. Who is this?

ROSE. My brother, of course. Henry, like I told you. (*To Nina*) It sounds so mysterious, but it isn't. He's much older. You know he builds ships, I mean during our wars. I'll tell him the whole story, Nick, and he'll know what to do.

NICK (*amused*). Of course he will.

ROSE. I'm going to drive over to my doctor's. He's going to wait for me on a hot Sunday. It'll be expensive — (*To Nina*) I had a heart murmur. They had to take me out of school for a year.

NINA. Recently?

(*Nick chokes back a laugh.*)

ROSE (*giggles*). That's charming — "recently." (*To Nick*) There's so much I wanted to consult you about. I waited up for you last night, but — well. Should I do *just* as you told me yesterday?

NICK (*who doesn't remember what he told her*). Sure.

ROSE. Everything?

NICK. Well —

NINA. I think, Mrs. Griggs, you'll have to remind Nick what he told you. Yesterday is a long time ago when you have so many ladies to attend to —

ROSE (*as Nick laughs*). I shouldn't have brought it up like this. Oh, Mrs. Denery, you might as well know: it's about a divorce, and Nick has been most kind.

NINA. I am sure of it.

ROSE. Just one more thing. What should I do about our boys? Should I telephone them or let my brother? One of our sons works on the atom bomb, you know. He's the religious one and it will be traumatic for him. What do you think, Nick?

NINA (*trying not to laugh, moves away*). Goodness.

NICK. I think you should go and have your breakfast. It's my firm belief that women only look well in hats after they've eaten.

ROSE (*to Nick, softly*). And I'm going to just *make* Henry commission the portrait — and for the very good price that he can afford to pay. You remember though that I told you she can't take the braces off her teeth for another six months.

NICK (*laughs*). Go along now, my dear.

ROSE. Thank you for all you've done. And forgive me, Nina. I'll be back tonight, Nick, before you go to bed because you'll want to know how everything turns out.

(*She exits through room.*)

NICK (*looks up at Nina*). There was a day when we would have laughed together. Don't you have fun anymore?

NINA. I don't think so.

NICK. She's quite nice, really. And very funny.

NINA. I suppose it's all right to flirt with, or to charm, women and men and children and animals but nowadays it seems to me you include books-in-vellum and sirloin steaks, red squirrels and lamp shades.

NICK. Are you crazy? Flirt with that silly woman? Come and eat your breakfast, Nina. I've had enough seriousness where none is due.

(*Through this speech, Carrie has come down the steps. She meets Sophie who is going through the hall to the dining room. Sophie is carrying a tray.*)

CARRIE. Good morning, dear. Is Frederick in the dining room?

SOPHIE. No. He has not come down as yet.

(*Carrie comes into the room, continues on to the porch.*)

CARRIE (*to Nick and Nina*). Good morning. Your maid said you wanted to see me, Nick.

NICK (*hesitantly*). Carrie, I hesitated all day yesterday. I told myself perhaps you knew, but maybe, just maybe, you didn't.

NINA. Oh, it sounds so serious.

CARRIE. It does indeed.

NICK (*carefully*). Don't you know that man's reputation, Carrie? You can't travel around Europe with him.

CARRIE. Travel around Europe with *him?* I'm going to Europe with Frederick. What do you mean, Nick?

NICK. I —

(*Sophie comes into room, goes out to porch. During next speeches, she pours coffee.*)

CARRIE. Please tell me.

NICK. I saw Frederick in the travel agency yesterday with a man I once met in Europe. Not the sort of man you'd expect to see Frederick with.

CARRIE. Are you talking about Mr. Payson?

NICK. Yes, I am. Well, I waited until they left the travel place and then I went in.

NINA. Why did you go in?

NICK. The man said he had booked your passage on the *Elizabeth* and now he had another for Mr. Payson and Fred had just paid for it — (*Carrie turns sharply*) I didn't know whether you knew, Carrie, or if I should tell you —

CARRIE. I didn't know. I thank you for telling me. (*After a second*) What did you mean, Nick, when you asked me if I knew Payson's reputation? I don't like to press you for gossip, but —

NINA. He didn't mean anything, Mrs. Ellis —

NICK. Oh, look here, Nina, you know he's part of Count Denna's set, and on the nasty fringe of that.

(*Sophie leaves the porch.*)

CARRIE. What does that mean: Count Denna's set and the nasty fringe of that?

NINA (*quickly*). It means very little. The Count is a foolish old man who gives large parties —

NICK (*to Nina*). Would you want your young son with such people at such parties?

NINA (*angrily*). I have no son. And I don't know: perhaps I would have wanted to leave him alone —

CARRIE. All people who have no children think that, Mrs. Denery. But it just isn't true. (*To Nick*) I don't know much about Mr. Payson but I've been worried for a long time that he's taken Frederick in. Frederick admires his writing, and — Yet I know so little about him. He stayed with us a few weeks in town last winter. He'd just come back from Europe then —

NICK. He'd just come back from a filthy little scandal in Rome. It was all over the papers.

NINA. You don't know it was true.

CARRIE. What kind of scandal? (*No answer. Softly*) Please help me. I don't understand.

NICK. Look, Carrie, there's nothing to understand. The guy is just no good. That's all you need to know. He's nobody to travel around Europe with.

CARRIE. How could Fred have — (*She hesitates for a minute*) It was kind and friendly of you to tell me. I am grateful to you both.

(*She goes slowly across the room and into the hall toward the dining room. There is a long pause: Nick takes a sip of coffee, looks at Nina.*)

NICK. What would you have done?

NINA. Have you ever tried leaving things alone?

NICK. I like Carrie. She doesn't know what the hell it's all about — and the chances are the boy doesn't either. I'm sorry for them. Aren't you? (*When she doesn't answer*) What's the matter, Nina?

NINA. I can smell it: it's all around us. The flower-like odor right before it becomes faded and heavy. It travels ahead of you, Nick, whenever you get most helpful, most loving and most lovable. Down through the years it runs ahead of us — I smell it — and I want to leave.

NICK (*pleasantly*). I think maybe you're one of the few neurotics in the world who didn't marry a neurotic. I wonder how that happened?

NINA. *I want to leave.*

NICK (*sharply*). Then leave.

NINA. You won't come?

NICK. I told you: we'll go Friday. If you want to go before, then go. But stop talking about it, Nina. Or we'll be in for one of your long farewells — and long returns. I don't think I can stand another. Spare yourself, darling. You pay so heavy, inside. (*Comes to her, puts his arms around her*) Friday, then. And in the meantime, gentle down to the pretty lady you truly are.

(*He kisses her. Exits. Nina stands quietly for a minute. Sophie comes onto the porch, begins to gather the dishes.*)

SOPHIE. Would you like something, Mrs. Denery?

NINA (*softly*). No, thank you.

(*She moves off, through the room and toward the staircase. As she starts up the stairs, Frederick comes down.*)

FREDERICK. Good morning.

NINA. Good morning, Mr. Ellis. (*Stops as if she wanted to tell him something*) I — er. Good morning.

(*She goes up as Sophie, who has heard their voices, leaves the dishes and comes quickly into the room.*)

SOPHIE (*calling into the hall*). Fred. Fred. (*He comes in*) Would you like to have your breakfast on the kitchen porch?

FREDERICK. Sure. Why?

SOPHIE. Your mother is — er — (*Points toward dining room*) She has found out that — Come.

FREDERICK. Denery told her he saw me in the travel agency. I was sure he would. There's nothing to worry about. I intended to tell her this morning.

SOPHIE. But perhaps it would be more wise —

FREDERICK (*smiles*). We'll be leaving here tomorrow and for Europe on the sixteenth. You and I won't see each other for six months. Sophie, you're sure you feel all right about my going?

SOPHIE. Oh, I do.

FREDERICK. We will visit your mother. And —

SOPHIE (*very quickly*). No, no, please do not do that. I have not written to her about us —

FREDERICK. Oh.

SOPHIE. You see, we have as yet no date of time, or —

FREDERICK (*smiles*). I don't think you want a date of time, Sophie. And you don't have to be ashamed of wishing you could find another way. But if there isn't any other way for you, then I'll be as good to you as I know how. And I know you will be to me.

SOPHIE. You are a kind man. And I will also be kind, I hope.

FREDERICK. It isn't any deal for you. You are a girl who should love, and will one day, of course.

SOPHIE (*puts her hand to his mouth*). Shssh. Such things should not be said. (*Cheerfully*) It will be nice in your house with you, and I will be grateful for it.

FREDERICK. I have no house, Sophie. People like me never have their own house, so to speak.

SOPHIE. Never mind. Whatever house. It will be nice. We will make it so.

(*He smiles, pats her arm.*)

FREDERICK. Everybody in the dining room? (*He starts for hall*) Might as well face it out.

SOPHIE. I would not. No, I would not. All of you face out too much. Every act of life should not be of such importance —

FREDERICK (*calling into dining room*). Mother. (*Sophie shrugs, smiles, shakes her head, and exits. Frederick comes back into room, pours himself a cup of coffee. After a minute, Carrie appears. She comes into the room obviously disturbed*) There's nothing to be so upset about.

CARRIE. You think that, really?

(*Mrs. Ellis appears in the hall.*)

FREDERICK. We're going to have a companion. That's all. Payson knows all of Europe and —

MRS ELLIS. Of course. You're lucky to get Mr. Payson to go along.

(*Both turn to look at her.*)

FREDERICK (*after a second, to Carrie*). What is it, Mother?

CARRIE. I can't say it. It's shocking of you to take along a guest without consulting me. You and I have planned this trip for three years and —

FREDERICK. I didn't consult you because the idea came up

quickly and Payson had to get his ticket before the travel office closed for the weekend —

CARRIE. *Payson* had to get *his* ticket?

FREDERICK. I thought you'd given up going through my check-books.

CARRIE. *Please don't speak that way to me.* We are not going to Europe.

FREDERICK (*after a second, quietly*). I am.

CARRIE. We are not going, Fred. We are not going.

MRS. ELLIS. Your mother's feelings are hurt. She had looked forward to being alone with you. Of course.

FREDERICK. We'll still be together.

CARRIE (*to Mrs. Ellis*). I don't wish to be interpreted, Mother. (*To Frederick*) There's no sense talking about it: we'll go another time.

FREDERICK. Will you stop acting as if you're taking me back to school? I will be disappointed if you don't wish to come, but I am sailing on the sixteenth. (*Then, quietly*) I've never had much fun. Never seen the things I wished to see, never met the people I wanted to meet or been the places where I could. There are wonderful things to see and learn about. We're lucky to have somebody who knows about them and who is willing to have *us* tag along. *I'm* not much to drag around — I'll come back, and you can take up my life again. Six months isn't much to ask.

MRS. ELLIS. Six months? Sad to ask so little.

CARRIE (*as if she recognized a tone of voice*). Mother, please. I —

MRS. ELLIS. Perhaps you won't want to come back at all. I wouldn't blame you.

CARRIE. Fred, don't make a decision now. Promise me you'll think about it until tomorrow and then we'll talk quietly and —

MRS. ELLIS (*to Frederick*). Don't make bargains with your mother. Everything always ends that way between you. I advise you to go now, or stay.

FREDERICK. I am going. There is nothing to think about. I'm going.

(*He exits, goes up staircase. There is a pause.*)

CARRIE (*angry*). You always do that, Mother. You always arrange to come out his friend and make me his enemy. You've been amusing yourself that way all his life.

MRS. ELLIS. There's no time for all that, Carrie. I warned you to say and do nothing. I told you to make the best of it and go along with them.

CARRIE. How could I do that? That man is a scoundrel and Fred doesn't know it, and won't believe it. What am I to do now?

MRS. ELLIS. You're to go upstairs and say that you are reconciled to his leaving without you but that Frederick is to make clear to his guest that his ten thousand a year ends today and will not begin again. Tell him you've decided young people have a happier time in Europe without money —

CARRIE. I couldn't do that. He'd hate me for it. Maybe we'd better let him go, and perhaps I can join him later. Time will — (*Sees Mrs. Ellis's face*) I will not cut off his allowance.

MRS. ELLIS. I didn't know it was you who wrote the check.

CARRIE (*with dignity*). Are you quite sure you wish to speak this way?

MRS. ELLIS. Relatively sure.

CARRIE. Then I will say that the money is his father's money, and not yours to threaten him, or deprive him, in any proper sense.

MRS. ELLIS. In any *proper* sense. There is no morality to money, Carrie, and immoral of people to think so.

CARRIE. If you stop his allowance, Mother, I will simply send him mine.

MRS. ELLIS. Then I won't give you yours. (*Carrie turns as if she were shocked. Mrs. Ellis, gently*) Yes, old people are often harsh, Carrie, when they control the purse. You'll see, when your day comes. And then, too, one comes to be bored with those who fool themselves. I say to myself, one should have power, or give it over. But if one keeps it, it might as well be used, with as little mealymouthness as possible. Go up now, press him hard, do it straight. (*Carrie turns slowly to exit*) Tell yourself you're doing it for his own good.

CARRIE (*softly*). I wouldn't be doing it otherwise.

MRS. ELLIS. Perhaps. Perhaps not. Doesn't really matter. I'm off to church now. You can skip church today, Carrie.

CARRIE. Thank you for the dispensation.

(*Rose comes from the direction of the dining room and into the room.*)

MRS. ELLIS (*to Carrie, as Carrie moves off*). Quite all right. You have God's work to do. (*She turns to watch Rose who is elaborately settling herself in a chair as if she were arranging a scene*) What are you doing, Mrs. Griggs? (*Rose nervously points to left window. Mrs. Ellis looks toward it, watches Rose fix her face*) Is it Robert Taylor you're expecting? (*Griggs comes in from the left windows. He has on riding pants and an old shirt*) Oh.

GRIGGS. Good morning.

MRS. ELLIS. Your wife's getting ready to flirt. You'd be safer in church with me.

(*She exits as Griggs laughs. He goes to coffee urn.*)

ROSE (*Meaning Mrs. Ellis*). Nasty old thing. (*Then*) I'm driving over to see him. I'm sorry I had to make such a decision, but I felt it was necessary now.

GRIGGS. Are you talking about your brother?

ROSE. Yes, of course. Now, I know it will be bad for you, Ben, but since *you're* being so stubborn, I didn't know what else to do.

GRIGGS. I think you should see Henry.

ROSE. But he's going to be very, very angry, Ben. And you know much influence he has in Washington.

GRIGGS. Tell him to use his influence. And tell him to go to hell.

ROSE (*giggles*). On a Sunday?

GRIGGS. Rose, no years will make you serious.

ROSE. You used to like me that way.

GRIGGS. So you always wanted to believe.

ROSE. How can I just walk into Henry's happy house and say Ben wants a divorce, and I don't even know the reason. I *ask* him and I *ask* him but he says there is no reason —

GRIGGS. I never said there was no reason. But it isn't a reason that you like, or will accept. If I were in love with another woman you'd rather enjoy that. And·certainly Henry would.

ROSE. It would at least be human. And I am not convinced it isn't so. I've done a good deal of thinking about it, and I've just about decided it's why you stayed in Europe so long.

GRIGGS. I didn't arrange World War II and don't listen to the rumors that I did.

ROSE. He said it at the time. He said he had known a good many professional soldiers but nobody had managed to make so much fuss about the war as you did, or to stay away so long. Henry said that.

GRIGGS. I guessed it was Henry who said that.

ROSE (*laughs*). But you didn't guess that it was Henry who got you the last promotion.

GRIGGS. Rose, stop that. You're lying. You always do it about now. Give Henry this reason for the divorce — tell him my wife's too young for me. For Henry's simple mind, a simple reason.

ROSE. I've wanted to stay young, I've —

GRIGGS. You've done more than stay young: you've stayed a child.

ROSE. What about your mother, Ben, have you thought of her? It would kill her —

GRIGGS. She's been dead sixteen years. Do you think this will kill her again?

ROSE. You know what I mean. She loved me and she was happy for our marriage.

GRIGGS. No, she didn't. She warned me not to marry — (*With feeling*) I began my life with a serious woman. I doubt if any man gets over that, or ever really wants any other kind of woman.

ROSE. *Your mother loved me.* You have no right to malign the dead. I say she loved me, I know she did.

GRIGGS (*wearily*). What difference does it make?

ROSE. You never think anybody loves me. Quite a few men have found me attractive —

GRIGGS. And many more will, my dear.

ROSE. I always knew in the end I would have to tell you although I haven't seen him since you came home. That I promise you. I told him you were a war hero with a glorious record and he said he wouldn't either any longer —

GRIGGS (*who is at the left window*). Henry's chauffeur is outside, Rose.

ROSE. He was very, very, very, very much in love with me while he was at the Pentagon.

GRIGGS. Good place to be in love. The car is outside, Rose.

ROSE. Even after we did it, he kept on saying that you didn't make love to a friend, more than a friend's, wife.

GRIGGS. Rose, don't let's talk this way.

ROSE. Does it hurt you? Well, you've hurt me enough. The third time you went to Europe was when it really began, maybe the second. Because I, too, wanted affection.

GRIGGS (*gently*). I can understand that.

ROSE. Ask me who it was. Ask me, Ben, and I will tell you. (*No answer*) Just ask me.

GRIGGS. No, I won't do that, Rose.

ROSE. Remember when the roses came from Teheran, I mean wired from Teheran, last birthday? That's who sent them. You didn't even like Teheran. You said it was filthy and the people downtrodden. But he sent roses.

GRIGGS. He sounds like a good man. Go to him, Rose, the flying time is nothing now.

ROSE (*angrily*). You just stop being nasty. And now I am going to tell you who it is.

GRIGGS (*begins to move toward door*). Please, Rose. We have had so many years of this — Please. Do I have to tell you that I don't care who it is?

ROSE (*she begins to move toward him*). I'd like to whisper it. I knew if I ever told you I'd have to whisper it. (*He begins to back away*) Ben, you come right here. Ben stand still. (*He starts to laugh*) Stop that laughing. (*Very loudly, very close to him*) It was your cousin, Ralph Sommers. There. (*She turns away*) There. You won't ever speak with him about it?

GRIGGS. You can be sure of that.

ROSE (*outside an automobile horn is sounded*). Oh, I'm late. I can't talk any more now, Ben. What am I going to tell Henry? Anyway, you know Henry isn't going to allow me to give you a divorce. You know that, Ben. (*Carefully*) And therefore I won't be able to do what you want, and the whole day is just wasted. Please tell me not to go, Ben.

GRIGGS (*as if he has held on to himself long enough*). Tell Henry that I want a divorce. But in any case I am going away. I am leaving. That is all that matters to me or need matter to you or him. I would prefer a divorce. But I am going, whatever you and Henry decide. Understand that, Rose, the time has come to understand it.

ROSE (*gently*). I am going to try, dear. Really I am. It's evidently important to you.

(*She exits through hall. Griggs sits down as if he were very tired. A minute later, Crossman comes from the direction of the dining room, carrying the Sunday papers. He looks at Ben, goes to him, hands him the front page. Ben takes it, nods, sits holding it. Crossman crosses to a chair, begins to read the comic section. A second later, Nina comes down the stairs, comes into the room, starts to speak to Ben and Crossman, changes her mind and sits down. Then Constance, in an old-fashioned flowered hat and carrying a large palmetto fan, comes into the room.*)

CONSTANCE. I'm off to church. Anybody want anything just ring for Leon or Sophie. Want to come to church with me, Ned? (*He peers over his paper, amazed*) All right. I just thought — Well, Nick told us that you told him last night —

CROSSMAN (*laughs*). I think perhaps I shall not again go out at night.

CONSTANCE. Oh, it's good for all of us to confide in somebody — (*She becomes conscious of Nina and Griggs, smiles awkwardly and then with great determination leans over and kisses Crossman*) Good-bye, darling.

(*Surprised, he gets up, stands watching her leave the room.*)

NINA (*after a minute, hesitantly*). I've got a car and a full picnic basket and a cold bottle of wine. Would you — (*Turning to Crossman and then to Griggs*) like to come along? I don't know where to go, but —

CROSSMAN. Got enough in your picnic basket for lunch *and* dinner?

NINA. I think so.

CROSSMAN. Got a mandolin?

NINA (*smiles*). No. Does that rule me out?

CROSSMAN. Almost. But we'll make do. The General whistles very well.

GRIGGS (*smiles, gets up*). Is one bottle of wine enough on a Sunday?

NINA (*laughs*). Not for the pure in heart. I'll get five or six more.

(GRIGGS *follows her out through hall. Crossman gets up, folds the comic section, puts it under his arm, exits through hall. As he exits, Sophie comes onto the porch. She begins to pile the breakfast dishes on a tray. She sees a half-used roll and a piece of bacon, fixes it for herself, goes out carrying the tray and chewing on the roll as the curtain falls.*)

Curtain

Act Two

Scene 2.

SCENE: *The same. Nine-thirty that evening.*

AT RISE: *Nick is lying on the couch. Next to him, on the floor, is an empty champagne glass. On the table, in a silver cooler, is a bottle of champagne. Constance is sitting at the table playing solitaire and humming with the record on the phonograph. On the porch, Sophie is reading to Mrs. Mary Ellis.*

NICK (*to Constance, irritably*). Please don't hum.

CONSTANCE. Sorry. I always like that so much, I —

NICK. And please don't talk. Mozart doesn't need it.

CONSTANCE. Haydn.

NICK. Mozart.

CONSTANCE. I'm sorry but it's Haydn.

NICK. You know damn well I know what I'm talking about.

CONSTANCE. You don't know what you're talking about. Go look.

NICK (*gets up, picks up his glass, goes to phonograph, shuts it off, looks down, turns away annoyed, picks up a champagne bottle, pours himself a drink, then brings the bottle to Constance*). Ready for another?

CONSTANCE. I haven't finished this.

(*Nick carries the bottle out to the porch.*)

MRS. ELLIS. For the fourth time, we don't want any. Please go away. We're having a nice time. We're in the part I like best.

NICK. A nice time? Will I think such a time is a nice time when I am your age? I suppose so.

MRS. ELLIS. No, Mr. Denery. If you haven't learned to read at your age, you won't learn at mine.

NICK (*laughs, pats her shoulder*). Never mind, I like you.

MRS. ELLIS. Yes? People seldom like those who don't like them.

NICK. You haven't forgotten how to flirt. Come on inside and talk to me. My wife disappears, everybody disappears — (*Stretches*) I'm bored, I'm bored.

MRS. ELLIS. And that's a state of sin, isn't it?

NICK. Unfortunately, it isn't. I've always said I can stand any pain, any trouble — but not boredom.

MRS. ELLIS. My advice is to try something intellectual for a change. Sit down with your champagne — on which you've been chewing since early afternoon — and try to make a paper hat out of the newspaper or get yourself a nice long piece of string.

NICK (*goes to Sophie*). Sophie, come in and dance with me.

MRS. ELLIS (*calls in*). Constance, whistle for Mr. Denery, please.

NICK (*to Sophie*). You don't want to sit here and read to Mrs. Ellis.

SOPHIE. Yes, sir, I do. I enjoy the adventures of Odysseus. And the dollar an hour Mrs. Ellis pays me for reading to her.

NICK. Give you two dollars an hour to dance with me.

MRS. ELLIS. It's not nearly enough, Sophie.

NICK (*pats Mrs. Ellis*). You're a corrupter of youth — you steal the best hours.

MRS. ELLIS (*shakes his hand off her shoulder*). And you're a toucher: you constantly touch people or lean on them. Little moments of sensuality. One should have sensuality whole or not at all. Don't you find pecking at it ungratifying? There are many of you: the touchers and the leaners.

NICK (*laughs, pats her again*). You must have been quite a girl in your day.

MRS. ELLIS. I wasn't. I wasn't at all. (*Nick wanders into the room. Mrs. Ellis speaks to Sophie*) I was too good for those who wanted me and not good enough for those I wanted. Like Frederick, Sophie. Life can be hard for such people and they seldom understand why and end bitter and confused.

SOPHIE. I know.

MRS. ELLIS. Do you? Frederick is a nice boy, Sophie — and that is all. But that's more than most, and good to have in a small way.

SOPHIE. Yes, I think so.

(*Mrs. Ellis smiles, pats her hand; Sophie begins again to read.*)

NICK (*near the phonograph, to Constance*). Dance with me?

CONSTANCE. I don't know how anymore.

NICK. Has it been wise, Constance, to lose all the graces in the service of this house?

CONSTANCE. Do you think I wanted it that way?

NICK. I'm not sure you didn't. You could have married Ned, instead of dangling him around, the way you've done.

CONSTANCE. Ned has come here each summer because, well, because I guess this is about the only home he has. I loved Ned and honored him, but — I just wasn't in love with him when we were young. You know that, and you'd have been the first to tell me that you can't marry unless you're in love — (*He begins to laugh*) What are you laughing at?

NICK. "Can't marry unless you're in love." What do you think the rest of us did? I was in love with you. I've never been in love again.

CONSTANCE (*very sharply*). *I don't want you to talk to me that way.* And I don't believe you. You fell in love with Nina and that's why you didn't come back — (*Desperately*) You're *very* much in love with Nina. Then and now. Then —

NICK. Have it your way. What are you so angry about? Want to know something: I've never been angry in my life. (*Turns to her, smiles*) In the end, we wouldn't have worked out. You're a good woman and I am not a good man.

CONSTANCE. Well, whatever the reason, things turned out for the best. (*Carefully*) About Ned. What did he say last night? I mean did he really talk about me?

NICK (*expansively*). He said he loved you and wanted you and had wasted his life loving you and wanting you. And that he wasn't coming here anymore. This is his last summer in this house.

CONSTANCE (*she turns, pained, startled*). His last summer? He said that?

(*Carrie comes quickly into the room.*)

CARRIE. Has Fred come back?

NICK. Well, where have *you* been? Come and have a drink and talk to me.

(*He moves to pour her a drink as she crosses to the porch.*)

CARRIE (*softly, to Mrs. Ellis*). I've been everywhere. Everywhere possible. I even forced myself to call on Mr. Payson.

MRS. ELLIS. And what did he say?

CARRIE. That Fred came in to see him after he left here this morning, stayed a few minutes, no more, and he hasn't seen him since.

MRS. ELLIS. Ah, that's good.

CARRIE. What's good about it? It means we don't know where he's been since ten this morning. (*Softly*) I don't know what else to do or where else to look. What should I do? Shall I call the police, what else is there to do?

MRS. ELLIS. Nothing.

CARRIE. How can I do nothing? You shouldn't have made me threaten him. We were wrong. It wasn't important that he wanted to go to Europe with a man his own age. What harm was there in it?

MRS. ELLIS. All his life you've been plucking him this way and plucking him that. Do what you like. Call the police.

NICK (*who has come to the door carrying a glass for Carrie*). Can I do anything, Carrie?

CARRIE. I don't know, Nick. I only found one person who had seen him, down by the water —

NICK. Is he — would he have — is that what you're thinking, Carrie?

CARRIE. I'm afraid, I'm afraid.

NICK (*quickly, the kind of efficiency that comes with liquor and boredom*). Then come on, Carrie. You must go to the police right away. I'll get a boat. Tell the police to follow along. Right away.

(*Carrie gets up. Starts toward Nick. Sophie gets up.*)

SOPHIE (*angrily, in French, to Nick*). Do not enjoy the excitement so much. Stop being a fool.

NICK (*amazed*). What?

SOPHIE (*in German*). I said don't enjoy yourself so much. Mind your business.

CARRIE. What? What is it, Sophie?

SOPHIE (*to Carrie*). Frederick is in the cove down by the dock. He has been there all day.

NICK (*to Sophie*). You said I was a fool. I don't like such words, Sophie. I don't.

CARRIE. You've let me go running about all day, frantic with terror —

SOPHIE. He wanted to be alone, Mrs. Ellis. That is not so terrible a thing to want.

CARRIE. How dare you take this on yourself? How dare you —

MRS. ELLIS. I hope this is not a sample of you as a mother-in-law.

SOPHIE (*gently, to Carrie*). He will return, Mrs. Ellis. Leave him alone.

NICK (*softly*). Sophie, I think you owe me an apology. You are by way of being a rather sharp little girl underneath all that shyness, aren't you? I'm waiting. (*No answer*) I'm waiting.

MRS. ELLIS. Well, wait outside, will you?

(*He stares at her, turns, goes in the room.*)

NICK (*very hurt, to Constance*). I don't think I like it around here, Constance. No, I don't like it.

(*He goes out left windows.*)

CARRIE. Since Frederick has confided in you, Sophie, perhaps you should go to him.

SOPHIE. He has not confided in me. Sometimes his troubles are his own.

(*She gets up, walks through room, sits down near Constance. On the porch, Mrs. Ellis leans over and whispers to Carrie.*)

CARRIE. Not tonight.

MRS. ELLIS. Why not tonight? We'll be leaving in the morning.

CARRIE. Because I've changed my mind. I think it best now that we let him go to Europe.

MRS. ELLIS (*gets up*). He will not want to go to Europe. Haven't you understood that much?

CARRIE. How do you know what he wants or feels —

MRS. ELLIS (*she comes into room, sits near Constance and Sophie. After a second Carrie follows her in*). Sophie, I think a decision had best be made now. There should be no further postponement.

CARRIE (*very nervous*). This isn't the time. Fred will be angry —

MRS. ELLIS (*to Sophie*). I don't want to push you, child, but nothing will change, nothing. I know you've wanted to wait, and so did Frederick, both of you hoping that maybe — But it will all be the same a year from now. Miracles don't happen. I'm telling you the truth, Sophie.

SOPHIE. Yes, Mrs. Ellis, and I agree with you. Nothing will change. If Frederick is willing for an early marriage then I am also willing.

CONSTANCE. Is this the way it is? *Willing* to marry, *willing* to *marry* —

SOPHIE. I do not use the correct word?

CONSTANCE (*to Mrs. Ellis and Carrie*). If that's the way it is, then I am not willing. I thought it was two young people who — who — who loved each other. I didn't ever understand it, and I didn't ask questions, but — Willing to get married. What have you been thinking of, why — (*Sharply, hurt*) What kind of unpleasant thing has this been?

MRS. ELLIS (*to Constance and Carrie*). Why don't you take each other by the hand and go outside and gather in the dew?

SOPHIE. Aunt Constance is sad that we do not speak of it in the romantic words of love.

CONSTANCE. Yes. I am. And shocked. When Carrie first talked to me about the marriage, I asked you immediately and you told me you were in love —

SOPHIE. I never told you that, Aunt Constance.

CONSTANCE. I don't remember your exact words, but of course I understood — You mean you and Frederick have never been in love? Then why have you —

SOPHIE. Aunt Constance, I do not wish to go on with my life as it has been. I have not been happy, and I cannot continue here. I cannot be what you have wished me to be, and I do not want the world you want for me. It is too late —

CONSTANCE (*softly*). Too late? You were thirteen years old when you came here. I've tried to give you everything —

SOPHIE. I came from another world and in that world thirteen is not young. I know what you have tried to give me, and I am grateful. But it has been a waste for us both.

CONSTANCE. Were you happy at home, Sophie?

SOPHIE. I did not think in such words. I was comfortable with myself, if that is what you mean, and I am no longer.

CONSTANCE (*gently*). I have been so wrong. And so careless in not seeing it. Do you want to go home now?

SOPHIE. No. My mother cannot — Well, it is not that easy. I do not — (*As if it were painful*) I do not wish to go home now.

CONSTANCE. It's perfectly simple for you to go home. Why, why isn't it?

SOPHIE. I do not want to say, Aunt Constance. I do not want to. (*With feeling*) Please do not talk of it any more. Please allow me to do what I wish to do, and know is best for me. (*Smiles*) Frederick and I will have a nice life, we will make it so. (*She exits.*)

CARRIE (*sharply*). Don't be too disturbed, Constance. I have decided that Frederick should go to Europe and this time I am not going to allow any interference of any kind.

(*Frederick appears in the hall, comes into the room.*)

FREDERICK. I'm not going to Europe, Mother.

CARRIE. I have had a bad day. And I have thought of many things. I was mistaken and you were right. You must go wherever you want — however you want to go.

FREDERICK. I am not going, Mother. Payson made that very clear to me this morning.

MRS. ELLIS. Don't, Frederick. It's not necessary. I know.

FREDERICK. But evidently Mother doesn't. . . . Payson made it clear to me that I was not wanted and never had been unless I supplied the money.

(*Constance rises, moves to the porch.*)

CARRIE (*after a second*). I — Er — I don't believe he meant that. You just tell him that it's all been a mistake and there will certainly be money for the trip. Just go right back and say that, Frederick —

FREDERICK (*very sharply*). Mother! I don't want to see him again! Ever.

CARRIE. You often imagine people don't like you for yourself. *I'll* go and tell Mr. Payson that it's all fixed now —

MRS. ELLIS. Carrie, you're an ass. (*To Frederick*) But I hope you haven't wasted today feeling bitter about Mr. Payson. You have no right to bitterness. No right at all. Why shouldn't Mr. Payson have wanted your money, though I must say he seems to have been boorish about not getting it. People like us should pay for the interest of people like him. Why should they want us otherwise? I don't believe he ever pretended to feel anything else about you.

FREDERICK (*softly*). No, he never pretended.

MRS. ELLIS. Then understand that you've been the fool, and not he the villain. Take next week to be sad: a week's long enough to be sad in. Plenty long enough.

FREDERICK (*smiles*). All right, Grandma. I'll take a week.

(*Sophie appears at the hall door.*)

SOPHIE (*to Frederick*). You have had no dinner? I have made a tray for you.

(*He turns, goes to her, takes her hand, goes out.*)

MRS. ELLIS. Are you going to interfere this time, Carrie? I hope not.

(*She goes out. Carrie stands for a minute near the porch. Then she goes out to Constance.*)

CARRIE. I don't like it either.

CONSTANCE (*wearily*). Whole thing sounds like the sale of a shore-front property. I don't know. Seems to me I've been so mixed up about so much. Well, maybe you all know what you're doing.

CARRIE. I don't know what I'm doing.

CONSTANCE. Why did you want the marriage, Carrie? I mean a month ago when you spoke to me —

CARRIE. I don't even know that.

CONSTANCE. You always seem so clear about everything. And so strong. Even when we were girls. I envied you that, Carrie, and wanted to be like you.

CARRIE (*laughs*). Clear and strong? Don't envy me, Con.

(*She exits toward hall and staircase. As she does, Nick comes in. He is now drunk.*)

NICK. Come on out, Carrie. It's a wonderful night. Take you for a sail.

CARRIE (*laughs*). Good night, Nick.

NICK (*as she goes up steps*). I'm lonely, Carrie. I wouldn't leave you if you were lonely. (*When she doesn't answer, he goes into room, looks around, sees Constance sitting on the porch, goes over, stands in the door looking out. After a second*) I wish I wanted to go to bed with you, Con. I just can't want to. I don't know why. I just don't want it.

CONSTANCE. Stop talking that way. You've had too much to drink.

(*She gets up, comes into room. He grabs her arm.*)

NICK. Now you're angry again. (*Puts his arms around her*) I'll sing you a lullaby. Will you like that?

CONSTANCE. Look, Nick, you've been rather a trial tonight. Do go to bed.

NICK. I'm not going to bed. I'm lonely. I'm —

(*The phone rings, Constance goes to it. Nick pours himself a glass of champagne.*)

CONSTANCE. Yes? General Griggs isn't in, Rose. Oh. Yes. Just a minute. (*To Nick*) Rose Griggs wants to talk to *you*.

NICK. What's the matter, she got some new trouble?

CONSTANCE (*annoyed*). Do you want the call or don't you?

NICK. Tell her I'm busy.

CONSTANCE (*in phone*). He's busy drinking, Rose. Shall I leave a message for General Griggs — Oh. (*She puts the phone down, annoyed*) She says it's absolutely and positively urgent that she speak with *you*. Not her husband. Absolutely and positively.

(*She exits through hall. Nick rises and goes to phone.*)

NICK. Look here, my dear, don't be telling people you want to speak to me and not to your husband. Sounds awful. (*Laughs*) Oh. A most agreeable doctor. Look, you don't have to convince me. Save it for your husband. Oh, come on. You're getting like those people who believe their own press agents. Anyway, I once knew a woman with heart trouble and it gave her a nice color. You didn't go to the doctor to believe him — (*Sighs, listens*) All right, of course I'm sorry. It sounds jolly nice and serious and I apologize. Oh. Well, that is kind of you. Yes, tell your brother I'd like to stay with him. Oh, by Friday, certainly. How old is your niece? Is she the one with the braces on her teeth? (*Nina appears from the hall entrance. She is followed by Griggs who is carrying the picnic basket*) No, I won't paint out her braces. That big a hack I'm not. Yes, we'll have plenty of time together. You're a good friend. (*To Nina and Griggs*) Had a nice day? (*Into phone*) No, I'm talking to your husband. Oh. Good-bye. Take care of yourself. (*He hangs up. To Griggs*) That was Rose. (*Gaily, to Nina*) I've had a dull day, darling. (*Crossman comes in*) Where'd you skip to?

NINA. We drove over to Pass Christian.

NICK. Did you put the car in the garage?

CROSSMAN (*gives Nina the keys*). Yes, all safe.

NICK. Did you drive, Ned? That heavy Isotta? (*To Nina*) Nobody who drinks as much as Ned should be driving that car. Or any car belonging to me.

NINA. And nobody as tight as you are should talk that way.

NICK (*laughs*). Have a drink, Ned.

(*He brings Crossman a glass.*)

CROSSMAN. Thank you, no.

(*Nick turns, hands glass to Griggs.*)

GRIGGS. No, thank you.

NICK. What the hell is this? Refusing to have a drink with me — (*To Crossman*) I'm trying to apologize to you. Now take the drink —

NINA. Nick, please —

NICK. Stay out of it, Nina. Women don't know anything about the etiquette of drinking.

CROSSMAN. Has it got etiquette now? (*As Nick hands him glass. Shakes his head*) Thank you.

NICK. Look here, old boy, I say in the light of what's happened, you've just got to take this. It's my way of apologizing and I shouldn't have to explain that to a gentleman.

(*He grabs Crossman's arm, playfully presses the glass to Crossman's lips.*)

CROSSMAN (*quietly*). Don't do that.

NICK. Come on, old boy. If I have to pour it down you —

CROSSMAN. Don't do that.

(*Nick, laughing, presses the glass hard against Crossman's mouth. Crossman pushes the glass and it falls to the floor.*)

NINA. Well, we got rid of that glass. But there are plenty more, Nick.

NICK (*sad, but firm, to Crossman*). Now *you've* put *yourself* on the defensive, my friend. That's always tactically unwise, isn't it, General Griggs?

GRIGGS. I know nothing of tactics, Mr. Denery. Certainly not of yours.

NICK. Then what the hell are you doing as a general?

GRIGGS. Masquerading. They had a costume left over and they lent it to me.

NICK (*to Crossman*). I'm waiting, Ned. Pour yourself a drink, and make *your* apologies.

CROSSMAN. You are just exactly the way I remember you. And that I wouldn't have believed of any man.

(*He turns, goes out.*)

NICK. What the hell does that mean? (*Calling*) Hey, Ned. Come on back and have it your way. (*Gets no answer, turns, hearty again*) Come on, General. Have a bottle with me.

NINA. Are we going to start again?

NICK. General, got something to tell you: your wife telephoned but she didn't want to speak to you.

GRIGGS. That's understandable. Good night, Mrs. Denery, and thank you for a pleasant day.

NICK. But she'll want to speak to you in the morning. Better stick around in the morning.

GRIGGS (*stares at him*). Thank you. Good night.

NICK (*following him*). I think you're doing the wrong thing, wanting to leave Rose. You're going to be lonely at your age without —

GRIGGS. If my wife wishes to consult you, Mr. Denery, that's her business. But I don't wish to consult you.

(*He exits.*)

NICK. Sorry. Forget it.

(*Nick turns, takes his drink to the couch, lies down.*)

NINA (*after a pause*). You know, it's a nasty business hating yourself.

NICK. Who's silly enough to do that?

NINA. Me.

NICK (*warmly*). Come on over here, darling, and tell me about yourself. I've missed you.

NINA. To hate yourself.

NICK. I love you, Nina.

NINA. Here we go with that routine. Now you'll bait me until I tell you that you've never loved any woman, or any man, nor ever will. (*Wearily*) I'll be glad to get out of this house before Constance finds you out. She can go back to sleeping with her dreams. You still think you can wind up everybody's affairs by Friday?

NICK. Oh, sure. Friday. Then we're going up to spend a month with Rose's brother, Henry something or other. In New Orleans.

NINA. What are you talking about?

NICK. Rose fixed it for me. I'm going to do a portrait of her niece, the heiress to the fortune. The girl is balding and has braces. (*Looks at her*) Five thousand dollars.

NINA. Are you crazy?

NICK. Not a bit.

NINA. It's all right to kid around here —

NICK. I *don't* know what you mean.

NINA (*violently*). Please don't let's talk this way. Just tell Mrs. Griggs that you've changed your mind —

NICK. I demand that you tell me what you mean.

NINA (*angrily*). How many years have we avoided saying it? Why must you walk into it now? (*Pauses, looks at him*) All right. Maybe it's time: you haven't finished a portrait in twelve years. And money isn't your reason for wanting to do this portrait. You're setting up a silly flirtation with Mrs. Griggs. I'm not going to New Orleans, Nick. I am not going to watch it all again. I can't go on this way with myself— (*Then softly*) Don't go. Call it off. You know how it will end. Please let's don't this time—We're not young anymore, Nick. Somewhere we must have learned something.

NICK (*carefully*). If I haven't finished every picture I started it's because I'm good enough to know they weren't good enough. All these years you never understood that? I think I will never forgive you for talking that way.

NINA. Your trouble is that you're an amateur, a gifted amateur. And like all amateurs you have very handsome reasons for what you do not finish—between trains and boats.

NICK. You have thought that about me, all these years?

NINA. Yes.

NICK. Then it was good of you and loyal to pretend you believed in me.

NINA. Good? Loyal? What do they mean? I loved you.

NICK. Yes, good and loyal. But I, too, have a little vanity— (*She laughs; he comes to her*) And no man can bear to live with a woman who feels that way about his work. I think you ought to leave tomorrow, Nina. For good and forever.

NINA (*softly*). Yes. Yes, of course.

(*She starts to exit. He follows behind her, talking.*)

NICK. But it must be different this time. Remember I said years ago—"Ten times of threatening is out, Nina," I said —the tenth time you stay gone.

NINA. All right. Ten times is out. I promise for good and forever.

NICK (*she is climbing the staircase*). This time, spare yourself the return. And the begging and the self-humiliation and the self-hate. This time they won't do any good. (*He is following her but we cannot see him*) Let's write it down, darling. And have a drink to seal it.

(*Constance comes into the hall. She hears the words, and stands, frowning, thoughtful. Then she turns out the lights on the porch, puts out all lights except one lamp, comes back into the living room and begins to empty the ashtrays, etc. Sophie comes into the room carrying pillow, sheets, quilts, a glass of milk, and crosses to couch. Without speaking, Constance moves to help her and together they begin to make the couch for the night.*)

SOPHIE (*after a minute*). Do not worry for me, Aunt Constance.

CONSTANCE. I can't help it.

SOPHIE. I think perhaps you worry sometimes in order that you should not think.

CONSTANCE (*smiles*). Yes, maybe. I won't say any more. I'll be lonely without you, Sophie. I don't like being alone, anymore. It's not a good way to live. And with you married, I'll be alone forever, unless — Well, Ned's loved me and it's been such a waste, such a waste. I know it now but — well — I don't know. (*Shyly, as a young girl would say it*) You understand, Sophie? (*Sophie stares at her, frowning. Then Constance speaks happily*) Sleep well, dear.

(*She comes to Sophie, kisses her, exits, closing door. Sophie finishes with the bed, brings her milk to the bed table, takes off her robe, puts it around her shoulders, gets into bed, and lies quietly, thinking. Then she turns as she hears footsteps in the hall and she is staring at the door as Nick opens it. He trips over a chair, recovers himself, turns on a lamp.*)

NICK (*sharply*). Constance! What is this — a boys' school with lights out at eleven! (*He sees Sophie*) Where's your aunt? I want to talk to her. What are you doing?

SOPHIE. I think I am asleep, Mr. Denery.

NICK. You're cute. Maybe too cute. (*He pours himself a drink*) I'm going down to the tavern and see if I can get up a beach party. Tell your aunt. Just tell her that. (*Going toward door*) Want to come? You couldn't be more welcome. (*She shakes her head*) Oh, come on. Throw on a coat. I'm not mad at you anymore. (*He comes back toward her, looks down at her*) I couldn't paint you, Sophie. You're too thin. Damn shame you're so thin. (*Suddenly sits down on bed*) I'm sick of trouble. Aren't you? Like to drive away with me for a few days? (*Smiles at her*) Nobody would care. And we could be happy. I hate people not being happy. (*He lies down. His head is now on her knees*) Move your knees, baby, they're bony. And get me a drink.

SOPHIE. Take the bottle upstairs, Mr. Denery.

NICK. Get me a drink. And make it poison. (*Slowly, wearily, she gets up, takes his glass, goes to bottle, pours drink. He begins to sing. She brings glass back to him. He reaches up to take the glass, decides to pull her toward him, and spills the liquid on the bed*) Clumsy, honey, clumsy. But I'll forgive you.

(*He is holding her, and laughing.*)

SOPHIE. Please go somewhere else, Mr. Denery.

NICK (*springs up, drunk-angry*). People aren't usually rude to me, Sophie. Poor little girls always turn rude when they're about to marry rich little boys. What a life you're going to have. That boy doesn't even know what's the matter with him —

SOPHIE (*very sharply*). Please, Mr. Denery, go away.

NICK (*laughs*). Oh, you know what's the matter with him? No European would be as innocent of the world as you pretend. (*Delighted*) I tricked you into telling me. Know that?

SOPHIE. You are drunk and I am tired. Please go away.

NICK (*sits down across the room*). Go to sleep, child. I'm not disturbing you. (*She stares at him, decides she can't move him, gets into bed, picks up a book, begins to read*) I won't say a word. Ssh. Sophie's reading. Do you like to read? Know the best way to read? With someone you love. Out loud. Ever try it that way, honey? (*He gets up, comes to bed, stands near her, speaking over her shoulder*) I used to know a lot of poetry. Brought up on Millay. My candle and all that. "I had to be a liar. My mother was a leprechaun, my father was a friar." Crazy for the girl. (*Leans over and kisses her hair. She pulls her head away*) Ever wash your hair in champagne, darling? I knew a woman once. (*Tips the glass over her head*) Let's try it.

SOPHIE (*sharply*). Let us not try it again.

NICK (*sits down beside her*). Now for God's sake don't get angry. (*Takes her shoulders and shakes her*) I'm sick of angry women. All men are sick of angry women, if angry women knew the truth. Sophie, we can always go away and starve. I'll manage to fall in love with you.

SOPHIE (*he is holding her*). Mr. Denery, I am sick of you.

NICK (*softly*). Tell me you don't like me and I will go away and not come back.

SOPHIE. No, sir. I do not like you.

NICK. People have hated me. But nobody's ever not liked me. If I thought you weren't flirting, I'd be hurt. Is there any aspirin downstairs? If you kiss me, Sophie, be kind to me for just a minute, I'll go away. I may come back another day, but I'll go all by myself — (*Desperately*) Please, Sophie, please.

SOPHIE (*sighs, holds up her side face to him*). All right. Then you will go, remember. (*He takes her in his arms, pulls her down on the bed. She struggles to get away from him. She speaks angrily*) Do not make yourself such a clown. (*When she cannot get away from him*) I will call your wife, Mr. Denery.

NICK (*delighted*). That would be fun, go ahead. We're getting a divorce. Sophie, let's make this night our night. God, Julie, if you only knew what I've been through —

SOPHIE (*violently*). Oh shut up.

(*She pulls away from him with great effort. He catches her robe and rolls over on it.*)

NICK (*giggles as he settles down comfortably*). Come on back. It's nice and warm here and I love you very much. But we've got to get some sleep, darling. Really we have to.

(*Then he turns over and lies still. She stands looking at him.*)

SOPHIE (*after a minute*). Get up, Mr. Denery. I will help you upstairs. (*No answer*) Please, please get up.

NICK (*gently, half passed-out*). It's raining out. Just tell the concierge I'm your brother. She'll understa — (*The words fade off. Sophie waits a second and then leans over and with great strength begins to shake him*) *Stop that.* (*He passes out, begins to breathe heavily. She turns, goes to hall, stands at the foot of the steps. Then she changes her mind and comes back into the room. She goes to the couch, decides to pull him by the legs. Softly*) I'll go away in a few minutes. Don't be so young. Have a little pity. I am old and sick.

(*Sophie draws back, moves slowly to the other side of the room as the curtain falls.*)

Curtain

Act Three

SCENE: *The same. Seven o'clock the next morning.*

AT RISE: *Nick is asleep on the couch. Sophie is sitting in a chair, drinking a cup of coffee. A minute after the rise of the curtain, Mrs. Ellis comes down the steps, comes into the room.*

MRS. ELLIS. I heard you bumping around in the kitchen, Sophie. The older you get the less you sleep, and the more you look forward to meals. Particularly breakfast, because you've been alone all night, and the nights are the hardest — (*She sees Nick, stares, moves over to look at him*) What is this?

SOPHIE. It is Mr. Denery.

MRS. ELLIS. What's he doing down here?

SOPHIE. He became drunk and went to sleep.

MRS. ELLIS. He has been here all night? (*Sophie nods*) What's the matter with you? Get him out of here immediately.

SOPHIE. I cannot move him. I tried. Shall I get you some coffee?

MRS. ELLIS. Are you being silly, Sophie? Sometimes it is very hard to tell with you. Why didn't you call Constance or Mrs. Denery?

SOPHIE. I did not know what to do. Mr. and Mrs. Denery had some trouble between them, or so he said, and I thought it might be worse for her if — (*Smiles*) Is it so much? He was just a little foolish and sleepy. (*Goes toward door*) I will get Leon and Sadie and we will take him upstairs.

MRS. ELLIS (*crosses to door*). You will not get Leon and Sadie. Rose Griggs may be president of the gossip club for summer Anglo-Saxons, but Leon is president of the Negro chapter. You will get this, er, out of here before anybody else sees him. (*She crosses back to bed, pulls blanket off Nick*) At least he's dressed. Bring me that cup of coffee. (*Sophie brings cup*) Mr. Denery! Sit up! (*Nick moves his head slightly. To Sophie*) Hold his head up.

(*Sophie holds Nick's head; Mrs. Ellis tries to make him drink.*)

NICK (*very softly*). Please leave me alone.

MRS. ELLIS (*shouting in his ear*). Mr. Denery, listen to me. *You are to get up and get out of here immediately.*

NICK (*giving a bewildered look around the room; then he closes his eyes*). Julie.

SOPHIE. He has been speaking of Julie most of the night.

MRS. ELLIS (*very sharply*). Shall I wake your wife and see if she can locate Julie for you, or would you rather be cremated here? Get up, Mr. Denery.

(*He opens his eyes, shuts them again.*)

SOPHIE. You see how it is? (*She tries to pull her robe from under him*) Would you get off my robe, Mr. Denery?

MRS. ELLIS. Sophie, you're a damned little ninny. (*Very loudly, to Nick*) Now get up. You have no right to be here. You must get up immediately. I say *you,* you get up. (*Shouting*) Get to your room. Get out of here.

NICK (*turns, opens his eyes, half sits up, speaks gently*). Don't scream at me, Mrs. Ellis. (*Sees Sophie, begins to realize where he is, groans deeply*) I passed out?

SOPHIE. Yes, sir. Most deeply.

NICK. Champagne's always been a lousy drink for me. How did I get down here? (*He turns over*) I'm sorry, child. What happened?

SOPHIE. You fell asleep.

NICK. Did I — God, I'm a fool. What did I — Did I do anything or say anything? Tell me, Sophie.

MRS. ELLIS. Please get up and get out of here.

NICK. I'm thirsty. I want a quart of water. Or a bottle of beer. Get me a bottle of cold beer, Sophie, will you? (*Looks around the bed*) Where'd you sleep? Get me the beer, will you?

MRS. ELLIS (*carefully*). Mr. Denery, you are in Sophie's bed, in the living room of a house in a small Southern town where for a hundred and fifty years it has been impossible to take a daily bath without everybody in town knowing what hour the water went on. You know that as well as I do. Now get up and go out by the side lawn to the boathouse. Put your head under water, or however you usually treat these matters, and come back through the front door for breakfast.

NICK (*laughs*). I couldn't eat breakfast.

MRS. ELLIS. I don't find you cute. I find only that you can harm a young girl. Do please understand that.

NICK. Yes, I do. And I'm sorry. (*He sits up, untangling himself from the robe*) What's this? Oh, Sophie, child, I must have been a nuisance. I am *so* sorry.

MRS. ELLIS. Get up and get the hell out of here.

(*The door opens and Rose, carrying her overnight handbag, sticks her head in.*)

ROSE (*to Mrs. Ellis, who is directly on a line with the door*). You frightened me. I could hear you outside on the lawn, so early. Oh, Nick. How nice you're downstairs. I never expected it — (*Her voice trails off as she sees Sophie and realizes Nick is on the bed*) Oh. (*Giggles, hesitantly*) You look like you just woke up, Nick. I mean, just woke up where you are.

MRS. ELLIS (*to Nick*). Well, that's that. Perhaps you wanted it this way, Mr. Denery.

(*She starts out as Leon appears carrying the coffee urn. Rose stands staring at Nick.*)

LEON (*very curious, but hesitant in doorway*). Should I put it here this morning, like every day, or —

MRS. ELLIS. Who told you, Leon?

LEON. Told me what, Mrs. Ellis? Sadie says take on in the urn —

MRS. ELLIS. Who told you about Mr. Denery being here?

LEON. Told me? Why Miss Sophie came in for coffee for them.

MRS. ELLIS (*after a second, shrugs, points to coffee urn*). Take it into the dining room.

LEON. You want me come back and straighten up, Miss Sophie?

MRS. ELLIS (*waves him out*). Mrs. Griggs will be glad to straighten up.

(*She exits.*)

ROSE (*softly to Nick*). You were here all night? I come back needing your help and advice as I've never before needed anything. And I find you —

NICK. Rose, please stop moving about. You're making me seasick. And would you go outside? I'd like to speak to Sophie.

ROSE. I am waiting for you to explain, Nick. I don't understand.

NICK. There is no need for you to understand.

ROSE. I'm not judging you. I know that there's probably a good explanation — But please tell me, Nick, what happened and then I won't be angry.

NICK. What the hell are you talking about? Now go upstairs, Rose.

ROSE (*softly, indignant*). "Go upstairs, Rose." After I work my head off getting the commission of the portrait for you and after I go to the doctor's on your advice, although I never would have gone if I had known, and I come back here and find you this way. (*Sits down*) You've hurt me and you picked a mighty bad day to do it.

(*The door opens and Constance comes in. She goes to Nick, stands looking at him.*)

CONSTANCE. Nick, I want you to go to that window and look across the street. (*He stares at her. Then he gets up slowly and slowly moves to the window*) The Carters have three extra guests on their breakfast porch, the Gable sisters are unexpectedly entertaining —

NICK. It can't be that bad, Constance.

CONSTANCE. It is just that bad.

NICK. I'm sorry. I was silly and drunk but there's no sense making more out of it than that.

CONSTANCE. I am not making anything out of it. But I know what is being made out of it. In your elegant way of life, I daresay this is an ordinary occurrence. But not in our village. (*The telephone rings. Constance picks up phone, says "Hello," pauses, "Hello, Mrs. Sims." Then her face becomes angry and she hangs up. She stands looking at the phone, and then takes it off the hook. Turns to Nick*) Please explain to me what happened. (*Points to telephone and then across the street*) I only know what they know.

SOPHIE. Mr. Denery came down looking for someone to talk to. He saw me, recited a little poetry, spoke to me of his troubles, tried to embrace me in a most mild fashion. He was uncertain of my name and continued throughout the night to call me Julie although twice he called for Cecile. And fell into so deep a sleep that I could not move him. Alcohol. It is the same in my country, every country.

CONSTANCE. You are taking a very light tone about it, Sophie.

SOPHIE (*turns away, goes toward couch, and through the next speeches will strip the bed and pile the clothes*). I will speak whichever way you think most fits the drama, Aunt Constance.

CONSTANCE. Will you tell me why you stayed in the room? Why didn't you come and call me, or —

NICK. Oh, look here. It's obvious. The kid didn't want to make any fuss and thought I'd wake up and go any minute. Damn nice of you, Sophie, and I'm grateful.

CONSTANCE. It was dangerous "niceness."

(*Sophie looks up, stares at Constance.*)

NICK. Constance, it's not all that much.

CONSTANCE. Isn't it? You've looked out of the window. Now go down to the drugstore and listen to them and I think you'll change your mind.

NICK. Look. A foolish guy drinks, passes out —

ROSE (*amazed as she turns to look at Sophie*). Why, look at Sophie. Just as calm as can be. Making the bed. Like it happened to her every night.

CONSTANCE (*turns, realizes Rose is in the room*). What are you doing here, Rose?

ROSE. Sitting here thinking that no man sleeps in a girl's bed unless she gives him to understand — (*Constance stares at her*) You can blame Nick all you like. But you know very well that a nice girl would have screamed.

CONSTANCE. How dare you talk this way? What ever gave you the right — I hope it will be convenient for you to leave today. I will apologize to the General.

ROSE (*softly*). That's all right, Constance. I must leave today, in any case. You see, I have to — You won't be mad at me for long when you know the story. Oh, I'm very tired now. Could I have my breakfast in bed? Doctor's orders. (*She goes out, passes Crossman who is coming in. In sepulchral tones*) Good morning, dear Ned. Have you heard — ?

CROSSMAN (*cheerful*). Good morning. Yes, I've heard. I'm not the one deaf man in town.

CONSTANCE. Ned, what should we do?

CROSSMAN. Is there always something that can be done, remedied, patched, pulled apart and put together again? There is nothing to "do," Con. (*Smiles to Sophie, amused*) How are you, Sophie?

SOPHIE. I am all right, Mr. Ned.

NICK. Ned, is it as bad as (*Gestures toward window and Contance*) Constance thinks?

CONSTANCE. What's the difference to you? You're just sitting there telling yourself what provincial people we are and how you wish you were in the Ritz bar with people who would find it amusing with their lunch. It has taken me too many years to find out that you —

CROSSMAN. All right, Con, what's the good of discussing Nick's character and habits now?

NICK. Whatever you think of me, I didn't want this. I know what it will mean to Sophie and I'll do anything that will help her —

SOPHIE. What will it "mean" to me, Mr. Ned?

CONSTANCE (*softly*). You're old enough to know. And I believe you do know.

SOPHIE. I want to know from Mr. Ned what he thinks.

CROSSMAN (*to Sophie*). I know what you want to know: the Ellis name is a powerful name. They won't be gossiped about out loud. They won't gossip about you and they won't listen to gossip about you. In their own way they'll take care of things. (*Carefully*) You can be quite sure of that. Quite sure.

SOPHIE (*after a second*). And that is all?

CROSSMAN. That is all.

SOPHIE (*softly*). Thank you, Mr. Ned.

CONSTANCE. Take care of things? She hasn't done anything. Except be stupid. The Tuckerman name is as good as the Ellis name —

CROSSMAN. Yes, yes. Sure enough.

(*Sophie exits. She passes Leon in the hall. He is carrying his hat.*)

LEON. Mrs. Ellis is cutting up about her breakfast. And Sadie's waiting for orders. We're messed this morning, for good.

CONSTANCE. Not at all. Tell Sadie I'm coming. (*She goes toward door*) What's your hat for, Leon?

LEON. Well, kind of a hot sun today.

CONSTANCE. Not in here. Rest your hat: you'll have plenty of time to gossip when the sun goes down.

(*She goes out.*)

NICK. Ned. Ned, you understand I never thought it — Is Constance being — I mean, is she being old-maid fussy or is it really unpleasant —

CROSSMAN. She loves the girl, and she's worried for her.

NICK. If I could do something —

CROSSMAN. You did; but don't make too much of it.

NICK. Thank you, boy.

CROSSMAN. Or too little. (*Nick groans*) Nobody will blame you too much. The girl's a foreigner and they don't like her. You're a home-town boy and as such you didn't do anything they wouldn't do. Boys will be boys and in the South there's no age limit on boyishness. Therefore, she led you on, or whatever is this morning's phrase. You'll come off all right. But then I imagine you always do.

NICK. You think this is coming off all right?

CROSSMAN. No, I don't.

NICK. I didn't even want her. Never thought of her that way.

CROSSMAN. That *is* too bad. Better luck next time. You're young — in spirit.

(*He exits into hall toward dining room as Hilda, carrying a jewel case, and hat box, comes down the steps. She has on her hat and gloves.*)

NICK (*who is sitting on a line with the door and sees her, speaks in German*). Where you going?

HILDA (*in German*). Good morning, sir. I am taking madame's luggage to the nine-thirty train.

(*She moves off as Nina appears. Nina has on a hat and gloves. On her heels is Rose in a fluffy negligee. Rose is talking as she follows Nina down the steps.*)

ROSE. Of course it was indiscreet but you're a woman of the world, Nina, and you know what young girls are with a tipsy man. Nina, do believe that I saw them this morning and he didn't have the slightest interest in her. Nina —

NINA (*turns to her, pleasantly*). I know it's eccentric of me, Mrs. Griggs, but I dislike being called by my first name before midnight.

ROSE. You shouldn't allow yourself such a nasty snub. I'm only trying to help Nick. I know him well enough to know that he didn't do a thing — (*Nina laughs*) He's been my good friend. I'm trying to be a friend to him.

NINA. You will have every opportunity.

NICK (*very angry*). Will you please not stand there in the hall discussing me?

ROSE. Oh! (*Looks at Nick, then at Nina, steps back into hall, calls toward kitchen*) Leon! Could I have my tray upstairs? (*As she goes past room and exits upstairs*) Anybody seen my husband this morning?

NICK. Nina. I just want to say before you go that they're making an awful row about nothing —

NINA. You don't owe me an explanation, Nick.

NICK. Nothing happened, Nina, I swear. Nothing happened.

NINA. Try out phrases like "nothing happened" on women like Mrs. Griggs.

NICK (*smiles*). I'm sorry as all hell but they sure are cutting up —

NINA. Well, it is a tasty little story. Particularly for a girl who is going to be married.

NICK. My God, I'd forgotten about the boy. I must say he's an easy boy to forget about. Now I'll have to take *him* out and explain —

NINA. Don't do that, Nick. He isn't a fool.

NICK (*looks around, thinking of anything to keep her in the room*). Shall I get you a cup of coffee, darling?

NINA. No. Darling will have it on the train.

NICK. Nina, I swear I didn't sleep with her.

NINA. I believe you. The girl doesn't like you.

NICK. Doesn't she? She's been very kind to me. She could have raised hell. That doesn't sound as if she doesn't like me. (*Nina laughs*) Don't laugh at me this morning. (*After a second*) What can I do for her, Nina?

NINA. You used to send hampers of white roses. With a card saying "White for purity and sad parting."

NICK. Stop being nasty to me. (*Then he smiles and comes toward her*) Or maybe it's a good sign.

NINA. It isn't. I just say these things by rote. (*Turns*) I don't know how long I'll be in New York, but you can call Horace and he'll take care of the legal stuff for us.

NICK (*close to her*). I told you last night that I would agree to the separation because I knew with what justice you wanted to leave me.

NINA (*coldly*). That's not at all what you said.

NICK. I was tight. It was what I meant to say —

NINA. You're lying. You said just what you meant to say: I was to leave. And not —

NICK. Stop, Nina. Take any kind of revenge you want, but — please — some other day. (*Leans down, puts his face against her face*) Don't leave me. Don't ever leave me. We've had good times, wild times. They made up for what was bad and they always will. Most people don't get that much. We've only had one trouble; you hate yourself for loving me. Because you have contempt for me.

NINA. For myself. I have no right —

NICK. No, nobody has. No right at all.

NINA. I wouldn't have married you, Nick, if I had known —

NICK. You would have married me. Or somebody like me. You've needed to look down on me, darling. You've needed to make fun of me. And to be ashamed of yourself for doing it.

NINA. Am I that sick?

NICK. I don't know about such words. You found the man you deserved. That's all. I am no better and no worse than what you wanted. You like to — to demean yourself. And so you chose me. You must say I haven't minded much. Because I've always loved you and known we'd last it out. Come back to me, Nina, without shame in wanting to. (*He leans down, kisses her neck*) Put up with me a little longer, kid. I'm getting older and I'll soon wear down.

NINA (*she smiles, touched*). I've never heard you speak of getting old.

NICK (*quickly*). Yes. The *Ile* sails next week. Let's get on. We'll have fun. Tell me we're together again and you're happy. Say it, Nina, quick.

NINA. I'm happy.

(*He takes her in his arms, kisses her. Then he stands away, looks at her, and smiles shyly.*)

NICK. There'll be no more of what you call my "homecomings." Old friends and all that. They are damn bores, with empty lives. If we could only do something for the kid. Take her with us, get her out of here until they get tired of the gossip —

NINA (*laughs*). I don't think we will take her with us.

NICK (*laughs*). Now, now. You know what I mean.

NINA. I know what you mean — and we're not taking her with us.

NICK. I feel sick, Nina.

NINA. You've got a hangover.

NICK. It's more than that. I've got a sore throat and my back aches. Come on, darling, let's get on the train.

NINA. You go. I'll stay and see if there's anything I can do. That's what you really want. Go on, Nicky. Maybe it's best.

NICK. I couldn't do that.

NINA. Don't waste time, darling. You'll miss the train. I'll bring your clothes with me.

NICK (*laughs, ruefully*). If you didn't see through me so fast, you wouldn't dislike yourself so much. You're a wonderful girl. It's wonderful of you to take all this on —

NINA. I've had practice.

NICK. That's not true. You know this never happened before.

NINA (*smiles*). Nicky, it always confuses you that the fifth time something happens it varies slightly from the second and fourth. No, it never happened in this house before. Cora had a husband and Sylvia wanted one. And this isn't a hotel in Antibes, and Sophie is not a rich Egyptian. And this time you didn't break your arm on a boat deck and it isn't 1928 —

NICK. This is your day, Nina. But pass up the chance to play it too hard, will you? Take me or leave me now but don't —

NINA. You're right. Please go, darling. Your staying won't do any good. Neither will mine, but maybe —

NICK. When will you come? I tell you what: you take the car and drive to Mobile. I'll get off there and wait at the Battle House. Then we can drive the rest of the way together. Must be somewhere in Mobile I can waste time for a few hours —

NINA (*gaily*). I'm sure. But let's have a week's rest. Now go on.

NICK (*takes her in his arms*). I love you, Nina. And we'll have the best time of our lives. And thank you. (*He kisses her*) They won't rag you, nobody ever does. We'll get the bridal suite on the *Ile* and have all our meals in bed. (*He moves away*) If you possibly can, bring the new portrait with you. I can finish it now. And try to get me the old portrait, darling. Maybe Constance will sell it to you — (*Nina laughs*) All right. Think what you want and I'll be what I am. I love you and you love me and that's that and always will be.

(*He exits. She stands quietly. Then she turns, goes to the bell cord, pulls it. After a second, Constance appears in the hall.*)

NINA. Leon, could I have breakfast on the porch?

CONSTANCE (*in the doorway. She is carrying a tray*). Yes, of course. I'll tell Leon to bring it.

NINA. I am very sorry, Constance.

CONSTANCE. I am sorry, too, my dear.

NINA. I don't know what else to say. I wish —

CONSTANCE. There's nothing for us to say. (*There is an awkward pause*) Well. I'll tell Leon. Old lady Ellis is having her second breakfast. She always does on her last day. I don't know why. (*She starts out as Carrie, followed by Frederick, comes down the steps. Carrie has on her hat, etc., as if she were ready for traveling. Frederick is carrying two valises)* Shall I send breakfast up to Nick?

NINA *(very quickly)*. No, no. I'll just have mine and —

FREDERICK *(calling to Constance)*. Where's Sophie?

CONSTANCE. I'll send her in.

FREDERICK. Don't sound so solemn, Miss Constance.

CONSTANCE. I didn't mean to.

(She disappears in the direction of the dining room. Frederick and Carrie come into the room.)

NINA. Mr. Ellis, I should be carrying a sign that says my husband is deeply sorry and so am I.

(He smiles at her. She turns, goes out on the porch, closes the door behind her.)

CARRIE. She's a nice woman, I think. Must be a hard life for her.

FREDERICK *(laughs)*. I don't think so. *(Turns as he hears Sophie in the hall)* Now remember, Mother. *(Sophie appears in the door. Frederick goes to her, takes her chin in his hand, kisses her)* I want to tell you something fast. I don't know how to explain it but I'm kind of glad this foolishness happened. It makes you seem closer to me, some silly way. You must believe that, although I can't make it clear. Now there are two things to do right away. Your choice.

SOPHIE. I have made bad gossip for you, Frederick. We must speak about that. Right away.

FREDERICK. There's no need to speak about it again. It's a comic story and that's all. And you must begin to laugh about it.

SOPHIE *(smiles)*. I did laugh but nobody would laugh with me. And nobody will laugh in New Orleans, either. Is that not so, Mrs. Ellis?

CARRIE. I think you should travel up with us, Sophie. Right now. Whatever is to be faced, we will do much better if we face it all together and do it quickly.

FREDERICK *(looks at her)*. You're putting it much too importantly. There's nothing to be faced.

CARRIE. I didn't mean to make it too important. Of course, it isn't —

SOPHIE *(puts her hand on Fred's arm)*. It is important to you. And you must not be kind and pretend that —

FREDERICK. I'm not being kind. I told you the truth. That's all, now or ever. *(Shyly)* As far as I'm concerned, it makes us seem less like strangers. I'd hope you'd feel the same way —

CARRIE (*quickly*). Run and pack a bag, Sophie. It's a lovely day for driving and we'll be in town for lunch. I think you and I will have it at the club — Now let's not talk about it anymore —

SOPHIE. No. It would be most mistaken of me to come now. My leaving here would seem as if I must be ashamed and you ashamed for me. I must not come with you today. I must stay here. (*Smiles*) It must be faced.

FREDERICK. All right. That makes sense. Mother and Grandma will drive up and I'll stay here —

SOPHIE (*very quickly*). No, no. You must not stay here. (*Points to window*) They knew you had made plans to leave today as usual. And so you must leave. We must act as if nothing had happened, and if we do that, and are not worried, it will all end more quickly. (*Goes to Frederick*) Believe me, Frederick. You know what I say is true. All must seem to be as it has been. (*To Carrie*) You tell him that, please, Mrs. Ellis.

CARRIE. I don't know. You belong with us now, Sophie. We don't want to leave you, or Constance. I think she should come along and —

SOPHIE. Oh, she would not do that. You know she would not. (*Smiles, very cheerfully*) Now. You are both very kind. But you know what I say is best for us all, and of no importance whether I come one week or the next. (*Takes Frederick's arm*) You have said I must laugh about it. I do laugh, and so it will be nothing for me to stay.

(*Mrs. Ellis comes to the door from the direction of the dining room.*)

CARRIE. Good-bye, Sophie. We will be waiting for you.

(*She exits, passing Mrs. Ellis without speaking.*)

FREDERICK (*unhappily*). You all seem to know what's right, what's best, so much faster than I do. I —

SOPHIE (*smiles, puts her hand over his mouth*). This is best. Please.

FREDERICK. Then let me come back this weekend. Can I do that?

SOPHIE (*she touches his face*). I think so. You are a nice man, Frederick.

FREDERICK (*kisses her*). And you're a nice girl to think so. See you in a few days. (*Turns to go out, passes Mrs. Ellis*) I feel happy, Grandma.

(*Mrs. Ellis nods, waits for him to exit. Sophie sits down.*)

MRS. ELLIS (*after a second*). Sophie.

SOPHIE (*smiles as if she knew what was coming*). Yes.

MRS. ELLIS. Did *Carrie* ask you to leave with us? (*Sophie nods*) Ah. That's not good. When Carrie gets smart she gets very smart. Sophie, Frederick meant what he said to you. But I know them both and I would guess that in a week, or two or three, he will agree to go to Europe with his mother and he will tell you that it is only a postponement. And he will believe what he says. Time and decisions melt and merge for him and ten years from now he will be convinced that you refused to marry him. And he will always be a little sad about what could have been.

SOPHIE. Yes. Of course.

MRS. ELLIS. Carrie never will want him to marry. And she will never know it. Well, she, too, got cheated a long time ago. There is very little I can do — perhaps very little I want to do anymore. Don't judge him too harshly, child.

SOPHIE (*smiles*). No, I will not judge. I will write a letter to him.

MRS. ELLIS. That's my girl. Don't take from us what you don't have to take, or waste yourself on defeat. (*She gets up*) Oh, Sophie, feel sorry for Frederick. He is nice and he is nothing. And his father before him and my other sons. And myself. Another way. Well. If there is ever a chance, come and see me.

(*She moves out. Sophie remains seated. After a second Constance comes in from the hall. She looks at Sophie.*)

CONSTANCE (*hesitantly*). Carrie tells me you'll be going up to town in a few weeks to stay with them. I'm glad. (*No answer*) Er. Why don't you go up to my room, dear, and lie down for a while? (*Points to porch*) *She's* on the porch. I'm going to ask the Denerys to leave today. I am sure they will want to, anyway. And the Griggses will be going and then just you and I —

SOPHIE. I will not be going to New Orleans, Aunt Constance, and there will be no marriage between Frederick and me.

CONSTANCE (*stares at her*). But Carrie told me —

SOPHIE. Now she believes that she wants me. But it will not be so.

CONSTANCE (*after a second*). I wish I could say I was surprised or angry. But I'm not sorry. No marriage without love —

SOPHIE. Yes. Yes.

CONSTANCE (*gently*). You're not to feel bad or hurt.

SOPHIE. I do not.

CONSTANCE. I'm — I'm glad. Mighty glad. Everything will work out for the best. You'll see. After everybody goes, we'll get the house and the accounts cleaned up and straightened out as usual. (*Gaily*) And then I think you and I will take a little trip. I haven't seen Memphis in years and maybe in a few months — (*Gently*) You know what? We can even sell, rent, the place, if we want to. We can pick up and go anywhere we want. You'll see, dear. We'll have a nice time.

SOPHIE (*almost as if she were speaking to a child*). Yes, Aunt Constance. (*Constance goes out. Sophie turns to watch Leon who, during Constance's speech, has come out on the porch and is serving breakfast to Nina. Sophie rises and goes out to the porch. She takes the coffee pot from Leon — he has finished placing the other dishes — nods to him, and pours Nina's coffee. Leon exits. Nina turns, sees Sophie, turns back*) You are a pretty woman, Mrs. Denery, when your face is happy.

NINA. And you think my face is happy *this* morning?

SOPHIE. Oh, yes. You and Mr. Denery have had a nice reconciliation.

NINA (*stares at her*). Er. Yes, I suppose so.

SOPHIE. I am glad for you. That is as it has been and will always be. (*She sits down*) Now could I speak with you and Mr. Denery?

NINA (*uncomfortably*). Sophie, if there is anything I can do — Er. Nick isn't here. I thought it best for us all —

SOPHIE (*softly*). Ah. Ah, my aunt will be most sad.

NINA. Sophie, there's no good my telling you how sorry, how — What can I do?

SOPHIE. You can give me five thousand dollars, Mrs. Denery. American dollars, of course. (*Demurely; her accent from now on grows more pronounced*) I have been subjected to the most degrading experience from which no young girl easily recovers. (*In French*) A most degrading experience from which no young girl easily recovers —

NINA (*stares at her*). It sounds exactly the same in French.

SOPHIE. Somehow sex and money are simpler in French. Well. In English, then, I have lost or will lose my most beloved fiancé; I cannot return to school and the comrades with whom my life has been so happy; my aunt is uncomfortable and unhappy in the only life she knows and is burdened with me for many years to come. I am utterly, utterly miserable, Mrs. Denery. I am ruined. (*Nina bursts out laughing. Sophie smiles*) Please do not laugh at me.

NINA. I suppose I should be grateful to you for making a joke of it.

SOPHIE. You make a mistake. I am most serious.

NINA (*stops laughing*). Are you? Sophie, it is an unpleasant and foolish incident and I don't wish to minimize it. But don't you feel you're adding considerable drama to it?

SOPHIE. No, ma'am. I did not say that is the way I thought of it. But that is the way it will be considered in this place, in this life. Little is made into very much here.

NINA. It's just the same in your country.

SOPHIE. No, Mrs. Denery. You mean it is the same in Brussels or London or Paris, with those whom you would meet. In my class, in my town, it is not so. In a poor house if a man falls asleep drunk — and it happens with us each Saturday night — he is not alone with an innocent young girl because the young girl, at my age, is not so innocent and because her family is in the same room, not having any other place to go. It arranges itself differently; you have more rooms and therefore more troubles.

NINA. Yes. I understand the lecture. Why do you want five thousand dollars, Sophie?

SOPHIE. I wish to go home.

NINA (*gently*). Then I will be happy to give it to you. Happier than you know to think we can do something.

SOPHIE. Yes. I am sure. But I will not accept it as largesse — to make you happy. We will call it a loan, come by through blackmail. One does not have to be grateful for blackmail money, nor think of oneself as a charity girl.

NINA (*after a second*). Blackmail money?

SOPHIE. Yes ma'am. You will give me five thousand dollars because if you do not I will say that Mr. Denery seduced me last night. (*Nina stares at her, laughs*) You are gay this morning, madame.

NINA. Sophie, Sophie. What a child you are. It's not necessary to talk this way.

SOPHIE. I wish to prevent you from giving favors to me.

NINA. I intended no favors. Nick did not seduce you and I

want no more jokes about it. (*Pleasantly*) Suppose we try to be friends —

SOPHIE. I am not joking, Mrs. Denery. And I do not wish us to be friends.

NINA (*gets up*). I would like to give you the money. And I will give it to you for that reason and no other.

SOPHIE. It does not matter to me what you would like. You will give it to me for my reason — or I will not take it.

(*Nina goes toward door, goes into the room, then turns and smiles at Sophie.*)

NINA. You are serious? Just for a word, a way of calling something, you would hurt my husband and me?

SOPHIE. For me it is more than a way of calling something.

NINA. You're a tough little girl.

SOPHIE. Don't you think people often say other people are tough when they do not know how to cheat them?

NINA (*angrily*). I was not trying to cheat you of anything —

SOPHIE. Yes, you were. You wish to be the kind lady who most honorably stays to discharge — within reason — her obligations. And who goes off, as she has gone off many other times, to make the reconciliation with her husband. How would you and Mr. Denery go on living without such incidents as me? I have been able to give you a second, or a twentieth, honeymoon.

NINA. Is that speech made before you raise your price?

SOPHIE (*smiles*). No. A blackmail bargain is still a bargain.

(*Crossman appears in the hall, Sophie sees him.*)

NINA. How would — How shall we make the arrangements?

SOPHIE (*calling*). Mr. Ned. (*Pleasantly, to Nina*) Mr. Ned will know what to do.

NINA (*after a second to Crossman*). I'd like to get a check cashed. It's rather a large check. Could you vouch for me at the bank?

CROSSMAN. Sure. The bank's around the corner.

SOPHIE. Would you like me to come with you, Mrs. Denery?

NINA (*smiles*). You know, I think perhaps it's wisest for you to stay right here. You and I in a bank, cashing a check, this morning, could well be interpreted as a payoff, or blackmail.

(*She goes out.*)

SOPHIE. I will be going home, Mr. Ned.

CROSSMAN. Good. (*Looks at her, turns to stare at Nina*) At least I hope it's good.

SOPHIE. I think it is more good than it is not good.

(He goes out. Rose comes down the steps. Her manner is hurried, nervous. She goes immediately to windows. She looks out as if she saw somebody coming. Then she turns and sees Sophie.)

ROSE *(very nervous)*. Oh. Good morning, Sophie.

SOPHIE. We have seen each other earlier this morning, Mrs. Griggs.

ROSE. Oh. It's like a nightmare to me, as if a year had gone by. I've asked for my breakfast tray twice and nobody pays any attention. And the doctor says that's the way it *must* be.

SOPHIE *(exiting)*. I will get it for you.

ROSE *(back at the window, speaks to Sophie who has left the room)*. Not you, Sophie. You have your own troubles, God knows. I don't know how any of us can eat anything today. *(Griggs, in riding pants and old shirt, comes in through the windows. Because she is upstage of the windows, he does not see her until she speaks)* I've been looking everywhere for you, Ben.

GRIGGS *(turns)*. Rose. You knew where I was.

ROSE. That was all we needed here today: a telephone call to the stables. Oh, Ben, it was I who found them. But you don't know about it —

GRIGGS. I've heard all about it.

ROSE. Terrible, isn't it?

GRIGGS. No.

ROSE. He's been a disappointment to me. I've been lying on the bed thinking about it. Nick Denery, I mean.

GRIGGS. I'm sorry.

ROSE. You know, Ben, I've just about come to the conclusion that I'm often wrong about people, mostly men.

GRIGGS. And what did you and Henry — ah — put together, Rose?

ROSE. It was so hot in town. Henry's got that wonderful air conditioning, of course, but it's never like your own air. I think Sunday's the hottest day of the year, anyway. Athalia's braces cost twenty-five hundred dollars at that Greek dentist's and believe me they don't make anybody look prettier —

GRIGGS. What point did you come to about my decision?

ROSE. Decision? Your decision —

GRIGGS (*tensely*). Please stop playing the fool. I'm afraid of you when you start playing that game.

ROSE. *You* afraid of *me?*

GRIGGS. Yes, me afraid of you. This very minute. Be kind, Rose, and tell me what has been decided for me.

ROSE (*softly, very nervous*). It wasn't like that. Before I saw Henry I went to see Dr. Wills. You know he won't ever see patients on Sunday.

GRIGGS. Not unless the fee is over a hundred.

ROSE. I've always been sorry you didn't like Howard Wills. He's known as the best man in the South, Ben. He gave up a beach picnic with that woman, you know. Only that famous a man could buck having an open mistress —

GRIGGS. I don't want to hear about Wills. Come to the point. What did you and Henry —

ROSE. I've been uneasy. I've sometimes been in pain, all summer. But I guess I knew because I guess I've known since that army doctor in 1934 — I didn't want to talk about it — (*Moves toward him, frightened*) I have bad heart trouble, Ben.

GRIGGS (*after a second, as if he were sick*). Don't play that trick, Rose. It's just too ugly.

ROSE. I am not playing a trick. Wills wrote you a letter about it. (*She reaches in the pocket of her robe, hands him a folded paper. He takes it from her, reads it.*)

GRIGGS (*violently*). How much did Henry pay Wills for this?

ROSE. It wasn't bought. Even Henry couldn't buy it.

(*She turns, goes toward door.*)

GRIGGS (*softly*). Tell me about it.

ROSE. There isn't much to tell. I've known some of it for years, and so have you. I just didn't know it was this bad, or didn't want to. Wills says I must lead a — well, a very different life. I'll have to go to the country somewhere and rest most of the day — not climb steps or go to parties or even see people much. I like people, I — Well, I just don't understand what I can do, except sit in the sun, and I hate sun — Oh, I don't know. He said worse than I am saying — I can't say it —

GRIGGS. Yes. (*After a second*) I'm sorry.

ROSE. I know you are. You've been my good friend. I'm frightened, Ben. I play the fool, but I'm not so big a fool that I don't know I haven't got anybody to help me. I pretend about our boys and what they're like but I know just as well as you do that they're not very kind men and won't want me and won't come to help me. And of course I know about Henry — I always have. I've got nobody and I'm not young and I'm scared. Awful scared.

GRIGGS. You don't have to be.

ROSE (*who is crying, very quietly*). Wills says that if I take good care I might be, probably will be, in fine shape at the end of the year. Please stay with me this year, just this year. I will swear a solemn oath — believe me I'm telling the truth now — I will give you a divorce at the end of the year without another word. I'll go and do it without any fuss, any talk. But please help me now. I'm so scared. Help me, please. One year's a lot to ask, I know, but —

(*Griggs comes to her, presses her arm.*)

GRIGGS. Of course. Of course. Now don't let's speak of it again and we'll do what has to be done.

(*She turns, goes out. He stands where he is. A minute later, Crossman comes in, stares at Griggs as if he knew something was wrong.*)

CROSSMAN. Seen Sophie?

GRIGGS (*as if it were an effort*). In the kitchen, I guess.

(*He watches as Griggs takes out a cigarette and lights it. Griggs's hands are shaking and as he puts out the match, he stares at them.*)

GRIGGS. My hands are shaking.

CROSSMAN. What's the matter?

GRIGGS. Worst disease of all. I'm all gone. I've just looked and there's no Benjamin Griggs.

CROSSMAN (*after a second*). Oh, that. And you've just found that out?

GRIGGS. Just today. Just now.

CROSSMAN. My God, you're young.

GRIGGS (*laughs*). I guess I was. (*Slowly, carefully*) So at any given moment you're only the sum of your life up to then. There are no big moments you can reach unless you've a pile of smaller moments to stand on. That big hour of decision, the turning point in your life, the someday you've counted on when you'd suddenly wipe out your past mistakes, do the work you'd never done, think the way you'd never thought, have what you'd never had — it just doesn't come suddenly. You've trained yourself for it while you waited — or you've let it all run past you and frittered yourself away. I've frittered myself away, Crossman.

CROSSMAN. Most people like us.

GRIGGS. That's no good to me. Most people like us haven't done anything to themselves; they've let it be done to them. I had no right to let it be done to me, but I let it be done. What consolation can I find in not having made myself any more useless than an Ellis, a Denery, a Tuckerman, a —

CROSSMAN. Say it. I won't mind. Or a Crossman.

GRIGGS. The difference is you've meant to fritter yourself away.

CROSSMAN. And does that make it better?

GRIGGS. Better? Worse? All I know is it makes it different. Rose is a sick woman. But you know I'm not talking only about Rose and me, don't you?

CROSSMAN. I know.

GRIGGS (*very slowly*). I am not any too sure I didn't partly welcome the medical opinion that made it easier for me to give up. (*Then in a low voice as if to himself*) And I don't like Rose. And I'll live to like her less.

(*He starts toward door. Constance appears in the hall carrying a tray. She is followed by Sophie who is carrying a carpet sweeper and a basket filled with cleaning rags, etc. Constance comes to the door. She speaks wearily.*)

CONSTANCE (*to Griggs*). Sorry about Rose's breakfast. I forgot it. Sophie is going to help Rose get packed. I don't mean to sound inhospitable but since you were going tomorrow, anyway — I'm just tired and it would be easier for us. Please forgive me but you're an old friend and you will understand.

GRIGGS (*smiles, pats her arm*). I'll take the tray.

(*He takes it from her, goes up the steps. Constance comes in the room, sighs, sits down.*)

CROSSMAN. Sophie. (*Sophie comes to him*) I was asked to give you this.

(*He hands her an envelope.*)

SOPHIE. Thank you, Mr. Ned.

CONSTANCE (*idly, without interest*). Secrets?

CROSSMAN. That's right. Secrets. Old love letters or something.

(*Sophie laughs, goes out.*)

CONSTANCE (*after a silence*). I hate this house today.

CROSSMAN. Well, they'll all be gone soon.

CONSTANCE. You won't go? Please.

CROSSMAN. I'll stay for a few days if you'd like me to.

CONSTANCE. Oh, yes. I need you to stay.

CROSSMAN (*points out of window*). Just act as if nothing had happened and they'll soon stop talking.

CONSTANCE. Oh, I'm not worrying about that. (*Pauses*) I feel so lost, Ned. As if I distrusted myself, didn't have anything to stand on. I mean, right now, if you asked me, I just wouldn't know what I thought or believed, or ever had, or — (*Shyly*) Well, what *have* I built my life on? Do you know what I mean?

CROSSMAN. Sure. I know.

CONSTANCE (*as if she had trouble with the words*). It's — it's so painful. (*Then as if she wished to change the subject*) Sophie will be going back to Europe. She just told me. She *wants* to go. Did you know that?

CROSSMAN. Is that so?

CONSTANCE. I was so sure I was doing the right thing, bringing her here. You see? That's part of what I mean by not knowing the things I thought I knew. Well. (*Pauses as if she were coming to something that frightens her*) Nick said you wouldn't be coming here next summer. Did you say anything like that, or was it one of Nick's lies? (*He does not answer her. She stares at him*) Why, Ned?

CROSSMAN. Hasn't anything to do with you, Con. Just think I'd be better off. You know, it's kind of foolish —two weeks a year — coming back here and living a life that isn't me anymore. It's too respectable for me, Con. I ain't up to it anymore.

CONSTANCE. Oh. It's what I look forward to every summer. What will I — (*Very quickly*) Where is Nick? I haven't seen him. I wish they'd leave —

CROSSMAN. They've gone.

CONSTANCE (*stares at him*). Without a word to me? Exactly the way he left years ago. I didn't ever tell you that, did I? We had a date for dinner. He didn't come. He just got on the boat. I didn't ever tell anybody before. (*Violently*) What a fool. All these years of making a shabby man into the kind of hero who would come back someday all happy and shining —

CROSSMAN. Oh, don't do that. He never asked you to make him what he wasn't. Or to wait twenty years to find him out.

CONSTANCE. No, he didn't. That's true. (*She rises, goes to the portrait and stands staring at it*) Do I look like this?

CROSSMAN. You look nice.

CONSTANCE. Come and look at it.

CROSSMAN. No. I don't want to.

CONSTANCE. Much older than I thought or — And I don't look very bright. (*Puts the picture away from her*) Well, I haven't been very bright. I want to say something to you. I can't wait any longer. Would you forgive me?

CROSSMAN. Forgive you? For what?

CONSTANCE. For wasting all these years. For not knowing what I felt about you, or not wanting to. Ned, would you have me now?

CROSSMAN (*after a second*). What did you say?

CONSTANCE. Would you marry me? (*There is a pause. Then Sophie comes from the direction of the dining room carrying a carpet sweeper and a cleaning basket. As she goes up the steps she is singing a cheerful French song. Constance smiles*) She's happy. That's good. I think she'll come out all right, always.

CROSSMAN (*stares at Constance; then slowly, carefully*). I live in a room and I go to work and I play a game called getting through the day while you wait for night. The night's for me — just me — and I can do anything with it I want. There used to be a lot of things to do with it, good things, but now there's a bar and another bar and the same people in each bar. When I've had enough I go back to my room — or somebody else's room — and that never means much one way or the other. A few years ago I'd have weeks of reading — night after night — just me. But I don't do that much anymore. Just read, all night long. You can feel good that way.

CONSTANCE. I never did that. I'm not a reader.

CROSSMAN (*as if he hadn't heard her*). And a few years ago I'd go on the wagon twice a year. Now I don't do that anymore. And I don't care. (*Smiles*) And all these years I told myself that if you'd loved me everything would have been different. I'd have had a good life, been worth something to myself. I wanted to tell myself that. I wanted to believe it. Griggs was right. I not only wasted myself, but I wanted it that way. All my life, I guess, I wanted it that way.

CONSTANCE. And you're not in love with me, Ned?

CROSSMAN. No, Con. Not now.

CONSTANCE (*gets up, goes to him*). Let's have a nice dinner together, just you and me, and go to the movies. Could we do that?

CROSSMAN. I've kept myself busy looking into other people's hearts so I wouldn't have to look into my own. (*Softly*) If I made you think I was still in love, I'm sorry. Sorry I fooled you and sorry I fooled myself. And I've never liked liars — least of all those who lie to themselves.

CONSTANCE. Never mind. Most of us lie to ourselves. Never mind.

Curtain

The Lark

ADAPTED FROM THE FRENCH PLAY
BY JEAN ANOUILH

The Lark was first produced at the Longacre Theatre, New York City, on November 17, 1955, with the following cast:

(*In the order of their appearance*)

WARWICK	CHRISTOPHER PLUMMER
CAUCHON	BORIS KARLOFF
JOAN	JULIE HARRIS
JOAN'S FATHER	WARD COSTELLO
JOAN'S MOTHER	LOIS HOLMES
JOAN'S BROTHER	JOHN REESE
THE PROMOTER	ROGER DE KOVEN
THE INQUISITOR	JOSEPH WISEMAN
BROTHER LADVENU	MICHAEL HIGGINS
ROBERT DE BEAUDRICOURT	THEODORE BIKEL
AGNES SOREL	ANN HILLARY
THE LITTLE QUEEN	JOAN ELAN
THE DAUPHIN	PAUL ROEBLING
QUEEN YOLANDE	RITA VALE
MONSIEUR DE LA TREMOUILLE	BRUCE GORDON
ARCHBISHOP OF REIMS	RICHARD NICHOLLS
CAPTAIN LA HIRE	BRUCE GORDON
EXECUTIONER	RALPH ROBERTS
ENGLISH SOLDIER	EDWARD KNIGHT
SCRIBE	JOE BERNARD

LADIES OF THE COURT: Ruth Maynard, Elizabeth Lawrence. MONKS and SOLDIERS: Michael Price, Joe Bernard, Michael Conrad, William Lennard, Milton Katselas, Edward Grower.

Produced by
KERMIT BLOOMGARDEN

Directed by
JOSEPH ANTHONY

Setting and lighting designed by
JO MIELZINER

Costumes designed by
ALVIN COLT

Music composed by
LEONARD BERNSTEIN

Scenes

Act One

The Trial

Act Two

The Trial

Act One

Before the curtain rises we hear the music of a psalm: the chorus is singing "Exaudi orationem meam, domine." *When the curtain rises the music changes to a motet on the words* "Qui tollis," *from the Mass.*

SCENE: *Another day in the trial of Joan. The stage is a series of platforms, different in size and in height. The cyclorama is gray in color and projections will be thrown on it to indicate a change of scene. At this moment we see the bars of a jail on the cyclorama.*

AT RISE: *Joan is sitting on a stool. Cauchon is standing downstage near the Promoter. The Priests are about to take their places on the Judges' bench. The Inquisitor sits quietly on a stool near the Judges. Joan's family stand upstage; the royal family stand in a group. Village Women cross the stage carrying bundles of faggots and English Soldiers and Guards move into place. Beaudricourt and La Hire appear and take their places upstage. Warwick enters and moves through the crowd.*

WARWICK. Everybody here? Good. Let the trial begin at once. The quicker the judgment and the burning, the better for all of us.

CAUCHON. No, sire. The whole story must be played. Domremy, the Voices, Chinon —

WARWICK. I am not here to watch that children's story of the warrior virgin, strong and tender, dressed in white armor, white standard streaming in the wind. They can make the statues that way, in days to come. Different politics may well require different symbols. We might even have to make her a monument in London. Don't be shocked at that, sire. The politics of my government may well require it one day, and what's required, Englishmen supply. That's our secret, sire, and a good one, indeed. (*Moves downstage to address the audience*) Well, let's worry about only this minute of time.

I am Beauchamp, Earl of Warwick. I have a dirty virgin witch girl tucked away on a litter of straw in the depths of a prison here in Rouen. The girl has been an expensive nuisance. Your Duke of Burgundy sold her high. You like money in France, Monseigneur, all of you. That's the French secret, sire, and a good one, indeed. (*He moves toward Joan*) And here she is. The Maid. The famous Joan the Maid. We paid too much. So put her on trial, and burn her, and be finished.

CAUCHON. No, sire. She must play out her whole life first. It's a short life. It won't take very long.

WARWICK (*moves to a stool near Cauchon*). If you insist. Englishmen are patient, and for the purposes of this trial I am all Englishmen. But certainly you don't intend to amuse yourselves by acting out all the old battles? I would find that very disagreeable. Nobody wishes to remember defeat.

CAUCHON. No, sire. We no longer have enough men to act out the old battles. (*Turns toward Joan*) Joan? (*Joan turns to Cauchon*) You may begin.

JOAN. Can I begin anyplace I want to?

CAUCHON. Yes.

JOAN. Then I'll start at the beginning. It's always nicer at the beginning. I'll begin with my father's house when I was very small. (*Her Mother, her Father and her Brothers appear onstage. She runs to join them*) I live here happy enough with my mother, my brothers, my father. (*We hear the music of a shepherd song and as she leaves the family group she dances her way downstage, clapping her hands to the music*) I'm in the meadow now, watching my sheep. I am not thinking of anything. It is the first time I hear the Voices. I wasn't thinking of anything. I know only that God is good and that He keeps me pure and safe in this little corner of the earth near Domremy. This one little piece of French earth that has not yet been destroyed by the English invaders. (*She makes childish thrusts with an imaginary sword, and stops suddenly as if someone has pulled her back*) Then, suddenly, someone behind me touched my shoulder. I know very well that no one is behind me. I turn and there is a great blinding light in the shadow of me. The Voice is grave and sweet and I was frightened. But I didn't tell anybody. I don't know why. Then came the second time. It was the noon Angelus. A light came over the sun and was stronger than the sun. There he was. I saw him. An angel in a beautiful clean robe that must have been ironed by somebody very careful. He had two great white wings. He didn't tell me his name that day, but later I found out he was Monseigneur the Blessed Saint Michael.

WARWICK (*to Cauchon*). We know all this. Is it necessary to let her go over that nonsense again?

CAUCHON. It is necessary, sire.

JOAN. Blessed Saint Michael, excuse me, but you are in the wrong village. I am Joan, an ignorant girl, my father's daughter — (*Pauses, listens*) I can't save France. I don't even know how to ride a horse. (*Smiles*) To you people the Sire de Beaudricourt is only a country squire, but to us he is master here. He would never take me to the Dauphin, I've never even bowed to him — (*Turns to the court*) Then the Blessed Saint Michael said Saint Catherine would come along with me, and if that wasn't enough Saint Marguerite would go, too. (*She turns back as if to listen to Saint Michael*) But when the army captains lose a battle — and they lose a great many — they can go to sleep at night. I could never send men to their death. Forgive me, Blessed Saint Michael, but I must go home now — (*But she doesn't move. She is held back by a command*) Oh, Blessed Saint Michael, have pity on me. Have pity, Messire. (*The chorus sings "Alleluia, Alleluia" to the shepherd's tune. She listens, smiles, moves back into the trial. Simply*) Well, he didn't. And that was the day I was saddled with France. *And* my work on the farm.

(*The Father, who has been moving about near the Mother, suddenly grows angry.*)

THE FATHER. What's she up to?

THE MOTHER. She's in the fields.

THE FATHER. So was I, in the fields, but I've come in. It's six o'clock! I ask you, what's she up to?

THE BROTHER. She's dreaming under the lady tree.

THE FATHER. What's anybody doing under a tree at this hour?

THE BROTHER. You ask her. She stares straight ahead. She looks as if she is waiting for something. It isn't the first time.

THE FATHER (*angrily to the Brother*). Why didn't you tell me? She has a lover.

THE MOTHER (*softly*). Joan is as clean as a baby.

THE FATHER. All girls are as clean as babies until that night when they aren't anymore. I'll find her and if she is with someone, I'll beat her until —

JOAN. I was with someone, but my lover had two great white wings and through the rain he came so close to me that I thought I could touch his wings. He was very worried that day, he told me so. He said the Kingdom of France was in great misery and that God said I could wait no longer. There has been a mistake, I kept saying. The Blessed Saint Michael asked me if God made mistakes. You understand that I couldn't very well say yes?

THE PROMOTER. Why didn't you make the Sign of the Cross?

JOAN. That question is not written in your charge against me.

THE PROMOTER. Why didn't you say to the archangel, *"Vado retro Satanas?"*

JOAN. I don't know any Latin, Messire. And *that* question is not written in your charge against me.

THE PROMOTER. Don't act the fool. The devil understands French. You could have said, "Go away, you filthy, stinking devil."

JOAN (*angry*). I don't talk that way to the Blessed Saint Michael, Messire!

THE PROMOTER. The Devil told you he was Saint Michael and you were fool enough to believe him.

JOAN. I believed him. He could not have been the Devil. He was so beautiful.

THE PROMOTER. The Devil *is* beautiful!

JOAN (*shocked*). Oh, Messire!

CAUCHON (*to The Promoter*). These theological subtleties are far above the understanding of this poor child. You shock her without reason.

JOAN (*to The Promoter*). You've lied, Canon! I am not as educated as you are, but I know the Devil *is* ugly and everything that is beautiful is the work of God. I have no doubts. I know.

THE PROMOTER. You know nothing. Evil has a lovely face when a lovely face is needed. In real life the Devil waits for a soft, sweet night of summer. Then he comes on a gentle wind in the form of a beautiful girl with bare breasts —

CAUCHON (*sharply*). Canon, let us not get mixed up in our private devils. Continue, Joan.

JOAN (*to The Promoter*). But if the Devil is beautiful, how can we know he is the Devil?

THE PROMOTER. Go to your priest. He will tell you.

JOAN. Can't I recognize him by myself?

THE PROMOTER. No. Certainly not. No.

JOAN. But only the rich have their priests always with them. The poor can't be running back and forth.

THE PROMOTER (*angry*). I do not like the way you speak in this court. I warn you again —

CAUCHON. Enough, enough, Messire. Let her speak peacefully with her Voices. There is nothing to reproach her with so far.

JOAN. Then another time it was Saint Marguerite and Saint Catherine who came to me. (*She turns to the Promoter*) And they, too, were beautiful.

THE PROMOTER. Were they naked?

JOAN (*laughs*). Oh, Messire! Don't you think our Lord can afford to buy clothing for His Saints?

CAUCHON (*to the Promoter*). You make us all smile, Messire, with your questions. You are confusing the girl with the suggestion that good and evil is a question of what clothes are worn by what Angels and what Devils. (*Turns to Joan*) But it is not your place to correct the venerable Canon. You forget who you are and who we are. We are your priests, your masters, and your judges. Beware of your pride, Joan.

JOAN (*softly*). I know that I am proud. But I am a daughter of God. If He didn't want me to be proud, why did He send me His shining Archangel and His Saints all dressed in light? Why did He promise me that I should conquer all the men I have conquered? Why did He promise me a suit of beautiful white armor, the gift of my king? And a sword? And that I should lead brave soldiers into battle while riding a fine white horse? If He had left me alone, I would never have become proud.

CAUCHON. Take care of your words, Joan. You are accusing our Lord.

JOAN (*makes the Sign of the Cross*). Oh. God forbid. I say only that His Will be done even if it means making me proud and then damning me for it. That, too, is His Right.

THE PROMOTER (*very angry*). What are you saying? Could God wish to damn a human soul? How can you listen to her without shuddering, Messires? I see here the germ of a frightful heresy that could tear the Church —

(*The Inquisitor rises. The Promoter stops speaking. The stage is silent. Ladvenu, a young priest, rises and goes to the In-*

quisitor. The Inquisitor whispers to him. Ladvenu moves to Cauchon, whispers to him.)

CAUCHON (*looks toward The Inquisitor; very hesitant*). Messire — (*The Inquisitor stares at Cauchon. Cauchon hesitates, then turns toward Joan*) Joan, listen well to what I must ask you. At this moment, are you in a State of Grace?

LADVENU. Messire, this is a fearful question for a simple girl who sincerely believes that God has chosen her. Do not hold her answer against her. She is in great danger and she is confused.

CAUCHON. Are you in a State of Grace?

JOAN (*as if she knew this was a dangerous question*). Which moment is that, Messire? Everything is so mixed up, I no longer know where I am. At the beginning when I heard my Voices, or at the end of the trial when I knew that my king and my friends had abandoned me? When I lost faith, when I recanted, or when, at the very last minute, I give myself back to myself? When —

CAUCHON (*softly, worried*). Messire demands an answer. His reasons must be grave. Joan, are you in a State of Grace?

JOAN. If I am not, God will help me in Grace. If I am, God will keep me in Grace. (*The Priests murmur among themselves. The Inquisitor, impassive, sits down.*)

LADVENU (*gently, warmly*). Well spoken, Joan.

THE PROMOTER (*sharply*). And the Devil would have the same clever answer.

WARWICK (*to Cauchon, pointing to the Inquisitor*). Is that the gentleman about whom I have been told?

CAUCHON (*softly*). Yes.

WARWICK. When did he arrive?

CAUCHON. Three days ago. He has wished to be alone.

WARWICK. Why was I not told of his arrival?

CAUCHON. He is one of us, sire. We do not acknowledge your authority here.

WARWICK. Only when you count our money and eat our food. Never mind, the formalities do not matter to me. But time does matter and I hope his presence will not add to the confusion. I am almost as bewildered as the girl. All these questions must be very interesting to you gentlemen of the Church, but if we continue at this speed we'll never get to the trial and the girl will be dead of old age. Get to the burning and be done with it.

CAUCHON (*angry*). Sire! Who speaks of burning? We will try to save the girl —

WARWICK. Monseigneur, I allow you this charade because the object of my government is to tell the Christian world that the coronation of the idiot Charles was managed by a sorceress, a heretic, a mad girl, a whore camp-follower. However you do that, please move with greater speed.

CAUCHON. And I remind you each day that this is a court of the Church. We are here to judge the charge of heresy. Our considerations are not yours.

WARWICK. My dear Bishop, I know that. But the fine points of ecclesiastic judgments may be a little too distinguished for my soldiers — and for the rest of the world. Propaganda is a soft weapon: hold it in your hands too long, and it will move about like a snake, and strike the other way. Whatever the girl is or has been, she must now be stripped and degraded. That is why we bought her high, and it is what we will insist upon. (*Smiles*) I'm coming to like her. I admire the way she stands up to all of you. And she rides beautifully — I've seen her. Rare to find a woman who rides that way. I'd like to have known her in other circumstances, in a pleasanter world. Hard for me to remember that she took France away from us, deprived us of our heritage. We know that God is on the side of the English. He proved himself at Agincourt. "God and my right," you know. But when this girl came along, and we began to lose, there were those who doubted our motto. That, of course, cannot be tolerated. "God and my right" is inscribed on all English armor, and we certainly have no intention of changing the armor. So get on with her story. The world will forget her soon enough. Where were we?

THE FATHER (*comes forward*). At the moment when I find her under the lady tree. (*He goes to Joan*) What are you doing? You were crying out to someone, but the bastard fled before I could catch him. Who was it? Who was it? Answer me. Answer me, or I'll beat you to salt mash.

JOAN. I was talking to the Blessed Saint Michael.

THE FATHER (*hits Joan*). That will teach you to lie to your father. You want to start whoring like the others. Well, you can tell your Blessed Saint Michael that if I catch you together I'll plunge my pitchfork into his belly and strangle you with my bare hands for the filthy rutting cat you are.

JOAN (*softly*). Father, it was Saint Michael who was talking to me.

THE FATHER. The priest will hear about this, and from me. I'll tell him straight out that not content with running after men, you have also dared to blaspheme!

JOAN. I swear to you before God that I am telling the truth. It's been happening for a long time and always at the noon or evening Angelus. The Saints appear to me. They speak to me. They answer me when I question them. And they all say the same thing.

THE FATHER. Why would the Saints speak to you, idiot? I am your father, why don't they speak to me? If they had anything to say they'd talk to me.

JOAN. Father, try to understand the trouble I'm in. For three years I've refused what they ask. But I don't think I can say no much longer. I think the moment has come when I must go.

THE FATHER. For forty years I've worked myself to death to raise my children like Christians, and this is my reward. A daughter who thinks she hears Voices.

JOAN. They say I can't wait any longer —

THE FATHER. *What* can't wait any longer?

JOAN. They tell me France is at the last moment of danger. My Voices tell me I must save her.

THE FATHER. You? — You? You are crazy. Crazy. You are a fool! A fool and a crazy girl.

JOAN. I must do what my Voices tell me. I will go to the Sire de Beaudricourt and ask him to give me an armed escort to the Dauphin at Chinon. I'll talk to the Dauphin and make him fight. Then I will take the army to Orléans and we'll push the English into the sea.

THE FATHER. For ten years I have dreamed that you would disgrace us with men. Do you think I raised you, sacrificed everything for you, to have you run off to live with soldiers? I knew what you would be. But you won't — I'll kill you first. (*He begins to beat her and to kick her.*)

JOAN (*screams*). Stop! Stop! Oh, Father, stop!

LADVENU (*rises, horrified*). Stop him. Stop him. He's hurting her.

CAUCHON. We cannot, Brother Ladvenu. We do not know Joan. You forget that we first meet her at the trial. We can only play our roles, good or bad, just as they were, each in his turn. And we will hurt her far more than he does. You know that. (*Turns to Warwick*) Ugly, isn't it, this family scene?

WARWICK. Why? In England we are in favor of strong punishment for children. It makes character. I was half beaten to death as a boy, but I am in excellent health.

THE FATHER (*he looks down at Joan who has fallen at his feet*). Crazy little whore. Do you still want to save France? (*Then, shamefaced, he turns to the Judges*) Well, messieurs, what would you have done in my place if your daughter had been like that?

WARWICK. If we had known about this girl from the very beginning, we could have reached an agreement with her father. We tell ourselves that our intelligence service is remarkable and we say it so often that we believe it. It should be their business not only to tell us what is happening, but what might happen. When a country virgin talked about saving France, I should have known about it. I tell myself now I would not have laughed. (*The Mother comes forward. She bends over Joan.*)

THE FATHER (*to the Mother*). The next time your daughter talks of running after soldiers, I'll put her in the river and with my own hands I'll hold her under. (*The Mother takes Joan in her arms.*)

THE MOTHER. He hurt you bad.

JOAN. Yes.

THE MOTHER (*softly*). He's your father.

JOAN. Yes. He is my father. Oh, Mama, somebody must understand. I can't do it alone.

THE MOTHER. Lean against me. You're big now. I can hardly hold you in my arms. Joan, your father is a good and honest man but — (*She whispers in Joan's ear*) I've saved a little from the house money. If you'd like one, I'll buy you a broidered kerchief at the very next fair.

JOAN. I don't need a kerchief. I won't ever be pretty, Mama.

THE MOTHER. We're all a little wild when we're young. Who is it, Joan? Don't have secrets from me. Is he from our village?

JOAN. I don't want to marry, Mama. That isn't what I mean.

THE MOTHER. Then what do you mean?

JOAN. Blessed Saint Michael says that I must put on man's clothes. He says that I must save France.

THE MOTHER. Joan, I speak to you in kindness, but I forbid you to tell me such nonsense. A man's clothes! I should just like to see you try it.

JOAN. But I'll have to, Mama, if I'm to ride horse with my soldiers. Saint Michael makes good sense.

THE MOTHER. Your soldiers? Your soldiers? You bad girl! I'd rather see you dead first. Now I'm talking like your father, and that I never want to do. (*She begins to cry*) Running after soldiers! What have I done to deserve a daughter like this? You will kill me.

JOAN. No, Mama, no. (*She cries out as her Mother moves off*) Monseigneur Saint Michael. It cannot be done. Nobody will ever understand. It is better for me to say no right now. (*Pauses, listens*) Then Saint Michael's voice grew soft, the way it does when he is angry. And he said that I must take the first step. He said that God trusted me and if a mountain of ice did rise ahead of me it was only because God was busy and trusted me to climb the mountain even if I tore my hands and broke my legs, and my face might run with blood — (*After a second, slowly, carefully*) Then I said that I would go. I said that I would go that day. (*Joan's Brother comes forward and stands looking at her.*)

THE BROTHER. You haven't got the sense you were born with. If you give me something next time, I won't tell Papa I saw you with your lover.

JOAN. So it was you, you pig, you told them? Here's what I'll give you this time — (*She slaps him*) And the next time — (*She slaps him again, and begins to chase him. He runs from her*) and the time after that. (*Joan's voice changes and she moves slowly about not concerned with him any longer but speaking into space*) And so I went to my uncle Durand. And my uncle Durand went to the seigneur of the manor. And I walked a long way west and a little way south and there was the night I was shivering with rain — or with fear — and the day I was shivering with sun — or with fear — and then I walked to the west again and east. I was on my way to the first fool I had to deal with. And I had plenty of them to deal with. (*She moves upstage, bumps into two Soldiers as Beaudricourt comes onstage.*)

BEAUDRICOURT. What is it? What's the matter? What does she want? What's the matter with these crazy fools? (*He grabs Joan and shakes her*) What's the matter with you, young woman? You've been carrying on like a bad girl. I've heard about you standing outside the doors ragging at the sentries until they fall asleep.

JOAN (*he holds her up. She dangles in front of his face*). I want a horse. I want the dress of a man. I want an armed escort. You will give them orders to take me to Chinon to see the Dauphin.

BEAUDRICOURT. Of course. And I will also kick you in the place where it will do the most good.

JOAN. Kicks, blows. Whichever you like best. I'm used to them by now. I want a horse. I want the dress of a man. I want an armed escort.

BEAUDRICOURT. That's a new idea — a horse. You know who I am and what I usually want? Did the village girls tell you? When they come to ask a favor it usually has to do with a father or a brother who has poached my land. If the girl is pretty, I have a good heart, and we both pitch in. If the girl is ugly, well, usually I have a good heart, too, but not so good as the other way. I am known in this land for good-heartedness. But a horse is a nasty kind of bargain.

JOAN. I have been sent by Blessed Saint Michael.

BEAUDRICOURT (*puts her down hurriedly, makes the Sign of the Cross*). Don't mix the Saints up in this kind of thing. That talk was good enough to get you past the sentries, but it's not good enough to get you a horse. A horse costs more than a woman. You're a country girl. You ought to know that. Are you a virgin?

JOAN. Yes, sire.

BEAUDRICOURT. You have lovely eyes.

JOAN. I want more than a horse, sire.

BEAUDRICOURT (*laughs*). You're greedy. But I like that sometimes. There are fools who get angry when the girl wants too much. But I say good things should cost a lot. That pleases me in a girl. You understand what I mean?

JOAN. No, sire.

BEAUDRICOURT. That's good. I don't like clear-thinking women in bed. Not in my bed. You understand what I mean?

JOAN. No, sire.

BEAUDRICOURT. Well, I don't like idiots, either. What is it you're up to? What else besides a horse?

JOAN. Just as I said before, sire. An armed escort as far as Chinon.

BEAUDRICOURT. Stop that crazy talk. I'm the master here. I can send you back where you came from with no better present than the lashes of a whip. I told you I like a girl to come high, but if she costs too much the opposite effect sets in — and I can't — well, I can't. You understand what I mean? (*Suddenly*) Why do you want to go to Chinon?

JOAN. As I said before, sire, I wish to find Monseigneur the Dauphin.

BEAUDRICOURT. Well, you *are* on a high road. Why not the Duke of Burgundy while you're at it? He's more powerful, and he likes the girls. But not our Dauphin. He runs from war and women. An hour with either would kill him. Why do you want to see such a fellow?

JOAN. I want an army, Messire. An army to march upon Orléans.

BEAUDRICOURT. If you're crazy, forget about me. (*Shouting*) Boudousse. Boudousse. (*A Soldier comes forward*) Throw some cold water on this girl and send her back to her father. Don't beat her. It's bad luck to beat a crazy woman.

JOAN. You won't beat me. You're a kind man, Messire. Very kind.

BEAUDRICOURT. Sometimes yes, sometimes no. But I don't like virgins whose heads come off at night —

JOAN. And you're very intelligent, which is sometimes even better than being kind. But when a man is intelligent *and* kind, then that's the very best combination on God's fine earth.

BEAUDRICOURT (*he waves the Guard away*). You're a strange girl. Why do you think I'm intelligent? Want a little wine?

JOAN. It shows in your face. You're handsome, Messire.

BEAUDRICOURT. Twenty years ago, I wouldn't have said no. I married two rich widows, God bless me. But not now. Of course, I've tried not to get old too fast, and there are men who get better looking with age — (*Smiles*) You know, it's very comic to be talking like this with a shepherd girl who drops out of the sky one bright morning. I am bored here. My officers are animals. I have nobody to talk to. I like a little philosophy now and then. I should like to know from your mouth what connection you see between beauty and intelligence? Usually people say that handsome men are stupid.

JOAN. Hunchbacks talk that way, and people with long noses,

or those who will die of a bitter egg that grows in their head. God has the power to create a perfect man — (*She smiles at him*) and sometimes He uses His power.

BEAUDRICOURT. Well, you can look at it that way, of course. But you take me, for example. No, I'm not ugly, but sometimes I wonder if I'm intelligent. No, no, don't protest. I tell you there are times when I have problems that seem too much for me. They ask me to decide something, a tactical or administrative point. Then, all of a sudden, I don't know why, my head acts like it's gone someplace else, and I don't even understand the words people are saying. Isn't that strange? (*After a second*) But I never show it. I roar out an order whatever happens. That's the main thing in an army. Make a decision, good or bad, just *make* it. Things will turn out almost the same, anyway. (*Softly, as if to himself*) Still, I wish I could have done better. This is a small village to die away your life. (*Points outside*) They think I'm a great man, but they never saw anybody else. Like every other man, I wanted to be brilliant and remarkable, but I end up hanging a few poor bastards who deserted from a broken army. Ah, well. (*Looks at her*) Why do I tell you all this? You can't help me, and you're crazy.

JOAN. They told me you would speak this way.

BEAUDRICOURT. *They* told you?

JOAN. Listen to me, nice, good Robert, and don't shout any more. It's useless. I'm about to say something very important. You will be brilliant and remarkable. You will shake a nation because *I* will do it for you. Your name will go far outside this village —

BEAUDRICOURT (*puts his arms around her*). What are you talking about?

JOAN (*she pulls away from him*). Robert, don't think any more about my being a girl. That just confuses everything. You'll find plenty of girls who are prettier and will give more pleasure — (*Softly*) and will not ask as much. You don't want me.

BEAUDRICOURT. Well, I don't know. You're all right.

JOAN (*sharply*). If you want me to help you, then help me. When I say the truth say it with me.

BEAUDRICOURT (*politely*). But you're a pleasant-looking girl, and it's nice weather, and . . . (*Laughs*) No, I don't want you any more than that.

JOAN. Good. Now that we have got that out of the way, let's pretend that you've given me the clothes of a boy and we're sitting here like two comrades talking good sense.

BEAUDRICOURT (*fills a glass*). All right. Have a little wine.

JOAN (*drinks her wine*). Kind, sweet Robert. Great things are about to begin for you. (*As he starts to speak*) No, no. Listen. The English are everywhere, and everywhere they are our masters. Brittany and Anjou will go next. The English wait only to see which one will pay the higher tribute money. The Duke of Burgundy signs a bitter treaty and the English give him the Order of the Golden Fleece. They invented just such medals for foreign traitors. Our little monkey Dauphin Charles sits with his court in Bourges, shaking and jibbering. He knows nothing, his court knows nothing, and all falls to pieces around him. You know that. You know our army, our good army of brave boys, is tired and sick. They believe the English will always be stronger and that there's no sense to it anymore. When an army thinks that way, the end is near. The Bastard Dunois is a good captain and intelligent. So intelligent that nobody will listen to him. So he forgets that he should be leading an army and drowns himself in wine, and tells stories of past battles to his whores. I'll put a stop to that, you can be sure —

BEAUDRICOURT (*softly*). *You'll* put a stop to —

JOAN. Our best soldiers are like angry bulls. They always want to attack, to act fine for the history books. They are great champions of bravery. But they don't know how to use their cannon and they get people killed for nothing. That's what they did at Agincourt. Ah, when it comes to dying, they're all ready to volunteer. But what good is it to die? You think just as I do, my dear Robert: war isn't a tournament for fancy gentlemen. You must be smart to win a war. You must think, and be smart. (*Quickly*) But you who are so intelligent, knew all that when you were born.

BEAUDRICOURT. I've always said it. I've always said that nobody thinks anymore. I used to be a thinker, but nobody paid any attention.

JOAN. They will, they will. Because you have just had an idea that will probably save all of us.

BEAUDRICOURT. I've had an idea?

JOAN. Well, you are about to have it. But don't let anything get in its way. Please sit quiet and don't, well, just — (*As *he is about to move she holds him down*) You are the only man in France who at this minute can see the future. Sit still.

BEAUDRICOURT. What is it that I see?

JOAN. You know your soldiers. You know they will leave you soon. You know that to keep them you must give them faith. You have nothing else to give them now. A little bread, a little faith — good things to fight with.

BEAUDRICOURT. It's too late —

JOAN. A girl comes before you. Saint Michael and Saint Catherine and Saint Marguerite have told her to come. You will say it's not true. But I believe it *is* true, and that's what matters. A farm girl who says that God is on her side. You can't prove He isn't. You can't. Try it and see. The girl came a long, hard way, she got as far as you, and she has convinced you. Yes, I have. I have convinced you. And why have I convinced so intelligent a man? Because I tell the truth, and it takes a smart head to know the truth.

BEAUDRICOURT. Where is this idea you said I had?

JOAN. Coming, coming just this minute. You are saying to yourself, if she convinced me, why shouldn't she convince the Dauphin and Dunois and the Archbishop? After all they're only men like me, although a good deal less intelligent. (*Very fast*) All right, that's settled. But now you're saying to yourself when it comes to dying, soldiers are very intelligent, and so she'll have a harder time with them. No, she won't. She will say English heads are like all others: hit them hard enough, at the right time, and we'll march over them to Orléans. They need faith, your soldiers. They need somebody who believes it to say that God is on their side. Everybody says things like that. But *I* believe it — and that's the difference. Our soldiers will fight again, you know it, and because you know it you are the most remarkable man in France.

BEAUDRICOURT. You think so?

JOAN. The whole world will think so. But you must move fast. Like all great political men you are a realist. At this minute you are saying to yourself, "If the troops will believe this girl has come from God, what difference does it make whether she has or not? I will send her to Bourges tomorrow with the courier."

BEAUDRICOURT. The courier does go tomorrow. How did you know that? He goes with a secret packet —

JOAN (*laughs, delighted*). Give me six good soldiers and a fine white horse. I want a *white* horse, please. I will do the rest. But give me a quiet white horse because I don't know how to ride.

BEAUDRICOURT (*laughs*). You'll break your neck.

JOAN. It's up to Blessed Saint Michael, to keep me in the saddle. (*He laughs. She doesn't like his laughter*) I will make you a bet, Robert. I'll bet you a man's dress that if you will have two horses brought now, and we both ride at a gallop, I won't fall off. If I stay on, then will you believe in me? All right?

BEAUDRICOURT (*laughs*). All this thinking makes a man weary. I had other plans for this afternoon, as I told you, but any kind of exercise is good for me. Come on.

(*He exits. Joan, smiling, looks toward Heaven. Then she runs after Beaudricourt. But she is stopped by a Soldier and suddenly realizes she is back in the trial. She sits quietly as the lights fade out on the Beaudricourt scene.*)

WARWICK. She made that idiot believe he wasn't an idiot.

CAUCHON. It was a man-woman scene, a little coarse for my taste.

WARWICK. Coarse for *your* taste. The trick of making him believe what she put into his head is exactly what I do in my trade and what you do in yours. Speaking of your trade, sire, forgive a brutal question but, just between ourselves, do you really have the faith?

CAUCHON (*simply*). As a child has it. And that is why my judges and I will try to save Joan. To the bitter end we will try to save her. Our honor demands that — (*Warwick turns away. Cauchon, sharply*) You think of us as collaborators and therefore without honor. We believed that collaboration with you was the only reasonable solution —

WARWICK. And so it was. But when you say reasonable solution it is often more honorable to omit the word honor.

CAUCHON (*softly*). I say honor. Our poor honor, the little that was left us, demanded that we fight for our beliefs.

WARWICK. While you lived on English money —

CAUCHON. Yes. And while eight hundred of your soldiers were at our gates. It was easy for free men to call us traitors, but we lived in occupied territory, dependent upon the will of your king to kill us or to feed us. We were men, and we wanted to live; we were priests, and we wanted to save Joan. Like most other men, we wanted everything. We played a shameful role.

WARWICK. Shameful? I don't know. You might have played a nobler part, perhaps, if you had decided to be martyrs and fight against us. My eight hundred men were quite ready to help.

CAUCHON. We had good reason to know about your soldiers. I remember no day without insults and threats. And yet we stood against you. Nine long months before we agreed to hand over a girl who had been deserted by everybody but us. They can call us barbarians, but for all their fine principles I believe they would have surrendered her before we did.

WARWICK. You could have given us the girl on the first day. Nine long months of endless what?

CAUCHON. It was hard for us. God had been silent since Joan's arrest. He had not spoken to her or to us. Therefore, we had to do without his counsel. We were here to defend the House of God. During our years in the seminaries we learned how to defend it. Joan had no training in our seminaries and yet, abandoned, she defended God's House in her own way. Defended it with that strange conflict of insolence and humility, worldly sense and unworldly grandeur. (*Softly*) The piety was so simple and sweet — to the last moment of the last flame. We did not understand her in those days. We covered our eyes like old, fighting, childish men, and turned away so that we could not hear the cries of anguish. She was all alone at the end. God had not come to her. That is a terrible time for a religious nature, sire, and brings doubt and despair unknown to others. (*Cauchon rises and turns away*) But it is then and there that some men raise their heads, and when they do, it is a noble sight.

WARWICK. Yes, it is. But as a man of politics, I cannot afford the doctrine of man's individual magnificence. I might meet another man who felt the same way. And he might express his individual magnificence by cutting off *my* head.

CAUCHON (*softly, as if he hadn't heard Warwick*). Sometimes, to console myself, I remember how beautiful were all those old priests who tried to protect the child, to save her from what can never now be mended —

WARWICK. Oh, you speak in large words, sire. Political language has no such words as "never now be mended." I have told you that the time will come when we will raise her a statue in London.

CAUCHON. And the time will come when our names will be known only for what we did to her; when men, forgiving their own sins, but angry with ours, will speak our names in a curse —

(*The lights dim on Warwick and Cauchon and we hear the music of a court song. A throne is brought onstage and as the lights come up slowly on the Dauphin's Court, the cyclorama reflects the royal fleur-de-lis. The Dauphin, Charles, is lolling about on his throne playing at bilboquet. Agnes Sorel and the Little Queen are practicing a new dance. Yolande is moving about. Four courtiers are playing at cards.*)

THE LITTLE QUEEN (*she is having a hard time learning the dance steps*). It's very hard.

AGNES. Everything is very hard for you, dear.

THE LITTLE QUEEN (*as they pass Charles*). It's a new dance. Very fashionable. Influenced by the Orient, they say.

AGNES (*to Charles*). Come. We'll teach you.

CHARLES. I won't be going to the ball.

AGNES. Well, *we* will be going. And we must dance better than anybody else and look better than anybody else. (*Stops, to Charles, points to her headdress*) And I'm not going in this old thing. I'm your mistress. Have a little pride. A mistress must be better dressed than anybody. You know that.

THE LITTLE QUEEN. And so must wives. I mean better dressed than other wives. The Queen of France in last year's shoddy. What do you think they will say, Charles?

CHARLES. They will say that poor little Queen married a king who hasn't a sou. They will be wrong. I have a sou. (*He throws a coin in the air. It falls and he begins to scramble on the floor for it.*)

THE LITTLE QUEEN. I can hear them all the way to London. The Duchess of Bedford and the Duchess of Gloucester — (*Charles, on the floor, is about to find his sou as the Archbishop and La Tremouille come in. Charles jumps back in fear.*)

LA TREMOUILLE (*to Charles*). You grow more like your father each day.

ARCHBISHOP. But his father had the decency to take to his bed.

CHARLES. Which father?

LA TREMOUILLE. You act so strangely, sire, that even I, who knew your mother, am convinced you are legitimate. (*Angrily, to Charles who is still on the floor*) Move. Move.

THE LITTLE QUEEN. Oh, please don't speak to him that way, Monsieur de la Tremouille.

ARCHBISHOP (*who has been glaring at the dancers*). You believe this is the proper time for dancing?

THE LITTLE QUEEN. But if the English take us prisoner, we have to know a little something. (*La Tremouille stares at her, exits.*)

YOLANDE. What harm do they do, sire? They are young — and there isn't much ahead for them.

ARCHBISHOP. There isn't much ahead for any of us. (*He moves off.*)

YOLANDE. Please get up, Charles. It is a sad thing to see you so frightened by so many men.

CHARLES. And why shouldn't I be frightened of La Tremouille and the Archbishop? I have been all my life. They could order every soldier in the place to cut me up and eat me.

AGNES. They're cheats, every woman in England. We set the styles — and they send spies to steal the latest models. But, fortunately, they're so ugly that nothing looks very well — (*Admires her own feet and hands*) with cows for feet and pigs for hands. We want new headdresses. Are you the King of France or aren't you?

CHARLES. I don't know if I am. Nobody knows. I told you all about that the first night you came to bed.

AGNES. The new headdress is two feet tall and has two horns coming from the side —

CHARLES. Sounds like a man. A small married man.

THE LITTLE QUEEN. And they have a drape at the back — they will cause a revolution, Charles.

AGNES. The English ladies — the mistresses, I mean, of course — won't be able to sleep when they see us. And if they can't sleep neither will the Dukes. And if the Dukes can't sleep they won't feel well and they won't have time to march on us —

CHARLES. They won't march on us. Nobody wants this dull

town. They're already in Orléans. So there isn't much sense counterattacking with a headdress.

THE LITTLE QUEEN. Oh, Charles, one has to have a little pleasure in life. And Mama — (*Pointing to Yolande*) and the Archbishop and La Tremouille, and all the wise people, tell us that the end is here, anyway, and this will be the last state ball —

CHARLES. How much do they cost?

AGNES. I flirted with the man — in a nice way — and he's going to let us have them for six thousand francs.

CHARLES. Where would I get six thousand francs, you little idiot?

THE LITTLE QUEEN. Twelve thousand francs, Charles. I'm here.

CHARLES. That's enough to pay Dunois' army the six months' wages that I owe them. You are dreaming, my kittens. My dear mother-in-law, please speak to these children.

YOLANDE. No. I wish to speak to you.

CHARLES. For two days you've been following me about looking the way good women always look when they're about to give a lecture.

YOLANDE. Have I ever spoken against your interests? Have I ever shown myself concerned with anything but your welfare? I am the mother of your Queen, but I brought Agnes to you when I realized she would do you good.

THE LITTLE QUEEN. Please, Mama, don't brag about it.

YOLANDE. My child, Agnes is a charming girl and she knows her place. It was important that Charles make up his mind to become a man, and if he was to become a man he had to have a woman.

THE LITTLE QUEEN. I am a woman and his wife in the bargain.

YOLANDE. You are my dear little girl and I don't want to hurt you, but you're not very much of a woman. I know because I was just like you. I was honest and sensible, and that was all. Be the Queen to your Charles, keep his house, give him a Dauphin. But leave the rest to others. Love is not a business for honest women. We're no good at it. Charles is more virile since he knows Agnes. You are more virile, aren't you, Charles?

AGNES (*too firmly*). Yes, indeed.

YOLANDE. I hope so. He doesn't act it with the Archbishop or La Tremouille.

AGNES. Things like that take a while. But he's much more virile. Doesn't read so much anymore. (*To Charles*) And since it's all due to me the very least you can do is to give me the headdress. And one for the Little Queen. (*Charles doesn't answer*) I feel ill. And if I feel ill it will certainly be for a whole week. And you'll be very bored without me. (*Eagerly, as she sees his face*) Sign a Treasury Bond and we'll worry afterward. (*He nods. She turns to the Little Queen*) Come, my little Majesty. The pink one for you, the green one for me. (*To Charles, as they exit*) We'll make fools of those London ladies, you'll see. It'll be a great victory for France.

CHARLES (*to Yolande*). A great victory for France. She talks like an army captain. I'm sick of such talk. France will be victorious, you'll be a great king — all the people who have wanted to make a king out of me. Even Agnes. She practices in bed. That's very funny. I must tell you about it someday. I am a poor frightened nothing with a lost kingdom and a broken army. When will they understand that?

YOLANDE. I understand it, Charles.

CHARLES (*softly*). Do you? You've never said that before.

YOLANDE. I say it now because I want you to see this girl. For three days I have had her brought here, waiting for you —

CHARLES. I am ridiculous enough without playing games with village louts who come to me on clouds carrying a basket of dreams.

YOLANDE. There is something strange about this girl, something remarkable. Or so everybody thinks, and that's what matters.

CHARLES. You know La Tremouille would never allow me to see the girl.

YOLANDE. Why not? It is time they understood that a peasant at their council table might do a little good. A measure of common sense from humble people might bring us all —

CHARLES (*sharply*). To ruin. Men of the people who have been at council tables, have become kings, and it was a time of massacre and mistake. At least I'm harmless. The day may come when Frenchmen will regret their little Charles. At least, I have no large ideas about how to organize death. (*He throws his ball in the air.*)

YOLANDE. Please stop playing at bilboquet, Charles.

CHARLES. Let me alone. I like this game. When I miss the cup, the ball only falls on my nose, and that hurts nobody but me. But if I sit straight on the throne with the ball in one hand and the stick in the other, I might start taking myself seriously. Then the ball will fall on the nose of France, and the nose of France won't like it. (*The Archbishop and La Tremouille enter.*)

LA TREMOUILLE. We have a new miracle every day. The girl walked to the village church to say her prayers. A drunken soldier yelled an insult at her. "You are wrong to curse," she said, "You will soon appear before our Lord." An hour later the soldier fell into a well and was drowned. The stumbling of a drunkard has turned the town into a roaring holiday. They are marching here now, shouting that God commands you to receive this girl.

CHARLES. He hasn't said a word to me.

LA TREMOUILLE. The day God speaks to you, sire, I will turn infidel.

ARCHBISHOP (*very angry*). Put up that toy, Your Majesty. You will have the rest of your life to devote to it.

LA TREMOUILLE. Get ready to leave here.

CHARLES. Where will I go? Where will you go? To the English?

ARCHBISHOP. Even from you, sire, we will not accept such words. (*As La Tremouille angrily advances on Charles, Yolande moves between them.*)

YOLANDE (*to Archbishop*). Allow him to see the girl.

ARCHBISHOP. And throw open the palace to every charlatan, every bone setter, every faith healer in the land?

LA TREMOUILLE. What difference does it make anymore? We have come to the end of our rope.

YOLANDE. If he sees the girl, it will give the people hope for a few days.

CHARLES. Oh, I am tired of hearing about the girl. Bring her in and have it ended. Maybe she has a little money and can play cards.

YOLANDE (*to La Tremouille*). We have nothing to lose, sire—

LA TREMOUILLE. When you deal with God you risk losing everything. If He has really sent this girl then He has decided to concern Himself with us. People who govern states should not attract God's attention. They should make themselves very small and pray that they will go unnoticed.

(*Joan comes in. She stands small and frightened, staring at Charles, bowing respectfully to the Archbishop. As she moves toward the throne, one of the Courtiers laughs. Joan turns to stare, and the Courtier draws back as if he is frightened.*)

CHARLES. What do you want? I'm a very busy man. It's time for my milk.

JOAN (*bows before him*). I am Joan the Maid. The King of Heaven has sent me here. I am to take you to Reims and have you anointed and crowned King of France.

CHARLES. My. Well, that is splendid, mademoiselle, but Reims is in the hands of the English, as far as I know. How shall we get there?

JOAN. We will fight our way there, noble Dauphin. First, we will take Orléans and then we will walk to Reims.

LA TREMOUILLE. I am commander of the army, madame. We have not been able to take Orléans.

JOAN (*carefully*). I will do it, sire. With the help of our Lord God who is my only commander.

LA TREMOUILLE. When did Orléans come to God's attention?

JOAN. I do not know the hour, but I know that he wishes us to take the city. After that, we will push the English into the sea.

LA TREMOUILLE. Is the Lord in such bad shape that he needs you to do his errands?

JOAN. He has said that he needs me.

ARCHBISHOP. Young woman — (*Joan kneels and kisses the hem of his robe*) If God wishes to save the Kingdom of France he has no need of armies.

JOAN. Monseigneur, God doesn't want a lazy Kingdom of France. We must put up a good fight and then He will give us victory.

ARCHBISHOP (*to Charles*). The replies of this girl are, indeed, interesting and make a certain amount of good sense. But this is a delicate matter: a commission of learned doctors will now examine her. We will review their findings in council —

LA TREMOUILLE (*to Charles*). And will keep you informed of our decision. Go back to your book. She will not disturb you any more today. Come, Madame Henriette —

JOAN. My name is Joan.

LA TREMOUILLE. Forgive me. The last quack was called Henriette.

ARCHBISHOP. Come, my child —

CHARLES. *No!* (*He motions to Joan*) You. Don't move. (*He turns toward La Tremouille, standing straight and stiff and holding Joan's hand to give himself courage*) Leave me alone with her. (*Giggles*) Your King commands you. (*La Tremouille and the Archbishop bow and leave. Charles holds his noble pose for an instant, then bursts into laughter*) And they went. It's the first time they ever obeyed me. (*Very worried*) You haven't come here to kill me? (*She smiles*) No. No, of course not. You have an honest face. I've lived so long with those pirates that I've almost forgotten what an honest face looks like. Are there other people who have honest faces?

JOAN. Many, sire.

CHARLES. I never see them. Brutes and whores, that's all I ever see. And the Little Queen. She's nice, but she's stupid. And Agnes. She's not stupid and she's not nice. (*He climbs on his throne, hangs his feet over one of the arms and sighs*) All right. Start boring me. Tell me that I ought to be a great king.

JOAN (*softly*). Yes, Charles.

CHARLES. Listen. If you want to make an impression on the Archbishop and the council, we'll have to stay in this room for at least an hour. If you talk to me of God and the Kingdom of France, I'll never live through the hour. Let's do something else. Do you know how to play at cards?

JOAN. I don't know what it is.

CHARLES. It is a nice game invented to amuse my Papa when he was ill. I'll teach you. (*He begins to hunt for the cards*) I hope they haven't stolen them. They steal everything from me around here and cards are expensive. Only the wealthiest princes can have them. I got mine from Papa. I'll never have the price of another pack. If those pigs have stolen them — No. Here they are. (*He finds them in his pocket*) My Papa was crazy. Went crazy young — in his thirties. Did you know that? Sometimes I am glad I am a bastard. At least I don't have to be so frightened of going crazy. Then sometimes I wish I were his son and knew that I was meant to be a king. It's confusing.

JOAN. Of the two, which would you prefer?

CHARLES. Well, on the days when I have a little courage, I'd risk going crazy. But on the days when I haven't any courage — that's from Sunday to Saturday — I would rather let everything go to hell and live in peace in some foreign land on whatever little money I have left.

JOAN. Today, Charles, is this one of the days when you have courage?

CHARLES. Today? (*He thinks a minute*) Yes, it seems to me I have a little bit today. Not much, but a little bit. I was sharp with the Archbishop, and —

JOAN. You will have courage every day. Beginning now.

CHARLES. You have a charm in a bottle or a basket?

JOAN. I have a charm.

CHARLES. You are a witch? You can tell me, you know, because I don't care. I swear to you that I won't repeat it. I have a horror of people being tortured. A long time ago, they made me witness the burning of a heretic at the stake. I vomited all night long.

JOAN. I am not a witch. But I have a charm.

CHARLES. Sell it to me without telling the others.

JOAN. I will give it to you, Charles. For nothing.

CHARLES. Then I don't want it. What you get free costs too much. (*He shuffles the cards*) I act like a fool so that people will let me alone. My Papa was so crazy they think I am, too. He was very crazy, did all kinds of strange things, some of them very funny. One day he thought it would be nice to have a great funeral, but nobody happened to die just then so he decided to bury a man who'd been dead four years. It cost a fortune to dig him out and put him back, but it was fun. (*He laughs merrily, catches himself, stares at Joan*) But don't think you can catch me too easily. I know a little about the world.

JOAN. You know too much. You are too smart.

CHARLES. Yes. Because I must defend myself against these cutthroats. They've got large bones, I've got puny sticks. But my head's harder than theirs and I've clung to my throne by using it.

JOAN (*gently*). I would like to defend you against them, Charles. I would give my life to do it.

CHARLES. Do you mean that?

JOAN. Yes. And I'm not afraid of anything.

CHARLES. You're lucky. Or you're a liar. Sit down and I'll teach you to play.

JOAN. All right. You teach me this game and I'll teach you another game.

CHARLES. What game do you know?

JOAN. How not to be too smart. (*Softly*) And how not to be afraid.

CHARLES (*laughs*). You'll be here a lifetime, my girl. Now. See these cards? They have pictures painted on them. Kings, queens and knaves, just as in real life. Now which would you say was the most powerful, which one could take all the rest?

JOAN. The king.

CHARLES. Well, you're wrong. This large heart can take the king. It can put him to rout, break his heart, win all his money. This card is called —

JOAN. I know. It is called God. Because God is more powerful than kings.

CHARLES. Oh, leave God alone for a minute. It's called the ace. Are you running this game? God this and God that. You talk as if you dined with Him last night. Didn't anybody tell you that the English also say their prayers to God? Every man thinks God is on his side. The rich and powerful know He is. But we're not rich and powerful, you and I — and France.

JOAN. That isn't what God cares about. He is angry with us because we have no courage left. God doesn't like frightened people.

CHARLES. Then He certainly doesn't like me. And if He doesn't like me, why should I like Him? He could have given me courage. I wanted it.

JOAN (*sharply*). Is God your nurse? Couldn't you have tried to do a little better? Even with those legs.

CHARLES. I am sorry to know that my legs have already come to your attention. It's because of my legs that Agnes can never really love me. That's sad, isn't it?

JOAN. No.

CHARLES. Why not?

JOAN. Because your head is ugly, too, and you can't be sad about everything. But what's inside your head isn't ugly, because God gave you sense. And what do you do with it? Play cards. Bounce a ball in the air. Play baby tricks with the Archbishop and act the fool for all to see. You have a son. But what have you made for him? Nothing. And when he's grown he, too, will have a right to say, "God didn't like me, so why should I like Him?" But when he says God he will mean you because every son thinks his father is God.

And when he's old enough to know that, he will hate you for what you didn't give him.

CHARLES. Give him? What can I give him? I'm glad to be alive. I've told you the truth: I am afraid. I've always been and I always will be.

JOAN. And now I'll tell you the truth: I am also afraid. (*With force*) And why not? Only the stupid are not afraid. What is the matter with you? Don't you understand that it was far more dangerous for me to get here than it is for you to build a kingdom? I've been in danger every minute of the way, and every minute of the way I was frightened. I don't want to be beaten, I don't want pain, I don't want to die. I am scared.

CHARLES (*softly*). What do you do when you get scared?

JOAN. Act as if I wasn't. It's that simple. Try it. Say to yourself, yes, I am afraid. But it's nobody else's business, so go on, go on. And you do go on.

CHARLES (*softly*). Where do you go?

JOAN (*slowly, carefully*). To the English, outside Orléans. And when you get there and see the cannon and the archers, and you know you are outnumbered, you will say to yourself, all right, they are stronger than I am, and that frightens me, as well it should. But I'll march right through because I had sense enough to get frightened first.

CHARLES. March through a stronger army? That can't be done.

JOAN. Yes it can. If you have sense and courage. Do you want to know what happened in my village last year? They tell the story as a miracle now but it wasn't. The Bouchon boy went hunting. He's the best poacher in our village, and this day he was poaching on the master's grounds. The master kept a famous dog, trained to kill, and the dog found the Bouchon boy. The boy was caught and death faced him. So he threw a stone and the dog turned his head. That was sense. And while the dog turned his head the boy decided the only way was to stand and fight. That was courage. He strangled the dog. That was victory. See?

CHARLES. Didn't the dog bite him?

JOAN. You're like the old people in the village — you really believe in miracles. Of course the dog bit him. But I told you the boy had sense, and sense saved his life. God gave man an inside to his head, and He naturally doesn't want to see it wasted. (*Smiles*) See? That's my secret. The witches' secret. What will you pay me for it now?

CHARLES. What do you want?

JOAN. The army of France. Believe in God and give me the army.

CHARLES (*moves away from her*). Tomorrow. I'll have time to get ready —

JOAN (*moves after him*). No, right now. You are ready. Come on, Charlie.

CHARLES. Perhaps I am. Perhaps I've been waiting for you and didn't know — (*Laughs nervously*) Shall we send for the Archbishop and La Tremouille and tell them that I have decided to give the army to you? It would be fun to see their faces.

JOAN. Call them.

CHARLES (*in a panic*). No. I am frightened.

JOAN. Are you as afraid as you ever can be, ever were or will be, then, now and in the future? Are you sick?

CHARLES (*holding his stomach*). I think so.

JOAN. Good. Good. Then the worst is over. By the time they get scared, you'll be all over yours. Now, if you're as sick as you can get, I'll call them. (*She runs upstage and calls out*) Monseigneur the Archbishop. Monseigneur de la Tremouille. Please come to the Dauphin.

CHARLES (*almost happy*). I am very sick.

JOAN (*moves him to the throne and arranges his hands and feet*). God is smiling. He is saying to Himself, "Look at that little Charles. He is sicker than he's ever been in his life. But he has called in his enemies and will face them. My, such a thing is wonderful." (*With great force*) Hang on, Charles. We'll be in Orléans. (*The Archbishop and La Tremouille enter, followed by Yolande and the Courtiers.*)

ARCHBISHOP. You sent for us, Your Highness?

CHARLES (*very sharply*). I have made a decision. The Royal Army is now under the command of Joan the Virgin Maid, here present. (*Roars out*) I wish to hear no word from you. None. (*They stare at Charles.*)

JOAN (*clapping her hands*). Good. Good, my Charles. You see how simple it is? You're getting better looking, Charles. (*Charles giggles. Then he suddenly stops the giggle and stares at Joan. She stares at him. She drops to her knees*) Oh, my God, I thank you.

CHARLES. There is no time to lose. We will need your blessing, sire. Give it to us. (*To La Tremouille*) Kneel down, sire.

(*La Tremouille, Yolande and the Courtiers drop to their knees. As the Archbishop pronounces the blessing, we hear the chorus sing the* Benedictus. *A Court Page gives a sword to the Dauphin. The Dauphin gives the sword to Joan. Warwick comes into the scene and moves downstage to address the audience.*)

WARWICK. In real life, it didn't work out exactly that way. As before, now, and forever, there were long discussions in the French fashion. The council met. Desperate, frightened, with nothing to lose, they decided to dress the girl in battle flags and let her go forth as a symbol. It worked well. A simple girl inspired simple people to get themselves killed for simple ideals.

(*Joan rises and moves away from the Dauphin. She puts her hand on the sword, and lowers her head in prayer.*)

Curtain

Act Two

Before the curtain rises we hear the music of a soldiers' song. The Soldiers sing of Joan and her victories.

AT RISE: *Joan, in full armor, moves across the stage to the music. She carries her sword high above her head in a kind of hero's salute to a group of admiring Village Women. She marches off as Cauchon, the Inquisitor, and the Judges take their places. Warwick moves down to address the audience.*

WARWICK. She was in the field. From that day laws of strategy no longer made any difference. We began to lose. They say that Joan worked no miracles at Orléans. They say that our plan of isolated fortresses was absurd, that they could have been taken by anyone who had courage enough to attack. But that is not true. Sir John Talbot was not a fool. He's a good soldier, as he proved long before that miserable business, and after it. By all military laws his fortified positions could not have been broken. And they could not have been broken except by — Well, by what? What shall we call it even now? The unknown, the unguessed — God, if that's the way you believe. The girl was a lark in the skies of France, high over the heads of her soldiers, singing a wild, crazy song of courage. There she was, outlined against the sun, a target for everybody to shoot at, flying straight and happy into battle. To Frenchmen, she was the soul of France. She was to me, too. (*Smiles, to Cauchon*) Monseigneur, I like France. Of course, you have your fair share of fools and blackguards. (*Somebody coughs nervously. Warwick laughs*) But every once in a while a lark does appear in your sky and then everything stupid and evil is wiped out by the shadow of the lark. I like France very much.

CAUCHON. Your guns prove your affection.

WARWICK. They prove nothing. I love animals but I hunt with guns. (*Sharply*) Too difficult to explain to a man of your simple piety, Monseigneur. So let's get on with the trial.

The lark has been captured. The King she crowned, the royal court she saved — for a minute, at least — are about to abandon their little girl. Their loyalty lasted through victory. When we took her prisoner, their luck ran out. They are returning as fast as they can to the old, stale political games. (*Charles and the Archbishop appear.*)

JOAN (*as she goes back to the trial*). Charles. (*No answer*) Charles.

CHARLES (*he turns toward her, then turns away again. He speaks to the Archbishop*). I didn't want to send the letter. I tell you I have a feeling that —

ARCHBISHOP. The letter was necessary, sire. We must be rid of the girl now. She is dangerous to us.

CHARLES. I didn't like the letter —

CAUCHON (*gently, to Joan*). Yesterday Charles disavowed you in a letter sent to all his cities.

JOAN. Charles. (*No answer. To Cauchon*) Well. He is still my King. And he is your King.

CAUCHON. No, he is not my King. We are loyal subjects of Henry of Lancaster, King of England, King of France. Joan, we love France as much as you do, but we believe the English Henry will put an end to this terrible war. That is why we have taken him as king. The man you call king is, for us, a rebel, claiming a throne that does not belong to him, refusing a good peace because it does not suit his ambitions. He is a puppet man, and we do not wish him as master. (*Sharply*) But I only confuse you. This is not a political trial in which you state your beliefs and we state ours. We are here only to return a lost girl to the bosom of the Sainted Mother Church.

JOAN (*pointing to Charles*). That puppet man is the king God gave you. He is a poor, skinny, miserable thing, but with a little time —

CHARLES (*to the Archbishop*). I object as much to being defended in this fashion as I do to being attacked.

ARCHBISHOP. Let them speak, sire. Turn away. It will be over soon. They will speed up the trial now. They will burn her at the stake.

CHARLES (*softly, as if he were sick*). I hate violence. It makes me sick —

ARCHBISHOP (*sharply*). Count yourself a lucky man. If the English do not condemn her to death, we will have to do it.

CHARLES. I will never do that, Monseigneur. After all, the girl loved me. I will never do that.

ARCHBISHOP. No, sire, certainly not. We will do it for you. (*They move off.*)

CAUCHON (*to Joan*). You are not stupid, Joan. You can understand what we think. You swear that you heard voices and you swear to the messages they sent you. But because we believe in another king, we cannot believe that it was God Who sent you to fight against us. We are priests but we are men. And man can not believe that God has turned against him.

JOAN. You'll have to believe it when we've beaten you.

CAUCHON. Ah, you answer like a foolish child.

JOAN. My Voices told me —

CAUCHON. How often have we heard those words? Do you think you are the only girl who has ever heard voices?

JOAN. No, I don't think that.

CAUCHON. Not the first and not the last. Every village priest has had his share of young girls in crisis. If the Church believed every sick child — (*Wearily*) You have good sense. You were commander in chief of the army.

JOAN (*with pride and sudden energy*). I commanded brave men. *They* believed in me, and *they* followed me.

CAUCHON. Yes. And if on the morning of an attack one of your brave men had suddenly heard voices that ordered him *not* to follow you, what would you have done with him?

(*Joan laughs and there is sudden, loud laughter from offstage Soldiers.*)

JOAN (*calls out toward the laughter*). The Seigneur Bishop is a priest. He has never been close to you, my soldiers. (*The laughter dies off. Amused, she turns back to Cauchon*) A good army fights, drinks, rapes — but they don't hear voices.

CAUCHON. A jest is not an answer. You know that a disobedient soldier in your army, in any army in this world, would be silenced. The Church Militant is also an army of this earth and we, its priests, do not believe in the Divine origin of *your* disobedience. Nobody believes in you now, Joan.

JOAN. The common people believe in me —

CAUCHON. They believe in anything. They will follow another leader tomorrow. You are alone, all alone.

JOAN. I think as I think. You have the right to punish me for it.

CAUCHON. You are strong and you are stubborn, but that is not a sign that God is on your side.

JOAN. When something is black I cannot say that it is white.

THE PROMOTER (*rises and speaks angrily to Joan*). What spell did you cast upon the man you call your King? By what means did you force him to give his armies to you?

JOAN. I have told you. I cast no spell upon him.

THE PROMOTER. It is said that you gave him a piece of mandrake.

JOAN. I don't know what mandrake is.

THE PROMOTER. Your secret has a name. We want to know what it is.

JOAN (*sharply*). I gave him courage. That is the only word I know for what was between us. When a girl says one word of good sense and people listen to her, that's proof that God is present and no strange spells or miracles are needed.

LADVENU (*softly*). Now there is a good and humble answer, Monseigneur. An answer that cannot be held against her.

THE PROMOTER. I do not agree. She is saying that she does not believe in the miracles as they are taught in our Holy Book. (*To Joan*) You declare that you deny the act of Jesus at the Marriage of Cana? You declare that you deny the miracle raising of Lazarus from the dead?

JOAN. No, Messire. Our Seigneur changed the water into wine and retied the thread of Lazarus' life. But for Him Who is Master of life and death, that is no more miracle than if I were to make thread for my loom.

THE PROMOTER (*with great anger, to the Judges*). Mark her words. Write them down. She says that Jesus made no miracles.

JOAN (*runs toward the Judges with great force*). I say that true miracles are not tricks performed by gypsies in a village square. True miracles are created by men when they use the courage and intelligence that God gave them.

CAUCHON. You are saying to us, *to us,* that the real miracle of God on this earth is man. Man, who is naught but sin and error, impotent against his own wickedness —

JOAN. And man is also strength and courage and splendor in his most desperate minutes. I know man because I have seen him. He is a miracle.

LADVENU (*quickly, nervously*). Monseigneur, Joan speaks an awkward language. But she speaks from the heart, and without guile. Perhaps when we press down upon her, we risk making her say here what she does not mean.

THE PROMOTER (*to Joan*). Do you believe that man is the greatest miracle of God?

JOAN. Yes, Messire.

THE PROMOTER (*shouts*). You blaspheme. Man is impurity and lust. The dark acts of his nights are the acts of a beast —

JOAN. Yes, Messire. And the same man who acts the beast will rise from a brothel bed and throw himself before a blade to save the soldier who walks beside him. Nobody knows why he does. He doesn't know. But he does it, and he dies, cleansed and shining. He has done both good and evil, and thus twice acted like a man. That makes God happy because God made him for just this contradiction. We are good and we are evil, and that is what was meant.

(*There is indignant movement among the Judges. The Inquisitor rises, holds up his hand. Immediately there is silence. They have been waiting for him to speak.*)

THE INQUISITOR. I have at no time spoken. (*To Joan*) I speak to you now. I represent here the Holy Inquisition of which I am the Vicar for France. I have arrived from the south of Spain, and have little knowledge of the French and English war. It does not concern me whether Charles or the Lancaster Henry rules over France. It does not concern me that the French Duke of Burgundy has joined the English, and thus Frenchman fights French brother. They are all children of the Church. Nor have I interest in defending the temporal integrity of the Church in these quarrels. (*Turns toward Cauchon*) We leave such matters to our bishops and our priests. (*Bows to Cauchon*) Nor time to be curious about the kindness and humanity which seem to move the judgment. (*Sharply, toward the Promoter*) Nor do we find interest in these endless dreams of the Devil that haunt the nights of the Promoter. The Holy Inquisition fights in the dark world of night, against an enemy it alone can recognize. (*Stops, moves toward Warwick*) We do not care that the princes of the earth have sometimes laughed at the vigilance with which we hunt the enemy, the time and thought that we give to the judgment of the enemy. The princes of the earth are sometimes swift and shallow men. They remove their enemies with a length of rope and, in the crudeness of their thinking, they believe the danger ended there. We hear the mocking laughter of such men and we forgive it. The Holy Inquisition concerns itself in matters unknown to temporal kings. Our enemy is a great enemy and has a great name. (*To Joan*) You know his name?

JOAN. No, Messire. I do not understand you.

THE INQUISITOR. You will understand me. Stand up. You will answer now to me. Are you a Christian?

JOAN. Yes, Messire.

THE INQUISITOR. The trees that shaded the village church threw shadows on the house of your father. The bells of the church brought you to prayer and sent you to work. The men we sent to your village all bring the same word: you were a pious girl.

JOAN. Yes, Messire.

THE INQUISITOR. You were a tender little girl. And you were a tender woman. You cried for the wounded in every battle —

JOAN. Yes. I cried for the wounded. They were French.

THE INQUISITOR. And you cried for the English. You stayed with a wounded English soldier who screamed through a night of pain. You held him until he died, calling him your child and giving him a hope of Heaven.

JOAN. You know that, Messire?

THE INQUISITOR. Yes. The Holy Inquisition knows much of you, Joan. Grave considerate talk was given to you. And they sent me here to judge you.

LADVENU. Messire Inquisitor, Joan has always acted with kindness and Christian charity, but this court has buried it in silence. I am happy to hear you remind them that —

THE INQUISITOR (*sternly*). Silence, Brother Ladvenu. I ask you not to forget that the Holy Inquisition alone is qualified to distinguish between theological virtues and that troubled brew that man so boastfully calls the milk of human kindness. (*Turns to the Judges*) Ah, my masters. What strange matters concern you all. Your business is to defend the Faith. But you see the kind eyes of a young girl and you are overwhelmed.

LADVENU. Our Lord loved with charity and kindness, Messire. He said to a sinner, "Go in peace." He said —

THE INQUISITOR. Silence, I said to you, Brother Ladvenu. (*Softly, carefully*) You are young. I am told your learning is very great and that is why you were admitted to this trial. Therefore I am hopeful that experience will teach you not to translate the great words into the vulgar tongue, nor embroider the meaning to suit your heart. Be seated and be silent. (*He turns back to Joan*) You were very young when you first heard your Voices.

JOAN. Yes, Messire.

THE INQUISITOR. I am going to shock you: there is nothing very exceptional about the Voices you heard. Our archives are full of such cases. There are many young visionaries. Girls frequently experience a crisis of mysticism. It passes. But with you — and your priest should have recognized it — the crisis was prolonged. The messages became precise and the Celestial Voices began to use most unusual words.

JOAN. Yes. My Voices told me to go and save the Kingdom of France.

THE INQUISITOR. A strange order to an ignorant peasant girl.

JOAN. Not so strange, Messire, because it turned out to be the truth.

THE INQUISITOR. I say a strange order to a girl who had seen nothing of war. The troubles of France could have been no more to you than tales told at twilight. And yet suddenly you went out into the great world of kings and battles, convinced that it was your mission to aid your brothers in their struggle to keep the land on which they were born, and which they imagine belongs to them.

JOAN. Our Lord could not want the English to kill us and to conquer us. He could not want us to live by their laws and wishes. When they have gone back across the sea, to their own land, I will not go and pick a quarrel with them. They can rest easy in their own house. I've always said that.

THE INQUISITOR (*sternly*). And I say your presumption is not suited to my taste.

LADVENU. She did not mean, Messire — she speaks in a youthful fashion.

CAUCHON (*softly*). Be still, Brother Ladvenu.

THE INQUISITOR (*to Joan*). It would have been more fitting for a pious girl to have spent her life in prayers and penitence and, in such manner, obtained from Heaven the promise that the English would be defeated.

JOAN. I did all that. But I think you must first strike and then pray. That's the way God wants it. I had to explain to Charles how to attack. And he believed me and Dunois believed me and La Hire — good men, wild bulls they were, and warriors. Ah, we had some fine battles together. It was good, in the dawn, riding boot to boot with friends —

THE PROMOTER. To the kill. Did your Voices instruct you to kill?

JOAN (*angrily*). I have never killed a man. But war is war.

CAUCHON. You love war, Joan.

JOAN (*softly*). Yes. And that is one of the sins from which God will have to absolve me. But I did not like pain or death. At night, on the battlefield, I would weep for the dead —

THE PROMOTER. You would weep at night for the dead but by morning you were shouting for a new battle.

JOAN (*moves to him, with great force*). I say God did not wish one Englishman to remain in France. That's not so hard to understand, is it? We had to do our work, that's all. You are wise men, you think too much. Your heads are filled with too much celestial science. You don't understand even the simplest things anymore — things that my dullest soldier would understand without talk. Isn't that true, La Hire?

(*She stumbles, moves away from the Judges, and falls to the ground. The lights dim on the trial and we hear again the whistling of the soldiers' song. La Hire, in full armor, appears upstage and moves toward Joan.*)

LA HIRE. The morning has come, Madame Joan. (*She sits up, shivers, stares at La Hire.*)

JOAN. The night was cold, La Hire. (*He sits beside her, warms her hands in his own. Joan looks toward the trial, then up, then back to La Hire, as if she were confused by the place and the time*) Good La Hire. Great La Hire. You've really come to help me as I knew you would.

LA HIRE (*he takes out an onion and begins to peel it*). Come to help you? I was sleeping fifty feet from you, Madame Joan, watching over you as I always do. (*She laughs and moves closer to him*) Don't come too close. I stink of wine and onions.

JOAN. No, no. You smell fine.

LA HIRE. Usually you tell me I stink too much to be a Christian. You say I am a danger to the army because if the wind is behind me the English will know where we are.

JOAN. Oh, La Hire, I was so stupid in those days. You know how girls are. Nothing ever happens to them, they know nothing, so they pretend they know everything. But I am not so stupid anymore. You smell good because you smell like a man.

LA HIRE. I can't stand a man who washes in the field because to me a man like that isn't a man. I was brought up on an onion in the morning. The rest can have their sausage. The smell is more distinguished, you tell me. I know you think a breakfast onion is a sin.

JOAN (*laughs*). Nothing that is true is a sin, La Hire. I was a fool. I tormented you. But I didn't know anything then. I didn't. (*Softly*) Ah, you smell so good. Sweat, onions, wine. You have all the smells a man should have. And you curse, you kill, and you think of nothing but women.

LA HIRE. Me?

JOAN. You. But I tell you that with all your sins you are like a bright new coin in the hand of God.

LA HIRE. Well, I have had a bastard life and when I go into battle, I say my prayers. I say, "God, I hope You'll help me as I would help You if You faced those God-damned" — (*Softly*) To tell you the truth, I'm frightened of what will happen to me if I get killed.

JOAN. Paradise will happen to you. They are looking forward to having you with them.

LA HIRE. That gives me heart, Madame Joan. I've wanted to go to Paradise. But if it's all full of saints and bishops, I might not be too happy —

JOAN. It's full of men like you. It's the others who are kept waiting at the gates — (*Suddenly*) The gates. The gates of Orléans. They're ahead of us — the day has come, La Hire. To horse, my boy, to horse. (*She climbs on her stool. La Hire stands next to her. They hold imaginary reins in their hands as they ride imaginary horses*) It's dawn, La Hire. The woods are still wet from the night, the trees are still dark and strange. It's fine to ride into battle with a good soldier by your side.

LA HIRE. Some people don't like it. Some people like to make a little garden out of life and walk down a path.

JOAN. But they never know what we know. (*As if she were puzzled and ashamed*) Death has to be waiting at the end of the ride before you truly see the earth, and feel your heart, and love the world. (*Suddenly, in a whisper*) There are three English soldiers. (*She looks back*) We've outridden the others. We are alone.

LA HIRE. Get off your horse, Madame Joan. Lead him back. You have never used your sword.

JOAN. No. Don't meet them alone, La Hire —

LA HIRE (*he draws his sword*). I'll kill them . . . God-damned English bastards. (*Sword in hand, he disappears.*)

JOAN (*kneels in prayer*). Dear God, he is as good as bread. I answer for him. He's my friend. (*She turns toward the Judges, angry, defiant*) The last word will not be spoken at this trial. La Hire will come to deliver me. He will bring three hundred lancers, I know them all, and they will take me from my prison —

CAUCHON. Yes. They came to deliver you, Joan.

JOAN (*running to him*). Where are they? I knew they would come —

CAUCHON. They came to the gates of the city. When they saw how many English soldiers were here, they turned and went away.

JOAN (*shaken*). Ah. They turned and went away. Without fighting? (*Cauchon turns away*) Yes. Of course. It was *I* who taught them to do just that. I would say to them, "Have a little sense. It doesn't cost a sou. Learn not to be brave when you are outnumbered, unless —" (*Violently*) That's what they did. They went to get reinforcements for me —

CAUCHON. No. Your friends will not return, Joan.

JOAN. That's not true. "Learn not to be brave when you are outnumbered," I said, "*unless* you can't retreat. Then you must fight because there is no other way —" (*Proudly*) La Hire will return. Because there is no other way to save me now.

CAUCHON. La Hire sells himself to whichever prince has need. When he discovered that your Charles was tired of war and would sign any peace, he marched his men toward Germany. He looks for a new land on which to try his sword. (*Comes to her*) You have been abandoned. It will sound strange to you, but the priests of this court are the only men who care for your soul and for your life. Humble yourself, Joan, and the Church will take your hand. In your heart, you are a child of the Church.

JOAN (*softly*). Yes.

CAUCHON. Trust yourself to the Church. She will weigh your deeds and take from you the agony of self-judgment.

JOAN (*after a long silence*). For that which is of the Faith, I turn to the Church, as I have always done. But what I am, I will not denounce. What I have done, I will not deny.

(*There is a shocked silence. Then there is great movement in the courtroom, as if this were the answer that would bring the judgment. The Inquisitor rises. The Priests are suddenly silent. The Inquisitor slowly moves before the Priests, peering into their faces. The Priests draw back, frightened.*)

THE INQUISITOR (*to one Priest*). Not you. (*To another Priest*) Not you. (*To a third Priest*) Not you. (*Pauses before Cauchon, stares at him*) And not you, Bishop of Beauvais. I have spoken of the great enemy, but not even now do you know his name. You do not understand on whom you sit in judgment, nor the issues of the judgment. I have told you that the Holy Inquisition is not concerned with royal rank or merchant gold or peasant birth. To us, a scholar in his room is equal in importance to an emperor in his palace. Because *we* know the name of the enemy. His name is natural man. (*There is silence, Ladvenu moves forward*) Can you not see that this girl is the symbol of that which is most to be feared? She is the enemy. She is man as he stands against us. Look at her. Frightened, hungry, dirty, abandoned by all, and no longer even sure that those Voices in the air ever spoke to her at all. Does her misery make her a suppliant begging God for mercy and for light? No. She turns away from God. She dares to stand under torture, thrashing about like a proud beast in the stable of her dungeon. She raises her eyes, not to God, but to man's image of himself. I have need to remind you, Masters, that he who loves Man does not love God.

LADVENU (*with great force*). It cannot be. Jesus Himself became a man.

THE INQUISITOR (*turns to Cauchon*). Seigneur Bishop, I must ask you to send your young assessor from this courtroom. I will consider after this session whether he may return or whether I will bring charges against him. (*Shouts*) Against him, or against any other. *Any* other. I would bring charges against myself if God should let me lose my way.

CAUCHON (*softly*). Leave us, Brother Ladvenu.

LADVENU. Messire Inquisitor, I owe you obedience. I will not speak again. But I will pray to our Lord Jesus that you remember the weakness of your small, sad, lonely — enemy. (*Ladvenu exits.*)

THE INQUISITOR. Do you have need to question her further? To ask all the heavy words that are listed in your legal papers? What need to ask her why she still persists in wearing man's dress when it is contrary to the commandments? Why she dared the sin of living among men as a man? The deeds no longer matter. What she has done is of less importance than why she did it, the answers less important than the one answer. It is a fearful answer, "What I am, I will not . . ." You wish to say it again? Say it.

JOAN (*slowly, softly*). What I am, I will not denounce. What I have done, I will not deny.

THE INQUISITOR (*carefully, as if he has taken the measure of an enemy*). You have heard it. Down through the ages, from dungeon, from torture chamber, from the fire of the stake. Ask her and she will say with those others, "Take my life. I will give it because I will not deny what I have done." This is what they say, all of them, the insolent breed. The men who dare our God. Those who say no to us — (*He moves toward Joan. Cauchon rises*) Well, you and all like you shall be made to say yes. You put the Idea in peril, and that you will not be allowed to do. (*Turns to the Judges*) The girl is only a monstrous symbol of the faith decayed. Therefore I now demand her immediate punishment. I demand that she be excommunicated from the Church. I demand that she be returned to secular authority there to receive her punishment. I ask the secular arm to limit her sentence to this side of death and the mutilation of her members. (*Cauchon moves to the Inquisitor as if to stop the judgment.*)

WARWICK (*to Cauchon*). A passionate man and so sincere. I think he means simply to throw the dirty work to me. I am the secular authority here. Why didn't your French Charles have her burned? It was his job.

CHARLES (*very disturbed*). I don't want to do it. I don't like killing.

(*A large, masked figure appears.*)

CAUCHON (*calls to the masked man*). Master Executioner, is the wood for the stake dry, and ready to burn?

EXECUTIONER. All is ready. Things will go according to custom. But I will not be able to help the girl this time.

CAUCHON. What do you mean help her, Master?

EXECUTIONER. We let the first flames rise high. Then I climb up behind the victims and strangle them the rest of the way. It's easier and quicker for everybody. But I have had special instructions this time to make the fire very high. And so it will take longer and I will not be able to reach her for the act of mercy.

CAUCHON (*moves to Joan*). Did you hear that?

JOAN. I've remembered a dream from years ago. I woke screaming and ran to my mother — (*Screams as if in pain*) Ah.

CAUCHON (*desperately*). Joan, for the last time I offer you the saving hand of your Mother Church. We wish to save you, but we can delay no longer. The crowd has been waiting since dawn. They eat their food, scold their children, make jokes, and grow impatient. You are famous and they have nothing better to do with their lives than bring garlands to the famous — or watch them burn.

JOAN (*as if she is still in the dream*). I forgive them, Messire. I forgive you, too.

THE PROMOTER (*furiously*). Monseigneur speaks to you like a father in order to save your miserable soul and you answer by forgiving him.

JOAN. Monseigneur speaks to me gently, he takes great pains to seduce me, but I do not know whether he means to save me or to conquer me. In any case, he will be obliged to have me burned.

CAUCHON (*comes to her*). For the last time I say: Confess your sins and return to us. We will save you.

JOAN (*she clings to his robe*). I wish to return to the Church. I want the Holy Communion. I have asked for it over and over again. But they have refused to give it to me.

CAUCHON. After your confession, when you have begun your penance, we will give it to you. (*There is no answer. Very softly*) Are you not afraid to die?

JOAN. Yes. I am afraid. What difference does that make? I've always been so afraid of fire. (*Gasps*) I've remembered a dream —

CAUCHON (*pulls her to him*). Joan, we cannot believe in the Divinity of your Voices. But if we are wrong — and certainly that thought has crossed our minds —

THE PROMOTER (*furious*). No, I say no. Even to you, my Bishop of Beauvais —

CAUCHON (*to Joan*). But if we are wrong then we will have committed a monstrous sin of ignorance and we will pay for it the rest of our eternal lives. But we are the priests of your Church. Trust our belief that we are right, as you trusted your good village priest. Place yourself in our hands. You will be at peace.

JOAN. I cannot follow what you say. I am tired. Oh, sire, I do not sleep at night. I come here and all is said so fast that I cannot understand. You torture me with such gentle words, and your voice is so kind. I would rather have you beat me —

CAUCHON. I talk to you thus because my pride is less than yours.

JOAN (*she moves away from him, as if she were sick and wanted to be alone*). Pride? I have been a prisoner so long — I think my head is sick and old, and the bottom of me does not hold any more. Sometimes I don't know where I am and my dungeon seems a great beech tree. I am hungry, or I was, and I want a taste of country milk —

CAUCHON (*desperately, as if he were at the end*). Look at me, Joan, keep your mind here. I am an old man. I have killed people in the defense of my beliefs. I am so close to death myself that I do not wish to kill again. I do not wish to kill a little girl. Be kind. (*Cries out*) Help me to save you.

JOAN (*very softly; broken now*). What do you want me to say? Please tell me in simple words.

CAUCHON. I am going to ask you three questions. Answer yes three times. That is all. (*With passion*) Help me, Joan.

JOAN. But could I sleep a few hours, sire?

CAUCHON. No! We cannot wait. Do you entrust yourself with humility to the Holy Roman and Apostolic Church, to our Holy Father, the Pope, and to his bishops? Will you rely upon them, and upon no one else, to be your judges? Do you make the complete and total act of submission? Do you ask to be returned to the bosom of the Church?

JOAN. Yes, but — (*The Inquisitor rises. Cauchon becomes nervous*) I don't want to say the opposite of what my Voices told me. I don't ever want to bear false witness against Charlie. I fought so hard for the glory of his consecration. Oh, that was a day when he was crowned. The sun was out —

CHARLES (*to Joan*). It was a nice day and I'll always remember it. But I'd rather not think it was a divine miracle. I'd rather people didn't think that God sent you to me. Because now that you're a prisoner, and thought to be a heretic and a sorceress, they think that God has abandoned me. I'm in bad enough trouble without that kind of gossip. Just forget about me and go your way. (*Joan bows her head.*)

CAUCHON. Do you wish me to repeat the question? (*Joan does not answer. Cauchon is angry*) Are you mad? You understand now that we are your only protectors, that this is the last thing I can do for you? You cannot bargain and quibble like a peasant at a village fair. You are an impudent girl, and I now become angry with you. You should be on your knees to the Church.

JOAN (*falls to her knees*). Messire, deep in your heart do you believe that our Lord wishes me to submit to the judgment?

CAUCHON. I so believe.

JOAN (*softly*). Then I submit.

(*There is great movement in the court. The Inquisitor rises; the Promoter moves to him.*)

CAUCHON (*very tired now*). You promise to renounce forever the bearing of arms?

JOAN. But, Messire, there is still so much to do —

CAUCHON (*angrily*). Nothing more will ever be done by you.

WARWICK. That is true, Joan.

CHARLES. And if you're thinking of helping me again, please don't. I won't ever use you anymore. It would be very dangerous for me.

JOAN (*broken now, almost as if she were asleep*). I renounce forever the bearing of arms.

CAUCHON (*in great haste*). Do you renounce forever the wearing of that brazen uniform?

JOAN. You have asked me that over and over again. The uniform doesn't matter. My Voices told me to put it on.

THE PROMOTER. It was the Devil who told you to put it on.

JOAN. Oh, Messire, put away the Devil for today. My Voices chose the uniform because my Voices have good sense. (*With great effort*) I had to ride with soldiers. It was necessary they not think of me as a girl. It was necessary they see in me nothing but a soldier like themselves. That is all the sense there was to it.

CAUCHON. But why have you persisted in wearing it in prison? You have been asked this question in many examinations and your refusal to answer has become of great significance to your judges.

JOAN. And I have asked over and over to be taken to a Church prison. Then I would take off my man's uniform.

THE PROMOTER (*to Cauchon*). Monseigneur, the girl is playing with us, as from the first. I do not understand what she says or why you —

JOAN (*angry*). One doesn't have to be an educated man to understand what I am saying.

THE PROMOTER (*turns to Judges*). She says that she submits to the Church. But I tell you that as long as she refuses to put aside that Devil dress, I will exercise my rights as master judge of heretics and witchcraft. (*To Cauchon*) Strange pressures have been put upon all of us. I know not from where they come, but I tell even you —

JOAN. I have said that if you put me in a Church prison I will take off this uniform.

THE PROMOTER. You will not bargain. Put aside that dress or, no matter who feels otherwise, you will be declared a sorceress.

JOAN (*softly, to Cauchon*). I am not alone in prison. Two English soldier guards are in the cell with me night and day. The nights are long. I am in chains. I try hard not to sleep, but sometimes I am too tired — (*She stops, embarrassed*) In this uniform it is easier for me to defend myself.

CAUCHON (*in great anger*). Have you had so to defend yourself since the beginning of this trial? (*Warwick moves to Joan.*)

JOAN. Every night since I've been captured. I don't have much sleep. In the mornings, when I am brought before you, I am confused, and I don't understand your questions. I told you that. Sometimes I try to sleep here in the trial so that I will stay awake in the night —

CAUCHON. Why haven't you told us this before?

JOAN. Because the soldiers told me they would be hanged if I said anything —

WARWICK (*very angry*) They were right. (*To Cauchon*) Detestable bastards. It's disgusting. They've learned such things since they came to France. It may be all right in the French Army, but not in mine. (*Bows to Joan*) I am sorry, Madame. It will not happen again.

CAUCHON (*to Joan*). The Church will protect you from now on. I promise you.

JOAN. Then I agree to put on woman's dress.

CAUCHON. Thank you, my child. That is all. (*He moves to the*

Inquisitor) Messire Inquisitor, Brother Ladvenu drew up the Act of Renunciation. Will you permit me to recall him here? (*With bitterness*) The girl has said yes, thus man has said yes.

THE PROMOTER (*to the Inquisitor*). Messire Inquisitor, you are going to allow this to happen?

THE INQUISITOR. If she said yes, she has fulfilled the only condition that concerns me.

THE PROMOTER (*turns to Cauchon*). This trial has been conducted with an indulgence that is beyond my understanding. (*To the Inquisitor*) I am told that there are those here who eat from the English manger. I ask myself now if they have arranged to eat better from the French manger.

THE INQUISITOR (*rises, moves toward Joan*). It is not a question of mangers, Messire Promoter. *I* ask myself how did it happen that this girl said yes when so many lesser ones did not bow the head. I had not believed it to be possible. (*Points to Cauchon*) And why was tenderness born in the heart of that old man who was her judge? He is at the end of a life worn out with compromise and debasement. Why now, here, for this girl, this dangerous girl, did his heart — (*He kneels, ignoring the others. As he prays, we hear only the words . . .*) Why, Oh Lord . . . ? Why, Oh Lord . . . ? Consecrate it in peace to Your Glory. . . . Your Glory —

CAUCHON (*as Ladvenu enters*). Please read the act.

LADVENU (*comes to Joan. With great tenderness*). I have prayed for you, Joan. (*Reading*) "I, Joan, commonly called The Maid, confess having sinned through pride and malice in pretending to have received revelations from our Lord God. I confess I have blasphemed by wearing an immodest costume. I have incited men to kill through witchcraft and I here confess to it. I swear on the Holy Gospels I will not again wear this heretic's dress and I swear never to bear arms again. I declare that I place myself humbly at the mercy of our Holy Mother Church and our Holy Father, the Pope of Rome and His Bishops, so that they may judge my sins and my errors. I beseech Her to receive me in Her Bosom and I declare myself ready to submit to the sentence which She may inflict upon me. In faith of which, I have signed my name upon this Act of Renunciation of which I have full knowledge. (*Ladvenu hands the pen to Joan. She moves it in the air, as if she had not heard and did not understand. Ladvenu takes her hand and puts it on the paper*) I will help you.

CAUCHON (*as if he were a very old man*). You have been saved. We, your judges, in mercy and mitigation, now condemn you to spend the remainder of your days in prison. There you will do penance for your sins. You will eat the bread of sorrow and drink the water of anguish until, through solitary contemplation, you repent. Under these conditions of penance, we declare you delivered of the danger of excommunication. You may go in peace. (*He makes the Sign of the Cross*) Take her away.

(*Cauchon stumbles and is helped by Ladvenu. A Soldier pushes Joan away from the trial. The Judges rise and slowly move off. Cauchon moves past Warwick.*)

WARWICK. There were several times, sire, when I thought I would have to interfere. My King must have what he paid for. But you were right and I was wrong. The making of a martyr is dangerous business. The pile of faggots, the invincible girl in the flames, might have been a triumph for the French spirit. But the apologies of a hero are sad and degrading. You did well, sire; you are a wise man.

CAUCHON (*with bitterness*). I did not mean to earn your praise.

(*He moves off. The lights dim on the trial as Warwick moves off. Four Soldiers appear with spears, and their spears become the bars of Joan's jail cell. Charles appears and stands looking at Joan through the bars.*)

CHARLES. I didn't want you to sacrifice yourself for me, Joan. I know you loved me, but I don't want people to love me. It makes for obligations. This filthy prison air is wet and stinks. Don't they ever clean these places? (*He peers into her cell, sees the water pail that sits beside her, and draws back*) Tell them to give you fresh water. My God, what goes on in this world. (*She does not answer him*) Don't you want to speak to me, Joan?

JOAN. Good-bye, Charlie.

CHARLES. You must stop calling me Charlie. Ever since my coronation I am careful to make everyone say sire.

JOAN. Sire.

CHARLES. I'll come and see you again. Good-bye.

(*He moves off. Joan lies in silence. Then she tries to drink from the water pail, retches, and puts her hand over her mouth as if she were sick.*)

JOAN. Blessed Saint Michael. (*She makes a strange sound, shivers*) I am in prison. Come to me. Find me. (*Cries out*) I need you now. (*Very loudly*) I told you that I was afraid of fire, long before I ever knew — or did I always know? You want me to live? (*When there is no answer*) Why do I call for help? You must have good reason for not coming to me. (*She motions toward courtroom*) They think I dreamed it all. Maybe I did. But it's over now . . . (*Warwick comes slowly into the cell.*)

WARWICK (*hesitantly*). You are weeping?

JOAN. No, Monseigneur.

WARWICK. I am sorry to disturb you. I only came to say that I am glad you are saved. You behaved damned well. I, er, well, it's rather difficult to say in my language, but the plain fact is that I like you. And it amused me to watch you with the Inquisitor. Sinister man, isn't he? I detest these intellectual idealists more than anything in the world. What disgusting animals they are. He wanted only to see you humiliate yourself, no matter your heart or your misery. And when you did, he was satisfied.

JOAN (*softly*). He had reason to be satisfied.

WARWICK. Well, don't worry about him. It all worked out well. Martyrs are likely to stir the blood of simple people and set up too grand a monument to themselves. It's all very complex and dangerous. Tell me, are you a virgin?

JOAN. Yes.

WARWICK. I knew you were. A woman would not talk as you do. My fiancée in England is a very pure girl and she also talks like a boy. You are the greatest horsewoman I have ever seen. (*When there is no answer*) Ah, well. I am intruding on you. Don't hesitate to let me know if I can ever do anything for you. Good-bye, Madame.

JOAN. Nobody else came to see me here. You are a kind man, Monseigneur.

WARWICK. Not at all. (*Motions toward courtroom*) It's that I don't like all those fellows who use words to make war. You and I killed because that was the way things turned out for us.

JOAN. Monseigneur, I have done wrong. And I don't know how or why I did it. (*Slowly, bitterly*) I swore against myself. That is a great sin, past all others — (*Desperately*) I still believe in all that I did, and yet I swore against it. God can't want that. What can be left for me?

WARWICK. Certainly they are not going to make you a gay life, not at first. But things work out and in time your nasty Charles might even show you a speck of loyalty —

JOAN. Yes, when I am no longer dangerous, he might even give me a small pension and a servant's room at court.

WARWICK (*sharply*). Madame, there will be no court.

JOAN. And I will wear cast-off brocade and put ornaments in my hair and grow old. I will be happy that few people remember my warrior days and I will grovel before those who speak of my past and pray them to be silent. And when I die, in a big fat bed, I will be remembered as a crazy girl who rode into battle for what she said she believed, and ate the dirt of lies when she was faced with punishment. That will be the best that I can have — if my little Charles remembers me at all. If he doesn't there will be a prison dungeon, and filth and darkness — (*Cries out*) What good is life either way?

WARWICK. It is good any way you can have it. We all try to save a little honor, of course, but the main thing is to be here —

JOAN (*rises, calls out, speaking to the Voices*). I was only born the day you first spoke to me. My life only began on the day you told me what I must do, my sword in hand. You are silent, dear my God, because you are sad to see me frightened and craven. And for what? A few years of unworthy life. (*She kneels. Softly, as if she is answering a message*) I know. Yes, I know. I took the good days from You and refused the bad. I know. Dear my God forgive me, and keep me now to be myself. Forgive me and take me back for what I am. (*She rises. She is cheerful*) Call your soldiers, Warwick. I deny my confession.

WARWICK. Joan. No nonsense, please. Things are all right as they are. I —

JOAN. Come. (*She holds out her hand to him.*)

WARWICK. I don't want anything to do with your death.

JOAN (*Smiles*). You have a funny gentleman's face. But you are kind. Come now. (*She calls out*) Soldiers! Englishmen! Give me back my warrior clothes. And when I have put them on, call back all the priests. (*Stops, puts her hands in prayer and speaks simply*) Please God, help me now.

(*The music of the* "Sanctus" *begins as the Judges, Cauchon, the Inquisitor, the Promoter, Charles, the People of the Court, return to the stage. Two Soldiers bring a crude stake. Joan herself moves to the stake and the Soldiers lash her to it. Other Soldiers and Village Women pick up the bundles of faggots and carry them offstage. The Executioner appears with lighted torch and moves through the crowd.*)

JOAN (*as they are about to carry her off*). Please. Please. Give me a Cross.

THE PROMOTER. No Cross will be given to a witch.

AN ENGLISH SOLDIER (*he has taken two sticks of wood and made a Cross. Now he hands his Cross to Joan*). Here, my daughter. Here's your Cross. (*Very angry, to the Promoter*) She has a right to a Cross like anybody else.

(*Joan is carried off stage. The lights dim and we see the shadows of flames as they are projected on the cyclorama. Ladvenu runs on stage with a Cross from the church and stands holding it high for Joan to see.*)

THE INQUISITOR (*calling to Executioner*). Be quick. Be quick. Let the smoke hide her. (*To Warwick*) In five minutes, Monseigneur, the world will be crying.

WARWICK. Yes.

THE INQUISITOR (*shouting to Executioner*). Be quick, master, be quick.

EXECUTIONER (*calling in to him*). All is ready, messire. The flames reach her now.

LADVENU (*calling out*). Courage, Joan. We pray for you.

CAUCHON. May God forgive us all.

(*Cauchon falls to his knees and begins the prayer for the dead. The prayers are murmured as the chorus chants a Requiem. The Soldiers and the Village People return to the stage: a Woman falls to the ground; a Soldier cries out; a Girl bends over as if in pain and a Soldier helps her to move on; the Court Ladies back away, hiding their faces from the burning; the Priests kneel in prayer.*)

CHARLES (*in a whisper as he leaves*). What does she do? What does she say? Is it over?

THE INQUISITOR (*to Ladvenu*). What does she do?

LADVENU. She is quiet.

THE INQUISITOR (*moves away*). Is her head lowered?

LADVENU. No, messire. Her head is high.

THE INQUISITOR (*as if he were in pain*). Ah. (*To Ladvenu*) She falters now?

LADVENU. No. It is a terrible and noble sight, messire. You should turn and see.

THE INQUISITOR (*moves off*). I have seen it all before.

(*The lights dim. Cauchon rises from his prayers. He stumbles and falls. Ladvenu and Warwick move to help him. He takes Ladvenu's arm, but moves away from Warwick, refusing his help. As the stage becomes dark, Cauchon, the Promoter, Ladvenu and Warwick move downstage and the light comes up on La Hire who stands above them. La Hire is in full armor, holding helmet and sword.*)

LA HIRE. You were fools to burn Joan of Arc.

CAUCHON. We committed a sin, a monstrous sin.

WARWICK. Yes, it was a grave mistake. We made a lark into a giant bird who will travel the skies of the world long after our names are forgotten, or confused, or cursed down.

LA HIRE. I knew the girl and I loved her. You can't let it end this way. If you do, it will not be the true story of Joan.

LADVENU. That is right. The true story of Joan is not the hideous agony of a girl tied to a burning stake. She will stand forever for the glory that can be. Praise God.

LA HIRE. The true story of Joan is the story of her happiest day. Anybody with any sense knows that. Go back and act it out.

(*The lights dim on the four men and come up on the Coronation of Charles in Reims Cathedral. The altar cloth is in place, the lighted candles are behind the altar, stained glass windows are projected on the cyclorama. The Archbishop appears, and the people of the royal court. Joan stands clothed in a fine white robe, ornamented with a fleur-de-lis.*)

WARWICK (*moves into the coronation scene, stares bewildered as Charles, in coronation robes, carrying his crown, crosses to the altar*). This could not have been her happiest day. To watch Holy Oil being poured on that mean, sly little head!

CHARLES (*turns to Warwick, amused*). Oh, I didn't turn out so bad. I drove you out of the country. And I got myself some money before I died. I was as good as most.

WARWICK. So you were. But certainly the girl would never have ridden into battle, never have been willing to die because you were as good as most.

JOAN (*comes forward, smiling, happy*). Oh, Warwick, I wasn't paying any attention to Charlie. I knew what Charlie was like. I wanted him crowned because I wanted my country back. And God gave it to us on this Coronation Day. Let's end with it, please, if nobody would mind.

(*As the curtain falls the chorus sings the* "Gloria" *of the Mass.*)

Curtain

Candide

A COMIC OPERETTA
BASED UPON VOLTAIRE'S SATIRE

Lyrics by Richard Wilbur
Score by Leonard Bernstein
Two additional lyrics by John Latouche

Candide was first produced at the Martin Beck Theatre, New York City, on December 1, 1956, with the following cast:

(In the order of their appearance)

DR. PANGLOSS	MAX ADRIAN
CUNEGONDE	BARBARA COOK
CANDIDE	ROBERT ROUNSEVILLE
BARON	ROBERT MESROBIAN
MAXIMILLIAN	LOUIS EDMONDS
KING OF HESSE	CONRAD BAIN
HESSE'S GENERAL	NORMAN ROLAND
MAN	BORIS APLON
WOMAN	DORIS OKERSON
DUTCH LADY	MARGARET ROY
DUTCH MAN	TONY DRAKE
ATHEIST	ROBERT RUE
ARAB CONJURER	ROBERT BARRY
INFANT CASMIRA	MARIA NOVOTNA
LAWYER	WILLIAM CHAPMAN
VERY, VERY OLD INQUISITOR	CONRAD BAIN
VERY OLD INQUISITOR	CHARLES ASCHMANN
BEGGARS	MARGARET ROY, ROBERT COSDEN, THOMAS PYLE
FRENCH LADY	MAUD SCHEERER
OLD LADY	IRRA PETINA
MARQUIS MILTON	BORIS APLON
SULTAN MILTON	JOSEPH BERNARD
PILGRIM FATHER	ROBERT RUE
PILGRIM MOTHER	DOROTHY KREBILL
CAPTAIN	CONRAD BAIN
MARTIN	MAX ADRIAN
GOVERNOR OF BUENOS AIRES	WILLIAM OLVIS
OFFICERS	GEORGE BLACKWELL, TONY DRAKE, THOMAS PYLE
FERONE	WILLIAM CHAPMAN
MADAME SOFRONIA	IRRA PETINA
DUCHESS	MAUD SCHEERER
PREFECT OF POLICE	NORMAN ROLAND
PRINCE IVAN (FAT MAN)	ROBERT MESROBIAN

Produced by
ETHEL LINDER REINER

in association with
LESTER OSTERMAN, JR.

Directed by
TYRONE GUTHRIE

Assisted by
TOM BROWN

Production designed by
OLIVER SMITH

Costumes designed by
IRENE SHARAFF

Scenes

Act One

Scene 1. Westphalia. Outside the castle of the Baron Thunder Ten Tronch.

Scene 1A. Travels from Westphalia to Lisbon.

Scene 2. The market square of Lisbon. The day of the famous earthquake.

Scene 2A. Travels from Lisbon to Paris.

Scene 3. Paris. The ballroom of a house in Paris.

Scene 3A. Travels from Paris to Buenos Aires.

Scene 4. Buenos Aires. The wharf in front of the Governor's palace; the Governor's palace, terrace and balcony.

Act Two

Scene 1. Same as Buenos Aires, Act One, Scene 4.

Scene 1A. Travels from Buenos Aires to Venice.

Scene 2. Venice. A gambling house.

Scene 3. Westphalia in ruins.

Act One

Scene 1.

SCENE: *Westphalia. Outside the castle of the Baron Thunder Ten Tronch.*

AT RISE: *Pangloss appears.*

PANGLOSS. I have been asked to tell you that this is Westphalia. It is a fine, sunny day. The sun shines on all wedding days, except when it doesn't. Now. The women of Westphalia are very pure women. (*The Women of the Chorus appear*) I am told there are women in this world who are not pure, but the uneducated say a great many foolish things, don't they? (*The Men of the Chorus appear*) Our men are brave. The war is over, but we still have six divisions of artillery ready to start another war. It was a long and bloody war, but if men didn't fight they would never know the benefits of peace, and if they didn't know the benefits of peace they would never know the benefits of war. You see, it all works out for the best. (*King of Hesse, escorted by Soldiers, appears*) This is the King of Hesse, our hereditary enemy. We destroyed his army last week and took him prisoner. We treat him with great courtesy. He has a nice room in the basement. He comes out every day for exercise, and seems most content. (*Hesse exits*) Oh, forgive me. I am Pangloss, Doctor of Heidelberg, Leipzig, and Würzburg Universities in Philosophy and Metaphysics. I have long been resident tutor to the Baron's house. It's been a good life. Although, between you and me, I sometimes miss the cloisters of the university and small talk in Greek. (*Gretchen comes toward him*) Good morning, Gretchen.

GRETCHEN. You owe me money.

PANGLOSS. Ah, well. If she didn't think of money, she wouldn't think at all. Which certainly proves that all is for the best in this best of all possible worlds. (*He sings*)

Look at this view! Mountains and towers!
Green meadows, too, bursting with flowers!
This is the heart of the best of all possible worlds.
Much the best part of the best of all possible worlds.

CHORUS (*sings*).

Yes, it's the heart of the best of all possible worlds.
Much the best part of the best of all possible worlds.

PANGLOSS (*sings, gesturing toward the Chorus*).

Our men are lean, handsome and active.
Where have you seen girls more attractive?
None have more grace in this best of all possible worlds.
No finer race in this best of all possible worlds.

CHORUS (*sings*).

No finer race in this best of all possible worlds.
No better place in this best of all possible worlds.

PANGLOSS (*sings*).

And best of all, we now convene
With keen anticipation,
To watch a happy wedding scene
And have a celebration.

CHORUS (*sings*).

A happy celebration.

PANGLOSS (*sings*).

All hail the groom
And bride, of whom
Our hearts could not be fonder.
The love that reigns in Heaven above
Is mirrored in the marriage of

(*Candide and Cunegonde enter. Pangloss continues singing*)

Candide and Cunegonde!

CHORUS (*sings*).

Candide and Cunegonde!

PANGLOSS (*sings*).

Wherefore and hence, therefore and ergo —

CHORUS (*sings*).

Wherefore and hence, therefore and ergo —

PANGLOSS (*sings*).

All's for the best in this best of all possible worlds.

CHORUS (*sings*).

All's for the best in this best of all possible worlds.

PANGLOSS (*sings*).
Any questions?
Ask without fear.
(*Touches his head*)
I've all the answers here.
CUNEGONDE (*sings*).
Dear master, I am sure you're right
That married life is splendid.
But why do married people fight?
I cannot comprehend it.
CHORUS (*sings*).
She cannot comprehend it.
PANGLOSS (*sings*).
The private strife
Of man and wife
Is useful to the nation:
It is a harmless outlet for
Emotions which could lead to war
Or social agitation.
CHORUS (*sings*).
A brilliant explanation!
PANGLOSS (*sings*).
Therefore, it's true.
No one may doubt it:
CHORUS (*sings*).
Therefore, it's true.
No doubt about it:
PANGLOSS (*sings*).
Marriage is blest in
This best of all possible worlds.
CHORUS (*sings*).
All's for the best in
This best of all possible worlds.
PANGLOSS (*sings*).
Next question?
Deep though it be,
There's none too deep for me!
CANDIDE (*sings*).
Since marriage is divine, of course,
We cannot understand, sir,
Why should there be so much divorce.
Do let us know the answer.

CHORUS (*sings*).

Do let us know the answer.

PANGLOSS (*sings*).

Why, marriage, boy,
Is such a joy,
So lovely a condition,
That many ask no better than
To wed as often as they can,
In happy repetition.

CHORUS (*sings*).

A brilliant exposition!

PANGLOSS, CANDIDE, CUNEGONDE (*sing*).

Wherefore and hence, therefore and ergo . . .

CHORUS (*sings*).

Wherefore and hence, therefore and ergo . . .

PANGLOSS (*sings*).

All's for the best in this best of all possible worlds.

CHORUS (*sings*).

All's for the best in this best of all possible worlds.

PANGLOSS, CUNEGONDE, CANDIDE (sing).

A brilliant exposition!
Q.E.D.
All's for the best.

ALL (*sing*).

A brilliant exposition in this best of all
Possible, possible, possible, possible worlds!
A brilliant exposition! Q.E.D.

(*The Baron Thunder Ten Tronch enters.*)

CUNEGONDE (*speaks*).

Good morning, dear Father.

BARON. A good morning, dear children, on your wedding day. (*Maxmillian enters. He is hung with medals*) Good morning, son. Where did you get the medals?

MAXIMILLIAN. Father, I have one of my headaches.

BARON. Have you had a headache for three years? Why didn't you join the army when I sent for you? (*Points to Candide*) My adopted son never left my side. He earned his medals.

MAXIMILLIAN. I sprained my ankle, Father. I have soft bones. I've explained it all before —

BARON. Candide didn't worry about his bones. He worried about mine.

MAXIMILLIAN. He has strong bones. Lower-class bones.

PANGLOSS. Baron, here are the marriage contracts in Latin, Greek and Westphalian dialect. A record for history.

MAXIMILLIAN (*to Cunegonde*). As your brother — and the future head of this house, God forbid Father ever dies, please God — I must once again protest your marriage to a man of unknown birth. And if you hadn't paid so much for your wedding dress, I could have had a new uniform.

CUNEGONDE (*laughs*). But it's a nice uniform. And certainly not touched by war.

BARON (*to Candide*). Come sign the marriage contracts, my boy.

CANDIDE (*coming to table*). Oh, sir, I can make no marriage settlement. You know I have nothing to give Cunegonde.

PANGLOSS. You have a pure heart. A woman wants nothing else.

CANDIDE (*to Baron*). You have been much too generous with Cunegonde's dowry. I cannot accept —

BARON. I haven't given her a damn thing.

CANDIDE. Thank you, sir. Thank you. And now I have a great favor to ask of you —

BARON (*very quickly*). I can't afford anything. I must look out for my old age. What is it?

CANDIDE. This is the happiest day of my life and it pains me to think we have a prisoner in the house. Could we invite the King of Hesse to have wine and cake with us at the marriage feast?

(*Baron nods, signals to a Soldier. The Soldier exits to fetch the King of Hesse.*)

PANGLOSS (*to Candide, as they move away*). Your old teacher is proud of you. Now make me happy. Throw yourself back through the years and repeat your lesson: tell me the golden rules of a high-minded Westphalian man.

CANDIDE. The heart of man is generous; the honor of a man is all he needs on life's journey; the poor must be respected since they are always with us; the beauty of noble thought; the treasure that is sweet, sacred womanhood —

PANGLOSS (*to a Pretty Girl who passes*). Good morning, Paquette.

PAQUETTE. You owe me money.

PANGLOSS (*to Candide*). Women are sometimes difficult. But if they weren't difficult perhaps nobody would pay any attention to them. Tell me, my boy, do you know much of women? Have you, I mean did you, perhaps, in a daring minute —

CANDIDE. What, sir? I don't know what you mean.

PANGLOSS (*delighted*). Oh, I am so glad. So glad. (*To another*

Pretty Girl) Hello, Irmentrude. You look charming — (*Quickly*) I paid you. (*She disappears.*)

PANGLOSS (*Hurries to Cunegonde*). Cunegonde, my dear little girl, make your old teacher happy. Repeat the words of a high-minded Westphalian lady and swear that you will live by them.

CUNEGONDE. The honor of a woman is all she needs on life's journey. Dr. Pangloss, is that really all a woman needs?

PANGLOSS. Nothing else.

CUNEGONDE. Do you like my dress?

PANGLOSS. Continue, dear girl: The treasure that is sweet, sacred womanhood —

CUNEGONDE. Treasure. Yes, sir. Do you think it will rain? If it rains, my hair won't curl — (*Pats Pangloss affectionately*) I'm a bad pupil. I always was. But don't be angry with me.

(*Pangloss smiles, kisses her, and moves to Maximillian.*)

PANGLOSS. Maximillian, I have a new medal for you. Come along. (*They exit.*)

BARON (*to Cunegonde*). And how's my pretty daughter? Nervous as a bride should be?

CUNEGONDE. No, Father. I am not nervous.

BARON (*as he exits*). Oh, my God. Neither was your mother.

CANDIDE. We're alone. We shouldn't be.

CUNEGONDE. Why not? What silly old customs. We'll be married in a few minutes. Would you like to see my veil?

(*She moves toward him. He draws back.*)

CANDIDE. Cunegonde, you know that I am forbidden to see the wedding veil —

CUNEGONDE. For a daring hero, you're not very daring.

CANDIDE. I respect you and I —

CUNEGONDE. You should respect me. I'm very pure.

CANDIDE. You need hardly tell me such a thing.

CUNEGONDE. I've never even thought about another man. I've never kissed another man.

CANDIDE (*amazed*). Of course not, Cunegonde.

CUNEGONDE. I think you should apologize, darling.

CANDIDE. I do. (*Bewildered*) Indeed I do.

CUNEGONDE. All right. I forgive. Now where are we going on our honeymoon?

CANDIDE. Well, we'll stay here and take a nice picnic basket — (*Sadly*) I can't take you anywhere, Cunegonde. You know I have nothing.

CUNEGONDE. I don't want anything, darling. And anyway, Father's rich.

CANDIDE. I won't take anything from your father. (*Desperately*) Cunegonde, I will work for you, I will give my life for you, but that isn't much to offer. I can't even give you a house of your own —

CUNEGONDE. Darling, darling. We've said all this before. I don't want houses or dresses or jewelry — they're all rather vulgar, aren't they? I'll live in this dress the rest of my life. These shoes will last me until death. I want nothing. Absolutely nothing but you.

CANDIDE (*sings*).

Soon, when we feel we can afford it,
We'll build a modest little farm.

CUNEGONDE (*sings*).

We'll buy a yacht and live aboard it,
Rolling in luxury and stylish charm.

CANDIDE.

Cows and chickens.

CUNEGONDE.

Social whirls.

CANDIDE.

Peas and cabbage.

CUNEGONDE.

Ropes of pearls.

CANDIDE.

Soon there'll be little ones beside us;
We'll have a sweet Westphalian home.

CUNEGONDE.

Somehow we'll grow as rich as Midas;
We'll live in Paris when we're not in Rome.

CANDIDE.

Smiling babies.

CUNEGONDE.

Marble halls.

CANDIDE.

Sunday picnics.

CUNEGONDE.

Costume balls.

CUNEGONDE.

Oh, won't my robes of silk and satin
Be chic! I'll have all that I desire.

CANDIDE.

Pangloss will tutor us in Latin
And Greek, while we sit before the fire.

CUNEGONDE.

Glowing rubies.

CANDIDE.

Glowing logs.

CUNEGONDE.

Faithful servants.

CANDIDE.

Faithful dogs.

CUNEGONDE.

We'll round the world enjoying high life;
All will be pink champagne and gold.

CANDIDE.

We'll lead a rustic and a shy life,
Feeding the pigs and sweetly growing old.

CUNEGONDE.

Breast of peacock.

CANDIDE.

Apple pie.

CUNEGONDE.

I love marriage.

CANDIDE.

So do I.

CUNEGONDE.

Oh happy pair!
Oh, happy we!
It's very rare
How we agree.

BOTH.

Oh happy pair!
Oh, happy we!
It's very rare
How we agree.
Oh happy pair!
Oh, happy we!
It's very rare
How we agree!

(*The people of the scene return to the stage.*)

CANDIDE (*moves to the King of Hesse*). I would like to make you welcome at my wedding feast. Can you forget old battles on this happy day?

HESSE. I am happy to forget old battles. I don't like battles. I hate war.

(*They shake hands and Candide moves away. The General of the Hessian army appears, hiding behind a pillar, and taps Hesse on the shoulder.*)

HESSE'S GENERAL (*in a whisper*). Your Majesty.

HESSE. Oh, my God, what are you doing here?

HESSE'S GENERAL. Your Majesty, precisely at noon you will be rescued.

HESSE. I don't want to be rescued. I don't want to go home. I like being a prisoner. Go away, please.

HESSE'S GENERAL. We will not pay your ransom. We have been in conference all night and have decided it is cheaper to fight.

HESSE. Please leave me alone. I'm sick of war —

HESSE'S GENERAL. The honor of Hesse calls for the destruction of Westphalia. Have a little honor, Your Majesty. (*He creeps off.*)

PANGLOSS. We shall now sing the first eighteen stanzas of the wedding chorale, omitting the eleventh, twelfth and thirteenth stanzas which have to do with fertility festivals. We shall use the Saint Stanislaus version.

CHORUS (*sings*).

We subjects of this Barony
Are gathered here in pride and glee
To hail the lovely bride-to-be
And graft upon her noble tree
The flower of chivalry.

(*The General of the Hessian army appears, signaling to his men. They invade Westphalia. Through the noise of battle, we hear the cries of Westphalian Ladies, the outraged shouts of Westaphalian Men. We see Cunegonde carried off by the General as Candide rushes to her defense. Ladies rush across the stage in panic as Hessian Soldiers pursue them. In the midst of the excitement, Pangloss climbs on the wedding table.*)

PANGLOSS. Gentlemen! Gentlemen! I have never before in my life used strong words, but I am forced to say this is unsporting. (*He is knocked off the table and disappears.*)

(*The last figures in the battle disappear. The stage is empty. After a second, the Baron and Maximillian appear, struggle toward each other and fall to the ground. Cunegonde, without her wedding dress, appears and falls to the ground trying to reach her father. Pangloss appears and struggles to reach the three figures.*)

PANGLOSS. Tut, tut, the good Baron. Tut, tut, the good Maximillian. (*He moves toward Cunegonde.*)

PANGLOSS. Cunegonde. Cunegonde. Poor, pretty child. (*He falls as Candide comes stumbling on.*)

CANDIDE (*calling*). Cunegonde, Cunegonde —

PANGLOSS. Candide — (*Candide runs to him*) Cunegonde is dead. Westphalia is destroyed. Don't cry, don't stay to mourn us. The world is beautiful — go forth and see it.

CANDIDE. My Cunegonde —

PANGLOSS. Yes, I know. But think of it this way: If she hadn't died she'd never have been born. There is some sweetness in every woe. The world will be good to you, kind to you. Go now.

(*Music begins. Candide moves slowly out of Westphalia. Lights dim and come up as Candide travels from Westphalia to Lisbon.*)

Scene 1A.

SCENE: *The frame of a house is rolled onstage.*

Inside the house a Woman and a Man are sitting at a table, eating their large dinner and throwing away the food that does not please them.

CANDIDE (*to the Man and the Woman*). Please, have you any work for me? (*No answer*) I have traveled a long way. Could I rest in your stables?

MAN. No.

CANDIDE. Could I have a little of your garbage?

WOMAN. Certainly not.

(*The house rolls offstage.*)

CANDIDE (*sings*).

My world is dust now,
And all I loved is dead.
Oh, let me trust now

In what my master said:
"There is a sweetness in every woe."
It must be so. It must be so.
The dawn will find me
Alone in some strange land.
But men are kindly;
They'll give a helping hand.
So said my master, and he must know.
It must be so. It must be so.

(*The frame of three houses is wheeled on stage. Candide knocks on first door. A woman appears.*)

CANDIDE. Bread, ma'am? (*She shuts the door. He knocks on second door. A Man appears*) A little water, sir? (*The Man makes an angry gesture. Candide moves on to third door. A Man hands him a loaf of bread. Candide stares at the bread, unbelieving*) Thank you, sir. You are a Christian.

MAN. How dare you? I am an atheist.

CANDIDE. I don't know what that is.

MAN. Never mind. Go your way. God bless you.

(*Candide moves away as the market square of Lisbon is wheeled onstage.*)

Scene 2.

SCENE: *The market square of Lisbon. The day of the famous earthquake. There are a variety of booths, a bear on a chain, and an animal cage presided over by a Man in Arab costume. A few of the Boothkeepers are eating their breakfast, getting ready for the Crowd.*

Candide comes wandering in and stares at those who are eating. He does not see Pangloss who, in beggar's rags, is sitting in a corner.

TWO GIRLS (*with a dog, sing*).
What a day, what a day,
For an auto-da-fé!
What a sunny summer sky!

TWO BARKERS (*sing*).

Big and small, one and all
Will be itching to buy,
Everyone in town
Is coming down
So raise the prices high!

Hurry hurry hurry
Hurry hurry hurry, right this way!

(*Candide joins the Crowd.*)

TWO OTHER BARKERS (*sing*).

Hurry hurry hurry
Hurry hurry hurry
Hurry hurry hurry, don't delay!

ALCHEMIST *and* JUNKMAN.

Pots and pans!
Metal cans!

JUNKMAN.

Bought or traded or sold!

ALCHEMIST.

I can turn them into gold!

ALCHEMIST *and* JUNKMAN.

Fans and pots
And whatnots

JUNKMAN

Trading new ones for old!

ALCHEMIST.

For a tiny fee
My alchemy
Can turn them into gold!

DOCTOR.

Here be powders and pills
For your fevers and chills.
I've a cure safe and sure
For whatever your ills.
For a fit of migraine,
Or a pox on the brain
Here's an herb that will curb any pain!

WINESELLER.

Here be bags full of wine.
Here be nectars divine

From the Volga, the Po,
And the Rhône and the Rhine.
Sherry sweet, sherry dry,
And a golden Tokay,
And a pale British ale you must try.

BEAR MAN.

See the great Russian bear
In his elegant lair,
As he trots a gavotte
With his nose in the air!
Then he does a pliée,
And a series of gay
Somersaults as he waltzes away!

CROWD (*running to bear booth*).

Can a great Russian bear
Have an elegant lair?
Can he trot a gavotte
With his nose in the air?
Can he do a pliée
And a series of gay
Somersaults as he waltzes away?

(*The bear dances.*)

JUNKMAN.

Any kind of metal
Any kind of metal
Any kind of metal bought and sold!

ALCHEMIST.

Any kind of metal
Any kind of metal
Any kind of metal turned to gold!

MAN *and* WIFE (*with junk cart*).

Silken hose, furbelows,
Ribbons, laces, and bows!
Buy a bonnet for your spouse!

TWO WHORES (*in Crowd*).

Sailor boy, sailor boy,
If you're looking for joy,
Step along before the crowd arrives
And have one on the house!

LETTERWRITER (*in Crowd*).

Here be paper and quill.
Let me draw up your will.

If a debt isn't met
I will write you a bill.
Every letter is planned
So that all understand
Every line of my fine flowing hand!

FISHWIVES (*in Crowd; sing in turn*).

Here be shrimp, here be fish,
Caviar by the dish!
I have garfish and starfish
And squid if you wish!
Here be mussels and ray!
And an octopus they
Caught today in the Bay of Biscay!

MAN (*carrying a box of fighting cocks*).

Here be fierce fighting cocks
Trammeled up in a box!
Every bird has a murderous
Spur on its hocks!
You will crow with delight
'Til a bird wins the fight —
Bet me which, and get rich if you're right!

(*Two toy cocks fight with each other.*)

ALL MEN MERCHANTS, BARKERS, ETC.

Hurry hurry hurry
Hurry hurry hurry
Hurry hurry hurry, come and buy!

ALL WOMEN WHORES, FISHWIVES, ETC.

Hurry hurry hurry
Hurry hurry hurry
Hurry hurry hurry, come and try!

CROWD.

What a day, what a day
For an auto-da-fé!
There's a gleam in every eye!

ALL.

What a day, what a day
For an auto-da-fé!
There's a bee in every bonnet
And a thumb in every pie!

CONJURER (*as he raises curtain on cage*). AAAAAAAYYYYYYY have an announcement!

(*The Crowd stops singing, moves toward him. In the animal*

cage we see the Infant. She is about twenty-five, but is very small and is dressed in child's costume. She is drinking from a glass which she hastily puts aside.)

Come look on the Infant Casmira.
Deep in a trance that has lasted for three days.
Only six years old, she has powers to see underground.
She will tell you the future, she never is wrong,
She never has made a mistake, and all for
Two real. Two shilling. Two kopeck. Two lira.
Awaken her with the sound of silver —

(*Crowd throws coins. The Infant Casmira begins to whirl about.*)

CROWD.

Is that a child?
She's rather wild to be a child!

INFANT CASMIRA.

Ha ha ha ha
Ha ha ha ha ha ha
Ha ha ha ha
Ha ha ha ha ha ha ha!

CROWD.

What does she say? What does she say?
What does she say?

INFANT CASMIRA.

Hoo hoo hoo hoo
Hoo hoo hoo hoo hoo hoo
Hoo hoo hoo hoo
Hoo hoo hoo hoo hoo hoo hoo!

CONJURER.

She say:
There is terrible trouble.
Pretty soon there is gonna be terrible trouble.
Ay ay ay, such a terrible trouble.
Ay ay ay ay!

CROWD.

What can it be? What can it be?
What can it be?

INFANT CASMIRA.

Ho ho ho ho
Ho ho ho ho ho ho
Ho ho ho ho
Ho ho ho ho ho ho ho!

CROWD.

What does it mean? What does it mean?
What does it mean?

INFANT CASMIRA.

Hee hee hee hee
Hee hee hee hee hee hee
Hee hee hee hee
Hee hee hee hee hee hee hee!

CONJURER.

She say:
She cannot see the trouble.
Because her eyesight is not enough clearly.
The only cure is to place two gold coins on her eyelids.

(Somebody in Crowd throws coins.)

Thank you. Now she will tell.

CROWD.

What does she see? What does she see?
What does she see?

INFANT CASMIRA.

Heh heh heh heh
Heh heh heh heh heh heh
Heh heh heh heh
Heh heh heh heh heh heh heh!

CROWD.

What is it now? What it is now?
What is it now?

INFANT CASMIRA.

Ha ha ha ha
Ha ha ha ha ha ha
Ha ha ha ha
Ha ha ha ha ha ha ha!

CONJURER.

She say:
That the earth gonna quake
And the ground gonna shake
All the town falling down
All the buildings will break
Is a terrible sound
Coming up from the ground
But she don't say the name of the town!

CROWD.

Ah!

We have to know! We have to know!
We have to know!

INFANT CASMIRA.

Hoo hoo hoo hoo
Hoo hoo hoo hoo hoo hoo
Hoo hoo hoo hoo
Hoo hoo hoo hoo hoo hoo hoo!

CONJURER.

She say:
Spirit voices are fading.
Two more gold coins placed against her eardrums
Will bring back her hearing.

(*Coins are thrown.*)

Thank you.

(*Infant passes out.*)

Sorry.
Thousand apologies. She is in trance again.
Come back tomorrow!
Another revelation tomorrow!

CROWD.

Ha ha ha ha, ha ha ha ha,
Wonderful child!
What a hoo hoo hoo hoo, hoo hoo hoo hoo
Wonderful child!
What a wonderful child! Wonderful child! Wonderful child!
What a child!

(*Crowd moves away from the Infant.*)

DOCTOR (*calling to people in the square*). I have philosophic aurate. I have mercury, the cure for many affairs of the heart.

(*At the mention of the word "mercury," Pangloss lying on the gibbet steps, rises and shuffles toward the Doctor.*)

I have a new stock of charmed nutmegs for the unloved, and fresh minted vinegar for ladies who have loved too well.

BEAR MAN. This bear is two hundred and ten years old, and a husband still.

SAILOR. Where's his wife?

BEAR MAN. Where is yours?

(*A Sailor is having his teeth examined by the Doctor. Pangloss stands watching.*)

DOCTOR. Here be a new salt sea solution to increase the duties of the male. For males who have over-increased their duties here be a mercury solution. Moral instructions enclosed.

(*The Doctor offers bottle to Pangloss.*)

Sir?

PANGLOSS. How much, good doctor?

DOCTOR. Five reis.

PANGLOSS. I have only one coin. But, perhaps, in the kindness of your heart, from one philosopher to another, for that is what I am, you would like to give me —

(*The Doctor tries to bat him with a broom. Candide gets in the way and is shoved against Pangloss.*)

CANDIDE. Excuse me, sir. I stumbled.

PANGLOSS. And if you had not stumbled against my head, I would no longer know that I had a head, so weak am I from hunger.

CANDIDE. And I hurt you because I am weak from hunger. The weak kick the weak. That's sad, isn't it?

PANGLOSS. Not at all. If the weak didn't kick the weak, then the strong would kick the weak and certainly that would hurt far more. Things are for the best in this best of all possible worlds.

CANDIDE (*picks up Pangloss, stares at him*). It cannot be. It cannot be. I have seen a miracle. What is your name? Who are you?

PANGLOSS. Candide! My boy —

CANDIDE. But I left you dead in Westphalia —

PANGLOSS. Three days after my death, I woke up. But no stone was left in the castle, no tree left standing — (*Softly*) All were dead around me.

CANDIDE. Dear, good master. You bear the marks of brave battle.

PANGLOSS (*shakes his head*). The marks I bear are the marks of love.

CANDIDE (*he cries*). But, dear master, how can anything so noble as love produce, forgive me, so disgusting an effect upon the human body?

PANGLOSS. You remember our pretty maid servant, Paquette?

CANDIDE. Indeed, master. You were very kind to her.

PANGLOSS. Yes I was. Some men, not philosophers, would think she repaid my kindness in an odd fashion. But I —

PANGLOSS (*sings*).

Dear boy, you will not hear me speak
With sorrow or with rancor

Of what has paled my rosy cheek
And blasted it with canker;
'Twas Love, great Love, that did the deed
Through Nature's gentle laws,
And how should ill effects proceed
From so divine a cause?

Sweet honey comes from bees that sting,
As you are well aware;
To one adept in reasoning,
Whatever pains disease may bring
Are but the tangy seasoning
To Love's delicious fare.

Columbus and his men, they say,
Conveyed the virus hither
Whereby my features rot away
And vital powers wither;
Yet had they not traversed the seas
And come infected back,
Why, think of all the luxuries
That modern life would lack!

All bitter things conduce to sweet,
As this example shows;
Without the little spirochete
We'd have no chocolate to eat,
Nor would tobacco's fragrance greet
The European nose.

Each nation guards its native land
With cannon and with sentry,
Inspectors look for contraband
At every port of entry,
Yet nothing can prevent the spread
Of Love's divine disease:
It rounds the world from bed to bed
As pretty as you please.

Men worship Venus everywhere,
As plainly may be seen;
The decorations which I bear
Are nobler than the Croix de Guerre,

And gained in service of our fair
And universal Queen.

CANDIDE. But, Master, you look so awful —

(There is a grotesque fanfare of rams' horns as the Grand Inquisitor, in fine robes, followed by two small Inquisitors, who are followed by two smaller Professors, march onstage. Two Guards bring on three Prisoners — two men and a woman — and push them into a corner.)

CANDIDE. What is happening?

PANGLOSS. The men of the Inquisition. I have always wished to visit with the educated gentlemen.

(He starts toward them but the Infant Casmira, lying on the floor of her cage, lets out a series of shrieks.)

FIRST SMALL INQUISITOR. There is that terrible child again.

GRAND INQUISITOR (*frightened*). What does she say?

CONJURER (*leans down, listens*). She says the earth will shake.

GRAND INQUISITOR. Nonsense.

(The earth begins to shake. People are thrown off balance, and fall to the ground. There are screams and angry, threatening shouts to the Inquisitor.)

GRAND INQUISITOR (*shouting*). Quiet! Have faith. We have taken council. We have found an unfailing remedy for earthquakes. Witches and wizards have moved among us: we will bring them to trial.

SECOND SMALL INQUISITOR (*calling to the Guard*). Bring on the prisoners.

(The Guard pushes forward a Middle-aged Man. The fanfare is repeated.)

What is the charge?

FIRST PROFESSOR. Eating ham and eggs and throwing away the ham, as his people did before him.

GRAND INQUISITOR. Most certainly such a deed contributes to the formation of an earthquake, as can be demonstrated sub codici Papae Marcelli.

(Music.)

THE THREE INQUISITORS (*to Crowd*).

Shall we let the sinner go or try him?

MALE CHORUS.

Try him!

THE THREE INQUISITORS.

Is the culprit innocent or guilty?

MALE CHORUS.

Guilty!

THE THREE INQUISITORS.

Shall we pardon him or hang him?

MALE CHORUS.

Hang him!

(*Bell rings.*)

MIXED CHORUS.

What a lovely day, what a jolly day,
What a day for a holiday!

(*Repeat words.*)

He don't mix meat and dairy:
He won't eat humble pie:
So sing a miserere
And hang the bastards high!

(*The Guards drag off the Middle-aged Man, as the Inquisitors mumble among themselves. An Old Man is pushed forward by a Guard.*)

GRAND INQUISITOR. What is the charge?

FIRST PROFESSOR. The overbuying of candles for the overreading of books in subversive association with associates.

OLD MAN. Great judge, I learned to read as a very young man. I can see now that I was a tool and a fool. I was poor, I was lonely —

FIRST PROFESSOR. Who are your associates? Be quick.

OLD MAN. Yes, sir. Well, there was Emmanuel, Lilybelle, Lionel, and Dolly and Molly and Polly, of course. And my Ma and my Pa and my littlest child. A priest, deceased, and my uncle and my aunt. The president, his resident, and the sister of my wife —

GRAND INQUISITOR. All right. All right. Thank you for your splendid cooperation.

(*There is a fanfare.*)

(*Music.*)

THE THREE INQUISITORS.

Shall we doubt the charges or approve them?

MALE CHORUS.

Approve them!

THE THREE INQUISITORS.

Shall we show this helpful witness mercy?

MALE CHORUS.

Mercy!

THE THREE INQUISITORS.

Shall we give him five or ten years?

MALE CHORUS.

Ten years!

MIXED CHORUS.

At first he lied and tricked us,
But now he's sung his tale.
So bid him Benedictus
And let him sing in jail!

(*A Woman is pushed forward by the Guards.*)

GRAND INQUISITOR. What is the charge?

FIRST PROFESSOR. Well, sir, the evidence is long —

GRAND INQUISITOR (*quickly*). Death by hanging.

PANGLOSS. Oh, I say. (*Advances*) Really, gentlemen. (*Bows*) I am a guest from a distant land —

GRAND INQUISITOR. Death by hanging.

(*The Guard moves toward the astonished Pangloss.*)

CANDIDE (*steps forward*). Good gentlemen! Professor Pangloss is a man of eminent standing, a mystic and a metaphysician —

SECOND PROFESSOR. Who is this boy with the foreign accent?

CANDIDE. I am one who believes in the goodness of man in the best of all possible worlds.

GRAND INQUISITOR. Death by hanging.

PANGLOSS. Gentlemen. Your methods are not legal ——

(*Music.*)

THE THREE INQUISITORS.

Are our methods legal or illegal?

MALE CHORUS.

Legal!

THE THREE INQUISITORS.

Are we judges of the law, or laymen?

MALE CHORUS.

Amen!

THE THREE INQUISITORS.

Shall we hang them or forget them?

MALE CHORUS.

Get them!

MIXED CHORUS.

When foreigners like this come
To criticize and spy,

We chant a Pax Vobiscum
And hang the bastards high!

(The Guards come forward in sanbenitos and put a paper mitre on the head of each Prisoner. The mitres and sanbenitos are painted with flames, devils without claws and tails. The Prisoners go toward the gibbet steps.)

ALL.

What a day, what a day,
Oh, what a day, what a day,
Oh, what a day,
What a perfect day for hanging!

(Bells begin to peal as the Prisoners are lined up at the gibbet steps.)

What a lovely day,
What a jolly day,
What a day for a holiday!

(Repeat three times.)

At last we can be cheery,
The danger's passed us by.
So chant a Dies Irae!
We've hung the bastards high!
Oh, what a day!

(Music ends.)

EXECUTIONER (*to the Prisoners as they go up the gibbet steps*). Three reis, please. And three more will grease your road to eternity.

PANGLOSS. I have two reis. Could I get a little bread for my friend and me? We are hungry.

EXECUTIONER. Bread is the heaviest thing you can eat. Gives you indigestion at a time like this.

CANDIDE (*to Executioner*). I have nothing. But then I have done nothing.

EXECUTIONER. That's the hardest way to die, boy. From my long experience I can tell you that the guilty die easier than the innocent. They have a decent sense of accomplishment.

(Pangloss and Candide disappear.)

CROWD (*singing*).

We've had a nice fiesta,
The heretics are dead.
It's time for our siesta,
So let's go home to bed.

GRAND INQUISITOR (*picks up his papers, books, etc., and addresses the crowd*). I declare now an hour of prayer. Go to your houses and make proper donations to the Inquisition — all donations are tax deductible — and fast until the dinner hour. The danger is over.

(*The earth quakes. People are thrown to the ground. The scenery falls apart.*)

Scene 2A.

SCENE: *Travels from Lisbon to Paris.*

CANDIDE (*appears, singing to himself*).

My master told me
That men are loving-kind;
Yet now behold me
Ill-used and sad of mind.
Men must have kindness I cannot see.
It must be me. It must be me.

My master told me
The world is warm and good;
It deals more coldly
Than I had dreamt it would.
There must be sunlight I cannot see.
It must be me. It must be me.

(*He moves across stage toward a group of Beggars. The Beggars stare at him.*)

FIRST BEGGAR. You didn't sound like a beggar coming down the road. Better learn to walk slower, boy, and save your feet.

CANDIDE. I'm not a beggar.

SECOND BEGGAR. You're a king?

FIRST BEGGAR. I don't think he's a king.

THIRD BEGGAR. You're a general?

FIRST BEGGAR. I don't think he's a general.

CANDIDE. I was a soldier —

THIRD BEGGAR. You don't look it.

CANDIDE (*with pain*). *I am not a beggar.*

FIRST BEGGAR (*gets up*). Let's move on to Paris: it's the beggar's city. There's always a party in Paris. (*They start off. Candide does not move. The First Beggar turns to Candide*) Want to come with us, *soldier?*

(*They move off. Slowly Candide follows them. The frame of a house is rolled on. A painted, elderly Lady is standing in the window.*)

LADY. *Bon soir, monsieur.* You are bemused with wine?

CANDIDE. Oh, no, sir. I am bemused with weariness.

LADY. I am not a sir. I am a madame.

CANDIDE. Please excuse me. My head goes about from hunger.

LADY. Come in. Do. Cleaned, you would be handsome. At six o'clock, of course, you must disappear. My lover is very jealous. . . .

CANDIDE. Your lover? I am indeed in Paris.

LADY. The outskirts of Paris.

(*The lights fade and come up on the ballroom of a fine Paris house.*)

Scene 3.

SCENE: *Paris. The ballroom of a house in Paris. The garden can be seen. Left stage, a group of screens form a boudoir.*

AT RISE: *The guests are waltzing about. Outside, in the garden, the Beggars and Candide are staring at the party.*

A MAN (*to his partner*). Who is giving this party?

HIS PARTNER. Two rich gentlemen. To introduce their niece, as one calls such women this year.

THE MAN. What's their names?

ANOTHER MAN. The Marquis something and the Sultan something. What difference does it make? The wine is good.

(*An Old Lady, dressed to the nines, carrying something high above her head, comes dodging and tripping and falling among the dancers. She is followed by two eager gentlemen, the Marquis and the Sultan.*)

MARQUIS (*nervous, to the Old Lady*). But where is she, where is madame? The guests have been waiting for an hour.

OLD LADY (*giggling*). She didn't have the proper garters. We had to send to the jeweler. . . . (*Coquettishly opens the box*) Would it please you both to have a little, little look?

MARQUIS. Oh, yes!

SULTAN. It would please me to have a look at the lady.

OLD LADY. Oh, be patient, dear. It's her first Paris party, and she is nervous. How well I remember my first Paris party. Not like this, I can tell you. You had to present proof of seven titled ancestors at the door. That was the night the Duke of Hamburg saw me and killed himself. . . .

SULTAN. So all right, already. (*Moves toward boudoir*) I'm going in.

OLD LADY (*hastily*). Be patient. This girl has come from the cloisters, pure and innocent. You've been very lucky, you boys.

MARQUIS (*to Sultan*). We've been very lucky, us boys.

SULTAN. I'm going to break down the door.

MARQUIS. No, no, cousin. We cannot go into her room unless she invites us.

SULTAN. We pay for this house, you and I, and we've been in that room before.

OLD LADY. That's different. She's not getting undressed. She's getting dressed.

(*She sweeps into the boudoir.*)

SULTAN. I say we do these things better in the East. The girl would have been ready on time, or she'd have been dead.

MARQUIS. Oh, charming women make their own rules. And you know that you have found her charming.

SULTAN. *Charming!* In one generation you have learned to talk like these people. Such words. Charming. She's a woman. You and I are cousins and so it is sensible to split the expense. We are partners in this woman as we are partners in business. So please remember to observe the proper hours and days. And do not fall in love, as you usually do with these women.

MARQUIS. Oh, no, not in love. After all, she's as much yours as mine. (*To guests*) Madame will be with us very soon. In the meantime, supper is in the yellow room.

SULTAN. Cost a fortune.

MARQUIS. Giant truffles, grilled breast of lake peacock.

SULTAN. Cost a fortune.

MARQUIS. Boiled caviar —

SULTAN. And stewed bank notes from the family business. (*Guests, Marquis and Sultan exit.*)

(*The lights dim in the ballroom, come up in the boudoir.*)

OLD LADY (*to a Girl, who is crying*). Now what's the matter?

GIRL. I'm crying.

OLD LADY. You cry the way other people eat . . . right on time.

GIRL. I am so ashamed of my present life.

OLD LADY. Ach! You never had it so good.

GIRL. I've told you over and over again that I am Cunegonde, Baroness Thunder Ten Tronch of Westphalia.

OLD LADY. Then how come I found you in a Paris gutter?

CUNEGONDE. Last night I dreamed of home. I remembered my wedding day.

OLD LADY. You *married?* You didn't tell me that when I introduced you to these two nice gentlemen.

CUNEGONDE. No, I'm not married. The war came on the day of the wedding.

OLD LADY. Is that so? Ah, well, that's the way it happened to most of us. Sometimes war. Sometimes the man changed his mind. Where's the bridegroom?

CUNEGONDE. Dead. Trying to save me from rape . . .

OLD LADY. Died to save you from rape? Oh, aren't men silly? (*Old Lady exits from boudoir.*)

CUNEGONDE. Here I am in Paris. I don't even know how I got here. My heart broken. And yet I am forced to glitter, forced to be gay. (*She sings.*)

Glitter and be gay,
That's the part I play.
Here am I in Paris, France,
Forced to bend my soul
To a sordid role,
Victimized by bitter, bitter circumstance.

Alas for me, had I remained
Beside my lady mother,
My virtue had remained unstained
Until my maiden hand was gained
By some Grand Duke or other.

Ah, 'twas not to be;
Harsh necessity
Brought me to this gilded cage.
Born to higher things,

Here I droop my wings,
Singing of a sorrow nothing can assuage.

(*Suddenly brighter.*)
And yet, of course, I rather like to revel, ha, ha!
I have no strong objection to champagne, ha, ha!
My wardrobe is expensive as the devil, ha, ha!
Perhaps it is ignoble to complain . . .

Enough, enough
Of being basely tearful!
I'll show my noble stuff
By being bright and cheerful!

Ha, ha ha ha . . .
(*Reciting, to music.*)
Pearls and ruby rings. . . .
Ah, how can worldly things
Take the place of honor lost?
Can they compensate
For my fallen state,
Purchased as they were at such an awful cost?

Bracelets . . . lavalieres . . .
Can they dry my tears?
Can they blind my eyes to shame?
Can the brightest brooch
Shield me from reproach?
Can the purest diamond purify my name?

(*Suddenly bright again; singing as she puts on enormous bracelets.*)
And yet, of course, these trinkets are endearing, ha ha!
I'm oh, so glad my sapphire is a star, ha ha!
I rather like a twenty-carat earring, ha ha!
If I'm not pure, at least my jewels are!

(*Puts on three more bracelets.*)
Enough, enough!
I'll *take* their diamond necklace
And show my noble stuff
By being gay and reckless!

Ha ha ha ha ha . . .

Observe how bravely I conceal
The dreadful, dreadful shame I feel.
Ha ha ha ha ha, ha . . .

(*Puts on a giant diamond necklace.*)

Ha!

(*When Cunegonde finishes she is so covered with jewels, she can hardly be seen. The Old Lady enters at the end of the aria and immediately begins to rip off the jewels.*)

CUNEGONDE. No! No! I'm cold.

OLD LADY. Only married women can afford to look like whores. (*The boudoir screens disappear as Cunegonde enters the ballroom. The guests have returned to the waltz. The Marquis and the Sultan come running forward. But the Sultan is faster and rougher, and the gentle Marquis is left behind. The Sultan takes Cunegonde into the waltz. When they have waltzed for a minute, Cunegonde sees Candide in the garden. She screams.*)

MARQUIS. What — what is happening, my darling?

SULTAN. What's the matter now?

OLD LADY (*as Cunegonde is about to faint*). Madame must be alone. Pray excuse her. She isn't well.

MARQUIS. She isn't well. Oh, cousin, she's so pure, so delicate.

SULTAN (*angry*). So pure, so delicate.

MARQUIS. But, cousin, she's ill, we must send the guests away. (*The guests begin to say good night, and are followed outside by the hosts. In the boudoir, Cunegonde is pacing about. The Old Lady beckons to Candide. Candide, bewildered, tries to run away.*)

OLD LADY. Come in, come in — You poor boy. Don't be afraid.

CANDIDE. Oh — I couldn't come in here. I'm only looking for work. I'm hungry.

OLD LADY. I've been hungry many times, in many places in the world. I was most highly born and reduced very early —

CANDIDE. Who are you? Whose house is this?

(*Cunegonde appears in the ballroom and Candide stands paralyzed in disbelief.*)

CANDIDE (*singing*).

Oh. Oh. Is it true?

CUNEGONDE (*singing*).

Is it you?

CANDIDE.

Cunegonde! Cunegonde! Cunegonde!

CUNEGONDE.

Candide! Candide! Can—

OLD LADY (*speaks, interrupting song*). Your cries of love are natural, but too loud. Remember your benefactors are in the garden.

CANDIDE (*sings*).

Oh. Oh. Is it true?

CUNEGONDE (*sings*).

Is it you?

CANDIDE.

Cunegonde! Cunegonde! Cunegonde!

CUNEGONDE.

Candide! Candide! Can—

CANDIDE.

Oh. Oh. Is it true?

CUNEGONDE.

Is it you?

CANDIDE.

Cunegonde!

CUNEGONDE.

Candide!

BOTH.

Oh — my — dear — love!

CANDIDE.

Dearest, how can this be so?
You were dead, you know.
You were shot and bayoneted, too.

CUNEGONDE.

That is very true.
Ah, but love will find a way.

CANDIDE.

Then what *did* you do?

CUNEGONDE.

We'll go into that another day.
Now let's talk of you.
You are looking very well.
Weren't you clever, dear, to survive?

CANDIDE.

I've a sorry tale to tell.
I escaped more dead than alive.

CUNEGONDE.

Love of mine, where did you go?

CANDIDE.

Oh, I wandered to and fro . . .

CUNEGONDE.

Oh, what torture, oh, what pain . . .

CANDIDE.

Holland, Portugal, and Spain . . .

CUNEGONDE.

Ah, what torture . . .

CANDIDE.

Holland, Portu . . .

CUNEGONDE.

Ah, what torture . . .

CANDIDE.

I would do it all again
To find you at last!

BOTH.

Reunited after so much pain;
But the pain is past.
We are one again,
We are one at last!

One again, one at last
One again, one at last
One, one, one, one,
One
At last!

(*The Sultan and the Marquis return to the ballroom.*)

SULTAN. In the name of Allah, who is this man?

CANDIDE. Cunegonde, who is this scoundrel?

MARQUIS (*running to Cunegonde, who is crying*). My darling girl, what has happened?

CANDIDE. Gentlemen, I do not understand your presence in this house — (*Turns, bewildered, to Cunegonde*) And come to think of it, what are you doing here, Cunegonde? Who are these men? Gentlemen, this lady is my fiancée. I must demand that you leave her house, this house, whatever house, immediately —

MARQUIS (*outraged, draws his sword*). Your fiancée! You miserable beggar. How dare you —

(*As he advances on Candide, the Old Lady appears with a sword and hands it to Candide. Candide, anxious not to fight, backs away.*)

CANDIDE. Gentlemen, I have no desire to go about the world dueling. I ask only that you leave peacefully — (*He defends himself from the sword of the Marquis*) I do not understand how Cunegonde came to be here, but let me take her away in peace. She will tell you that we have loved since we were the smallest of children —

MARQUIS (*in love's pain, turns to the Sultan*). I can't believe she started so young. It's disgusting.

(*The Old Lady pushes Candide into the Marquis. The Marquis falls.*)

SULTAN. I will avenge you, my cousin. Our family, despite occasional bickerings and law suits, are as one. (*To Candide as they duel*) Do you know that you have killed the President of the Western division of the Far Eastern section of the banking house of —

(*The Old Lady trips the Sultan. He falls onto Candide's sword, and drops to the floor.*)

CANDIDE (*stands horrified. He throws down his sword and moves toward Cunegonde*). I have killed two men. I don't know why or how. I have killed because of you, and yet I don't even understand why you are here. Answer me, Cunegonde.

OLD LADY. There is no time for all that. These men are of great importance. I have seen enough trouble in my miserable life to tell you that we will all be arrested and executed for this. We must move with speed.

(*She picks up furs and jewel box.*)

CANDIDE. No. I must pay the penalty for what I have done. But before I do, I want you to tell me —

CUNEGONDE (*crying out*). Nothing. Nothing. I am here by accident. The house was empty, and I was starving, and they gave me a little food. (*The Old Lady throws her the jewel box. She catches it*) That is all. They treated me with the greatest respect — How dare you think anything else?

CANDIDE. What are those?

CUNEGONDE (*very nervous*). Jewels. My mother, the Baroness, gave them to me. You have seen her wear them —

CANDIDE. What are you saying, Cunegonde? Your mother had a little silver comb, nothing more.

CUNEGONDE. You have insulted me, Candide, and hurt me, too —

OLD LADY. Death stares us in the face, and you are insulted. Be still and allow me to think —

(A procession of Pilgrims is seen in the garden. They are moving to march music.)

PILGRIM FATHER. We are off to the new world. Any and all who wish to slough off the woes of this evil society may join us on our ocean journey to a new life. All who wish to join this loving band, come as sisters and brothers in faith —

(The procession moves off.)

OLD LADY. Come! Come! We will escape by mixing with this pious group.

CUNEGONDE (*stamping her foot*). But I don't wish to mix with a pious group. I don't wish to go to the new world —

(There is the sound of a police whistle.)

OLD LADY. Police! Be quick —

(A curtain, on which a ship is painted, is dropped on the Paris scene and the Pilgrim procession appears before it. The Old Lady, Cunegonde and Candide run to join them.)

Scene 3A.

SCENE: *A ship painted on a curtain.*

The Pilgrim procession is walking toward a gangplank.

PILGRIM FATHER (*sings*).

Come, pilgrims, to America!
Come, see the new domains of God!

ALL (*sing*).

Come, pilgrims, to America!
Come, see the new domains of God!

PILGRIM MOTHER (*sings*).

Leave France's wicked sod!
Come and dwell where Satan's hoof has never trod!

ALL (*sing*).

Come, pilgrims, to America!
Where Satan's hoof has never trod!

Alleluia. Alleluia. Alleluia. Alleluia.
Alleluia. Alleluia. Alleluia. Alleluia.

PILGRIM FATHER (*sings*).
We sail to seek God's pardon
Where innocence shall be restored
In that new Eden garden
Where man has not defied his Lord.

PILGRIM MOTHER (*sings*).
Make haste and come aboard!
Come before your hearts in error harden.

ALL (*sing*).
Come, pilgrims, to America!
Where innocence shall be restored!

CUNEGONDE *and* CANDIDE (*urged on by the Old Lady, sing with the Pilgrims*).
Alleluia. Alleluia. Alleluia. Alleluia.

ALL (*sing*).
Alleluia. Alleluia. Alleluia. Alleluia.

CAPTAIN (*speaks*). Welcome, travelers. You sail safe on a ship of the greatest comfort. Your staterooms are furnished in imported antique luxury.

PILGRIM FATHER (*sharply*). We wish no luxury. We sail to raise the rocks of America into hills of freedom.

PILGRIMS. Amen.

CAPTAIN (*to Cunegonde*). *You* will raise rocks, madame?

CUNEGONDE. Er . . .

OLD LADY (*quickly*). Certainly. That's why we have brought our furs.

CAPTAIN (*to Candide*). One thousand louis, monsieur, for you, your wife, and her duenna.

CANDIDE. Unfortunately, the lady is not my wife. She will be, however . . .

CAPTAIN. I'm afraid my ship couldn't accommodate itself to an arrangement of that character.

CANDIDE. No such thought was in my mind. We will occupy two staterooms, I assure you. What arrangement? I don't understand —

CAPTAIN (*calling*). Tickets! Tickets! Two thousand louis.

CUNEGONDE. We have no money. There wasn't time. We had to escape. . . .

OLD LADY (*hastily holds out a fur coat*). This coat of pampampalanium is worth five thousand louis without buttons or lining.

CAPTAIN. I will accept it. You will have no need of it in Mississippi.

PILGRIM FATHER. Mississippi? We were told you sail for the English colony of the north. . . .

CAPTAIN. Yes, yes, of course. We stop at Mississippi for those who wish to disembark there. That seldom happens, so we sail quickly on. (*As a few of the Pilgrims seem to hesitate*) All aboard, ladies and gentlemen. My ship has the best of food, the wittiest of company.

A PILGRIM. Wittiest of company?

PILGRIM FATHER. We spend our time in prayer.

CAPTAIN. Excellent. I know many a witty prayer. All aboard! All aboard for the new world. May you get what you deserve.

(*They move offstage as the curtain rises on Buenos Aires.*)

Scene 4

SCENE: *Buenos Aires. The wharf in front of the Governor's palace; the Governor's palace, terrace and balcony.*

AT RISE: *The Pilgrims, in chains, are being herded off the ship. Martin, a beggar street cleaner, is moving about.*

CAPTAIN (*striding off ship*). Hello, Martin. You look bad.

MARTIN. I hope so. And I'm sorry to see you looking very well. An evil occupation makes good circulation; evil connections make good complexions. (*He stares at Pilgrims*) No black slaves this time?

CAPTAIN. Times are hard. I take what I can get. I won't get much for this lot. White slaves are impractical — they show the dirt.

PILGRIM FATHER (*he is a wreck, but he is still the leader*). We demand the removal of these chains. Bring us to the representative of France in this land of Canada. . . .

(*The Captain laughs, strides off.*)

MARTIN (*to Pilgrims*). You're not the first he has brought this far afield. This miserable dump is called Buenos Aires.

That's the Governor's palace. The Captain is about to put you up on the auction block. (*There is a stunned silence. Then the Pilgrim Father collapses. The others begin to moan and cry and pray*) Oh, don't carry on so loud. All men are in slavery in this worst of all possible worlds. We choose it for ourselves.

CANDIDE (*stumbling to his feet*). Who are you?

MARTIN. A foreigner. A scholar. A beggar. A street cleaner. A pessimist.

CANDIDE (*puzzled*). Once I knew a man — he looked very like you, sir. He was a great man, kind and wise. He was an optimist and yet he used almost the same words that you . . .

MARTIN. If he was an optimist, he was neither kind nor wise, as you must know from the chains around your wrists.

CUNEGONDE. Chains. Chains. I who was born in a castle, daughter to a baron. We had seven German meals a day. I'm hungry. My mother had a sponge bath whenever she called for it, with three maids to do the soaping and one for odds and ends. My brother was white and blond. . . .

OLD LADY. I don't believe a word you say. I never have. Your German castle would not have served as stables for my father's falcons. Ask me who I am. Ask me. (*Nobody asks her*) I am the daughter of the Princess of Palestrina and a man so highly placed, of such piety, that even now I cannot disclose his name. I was beautiful, very spiritual, yet in my sixteenth year, from Constantinople to Odessa, round and round the Crimea, up and down the Black Sea . . . (*Screams*) Ask me what happened to that lovely little princess . . .

CUNEGONDE (*very angry*). A princess! (*To others*) She's my servant. I picked her out of a Paris gutter. . . .

OLD LADY (*very, very angry*). Where you were lying next to me until two rich men came along and took you to their house.

CANDIDE (*softly*). Cunegonde, every hour of this long voyage I have asked you to tell me how it was that I found you in Paris dressed in jewels, living in that great house. I know you are a virtuous woman, but please explain to me. . . .

OLD LADY. Oh, what a foolish man you are. Here we are about to be sold into slavery and you think of nothing but her virtue. Virtue. (*She laughs loudly*) Well, that was my last laugh.

CUNEGONDE (*shrieking*). You crone. You filth. You misery.

(*Cunegonde and Old Lady fight.*)

MARTIN. I've seen so much evil in my life that simply to keep my balance I am sometimes forced to believe there must be some good in this world. (*Bows to the ladies*) I am grateful to you for reminding me there isn't.

(*The Captain enters.*)

CAPTAIN. Rise up, my slaves, and march to the auction block. Welcome to the land of opportunity.

(*Martin moves behind the Captain and cuts the large key chain hanging from the Captain's arm. He throws the keys to the Pilgrims. They unlock their chains as the Captain, unaware of the loss of the keys, exits.*)

PILGRIMS. Thank you. Thank you.

MARTIN. It is typical of the insanity of man that in a minute of danger he stops to stay thank you to one who hates him.

PILGRIM FATHER. Thank you! Thank you!

(*Pilgrims run off. Four Officers come onstage. Candide and Cunegonde hide. Martin exits. One of the Officers is Maximillian.*)

FIRST OFFICER (*to Maximillian*). And how is His Excellency this morning?

MAXIMILLIAN. He's in a bad humor. He's bored. He's writing a book on the ugliness of C flat. Last week he was writing a book on the beauty of C flat.

SECOND OFFICER. What's C flat?

MAXIMILLIAN. Oh, dear boy, you Spaniards in exile are so uncultured. In Westphalia, I had a tutor from the day I was born. . . .

(*A handsome, middle-aged man appears on the balcony. He is the Governor of Buenos Aires.*)

GOVERNOR. Good morning, gentlemen. I had a wakeful night. I have analyzed every note in the scale and found them wanting. B double flat used to give me a little pleasure but even that went last night. . . .

(*Cunegonde sees Maximillian and screams. Maximillian sees her and screams. They walk toward each other in disbelief.*)

CUNEGONDE. I am Cunegonde. I had a brother. He was killed in Westphalia. His name was Maximillian.

MAXIMILLIAN (*pulls her to him*). My sister. My dear, dead sister. Weren't you dead?

CUNEGONDE. Yes, I was. It's a long story.

MAXIMILLIAN (*moves away from her*). You have fleas, Cunegonde.

GOVERNOR. That . . . that thing is your sister? Dear boy, why did you bore me with those fantasies of your noble birth?

MAXIMILLIAN. Your Excellency! My sister and I are descended from King Seidesberger and Queen Desolate of Westphalia. . . .

GOVERNOR. Oh, don't start all that again.

MAXIMILLIAN. Now you have really hurt my feelings. Please call your servants to attend my lady sister. Have the largest rooms prepared to suit her station. . . .

GOVERNOR (*laughing*). Most certainly. Bring this . . . Bring her in. (*Officer leads Cunegonde to the palace. The Governor, about to exit from balcony, calls down*) Have your sister bathed. Three or four times. Then have her peeled and painted.

CUNEGONDE (*speaks softly to Maximillian, pointing to Candide*). Dear brother, look who's there.

MAXIMILLIAN. Candide!

CANDIDE. Maximillian!

(*Candide, smiling happily, comes forward; Maximillian, with cries of surprise, moves to meet him. The Officers exit across stage with Cunegonde and the Old Lady.*)

MAXIMILLIAN. A miracle, dear brother.

CANDIDE. A miracle, dear brother.

(*They cry. Martin reenters and continues his sweeping.*)

MAXIMILLIAN. But my sister was dead. And you were dead. And Pangloss was dead. . . .

CANDIDE. No, no. Not in Westphalia. He died again in Lisbon.

MAXIMILLIAN. Oh. . . .

CANDIDE. Ah, there is so much we must tell each other. I will go backwards in the telling. Cunegonde was —

MAXIMILLIAN. I was taken to the burial ground after the Hessian victory. But a good farm woman saw that my eyelids fluttered and she conceived the most tender feelings for me.

CANDIDE. Maximillian, Cunegonde was, is —

MAXIMILLIAN. Later, a Spanish duchess conceived the most tender feelings for me. I traveled under her protection. Protection! A fine story I could tell you. . . .

CANDIDE. Cunegonde's memory is now confused, I believe, with the horrors she has seen. I don't know what to think of the stories she tells me —

MAXIMILLIAN. . . . And here I was, suddenly in Buenos Aires. (*Delighted*) My poor Candide. But I shall make your fortune. And my sister will live in the palace —

CANDIDE. We will be married on the morrow.

MAXIMILLIAN (*amazed*). I don't want to marry you.

CANDIDE. Your sister and I will be married on the morrow.

MAXIMILLIAN (*furious*). You still have the impudence to wish to marry a noble lady? You, of unknown birth, now a broken beggar . . .

CANDIDE. Maximillian! (*Gently*) That's not a very kind thing to say. Dr. Pangloss said that all men are created equal. I love your sister and she loves me. The marriage will take place immediately.

MAXIMILLIAN. You low-born climber. (*Advances on Candide in order to strike him with a glove*) I will send you to the slave block. I will throw you to the jungle.

(*Candide takes the glove from Maximillian and attempts to slap him. But before he is slapped, Maximillian drops quietly. Candide stands appalled, staring at the body.*)

CANDIDE (*moaning*). Oh, Maximillian, Maximillian. What have I done?

(*The Old Lady saunters out of the palace. She is now done up in fantastic feathers and jewels, and looks worse. She is fanning herself in a great-lady manner. She stands staring at Candide as he bends over Maximillian.*)

OLD LADY. He looked like the fainting kind.

CANDIDE. I have killed him.

OLD LADY (*crossing to Maximillian's body*). Killed him? . . . He was our protector. The situation here was obvious, although nothing is ever obvious to you. . . .

CANDIDE. What kind of man have I become? I have killed three times. Each time for love. What has love done to me?

OLD LADY (*to Candide as she hears the Governor approaching*). Hide. Hide. They will arrest you.

(*She looks around for a hiding place. Martin motions to a safe place in back of the palace. She grabs Candide, pulls him into hiding. After a second, the Governor appears. The Governor crosses to Maximillian's body.*)

GOVERNOR (*to Martin*). I loved this boy. Street cleaner! Tidy up here, please.

(*Martin comes to Maximillian, covers him with canvas, and begins to drag his body offstage. Three Officers appear.*)

FIRST OFFICER. Your Excellency, the young lady is now ready to meet you.

SECOND OFFICER. She says her name is the Baroness Cunegonde.

THIRD OFFICER. She claims that her family . . .

CUNEGONDE (*enters in a handsome dress*). I am not accustomed to appearing alone. Where is my duenna? . . . I've never in my life been alone with men — (*She sees the Governor, and bows*) Oh. Your Excellency.

GOVERNOR. Baroness Cunegonde, you look charming.

CUNEGONDE. Where is my brother?

MARTIN. Excuse me, madame. I have a message for you. Your brother has been called away. But you will meet again (*Softly*) . . . in the end.

(*He drags Maximillian's body offstage, as Old Lady appears.*)

CUNEGONDE. Oh. How nice. Thank you. Then I will move my baggage to his palace and wait his return. (*Remembering*) But I have no baggage.

GOVERNOR. And your brother has no palace. But I offer you my house.

CUNEGONDE. Thank you, sir. My duenna is with me, and my fiancé.

GOVERNOR. That is rather a large number of people. Perhaps we could put your duenna and your fiancé in a hotel.

CUNEGONDE. I don't understand, sir.

GOVERNOR. How long will it take you to understand?

CUNEGONDE. I don't understand, sir.

GOVERNOR. It's really not very hard if you keep your mind on it. I am offering you a wing of my house and a wing of my heart.

CUNEGONDE. I don't understand, sir.

GOVERNOR (*sighs*). Perhaps it will all take too long.

(*He starts back into palace.*)

OLD LADY (*desperate*). I think I understand. You are offering this innocent girl a wing of your heart. . . .

GOVERNOR. Yes. Because my heart has wings and flies about. I think it best to tell you that now.

CUNEGONDE. I don't understand, sir. . . .

GOVERNOR. I'll try once more. (*He sings*)

Poets have said
Love is undying, my love;
Don't be misled;
They were all lying, my love.

Love's on the wing,
But now while he hovers,
Let us be lovers.
One soon recovers, my love.

Soon the fever's fled,
For love's transient blessing.
Just a week in bed,
And we'll be convalescing.

Why talk of morals
When springtime is flying?
Why end in quarrels,
Reproaches and sighing,
Crying
For love?

For love undying, my love,
Is not worth trying, my love.
Never, my love,
Mention forever, my love.

Let it be lively,
Let it be lovely,
And light as a song,
But don't let it last too long!

OLD LADY (*speaking very quickly*). His Excellency is asking for your hand —

CUNEGONDE (*deeply hurt*). Hand? Oh, oh, sire — you must not take advantage of my innocence. . . .

OLD LADY. The great gentleman is proposing marriage.

GOVERNOR (*laughs*). I should like you to be my wife.

(*Old Lady waves to Cunegonde, nodding her head with violence.*)

CUNEGONDE (*softly*). Leave me, sire. I must have time to think it over.

(*The Governor bows, and exits.*)

OLD LADY (*to Cunegonde*). We are starving and have just been removed from chains. The greatest lord in South America wishes to marry you, and yet you . . .

CUNEGONDE. But I love Candide. I can't marry another man.

OLD LADY. Candide will be hunted down and executed for the murder . . . (*When Cunegonde looks bewildered and frightened*) . . . of the Marquis and the Sultan. The Paris police are on their way here now. It is your duty to marry the Governor and save Candide.

CUNEGONDE. But I don't love this man and I don't want to be unfaithful. . . .

OLD LADY. Look. Think of it this way. Marrying another man is no more unfaithful than sleeping with another man.

CUNEGONDE. Oooh! Is that true? You are so worldly.

OLD LADY. You have to live. You have to get along as best you can. (*She sings and begins dancing to the music of a tango*)

I was not born in Buenos Aires.
My father came from Rovno Gubernya.
But now I'm here . . . I'm dancing a tango:
Di dee di!
Dee di dee di!
I am easily assimilated.
I am so easily assimilated.

I never learned a human language.
My father spoke a High Middle Polish.
In one half-hour I'm talking in Spanish:
Por favor!
Toreador!
I am easily assimilated.
I am so easily assimilated.

It's easy, it's ever so easy!
I'm Spanish, I'm suddenly Spanish!

And you must be Spanish, too.
Do like the natives do.
These days you have to be
In the majority.

TWO LOCAL SEÑORES (*enter, and serenade the Old Lady*).

Tus labios rubí
Dos rosas que se abren a mí,
Conquistan mi corazón,
Y sólo con
Una canción.

(*Old Lady sings, imitating them*).

Tus labios rubí
Drei-viertel Takt, mon très cher ami,
Oui oui, sí sí, ja ja ja, yes, yes, da, da.
Je ne sais quoi.

SEÑORES (*sing as a crowd begins to gather*).

Me muero, me sale una hernia!

OLD LADY (*sings*).

A long way from Rovno Gubernya!

ALL (*including Cunegonde, who has caught the spirit*).

Tus labios rubí
Dos rosas que se abren a mí
Conquistan mi corazón
Y sólo con
Una divina canción . . .
De tus labios rubí
Rubí! Rubí!

(*Everybody is dancing. At the end of the dance Cunegonde is cheerful.*)

CUNEGONDE (*speaking*). Yes.

OLD LADY. What?

CUNEGONDE. I've made up my mind. I will marry the Governor. I will save Candide. My heart breaks.

(*Cunegonde runs into the palace. The crowd exits. The Old Lady smiles and nods. Martin reappears. Candide returns from his hiding place.*)

OLD LADY (*to Candide*). You must leave. They will arrest you.

CANDIDE. I can't leave Cunegonde.

OLD LADY. Go make your fortune and come back for us. Cunegonde will be safe. The Governor suggested that she stay and read to him at night. I think he's blind. Go quickly.

CANDIDE. That's very kind of him, but . . .

OLD LADY. Go quick. Quick. Go.

(*She exits.*)

CANDIDE. Where shall I go?

MARTIN. What difference does it make where anybody goes? Be on your way, boy.

CANDIDE. There is no place for me. Wherever I go I am beaten and starved. I mean no harm to anybody and yet I have murdered three men in the name of love. I am alone now. . . .

MARTIN. So are we all. It is the worst of all possible worlds, and if it wasn't, we would make it so.

CANDIDE. No, no. Although I have seen a great deal of evil, it is my conviction that man is . . . (*He chokes on the words*) honest and kind and . . . well . . . and . . . well, there must be a place where he *is* honest and kind and good and noble and . . .

MARTIN. There is such a place. And if I thought you believed that foolishness I would send you there. They would like you.

CANDIDE. I do believe that foolishness. I mean, I do believe what I believe, but I don't believe there's such a place in this world. I mean there is such a place, of course, but I haven't found it — (*Almost in tears*) Oh, I am tired. And I don't understand anything anymore.

MARTIN. In the highest peak of the Andes there is a country called Eldorado. I was born there. For hundreds of years . . . (*Points to palace*) their armies have been trying to find it. They break their backs on the mountains, and the people of Eldorado come out to stare at the soldiers. They do not understand what a soldier is, nor do they care that he came to kill them. They give him a house, send him to school, give him useful work, and make him smile. No enemy soldier has ever wanted to come back.

CANDIDE. Paradise.

MARTIN. No, no. Not Paradise. They would think Paradise a sick man's dream.

CANDIDE. Why did you leave such a place?

MARTIN. They put me out. They said I was the first man ever born there who wasn't happy. They said I was diseased and could not stay with them. They asked me to go. Perhaps they were right. I don't believe that man is honest, or kind, or good.

CANDIDE. Oh, I do, sir. I do believe it. I haven't anything else to believe in. Would they take me?

MARTIN. Yes. They will take any man who comes in peace. (*Throws him a compass*) Go up the Andes and turn left. Here is an emerald compass that points straight to a diamond hill. There's an elephant at the door. He will carry you in. Give him my regards.

(*The Governor, Cunegonde and the Old Lady appear on the balcony.*)

CANDIDE (*sings*).

Once again I must be gone,
Moving on to Eldorado.
Shall my hopes be answered there?
Is that land so good and fair?

Though that Eden well may be,
Though it shine however brightly,
Still no bright yonder can delight me;
Cunegonde won't be there to share it with me.

CUNEGONDE (*sings*).

Though it may seem
I am discarding Candide,
Truly my scheme
Is for safeguarding Candide.
Though I abhor
This loveless connection,
I'll feign affection
For your protection, Candide.

GOVERNOR (*sings*).

Why should I wed?
Marriage is awful, you know.
Passion is dead
Once it is lawful, you know.
No, I'll not wed.
That would be the worst thing.
After the first fling
Women are awful, you know.

OLD LADY (*sings*).

Haven't I got brains?
I'm devilishly witty!
We were just in chains, and now we're sitting pretty!

CUNEGONDE.

Farewell my love
Ah farewell my love
Aaaaaaaaah!

OLD LADY.

If you've got brains and you're clever and witty
You can make out and wind up sitting pretty!
Aaaaaaaaaaaaah!

GOVERNOR.

No, for passion is dead when it's lawful you know.
No, no, no, marriage is awful you know.
Aaaaaaaaaah!

CANDIDE.

Farewell my love farewell!
Farewell Cunegonde farewell farewell!
Aaaaaaaaaaaaah!

MARTIN (*speaks*). Well, they all believe what they are screaming. We'll see.

CUNEGONDE.

Though it may seem I am discarding Candide
Truly my scheme is for safeguarding Candide
Though I abhor this loveless connection
Farewell to my love
Farewell to my love
Farewell to my love
Farewell to my love

OLD LADY.

Haven't I got brains
I'm devilishly witty
We were just in chains
And now we're sitting pretty
Sitting pretty
You've got to have brains
You've got to have brains
You've got to have brains to live

GOVERNOR.

Why should I wed
Marriage is awful you know
Passion is dead once it is lawful you know
Women are awful after the first fling
No, no, I'll not wed
No, no, I'll not wed
No, no, I'll not wed, no.

CANDIDE.

Though that Eden may well be
Though it shine however brightly
What bright yonder can delight me
Farewell to my love
Farewell to my love
Farewell to my love.

(*At the end of the quartet, Candide lifts the compass, raises it, smiles and runs off.*)

Curtain

Act Two

Scene 1.

SCENE: *Same as Buenos Aires, Act One. But now we see into a room of the palace. Sailors are loading a boat. There is a group of miserable-looking Peons sitting downstage.*

AT RISE: *The Old Lady is sitting on the steps. Off the balcony, in the room, the Governor and Cunegonde are playing chess. The Governor is waiting for Cunegonde to move her chess piece. The room is filled with fine pictures and fine books.*

CUNEGONDE (*at chess table*). Hot, isn't it?

GOVERNOR. No.

CUNEGONDE. It was cold yesterday, wasn't it?

GOVERNOR. No.

CUNEGONDE. It will rain tonight, won't it?

GOVERNOR. Wherever you are, it's raining all the time.

OLD LADY. Hoihh!

SAILOR. What's the matter, lady?

OLD LADY. I'm homesick for everywhere but here. (*She sings*)

No doubt you'll think I'm giving in
To petulance and malice,
But in candor I am forced to say
That I'm sick of gracious living in
This stuffy little palace.
And I wish that I could leave today.
I have suffered a lot
And I'm certainly not
Unaware that this life has its black side.
I have starved in a ditch,
I've been burned for a witch,
And I'm missing the half of my backside.
I've been beaten and whipped

And repeatedly stripped,
  I've been forced into all kinds of whoredom;
But I'm finding of late
That the very worst fate
  Is to perish of comfort and BOREDOM.

GOVERNOR (*speaking*). Quiet.

CUNEGONDE (*sings to Governor*).

It was three years ago
As you very well know
  That you said we would soon have a wedding;
Every day you forget
What you promised, and yet
  You continue to rumple my bedding.
I'll no longer bring shame
On my family name.
  I had rather lie down and be buried;
No, I'll not lead the life
Of an unwedded wife.
  Tell me, when are we going to be MARRIED?

GOVERNOR (*speaking*). Quiet.

OLD LADY (*sings*).

I was once, what is more,
Nearly sawed in four
  By a specially clumsy magician;
And you'd think I would feel
After such an ordeal
  That there's charm in my present position.
But I'd far rather be
In a tempest at sea,
  Or a bloody North African riot,
Than to sit in this dump
On what's left of my rump
  And put up with this terrible QUIET.

CUNEGONDE (*joining in*).

When are we going to be MARRIED?

OLD LADY (*sings*).

Comfort and boredom
  and QUIET. . . .

CUNEGONDE (*sings, crescendo*)

When are we going to
  be —

GOVERNOR (*sings*).

QUIET!

CUNEGONDE (*speaking to the Governor*). I had a dream.

GOVERNOR. Great mistake.

CUNEGONDE. And in my dream, my dear mother, the Baroness, came to me. She is now a princess of Heaven. And you know what she told me? She told me that you must marry me.

GOVERNOR (*rings a bell. In a minute, two Officers will appear in answer to the bell*). Tell your mother to go back where she came from and to take you with her.

CUNEGONDE. My mother said that if you do not marry me this week, I must leave you.

OLD LADY. I have told you over and over again that such talk does not lead to marriage. Why don't you learn to cook?

CUNEGONDE (*softly to Old Lady*). He adores me. He will never allow me to leave. (*To Governor*) And so I will pack the few miserable clothes that you have bought me, and take passage on the boat that leaves next week.

GOVERNOR (*who has been whispering to the Officers*). No need to wait, sweetheart. The cotton boat goes immediately.

(*The Officers, with great speed, put heavy sacks over Cunegonde and the Old Lady and bundle them off. A Peon rises suddenly and begins pointing. The others rise in great excitement. Martin comes in to join the crowd. Candide enters. He is bowed down with gold and jewels.*)

CANDIDE. Good evening, good folk. (*To Martin*) My dear good friend. How glad I am to see you.

A WOMAN (*in crowd*). Look at that. A rich man kisses a beggar.

A PEON (*frightened*). Where does such a man come from?

ANOTHER WOMAN. Look at the jewels on him. Maybe he ain't human.

A PEON. What's in the bags, stranger?

CANDIDE. Gold. And I'd like to share it with you.

A WOMAN. I told you he wasn't human.

(*Candide smiles, dips into a bag and gives out large gold coins. The crowd draws back as if frightened. Then they pick up the gold with cries of pleasure.*)

A WOMAN. Kind stranger.

A MAN. Blessings from the poor.

A WOMAN. A man of charity.

(*The noise has brought the Governor to the balcony.*)

A WOMAN. This ain't gold. Ain't got no picture of a king. Ain't got no picture of a big-nosed general.

MARTIN. They don't need a king or a big-nosed general in Eldorado. They've never been at war, nor pronounced its name.

A WOMAN (*to Candide*). You left such a place? To come back here?

CANDIDE. Yes. I came back to find the woman I love.

A WOMAN. My God. He's crazy.

A MAN. There's no such place where they don't have soldiers and war.

CANDIDE. There is such a place. (*He sings*)

Up a seashell mountain,
Across a primrose sea,
To a jungle fountain
High up in a tree;

Then down a primrose mountain,
Across a seashell sea,
To a land of happy people,
Just and kind and bold and free.

CHORUS (*sings*).

To Eldorado . . .

CANDIDE (*sings*).

They bathe each dawn in a golden lake,
Emeralds hang upon the vine.
All is there for all to take,
Food and God and books and wine.

They have no words for fear and greed,
For lies and war, revenge and rage.
They sing and dance and think and read.
They live in peace, and die of age.

CHORUS (*sings*).

In Eldorado . . .

CANDIDE (*sings*).

They gave me home, they called me friend,
They taught me how to live in grace.
Seasons passed without an end
In that sweetly blessed place.

But I grew sad and could not stay;
Without my love my heart was cold.
So they sadly sent me on my way
With gracious gifts of gems and gold.

CHORUS (*sings*).

From Eldorado . . .

CANDIDE (*sings*).

Good-bye, they said, we pray you
May safely cross the sea.
Go, they said, and may you
Find your bride-to-be.

Then past the jungle fountain,
Along a silver shore,
I've come by sea and mountain
To be with my love once more.

CHORUS (*sings*).

From Eldorado . . .

CANDIDE (*sings*).

To be with my love once more.

(*The crowd exits as the two Officers cross stage carrying Cunegonde and the Old Lady, who are covered up completely and wrapped as bundles. There are muffled cries from within the bundles.*)

CANDIDE. What was that? It was a woman's voice.

GOVERNOR (*appears on balcony*). There are no female bales of cotton, sir. Perhaps the sun has tired you.

CANDIDE (*bows to Governor*). I wish to ask audience of Your Excellency. I have come to find the Baroness Cunegonde.

GOVERNOR. Oh, yes . . . Allow me the honor of joining you. (*He disappears.*)

CANDIDE. That's funny talk. It's no honor to join me.

MARTIN. That's the way the rich talk to the rich.

CANDIDE. The people of Eldorado made me very rich with gold and jewels. But I won't ever talk like that. I am a simple man —

MARTIN. Yes, you are. But His Excellency is not simple. I advise you to take care.

CANDIDE. Nothing to take care about. As soon as Cunegonde joins me, we will all take ship for home. Life will be good for us now —

MARTIN (*softly*). You mean to take me with you?

CANDIDE. You are my friend and my benefactor. What I have is yours, now and always.

MARTIN (*deeply upset. His voice rising*). Are you a man who remembers those who helped you? Are you a kind man, are you a just man? — (*Screams in pain*) If you are a good man,

I don't want to know you. It's too late, I am too old. I don't want to start thinking all over again —

CANDIDE. I am not a good man. So please don't cry.

GOVERNOR (*reappears, with Officer, who is carrying a wine tray*). Now, sir, a glass of wine. It's a modest wine because it has nothing to be immodest about.

CANDIDE. Thank you. I have come only to fetch the Baroness Cunegonde —

GOVERNOR. What lovely emeralds. I like emeralds.

(*At a signal, two more Officers appear.*)

CANDIDE. Would you bring me to the Baroness Cunegonde?

GOVERNOR. What lovely emeralds. *I like emeralds.*

MARTIN (*carefully to Governor*). My friend would like to contribute to your favorite charity. (*To Candide*) You never pay the rich. You endow a favorite charity.

(*He gives a bag of gold to the Governor.*)

GOVERNOR. Thank you. This gold will go to the Royal Insane Asylum. Now. The Baroness Cunegonde would not consent to stay here. I begged her to remain in my care — although I am a Governor and not a governess, as a rule — but when she found you were gone, she demanded to follow you to Europe.

CANDIDE (*deeply upset*). To Europe! We must find a ship! (*Spanish Ladies and Officers enter*) We must find a ship! Immediately.

GOVERNOR. The last ship sailed a few minutes ago. But be patient. In a few months —

CANDIDE. No, sir. I can't be patient. I will buy a boat. I will buy ten boats —

FIRST OFFICER. A boat, sir?

GOVERNOR. There is no boat in this harbor, except my pleasure schooner, the *Santa Rosalia*.

FIRST OFFICERS. But Your Excellency, the *Santa Rosalia* is a shell. It has not been used for many years . . .

GOVERNOR. Nonsense! The *Santa Rosalia* is *entirely* seaworthy.

FIRST LADY. A fine boat.

SECOND LADY. A famous boat.

CANDIDE. I will buy your boat. Here are ten thousand pieces of gold.

GOVERNOR. Who can refuse a lover? But I am not a merchant, and I do not sell boats.

CANDIDE. Oh, I could not accept so large a gift, sir.

GOVERNOR. I understand your feelings. Put twenty thousand pieces of gold on the steps. Buenos Aires needs *two* insane asylums.

(*Puzzled, Candide puts down two bags of gold.*)

SECOND OFFICER. Have a pleasant trip.

THIRD OFFICER. The wind and tide are favorable.

LADIES. Bon voyage.

GOVERNOR. My regards to the Baroness Cunegonde.

(*Martin and Candide exit.*)

GOVERNOR (*sings*).

Bon voyage, dear fellow,
Dear benefactor of your fellowman!
May good luck attend you.
Do come again and see us when you can.

CHORUS (*sings*).

Bon voyage, dear fellow,
Dear benefactor of your fellowman!
May good luck attend you.
Do come again and see us when you can.

GOVERNOR (*sings*).

Oh, but I'm bad. Oh, but I'm bad.
Playing such a very dirty trick on such a fine lad!
I'm a low cad, I'm a low cad:
Always when I do this sort of thing it makes me so sad,
  Ever so sad!
  Oh, but I'm bad!
  Ever so bad!

ALL (*sing*).

Bon voyage!

MEN OF CHORUS (*sing*).

Bon voyage, we'll see ya.
Do have a jolly trip across the foam.

WOMEN OF CHORUS (*sing*).

Santa Rosalia,
Do have a safe and pleasant journey home.

FULL CHORUS (*sings*).

Bon voyage!

GOVERNOR (*sings*).

I'm so rich that my life is an utter bore:
There is just not a thing that I need.
My desires are as dry as an applecore,
And my only emotion is *greed*.

Which is why, though I've nothing to spend it for,
I have swindled this gold from Candidi-di-di-di-dide,
Poor Candide!

GOVERNOR (*looks out to sea, speaks*). Oh, dear, the water's up to his neck — well, there goes his head. (*He sings*)

But I never would swindle the humble poor,
For you can't get a turnip to bleed.
When you swindle the rich you get so much more,
Which is why I have swindled Candide.
Oh, dear, I fear.
He's going down, he's going to drown!
Ah, poor Candide!

ALL (*sing*).

Bon voyage, best wishes.
Seems to have been a bit of sabotage.
Things don't look propitious,
Still from the heart we wish you bon voyage.
Bon voyage!!!!

(*The song ends as the scene at Buenos Aires blacks out and the lights come up on a raft in the middle of the ocean.*)

Scene 1A.

SCENE: *Travels from Buenos Aires to Venice.*
AT RISE: *Martin and Candide are on the raft. Candide is rowing, Martin is fishing with a strip of cloth.*

CANDIDE. He sold us a boat that was nothing but a shell and sank immediately. Did he wish to kill us, and why? He was a rich man and yet he cheated us. What for? He was such a cultured fellow — it cannot be true.

MARTIN (*wearily*). It cannot be true, but it is true.

CANDIDE. I don't understand. When I was poor and people were mean and cruel to me, I told myself that the rags of the poor smell bad, and bad smells make people frightened, and fright makes people angry, and anger makes people —

MARTIN. And that if ever you were rich you would smell sweet, and thus your troubles would be at an end. Well, you are still very rich and you will still have trouble because now you cannot be ignored, and no man will rest until he has stripped you. Or he will wait, frightened, for you to strip him.

CANDIDE. But what is the use of money unless it buys happiness?

MARTIN. Even on a log, starving, in the middle of an ocean, you talk like a sun-touched child. I'll make you into a pessimist before this voyage is over. Or nature will.

CANDIDE. I love nature, or I used to.

MARTIN. Then tell your love that we are starving and have not eaten for two days.

CANDIDE. We will survive.

MARTIN. Why do you wish to survive?

CANDIDE. Because I am convinced that there is as much good as there is evil in the world, and I am determined to find the good in others and in myself —

MARTIN. As much good as there is evil. In a world where men march across continents to kill each other without even asking why. Where the scientist strives to prolong life and at the same minute invents weapons to wipe it out. Where children are taught the rules of charity and kindness until they grow to the age where they would be punished if they put the rules into practice. Where half the world starves and the other half diets — (*A shark's head appears, and Martin looks at it with interest*) A pretty fish. It has strange eyes.

CANDIDE (*in doubt*). Yes, much of what you say is true, and many of my dreams have faded. But I still believe in the essential goodness of the human heart —

MARTIN. The human heart is cowardly and hypocritical, and is not a heart at all: it is more vicious than the monsters of the sea that rise around us now. We would be safer in the arms of a shark than in the arms of a brother —

(*The shark reappears and yanks Martin from the boat. Martin quietly disappears into the sea. Candide, not knowing that his friend has gone, continues to speak.*)

CANDIDE. You've had a bad life, my friend, but I still have enough Eldorado gold and gems to put charity to the test. Sometimes I wonder if I should ever have left there — Ah, well, we'll never have to grovel or beg, you and I, and we'll give to those who need it and sit ourselves down to live and think in peace. There is much that worries me, I admit to you, and I am not the optimist I once was. But we'll live quietly when we find my Cunegonde, and you'll feel better when you hear the laughter of my babies — (*He discovers Martin is not there and begins to shout*) Martin! Martin! Where are you?

(*Pangloss climbs aboard the raft.*)

CANDIDE. Dr. Pangloss . . . I left you in Lisbon. I thought you were dead.

PANGLOSS. I was dead. But the wife of a doctor, a pretty woman — pretty for a doctor's wife — saved me. She was very much in love with me, sweet girl, and we ran away together. But we were captured by pirates, and I have been a miserable galley slave for many years — (*He starts to cry. Candide holds him in his arms*) When you've swallowed a lot of water, you cry very easily. I am so hungry. (*Bright as a scholar*) Salt water is a purgative, my boy — for the body and for the mind.

CANDIDE. You'll be safe now. You'll have all you want to eat, and a carriage to ride in — (*As if to a child*) What would you like most? I am a very rich man.

PANGLOSS. I would like most to hear you repeat the golden rules of a high-minded Westphalian man.

CANDIDE. Honor, the generous heart of all mankind — No, sir, I *can't* say those words anymore.

PANGLOSS (*softly*). You break the heart of an old man.

CANDIDE (*struggling*). The heart of mankind is a generous heart. The honor of a man is all he needs on life's journey. The poor must be respected —

(*Pangloss smiles with pleasure. The lights dim as the raft moves off and Venice comes into place.*)

Scene 2.

SCENE: *Venice. A gambling house.*

AT RISE: *People are already at the gaming tables. The tables are presided over by Ferone, the owner of the gambling house. The guests are masked. From time to time the masks will be removed. Among the people at the table is Signora Sofronia, who is the Old Lady. She is very dressed up.*

CROUPIER. *Faites vos jeux, messieurs, dames.*

(The guests sing the words, "Money, money, money." The wheel turns and all heads turn with it. The wheel stops and there are cries from the losers. Signora Sofronia steps out, her arms loaded with chips.)

FERONE *(to all, as he moves forward to Sofronia).* Sixteen. And only one lady bet on the number. Allow me to congratulate you, Signora Sofronia.

CROUPIER. *Faites vos jeux — messieurs, dames.*

(The guests return to gambling.)

FERONE (*taking the chips from Sofronia*). I told you *not* to play sixteen. Have a little sense. You can't win every time. They are already suspicious of you. (*A chip drops. Sofronia scrambles on her hands and knees for it. Ferone puts his foot on the chip*) Get up. You're not in Rovno Gubernya. (*He hurries to greet a new group*) Signor Duca. (*To an Elderly Lady, who has entered with four very Tall Girls*) Madame La Duchesse. You were not with us last night.

LA DUCHESSE. No, I was with my astrologer. And tonight, with his advice, I shall win back the fortune I've lost to you. (*Prefect of Police enters and crosses between them. She points to him*) Isn't that the Prefect of Police?

FERONE. Yes, madame.

LA DUCHESSE. Strange. Last week he lost his fortune and killed himself. I went to the funeral. Very puzzling isn't it? Ah, well. (*Introducing the very Tall Girls*) My English cousins.

FOUR TALL GIRLS (*all together*). Hudda da.

LA DUCHESSE. They're so shy. Their father owns Africa. They're too young to play. Give them a little sugar water. I will play on number fifteen.

CROUPIER. *Faites vos jeux, messieurs, dames.*

FERONE (*to Tall Girls, as La Duchesse moves away*). Dull for you to stand around.

A TALL GIRL. Nowt tat tall.

FERONE. May I lend you a few chips?

FOUR TALL GIRLS (*all together*). How madly divine. What are chips?

FERONE. Chips are money.

FOUR TALL GIRLS. Aww.

FERONE. I wish you great luck.

FOUR TALL GIRLS (*all together*). Chips are money. How divinely mad. (*They hurry to the table.*)

FERONE (*to Sofronia*). Put your foot under the table and press the pedal to the left. *Left.* (*She moves to the table.*)

CROUPIER. *Faites vos jeux —*

(*The wheel turns. This time most of the guests scream in delight. Ferone leaves the table angrily. Sofronia joins him.*)

SOFRONIA. I did just as you told me. I put my foot on the pedal and pressed to the *right*. What happened?

FERONE. What happened is that you're a fool.

SOFRONIA. Who, me?

FERONE. I told you to press to the *left*. One more mistake and you'll be out of here.

SOFRONIA (*sings*).

I have always been wily and clever
At deceiving and swindling and such,
And I feel just as clever as ever,
But I seem to be losing my touch.
Yes, I'm clever, but where does it get me?

(*Indicates Ferone*)

My employer gets all of my take;
All I get is my daily spaghetti,
While he gorges on truffles and steak.

What's the use?
What's the use?
There's no profit in cheating.
It's all so defeating
And wrong,
Oh, so wrong!
If you just have to pass it along.

FERONE (*sings*).

That old hag is no use in this gyp-joint;
Not a sou have I made on her yet,
And the one thing that pays in this clip-joint
Is my fraudulent game of roulette.
But I have to pay so much protection

(*Indicates Prefect of Police*)

To the chief of police and his men
That each day when he makes his collection
I'm a poor man all over again.

OLD LADY *and* FERONE (*sing together*).

What's the use?

What's the use
Of dishonest endeavor
And being so clever?
It's wrong,
Oh, so wrong!
If you just have to pass it along.

PREFECT OF POLICE (*sings*).
It's a very fine thing to be prefect,
Shaking down all the gamblers in town.
My position has only one defect:
That there's somebody shaking *me* down.
(*Indicates a Fat Man*)
For this fellow unhappily knows me,
And he's on to the game that I play,
And he threatens to shame and expose me
If I do not incessantly pay.

OLD LADY, FERONE, *and* PREFECT OF POLICE (*sing together*).
What's the use?
What's the use
Of this sneaky conniving
And slimy contriving?
It's wrong,
Oh, so wrong,
If you just have to pass it along.

FAT MAN (*sings*).
I could live very well by extortion,
But I simply can't keep what I earn,
For I haven't a sense of proportion,
And roulette is my only concern.
I've a system that's fiendishly clever,
Which I learnt from a croupier friend,
And I *should* go on winning forever —
But I *do* seem to lose in the end.
OLD LADY, FERONE, PREFECT OF POLICE *and* FAT MAN (*sing together*).
What's the use?
What's the use —
OLD LADY (*sings*).
Of this cheating and plotting?
You end up with notting!

(They continue singing, repeating the refrains. At the end of the song, Sofronia moves off to small bedroom, rings a bell, and collapses. In a second, Cunegonde appears, carrying a foot bath. She is dressed as a scrub woman. She kneels, and takes off Sofronia's shoes.)

SOFRONIA. When you've been born a princess your feet always hurt.

CUNEGONDE (*weary, without interest*). So you've told me before. I don't believe you were born a princess.

SOFRONIA (*as she puts her feet in bath*). What difference does it make?

CUNEGONDE (*takes off her shoes, puts her feet into foot bath. Points out to the gambling room*). How did you do tonight?

SOFRONIA. Fine. Fine. In a few weeks we'll have a nice little nest egg, and we'll leave.

CUNEGONDE. Where'll we go?

SOFRONIA (*cheerful, but without conviction*). What do you mean, where'll we go? We'll buy a refined wardrobe, a carriage with a crest, put a footman on the box — What do you mean, where'll we go? The world is open, waiting for us.

CUNEGONDE. It hasn't acted that way.

SOFRONIA. We'll drive to Rome. I have relatives there, most highly placed. (*Cunegonde laughs. Sofronia bristles, then laughs with her*) Listen, my girl, we're lucky. We slept on mattresses this week.

CUNEGONDE. There was a time when I didn't think that so lucky.

SOFRONIA. Now none of that talk. What do you think most people get in this world — what they want? You do the best you can.

CUNEGONDE. Yes, you've told me that before.

SOFRONIA. Tomorrow will come. And it will be better.

(The lights dim in the bedroom and come up in the ballroom as Candide and Pangloss enter the room. They are in fine clothes, and Candide carries his gold in jeweled bags. They are given masks by an attendant. Ferone comes forward.)

CROUPIER. *Faites vos jeux, messieurs, dames.*

PANGLOSS. Our apologies for intruding.

FERONE. Yes, sir?

PANGLOSS. We are searching for a lady, and our private informants tell us that she may be in Venice, and that here, where the highest of society gathers —

FERONE. What is the name of the lady?

CANDIDE. The Baroness Cunegonde.

(*Ferone shakes his head.*)

FERONE. I'm afraid the name means nothing to me.

PANGLOSS. Ah, well. We'll continue on. We've posted large rewards in Brussels, in Paris, in Bordeaux, in Milan, all over Venice — (*To Ferone, indicating Candide*) His great fortune will bring him no pleasure until he finds the lady.

FERONE. His great fortune brings him no pleasure? (*Quickly*) Wait. Perhaps the lady is here. Names do not stay with me. Do be at home. What does the Baroness look like?

PANGLOSS. It has been a long time since my friend has seen her.

CANDIDE (*smiles*). She will not have changed. She is blonde, delicate, charming —

FERONE. Then certainly she is here. She must be here. Ah, ladies — a distinguished stranger — (*He pushes forward the four Tall Girls*) The Ladies Mary Cutely, Mary Toothly, Mary Soothly, and Mary Richmond. Is it possible —

(*Candide shakes his head. The Marquis and the Sultan, of the Paris episode, pass by. Candide stares at them, starts to follow them, then turns back, very puzzled. Ferone has moved into the bedroom. Pangloss moves toward the roulette table.*)

CROUPIER. *Faites vos jeux — messieurs, dames.*

LA DUCHESSE. Ten thousand on number fifteen.

FAT MAN. Twenty thousand on six.

DUKE OF NAPLES. Twenty-five thousand on eleven.

A LADY. Twenty-five thousand on twelve.

PANGLOSS. My! A lifetime in a minute. I bet five lire on number five.

DUKE OF NAPLES. No bets under a thousand are allowed here.

PANGLOSS. Oh, goodness. Oh, my.

CANDIDE. Here's a hundred thousand. Play if it gives you pleasure.

FERONE (*in bedroom, stares at Sofronia and Cunegonde, who are still bathing their feet*). Is this what I pay you for?

SOFRONIA. You ain't paid us.

FERONE. Now listen, there's a country boy out there, all dressed up and loaded with gold. Give him a sad story about your life. Tell him all about your mother and father — any nonsense. If you can't take him, you'll be out of here tonight. Both of you. Get to work. Be smart. (*He leaves.*)

SOFRONIA. Smart. He has to tell us to be smart.

CUNEGONDE. Ah. I'm sick of being smart. It ends up being hungry.

SOFRONIA. You stop that talk. Just do your part. We'll be in Rome in the morning.

(*Lights dim in bedroom, come up again in ballroom.*)

CANDIDE (*speaks to Pangloss and points to the Sultan and the Marquis*). I have seen ghosts or the sons of ghosts. I killed those men in Paris in a duel.

PANGLOSS. Is that so?(*Holds out chips*) Look. I am winning. But I don't feel it's proper to chance your money —

CANDIDE. Be happy, my friend. You deserve it.

(*Pangloss hurries back to the table, delighted.*)

DUKE OF NAPLES (*at table*). I place the Duchy of Naples on number four.

FERONE. Your pardon, my Duke. But Naples belongs to your mother.

DUKE OF NAPLES. My mother died at dinner. Or if she didn't, she will die at breakfast.

PANGLOSS. My goodness! What a way to speak of your mother.

DUKE OF NAPLES (*to Pangloss*). Lend me five thousand. You must come and spend Easter with us.

PANGLOSS (*gives him money*). How kind of you.

FERONE. The Duchy of Naples to be covered.

SULTAN (*to the Marquis, as they bump into Candide*). I have seen that man before.

MARQUIS. And I. But I can't remember where. In any case, it is a pleasant picture that comes down memory's lane.

(*Candide stands staring at them, but they move away.*)

CROUPIER. Number five wins again.

DUKE OF NAPLES (*to Pangloss*). My dear friend, lend me another ten thousand.

PANGLOSS. With pleasure. What a charming game this is! I now have thousands of lire and wish to place it all on number five. Then I'll buy cakes for everybody.

FERONE (*to Sofronia*). This gentleman is in search of a lady. Will you help him, Madame Sofronia?

SOFRONIA (*who is masked, to Candide who is masked*). I certainly will. (*She pushes Candide into bedroom*) You got troubles? You should know about me. You got a mother and a father? (*Before he can answer*) You got uncles? No? So you got no troubles.

OLD LADY (*sings*).

I've got troubles, as I said.
Mother's dying, Father's dead.
All my uncles are in jail.

CANDIDE (*sings*).

It's a very moving tale.

(*Cunegonde, wearing mask, enters with liquor tray.*)

SOFRONIA (*continues singing*).

Though our name, I say again, is
Quite the proudest name in Venice,
Our afflictions are so many,
And we haven't got a penny.

CANDIDE.

Madam, I am desolate
At your family's tragic state
Any help that I can give . . .
Please do tell me where they live.

I shall look them up tomorrow
And alleviate their sorrow
With a check made out to bearer.
In the meantime, buona sera.

SOFRONIA.

I've got troubles, as I said.
Mother's dying, Father's dead.
All my uncles are in jail.

CANDIDE.

It's a very moving tale.

SOFRONIA.

Although our name, I say again, is
Quite the proudest name in Venice,
All my uncles are in jail.

SOFRONIA *and* CANDIDE (*sing*).

It's a very moving tale.
Ah, what a moving tale!

(*Outside, in the gambling room, Pangloss is being generous to the pretty ladies.*)

PANGLOSS (*sings*).

Millions of rubles and lire and francs!
Broke the bank, broke the bank.
Broke the best of all possible banks.
Pieces of gold to the ladies I throw.
Easy come, easy go.
Shining gold to the ladies I throw.

See them on their knees before me.
If they love me, can you blame them?
Little wonder they adore me.
Watch them woo me as I name them:

(*As he names each lady he gives her gold coins.*)

Lady Frilly, Lady Silly,
Pretty Lady Willy-Nilly,
Lady Lightly, Lady Brightly,
Charming Lady Fly-by-Nightly.

My Lady Fortune found me.
What a joy to have around me
Lovely ladies, six or seven.
This is my idea of Heaven.

Fortune, keep the wheel a-spinning, spinning,
They adore me while I'm winning!

Lady Frilly, Lady Silly,
Pretty Lady Willy-Nilly,
Lady Lightly, Lady Brightly,
Charming Lady Fly-by-Nightly.

Fools love only one or two,
Ladies, I love all of you.

OLD LADY *and* CUNEGONDE (*in bedroom*).

I've got troubles, as I said.
Mother is dying, Father's dead
All my uncles are in jail

PANGLOSS.

Lady Frilly, Lady Silly,
Pretty Lady Willy-Nilly,
Lady Lightly, Lady Brightly,
Charming Lady Fly-by-Nightly.
My Lady Fortune found me

CANDIDE (*in bedroom*).
It's a very moving tale.

OLD LADY *and* CUNEGONDE.
Although our name, I say again, is
Quite the proudest name in Venice,
All my uncles are in jail.

OLD LADY, CUNEGONDE *and* CANDIDE.
It's a very moving tale . . .

CUNEGONDE, OLD LADY *and* CANDIDE.
She's got troubles . . .

What a joy to have around me
Lovely ladies, six or seven.
This is my idea of Heaven.
Fortune, keep the wheel a-spinning, spinning,
They adore me while I'm winning!

PANGLOSS *and* TALL GIRLS.
Lady Frilly, Lady Silly,
Pretty Lady Willy-Nilly,
Lady Lightly, Lady Brightly,
Charming Lady Fly-by-Nightly.
Fools love only one or two,
Ladies, I love all of you.

(*In the bedroom, Candide, his back to the wall, is pinned down by Cunegonde and Sofronia. He tries to move, but he is a prisoner. Sofronia turns Candide about and Cunegonde tries to snip off his bags of gold. The try is not successful. But Cunegonde and Sofronia are determined, and caution is thrown to the winds. Candide moves to the now empty gambling room and is pursued by Cunegonde and Sofronia. In the scuffle, the masks are knocked off. Candide, Cunegonde and Sofronia stand staring at each other.*)

CANDIDE (*very softly*). Cunegonde. (*He turns to stare at Sofronia, then turns back to stare at Cunegonde*) My pretty, my sweet, my pure Cunegonde. I loved you and sought you and I've found you. (*Takes off the bags of gold and throws them down*) This is what you want. I give it to you.

(*He crosses room, and exits. Ferone enters, picks up bags, looks at Cunegonde. She is crying.*)

FERONE. You are fools, both of you. The game is to get what you want without the man knowing you got it. He will go to the police. . . .

CUNEGONDE (*sadly*). No. This man won't go to the police.

FERONE (*to Sofronia*). Get out. You're not worth your supper. Get out.

PANGLOSS (*comes into the empty gambling room*). Now where has everybody gone? Hello, Cunegonde. Oh, dear child, how you have changed. (*Peers at Cunegonde. She exits. He speaks to Sofronia*) Oh, madame. A most disturbing series of events has come my way. I was standing with my arms full of money. I was robbed. And now the gaming table has strangely disappeared —

SOFRONIA (*wearily*). Yes. It's all moved to another room. And you will not be admitted. (*Bitterly*) Be smart. Come back tomorrow night and try again. (*She exits.*)

PANGLOSS. But I loaned a lot of money to a nice gentleman and a lady. . . . Oh, I am sure they are looking for me now. (*Calling out*) Gentlemen. This is Dr. Pangloss. I'm in here. Could you return the money now? (*Long pause. Sadly*) I'll wait. I'm sure they are looking for me.

(*The lights dim as Venice moves off and Westphalia comes into place.*)

Scene 3.

SCENE: *Westphalia in ruins.*

AT RISE: *Maximillian is onstage alone. Candide, Cunegonde, Old Lady and Pangloss come in. They do not see Maximillian.*

PANGLOSS (*to Cunegonde, who looks around and then starts to cry*). Now, now. The place doesn't look very nice, but there's always something homey about coming home.

MAXIMILLIAN. Well, look who's come here. Cunegonde. My God, you're ugly,

CUNEGONDE. My own brother. Deserted me — you deserted me in Buenos Aires. What are you doing here?

MAXIMILLIAN. Resting. I didn't desert you in Buenos Aires. (*Points to Candide*) He killed me.

OLD LADY (*to Candide*). What's the matter with you, you can't even kill this fool?

MAXIMILLIAN (*to Cunegonde*). Your lover killed me —

CUNEGONDE. He's not my lover. How dare you talk such filth? Never been my lover —

OLD LADY. Once they were going to give a medal to a man who hadn't been your lover. They looked and looked —

(*Cunegonde swipes at the Old Lady.*)

CUNEGONDE (*peers at Maximillian*). What did you do with your teeth?

MAXIMILLIAN. Sold them. I had many an adventure, I can tell you —

CUNEGONDE. Don't tell me. A man who would sell his teeth would sell his sister. (*Shouts to Heaven*) Our sainted mother knows that you sold your own sister. (*Shrieks*) Mother, look down at your son and make him give me the money —

MAXIMILLIAN (*to Pangloss, pointing to Cunegonde and Candide*). Have they both gone crazy?

PANGLOSS. Candide has not spoken these many weeks. I think he's upset.

CUNEGONDE. I've come home to die. (*Nobody answers*) I'm dying.

OLD LADY. So die.

MAXIMILLIAN. Dig me a little grave, sister. I'm so tired.

CUNEGONDE. I'll make you curses. You stole my fortune, tore the pearls from our mother's breast and gave them to women —

OLD LADY. Really? I never would have guessed that.

CUNEGONDE. Bring me a winding sheet.

OLD LADY. Don't be so modest.

PANGLOSS. I want only to cover my head. A head that was honored by Heidelberg should not be injured by the damp. I should, of course, like a stone over my grave, and one word — teacher — carved thereon. Then, in smaller letters, add that the deceased had nine degrees, three of them doctorates in —

CANDIDE (*quietly*). In lies. You were my master, and I loved you, and you taught me lies. I was a stupid boy, and you must have known it. (*With great force*) A man should be jailed for telling lies to the young.

PANGLOSS (*shocked*). Candide.

CANDIDE. Go away and lie to the trees.

PANGLOSS. Candide.

CANDIDE. You are a useless old man. Go away from here.

(*Pangloss goes slowly off.*)

MAXIMILLIAN (*to Candide*). You are ill-born. Nobody but the ill-born would speak that way to a man older than himself.

CANDIDE. I killed you once. A man could grow to like killing you. So get out before I do it again.

(*Frightened, Maxmillian moves off.*)

OLD LADY. Glad he's gone. Never did a day's work in his life.

CANDIDE. And did you? (*He begins to make a fire.*)

OLD LADY. Are you making a fire?

CANDIDE. Yes.

OLD LADY. What are you going to cook?

CANDIDE. Nothing for you. You'll get along, you always have. But not here. Get out.

OLD LADY. I've told you what happened to me. I've told you of my past —

CANDIDE. Yes, you had trouble. And so you lived on the world. I'm sick of your past — and mine. Get out. (*She goes slowly off.*)

CUNEGONDE. I'm hungry.

CANDIDE. So am I.

CUNEGONDE. I'm a woman —

CANDIDE. Do they get hungrier than men? Yes they do. In that fairy tale we lived in.

CUNEGONDE. I feel so tired —

CANDIDE. I followed you around the world, believing every foolish tale you told me, killing men for something called your honor.

CUNEGONDE. I was alone, I was frightened. I —

CANDIDE. Yes, I think that's true. I don't blame you, Cunegonde. My head was full of nonsense. But now I am tired of nonsense. I want to live. So go away and let me live.

(*Cunegonde rises and goes slowly off. Pangloss comes in. He is holding up a fish.*)

PANGLOSS (*timidly, to Candide*). I just came back for a minute. I brought you a little fish. I took a short course in oceanography at Leipzig. I used to be good at such things. Did you ever know that?

CANDIDE. I never knew you were good at anything.

PANGLOSS. I think I could summon back a little knowledge of . . . er . . . of the common things of life, if I tried. . . .

CANDIDE. Try hard.

PANGLOSS. You see . . . er . . . well . . . I was early taught that everything was for the best in this best of all possible worlds. I don't think I ever believed it, but it's most difficult to get rid of what you once thought, isn't it?

CANDIDE (*puts a pot on the fire*). Most difficult. But let's not philosophize about not philosophizing. Let's make a place to sleep.

(*The Old Lady and Maximillian come in. She is bowed down under twigs and branches and looks like a moving forest. Maximillian is carrying a homemade broom.*)

MAXIMILLIAN. I never carried anything before.

CANDIDE (*to Maximillian*). What are you doing here?

OLD LADY. He's going to work hard. He's promised me. You can't put him out. He'll die. He's so silly. And anyway, I've always wanted a son. (*Maximillian is sweeping the air with the broom. She hits him*) The air ain't dirty. Sweep the ground. (*Hastily, to Candide*) I've got wood for a fire, and dandelions and fiddleheads for our dinner. (*Points at Pangloss, who is having a bad time cleaning the fish*) Look who is doing what all wrong.

CANDIDE. Go to work and mind your business.

OLD LADY. I'm going to make us all some sensible shoes. If you're born a princess as I was, of course, your feet always hurt. Even through war and rape and . . .

(*Candide stares at her. She is silent. Cunegonde enters. There are leaves in her hair and she is clean. She has done her best to be pretty again.*)

CUNEGONDE (*she is carrying a giant mushroom, timidly*). I brought something for our dinner. I'm clean. (*Nobody answers. She throws the mushroom into the pot*) Mushrooms are good in a stew.

OLD LADY (*hauling the mushroom out of the stew, shrieking*). It's a poison mushroom, you silly woman. This is not the last supper. Can't you do anything in this world except get other people in trouble?

CUNEGONDE (*timidly*). Yes. I can cook. . . . (*She goes to the stew pot, stirs it, knocks it over. She sinks on the ground in shame*) She's right. There's nothing I can do. Nothing.

CANDIDE (*smiles*). Still boasting, aren't you? (*He comes to her*) Marry me, Cunegonde.

CUNEGONDE (*sadly, softly*). It's too late. I'm not young, I'm not good, I'm not pure.

CANDIDE. And I am not young, and not worth much. What we wanted, we will not have. The way we did love, we will not love again. Come now, let us take what we have and love as we are.

PANGLOSS. I'd love to do a ceremony. I had three weeks of divinity school in the Würzburg Gymnasium. Now you must say after me, "Love between men and women is the highest order of love between men and women. Thus we promise to think noble and do noble. . . ."

CANDIDE (*with force*). No. We will not think noble because we are not noble. We will not live in beautiful harmony because there is no such thing in this world, nor should there be. We promise only to do our best and live out our lives. Dear God, that's all we can promise in truth. Marry me, Cunegonde. (*He sings.*)

You've been a fool and so have I,
But come and be my wife,
And let us try before we die
To make some sense of life.
We're neither pure nor wise nor good;
We'll do the best we know;
We'll build our house, and chop our wood,
And make our garden grow.
And make our garden grow.

CUNEGONDE (*sings*).

I thought the world was sugar-cake,
For so our master said;
But now I'll teach my hands to bake
Our loaf of daily bread.

CANDIDE *and* CUNEGONDE (*sing*).

We're neither pure nor wise nor good;
We'll do the best we know;
We'll build our house, and chop our wood,
And make our garden grow.
And make our garden grow.

(*Cast begins slow entry.*)

PANGLOSS, MAXIMILLIAN, OLD LADY, CUNEGONDE, CANDIDE *and* GOVERNOR (*sing*).

Let dreamers dream what worlds they please;
Those Edens can't be found.
The sweetest flowers, the fairest trees
Are grown in solid ground.

ENTIRE COMPANY (*sings*).

We're neither pure nor wise nor good;

We'll do the best we know;
We'll build our house, and chop our wood,
And make our garden grow.
And make our garden grow.

Curtain

Toys in the Attic

For Richard Wilbur

Toys in the Attic was first produced at the Hudson Theatre, New York City, on February 25, 1960, with the following cast:

(In the order of their appearance)

CARRIE BERNIERS	MAUREEN STAPLETON
ANNA BERNIERS	ANNE REVERE
GUS	CHARLES MCRAE
ALBERTINE PRINE	IRENE WORTH
HENRY SIMPSON	PERCY RODRIGUEZ
JULIAN BERNIERS	JASON ROBARDS, JR.
LILY BERNIERS	ROCHELLE OLIVER
TAXI DRIVER	WILLIAM HAWLEY
THREE MOVING MEN	CLIFFORD COTHREN
	TOM MANLEY
	MAURICE ELLIS

Directed by
ARTHUR PENN

Setting and lighting designed by
HOWARD BAY

Costumes designed by
RUTH MORLEY

Scenes

The Berniers house in New Orleans.

Act One

Six P.M. on a summer day.

Act Two

Eight A.M. the following morning.

Act Three

Shortly after.

Act One

SCENE: *The Berniers' living room, the entrance porch to the house, and a small city garden off the porch. The house is solid middle-class of another generation. The furniture is heavy and old. Everything inside and outside is neat, but in need of repairs. The porch has two rocking chairs and is crowded with plants. The garden has a table and chairs that have been painted too often and don't stay together very well. It is a house lived in by poor, clean, orderly people who don't like where they live.*

AT RISE: *Anna Berniers, carrying her gloves and purse and still wearing her hat, pushes open the blinds of the windows that give on the garden. She lifts a large camellia pot and puts it outside. She pours a glass of water on the plant and moves back into the room to take off her hat. Anna is a nice-looking woman, calm and quiet. She is about forty-two. Carrie Berniers appears from the street, climbs the porch steps, and sits down in a porch chair. She is about thirty-eight, still pretty, but the prettiness is wearing thin and tired. She fans herself, rocks back and forth, the chair creaks and sways, and, wearily, she rises and moves to the other chair.*

CARRIE (*as she hears Anna moving about in the kitchen*). That you, Anna?

ANNA (*her voice*). Just got home.

CARRIE. Hot.

ANNA. Paper says a storm.

CARRIE. I know. I'll take the plants in.

ANNA. I just put them out. Let them have a little storm air.

CARRIE. I don't like them out in a storm. Worries me. I don't like storms. I don't believe plants do, either.

ANNA (*appears in the living room with a broom and dust rag; speaks out toward the porch*). Did you have a hard day?

CARRIE. He let me leave the office after lunch. "You're looking a little peaked, Miss Berniers, from the heat." I said I've been looking a little peaked for years in heat, in cold, in rain, when I was young, and now. You mean *you're* hot and want to go home, you faker, I said. I said it to myself.

ANNA. We had a private sale at the store. Coats. Coats on a day like this. There was a very good bargain, red with black braid. I had my eye on it for you all last winter. But —

CARRIE. Oh, I don't need a coat.

ANNA. Yes, you do. Did you go to the park? I wanted to, but the sale went so late. Old lady Senlis and old lady Condelet just sat there, looking at everything, even small coats. How can rich people go to a sale on a day like this?

CARRIE. I feel sorry for them. For all old ladies. Even rich ones. Money makes them lonely.

ANNA (*laughs*). Why would that be?

CARRIE. Don't you feel sorry for old ladies? You used to.

ANNA. When my feet don't hurt and I don't have to sell them coats at a sale. Was it nice in the park?

CARRIE. I didn't go to the park. I went to the cemetery.

ANNA (*stops dusting, sighs*). Everybody still there?

CARRIE. I took flowers. It's cool there. Cooler. I was the only person there. Nobody goes to see anybody in summer. Yet those who have passed away must be just as lonely in summer as they are in winter. Sometimes I think we shouldn't have put Mama and Papa at Mount Olive cemetery. Maybe it would have been nicer for them at Mount Great Hope with the new, rich people. What would you think if we don't get buried at Mount Olive with Mama and Papa?

ANNA. Anyplace that's cool.

CARRIE. I bought you a small bottle of Eau d'haut Alpine. Cologne water of the high Alps, I guess. (*Holds up a package*) Your weekly present. What did you buy me, may I ask, who shouldn't?

ANNA. Jar of candied oranges.

CARRIE. Oh, how nice. We'll have them for a savory. Do you know I read in our travel book on England that *they* think a proper savory is an anchovy. Anchovy after dinner. They won't make me eat it. What are you doing?

ANNA. Nothing. I'm going to clean.

CARRIE. Oh, don't. Sunday's cleaning day. Was this house always so big?

ANNA. It grew as people left it.

CARRIE. I want to tell you something I've never told you before. I never, ever, liked this house. Not even when we were children. I know *you* did, but I didn't.

ANNA. You know I liked it?

CARRIE. I don't think Julian ever liked it, either. That's why we used to have our supper out here on the steps. Did you ever know that's why I used to bring Julian out here, even when he was a baby, and we'd have our supper on the steps? I didn't want him to find out about the house. Julian and I. Nice of Mama and Papa to let us, wasn't it? Must have been a great deal of trouble carrying the dishes out here. Mama had an agreeable nature.

ANNA. I carried the dishes out.

CARRIE. Did you? Yes, so you did. Thank you, Anna. Thank you very much. Did you mind eating with Mama and Papa — (*Points off*) — in that awful oak tomb?

ANNA. Yes, I minded.

CARRIE. Well, it sure was a nice thing to do. I never knew you minded. Funny how you can live so close and long and not know things, isn't it?

ANNA. Yes, indeed. I called Mr. Shine today. He said he hadn't had an inquiry in months. He said we should reduce the price of the house. I said we would, but there wasn't anything to reduce it to.

CARRIE (*gets up, goes into the living room*). Oh, somebody'll come along will like it, you'll see.

ANNA. Nobody's ever liked this house, nobody's ever going to.

CARRIE. You always get mean to the house when something worries you. What's the matter?

ANNA. And you always go to the cemetery.

CARRIE (*opens the waist of her dress*). Just cooler. I so much like the French on the graves. *Un homme brave, mort pour la cité pendant la guerre* — Sounds better in French. A man gallant is so much more than just a gallant man. Nobody in our family's ever been killed in a war. Not Grandpapa, not Papa — Why, don't you think?

ANNA. Some people get killed, some people don't.

CARRIE (*laughs*). Papa always said he was scared to death and ran whenever he could. But Papa said just anything. Julian didn't like it when he said things like that. No little boy would. Papa shouldn't have talked that way.

ANNA. Papa's been dead twenty-two years, Carrie. You should have taken it up with him before this.

CARRIE. No letter for two weeks. I went to the main post office today, and said I was sure there'd been some confusion. Would they please call the other Berniers and see if a letter was there. And Alfie said, "Carrie, there are no other Berniers in New Orleans. There are some live in Biloxi, Mississippi, with a hardware store, but the central government of the United States does not give money to Louisiana to make calls to Mississippi, although maybe you could change that if you said it was Julian who had written the letter he didn't write." I was angry, but I didn't show it. How do you know it's Julian I am talking about, I said. We're expecting letters from Paris and Rome in reply to inquiries about our forthcoming tour.

(*She stops suddenly, run down.*)

ANNA. Julian's busy. That's all.

(*Gus, a colored man of about thirty-five, carrying a block of ice, comes up the porch steps.*)

GUS. You home?

ANNA. We're home.

(*Gus goes off toward the kitchen.*)

CARRIE (*goes toward the piano*). I bought a book called *French Lessons in Songs.* I don't believe it. Never been two weeks before in his whole life. (*Softly, slowly*) I telephoned to Chicago and the hotel manager said Julian and Lily had moved months ago. Why didn't Julian tell us that?

ANNA (*quietly*). I knew. I knew last week. Two letters came back here with address unknown. Carrie, Julian's married, he's moved away, he's got a business to take care of, he's busy. That's all.

CARRIE. He's never been too busy to write or phone to us. You know that.

ANNA. I know things have changed. That's as it should be.

CARRIE. Yes, of course. Yes.

GUS (*puts his head into the room*). Icebox all on one side. Miss Anna, you all sure need a new icebox. You all ought to treat yourselves.

ANNA. You know, Gus, colored people are getting to talk just like white people. Kind of a shame.

GUS. Ought to treat yourselves. Get a new little house, new little icebox. No more Julian to worry about. Just yourselves now to treat good.

CARRIE. It's true. You getting to talk just like that white trash in my office. Just yourselves now and all that. (*With force*) Well, what do you think? We *are* going to treat ourselves good. We're going to sell this house and never come back. We're going on a great, big, long trip. For a *year,* or five. What do you think of that?

GUS (*to Anna*). Ought to get yourselves a nice cat. I'll water the yard for you. Where are you going this time?

CARRIE. Where we were always going. To Europe.

GUS. You told me that last year. And I stopped the ice. And you told me around seven years back when Julian went on his other business trip, and I stopped the ice then — (*He laughs*) When I stop it now?

CARRIE (*angry, too upset*). Very soon. *Very* soon. You hear me, Gus? *Very* soon. And if you just don't believe me you come around to church Sunday and hear us take a solemn oath right in church. We don't break a solemn oath in church.

GUS. That's good. Lot of people do.

CARRIE. How dare you, Gus? When I say a solemn oath in church?

ANNA (*to Gus*). There's food in the icebox. Help yourself.

CARRIE. Remember, Gus, when Julian and I used to eat out there and you and your sister and brother'd walk past and stare at us, and Julian would go tell Mama we wanted more food, and he'd bring it to you himself?

GUS. Yes'm. Came in handy. Just like now.

(*He exits from the porch. He picks up a garden hose and disappears to the rear of the house.*)

CARRIE (*looks at Anna*). Why did I tell him that about Europe?

ANNA. I don't know.

CARRIE. Let's get out our travel books this evening and write out all our plans.

ANNA. No. Don't let's ever speak about it, until we're ready to go, or think about it, or listen to each other, or tell Gus — I don't want to write things down again.

CARRIE. It was you who wanted to wait last time. After the wedding.

ANNA. It was you, Carrie.

CARRIE. For a very good reason. Could we give them a smaller wedding present? Lily is a very rich girl and the one thing a very rich girl knows about is sterling silver. Her mother gave them ten thousand dollars. What would Lily have thought of us?

ANNA. I don't know. I don't think she cares about things like that. Lily was so in love with Julian —

CARRIE. Oh, I imagine even in love you take time off to count your silver. We could still go to Europe this year. Do you want to? How much money have we got? Did you make the deposit this week?

ANNA. Twenty-eight hundred and forty-three dollars. No, I didn't have time.

CARRIE (*quickly*). Oh, it's too hot tonight. Should we treat ourselves and go out for supper? It's been so long since we ate in a restaurant. Let's start doing our French lessons again because we'll need them now for the trip — (*She moves to the piano and plays and sings the next speech*) *"Une chambre pour deux dames."* Have you one room for two ladies? *"Ah non! Trop chère!"* Oh no! Too expensive! *"Merci, M'sieur. Trop chère."* We'll stay in Paris, of course, for just as long as we want. Then we'll go to Strasbourg, have the famous pâté, and put flowers on the graves of Mama's relatives.

ANNA. I'll have the pâté. You put flowers on the graves of Mama's relatives.

CARRIE. Remember the night Julian told us about the marriage? He said that night we would all go to Europe together, the way we always planned. Mama would want us to put flowers on the graves in Strasbourg. She would, Anna, and so we must.

ANNA. I don't know what the dead would like. Maybe Mama's changed.

CARRIE. As soon as we do set a date for departure, I'll have my evening dress fixed. No, I won't. Pink's no good for me now. I've kind of changed color as I got older. You, too. Funny. To change color. *"C'est trop chère, M'sieur."* I don't want to go if we have to say that all the time.

ANNA. We've always said it, we always will say it. And why not?

CARRIE. I just think it would be better not to go to Europe right now.

ANNA (*laughs*). We weren't going.

CARRIE. Save enough until we can go real right. That won't take long. Maybe just another year.

ANNA. A year is a long time — now.

CARRIE. If you want to go, just let's get up and go. (*In sudden, false excitement*) Come on. Let's do. I can't tell you how much I want to go — (*Points to the piano*) That and a good piano. Every time there's a wishbone I say I want a good life for Julian, a piano, a trip to Europe. That's all. You know, even if we can't go to Europe we could afford a little trip to Chicago. The coach fares are very cheap —

ANNA. I don't think we should run after Julian and Lily and intrude on their lives.

CARRIE. Who's doing that? What an unpleasant idea. (*As Anna starts toward the kitchen*) We haven't got twenty-eight hundred and forty-three dollars. I took out a thousand dollars yesterday and sent it to Chicago. I didn't know then that Julian had moved from the hotel. But I am sure they'll forward the money — I signed the wire with love from Anna and Carrie, so he knows it comes from you, too.

ANNA (*slowly*). I don't think you should have done that.

CARRIE. But I knew you would want to send it —

ANNA. How do you know what I want?

CARRIE (*slowly, hurt*). Shouldn't I know what you want for Julian? (*When Anna does not answer*) I'm sorry our trip will have to wait a little longer, but —

ANNA. I'm sorry, too. But it's not the trip. Nor the money. We are interfering, and we told ourselves we wouldn't.

CARRIE. But if he needs money —

ANNA. Needs it? Julian has a good business. Why do you think he needs it?

CARRIE. He's always needed it. (*Quickly*) I mean I don't mean that. I mean it's because the letter didn't come. Anyway, even people with a good business can use a little money — You think I did wrong?

ANNA. Yes, I do.

(*She exits*)

CARRIE (*calling after Anna*). Julian won't be angry with me. He never has been. I'll just telephone to him and say — (*She makes a half move to the phone*) But there's no place to phone to. Anna, what do you think?

(*There is no answer. After a second she moves back to the piano and begins to play. During her speech Albertine Prine and Henry Simpson appear in the garden. Albertine Prine is a handsome woman of about forty-five, dressed with elegance, but in no current fashion. She speaks carefully, as if she were not used to talking very much. Her movements are graceful and quiet. Henry is a colored man of about forty-five. He is dressed in a summer suit, but he carries a chauffeur's cap. Mrs. Prine stops as she hears the piano.*)

ALBERTINE. Is the older one Miss Caroline?

HENRY (*laughs*). They call her Carrie. No. Miss Anna is the older one.

ALBERTINE. You laugh at me. But I only met them twice before the marriage. Two long dinners. Many savage tribes have a law that people must eat alone, in silence. Sensible, isn't it? (*She moves toward the porch steps, then stops*) Perhaps it would be best if you went in. I'm not good at seeing people anymore, and there will be much chatter. (*He doesn't answer her. She laughs*) Very well. But I am sure it's hot in there. Would you tell them I'm out here?

HENRY (*gently*). *You* have come to call on *them.*

ALBERTINE. Nice to live this close to the river. I still like it down here. Soggy and steaming. The flowers aren't strong enough to cover the river smells. That's the way it should be. Very vain of flowers to compete with the Mississippi. My grandmother lived on this street when I was a little girl, and I liked it then. I used to pretend I slept under the river, and had a secret morning door up into this street. What are you holding?

HENRY. A chauffeur's cap.

ALBERTINE. You win many battles. Never mind. Wear it if you must. Put it on now and say I am here.

HENRY. No. Just go and ring the bell.

(*She moves up the porch steps. Anna comes back into the room, dressed in an apron and carrying a tray.*)

ANNA (*to Carrie*). I'm making jambalaya for you.

CARRIE. Isn't that nice?

(*The bell rings. Carrie jumps and runs to the door.*)

ALBERTINE (*to Carrie*). Hello, Miss Anna.

CARRIE (*amazed*). Mrs. Prine. Mrs. Prine. Do come in. (*She moves ahead of Albertine, calling*) Mrs. Prine is here. Isn't that nice?

ANNA (*moves forward*). Mrs. Prine, it's gracious of you to come. We should have come to call on you.

CARRIE (*flustered*). We're relatives now, after all. We did phone, three times. But, of course, you never got the messages.

ALBERTINE (*to Carrie*). Yes, I did get them, Miss Anna.

ANNA. *I* am Anna.

ALBERTINE. Forgive me.

ANNA (*turns to Carrie*). And this is Carrie. Close your dress.

CARRIE. Oh, my goodness. (*She turns away and nervously buttons her dress*) You must forgive me —

ANNA. How are you, Mrs. Prine? Are you spending the summer across the lake?

ALBERTINE. No. I've closed the lake house. Now that Lily is married, I stay right here in summer. I don't like the country.

CARRIE. Not like the country. My. I never heard anybody say a thing like that before. It takes courage to just up and say you don't like the country. Everybody likes the country.

ALBERTINE. Do they? I see so few people.

ANNA (*quickly*). You must be lonely without Lily.

ALBERTINE. No.

CARRIE. Oh. Goodness.

ALBERTINE. I've come at your supper time —

ANNA. And we'd like to share it with you.

CARRIE. Oh, please do stay. I'll just go and primp myself —

ALBERTINE. No, thank you. I eat at midnight. It's my bad habit to live at night and sleep the days away.

CARRIE. Lily said that — Well, she just said that.

ALBERTINE. I suppose it was hard on a child, a young girl, not to have her mother available during the day. But perhaps it was just as well. What time do you expect Lily and Julian?

CARRIE. Expect them? Expect them? We haven't heard for seventeen days —

ALBERTINE. Lily left a message that they'd be here tonight. I came to say —

ANNA (*as Carrie turns to her*). They'd be *here* tonight? We've had no word, Mrs. Prine.

CARRIE (*in great excitement*). The Chicago train comes in at seven. Have we time to get to the station? I'll phone. It's never on time. I'll get dressed right away. Are there enough shrimps? Is there crayfish bisque left? We can still buy some wine — Get dressed, Anna —

ALBERTINE. Miss Carrie, they are not on the Chicago train.

CARRIE. You said you had a message —

ALBERTINE. Yes, Lily spoke with Henry on the phone. She said they would be coming here tonight.

CARRIE. Then they *must* be on that train —

ALBERTINE. No. The call was not from Chicago. The call came from here.

CARRIE (*carefully*). It could not have come from here.

ALBERTINE. I am sure of it, Miss Carrie, because I saw Lily two nights ago.

CARRIE. Saw her? Here? Here? (*After a second*) What did Lily say?

ALBERTINE. I didn't speak to her. She was moving back and forth in front of the house as if she wished to come in and didn't wish to come in.

CARRIE (*after a pause*). You saw your daughter, after a whole year, walking in front of your house and you didn't speak to her? I don't understand, Mrs. Prine.

ALBERTINE. That's quite all right.

ANNA (*softly*). But we need to understand.

ALBERTINE (*turns her head, looks at Carrie and then at Anna*). Strange. Sometimes I can't tell which of you is speaking. (*To Carrie*) Your manner, Miss Carrie, is so, well, so Southern. And then, suddenly, you are saying what I had thought Miss Anna might say. It is as if you had exchanged faces, back and forth, forth and back.

CARRIE (*sharply*). Did you see Julian?

ALBERTINE. There. That's what I mean. No. Julian was not with Lily. I have simply had a message saying they would be here this evening. I have told you all I know.

CARRIE (*to Anna*). What should we do? (*To Albertine*) What are you going to do?

ALBERTINE. I will go home now and ask you to tell Lily that I will come again in the morning. Please tell them that the house is mostly closed up, but by tomorrow I can make them comfortable.

CARRIE. Oh, no. Julian will want to be here.

ALBERTINE. Ah, I am sure they prefer to stay here, but —

ANNA. There must be a good reason why Julian hasn't told us he is in town. If we seem upset, Mrs. Prine, it is because we are not accustomed to —

ALBERTINE. — daughters who walk in the night and mothers who do not speak to daughters who walk in the night. I really don't know why Lily didn't come in to me, nor why I didn't ask her. Good night. Thank you. (*She moves out, followed by Anna, followed by a dazed Carrie. Henry is waiting in the garden. Albertine moves toward him, then turns toward the porch*) I think you have met Henry Simpson. Miss Anna and Miss Carrie Berniers, Henry.

HENRY. Good evening.

(*Albertine takes his arm and they exit.*)

CARRIE (*softly*). Is *that* the man Lily calls Henry? *That* man was there in a white coat when we went for dinner, but I didn't know that was the Henry. You mean he's a nigger? I never heard anybody introduce a nigger before. I'm sorry I didn't say something. I never think of things in time. (*She turns, sees Anna has gone back to the living room, and moves to join her*) That man Lily called Henry is a nigger. Is he a chauffeur? What is he? Last time, he was a butler. Introduces us to a nigger — (*Sits down, desperate*) Do you believe that strange woman? Do you believe they're in town?

ANNA. Maybe Lily's pregnant. They arrived and wanted to go to a doctor first so they could tell us the good news. I'm sure something like that —

CARRIE. She's not pregnant.

ANNA. How do you know?

CARRIE. Girls like Lily don't have babies right away. Too full of good times the first year of marriage, I can tell you that.

ANNA. What do you know about the first year of marriage?

CARRIE. I just know.

ANNA. How? From books you don't read anymore?

CARRIE. You're saying that again. Teasing me again. No, I don't read much anymore, and I don't play the piano, or put ice on my face, or walk for wild flowers — (*Very loudly, as if she were going to cry*) I get tired now after work and that terrible man. All I want to do is have a little something to eat and play casino, and — Don't you like to play casino with me, is that what you're saying?

ANNA. Not every night. I like to read —

CARRIE. You don't ever have to play casino again. Read whenever you like, but don't nag me about it. You used to do it with Julian, too. Some people read and some people learn other ways — I think she's crazy, that Mrs. Prine. And you know what? I don't believe they're in New Orleans without coming here. (*Lamely*) Do you? What do you think?

ANNA. I think it's happened again. And he feels bad and doesn't want to tell us.

CARRIE. Well, that's natural enough. Who wants to come home and say they've failed? What do you mean? *What's* happened again?

ANNA (*gently*). You understood me.

(*She exits toward the kitchen.*)

CARRIE. I don't think it's nice to guess this way. We don't know anything, and yet here we are — (*But Anna has left the room*) A great many men take a long time to find themselves. And a lot of *good* businessmen just aren't worth bowing to. Goodness. Look at the people in my office. Dull, stupid — ugly, too. I don't like ugly people. I just can't help it, and I'm not ashamed anymore to say it. (*Anna comes back carrying a tray of food*) Are you going to *eat?*

ANNA. I always have. I think it's best to continue.

CARRIE. You're just as worried and nervous as I am. You always talk cold when you get nervous. Anna. Please. When he comes, don't be cold. Please. It will hurt him —

ANNA. Why do you so often make it seem as if I had been severe and unloving? I don't think it's true.

CARRIE. I don't do that. It's you who gave him everything, long before I was old enough to help. But sometimes you go away from us both, and, well, it worries Julian when you do that.

ANNA (*takes a bankbook from her pocket*). Here is the savings bankbook. Give it to him.

CARRIE (*deeply pleased*). Oh, thank you. I'll give it to him when we're alone and Lily doesn't see. (*Anna sits at the table, and puts food on Carrie's plate. Carrie moves about*) It's only for a short time. We'll have it back. After all, in a sense, this money is his. We lent it to him and he paid us back. This is the very money he paid us back, Anna. So, in a sense, it's his.

ANNA. Do come and eat.

CARRIE. You're thinking that what I just said is foolish. You're thinking that we never understood where he got the money to pay for your operation —

ANNA. You know very well where he got it: he played in a dangerous poker game.

CARRIE. I'm not so sure. I often wondered —

ANNA. The shrimps are getting cold. (*She begins to eat.*)

CARRIE. I can't eat. I don't know how you can. (*Sighs, then brightens*) You know, it sounds strange, but I am positive he will make a fortune someday.

ANNA. A fortune isn't necessary. A job is.

CARRIE. All those self-made men at the office. Like Mr. Barrett. No interest in anything. Making fun of opera and poetry and women. Mean, too, ever since he tried to put his hands on me years ago. Pig. Things can go wrong for a long time and then suddenly everything in a man's life clears up — Have you a headache, Anna? Do your eyes worry you to-night? Can I get you something?

ANNA. I haven't a headache. And if I had I wouldn't know the remedy. A prescription put up fresh each time Julian fails.

CARRIE. Oh, don't be sad. I'm not. I feel cheerful. Place and people and time make things go wrong, and then all of a sudden — (*There is the offstage noise of a car. She jumps up, runs to the window, stares out, nods at what she sees. Slowly, suddenly cool and calm, she turns back to Anna*) I am going to wait on the porch. Please don't show what you feel. Welcome him as he should always be welcomed in this, his house.

(*She moves to the porch. Julian's voice is heard offstage.*)

JULIAN. Is that my Carrie on the porch?

CARRIE (*laughs with enormous pleasure*). Yes, that's your Carrie on the porch. I can still jump. Shall I jump and you will catch me? (*In the middle of her speech, as she begins a jump movement, a Taxi Driver appears carrying a very large number of packages and valises*) Oh.

(*Julian and Lily Berniers appear. He is a handsome, tall man of about thirty-four. Lily is a frail, pretty girl of about twenty-one. She moves behind him. Julian's arms and hands are filled with valises and packages.*)

JULIAN. Don't jump. I have no hands to catch you. (*Grinning, he moves up the steps as Carrie waits for him. He puts the valises down and takes her in his arms, lifting her from the ground*) Darling Carrie-Pie.

CARRIE. Julian.

(*He kisses her, puts her down. She clings to him a minute and follows him as he moves quickly into the house and toward Anna. Lily follows Carrie. Anna stands waiting for him, smiling warmly. When he kisses Anna it is quite different — no less warm, but different — from his greeting to Carrie. Anna moves away from him and toward Lily.*)

ANNA. My dear Lily, how good to see you.

CARRIE (*to Julian*). One year and six days. (*As she hears Anna's greeting to Lily*) Lily! I didn't see you. (*Kisses Lily. Lily smiles and kisses her*) Forgive me. One year and six days. I was so excited that I didn't see you —

JULIAN (*to the Taxi Driver, who comes in carrying the valises and packages*). Bring them in. Bring them in. I'm hungry, Anna. Hungry for your cooking. Not a good restaurant in Chicago. Would *not* know a red pepper if they saw one.

CARRIE. There's crayfish in the icebox, thank God, and jambalaya on the table —

JULIAN. Then go and get them. I'm weak. *Very,* very weak.

ANNA (*laughs*). You don't look it.

CARRIE. Sit down, dear —

(She starts to run off to the kitchen. Before she does, Julian hands the Taxi Driver several bills. She peers at them. Julian laughs.)

JULIAN. Don't be nosey. He deserves them. No porters at the station because the train came in early.

TAXI DRIVER (*stares at the bills*). Thank you, sir. Thank you — (*Puzzled*) The train came in —

JULIAN (*Quickly*). All right. Good-bye. (*Gives him another bill*) Buy your baby something from me.

TAXI DRIVER. Thank you, sir. But I have to say in frank and complete honesty that I haven't got a baby.

JULIAN (*gives him another bill*). Then take this and get one and name it Julian.

(The Taxi Driver laughs and exits.)

ANNA. You still say that to waiters and taxi drivers. That means you've been in a poker game. And what train came in early?

CARRIE (*very quickly*). Anna, go get the crayfish. And make fresh, hot coffee. Lily, shall I take you to your room? Oh, my no, it needs cleaning. Well, just sit down. Anna, get the crayfish for Julian.

ANNA. There are no crayfish.

JULIAN (*is eating the dinner on the table with great pleasure*). We'll go out later and have them with champagne. (*To Anna*) The same dress?

ANNA. The same dress. You look tired, Lily. Can I get you something?

LILY. I am tired. Julian doesn't like me to be tired.

JULIAN. I don't like anybody to be tired. But it was a long trip, darling — (*As if he is prompting her*) Wasn't it a long trip, Lily?

LILY. Yes. When it happened. It was long when it happened.

JULIAN. Lily.

LILY (*quickly, to Carrie and Anna*). It was a very long trip. Longer than going.

ANNA. The wedding day. My how it rained. And Julian put his new coat round your pretty dress and the drawing room was full of flowers. Remember?

LILY (*smiling, suddenly uplifted, happy*). Did it rain? I don't remember. It was all days to me: Cold and hot days, fog and light, and I was on a high hill running down with the top of me, and flying with the left of me, and singing with the right of me — (*Softly*) I was doing everything nice anybody had ever done nice.

ANNA (*touched*). Nice.

LILY. What were you doing when I was doing all that, Julian?

JULIAN (*his mouth very full*). Being my kind of happy.

LILY. You're always happy.

JULIAN. I am glad you think that, darling.

ANNA. You've given us no news. How is the shoe factory?

JULIAN. What shoe factory?

(*There is a long silence. He is grinning and eating. Anna moves toward the window, and takes in a plant. Carrie, standing behind Julian, holds up her hand in an attempt to stop Anna's questions. Anna sees it and ignores it.*)

ANNA (*Carefully*). The shoe factory that you bought in Chicago.

JULIAN. Oh, *that* shoe factory. It's gone.

ANNA. Don't be flip with me, Julian.

CARRIE (*Gesturing wildly*). He's not. He's just trying to explain —

JULIAN (*turns, sees Carrie, laughs, catches the gesturing hand*). No, I'm not. I'm not trying to explain anything. (*To Anna*) I was being flip. I forget that you worry about the money I lose.

ANNA. It's not the money — It's that you don't seem to care. And the money was —

JULIAN. Lily's money.

LILY. My money? Doesn't matter about my money. I don't want money.

CARRIE (*to Lily*). You mustn't worry about it. Not worth it.

LILY. I'm not worried about money, Miss Carrie.

CARRIE. I suppose rich people always worry about money. People like us have to learn there are more important things.

LILY. I said I wasn't worried about money, Miss Carrie.

CARRIE. Well, you mustn't.

JULIAN (*to Anna*). The factory was a crooked sell. The machinery wasn't any good. I didn't know anything about shoe machinery and I never should have thought I did. Man who sold it to me faked the books. That's all.

CARRIE (*softly*). That could happen to anybody.

JULIAN (*laughs*). No. Not to anybody. Just to me.

CARRIE. That's not true. And you mustn't ever believe it.

JULIAN. Darling Carrie. Hiding her hopes that I would come home with Chicago over my shoulder, dressed in gold, bringing candied oranges to hang in your hair. Well, that's just what I've done. Your hair don't look nice, Carrie-Pie.

ANNA (*rises, crosses to the pile of dishes to carry them out*). We can help you.

CARRIE. Yes, indeed we can. Julian, come in the kitchen and help me wash the dishes.

JULIAN. No, ma'am. And you're never going to wash dishes again.

ANNA. I don't wish to ask questions that you might not like, Julian. But it's uncomfortable this way. Your mother was here, Lily. She said she had seen you, had a message from you. She said she would come back tomorrow. (*To Julian, who has turned to stare at Lily*) So this is not your first night in town. You need not explain, but I thought we should.

JULIAN. We've been in New Orleans for a week, at the hotel. I had a good reason for that. It was no neglect of you. I even came by and stared in at you — (*Points outside*) — the first hour back. You were playing casino and Anna was yawning. You look tired, both of you. You need a long, long good time. (*To Anna*) This time, no need to be sad. I used to tell you: never was any good; never came out anywhere.

ANNA. I am sad that you think it all so easy, so unimportant, so — "Never came out anywhere." I guess not, although I don't think those words mean very much.

CARRIE (*to Anna, in a voice used once before*). I won't have that kind of talk. This is a happy, joyous night. Julian is home and that's all we need to know. It's a happy, joyous night.

(*Anna exits.*)

LILY (*to Julian*). I didn't see my mother, I didn't go in. And I only sent the message today. I knew we'd arrive here, anyway, so — (*Softly, when there is no answer*) — I disobeyed you. But not much. Have I done harm?

JULIAN. No.

(*Carrie, listening, pretending she isn't, is idly playing on the piano with one hand.*)

LILY. I know you told me not to see anybody. But you didn't tell me why or anything. You just kept leaving the hotel. I want to see my mother. I want to talk with my mother.

JULIAN (*smiles*). I'm glad to hear that. I've never heard you want that before.

LILY. Are you angry with me?

JULIAN (*smiles at her, shakes his head, moves away*). Carrie, stop that awful sound, darling. Just wait for the good piano —

CARRIE (*laughs*). No, I'd only find out I couldn't really play.

(*Julian has moved out to porch and is hauling in valises. Lily rises and follows him.*)

JULIAN (*calling to Carrie*). You all been to the opera?

CARRIE. No. We'll wait until Europe.

JULIAN (*laughs*). Still talking about Europe?

CARRIE. Oh, we'll go someday. You'll see.

JULIAN (*bringing in valises*). Someday soon?

(*He goes out again for more.*)

CARRIE. In a few years. Plenty of time. We're not that old.

(*She moves quickly out of the room.*)

JULIAN. Yes, you are. Old enough to have fun. Have to crowd it in now, Carrie, both of you. Crowd it in fast. (*Smiling at Lily*) You, too. Twenty-one is very, very old.

LILY. Tell me you're not angry with me.

JULIAN (*his arms heavy with valises*). I am not angry with you. Have I ever been angry with you? Why do you ask me that so often?

LILY. Julian, who is the lady you talked to on the train?

JULIAN (*too lightly*). Which lady? — I talk to everybody.

LILY. The not such a young lady with the sad face.

JULIAN. Most ladies on trains are not young and have sad faces. I often wondered why. (*He tries to pass her*) Move, darling.

LILY. The one you were with today and yesterday and —

JULIAN (*turns, stares at her*). Where did you see me?

LILY. I don't know. Just on the street. In front of the hotel —

JULIAN. No, you didn't.

LILY. No, I didn't. That's the first lie I ever told you, Julian.

JULIAN. Then it's one more than I ever told you.

(*Carrying the valises, he moves into the living room. Lily follows him.*)

LILY. I saw you in Audubon Park. On a bench. By the ducks.

JULIAN. Have you told anybody?

LILY. No.

JULIAN. Don't. The lady would be in trouble. And so would we.

LILY. And in that little restaurant. At a table —

JULIAN. Oh, Lily.

LILY. I didn't mean to walk after you, to follow you. But I was so lonely in the hotel room, locked up the way you asked me to be.

JULIAN. All right, darling, all right. Don't follow me, Lily, ever again. That's not the way to be married. (*Lily hesitates, as if to say something, then exits*) Hey, everybody. Come and get your presents. Hey, where is everybody?

CARRIE (*appears in the garden, runs up the porch, speaks in a whisper*). Julian. I want to speak to you. Come here.

JULIAN. Can't. You come here.

CARRIE. Sssssh. (*He comes to the porch. She sits down on the porch steps*) Come here. I've got a nice secret. And this is where we always told nice secrets.

JULIAN. You come here. *I* got nice secrets. Where's Anna? Anna!

CARRIE. Ssh. Ssh.

JULIAN (*sits beside her*). What's the matter with you?

CARRIE (*gives him the savings bankbook*). No need for Lily to see. You'll just tell her it's yours. More than twenty-eight hundred dollars. And we don't need any of it, not any of it, so don't say anything — (*He takes her hands, kisses them. She is very moved. Softly, embarrassed*) Don't say anything, please. And if that isn't enough, we can manage other things, too.

JULIAN (*stares at the book, then rises and calls out*). Anna!

CARRIE. Anna doesn't want any thanks —

(*Anna comes into the room.*)

JULIAN (*enters the room, holds out the bankbook*). God bless you. All my life it's been this way.

ANNA (*smiles*). You are our life. It is we who should thank you.

(*He takes her in his arms.*)

JULIAN. How many, many times.

CARRIE (*comes into the room*). You paid it back, always.

JULIAN. You know I didn't. But this time I will.

CARRIE. Of course you will. But Lily doesn't have to know about all this — So ssh.

JULIAN. Stop ssshing me and come here and sit down and stop talking. (*He puts Carrie in a chair and motions to Anna to be seated. Then he leans down to unwrap the boxes and open the valises. The boxes are dressmaker boxes, and he pulls from them two fancy evening dresses. They are too grand for anything less than a ball. Carrie leans forward, stares at them*) For a ball. Wear them the second time at the opera, if you like. But I don't think dresses like these should be worn twice in the same city, do you? Everybody in Paris will talk, and we can't have that. (*He opens another box*) Maybe you can wear them again when you get to Strasbourg. (*Points his finger at Carrie*) Not to the cemetery. I bet the opera house there is drafty — (*He has taken out two fur pieces and arranged them over the dresses*) No, no. I've got things mixed up. (*He begins to fumble in another box*) Or so the lady said. The furs are for breakfast or something. (*He is now holding up two fur-trimmed opera coats. They are royal in feeling*) *These* are for the dresses. And maybe they can be worn the second time. (*He moves to arrange them over Anna and Carrie. Carrie's is much too large and she looks drowned. He points to the other boxes and valises*) Suits for traveling. Dresses for informal evenings, whatever that is. (*Pulls out frothy, very youthful negligees*) For flirtations on Italian terraces. (*Drapes them over Anna and Carrie. He goes to Carrie with a large, rather flashy necklace*) Garnets. Your birthstone. Next time, pearls. (*He drapes over Anna's arm a large gold mesh bag*) Remember when old lady Senlis used to come along swinging her gold mesh bag, and your eyes would pop out wondering what was in it? Look and see what's in this one.

ANNA (*softly*). What is all this, Julian?

JULIAN. It is that we're rich. Just open your gold mesh bag with diamond initials — Anna, *diamond* initials — and see what's inside.

CARRIE (*loud, nervous giggle*). The only thing could be, is a certificate to an insane asylum.

JULIAN (*takes an envelope from the purse*). You're wrong. A certificate to a boat called the *Ottavia*, sailing day after tomorrow. Two rooms, one of them a parlor. Think of that, a parlor on a boat. (*He takes the envelope to Carrie*) Look at it, look at it. Of course, we had always planned to go together. But I won't be able to go with you, darling, not this time, big business here, and all that. But we'll join you in a few months —

CARRIE (*dully*). We'll wait for you.

JULIAN. No, you won't. No more waiting for anything.

ANNA (*softly*). Where does all this come from, Julian?

JULIAN. All over town. I just went in places and said bring out the best for two pretty ladies who are on their way. On their way.

ANNA. You know what I mean.

JULIAN. I know what you mean. They were bought with my money. Mine. Yours. Ours. We're rich. How do you like that, how do you like it?

CARRIE. We'll like it fine — when it happens. (*Giggles*) Rich. Us!

JULIAN. What are you doing?

CARRIE. Trying to make a neat package.

JULIAN. Stop it. (*When she doesn't*) I said to stop it. Nothing's going back this time. Listen to me. Now listen to me. We're rich. (*Lily comes into the room. She is in underwear and is carrying a hairbrush. He smiles at her*) Aren't we rich?

LILY. Mama's rich, I guess.

JULIAN. No, us, us. I've been telling you for a week.

LILY. There are three men at the back door. From a trucking company —

JULIAN. Tell them to bring them in, darling. (*She exits*) Right in here. Now you're going to see something.

CARRIE (*stares at the boat tickets*). Are these real boat tickets? I mean, stamped and bought?

JULIAN. Bought and stamped. Look. It's going to be this way. The first money is for us to have things. Have fun. After that, I promise you, we'll invest. And like all people with money, we'll make more and more and more until we get sick from it. Rich people get sick more than we do. Maybe from worry.

ANNA. Poor people, too. Like me, right now. (*Very sharply*) Where did you get this money, Julian?

CARRIE. Oh, now don't start that tone. You know very well he's been in a poker game.

JULIAN. No, she doesn't know that, and you don't either. (*Two*

Moving Men appear, carrying a fancy, highly carved spinet. There is a big sign on the spinet lettered Carrie) Come in. Just put it down. (*Motions to Carrie*) By that lady.

(*The Men carry the spinet to Carrie and place it near her.*)

CARRIE. My God.

(*Another Moving Man comes in wheeling a large refrigerator on a dolly. The first two Men move to help him.*)

JULIAN. And put that by this lady. (*He motions toward Anna. They wheel the refrigerator and place it almost in front of Anna. Lily comes back into the room*) Good. (*He pulls out several large bills*) Thank you. Buy the babies something from me. (*To the head Moving Man*) Name the next one Julian.

MOVING MAN. There ain't going to be no next one. Thank you.

(*They exit.*)

LILY. Why do you always say that? We'll name our son Julian. Don't you believe —

JULIAN (*laughs*). Insurance. That's all.

CARRIE (*to Lily*). You're in your slip. In front of men.

JULIAN. Can't harm them.

CARRIE. I never heard of such a thing. Answering the door in your underwear. Don't you mind?

JULIAN. I mind that you haven't looked at your piano. Think, Carrie, a fine new piano, what you always wanted, right in front of you — Play it. Play it for me, Carrie, the way we used to always say.

(*She puts out her hand, touches a note, takes her hand away and puts it over her face.*)

JULIAN (*softly, smiling*). I know. Take your time.

ANNA. What is all this? Answer me, please, Julian.

JULIAN. I'm going to tell you all about it someday soon. I can't now. But I'll tell you this much, I didn't play poker. All I did was sell some real estate.

ANNA. You never owned any real estate.

JULIAN. No. But I do now, see?

ANNA. No, I don't see. I don't see at all.

JULIAN. Once I liked somebody and they liked me, and she thought I was kind to her. So years go by and she hears about a good thing, and gives me the tip on it. And the tip works. Boy, how it worked. Now let it go. I'll tell you soon, but in the meantime I gave my word because she could be in bad trouble. Now stop worrying, and sit back — (*He guides Anna's hand to refrigerator door, opens it, pulls an envelope from it*) I finished the deal and collected the money at two o'clock today. At two-eighteen, I rang the bells of Mr. Maxwell Shine. And so here's the mortgage to the house. (*Kneels; softly*) Look, Anna, first time in our lives, first time in our father's life. You have a house, without worry or asking him to wait. Remember when I was a kid and the time you took me with you and you made me tell Mr. Shine how I wouldn't have anyplace to live unless — Christ God, how I hated — Do you remember?

ANNA. I remember.

JULIAN. Well, there'll never be such things to say again. Not for any of us. (*He rises and shouts*) Not ever, ever. (*To Carrie*) I wrote your Mr. Barrett a letter last night. I wrote it three times. "Your petty angers, the silk stockings at Christmas that were always cheaper than a decent salary. Miss Caroline Berniers will not return to work." (*Carrie rises, makes a sound in her throat, stands staring at him. He turns to Anna*) For you I just wrote that Miss Anna Berniers was resigning from the coat department because she was leaving for an extended European tour. (*He sits down. Anna lifts her head and stares at him. There is a long silence*) Well. Say something.

ANNA. I can't say something.

JULIAN. I know, I know. All came so fast. Well, we don't have to say things to each other, never did. Just sit back and have fun. That's all I want. (*To Lily*) And for you — Give me the wedding ring. (*Sharply she pulls back from him*) Give it to me. (*He takes the ring from her finger*) Twenty dollars in a pawnshop, and I polished it, and prayed you wouldn't mind, or say anything. (*He takes from his pocket, and puts on her finger, a very large diamond ring*) With this, I you wed again, and forever.

LILY. Please give me my ring.

JULIAN (*now he holds up her hand so that she can see her new diamond ring*). Look, darling, look at it. Superstitious? (*He looks at Lily, then at Carrie, then at Anna*) Please don't cry or look it, all of you. (*He takes an envelope from his pocket, goes to each of them as he speaks, lets them look into the envelope*) One hundred and fifty thousand dollars, less peanuts — (*Motions to the packages*) — for this. Seventy-five thousand for my partner, seventy-five thousand for me. My lawyer said I shouldn't carry all that cash around, rich people don't carry cash, not more than ten or twenty dollars, so other people pay the bills. But I said I'll carry this, I like it — Hey, did you hear — my lawyer. *I've* got a *lawyer*. What do you think of that? (*Carrie has paid little attention to the money in the envelope, but Anna is staring at it*) Ain't counterfeit. Twenty five-thousand-dollar bills; fifty one-thousand-dollar bills — You'll believe it all by tomorrow. Big, successful Julian, the way you wanted me. The man who was never good at anything except living on his sisters, and losing his wife's money. I never minded failure much, you minded. But you know what? I like things this way: Making bargains, talking big — I don't take my hat off in elevators anymore — (*Laughs with great pleasure and picks up a large package*) Now to *important* business. Last night I drew up a budget list, you know, the way we used to. Only where we put carfare for the week, I put champagne, and where we put lunch money, sixty cents each, I put caviar. You'll like caviar.

CARRIE. I hate caviar. The one time I ever ate it, I hated it. Just hated it.

JULIAN (*holds up the package*). Champagne. *And* caviar, Carrie-Pie. You'll learn to like it. (*He starts toward the kitchen*) We're going to have a champagne-caviar party just for us. Sit down and play the piano.

(*He exits.*)

CARRIE (*softly*). Since when do you give me orders? (*Very loudly*) I said since when do you give me orders? (*Anna puts up a hand, as if to quiet her*) I don't believe it all. I don't believe it. (*When Anna doesn't answer her*) We have no jobs. (*To Lily*) What is this all about?

LILY. I want my ring. I was married in my ring.

CARRIE. I asked you a question, Lily.

LILY. I didn't hear you.

CARRIE. What is this all about? Where did Julian get this money?

LILY. I don't know, ma'am. A lady came to Chicago and phoned him, and he went to see her, and everything changed and he said we were coming here, and she was on the train, and he didn't want me to know. She calls him every night at six o'clock.

CARRIE. I'm not talking about women. That's not my business.

I'm talking about this — (*She motions around*) Europe day after tomorrow! Has he gone crazy? What does he think we are, fine ladies with maids and secretaries who can move whenever they like? Whore's clothes. I wouldn't be seen in this. Not seen. (*Turns on Anna*) For God's sake take off that stuff. What are you doing?

ANNA (*who is reading the mortgage document*). Trying to understand.

CARRIE (*in a whisper*). Does it really say —

ANNA. Yes. It really says we own this house.

CARRIE. This house. This awful house. He's changed. He even talks different. Didn't he know we hated this house, always, always, always.

ANNA. You used to tell him how much we liked it, and the garden, and the street, and the memories of Mama and Papa.

CARRIE. You know very well I said all that to keep him from being ashamed of the house and what we didn't have —

ANNA (*hands her the paper*). Well. We've been rewarded.

LILY. I want my ring. I was married in my ring. (*She holds up her hand*) This is a vulgar ring.

CARRIE (*points to a tiny pin she is wearing*). Topaz is my birthstone. How could he forget when he gave me this pin with the first job he ever lost. I even wear it at night —

LILY. I want my married ring.

CARRIE. You said that before.

(*Lily runs toward the table, picks up the ring. As she does, the phone rings, and she continues the run that will bring her to the phone.*)

LILY. Hello. (*A slight pause*) No, ma'am. No, he isn't. This is his wife. What is *your* name?

(*She stares at the phone and then hangs up. After a second, she puts on the old ring and, with a violent movement, throws the diamond toward the window. It hits the window and drops. Julian comes into the room carrying an ice bucket, two bottles of champagne, glasses and two large jars of caviar.*)

JULIAN. I heard the phone. Didn't the phone ring?

ANNA (*after a second*). No.

JULIAN (*pouring*). Now. (*To Carrie, points to the piano*) Why aren't you playing? And you took off — Put the pretty clothes on so I can be proud.

CARRIE (*sharply*). All of them?

LILY. The phone did ring. It was that lady who calls every

evening. I told her you weren't here. I don't know why I said it, but I did.

JULIAN. I have business with that lady. I've told you that before. I was to meet her this evening. It's not easy for her to call me and I can't call her. Did she say she'd call back tonight? (*Lily shakes her head*) Why did you tell her I wasn't here?

LILY. I didn't know I was going to do it. Please forgive me. It wasn't nice.

JULIAN. Not nice, wasn't it? You know what I think it wasn't? Respectful. (*He moves toward Carrie*) Re-spect-ful — Respectful. I don't think I can spell that word. I never used it before. But I like it. (*He hits his chest*) A man. Respect. That's what you always said, success isn't everything but it makes a man stand straight, and you were right. (*He hands a glass of champagne to Anna and offers caviar. He speaks to Carrie*) You want to know something? I bring you a piano, I ask you to play it for me, you don't. I don't think that's respectful. (*He laughs*) I like that word. (*Carrie sits down at the piano and begins to play. She fumbles, as if she is thinking of something else, then plays a waltz. Julian moves to Lily, gives her a glass, whirls her around, kisses her hair*) I forgive you, my infant bride. (*He looks at her hand*) Where's your ring?

(*Anna rises, crosses, and picks up the ring.*)

LILY. I don't know.

JULIAN. You don't know.

ANNA. I have it. I was looking at it.

(*Julian smiles, kisses Lily's hair. The music stops sharply and he turns to Carrie.*)

JULIAN. More, more. It's a party. We're having a party. (*To Anna*) Dance?

(*He pulls her to her feet, whirls her around, the long evening coat tangled in her legs.*)

CARRIE. Anna. You look like a fool. Like a real fool.

JULIAN. What's the matter? (*Moving to Carrie. He hands her a glass of champagne. Staring at him, she sips it*) Good? (*He spoons out a large amount of caviar, sings*) *Avez-vous les chambres, Monsieur Hotel-keeper? Non, ils ne sont pas trop chères."* Nothing is too expensive now. Send up two pounds *de* caviar *pour* breakfast *pour ma soeur et moi.* (*He leans over her with the caviar*) Now.

(He forces her mouth open. Julian laughs.)

CARRIE. You're laughing at me. You've never laughed at me before. *(She rises, shrilly)* You're laughing at me.

JULIAN. No, I wasn't. I'm just happy. I'm giving a party — *(He looks at Anna, who turns her head away; then at Lily, who looks sad and tearful)* What's the matter with everybody? *(He drinks his champagne. He pours himself another drink, bolts it, stares at them)* We're not having a very nice party. What's the matter?

Curtain

Act Two

SCENE: *The same as Act One. Early Thursday morning.*

AT RISE: *The spinet and the refrigerator are as they were the night before. Anna, in a housedress, is lowering the plants from the window into the garden. On a chair is a large, old-fashioned trunk-type suitcase; near the suitcase are two pairs of shoes. Anna sits down, and begins to polish the shoes with rag and paste. Carrie enters carrying a coffee pot. She is dressed and has on her hat. She sits down and pours herself a cup of coffee.*

CARRIE. Is your headache better?

ANNA. I didn't have a headache.

CARRIE. You said you did.

ANNA. No, I didn't.

CARRIE. Last night, before you went to bed, you said your eyes were bothering you, you had a headache.

ANNA. No.

CARRIE. I think everybody's going crazy. I really do. No wonder you can't remember what you said. I don't think I slept an hour. I'd close my eyes, and say I don't believe it, when I get up — (*Points to the spinet, the boxes, etc.*) — that thing, and that, won't be there, and it will be years ago. He stayed out in the garden drinking by himself till late last night. (*Points inside*) Still asleep?

ANNA. I suppose so.

CARRIE. How could *you* have slept last night? Mama use to say you could sleep through anything.

ANNA. Mama believed that lack of sleep was a sign of good breeding. Do you remember the time she said she hadn't slept for two years? Yes, I heard Lily, if that's what you mean.

CARRIE. She rattled around half the night. She went out, she came back, she went out. She's a very strange girl. I remember thinking that the first time I ever met her. (*Points around the room*) And she doesn't know any more about all this than we do. That's not natural in a good marriage. In a good marriage a man doesn't have secrets from his wife.

ANNA. How do you know?

CARRIE. It's not natural in a good marriage, I can tell you that.

ANNA. We don't know anything about a good marriage or a bad one. I read somewhere that old maids are the true detectives of the human heart. But I don't want to be a detective of other people's hearts. I'm having enough trouble with my own.

CARRIE. I know you are. I know you're just as worried as I am. I know that's why you're having headaches again.

ANNA. I said I didn't have a headache.

CARRIE. I'll get you something for it. Julian pampers Lily as if she were a child. He never treated us that way, always boasted of our good sense.

ANNA. He didn't marry us.

CARRIE. Nobody wants a child for a wife.

ANNA. There's no sense telling your opinions about marriage to me. I don't know anything about it.

(*She gets up, carries a pair of shoes to the valise, wraps them in paper, and packs them.*)

CARRIE. What are you doing?

ANNA. Put your clothes out. I'm going to wash and iron today.

CARRIE. What for?

ANNA (*turns to stare at her*). Europe.

CARRIE. We'll miss the eight-thirty streetcar. (*When there is no answer*) We'll miss the eight-thirty streetcar. (*When there is no answer*) I know what Julian said. But I get the mail before Mr. Barrett, and if Julian did write such a letter I'll just throw it out. You better go down to the store and get somebody to do the same for you. (*Very sharply, when Anna does not answer*) *We have no jobs.* They're not easy to get and we're not young. You told me all my life what that would mean to us. You said that as long as we could work and save a little then we could get sick when we get old, and take care of Julian, and not end as Mama and Papa did.

ANNA. Julian has come home rich. We can get sick now.

CARRIE. Rich! Do you really believe this foolishness? Julian rich! God knows what he's been up to. God knows when and how it will blow up. Doesn't it worry you?

ANNA. Yes. It worries me. But I think we should go to Europe. He wants us to go.

CARRIE. What do you mean, he wants us to go? You make it sound as if we're in his way.

ANNA. I don't know what I mean.

CARRIE. Go to Europe. What are you talking about? What's going to happen when trouble comes if we're not here to take care of it?

ANNA. Why do you think trouble will come?

CARRIE. Because it always has. You know very well what I mean. Well, you go to Europe and I'll go to work.

ANNA (*laughs*). All right.

CARRIE. If Mr. Samuel Barrett has seen the letter, I'll apologize. Mr. Barrett likes people to apologize. Nineteen years of faithful work matter for something. (*Giggles*) Ho, ho. I'd like to see you in Europe alone.

(*Lily appears from the bedroom. She has on a dress and over the dress she has on a nightgown. She stares at Carrie and Anna as if she didn't know who they were.*)

ANNA. Morning. (*She rises to pour Lily a cup of coffee*) Julian want his breakfast?

LILY. I don't know. (*She points to the left side of the room*) He slept in there.

CARRIE. Mama and Papa's room.

LILY. He thought I was asleep when he went in there, but I wasn't.

CARRIE. No, you certainly weren't. You moved around most of the night. Are you dressed or undressed? Well, I'm off to work.

LILY. My. It's awfully hot to go to work.

CARRIE. Yes. And sometimes it's awfully cold.

(*She exits toward the porch. As she moves out, Mrs. Prine appears in the garden. Henry stands outside the garden fence. During the scene between Lily and Albertine, he will occasionally be seen moving back and forth.*)

ALBERTINE. Good morning.

CARRIE. Good morning.

(*Carrie hurries off. At the sound of her mother's voice, Lily runs to the porch, stares at her mother and runs back into the room.*)

LILY. Oh. Where are my shoes? (*Stares down at herself, sees that she is barefoot, hesitates*) Oh. (*Runs out again to the porch and down to the garden*) Mama. I don't know why I did that.

(*Albertine moves toward her and they kiss.*)

ALBERTINE. I come calling much too early. I forget that other people sleep at night.

LILY. I didn't.

ALBERTINE. I know.

LILY. What did Henry tell you?

ALBERTINE. That you were out, er, visiting, and wanted to speak with me.

LILY. Yes. I didn't want Henry to come and get me. I didn't need his help.

ALBERTINE. He said the neighborhood worried him at two o'clock in the morning.

LILY. How did he know where I was?

ALBERTINE. You told him on the phone.

LILY. Did I? I don't remember — I was mean to Henry. Did he tell you that?

ALBERTINE. No.

LILY (*after a second*). I'm sorry I spoke that way.

ALBERTINE. How are you, Lily? I haven't seen you in a whole year. The garden wing of the house is being cleaned for you. You are very welcome, and I've come to say that to Julian.

LILY. Thank you. It's nice that you want us. Do you?

ALBERTINE. You are thinner, Lily. Have you been well?

LILY. Do you?

ALBERTINE. Do I what?

LILY. Do you really want me to come home again?

ALBERTINE. I'll come later. You must be tired from your — night's exercise.

LILY (*quickly*). Mama, don't go. Please. I need help. Your help. I'll start at the start and try not to take long and say things nice and clear —

ALBERTINE. There's no need. Don't distress yourself. I've guessed your trouble and I've brought you a check. (*She takes a check from her bag and puts it on the garden table*) Will you and Julian come and dine at eight? Then you'll decide if you wish to move in, or if, in this heat, you prefer the lake house. I've always meant to give you the lake house, Lily, and tomorrow we'll go around and have Warkins do the papers. (*When there is no answer*) At eight?

LILY. What does Mrs. Warkins look like? Does she speak in a low voice?

ALBERTINE. I don't know. I haven't seen her in years, and then only once or twice.

LILY. You haven't seen anybody in years, except Henry, of course. How old is Mrs. Warkins?

ALBERTINE. I know little about her, Lily. It's bad enough to know Warkins. I remember her as a tall woman with a sad face. Possibly from being married to a lawyer.

LILY. Is she in love with Mr. Warkins?

ALBERTINE (*smiles, shrugs*). That is a remarkable idea. Thank God I've never been in a position to find out. Let's waste time saying things like each to his own taste, and shaking our heads in gossip, but let's do it another time.

LILY. Please don't smile and shrug, Mama. It always makes me nervous. You are angry because I was mean to Henry last night, and he told you.

ALBERTINE. He told me nothing.

LILY. *I was mean to Henry.* That was bad of me, wasn't it?

ALBERTINE (*wearily, softly*). I don't know.

LILY. Well, tell him I'm sorry.

ALBERTINE. You have been saying you are sorry, in space, for many years.

LILY. You *are* angry now.

ALBERTINE. Oh, Lily.

LILY. I don't know what makes me speak so wrong. All I want is to tell you, and have you help me. But I get things out of order — Mama, I'm in trouble.

ALBERTINE. I know Julian lost the factory. Well, perhaps he doesn't belong in a large city. He'll find something here. In the meantime — (*She picks up the check and hands it to Lily.*)

LILY. What is it, Mama?

ALBERTINE (*slowly, too patiently*). I told you. It's a check. A check is for money. Money. It's five thousand dollars. It's yours. Oblige me by not speaking of it again.

LILY. Don't be angry with me.

ALBERTINE (*after a second*). Oh, Lily. Something always happens between us.

LILY. If I could only speak in order, then I wouldn't —

ALBERTINE. Don't fret. Everybody talks too much, too many words, and gets them out of order.

LILY. I know you think that. I know you do. That's what makes it so hard. It's that you never talk much, and you look down on people who don't do it very well.

ALBERTINE. You said you were in trouble. Do you wish to tell me about it?

LILY. You speak so severely, Mama.

ALBERTINE. Please, Lily, let us cease this talking about talking. Tell me or do not tell me.

LILY (*quickly, loudly*). Mama, we're rich.

ALBERTINE. Who?

LILY. Julian.

ALBERTINE. When you say rich, do you mean *money* rich or spiritual rich, or moral rich or —

LILY. You're teasing me. Money rich.

ALBERTINE. Well, isn't that nice. Julian didn't lose the factory?

LILY. Yes, he lost it. We got rich some other way. There were phone calls from a lady and Julian would talk so I couldn't understand, and then we came here, and it all has to do with the lady, I think, and something else —

ALBERTINE (*very quickly*). Never mind. Never mind. He'll probably tell me. What good news, Lily. I must say I hadn't expected it. Forgive my bringing the check. How impertinent of me to take for granted that Julian needed it. Don't tell him, just tear it up. Tonight we'll have a celebration — if I still know how. Shall we dine at Galatoire's? (*When there is no answer, she stares at Lily*) What trouble are you in?

LILY. First we lived in a big hotel in Chicago, and I didn't like it, and didn't have anything to do. Then we moved to a little, poor hotel and I learned to cook in the bathroom, and Julian and I were close together, and he didn't have his friends anymore, and he was sad and sweet and often he stayed with me all day, in bed, and we'd read or sleep, and he'd tell me about things. We were never really hungry, but I'd have to watch the meat and give him my share when he wasn't looking because he likes meat, and I was very happy.

ALBERTINE. How often the rich like to play at being poor. A nasty game, I've always thought. You had only to write me.

LILY. It wasn't a game, it wasn't. It was just after he lost all his money in the factory —

ALBERTINE. *Your* money in the factory. You like being poor and you're not going to be. Is that the trouble you are in? I can't be sorry for you, Lily. I don't think Julian would have liked the meat game for very long; and neither would you if the shortage had lasted much longer. (*Laughs*) Cheer up. Good fortune isn't as bad as it seems.

LILY. You're laughing at me, and you shouldn't. Julian will leave me now.

ALBERTINE. Why?

LILY. He is different. Things have changed.

ALBERTINE. Marriages change from day to day and year to year. All relations between people. Women, of course, have regrets for certain delicate early minutes, but — There is no answer to that.

LILY. Did you, Mama? Did you have those regrets?

ALBERTINE. I don't remember. I don't think so. Your father and I had very little together. And so we had little to regret.

LILY. I don't mean my father.

ALBERTINE (*after a long silence*). I came here because you were in trouble, or so you said. Not because I am. When I come to you for that reason, feel free to say what you wish. Until then, please do not.

LILY. Julian couldn't have me last night, and when I cried he said please not to, that — And so I went out and walked and walked. I had never seen that street before. I heard noise way up, and I went in. There were people and a woman stood before them on a box. The people talked about themselves right out loud. One woman had lost a leg but she said it was growing back and she proved it.

(*There is a long pause.*)

ALBERTINE. My. Are you dozing off?

LILY. And a man stood up and said how he used to drink and use a gun. And the lady on the box kept saying, "Truth, truth is the way to life, and the one way, the only way. Open your hearts with this knife and throw them here." (*Throws up her arm*) She had a knife in her hand —

ALBERTINE. Do sit down, Lily.

LILY. And she kissed the knife —

(*She kisses her hand in imitation.*)

ALBERTINE. Strange tastes people have. Don't kiss your own hand again, please.

LILY (*sits down, speaks quietly*). Everybody left and there I was. The woman said, "You want me, child?" And I said, "Could I buy your knife?" "No," she said. "The knife is not for sale." But I wanted it more than I ever wanted anything and, well — (*Smiles, slyly*) — finally, we swapped something — And when it was in my hand, for the first time in my life, I just said everything, and asked. The lady said the knife of truth would dress me as in a jacket of iron flowers and though I would do battle, I would march from the battle cleansed. Then I fell asleep —

ALBERTINE. Your many religious experiences have always made me uneasy, Lily —

LILY. When I woke up I knew that I must begin my struggle up the mountain path of truth by asking you —

ALBERTINE. You telephoned at two this morning to speak with me about a journey up a mountain path of truth?

LILY. And Henry came instead, and made me get in the car, and brought me *here*. He stood in the way — But he can't. Because I must ask truth, and speak truth, and act truth, now and forever.

ALBERTINE. Do you think this is the proper climate? So hot and damp. Puts mildew on the truth.

LILY. Did you sell me to Julian, Mama?

(*Albertine rises, comes to Lily, stares at her, and takes her by the shoulders.*)

ALBERTINE (*softly*). Lily, take hold of yourself. Take hold.

LILY. Answer me.

ALBERTINE. You are my child, but I will not take much more of this.

LILY (*in a cry*). Mama, Mama, I didn't mean to hurt you. (*Puts her hand on Albertine's chest*) But it's so bad for me. Julian may leave me now, and he's all I ever had, or will, or want — Mama, did he marry me for money?

ALBERTINE. He married you because he loved you. Shame on you, Lily. You are looking for pain, and that makes me sad and always has.

LILY. I told you there is another woman. I saw them. I followed them and they went places where people wouldn't see them and they talked. And she has something to do with his getting rich.

ALBERTINE. Do you intend him never to speak to another woman? I don't know what you are talking about, getting rich, but it's good for people to have money of their own. The day comes when they don't like taking it from others. I know people thought of Julian as a charming man who didn't care about such things. But I never thought so.

LILY. Last night when I lay waiting for him, and he knew it, he said he'd had too much champagne and he wanted to sleep alone. It's been like that since the lady came to Chicago.

ALBERTINE. You've learned women's chitchat very fast. I'm not good at this, but since we've started I can tell you everybody wants to sleep alone sometimes — (*Laughs*) — maybe most of the time.

LILY. He liked to come to bed with me. You didn't know that, did you?

ALBERTINE. I have not read it in the newspaper. But, as you know, I'm a large stockholder, and if you'd like it reported in detail — (*She breaks off, puts her hand over her eyes*) Forgive me.

LILY. You'd never believed anybody could want me. I didn't believe it, either. I was so scared at first that I — But there I was, good for the man I loved. He said I was better than anybody, and that I must learn to cook because he'd always believed that a woman who was good in the bedroom was good in the kitchen — (*She laughs happily*) And I did learn. What do you think of that?

ALBERTINE. I think well of it.

LILY (*softly*). I was beloved, Mama, and I flourished. Now I'm frightened. Help me.

ALBERTINE (gently). How can I help you when I don't understand what you're talking about? Are you really saying that if Julian stayed dependent on you, all would be safe, but if he has money for himself, and need not crawl to you —

LILY. That's an ugly way to speak, Mama.

ALBERTINE. On your struggle up the mountain path, you will find that truth is often ugly. It burns. (*After a second*) I don't believe there is any other woman, but in any case, be wise enough to wait and find out.

LILY. I don't want to be wise, ever, Mama, ever. I'm in love.

ALBERTINE. Then be happy that Julian has finally had a little luck. Lily, he would have come to hate your money. *That* was the danger I feared for you.

LILY. I never wanted us to have money. I hate money. You know that, Mama.

ALBERTINE. Then be very careful. Same thing as loving it.

(*The phone rings and Lily wheels and makes a dash for the house. At the same minute, Anna, who has been moving in and out of the room, packing the valise, turns from the valise and crosses to the phone. Lily falls over the porch steps and rolls to the ground. Henry runs toward her.*)

LILY. Anna! Anna!

ALBERTINE. Lily.

ANNA (*into the phone*). I will wake him. Just a minute.

(*She moves out. Albertine moves to help Lily rise.*)

LILY (*calling to Anna*). That's the woman. I want to speak to her. I want to ask her —

(*She makes a sudden, violent movement up the porch steps.*)

ALBERTINE. No. (*Very sharply*) No.

(*Henry touches Lily's arm as if to keep her from moving.*)

LILY (*to Henry*). Leave me alone. I told you that last night. I told it to you years ago when I rolled down the hill. I meant to roll down the hill and kill myself, but you didn't know it.

HENRY. I knew it.

(*Julian appears in the living room, dressed in a robe, the envelope of money in his pocket. He moves to the phone.*)

JULIAN. Hello. Sorry about the call last night. I was dying to tell you the good news, but of course I couldn't call you back. Did the cough medicine work? Did you have a good night's sleep? This is the great day, so stop worrying. Everything went fine. Got it right here in my pocket, nice clean bills. Eleven o'clock, waving a fortune at you. Where we agreed. (*He listens, smiling*) I did everything the way you told me, only better. Don't worry about me. He just beats women. (*Gently, affectionately*) I'll be there. Good-bye, my dear. (*Anna enters the living room carrying a glass of juice and a dress. Julian takes the juice from Anna, kisses her*) What's good for breakfast?

ANNA. Pancakes?

JULIAN (*looks around at the old dress she is packing*). Why are you taking all that old stuff? Throw out everything old. (*Stares at Anna*) What's the matter with you? You look terrible.

ALBERTINE (*through the window*). Morning, Julian.

(*Anna exits toward the kitchen.*)

JULIAN. Well, look who's here. Hello. (*He starts out for the porch, stops, kicks aside a few packages, grabs a small one and runs out*) A present for you.

ALBERTINE. Thank you.

(*He turns to Lily.*)

JULIAN. Hello, darling. (*Stares at her*) What's the matter with you? (*Lily shakes her head. He kisses her, and moves toward Albertine, with whom he shakes hands. He sees Henry and they shake hands.*) How's the fishing? Been up the bayou?

HENRY. Been up. But nobody got anything. Except crayfish.

JULIAN. Anybody asked what I missed most in Chicago, I'd have said a bayou, a bowl of crayfish, a good gun for a flight of wild ducks coming over — Going to buy a little place up there, first thing. You're welcome all the time. (*Sees that Lily has not moved and is staring at the ground*) What's the matter, Lily? (*When she doesn't answer, he speaks to Albertine*) I sure manage to depress my ladies. Never used to be that way. Do I depress you?

ALBERTINE (*laughs*). I'm very glad to see you.

(*She has now unwrapped the package and taken out a flame-red lace mantilla supported by a giant comb. She arranges it on her head.*)

JULIAN. What's it meant for?

ALBERTINE. I don't know.

JULIAN. When do you wear it?

ALBERTINE. I'll wear it for reading in bed. How very nice of you to bring it to me.

JULIAN. How nice of *you*. You put it on. Nobody else — (*turns to Lily*) Lily, did you show your mama your new ring? (*Lily shakes her head*) Oh. Go and get your ring and show your mama. (*Lily hesitates and then moves inside. He smiles ruefully at Albertine, points to the mantilla*) Silly present, isn't it? It cost a lot.

ALBERTINE (*laughs*). Nice to buy, nice to get, silly presents. Who wants a roast of beef?

(*She removes the mantilla and carefully folds it.*)

JULIAN (*smiles with pleasure*). That's what I thought — (*Confidentially, points inside*) I think I bought, got, brought — Well, they're sort of upset and they don't think I know it. I should have had sense enough to know that when you've been poor and wanted things you couldn't have, your stomach gets small and you can't eat much right away. I brought too much, and everything too grand, and, well. Guess they got a little sick. They're so happy that it comes out unhappy. You know how it is?

ALBERTINE. I don't think so.

JULIAN. It's a crazy old world. For years, they — (*Points inside*)

— tell me about what's going to be, what I'm going to do, you know, get rich and big time. The more I fail, the louder they cheer me with what we're all going to have, want. And so all my life I dream about coming up those steps carrying everything, and I make up what they will say, and what I will say — (*Smiles*) Well, when it came, I guess it was hard to believe, maybe even frightened them, I never thought of that, and I just bought anything if it cost a lot, and made Carrie sick on caviar, and everybody acted scared, and like they were going to cry. Natural enough. You know?

ALBERTINE (*carefully*). No, I don't know. You've had good fortune and brought it home. There's something sad in not liking what you wanted when you get it. And something strange, maybe even mean. (*Sharply, as if in warning*) Nobody should have cried about your good fortune, nobody should have been anything but happy.

JULIAN. No, no. You don't understand. They're happy. They just haven't had time — I scared them, Europe and a house and fancy things all in a day. Who wouldn't be scared? They thought I'd come home broke — God knows I always had — You don't know about that, but *they* do, and they got ready to give me all they had, and tell all the same nice lies about how the next time. And then there I come, strutting like a kid — (*Laughs with great pleasure*) Rich. Rich. Rich. (*As a child would say it*) I'm as good as you now. Isn't that true?

ALBERTINE (*laughs*). I'm not sure.

JULIAN. We'll have to have long talks and consultations.

ALBERTINE. About money? I don't think so. I like it very much. But it makes dull talk.

JULIAN. Oh, I just bet you don't really think that. (*He pokes her with his finger; she stares at him and sits very straight*) That's just the way *you* people want *us* to think. Not dull at all. Why, I had more fun this week — Know what I did?

(*He pokes her again. She reacts sharply and Henry laughs. She turns to look at Henry and then turns back to Julian, smiling.*)

ALBERTINE. Henry doesn't like people to poke me, do you, Henry?

HENRY. I never saw anybody do it before.

JULIAN. I went to see a man I hated the two times I ever saw him and the many times I heard about him. Once when he teased me as a boy, and once when he made fun of me as a man. (*He stops, remembers, sighs*) I guess he's the only man I ever hated. Well, I went right in his office and said I got something you want, and I'll take a hundred and fifty thousand dollars for it. After he said all about being crazy, and to get the hell out, he said, "Get your money from women — your sisters or your wife. You married her for it" — (*Julian rises, speaks softly to Albertine*) Did people think that? Did they?

ALBERTINE. I don't see people. I never thought it.

JULIAN (*leans down, kisses her hand*). Maybe I'll knock you down later, I said to him, but right now let's keep our minds on a hundred and fifty thousand dollars delivered a week from today. (*To Albertine*) Want to see?

(*He takes the envelope from his pocket and holds it open for her.*)

ALBERTINE (*laughs*). It does look nice. I don't think I ever saw anything larger than a hundred-dollar bill.

JULIAN. I tell you, the rich don't have any fun with money.

ALBERTINE. Smells rather nice, too.

JULIAN. I put cologne water on it. (*As he puts the envelope back in his pocket*) One hundred and fifty thousand dollars. Do people like you think it's a lot of money?

ALBERTINE. It's money. (*Very deliberately pokes him*) People like me think it's a good beginning. It's not a great fortune, but if you want one it will start you off.

JULIAN. You know, I think so, too. (*Smiles at her*) Isn't it funny? I liked you, but I never talked easy with you before. Now you just seem to me like anybody else.

ALBERTINE. I'm sorry.

JULIAN (*leans over and kisses her cheek*). I didn't mean it quite like that. I just mean that you always scared me, and now you don't. I guess most people like you scared me. (*Smiles*) I was kind of, well, kind of broken. I knew it, but I showed off to keep — (*He points inside*) — them from — (*He turns to Henry*) It's bad for a man to feel gone. (*Then, very gaily*) Like a miracle. I go in to see this bastard shaking, and I come out knowing I did fine, knowing I'm going to be all right forever. You understand it wasn't just the money?

ALBERTINE (*laughs*). I don't understand very much. Why don't you wait and tell me when you can?

JULIAN. All I mean, you do something right. *Just right.* You know a man's got to have what you've got — very different from trying to get a job or selling something he don't want.

I just sat there calm and smiling until he got through trying to find out how I, *I,* bought two acres of swamp land before he did, and how I could know how much he needed it. I thought to myself, so this is the way the big boys do it, you poor fool for being so scared all your life. So I said, "Get through, will you, I got a board of directors meeting and have no more time for you." (*Laughs with pleasure*) I don't know where I got that from. Maybe the movies. "You and my lawyer can attend to the rest, so agree or don't agree, I don't want to be in the room with you too long." He got white but he didn't say anything, so I got up and started out and he said, "All right. Give us two weeks to draw the papers" — My lawyer said, "Fair enough, sir," and I guess it was the "sir" that made me angry because I said, "No. I'll take it next Tuesday at two o'clock. Have it ready." And I walked out the happiest man in town. I paid back my life some way or other — (*Gus appears carrying ice*) You can lose for just so long — When you win, everything on you grows bigger, know what I mean?

(*He laughs and pokes Albertine.*)

ALBERTINE. And I grow black and blue.

GUS. Hi. Home to stay?

JULIAN. Gus, just look at that new icebox. (*Gus turns, stares in through the porch door*) Bought it more for you than for them.

GUS. In Chicago they keep it in the parlor?

JULIAN. Gus, my old friend Gus. You're going to have that farm, kid. Go find it and start with this.

(*He hands Gus several large bills. Gus looks at them, but doesn't take them.*)

GUS. You at that again?

JULIAN. This time I made it. Throw the ice away — (*He shoves the money into Gus's hand.*)

GUS. Julian, I don't want that kind of trouble again.

JULIAN. Nobody'll come for it this time. I'm telling you the truth. And there's as much more as you want. Now get going and find the farm.

GUS. Who the hell wants a farm? Got enough trouble. Where'd you make up the farm from?

(*He goes around the garden and disappears.*)

JULIAN. He said since we were kids about a farm — People talk about what they want, and then — How's that?

ALBERTINE. I guess most of us make up things we want, don't get them, and get too old, or too lazy, to make up new ones. Best not to disturb that, Julian. People don't want other people to guess they never knew what they wanted in the first place.

JULIAN. That's real sad. I know what I want and *I'm* going to be happy getting it.

ALBERTINE. Well, I like nice, rich, happy relatives, although I never had any. But I have bad news for you, Julian — it's not simple being happy, and money doesn't seem to have much to do with it, although it has to do with other things more serious.

(*Carrie comes in, moving slowly. She stops when she sees the group.*)

JULIAN. Morning. Where you been?

CARRIE. I — I've been downtown.

JULIAN. Buying things, I hope. (*To Albertine*) My sisters are going to Europe tomorrow. Isn't that fine, after years of —

CARRIE. Your sisters are not — (*Then, softly*) come inside, please.

JULIAN. What's the matter?

CARRIE (*starts toward the steps, sharply*). Come inside.

JULIAN (*playfully, but with meaning*). Carrie, stop talking like that. You got a new man on your hands. You got to talk to me different now, like I'm a tycoon. (*To Albertine*) What's a tycoon? How much, I mean?

ALBERTINE. Miss Carrie can tell you. She works for one.

JULIAN. Barrett? Is he? I don't want to be like Barrett —

CARRIE. He knows what you think of him. He'd already read your letter when I got there. I can't tell you what I felt. All I could think to say was that it was a joke and you'd be down later to apologize.

JULIAN (*after a second*). Did you? Did you really say that? Don't ever say that again, Carrie. That's one of things I don't ever have to do anymore. That's one of things money's going to buy us all.

CARRIE. I want to see you alone, Julian.

JULIAN. I don't think you should have gone to see him at all. We'll talk about it another time. I'm busy today. (*She wheels around, angry. Julian is grinning at Albertine*) How you like me? See? Got no time for small matters.

CARRIE. Small matters? After nineteen years. He said he didn't believe you wrote the letter. He said I wrote it, that it was like me, that he always had known about — (*She gasps*) — things in me. After nineteen years of loyalty — I want you to get dressed and go tell him that if you owe him an apology, he owes me an apology for the awful words he said —

JULIAN (*to Albertine*). That's how tycoons act toward loyal ladies?

ALBERTINE. I don't know how they act toward loyal ladies.

CARRIE. Julian —

ALBERTINE. I do know tycoons are not romantic about money and the happiness it buys.

JULIAN. Ah, can't I be romantic for a month?

(*Carrie moves into the living room and stands waiting.*)

ALBERTINE. All right. We'll give you a month. After a month I suggest venality. You'll find more people understand it and are less suspicious of it. Right now it's my impression that everyone around here thinks you held up a bank.

JULIAN. No, a poker game. Or a jewel robbery. Hey, Lily. Lily! Come and show your mama your ring. Lily! (*To Albertine*) *You* don't think I stole the money, do you?

(*He looks at his watch, then moves quickly toward the porch as Lily appears.*)

ALBERTINE (*because Julian is going up the steps of the porch, and because she speaks very softly, he does not hear her*). No. I think I know where you got it.

JULIAN (*as he passes Lily, he picks up her left hand*). Go show your mama — Where's your ring?

LILY. Somewhere.

JULIAN. Where is somewhere?

LILY. Don't be angry, please —

JULIAN. Why not? (*He moves into the room, sees Carrie, smiles*) Seen a large diamond ring?

CARRIE. Up to yesterday we never had such problems. Julian, he said bad things to me. Julian. (*He doesn't answer, and starts to leave the room*) Julian. Please answer me.

JULIAN. Answer you what?

CARRIE. Once, and not long ago, you'd have known by my face, and you'd have kissed me and said, "What is it, my Carrie?"

(*Behind Carrie, Anna appears carrying a breakfast tray. She stops.*)

JULIAN (*gently*). What is it, my Carrie?

CARRIE. I want to talk to you — Let's go by ourselves, the way we used to —

JULIAN. I'm due downtown —

CARRIE. You have no time for me. We're coming apart, you and I —

JULIAN. What are you talking about?

CARRIE. You've come home in all this mystery, and not said a word with me alone —

JULIAN. When I take you to the boat tomorow, I'll tell you all about "this mystery — "

CARRIE. I want to speak to you now. Now.

JULIAN (*softly*). Did you always use that tone with me? Did you? (*To Anna*) Did you? (*When she doesn't answer*) Say something, so I can tell the way you talk to me.

ANNA. Breakfast.

JULIAN (*takes the tray from her*). Will you press a shirt for me? (*She nods and moves off with him.*)

CARRIE. You're saying no to me, when I need you?

JULIAN. I'm not saying no to you. I'm saying that I'm busy. (*He sings as he exits.*)

ALBERTINE (*to Lily, who is on the porch*). What did you do with the ring?

LILY. I don't want it.

ALBERTINE. He will be hurt. Pretend that you do want it.

LILY. I don't want it.

(*Carrie, nervously moving about, comes to stand at the window and to listen to the voices in the garden.*)

ALBERTINE. There are many ways of loving. I'm sure yours must be among them. Put white flowers in your hair, walk up your mountain path of truth with a white banner in your hand, and as you drop it on his head, speak of love.

LILY. I gave her the ring and she gave me the knife.

ALBERTINE. I beg your pardon?

HENRY (*quickly*). I know what she means.

LILY. I gave the lady the ring and she gave me the knife. I didn't want the ring, and I didn't think Julian would care. But I will go and tell him the truth now and —

(*She starts into the room.*)

ALBERTINE. You asked my advice and here it is: You do too much. Go and do nothing for a while. Nothing. I have seen you like this before. (*With force*) I tell you now, do nothing.

(*To Henry*) You know the address of the upstairs knife lady?

LILY. Mama, don't make fun of her —

ALBERTINE. No, indeed. We will try to find your ring. Decide whether your costume is meant for day or night, and rest yourself. (*Softly*) Lily, don't tell Julian about the ring. (*Lily nods and enters the house. She sees Carrie, smiles at her, and exits toward the kitchen. Anna appears carrying a shirt and crosses the room toward the kitchen*) Well, there it is.

HENRY. You are not wise with Lily.

ALBERTINE. No. I never was. Well, it's been a good year, hasn't it? The best I ever had.

HENRY. Nothing has happened.

ALBERTINE. I know Lily. You do, too.

HENRY. She is jealous and scared —

ALBERTINE. And nothing I say will stop her from being foolish. And of course there is another woman. But Julian isn't sleeping with her. (*Laughs*) They raised him to be a very, very moral man.

HENRY. Very, very moral men sometimes sleep with women. I think.

ALBERTINE. But it shows on them. Do you think he's sleeping with another woman?

HENRY. He's not sleeping with her, and he won't. But he used to.

ALBERTINE. Yes? (*When there is no answer*) Cy Warkins is the man he's talking about, Cy Warkins who bought what he calls his two acres of swamp land. I'm not sure why Cy wanted it so much, but if it's down by the river I can make a good guess. Warkins owns fifty percent of the stock of the interstate agreement to take the railroad route along the docks. (*Laughs*) If my guess is right, he must have been surprised that Julian knew about the best-kept secret in years. I regret not being there when Julian told him. But who told Julian? Mrs. Warkins? (*Henry does not answer*) She never liked Warkins and that was the only thing I ever knew about her. But she must be forty now. (*When there is no answer*) But of course she wasn't always forty. (*She points inside*) They knew each other? And she told him about the railroad? I'm not gossiping, you know that.

HENRY. I think that's what happened. She was in love with Julian once. She hates Warkins and has wanted to leave for years. Maybe this is the money to leave with.

ALBERTINE (*softly, in a new tone, as if it is forced out of her, and she is ashamed*). How do you know about Mrs. Warkins? Please.

HENRY. I don't know about her anymore, but I used to. She's a cousin to me.

ALBERTINE (*stares at him, and then laughs*). She's part colored? Isn't that wonderful! Did Warkins know when he married her?

HENRY. He doesn't know now. But Julian did, and didn't care. She's a foolish woman and grateful for such things.

ALBERTINE. That's understandable, God knows.

HENRY. Not to me. I am not grateful, nor ungrateful, nor any word like that.

ALBERTINE. Nor should you be. You are in a bad humor with me this morning. You are disapproving. What have I done or said?

HENRY (*softly*). You look tired.

ALBERTINE (*rises, goes to him*). So many people who make things too hard for too little reason, or none at all, or the pleasure, or stupidity. We've never done that, you and I.

HENRY. Yes, we've done it. But we've tried not to.

(*Albertine touches his hand. Henry smiles and puts her hand to his face. Albertine turns and, as she does, she sees Carrie in the window. Albertine pauses as if to ask herself what Carrie could have heard.*)

ALBERTINE. Are you writing a book, Miss Carrie?

CARRIE (*softly*). This is our house, Mrs. Prine.

ALBERTINE (*sighs*). Indeed.

(*Henry takes her arm and they move off. Lily comes running into the room, holding her right hand in her left hand. She is followed by Anna, who carries a bottle and gauze bandage. Lily runs toward the hall, calling out.*)

LILY. Julian, I — I cut my hand.

ANNA. Lily.

LILY. Julian. I cut my hand. (*Then she turns and calls out loudly toward the garden*) Mama. Mama. I cut my hand.

CARRIE. Your mama has left with her friend.

(*Julian appears, rubbing his wet hair with a bath towel.*)

JULIAN. What's the matter?

LILY. I cut my hand.

JULIAN (*he picks up Lily's hand, holds it for Anna to bandage*).

It's a deep one. (*To Anna*) You ought not to have rusty knives in the kitchen.

(*Anna looks up as if she is about to speak, but changes her mind.*)

LILY. Ouch. (*She turns her hand toward Julian. He kisses it and she gently touches his face. She rubs her thigh*) And last night I fell in here and hit my leg. You could cure that, too. Please. Make me cured, Julian. Let's go to bed and maybe you'll be pleased with me — Maybe. (*She puts his hand on her breast. Anna turns away; Carrie stands staring at them*) And if you're pleased with me, then all the bad will go away, and I will pray for it to be that way. But if you're not, I'll understand, and won't ask why — (*She laughs gaily, slyly, and presses his hand on her breast*) But *if* you are pleased with me, darling — (*Julian leans down to kiss her*) I have missed you.

(*He picks her up in his arms and begins to move out of the room.*)

CARRIE (*sucks in her breath; loudly*). I read in a French book that there was nothing so abandoned as a respectable young girl.

JULIAN (*laughs*). That's true, thank God. (*He leans down to kiss Lily's hair*) Otherwise nobody could stand them.

(*Lily laughs merrily.*)

CARRIE (*comes toward them*). You didn't fall in here last night. When I turned on the light —

LILY. Yes, ma'am. I fell. I didn't see the spinet —

(*Julian, carrying Lily, exits.*)

CARRIE. You did not fall against the spinet. You were on this side of the room, hitting —

ANNA. Carrie.

CARRIE. She was hitting herself against that table. Just doing it. I saw her. I tell you, I saw her.

ANNA. I believe you.

CARRIE. He doesn't know she went out last night. He doesn't know she gave her ring away — to some woman — She's told him lies. She lies to him, she tricks him. I think she's a crazy girl — (*Points to the garden*) And that woman knows it. I think there's a crazy girl in there —

ANNA (*softly, as if to herself*). She cut her hand, quite deliberately and calmly, with a knife she took from her valise. She said a kind of prayer over the knife —

CARRIE (*moves swiftly toward Anna*). You saw her do that? You saw her cut herself? I tell you she's crazy.

(*She moves toward the door, right.*)

ANNA. No.

CARRIE. How can you stand what's happening here? He comes home with all this money nonsense. He's married to a crazy girl. I think he's in bed with a girl who —

ANNA. — he wanted. It's not our business.

CARRIE. It is our business that our brother sells something to Mr. Cyrus Warkins for a fortune Mr. Cyrus Warkins doesn't want to pay. Warkins is a powerful and dangerous man in this town, and Julian would be a baby in the hands of such a man —

ANNA. What are you talking about?

CARRIE. I don't know all it means. (*Points out to the garden*) But I heard them say this money, or whatever, has to do with Warkins' wife.

ANNA. He slept with Charlotte Warkins ten years ago. It's been over that long.

CARRIE. How do you know such a thing? How do *you* know?

ANNA. Because he told me.

CARRIE. I don't believe you. You're a liar.

ANNA. Be quiet, Carrie.

CARRIE. You've made it up, you always made up things like that. It didn't happen. He was an innocent boy — (*Anna laughs. Carrie unbuttons the neck of her dress as if she were choking*) He would never have told *you*. He would have told me. He was closer to me — There he is, another man, not our brother, lost to us after all the years of work and care, married to a crazy little whore who cuts her hand to try to get him into bed — (*Points to the garden*) The daughter of a woman who keeps a nigger fancy man. I'll bet she paid Julian to take that crazy girl away from her —

ANNA. Stop that talk. You know that's not true. Stop talking about Julian that way.

CARRIE. Let's go and ask him. Let's go and ask your darling child. Your favorite child, the child you made me work for, the child I lost my youth for — You used to tell us that when you love, truly love, you take your chances on being hated by speaking out the truth. (*Points inside*) Go in and do it.

ANNA. All right. I'll take that chance now and tell you that you want to sleep with him and always have. Years ago I used to be frightened that you would try and I would watch you and suffer for you.

CARRIE (*after a second, in a whisper*). You never said those words. Tell me I never heard those words. Tell me, Anna. (*When there is no answer*) You were all I ever had. I don't love you anymore.

ANNA. That was the chance I took.

Curtain

Act Three

SCENE: *The same. An hour later.*

AT RISE: *Carrie is as she was. Anna's suitcases are on the porch. She enters, puts another suitcase below the piano, and exits. Offstage, there is loud whistling, from Julian. Carrie crosses to the spinet and begins to pick out the melody he is whistling. He enters, dressed except for his shirt, and carrying his coat. He is singing and he smiles pleasantly at Carrie.*

JULIAN (*singing*).

This is the big day, this is the great day
This is the Berniers day.
Never been one, no, never never,
Never been such a Berniers day.
Never been such a day before.
Going to be more and plenty more.
Oh, it's money day, the end of trouble day,
And going to be more and plenty more.
Never been such a day before.
Not for Mama, not for Papa,
Not for Sister, not for Brother —
Going to be more and plenty more.

(*Shouts off*) Anna! Where's my shirt?

CARRIE (*softly*). Do you know that all I want in this world is what will be good for you?

JULIAN. And I for you. (*Anna appears carrying his shirt. He crosses to take it from her, puts it on, and sings to Anna.*)

Now every day she going to be
She going to be a Berniers day.
Say every day she going to be
She going to be a Berniers day,
And for Mama and for Papa
And for Sister and for Brother
Going to be just a Berniers day.

(*To Anna*) It's the best day of my life since I won the bag of marbles from old Gus. You made me give them back. You said he was a poor colored boy. But I was a poor white boy so I didn't know what you were getting so fancy about. Well, I'm on my way to the best day. (*To Carrie, pointing to valise*) Getting packed? Getting excited?

CARRIE (*pats the spinet*). I'll practice today and tonight I'll give a little concert for you and we'll sing all the pieces you used to like.

(*Anna begins to move out of the room.*)

JULIAN. Er. We'll be leaving today. (*Anna stops, turns. Carrie rises*) We'll be going. (*Nervously*) And *you'll* be leaving tomorrow, so just one day. 'Course I'll wait until tomorrow if you need me —

CARRIE. Where are you going?

JULIAN. Maybe a camping trip, maybe New York —

CARRIE. A few weeks?

JULIAN. I don't know. No. A year or so. And then back here, of course. This is where I belong. Where I want to be, where I was meant to be. (*Overcheerful*) And by that time you world travelers will be back and —

CARRIE. *You* want to go? Or *Lily* wants to go?

JULIAN. Never seen New York, either of us.

CARRIE. Lily wants to go.

JULIAN. I don't know. I just decided. We'll come back, don't worry, and — (*He crosses to the chest and takes out savings bankbook.*)

CARRIE. Why did you suddenly decide to go? Why?

JULIAN (*holds up the bankbook*). Some people got a family Bible. We got a savings bankbook. (*Softly, to Carrie*) Don't look like that. (*Points inside*) She's young and — I don't think she wanted to come back. I didn't think about it before but — And maybe we should be alone for a while. That's all. (*Points to the bankbook.*) Twenty thousand going in here this morning. Twenty thousand dollars. That going to be enough? (*Laughs with pleasure*) For six months maybe? Enough?

ANNA. I don't know anything about twenty thousand dollars.

JULIAN. You got to learn fast. Fast, I say. What was the word Mama used to use?

CARRIE (*in a cry*). Julian, don't go —

ANNA (*very fast*). *Faner. Elle commence a se faner.* The leaf came in the spring, stayed nice on the branch in the autumn until the winter winds would blow it in the snow. Mama said that in that little time of holding on, a woman had to make ready for the winter ground where she would lie the rest of her life. A leaf cannot rise from the ground and go back to the tree, remember that. I remembered it. But when it came there was nothing I could do.

JULIAN (*gently, touches her*). Mama was mean.

CARRIE (*shrilly*). Anna always says something about Mama when things are wrong. Always. Mama wasn't mean to you. Just to us.

JULIAN. Did you think I liked it that way? Did you? Mama had a tough time, I guess. That makes people mean. (*Softly, to Anna*) You're still on the tree, still so nice and pretty, and when the wind does come, a long time from now, I'll be there to catch you with a blanket made of warm roses, and a parasol of dollar bills to keep off the snow. Dollar bills make a mighty nice parasol, I just bet you. (*Smiles*) For another good lady, too. (*As if to himself*) Well, I'm off to give them to her. I'll walk right down Sailor's Lane and she'll be waiting for me. I'll take her arm, we'll have a cup of coffee, and I'll try to say thank you. No, I won't. People are always saying thank you so they can forget what they said it for. (*Holds up one envelope*) I'll just hand this to her and say, "Have a good life, baby," and then I'll walk her down to the depot and put her on the train. A happy day. (*Holds up other envelope*) Then I'll go around and bank our share. That'll make me respectable, won't it?

ANNA (*after a second*). Is she *fanée?*

JULIAN. Yes. A long time ago.

ANNA. Then wish her well from me.

JULIAN. I will.

CARRIE. Is the lady going to New York?

JULIAN. I don't know where she's going. I guess so. Doesn't everybody go to New York? (*Lily, on the last of Carrie's speech, comes into the room. Julian turns and grins at her*) Want to go to New York, or a fishing trip to Canada, or the Grand Canyon, or — Today?

LILY. With you?

JULIAN (*crosses to her, holds her face with his hand*). How would you like that? Time we found a place. Wherever.

LILY. You and me?

JULIAN. You and me.

LILY. In a room?

JULIAN (*laughs*). In a room, or a boat, or a tent —

LILY. Just you and me. And will the not happening, happen to us again?

JULIAN (*sharply*). Lily, stop that. I was tired and I had too much to drink last night. And I was nervous the last few days and am now. Any man will tell you that happens. (*Then, smiling*) Only you must never talk such things with any man, hear me?

LILY (*giggles*). I won't.

(*She drops the knife from her right hand. She looks down at it as if surprised.*)

JULIAN (*leans down, picks up the knife, stares at it*). What in the name of God is this?

LILY. The knife of truth. Will you swear on it? Swear that you will keep me with you whatever —

JULIAN. For Christ's sake, Lily. What the hell's the matter with you? (*He drops the knife on the table*) Stop talking foolish and stop playing with knives. Maybe kiddies should marry kiddies. But I'm thirty-four. Stop talking about last night and what didn't happen, because it's the kind of thing you don't talk about. Can't you understand that? (*Gently*) Now go pack your bags and go tell your mama we're going away.

LILY (*laughing with pleasure*). Can I say we're going away forever? Just us.

JULIAN. Forever. Just us. (*Turns, sees Carrie and Anna, and stops*) I mean we'll come back here, or the folks will come to us — (*Very fast*) You'll see. You'll come to visit us, we'll come to visit you — Buy us a little house up the bayou. Sometimes I wish I had gone on up the bayou years ago —

ANNA. You did.

JULIAN. Maybe I should have stayed. They said I was better with a muskrat boat than any Cajun, better with a gun. A nice little shack and a muskrat boat, all the bobwhite you could ever want — (*After a second*) Fine morning to be talking like this.

ANNA (*sharply*). Go on.

LILY (*she runs toward Julian, holds him; he puts his arms around her*). Will you be coming back for me?

JULIAN. What? What are you talking about? Lily, for Christ's sake. (*He kisses her, moves away; stops, looks pleadingly at all of them*) What's the matter? Please. It's the best day of my life. Please somebody look happy.

ANNA. Go on. (*He smiles, moves out at a run. Lily follows him to the porch. He turns and kisses her and runs off. After a second, Lily sits down on the porch, as though she is very tired. Anna speaks to Carrie*) I wanted to be around the children he will have. I wanted something nice to grow old for. I held on to that and prayed for it. (*Very softly*) This time he will go forever.

CARRIE. I don't believe it. You must have your headaches again. He will not go forever, or even for long —

ANNA. This time I say he will go forever. You lusted and it showed. He doesn't know he saw it, but he did see it, and someday he'll know what he saw. (*With great violence*) You know the way that happens? You understand something, and don't know that you do, and forget about it. But one night years ago I woke up and knew what I had seen in you, had always seen. It will happen that way with him. It has begun.

CARRIE. I told you I didn't love you anymore. Now I tell you that I hate you. We will have to find a way to live with that.

ANNA. I don't think so.

(*She moves out to the porch on her way to the garden.*)

LILY. Will he come back for me, Miss Anna?

ANNA. What's the matter with you, child? You must go and dress and pack your things. Julian won't be long and he'll want you to be ready. Shall I call your mother?

LILY. She talked cold to me. (*She imitates her mother*) "Try not to excite yourself, Lily. Try to make yourself clear, Lily." But when she talks to Henry — (*In another voice; soft and gentle*) "Lily has gone to bed. Sit down. What shall we read tonight?" (*In her own voice*) And one night she said to him, "Oh, God, make the time when we can be alone; make it come before we are both too old to have pleasure from peace." (*Softly*) She would have paid anything for that time. Did she? Did she pay Julian? It that why he took me?

ANNA (*very sharply*). How dare you speak that way of Julian? What a bitter thought about a man who loves you.

LILY. No. Who would want me for any other reason?

ANNA (*as she moves away*). Your modesty does not excuse you.

LILY. I love him, Miss Anna. If he said he loved somebody else

— Well, I'd just go away and he'd be rid of me. But this way — I know you understand.

ANNA. A woman who marries a man she loves should have a little more happiness from it and talk a little more sense. That's all I understand.

LILY. I've upset you, Miss Anna.

ANNA. Yes. You're an expert.

(*She disappears around the garden. Carrie has been sweeping the living room. She now moves to sweep the porch.*)

LILY. Cleaning day? (*Carrie does not answer*) Do you like to sweep? I like to mop.

CARRIE. Have you done it often? Twice, say?

LILY. I'm sorry you don't like me. I wanted you to.

CARRIE (*gestures inside*). I would like to sweep the porch. Would you —

LILY. Last night, in bed, Julian was thinking, I watched him. And thinking isn't the way to make love.

CARRIE. I don't know much about gentlemen in bed and I don't want to learn from you.

LILY. Haven't you ever slept with a man?

(*Carrie turns and stares at Lily.*)

CARRIE. Shall we have a pillow fight or make fudge? I don't like these girlish confidences.

LILY. I only thought you might like to know he was thinking of you, although, of course, I can't be sure. And maybe of Miss Anna, but most probably not.

CARRIE. You'll be leaving here in an hour. Be satisfied with that victory and don't trust me.

LILY. Oh, Miss Carrie. I wanted you to like me.

CARRIE. There is no need to worry about me anymore.

LILY. Oh, I do. And I will. I'm frightened of you.

CARRIE (*angrily*). Your favorite word. Did it ever occur to you that other people are frightened, too?

LILY. You? No. No, indeed. Of what, Miss Carrie?

CARRIE. Of my hair which isn't nice anymore, of my job which isn't there anymore, of praying for small things and knowing just how small they are, of walking by a mirror when I didn't know it would be there — (*She gasps*) People say "Those Berniers girls, so devoted. That Carrie was pretty, and then one day she wasn't; just an old maid, working for her brother." They are right. An old maid with candied oranges as a right proper treat each Saturday night. We didn't see people anymore, I guess, because we were frightened of saying or hearing more than we could stand. (*Very angrily*) There are lives that are shut and should stay shut, you hear me, and people who should not talk about themselves, and that was us.

LILY. Why don't you come away with us, Miss Carrie?

CARRIE. Stop sticking your baby pins into me. Go inside and pray that another woman won't do it to you. I want to clean the porch.

LILY. There is another woman. I've seen her. Nobody believes me.

CARRIE. I believe you.

LILY. I don't know who she is. Do you?

CARRIE. Your mother knows. Ask her.

LILY (*giggles*). I just bet that's true. But Mama won't tell me because she doesn't like me and doesn't tell me things. (*Runs to Carrie*) You know what does the harm? I keep thinking that Mama paid Julian to marry me. And then sometimes I think that's not true; he does love me. God made him love me because God knew how much I needed him. (*Smiles; ingratiating*) He just worships you, Miss Carrie, and I know he confides in you. Did he ever tell you Mama paid him? (*Grabs Carrie's arm and, in the force of the movement, throws Carrie off balance*) Tell me. Be good to me. Tell me.

CARRIE (*pulls away*). I tell you what I think: You're going to drive him crazy. (*She starts to move off. Lily grabs her.*)

LILY. Did my Mama —

CARRIE (*angry*). I don't know what she did. All he told us was that he had fallen in love and was going to be married.

LILY (*in a transport of pleasure*). Oh. Miss Carrie! Miss Carrie! (*She pirouettes*) He told you he was in love! Isn't that nice?

CARRIE. I remember wondering why he had picked that Sunday to tell us. Anna was going to the hospital the next morning for her eye operation. None of us had ever been in a hospital before, and we didn't know about the costs, and being in a ward, and all of that. So Julian came home and told about you, and then he said that Anna was going to have the best room in the hospital and he had called the great Dr. Kranz in Philadelphia, and the great Dr. Kranz was already on the train. He wouldn't let Anna say a word, said he won the money in a poker game. I don't know — Anna was more worried about that than about her eyes. And she fussed and fussed and never liked the fancy room and the uppity private nurses. But Dr. Kranz did a wonderful operation and when she came out of it, the first thing she said to Julian was, "My eyes were not made to make all this trouble for you." And he said a beautiful thing to her, he said, "Look, I'd give my both arms and one leg for you, but not two legs, so maybe I don't love you as much as I think," and how we all laughed. (*She smiles at Lily*) A few days later he brought you to see Anna. Do you remember?

LILY (*who has been staring at Carrie*). Yes.

CARRIE. I was happy that Julian was to be married.

LILY. You said so. (*Very loudly, as if out of control*) I didn't believe you.

CARRIE. Oh, I could have stopped the marriage, even you must have guessed that.

LILY. Even I. But you didn't stop it because you knew my mother had paid Julian — I'm glad I helped Miss Anna, I really am — would go on paying him, and you didn't have to worry about a little girl who didn't mean anything more to anybody than a bank check.

CARRIE. I have said none of that. You have been looking for it, and you would have found it in anything I, or anybody else, could say.

LILY. I don't mind, not much. It's better to know. I will take Julian any way I can have him. *If* I can have him. I feel most bad and sad, Miss Carrie, because what he married me for, he doesn't need anymore. Isn't that true?

CARRIE. I don't know. Take your questions to Mrs. Cyrus Warkins. She'll be in New York. You can have many a cozy evening.

LILY. She's coming with us?

CARRIE. No. She's going on the morning train.

LILY. I see. Is she a tall, dark lady?

CARRIE. I've never seen her. But Henry is tall and dark and she's his cousin, so perhaps. Your mother was very amused that the great lawyer Warkins had married a part nigger and didn't know it.

LILY. Does Julian love her?

CARRIE. I used to think I knew about Julian. I didn't. Ask your mother and her fancy man. They said Julian and the woman were together years ago. And my sister confirms the alliance.

LILY (*giggles too loudly*). Together? Alliance? Together in bed?

Alliance in bed? What a funny way to say it. Julian told me that you talked like an old maid when you were twelve years old, and that Gus used to say you kept your vagina in the icebox, that he'd seen it there and shut the door fast.

CARRIE (*very loudly*). Stop that filthy talk. Julian never said a thing like that —

LILY. Oh, please, I didn't mean to offend you. Julian said it in fun. Afterwards in bed, we always talked fun. That's almost the best time, when you laugh and say things you'd never say anyplace else, and it's all in honor bright. It's then that you ask about other girls, everybody does, Julian told me, and every man thinks it's a big bore he's got to get through for the next time, if you know what I mean. Julian said there was only one woman that ever mattered, long ago, and I wasn't to worry — (*She laughs*) — and that she was married to a bastard who beat her, and if he ever made money he'd give it to her to get away. (*She smiles*) So now she's coming with us. What will they do with me? (*She screams*) It pains me. I can't tell you. I'll ask her not to come. (*She turns and runs up the porch and into the room, toward the phone*) I'll tell her I don't blame her, of course, and I'll swear on my knife of truth that if I have just one more year — (*Grabs the phone book, drops it, holds it out to Carrie*) Please find it for me.

CARRIE. Mrs. Warkins isn't home. She's waiting for Julian.

LILY (*runs toward the porch*). I'll run.

CARRIE. Put your clothes on first. You've got a long way to go in your underwear.

LILY (*stares down at her nightgown*). Please, you go, Miss Carrie.

CARRIE. Oh, I don't think so.

LILY. Say I'm not angry, not anything like that. Say I know what it is to love and if at the end of a year, she wants and Julian wants — Well, then. Then.

CARRIE. I don't think I could say those things.

LILY. You don't talk the way you did. You talk real mean.

CARRIE. In the last day I lost my brother, my sister, my job. That's all I had to lose. Perhaps it's the fear of losing that makes us talk nice or better. (*Very loudly, sharply*) Don't you think? Don't you think maybe?

LILY. Do I talk different?

CARRIE. You are still the baby-rich girl, teething on other people. In a few years I think you'll have to start doing something for yourself.

LILY. A few years? A few days will be too late, a few minutes —What time is it? What time is Julian going to take her away?

CARRIE (*carefully*). I did not say he was going to take her away. He has gone to meet Mrs. Warkins, evidently to give her a share.

LILY. What time is it? I know Mr. Cyrus Warkins, he's Mama's lawyer. Mrs. Warkins is a sad lady, if she's the one who was on the train.

CARRIE. She's ailing, I've always heard, and doesn't go into society. But I suppose the real reason is that she's part nigger and thought somebody would find out. Julian didn't mind. Imagine that. He didn't mind.

LILY. Why should he? I don't mind Henry's being colored. I like Negro people, and Jewish, and once I liked two nuns. I hate Henry because he's Henry.

(*There is a long pause; as if Lily has dozed.*)

CARRIE (*watching Lily, sighs*). Your mind wanders, doesn't it? Go pack your bags now.

LILY. You're a fine lady. He'd listen to you. Miss Carrie, please call Mr. Cyrus Warkins.

CARRIE. I will not call Mr. Cyrus Warkins. His wife is not going to New York with me.

LILY. Mama should call him. Where's Mama? She went for my ring. Will Mr. Warkins listen to me? Nobody does. (*She runs to pick up the phone book, opens it, and drops the book*) Don't you want to help me? It's hot.

CARRIE. Wait for your mama.

LILY. You're teasing me. It's not nice to tease me and to pretend that you're not. (*As Carrie moves away*) Miss Carrie, please.

CARRIE (*sharply*). What do you want of me? What is that you want?

LILY. I don't want to be in the room alone. (*Points down to the telephone*) It's for the best, the best for everybody, isn't it?

CARRIE. What's the sense of answering you? You just go on talking and talking.

LILY. No, please. Please. Isn't it best for everybody?

CARRIE. I don't know about everybody. I'm not used to thinking that way. I just think about what's best for us, for Julian.

LILY. That's what I want, too. What's best for Julian. Please tell me.

CARRIE (*carefully, as if anxious to impress the words*). I don't know that I can. The people in the bank always talk of Mr. Warkins as a low-high-born man, tough and tricky, with plenty of riffraff friends to do his dirty work. Julian isn't fit to deal with such a man and God knows what could happen. Warkins is not a man to joke with.

LILY (*after the words "what could happen," Lily has picked up the phone and given the operator the number "Lafitte 1707." Her voice is firm*) Tell Mr. Warkins that Lily Berniers, Lily Prine, must speak to him immediately and does not wish to be kept waiting. (*Waiting, she smiles at Carrie*) I think that's the way Mama would say it. Oh, hello, Mr. Cyrus, this is Lily. (*She puts the phone down, wipes her hand on her nightgown, picks up the phone, waits*) Mr. Cyrus, you mustn't blame anybody if I tell you something. Will you promise a sacred promise on the life of your child?

CARRIE. He hasn't got a child.

LILY. But you haven't got a child. (*Pause*) Then why did you make a sacred promise on a child you haven't got? You mustn't joke with me, Mr. Cyrus, you must not. Oh. I see. Well, please tell your wife I'm not mad a bit. That's first. Just ask her to give me one more year with Julian and then I'll promise — Well, that's all. Just ask her that. (*She listens*) I wouldn't like to say because I don't understand much myself. Why does it matter? I don't see why it should. Oh. Well, Miss Carrie heard — (*Carrie wheels about*) A *lady* heard Henry say it. Henry? Why, the Henry of my mother — you know. Just that once, a long time ago, Julian had been — and that maybe she was helping him now. I don't know how Henry knew. (*After a second*) Oh, yes. I do. Henry is cousin to Mrs. Warkins. Yes, cousin. (*She waits, looks puzzled*) Mr. Cyrus? Mr. Cyrus? No, I don't think your wife's coming here. If she were, I could have asked her myself. I thought you could go right away, before she gets on the train — (*To Carrie*) He wants to know where he can find her to give her my message. (*Into phone*) I don't know.

CARRIE. Something about Sailor's Lane near the depot.

LILY. Something about Sailor's Lane near the depot. Yes. Nobody's done anything bad, you understand, Mr. Cyrus, and tell her I know that, but I'd just like to ask to have Julian for one more — Mr. Cyrus? Well, thank you. (*She puts the phone down, sits, smiles*) He says he sure will go talk to her.

(*Carrie sighs, waits, and then turns away. Anna comes into the room, dressed in a suit. She looks at Lily, who does not notice her. She crosses to the table and picks up the envelope with the boat tickets*).

ANNA. We can't go together now. What would you like to do about these boat tickets?

CARRIE. We can't go together *now?* I don't know what you mean. Were we ever going?

ANNA. I thought so. When Julian brought these home to us, he thought so.

CARRIE. How strange you are. Did Julian think that? I suppose so: one piece of nonsense makes for ten. We never in our lives had any intention of going, you know that as well as I do.

(*Anna picks up the valise, takes it to the porch and exits*).

LILY. I did right, just exactly. Didn't I? And I'll take the knife of truth and swear to keep my word —

CARRIE. Yes. But do it someplace else. It would be nice to see you in a dress. Why don't you try it?

LILY. Oh. All right.

(*She exits. Carrie sits down, as if exhausted. She looks at her watch. Anna comes back into the room, wearing a hat and carrying a coat.*)

ANNA. You never wanted to go to Europe? Never meant to go?

CARRIE. How do you know such things? You go on talking the way you always talked, saying you like or want what you always said. (*Anna doesn't answer. Carrie begins to recite in a make-fun singsong.*)

"On the fairest time of June
You may go, with sun or moon
Or the seven stars to light you
Or the polar ray to right you," —

Do you still like it, all the nights you read it to us?

ANNA. Yes. (*Slowly*) I don't know. I suppose it doesn't mean much to me anymore.

CARRIE. I can hear you, all your cultured evenings.

(*Mimics Anna's voice*)

"To see the laurel wreath on high suspended,
That is to crown our name when life is ended."

ANNA (*standing near the piano, she plays*). And you this? So deeply felt, your favorite.

CARRIE. Was it?

ANNA (*smiles*). And the candied oranges I brought each week?

CARRIE. I was sick of them ten years ago.

ANNA (*softly*). Well, people change and forget to tell each other. Too bad — causes so many mistakes. (*She crosses to the table, takes a ship's ticket from the envelope, puts the envelope back on the table*) I've taken my ticket, left yours in the envelope. You'll explain about that to Julian.

CARRIE. What are you talking about?

ANNA. I'll spend the night at a hotel. I'm going to Europe tomorrow.

CARRIE (*moves toward her, stares at her, starts to laugh*). You will be lonely.

ANNA. That's all right. I always have been.

CARRIE. You will look very silly, a middle-aged, scared-to-death woman, all by herself, trying to have a good time.

ANNA. You will stay here until you sell the house?

CARRIE. I don't believe you mean to go anywhere. It's just too crazy. You've never been anyplace in your life.

ANNA (*moves toward the door*). We have said good-bye.

CARRIE. You're showing off. You're just plain showing off. You're not going anywhere — (*As Anna reaches the door*) You can't go before Julian. It would kill him to know that anything was wrong between us.

ANNA. You don't love me, but you want me to stay with you.

CARRIE. We will find a way to live.

ANNA. No.

CARRIE. You need me. You always have. Julian, everybody, always thought you the strong and sturdy —

ANNA. And you the frail, the flutterer, the small. That's the way you wanted them to think. I knew better. Our patched-together supper, a little talk, sometimes a book, long ago on the piano, a game of casino, your bath, then mine, your room and my room, two doors closed.

CARRIE. All those years of nights, all the things you knew and never said. Does everybody live like that, or just two old maids?

ANNA. I loved you and so whatever I knew didn't matter. You wanted to see yourself a way you never were. Maybe that's a game you let people play when you love them. Well, we had made something together, and the words would have stayed where they belonged as we waited for our brother to need us again. But our brother doesn't need us anymore, and so the poor house came down.

CARRIE. I think our brother will need us. Now or someday. And we must stay together for it. (*Softly*) You're the kind of woman with no place to go, no place to go. (*Smiles*) You see? Some of those nights I thought about you, too. We must find a way to live.

ANNA. I don't wish to find a way to live with you. I am a woman who has no place to go, but I am going, and after a while I will ask myself why I took my mother's two children to be my own.

CARRIE. Go unpack your bags.

ANNA (*with great force*). Pretend it's last week. You've just told the girls in the bank that you can't have coffee, you have to hurry home, that Anna will be mad at you for being late, that Anna gives the orders to the soft and tender you. Go back and pretend it's still last week. (*She moves out to the porch, picks up a camellia plant and carries it down the steps. Mrs. Prine appears. Henry is with her, he waits beyond the garden fence*) Will I look very foolish carrying a camellia plant to Europe?

ALBERTINE. I don't think so. It's most becoming. Soft around the face.

(*Lily appears. She is dressed, has on her hat, and is neat and cheerful.*)

LILY (*to Anna*). Are you coming to New York with us? I would like that, Miss Anna.

ANNA. You shouldn't like it, and I'm not coming with you. (*She moves around the side of the house*) I guess two plants ain't more foolish than one.

LILY. Good-bye, Mama. We're going away. Good-bye. (*Smiles*) I know that will make you happy.

ALBERTINE. Here's your ring, Lily.

LILY. Oh. Thank you. I had forgotten — Oh. Madame Celeste gave it to you?

ALBERTINE. Madame Celeste sold it to me.

LILY. That's not fair, is it? Now I must give her back the knife of truth. (*She turns as if to leave*) I'd like to keep it, but she'd never sell it.

ALBERTINE (*very sharply*). Sit down. (*Lily sits down; Albertine sits opposite her, and speaks very quietly, but as if the words had been rehearsed*) I've had enough of whatever you're doing. However innocent is your innocence, I've had enough. More important, it is leading you into dangerous alleys. Not even for you will I again spend time in what you call an upstairs room with a morphine addict who holds séances to cover up what she sells.

LILY (*in a fury*). I don't believe you, I don't believe you, I don't believe you. You want to take my friend from me —

ALBERTINE. I am tired. I am sad. It is not good to know that my child swore fidelity to such a woman, and gave her wedding ring as proof.

LILY. My friend is a sweet friend. I gave her my ring because she loved me and gave me courage —

ALBERTINE. You are a pure girl and I believe you. Now listen: I am going to give you a good-bye present. Try to make use of it: the pure and the innocent often bring harm to themselves and those they love and, when they do, for some reason that I do not know, the injury is very great.

LILY (*who hasn't heard a word*). You have talked this way about my friend because you want to bring me pain. Henry makes plans to pain me — (*Outside the fence, Henry turns*) As you lie in bed with him, Henry makes the plans and tells you what to do.

ALBERTINE (*pleasantly, turns toward Henry*). Is that what we do in bed? (*To Lily*) You think that's what we do in bed? You're wrong. It's where I forget the mistakes I made with you.

HENRY. Stop it.

ALBERTINE (*ignores him; as if she is out of his control*). If something is the matter with you, come home and I will care for you, as I should, as I should. But if nothing is the matter with you, have pity and leave me alone. I tried with you all your life, but I did not do well, and for that I ask your pardon. But don't punish me forever, Lily.

LILY (*softly*). Is something the matter with me, Mama?

(*Henry moves toward Albertine and holds up his hand. Albertine stares at him, then nods.*)

ALBERTINE (*very gently*). No, darling. Certainly not.

LILY. If Julian leaves me —

ALBERTINE. Julian loves you, Lily.

LILY. I have sent a message and will keep my word. If Mrs. Warkins will give me one year —

ALBERTINE (*after a second*). You sent a message to Mrs. Warkins? Why?

LILY. Oh, because. I spoke to Mr. Warkins and told him to ask her to wait for Julian for one more year. (*Albertine moves forward. Henry moves toward her. Albertine turns and stares at Henry*) After that, if Julian doesn't want me — Where would I ever go, who would ever want me? I'm trouble, we all know that. I wouldn't have anywhere to go.

ALBERTINE (*after a long pause*). You will come home to me. You are my child.

LILY (*warmly, sweetly*). Thank you, Mama. Nice of you. But I couldn't go home to you anymore, as long as —

HENRY. If it ever happens, I won't be there. I won't be there.

LILY. Oh, thank you, Henry. That will be fine.

(*On the first part of Lily's speech, Henry sees Julian in the street. Henry makes a sudden move toward him, stops. Julian appears, stumbling toward the house. His face and hands are cut and bruised. He has been beaten, and one leg is injured. He moves toward the garden in great pain; his face is so stern that the people who see him know that to assist him would be to undignify him. Anna, who has seen him from the back of the house, starts toward him, then moves swiftly back as if on an errand. Lily does not move, but makes a loud sound. Julian tries to go up the steps of the porch, slips, and then clings to pillar of the porch. Carrie moves toward him, and then backs into the room. Henry goes toward Julian, but Julian puts up a hand, and Henry halts.*)

JULIAN. I took Charlotte to her brother's house. She'll be all right, but not her face. She's safe there, I think — Do you know what Charlotte I'm talking about?

HENRY. Yes.

JULIAN. She'd better not stay where she is. Just in case. Not in this town.

HENRY. All right.

(*Painfully, slowly, Julian moves into the room. Carrie, standing near the phone, points toward it.*)

CARRIE (*softly*). Doctor?

JULIAN. No. (*Anna comes in carrying a basin and bandages*) My friend. My poor friend. All she wanted, saved for, thought about — (*He gasps as if he is sick*) — to get away forever. Sanding there, standing in the alley, they slashed us up.

ALBERTINE (*who is standing on the porch; softly*). Who?

JULIAN. I don't know who. I saw two men and then I didn't see anything else. Two thugs he sent —

ALBERTINE. Who sent?

JULIAN (*in a shout*). Mr. Cyrus Warkins sent his men to meet us. (*He takes the money envelope from his coat pocket where it has been arranged as if it were a handkerchief, crumbles it, and throws it to the ground*) Nobody knew she came to Chicago to tell me, nobody knew she put up the money for the land, nobody knew her name. Tell her I swear it, I swear it. (*To Anna, who comes toward him with bandages*) Go away. (*To Henry*) I told *nobody*. Tell her I swear it on my life —

HENRY. No need to tell her that.

JULIAN. *But somebody did know. Somebody told him.* My friend — wanted to help me, took a dangerous chance and did — (*Softly*) You should see her. You should see her. Make her know I never spoke her name.

ALBERTINE. She will not think you did. I am certain she will not think you did.

JULIAN (*points to the envelope*). That's what's left of the money.

ALBERTINE. Shall I go to the police for you, Julian?

JULIAN. I went. High up, to Drummond.

ALBERTINE. Then perhaps —

JULIAN. No. I don't know what the thugs looked like — No matter what I said I could see Drummond saying to himself that I made it up, never could have had fifty dollars in my pocket, not less a hundred fifty thousand —

ALBERTINE. Shall I go to Warkins?

JULIAN. What for? Is he going to tell you who told him, who he hired to beat us up — What for?

ALBERTINE. I don't know.

JULIAN. Christ, what a mess-ass I am. She handed me the whole deal, told me every move to make, a baby could have done it.

(*His leg collapses and he falls to the floor. Slowly, painfully he lifts himself, moves toward the chair and table. Albertine turns away, as if the sight is painful. As Julian falls to the floor, Lily makes a dash to the porch. Albertine moves toward her; puts out a hand to hold her.*)

LILY. Mama, I did it.

ALBERTINE. Are you very sure you love him?

LILY. Mama, I did it. God forgive me.

ALBERTINE. Go in and sit by him. Just sit by him and shut up. Can you do that? Can you have enough pity for him not to kill him with the truth? Can you love him enough to go by him, sit down — (*Very softly, with great violence*) — *and be still?* (*Lily nods*) Then go and do it.

(*Lily moves into the house and timidly approaches Julian.*)

JULIAN. I don't look nice. Take off your hat, baby. We ain't going nowhere. There ain't nothing to go with.

LILY. May I wash your face?

JULIAN. Don't look like that. I'm all right. Nobody ever beat me up before, or slashed a friend.

CARRIE. Things can happen.

JULIAN. What did you say?

CARRIE. I said bad things happen to people. Doesn't mean anything.

JULIAN. I mean the way you said it. Say it that way again.

CARRIE. I don't know what you mean. Why don't you go rest yourself, darling. Good hot bath —

JULIAN (*turns to stare at her*). Why you start to purr at me? As if I'd done something good — (*Moves toward her*) You're smiling. What the hell's there to smile at? You *like* me this way? (*After a second, turns to stare at the room*) Pretty, all this. And the mortgage, and the tickets to Europe, and all the fun to come. Pretty, wasn't it?

CARRIE. We didn't want them. (*To Anna*) Did we?

ANNA. No, we didn't want them.

JULIAN. Don't talk that way. Won't do me any good. Assing it up all my God-damned life, all my life it's been the same. (*With violence*) Nobody ever beat me up before. Nobody's ever going to beat me up again.

(*There is a pause. Lily, who has been washing Julian's face, turns away. Carrie sighs and moves to the porch door. Then, as if a decision has been made, she moves out to the porch and leans down to pick up Anna's luggage.*)

ALBERTINE (*very sharply, to Carrie*). Mean to see a man stoke his pride. The meanest sight in the world. Don't you think?

CARRIE. Let's be glad nothing worse happened. We're together, the three of us, that's all that matters.

ALBERTINE. I counted four.

CARRIE. I mean the four of us.

ALBERTINE. Someday you will tell him about Lily? Then there

will be three of you. Before you tell him, let me know. I will want to come for her.

CARRIE (*points inside*). All that stuff has to go back, and the debts, got to find ourselves jobs. So much to do.

(*Carrie picks up the valises and moves into the room.*)

JULIAN. Old saying, money is a real pure lady and when the world began she swore herself an oath never to belong to a man who didn't love her. I never loved her and she guessed it. Couldn't fool her, she got good sense. (*Softly, desperately*) Nobody ever beat me up before. Maybe once it starts —

CARRIE. There's bad luck and there's good luck. That's all.

JULIAN. I guess so. Well, I've had the bad. Maybe I got a little good luck coming to me. Other men make it easy. Plenty of room in this world for everybody. Just got to fight for it. Got to start again, start again.

(*He rises. Lily moves to help him.*)

CARRIE. I'm going to get something nice to make soup with. You always liked a good soup when you didn't feel well. Meat and marrow, the way you like it. (*As she gets to the porch door*) Tomorrow's another day. (*Julian, leaning on Lily, moves out. Carrie, leaving the house, passes Henry and Albertine in the garden*) Good-bye, Mrs. Prine.

(*She exits. After a second Henry puts his hand on Albertine's shoulder.*)

HENRY. Good-bye.

(*Henry exits. Anna crosses to pick up her large valise at the same time Albertine rises to follow Henry.*)

Curtain

My Mother, My Father and Me

BASED UPON THE NOVEL HOW MUCH?
BY BURT BLECHMAN

For Blair

My Mother, My Father and Me was first produced at the Plymouth Theatre, New York City, on March 21, 1963, with the following cast:

(In the order of their appearance)

BERNARD HALPERN	ANTHONY HOLLAND
RONA HALPERN	RUTH GORDON
HERMAN HALPERN	WALTER MATTHAU
HANNAH	HELEN MARTIN
FILENE	BARBARA MOSTEL
MRS. JENNY STERN	LILI DARVAS
MRS. PARKER	ELAINE SWANN
WAITER	DON BILLETT
BUTLER	HARRY SMITH
DR. O'HARE	LEONARD HICKS
MR. PARKER	MILO BOULTON
MRS. LAMB	DOROTHY GREENER
BINKIE-PIE	HENRY GIBSON
MRS. COMPTON	LEONA POWERS
MRS. LAZAR	SUDIE BOND
MRS. KAUFMAN	EDA HEINEMANN
MISS EVELYN	AVRIL GENTLES
MR. LAZAR	JOE E. MARKS
DR. ZACHARY KATZ	MARK LENARD
TONIO CRAZZO	TOM PEDI
MR. KELLY	HEYWOOD HALE BROUN
MRS. KNOPF	DOROTHY GREENER
STYRON	MELVIN STEWART
NEGRO WOMAN	ROYCE WALLACE
DOORMAN	DON BILLETT
GIRL	JANE LAUGHLIN
WOMAN	VIRGINIA MADDOCKS
MAN	HARRY SMITH

Directed by
GOWER CHAMPION

Settings and lighting designed by
HOWARD BAY

Costumes designed by
DOROTHY JEAKINS

Scenes

The action of the play takes place in New York City.
The time is the present.

Act One

Before the curtain rises there is the sound of Berney Halpern playing the guitar as he sings a folk song.

SCENE: *The Halpern living room, Berney's room, and Jenny's skylight room. (The front stage is kept clear for other scenes.) The living room is crowded with too much of everything: draperies over draperies at the windows; too many pillows on the couch; too many boxes, ashtrays, lamps — three are on one table — too many candlesticks. Sometimes for lack of space, or because Rona Halpern got bored with them, ornaments are piled on ornaments and will, from time to time, fall off and crash.*

Berney's room, stage right, is more than crowded: it is almost impossible to move in it. There is photography equipment, instruments for making jewelry, an exercise machine, two typewriters, mounds of clay, the half-finished torso of a very lush woman, an Indian headdress, bows and arrows, a large picture of an Indian warrior, a tape recorder and a canoe. A dog is sleeping in the canoe.

AT RISE: *Mr. Halpern is sitting in front of a television located in a fancy fake Louis XIV cabinet. He is reading a newspaper. Rona is trying on hats; she has on a vast mink affair and is looking at herself in the mirror. Berney finishes his song, shakes his head, fumbles for new chords, is not pleased, and pushes the guitar away.*

RONA (*calling to Berney*). Berney, that was lovely. A lovely song. I'm crying. I said, I'm crying. Your father's crying, too. (*To Herman*) Tell the boy you're crying.

(*Herman looks up, sees the hat, and screams.*)

HERMAN. What's that?

RONA. They were reduced, they were reduced.

HERMAN. They should be.

RONA. If you buy furs in the spring, they're reduced. It's very wise, Herman, to buy furs in the spring.

HERMAN. Maybe. For those who can pay for them.

RONA. Those who can pay for them don't need to bother. It's people like me who have to walk their feet off, and all the trouble and work —

HERMAN. Well, go to the work of taking them back.

(*Hannah, who is a good-looking black woman, appears at the door*)

RONA. Coffee over there, Hannah.

HANNAH. Why?

RONA. Coffee over there, in the drawing-room part of the living room.

HANNAH. Ever since you met the Goys from that flea walk-up down the block.

(*She exits.*)

RONA. Flea walk-up! Six-hundred-a-month fleas. Herman, do you know there's a big movement to made-over houses? The Parkers pay six hundred a month. Sometimes I think we should have another bedroom.

HERMAN. What's another bedroom for? A three-bedroom apartment. Rona, you better right now understand that Florentine Footwear, we ain't paid a creditor. I'm telling you, Rona —

HANNAH (*appears in the doorway. She is carrying a silver coffee service. She puts it on the table*). Mrs. Halpern, you want it over there, carry it over there.

(*Rona smiles, sighs patiently, and takes the tray from Hannah. The price tags are still on each piece of silver.*)

MR. HALPERN. What the hell's that?

RONA. A bargain. The pot's got a little dent. So the nice young man said to me a dent in silver there *must* be to make an antique, so —

MR. HALPERN. Rona, I tell you, I ain't got it now. I ain't got it.

(*Berney's guitar-playing starts again.*)

RONA. All right, Herman. Drink your Sanka from it tonight. Enjoy a little beauty. I'll take it back tomorrow. I don't like it anyway. Don't get the price tags dirty. (*She goes to Berney's door*) Berney, a little pot roast on a plate?

BERNEY. No, Mother. You know I never eat before.

MR. HALPERN. Before what?

RONA. The folk-song festival. (*As Mr. Halpern makes a face*) Herman, Berney is finding himself.

(*Berney picks out new chords; they aren't right, and he shakes his head.*)

MR. HALPERN. Finding himself. At twenty-six, finding himself with a ukulele. At twenty-six, I supported my two sisters, my aunt and my mother.

RONA. *Your* mother! My mother is as good as your mother. Better. Mama's my own flesh and blood. Mama's your mama-in-law. My son's grandmother. We have to be good to her in her hour —

HERMAN. And what if she accepts?

RONA. She's not going to accept. Mama's not that way. Charity she'll never take. No charity.

MR. HALPERN. What's the matter with charity? You find a little charity, I'll take it. Where she going to stay? Where you going to put her?

RONA. I tell you, she's never going to come.

MR. HALPERN. In my bed? So I go to the Waldorf Astoria hotel and I say to them give me a suite, my wife wants her mother in my bed. A suite? Give me four rooms. No. My business is bankrupt. Give me *six* rooms so when I blow my head off, it can flop around in a little comfort.

RONA (*graciously, gently*). Herman.

MR. HALPERN (*excited*). What's that on your finger?

RONA. *Semi*-precious, *semi*-precious. They had a special sale for their charge customers —

HERMAN. How much is semi-precious?

BERNEY (*into the tape recorder*). My mother. My father. Chapter Twenty-two. For the first time in this manuscript I speak of myself. That was the advice given me by Mr. Jackson Bellamy, my instructor, in the Writers' Advanced Laboratory course. Use your life as Tolstoy used his experience in the Crimea — Well, I was born. Well — to hell with it. (*He speaks to the dog*) Dolly. (*The dog rises and comes to him*) Hold me, Dolly.

RONA. Mama's not going to come. All her life she's said young people should live by themselves. She wouldn't come after Papa's funeral, she won't come now. But it don't look nice this way, not to offer. My own mother.

BERNEY (*trying out his new song, his new chords*).

The life of a nigger ain't no good.

The life of a nigger ain't no good.
My man he's on the corner smokin' up the money,
Creepin' up the girls,
Knifin' in the night,
Beddin' in the day —

HANNAH (*comes into Berney's room*). What right you got singing and calling people niggers?

BERNEY. The song tries to tell the world of the enforced degradation of the Negro people.

HANNAH. You ain't no good. You take nigger right out of your Jew-boy mouth, you hear me? Degradation yet. Mind your business, you Berney.

(*She slams the door and exits.*)

BERNEY. The degradation that results from poverty and degradation. (*But Hannah is gone*) Chapter Twenty-three. That's the way it goes around here. The rescuing of a minority is a dangerous dung hole for the liberal. Deep in the womb of this world, the earth's womb, the world's womb, the womb of this world, the womb's womb — (*He thinks, can't find the right word, goes back to his guitar.*)

The life of a nigger ain't no good —
The life of a nigger ain't no good —

RONA. Lovely, Berney. Very sad. Would you like me to come with you, your Mama come with you to the folk-sing?

BERNEY. No.

RONA (*to Herman, in a whisper*). Say something to the boy.

HERMAN. Your mandolin sounds nice, Berney. (*Softly*) God forgive me.

BERNEY (*puts the guitar down. The dog jumps down, but Berney grabs her. Berney speaks into the recorder*). The duty of an artist is to face the truth. My chords are not good.

(*He sits, holding the dog. The doorbell rings. Rona rises, opens the door for a tall, thin girl of about twenty. She has long blond hair and her face barely shows through it. She walks past Rona and continues through the living room to open Berney's door.*)

RONA. Good evening. This is Berney's father, my husband. This is Berney's father, my husband —

(*But by this time the girl is in Berney's room.*)

HERMAN. Who's that?

RONA. Her name is Filene.

HERMAN. Filene? *Filene?* (*Excited*) Do you know what that

means? It means he's getting a little sense. Where'd he find her?

RONA. She just comes and goes. She's Greek.

HERMAN. Greek. The store ain't Greek.

RONA (*with interest*). The store? What store?

HERMAN. I don't think it's Greek. Maybe. It could be Greek. The first store ever thought of a basement. Takes expensive stuff, buys it in big lots, somtimes from France even, reduces it each week so sometimes it's down to nothing —

RONA (*excited*). *Where? Where* is it?

HERMAN. Boston.

RONA (*miserable*). Boston.

HERMAN (*opens Berney's door*). What's your father do, dear?

FILENE. Nothing.

HANNAH (*offstage*). Why you always come through the kitchen door?

(*Jenny, Rona's mother, comes into the living room, followed by Hannah.*)

RONA. Mama! What's the matter, Mama? How did you get in —

HANNAH. The way she always gets in. (*To Jenny*) I'm sitting there, eating my leftovers —

RONA. Mama, darling. Out at night. What are you doing out at night? Sit down, Mama.

(*Jenny crosses the room to Berney's door. She has three packages. She unwraps one package as she speaks to Berney.*)

JENNY (*opens the door*). Berney. (*Stares at Filene*) Hello, son. (*She holds up a bird in a cardboard cage*) Berney, I brought a little present. Call it Sam, please. I'd like it to be Sam.

BERNEY (*backs away*). Grandma, please. Grandma. I'm allergic.

RONA. That's kind of you, Mama, to waste your money. He's allergic. Berney, you all right? Mama, if you come out at night, you should eat dinner with us. Every night you're welcome.

JENNY. I don't like the cooking. (*She hands Herman a hideous necktie from a package*) Here, Herman.

HERMAN (*stares at the tie*). Thank you, Mrs. Stern.

(*Jenny unwraps a small, ugly fur piece, hands it to Rona.*)

RONA (*appalled*). Mama. My goodness.

HERMAN (*with a forced laugh*). You rich now, Mrs. Stern?

JENNY. I sold the candlesticks.

RONA. My heritage! You sold my only heritage!

JENNY. You got plenty candlesticks, Rona.

RONA. Where did you sell them, Mama? I'll go first thing in the morning and pay anything —

HERMAN. Rona!

JENNY. You think I like to sell? When your Papa brought them across an ocean?

RONA (*to Herman*). Did you send Mama her allowance last week? Did you forget?

JENNY. So I keep the bird. I like her. (*To the bird, singing*) Sam. Sammy.

RONA. Mama, it is bad luck to name a bird after a dead person. It's not nice.

JENNY. Bad luck came the day your Papa died. Bad luck stays now, and I don't even see him anymore. Herman, do you think I could have back the insurance money now?

HERMAN. Have a candy, Mrs. Stern.

RONA. Mama, you shouldn't come out alone. Herman, write Mama a check for the insurance money right away. (*She does not expect an answer and she gets none*) Mama, come live with us. (*When Jenny pays no attention*) People will talk. You'll fall again and they'll say why doesn't her daughter have the decency to take her in.

JENNY (*excited*). No. No. I want to stay in my place. Sam's place.

RONA. Papa is deceased.

JENNY. Not for me. Good-bye, Rona. Good-bye, Herman. (*To the bird*) Come on. Papa would have liked me to have a bird.

RONA. Mama, it breaks my heart that you won't consider living with us.

JENNY (*calling*). Berney, come tomorrow to visit.

RONA. Mama, we want you so much. We need you. I need you, Herman needs you —

HERMAN (*after a gesture from Rona*). Certainly do, Mrs. Stern.

RONA. But I know how it is. You'd never, never leave the nest you shared with Papa. But remember if you change your mind in the years to come, you're always welcome. We're your family and we want you with us.

(*Jenny, on her way to the door, half slips, half falls, tries to keep the bird upright, manages, and stands straight, weak, before they can reach her.*)

JENNY. Yeah. I'm sick. I can't live by myself anymore. I'll come. Thank you.

(*Jenny exits. There is silence, then Jenny's words register on Rona and she screams. Then Herman screams. The dog barks, we hear Berney's guitar, then Berney's voice.*)

BERNEY. Folks, I would like to do my version of —

(*Herman has lowered himself into a chair and is sitting quietly.*)

RONA. Herman, don't. It's not healthy. Get up. (*She runs off stage left, to a kind of ironing room with a skylight. It is very small, very crowded. It has an army cot, discarded hobbies of Berney's, bags of clothes and old rugs in it*) Help me. Help me. Herman! Hannah! (*She begins to pull things out of room, yells to Herman*) It's my own mother. I'm sick. I don't feel well. Help.

HANNAH. What are you doing in the ironing room? What you doing, Mrs. Halpern?

RONA. Hannah, my mother. My own flesh and blood. She's coming. You know how you feel about your own mother.

HANNAH. I don't feel nothing about my own mother. I ain't never seen her, and I ain't never wanted to.

RONA. Your own mother. Mama will help around the house, Hannah. She likes to work.

HANNAH. Mrs. Halpern, I'm warning you, I don't take care of no old lady.

(*Rona continues to pull and push at the clutter of the small room.*)

BERNEY (*after his song is finished, to Filene*). How was it?

FILENE. Somewhere between Stinkburg and Memphis.

BERNEY. Good-bye, Filene.

FILENE. Good-bye, Berney.

(*She exits.*)

BERNEY (*into the recording machine*). I have tried music and it has failed me. I will not touch the guitar again. I have always known that I wished to be a doctor. I knew it at fourteen with my tonsils. I wish to be of service —

(*Rona comes back into the living room.*)

RONA. Now, Herman, Mama won't be any expense. I'm going to market myself, much cheaper that way, you'll see, and I promise you I'm going to take back the hats, and the silver service, *and* that little black dress, and that radio we only used for a week — and I'm not going to buy anything else. (*She steps out of the living room, carrying two parcels. She crosses the stage, disappears for a second and appears again, now carrying five packages. She moves across the stage, disappears, and appears again, burdened down with packages. During her crosses, Mrs. Parker, seated at a restaurant table, moves onstage. Rona moves to join Mrs. Parker*) So sorry, Mrs. Parker. I started to take some things back to be credited, but I bumped into a glove sale, and French girdles, and ice skates for Berney —

MRS. PARKER. Quite all right. How are you? I've been very uncomfortable alone. Men have been staring at me. That man over there is just a disgrace. (*Calls off*) Two double martinis, please.

RONA. Which man?

MRS. PARKER. The man with the other man.

RONA (*cranes*). Which man with the other man?

MRS. PARKER. Mrs. Halpern! Please! Don't crane at men.

RONA. What a nice restaurant. I've never been here before. I didn't have any trouble getting in. They knew your name right away.

MRS. PARKER. Yes, of course.

(*The Waiter arrives with the drinks. Mrs. Parker drinks hers in one gulp. Rona tries the same thing, manages half.*)

MRS. PARKER (*to the Waiter*). Wa-it a minute. Just wa-it a minute. Bring a menu and another round.

RONA. What a pretty dress. You have such nice clothes.

MRS. PARKER. Takes time and care and an occasional trip to Paris.

RONA. Paris. I've never been. My son and I have long been planning a year in Europe —

MRS. PARKER. I wish that man would stop staring.

RONA. Which man?

(*She cranes again.*)

MRS. PARKER. Mrs. Halpern, please! He's very attractive. Well, I suppose there'll come a day when I'll miss that kind of open admiration. I often wish I hadn't been a beauty. My mother was a famous beauty in Providence, Rhode Island.

RONA. Well, of course, I never was beautiful, but I've been attractive to a good many men, or so they've said.

MRS. PARKER (*severely*). Promiscuity isn't the answer.

RONA. Oh, I didn't mean that. I should say not. I'm just not used to cocktails at lunch. I almost never have lunch. With anybody I mean. I just stop in at one of the department-store restaurants —

MRS. PARKER. There should be better things in life than shopping every day, Mrs. Halpern.

RONA. Oh, I don't mean I shop every day. Sometimes a concert, or a grand opera, and the museums and libraries. I'm so glad we've got to know each other, and right around the corner — (*The martinis arrive. Rona stares at hers*) Oh, I've never had *two* martinis — (*Mrs. Parker downs hers.*)

MRS. PARKER. Only alcoholics talk about what they *don't* drink. It's a sure sign.

RONA. Is that so? Then I'll certainly have to drink this —

(*She drinks her martini. Mrs. Parker stares at her.*)

MRS. PARKER. Did I hear you say your husband was dead?

RONA. Dead? No, indeed.

MRS. PARKER. Well, that kind of indignation shows something, all right, all rightey. Do you like your husband?

RONA (*giggles in disbelief*). What'd you say? Herman? I adore Herman. (*They fall into a depressed silence*) You must come over for bridge. I'd like to meet your husband.

MRS. PARKER (*who is a touchy drunk*). Would you just? I dare say. A lot of women would.

RONA. I didn't mean —

MRS. PARKER. You never know what you mean until you go to an analyst.

RONA (*impressed*). Do you go to an analyst? I've always wanted to know what it's like, what happens —

MRS. PARKER. Complicated. Very joyful, very painful. We're working on my drinking. He wants me to have a child.

RONA. Do they — my God! You mean, he, I mean the doctor, you mean *openly?* He fell in love?

MRS. PARKER. Oh, no, no. By my husband. Analysts are forbidden connection with the patient. Although, of course, he is a little in love with me. We talk about it every day and he says it is just in my mind because *I'm* in love with *him*.

RONA. Oh, how wonderful. Must be wonderful to have someplace to go every day, somebody to talk to. Strange time of life for a woman — between a lake and a pond, as they say. I mean an ocean and a pond. How much does it cost?

MRS. PARKER. Forty.

RONA. Forty what?

MRS. PARKER. Forty dollars.

RONA. For a whole course?

MRS. PARKER. Forty dollars an hour.

RONA. My. Like Miami Beach. But then that's for two in a room. I guess in analysis they don't allow two on a couch.

MRS. PARKER. I don't know what you're talking about, Mrs. Halpern.

RONA. I'm not used to cocktails at lunch. But my mother is coming to live with us —

She's moving in today. It's not going to be easy, but a mother is a mother.

I still don't see the man, Mrs. Parker. I really don't.

I said my mother was coming to live with us.

I wouldn't either. I mean —

The arms of a man? That's a good one.

Oh, nobody has an easy life, I guess.

And if you don't honor your mother, then who are you going to honor?

MRS. PARKER (*to any man*). Please don't stare at me. I don't like it and don't want it.

It's getting hard to eat lunch in a respectable restaurant.

What?

You still live with your parents? I left my parents early. I wouldn't even go to college.

I said, Daddy, what is there to be learned that cannot be learned in the arms of a man?

My Daddy, my adoring Daddy, slapped my face. Of course, now that I go to an analyst, I know why. He's dead, my Daddy.

Really? (*Laughs*) You're going to drive me to another drink.

(The lights dim and come up in the Halpern apartment as Jenny enters. She is carrying a cheap fishing rod, Sam the bird,

and a man's overcoat. She pushes and pulls at a large valise. She is exhausted and sits down.)

JENNY (*calling*). Rona. Rona. (*No answer*) I had promised the furniture to Mrs. Connor, you hear me, Mr. Halpern? (*No answer*) I wanted her to have my things so sometimes I could go and look —

(*Hannah comes into the room, carrying glasses and dishes for the dinner table. She jumps when she sees Jenny.*)

HANNAH. For God's sake. Creeping around again. I tell you, Mrs. Stern, I want you to stop scaring me.

JENNY (*cheerfully*). I'm here. I've come. (*Less cheerful*) Nobody home?

HANNAH. Why you didn't wait for them to come fetch you? What you doing sneaking around streets by yourself?

JENNY. I waited till there was no place to sit anymore. Mr. Halpern sold my furniture, the man said. I don't believe it.

HANNAH (*laughs*). Mr. Halpern sell anything, Mrs. Halpern buy anything.

JENNY (*has crossed to the dinner table and looked under the tablecloth that Hannah has just laid out*). Table's dirty. I'll get a wet rag. Only way to take off dirt.

HANNAH (*furious*). You an expert on dirt now?

JENNY. Yes, I'm an expert on dirt. We live in many poor places, and always everybody says Mrs. Stern's apartment only apartment fit for white people.

HANNAH. Your daughter comes home, I say give me my wages and find yourself a Jew-type nigger to put up with your mother and her insults —

JENNY. What insults? I mean white like clean. Excuse me, Miss Hannah, I sometimes now don't know what I say.

(*Hannah moves toward the kitchen, Jenny follows her. Hannah, at the door, swings on Jenny.*)

HANNAH. Stay out of the kitchen, Mrs. Stern. I'm telling you.

(*Jenny sits down. In a minute she rises, rearranges the dinner table, stops when she hears a noise in Berney's room. She goes to Berney's door, raps, gets no answer, opens the door. Berney enters through the front door, walks past Jenny into his room, closes the door behind him, sits down. Then he decides to come out again.*)

BERNEY. I go in. I say I want to enroll in medical school. I would like to discover cures for cancer, the common cold and insanity. I want to give my life to the mutilated— When I turned around he was on the phone. "Excuse me," he said, "this is a busy day." All right, Grandma, that's why I didn't come for you. I wanted to find myself—it didn't work.

JENNY. Maybe you should take a nice hike. Leave home. Go somewhere.

BERNEY. Where nobody knows me? (*Rona enters with some packages*) But they'd soon find out I can't do anything. You know that.

RONA. Berney, what's the matter? What kind of talk is that? Mama, why are you depressing Berney? That's not nice. (*Berney has gone to his room and slammed the door*) Now. Sorry to be late. I rushed. (*She puts the packages near the table*) Wait till you see your darling room. I bought a bed for myself and you're to have mine. God knows what we're going to do for storage space. (*She goes to Berney's door*) What's the matter, dear? (*No answer*) I should have gone to that old medical place with you. (*Herman comes in, looking tired and discouraged*) Herman, here's Mama. Make her welcome.

HERMAN. Hello, Mrs. Stern. Welcome. They take care of you all right?

(*Hannah comes in carrying more dishes. She exits.*)

RONA (*who has unpacked the silver coffee service; to Herman*). I didn't have time to take them back today, with Mama and all. We might as well enjoy a little beauty for one more night. Don't scowl, Herman. Tomorrow. Mama, want to wash?

JENNY. Wash what?

RONA. Oh, you know, before dinner and things.

JENNY. I'll wash the dishes after dinner.

RONA. Now, Mama, you mustn't ever do that. You must learn to live like a lady. That's what we have the colored girl for.

JENNY. I'll be the colored girl.

HERMAN. Rona, that's not a bad idea. Your mother is a lady who likes to work, makes her feel less like we're sacrificing, isn't that right, Mrs. Stern? Make you feel less like a charity case if you took over the kitchen?

RONA (*very loud, very sharp*). Herman! Hannah! Dinner. (*She sits down at table*) Berney! Dinner.

(Herman carries his drink to the table. Hannah appears carrying a tray.)

RONA. Mrs. Parker goes to an analyst. Drinks. He does very well, Mr. Parker. You'd have a lot in common, Herman. (*They are now seated. A place and chair have been forgotten and Jenny has not moved to the table*) My God! Mama! Come, come, Hannah. A place for my mother. (*She hits Herman. He jumps*) Apologize, Herman.

HERMAN. For what? I sit down where I always sit — I have no right to sit where I always sit?

(Rona points wildly at Jenny. Hannah appears with a place setting but no chair.)

RONA. Mama should sit at the head. Mama is the oldest. Come, Mama, you sit at the head.

HERMAN. How can a round table have a head? Explain that.

RONA. Explain, explain. A businessman. The human heart is a ledger? In spirit, Mama sits at the head. Spirit. Spirit, Herman. Berney, dear! (*Irritably*) Do sit down, Mama. *Sit down, please.* (*Jenny, finding no other chair, sits in Berney's chair. Rona whispers to Jenny*) Not in Berney's chair, dear. (*Jenny rises. Rona sees there is no other chair*) Herman! A chair for my mother! A chair for your mother-in-law!

HERMAN. Oh.

(Rises to get another chair, meets Hannah carrying the food. They get in each other's way. Finally Hannah puts the food on the table and Herman gets the chair.)

RONA (*looking into the platter, claps her hands*). A beef Bourg — (*Calls*) A beef Bourgin — (*Calls*) Berney! Just like you taught Hannah to make it. Berney reads. (*Vaguely*) But I thought I bought lobsters —

HANNAH. You did. But I told you before, Mrs. Halpern, I ain't fooling with lobsters. You want to fool with them, they're in the garbage.

(She exits.)

HERMAN (*softly*). Lobsters in the garbage.

RONA (*quickly*). Beef Bourgin is beef Burgundy. The French upper classes frequently take their styles from their peasants. Food, hats —

(Berney comes to the door, carrying his camera. As Rona is about to pass out the plates, Berney takes them from her and arranges them for a photograph. Herman, annoyed that his plate has been pulled from him, glares.)

BERNEY. Don't worry, Papa. You'll get it back.

RONA (*points to the camera*). For a magazine. (*Jenny has tasted the meat and is making faces*) What's the matter, Mama? (*Jenny spits out the meat, hurriedly covers it with a napkin, rises*) Where are you going?

JENNY. I want bread.

RONA. Mama, you must *not* get up for your own things. (*Jenny sits down again. Rona rings the bell*) Don't you like beef Bourg? Very expensive, the best sirloin.

HERMAN. When Rona markets, she don't say give me a chicken, a soup meat. She says is steak expensive today? Yes? Then I take it. No. Wait. What's *more* expensive than steak? Lobster? I take it. No, wait. I take both, one for the garbage, the can is hungry. No, wait. Raise the price of the steak, and then I take it, if, if, *if*, I *beg* you, you also raise the price of the lobster. (*To Berney, who is photographing him*) Stop it!

RONA. Herman, the lobster is beloved by Berney. Berney loves lobster.

BERNEY. Grandma, turn this way, please. (*She turns, smiles*) No. No. Don't smile.

JENNY. You want me to cry?

BERNEY. I don't want fake pictures. I want life as it is.

HERMAN. Life as it is. A fine thing to want. Believe me, I'd take a little of what life ain't. A business without troubles, or maybe just a father with lobsters.

RONA. Herman, I haven't had an easy day. Have some Hollandaise. You like the Hollandaise, Berney?

BERNEY. No, thank you.

RONA. You don't like the dinner?

BERNEY. *Nouveau, nouveau, nouveau.*

HERMAN. What's that?

BERNEY. *Nouveau riche*. We're new rich.

HERMAN. What did I hear you say? What are we? (*He bursts into a manic laugh*) What are we? Come down to the office and look at the books. Come down to the office and —

BERNEY (*smiles*). All right. I'll come tomorrow at nine.

HERMAN (*quickly*). No. Don't come. Forget it.

JENNY. Could I have some bread?

RONA. Where is Hannah?

(*She rings the bell long and loud. They sit in silence. Bored,*

Mr. Halpern turns on the TV. After a second, the TV voice comes on.)

TV VOICE. And Jackie Kennedy was in our village today with her sister, the princess. They went to six museums —

(*Berney turns off the machine.*)

HERMAN. What was the matter with that? You don't like Jackie?

RONA. My, it must be lovely to buy anything you want, your husband begs you to have it.

HERMAN. Turns off Jackie. How you like that? What's wrong with you and women, Berney, what gives out so wrong?

RONA. Herman, Mama doesn't like that kind of talk. You don't like sex talk do you, Mama?

JENNY. I don't care. With Sam and me there was peace when you broke the bread. Can I have some bread, Rona, please?

RONA (*shouts*). Bread, Hannah, *please*. (*Berney puts his hands over his ears*) I know, dear, but what are you going to do? Negro people forget things.

BERNEY. So do Jewish people.

(*Hannah appears with two small pieces of bread, hands them to Jenny.*)

JENNY. Two little pieces?

HANNAH. They diet around here. That's all there is.

RONA. Tomorrow, Mama, I'll buy two loaves, six loaves —

HERMAN. Buy ten and throw out eight.

JENNY (*chewing on the bread*). Lousy. Tomorrow I make the bread. (*She has been staring at the walls*) Walls are dirty. You never clean?

HERMAN. No. We buy new walls.

RONA. I don't feel well, Herman.

JENNY. A family should eat in peace, tell a joke, have a good loaf bread. I'm hungry.

RONA (*near tears*). Mama, all you've done since you got here is complain. Mama, we're doing our best for you. (*Crying*) Our best.

JENNY. Cry, cry. When she was a little girl, it was the same. And Sam would kiss her and give a cookie or candy — (*Rises*) I go help with the dishes. I be a little good to somebody.

(*She exits.*)

RONA (*after a minute*). It's not going to be easy. (*To Herman*) She's my own mother. The way I am to you, Berney.

(*They eat in silence.*)

HANNAH'S VOICE (*from the kitchen*). I tell you, Mrs. Stern. I tell you. Kitchen ain't made for two. Just take yourself to bed —

(*There is the sound of plates crashing. Jenny appears, carrying two broken plates.*)

RONA (*shrieks*). The Meissen. Belongs to Altman's.

HANNAH (*at the doorway*). You want my job, you take it. You hear, Mrs. Halpern? Anybody want my job for their old ma, they take it.

JENNY. I'll pay.

RONA. All right, Mama, all right. Hereafter, just break things belong to us.

HERMAN. How she going to find things belong to us?

RONA. Go to bed now. Don't cry so much, Mama.

JENNY (*who is not crying*). I never cry. Never in my life. Not even the day when Sam dies. Last Wednesday, I want to cry. But I don't cry because I hear Sam say, "Jenny, you never cry — "

(*Her face is screwed for tears.*)

BERNEY (*has focused his camera*). Look this way, Grandma. Your face is very fine when —

JENNY (*turns, sees the camera, and grins*). No. Life is too sad for crying.

(*As she grins, Berney makes a clucking sound of disappointment, and Jenny exits. Rona sighs, she takes Berney's hand.*)

RONA. Ready?

BERNEY. For what?

RONA (*surprised*). The Italian movie.

BERNEY. Saw it this afternoon.

RONA. We planned, Berney.

BERNEY. Got to work tonight.

HERMAN. What did you say?

BERNEY. I said work, work. I said the word work. Not the word money, just the word work.

(*He moves toward his room.*)

RONA (*to Berney*). We could go to that movie nobody understands. (*But Berney has closed his door*) Movie, Herm?

HERMAN. I am going to Manhasset, Long Island, New York.

RONA. They've never asked us before. You mean you're going without me?

HERMAN. They didn't ask me either. Have they ever asked me?

I'm going because I've got to go. We're near bankrupt, Rona.

RONA. Oh, don't start that, dear. Is he as rich as they say?

HERMAN. A private waterfall on the kitchen side, an inside pool for the winter, and he ain't even here in winter. Makes no sense. Three skyscrapers, a nice slum in Detroit. His wife won't sleep with him.

RONA. Won't sleep with him? That's disgusting. A woman denies a rich man like that.

HERMAN (*softly*). It's all right to deny a poor man.

RONA (*very quickly*). I've said before, there comes a time in human relations when another kind of love —

HERMAN. Another kind of love, he don't have to bother with. He's got a Hungarian in Manhasset, walking distance, but he rides, and a Chink in Florida.

RONA (*clucks in disapproval*). Disgusting. Well, I hope you get the loan, dear.

HERMAN. I've got to get it.

RONA. I'm off. Days alone, nights alone. Ah, well.

(*She exits. Herman picks up his hat and exits. The lights dim in the apartment and come up on an elaborate fireplace mantel and chair. On the mantel there are silver cups awarded for racing and sailing. The picture over the mantel is El Greco's St. Bernardino of Siena. From a room several rooms away, there is the sound of laughter and a dance band. Herman, on his way into the room, meets the Butler.*)

BUTLER. Who shall I say is calling, sir?

HERMAN. Mr. Herman Halpern. I'm Mr. Heim's cousin — we grew up together. Not in any place like this, I can tell you. (*Waves toward the music*) A party?

BUTLER. Yes, sir. I —

HERMAN. Shall I come along with you? Er. I'm his cousin, you know —

BUTLER. I am not sure where he is, sir. I'd better announce you.

(*He starts out.*)

HERMAN (*nervous*). Guess I never knew you had to announce a relative. Tell Mr. Heim it's an emergency. Tell him I wouldn't be here if —

BUTLER. Yes, sir.

(*He exits.*)

HERMAN (*looks around, listens to the music*). Come on in, meet my friends, dance a little — Can't, Moe, I'm not dressed for all those rich people. But the very next ball, I'd sure like to come — (*He begins to dance with an imaginary woman*) Janet? May I call you Janet? We're cousins, you know, although we haven't met in thirty years since that stinky wedding you had with Moe. Okay. Your feet hurt. You fat fool. (*He stops dancing, looks around*) Look, Moe, I sure been proud of you all these years. Everybody in the shoe business knows I'm related to Moe Heim. I did telephone you, many times, but I guess you never got the messages — Well, sure, I should have kept on calling, but everybody's got their pride. Anyway, Moe, we'll make up for past time. Still like to fish? Remember high school and the trips to Bear Mountain? Twenty-five thousand, Moe, I'll say it quick. Just for sixty days. (*He turns away, refused*) How can twenty-five thousand be a lot for you? Okay. (*He sits in chair, looks at his watch*) Trophy room. (*Points to silver cups*) Who'd you bribe for those, M. Heim and Sons? *You* ain't got no sons. I got a son. You're frigid, always was. Look at you. So small your feet don't touch the floor. Small men always got to push, I guess. And you pushed all right. *You're* Heim, and *you're* your sons, and you're the construction firm of Perottie and McCarthy who does your building for *yourself*. (*Leans forward, earnestly*) Look here, Moe, when they say that's crooked, I say it's not. What's crooked one generation, is a charity foundation the next. You got to. Even me. You laugh, the scale's so little, but we got one, a tax dodge, like they say. In the name of Frank James. Don't know where we got the name, so long ago — (*He settles back. There is silence*) So one man comes out fine, another man don't make it. Little slice of difference. Um. We had the same great-grandfather. (*Points to the El Greco*) Not him. Same great-grandfather. With our people that's like brothers, the rabbi says. Berney should have been a rabbi, a scholar — Look, Moe. How about ten thousand? That can't mean much to you. To me, it means a little peace. With my heart. My heart's cutting up. (*Under his breath*) A man's in a fine state when he has to invent his own heart being bad. God forgive me.

(*The Butler enters.*)

BUTLER. Mr. Heim is in a board meeting, sir. He sends his regrets and says that he will be calling you.

HERMAN. Yeah. Thank you. Tell him when I have a board meeting, we can't afford a dance band.

BUTLER. Yes, sir.

(He exits as the lights fade and come up in Berney's room and in the living room. Jenny is scrubbing the walls. Berney is standing before an easel. He is painting a portrait of Filene. Filene, sitting with her back to us, is naked. Her head is lolling on the back of the chair; very occasionally it swings to the record on the phonograph. Filene scratches her back.)

BERNEY. Filene, please don't scratch so much.

FILENE. Why not? *(No answer)* Why not?

BERNEY. Because it doesn't go with what's here, what I want.

FILENE. Want where?

BERNEY *(points to the easel)*. Here.

FILENE. Oh. *(She scratches her back)* Once when I was in bed, a man tried to tell me when to scratch and I broke his arm. Ever had your arm broken in bed?

BERNEY. No.

FILENE. Ever had your heart broken in bed?

BERNEY *(embarrassed)*. Could be.

FILENE. Yak. Ever been in bed?

BERNEY *(worried, giggles, points to the bed)*. Every night.

FILENE. You mean the same bed every night? What a world. *(She listens to the music, then softly begins to chant)* Full of boobs, kooks, finks, hips, square-squares, crackpotolas, apes, goodyniks, the knifeboys, the pillow fighters, old uncles and young buncles, gunzels, purple warps —

BERNEY *(very nervous)*. You don't say a word for a week. Then.

FILENE *(smiles dreamily)*. That's the way it is. Nothing and then a lot.

(Stretches. He sees her breasts.)

BERNEY *(very nervous)*. Filene. Take you home? Filene. Take you home?

FILENE. Where dat? Where home? No, Jack. It's oke here.

BERNEY *(miserably)*. Filene, get up, will you? *(No answer)* Filene. Filene, I want to go to bed. I'm sleepy. *(No answer)* I could lend you a dollar.

(Gingerly, he leans over and pokes her.)

FILENE. Read me a poem. I won't listen.

BERNEY. "Life is a blind, solitary walk to the grave. Alone, as separate in the day as in the night. Alone, alone, alone." It was called "Alone" and I sent it to Bennett Cerf with a note saying I was fourteen and I understood he was sympathetic. Oh, I'm glad really. One only finds oneself through fire. The mind burned, the body scorched, walking toward the next flame, head back —

FILENE. Who you get to play that with you?

BERNEY. I'll take you home —

FILENE (*turns over*). Put a flame to me, Jack. Burn me down.

BERNEY. Look here, Filene, I was talking about work, creation, walking through life's burning forest to the end. (*She snores*) Filene, please get up now. (*She turns over*) Oh, Christ.

(*The front door opens. Rona crosses straight to Berney's door, does not see Jenny.*)

RONA. A fine movie, very different. I don't think they did meet in Marienbad. Oh, Berney, we must see Europe. (*No answer*) A glass of milk with Mother?

(*Berney, on her first words, has leaped to Filene and is shaking her.*)

FILENE (*giggling*). Hey, that kind of thing costs money.

BERNEY (*passionate whisper*). Get up. My mother's here.

FILENE. That kind of thing costs more.

RONA. Berney, it's Mother. (*She tries the door. It is locked. She is shocked*) Locking Mama out? (*Frightened, calls*) Herman!

JENNY (*from the chair on which she is standing*). He ain't home.

RONA. Berney never locks the door. He's frightened of locked doors. (*On a late take, sees Jenny*) Mama! Mama! What are you doing? (*Sniffs*) Berney! Berney! I smell smoke. Fire!

FILENE (*who has been pulled from the bed by Berney and is now being forced into her raincoat*). Fire crazy, all of you.

BERNEY (*desperate*). Filene, *please* —

JENNY (*shouts, pointing to kitchen*). My bread. In the oven. My bread —

(*In trying to get off the chair, she topples, hangs onto the draperies, pulls them down with her. Berney's door opens and Filene enters the living room. She has on her raincoat, nothing under it. She is followed by Berney.*)

RONA (*softly*). My God. In your mother's house. You have besmirched your mother's house. Besmirched. Your mother.

(*She begins to cry.*)

FILENE. I tell you, there's nothing so crazy on earth as a middle-class American woman. Look, honey. (*She turns to Rona, throws open her coat and is, of course, naked. Rona screams*) Naked. I say to myself, if a turnip or a dog has no dress, *I* do not want a dress. When turnips and dogs get a nice dress, then I'll get a nice dress.

(*Herman comes in.*)

HERMAN (*abstractedly to Filene as she exits*). Hello.

RONA. Herman, Herman —

HERMAN. He wouldn't even see me.

RONA. Oh, Herman, pay attention to your family. Your son. Berney. A girl in his mother's bed. (*Shouts to Berney who has returned to his room*) Your father out getting money for his family. His son, in the house of his father, sleeping with a girl —

BERNEY (*wearily, through the door*). I didn't, Mama.

HERMAN. I believe him.

RONA (*to Herman*). Take his side against mine. Throw me out. Let his girls come marching through, one after the other — (*To Berney*) I don't want to go to Europe with you.

HERMAN. What's burning?

JENNY. My bread.

RONA (*shrieks at the sight of the blob Jenny has made on the wall*). Mama! Mama! Look at my own Mama. My own Mama.

JENNY. Tomorrow I make new bread.

(*She exits.*)

RONA. Herman, I need help. A doctor.

HERMAN. Me, too.

RONA (*points to Berney's room*). Make him say good night to his own mother.

HERMAN (*calls*). Say good night to your own mother.

RONA. A week in a hospital, a good rest, with nurses —

HERMAN (*angrily to Berney*). Say good night quick.

BERNEY. Good night.

RONA. I don't want to hear. (*Calls*) That will be for the best. Berney. I'll go to Europe by myself.

HERMAN. *Which* Europe?

(*The lights begin to dim in Berney's room. Berney lies down. Rona and Herman sit in the living room. Berney's hall door opens and Jenny sticks her head in.*)

JENNY (*looks at him, whispers*). So don't feel so bad. A girl is nature.

BERNEY (*shocked*). Grandma! You don't think —

JENNY. So what's to think? A big boy. You like the lady, she likes you.

BERNEY. I don't like her and she doesn't like me.

JENNY. So next time you like her, maybe.

BERNEY. Good night, Grandma.

JENNY. Take a bus, Berney. Maybe California. You get a nice job, make friends. There comes a time when a man should leave his mama —

BERNEY. I will. I will. Good night, Grandma, I'm tired.

JENNY. You're always tired.

(*Jenny exits.*)

HERMAN. I'm tired. Some evening. Come to bed, Rona.

RONA. You can sleep with what's happened here? How? I'm feeling bad, badly, Herman. I need somebody to talk to, somebody to help me. I'm going to call Mrs. Parker and ask her the name of her doctor. (*As he starts to protest*) Herman, a doctor is cheaper than a hospital — (*The lights begin to dim as Rona exits. The lights come up on Rona and Dr. O'Hare. Rona is lying on a couch. Dr. O'Hare is sitting behind her. He is an attractive man in his late thirties*) I try, Doctor. I tried yesterday, too. I want to talk. Who doesn't at forty an hour? I've been coming five days now. Do I pay you today? (*No answer*) Do I pay you today?

O'HARE. Yes, Mrs. Halpern.

RONA. Call me Rona, do. Do you reduce your fee after the first year? (*Gets no answer*) Isn't it unusual, Dr. O'Hare, for an analyst to be a Roman Catholic? Or did you say you weren't? Still, Sandor O'Hare sounds Catholic. I like your name. (*Giggles*) It's stylish. Did you make it up? Does Mrs. Parker, I mean, does she talk about her innermostly, well, you know what I mean, men? (*No answer*) Dr. O'Hare, you never answer my questions.

O'HARE. I don't discuss my patients, Mrs. Halpern.

RONA. That's honorable. That's the way it should be. But does she talk about, I mean, more easily? I think maybe it would be easier for me if you were a woman. A woman analyst. Still, I don't trust women scientists; if they were attractive they wouldn't need to work and I've never trusted an unattractive woman. They're bitter. Well, if Mrs. Parker's told you the truth, she's sleeping with her cousin. (*She turns to watch the effect of this; it has none, she turns back*) But she wants to sleep with you. I don't. So you don't have to worry about me. I daresay you have your hands full with Mrs. Parker. Do you approve of a woman sleeping with her cousin? (*No answer*) I *have* to know that, Dr. O'Hare, I really do.

O'HARE. I am not in the business of approving or disapproving, Mrs. Halpern. I am here to examine the facts.

RONA. Well, I don't understand your allowing her to sleep with her cousin. Did you *tell* her to sleep with her cousin? You don't tell me to sleep with my cousin. (*Laughs*) God forbid, as they say, you should see him. Mrs. Parker doesn't *want* to sleep with her cousin, she does it for companionship. SHE *wants to sleep with you.* I know that. And I know you won't sleep with her. I think you're right. (*No answer*) Won't you ever talk to me, Dr. O'Hare, for forty an hour? My husband says we can't afford this and he hopes that later on, in a month or two —

O'HARE. I've explained that I don't discuss Mrs. Parker with you and I don't discuss you with Mrs. Parker.

RONA. What is there to discuss about me? *I* don't sleep with my cousin. *I* don't sleep with other men.

O'HARE. You don't sleep with your husband, either, Mrs. Halpern.

RONA. That's not a kind thing to say. You mean to say that you think it's nicer to sleep with your cousin than *not* to sleep with your husband?

O'HARE. Analysis is not concerned with what is nice, it is concerned with what is true. Some women want to sleep with their fathers, some with their cousins (*Carefully*) and some with their sons.

RONA (*rears up from the couch. In shock*). Their sons! What kind of talk is that? That's disgusting talk, if I say so myself. You've hurt my feelings, Dr. O'Hare — (*She starts to cry softly. He rises, looks at his watch, pats her on the shoulder. She grabs his hand, takes it to her breast*) I know you didn't mean it. I know what you feel about me. I knew from the first consultation. But I've only known you a week, and we haven't even had dinner together —

O'HARE. Mrs. Halpern. Please listen to me carefully. You do not know what I feel. You are my patient here and nothing else.

RONA (*throwing his hand from her*). I can find better things to do with forty an hour than be hurt and insulted every minute —

O'HARE. I have come to the conclusion you should find better things to do. Good-bye, Mrs. Halpern.

RONA (*her voice rises*). How dare you? Because I refuse you, you insult me. I will have to tell my husband, Dr. O'Hare, that you approve of mothers and sons, cousins and, and, cousins and mixing. I don't think I should pay you for this session, as you call it. (*The couch begins to move off stage*) Your watch is incorrect. I am paying for three minutes more and three minutes I stay.

(*As Rona's voice fades, the lights come up in Berney's room. Jenny is sitting in a chair. Berney is testing a bow and arrow.*)

JENNY. What is it? Where you use the — the —

BERNEY. *Use* it? Not everything is for use. I just like it.

JENNY. You play a little on the guitar for me?

BERNEY. I've given up the guitar.

JENNY (*after a minute*). Um. You want I should pose a little for the camera?

BERNEY (*picks up the camera*). See this? I'm in the park, on a bench. Two little blond girls, four, five, maybe, kiss each other, kiss again. Then suddenly, they are on the ground and they got like little switch-blade knives, and they're fighting like hell, and using the knives like experts — (*He rises*) I never saw anything like it. I take my camera. The great shot of the world, unrehearsed infant murderers. I click away. A man comes along to watch, a mother comes running, one kid is bleeding. The man says, "Boy, you got there pictures anybody would buy, any art mag. Boy, I envy you —" Then he laughs. Then he says, "Next time take the cover off the lens." The cover was on the lens, and that's the history of my life.

JENNY. The camera, the guitar, the dictating machine, the phonograph. At your age a man should have something that's alive — a girl, Berney.

BERNEY. Oh, Grandma. It's my nap time.

JENNY. You just get up from another nap. You sleep, you sleep. Maybe you should go where there ain't so much steam heat. A cold climate, Berney —

BERNEY. Siberia? Would you like me to hitch a ride to Siberia?

JENNY. What's so wrong with Siberia? Snow is healthy. You open a little bookstore, you meet a big, strong girl who can carry you when it freezes too bad —

BERNEY. That's what you think of me, Grandma? A big, strong girl to carry me. Pretty picture of a man.

JENNY. Pretty picture. Is a pretty picture *here?* Sleep, eat, take a nap with a dog, the Mama, the Papa, the —

BERNEY (*angry*). Grandma, I'm trying to find out what I'm about, what the world's about —

JENNY. While you sleep? Go away, Berney, I say go away.

BERNEY. I'm going. Soon. Now leave me alone.

(*There is a long pause.*)

JENNY. Tell me a nice story. Tell me about those people. When you were little you used to say you would go to live with them, save them —

BERNEY. I wish I had gone.

JENNY. Yeah. They still fight, they still stand up so straight?

BERNEY. Oh, Grandma, the Indians haven't fought for a hundred years. They sit now. Just sit. No place for them in our fine modern world. We took their lands, killed their animals, cut down their mountains, put filth in their rivers. They are charity patients now, like you and me. That's what happens when the bully boys move in.

JENNY. Ach. Too bad.

BERNEY. Anything for dough. Anything. But they'll rise up one day — (*His face glows with a childish dream*) One day, there'll be another chief, a man of noble spirit, who gives his life to, to —

JENNY. You used to say *you'd* go be their chief.

BERNEY (*laughs*). Did I?

JENNY. Don't be ashamed. Sometimes baby talk is best talk. (*Pause. Berney seems to doze. In an effort to keep him interested*) What were the names I couldn't say?

BERNEY. The Wichitas, the Crows, Mohawks, the Wyandotts, Chinooks in the Montanan lands. (*He begins to be pleased with the sounds of the names*) The wise man Pontiac, betrayed; the Prophet Delaware; the buffalo, the bison, the hare, the bear, the shaggy pony, the willow wands, the arrow roots —

JENNY. What was the woman called? The girl?

BERNEY. Once I dug up an arrow root and boiled it and got

sick. Remember? And I practiced with the bow and arrow in Asbury Park and killed that rabbit — (*After a second*) I didn't kill it. I missed it.

JENNY. And Grandpa bought you a little drum and you'd sit — (*She begins to tap on the table. After a second Berney smiles and begins to speak to the rhythm of her tapping.*)

BERNEY. The river of Tombigbee, the mountain of Pastercene, Kamchouchee the giant moose who wouldn't die and the Simolee magic arrow that killed him; the girl, Tlingee, who braved the giant moose to save young warrior, River Black Wolf, her left breast torn open —

JENNY. That's the right kind of girl, Berney.

BERNEY (*caught now in happy memory*). The eagle and the whale Zuni, the eagle and the whale Zuni, wild hemp to catch the deer, the Pah-pol-se-kah-way, the wild black mare of Geronimo —

(*The noise of Berney shouting and Jenny drumming grows very loud as the lights go up in the living room. Rona, Herman and Mr. and Mrs. Parker are playing bridge, or trying to. Mr. Parker has opened his mouth to bid, can't be heard, and is obviously annoyed. Rona gives a nervous, indulgent chuckle.*)

MRS. PARKER (*to Mr. Parker*). I didn't hear your bid, darling.

MR. PARKER. That's because darling is waiting for the noise to stop. (*To Herman*) Bourbon and branch while we wait.

MRS. PARKER (*to Rona*). How old is your son?

RONA. Twenty-six. I was seventeen when he was born.

(*Herman, pouring drinks, laughs.*)

MRS. PARKER (*listens to the tom-tom*). Twenty-six. With a tom-tom. Therapy?

MR. PARKER (*to Herman*). Do much investing? In the Street?

HERMAN. Time to time. Too much tied up in shoes right now. And shoes stink. You boys in the Street sure sent things down.

MR. PARKER. Not my boys. The Kennedy boys. Lay the whole thing where it belongs.

MRS. PARKER (*leans forward firmly*). *I* am going on thinking Jack Kennedy is good-looking. This is a free country.

MR. PARKER (*shouts*). Four clubs. (*As he waits*) Kennedy and Rock Hudson. The dream of American women who are in the middle of the menopause.

RONA (*shocked*). My goodness, Mr. Parker! (*Smiles*) Arguments about Jack and Jackie. I've come to the conclusion they are causing a lot of trouble in the average American home. I guess nobody ever wanted to, you know, with the Eisenhowers.

MR. PARKER. Dear lady. How right you are. (*He strokes her arm*) You have something there. Something valuable. I'm going to speak to the boys about it. Take sex out of American life. Sex has no place in public life. (*Laughs*) I believe in a cozy little motel room. How about you, Halpern?

HERMAN (*puzzled*). What? Pass.

MRS. PARKER (*leans over, stares at Parker's stroking of Rona's arm*). Before you go to the motel, I bid four hearts.

(*The tom-tom noise grows very loud. Rona rises, crosses to Berney's door.*)

RONA. Berney, dear, I want you to meet Mr. and Mrs. Parker. (*She opens Berney's door*) Mrs. Parker's been to Europe five times and Athens. (*Stares at Jenny*) Mama. What *are* you doing? You cannot go on disturbing Berney when he is working. Mama, go to bed immediately, and, Berney, please come and meet — (*Berney rises, closes the door. Rona returns to table*) It's his grandmother making the noise. Crazy about him, you know.

MRS. PARKER. His *grandmother* on the *tom-tom?*

(*Three people enter and move across the room to Berney's door. They are Filene, Mrs. Lamb, a woman of about forty, and Binkie-Pie, a very small, thin young man. Binkie-Pie is carrying a briefcase. They cross the room, led by Filene.*)

RONA (*screams at the sight of Filene*). Herman! That girl!

FILENE (*turns, curtsies and in an elaborate Southern accent*). Evening, folks. My name's Susannah-Dear Bunchlet from Camolia, Alabama. University of Mississippi graduate. My father was living off an old nigger lady and raping me in the afternoon, so I shot him and left home.

MR. PARKER (*to Filene*). Hello, there.

FILENE (*correcting him*). *Hello, Miss Susannah-Dear Bunchlet.* My friends, Mrs. Fritzie Lamb and Binkie-Pie.

(*They open Berney's door and disappear.*)

RONA. Berney! You promised me! That girl. Herman! Make them leave. He promised me he would never see her again —

(*In Berney's room, the guests settle themselves. Nobody in the room speaks to Jenny, although she mumbles hello to everybody. Mrs. Lamb takes out a gin bottle, puts it on the table.*)

BINKIE-PIE (*opens his manuscript and begins to read*). I guess she was dead okay. I don't know. We took the lousy hundred and began to drive. I don't remember much about it except the rusty needle hurt my arm. Around Milwaukee, he said, "Come on." And I said, "You know a drugstore in Milwaukee, do you?" And he said, "Come on." And I said, "No, I don't want to." And he said, "You don't want to? What the hell's *want* got to do with it? If you don't want your own brother, then you don't want anybody, you dirty little gunzel —"

RONA. Herman, I am not going to allow girls in his room —

MRS. PARKER. So? That's it? That's a hard one for a doctor to cure. No wonder Sandor gave you up.

RONA. Sandor didn't give me up. I left. You call him Sandor? I thought that was forbidden.

MR. PARKER. Nothing is forbidden, is it, Mary Ellen?

MRS. PARKER. Ritchie, all these years I've been telling you only amateurs discuss their analysis.

MR. PARKER. And, kid, you ain't no amateur. Not after five years and thirty-five thousand dollars.

HERMAN (*softly*). Thirty-five thousand dollars on a person's *head*. I'm in the wrong end of the business.

RONA (*who is staring at Berney's door and has several times advanced toward it*). Today I heard about a doctor who charges fifty an hour.

HERMAN. Where'd you hear about him? Did you spend the day in Tiffany's? (*Herman rises, deeply disturbed*) Rona. Tomorrow I have a date with the Revenue boys. Today, Macy's refused the shipment with the buckles. (*Desperately to Parker*) Did you ever hear of a man near bankruptcy whose son doesn't work, who supports his crazy mother-in-law, whose wife goes to Tiffany's for a doctor —

RONA (*to Mr. Parker*). My husband's nightly joke is bankruptcy. Year in, year out.

MR. PARKER. I know, Mrs. Halpern. Only the very rich can afford to talk about bankruptcy. Never fails. Only the very rich. That's what we say in the Street. I can tell your old man is well heeled or he couldn't afford you. Anything so pretty comes high.

RONA. I don't come very high, Mr. Parker. When I was young,

I did have dreams of glory. I looked like Grace Kelly, so they said —

MRS. PARKER. You know, Mrs. Halpern, before I met you, I never knew Jewish people had neuroses. (*Clucks*) With all your other troubles. Israel and all.

HERMAN. Oh, we got everything. What other people got, we got more.

RONA (*to Mrs. Parker*). Women who have not had children never really understand other people's problems.

MRS. PARKER (*who is tight now*). Oh, I understand, all right. One no trump.

HERMAN. Pass.

MR. PARKER. Pass.

RONA. Pass.

MRS. PARKER. Three no trump.

MR. PARKER. You're at the raising-yourself stage.

(*As they play, a phonograph record is heard in Berney's room.*)

BINKIE-PIE (*reading*). His hair was greasy and thin, but I mixed it with a little blood, thinking that's the way he would have liked it at the end. But it turned out his family owned the town and in front of the funeral parlor the next day the pushers were more than the mourners, although pushers can be pretty good mourners when they do mourn. I said to my brother, my other brother, this ain't wise, Seymour —

BERNEY (*softly*). Good. Very good.

BINKIE-PIE. Thank you.

BERNEY (*points to phonograph*). I mean Handel.

MRS. LAMB. Handel? He's dead. Death's for suckers.

JENNY. Well, I guess there've been a lot of suckers. (*She rises*) Good night, folks.

(*Nobody answers. She moves out.*)

BINKIE-PIE (*resumes reading*). We rode and we rode and we rode and we rode and we rode and we rode and so it went. I was asleep, and the fix was wearing thin, and so I never saw it happen. But I always get stuck with the doings, and I don't like it. And so, we rode and we rode —

(*The lights have dimmed and come up in Jenny's room as she opens the door. Hannah and a black man jump up from the bed. Jenny screams, the man rushes by her.*)

HANNAH. Stop your noise, Mrs. Stern. Ain't you ever seen a man before?

JENNY. You're in my room.

HANNAH. My rest room before you came. You take my rest room. Can't two people rest themselves, have a little talk —

JENNY (*very upset*). You weren't talking.

RONA (*appears at Jenny's door*). What's the matter? I've never had such an evening. Where is the lobster salad, Hannah? Look at you. All rumpled. And you screaming, Mama —

JENNY. There was a man in my bed.

RONA. A man? Hannah!

HANNAH (*to Rona*). You see a man? You see anybody? Any more insultin' old talk from your Ma and I walk. Your Ma got some crazy dream.

RONA. Ssh. Now put on your new apron —

(*Hannah flounces off.*)

JENNY. I saw her husband last week and that wasn't her husband.

RONA. She hasn't got a husband. Mama, you were dreaming. Now go to bed and please stop yelling.

JENNY. *I don't want a man in my bed.*

RONA. Mama, please stop this foolishness and have a little pity on me. Nightie night.

JENNY (*screaming*). *There was a man in my bed.*

RONA (*screaming*). There was not.

JENNY. There was.

RONA. Stop that crazy sex talk. It's disgusting.

HANNAH (*in the hall*). I ain't going to stand for crazy old ladies —

RONA (*as she joins Hannah in the hall. Jenny listens*). You think having Mama here is easy on me? I'm going to give you a nice coat this Christmas, Hannah —

HANNAH. By Christmas, either your batty old Ma goes out of here or I go.

RONA. Ssh. Many things can happen by Christmas.

(*Jenny goes into her room, sits down.*)

JENNY. Many things can happen by Christmas. So we don't wait for Christmas. We go look for a nice baby. It says in the newspaper, they want responsible woman to sit with baby. I'm responsible woman. Berney will write a nice reference letter — (*She sighs*) Yesterday, again I ask for the insurance money. When Mr. Halpern pays, we give half to Berney. He goes away from here. Then we say to the family, it's been a good job, you nice people, fine baby, but we leave you now. We go where there is no snow. Where there is no snow, there we go. (*She rises, takes a Sterno stand and stove, lights it, puts water from a bottle into a pan, puts it on the stove, gives the bird a biscuit, eats one herself. After a pause*) How do I know how it happened like this? Who knows how what happened to them?

(*In the living room, Hannah is passing around the lobster salad.*)

MR. PARKER. Hard to believe now. Me with a pack on my back, ten-mile marches. I tell you, Halpern, a war should happen to every generation, and I'm not frightened to say so. I'm convinced the market went down because the small investor's got no confidence there'll be a war. No confidence. Well, I'm still young enough, if they hurry with this one — (*To Hannah*) Hello.

HANNAH. Hello there.

HERMAN. Shoes were good during the war. Everything was better.

MR. PARKER (*to Hannah*). Hello again.

HANNAH. Hello again.

MRS. PARKER (*looks down at the plate Hannah has handed her*). Oh, I was hoping it would be hot pastrami. Because you were Jewish people. I love hot pastrami.

MR. PARKER (*as Hannah is about to exit; in vaudeville Negro accent*). You a good-looking big lady.

HANNAH (*amused*). Eat your nice lobster salad. Build up your energy. (*To Rona*) I'm going home, so don't get no more ideas. (*She has reached the door. Sniffs*) The super says next time your Ma cook in that room, he going to notify the fire department. (*She moves to Jenny's door*) Mrs. Stern! Fire department coming.

(*Very frightened, Jenny jumps. As she jumps, she knocks over the Sterno can.*)

HANNAH (*delighted*). Fire! Fire!

(*Rona and Herman, followed by the Parkers, rush to the door. Jenny locks the door.*)

RONA (*rattling on the door*). Mama! Mama! What are you doing? Unlock the door this minute. (*She pushes at the door, can't budge it*) Herman, break the door. Break the door. Mama! Have you gone crazy? You'll kill us all —

HERMAN (*pushes on the door*). Mrs. Stern! Open the door!

Act Two

SCENE: *The parlor–waiting room of the Golden Age Nursing Home.*

AT RISE: *Jenny is sitting in a chair, dressed in a robe with a coat over it. She looks dazed. Two elderly ladies, Mrs. Lazar and Mrs. Compton, are sitting to one side of the room, listening to a music amplifier that is wired for the building. The piped music is over-cheerful. Mrs. Halpern and Berney are sitting on a couch. Mrs. Halpern is holding Berney's hand. Near them is a high table. Berney's camera case is on the table. Mrs. Compton is taking something apart with great care and interest. In a little while, we will find out that it is Berney's new camera. Mr. Halpern is in the phone booth.*

HERMAN. Tonio, I am coming as soon as I can. All right, put him on the phone. (*Into the phone, in a charming voice*) Yes, Mr. Kelly. Yes, sir. Our account books are open to you, always have been. No, sir, I don't know where they are, can't keep track of every scrap of paper. (*Softly*) Do you know where I am? Do you? (*With emotion*) I'm in a *hospital.*

MRS. LAZAR. Not a hospital. The Golden Age Nursing Home.

HERMAN. My old mother is sitting here dying and you're asking me to leave her. The Internal Revenue Department is asking me to leave my dying mother. No, she wasn't dying yesterday. *I* was sick.

MRS. LAZAR (*to Rona, pointing to Jenny*). *His* mother?

RONA (*Elaborately polite*). No, Madame. *My* mother.

MRS. LAZAR (*leans forward to speak to Herman in the booth*). *Her* mother. Not *your* mother.

HERMAN (*into the phone*). You think I like it? You think I don't want to? I'll be down. (*He exits, faces Rona so others cannot hear*) It's bad. They've discovered. I've got to go.

RONA. Herman, haven't I enough to bear? Isn't it your duty—

HERMAN. I'm telling you, Rona, there's trouble. Trouble and I mean trouble. Do the best you can. Get it as cheap as you

(Binkie-Pie rises, picks up his manuscript, leans over and uses it to conk Berney over the head. Berney sits down. Filene, Binkie-Pie and Mrs. Lamb file out. Jenny calls again and the phonograph record slowly ends.)

Curtain

HANNAH. Fire! Fire! We're going to burn up right here.

MR. PARKER (*to Hannah*). Hello there.

RONA. I can't stand much more.

HANNAH. A lunatic woman! A lunatic!

MR. PARKER. A very exciting evening.

RONA. My *evening coat's* in there! (*Screaming at Herman*) You were in the army. Push, push.

JENNY (*has put the fire out, is sitting, trembling, on the bed*). Go away. I make a little tea. Now I drink a little tea. Go away.

(*Mr. Parker takes over and the door caves in. They all rush into the tiny room. Rona leaps for Jenny. Jenny hits Rona's arm. Rona screams. Hannah follows to the attack.*)

HANNAH. You bring your stove and come out of here! I ain't working around no fire bug. Your Ma should be in a loony joint, that's where. You just give me that stove —

(*Jenny, protecting her Sterno, lifts the bread knife to Hannah. Over Rona's cries about her arm, and Hannah's successful struggle with the knife, the lights go down in Jenny's room and go up in Berney's room. Filene is sitting quietly. Binkie-Pie has finished reading, and Mrs. Lamb is standing behind him, massaging his eyes.*)

BERNEY (*points to the very thick manuscript*). Why did you write a novel? Why? Tell me that?

MRS. LAMB. Binkie-Pie, let's go. (*To Berney*) You're a dirty Spick.

BERNEY. The novel died the day *Ulysses* was published. It can't be done again until a new world is born. *We* are a society of worms. You can write poetry about worms, but you can't write novels.

(*His words are drowned out by Hannah, Rona, the Parkers and Herman as they retire from Jenny's room and lock Jenny inside.*)

HANNAH (*yelling*). A knife woman! A knife woman!

RONA. You hit your daughter! You hit your own daughter!

HANNAH. Somebody get the straitjacket.

JENNY (*calling, desperately, weakly*). Berney! Berney!

BERNEY (*strutting now, in lecture fashion*). Dope, murder, drink. Not enough. Homosexuality. Bah. Homosexuality is for squares. Invent something else and then maybe you can write a novel. Maybe.

can and make up your mind I can't pay it for long, please God. I ain't got it, so don't go getting any impression she's going to stay here forever — (*Rona motions to Jenny and the ladies, embarrassed*) If it's more than fifty a week, say no. Out of town, we can do better. I'll ask around —

RONA (*loudly, so Jenny can hear*). Nothing is too good for Mama. And certainly *not* out of town. How would Berney and I come every day to see her? Isn't that so, Mama? (*In a furious whisper to Herman*) It's going to be more than fifty and you know it. Up and down, up and down I've gone, you've made me, humiliating myself, and nothing I can find for fifty.

HERMAN (*tensely*). I can't pay. I can't pay.

RONA. Then what are we going to do? Tell me. Have private nurses like the doctor said we should?

(*The phone in the booth rings. Herman jumps. Mrs. Lazar springs for the booth.*)

HERMAN. Tell them I've left.

(*He rushes out. The lights dim down and come up in the Doctor's office. The Doctor is at his desk, facing away, speaking into the phone. Miss Evelyn ushers Rona in, indicates a chair. Rona sits.*)

DR. KATZ (*into the phone*). *Mais, je regrette. Non. Ce n'est pas possible.* It is not possible. We are full up, with a waiting list of —

MISS EVELYN (*to Rona*). Seventy-three applicants, one of them the mother of the Princess.

DR. KATZ. *Ah, c'est bon. C'est bon. C'est dommage.* A shame.

(*He pauses, puts the phone down, wheels his chair to face Rona but does not look at her: he is in deep thought. Dr. Katz is about thirty-eight, and has been told he is handsome.*)

MISS EVELYN (*timid about interrupting him*). Doctor, this is Mrs. Herman Halpern. (*To Katz*) *Sensibilu non. Combolobergere.* (*To Rona*) Dr. Katz speaks French, Turkish and German.

(*She exits. There is a pause. Dr. Katz raises his head.*)

DR. KATZ. Yes?

RONA. I'm Mrs. Halpern, Doctor, and my mother —

DR. KATZ. You are so young.

RONA. Oh.

DR. KATZ. What's your problem, dear?

RONA. Well, my darling mother. She has been ill. Our doctor said she must have expert care and nurses, and —

DR. KATZ. Of course. My name is Zachary Katz. Dr. Zachary Katz. But I want *you* to call me *Zatz.*

RONA. Oh. Well, I came to inquire because it's impossible at our very modest home —

DR. KATZ. Let me hear you say Zatz.

RONA (*smiles*). Zatz. And my husband is having temporary financial entanglements —

DR. KATZ. Again.

RONA. Zatz. I feel so —

DR. KATZ. Guilty? You must not. No, you must not. There comes a time when we have completed our round of duties to our parents. We must live our own lives, content in the belief that the old are happier away from us, happy in our sacrifice to pay for their excellent care in proper hands.

RONA. That's just it, Dr. Katz.

DR. KATZ (*roars*). Zatz.

RONA (*giggles*). Zatz.

DR. KATZ. Say to yourself, from this minute of my life Zatz is my friend, my confessor, my staff and my aid. Say it, dear, and you will feel lighter.

(*He rises, holds out his hands.*)

RONA (*she rises, goes toward him*). Zatz is my friend, my confessor, my —

(*The lights dim down, go up in the waiting room. Berney has his eyes closed. Jenny has not moved. Mrs. Compton has completed the dismantling of the camera.*)

MISS EVELYN. Who's for lunch? *So* good. I saw it. Lunch, lunch. (*She goes to Jenny*) Let me help you, Mrs. Stern, to your bed and your nice, hot lunch.

JENNY (*in a panic*). I ain't staying for lunch. Good-bye. Berney!

BERNEY (*wakes up*). I think I'm getting the flu, Grandma. (*Mrs. Lazar rises, Mrs. Compton rises. Mrs. Compton neatly gathers up the camera parts and puts them in Berney's lap. Berney stares at them, stares at Mrs. Compton*) My Leica! My new Leica!

MRS. COMPTON. I'll finish it after lunch.

MISS EVELYN (*trying to urge Jenny along*). Come along, dear.

JENNY (*frightened*). No. No. I will go now and — Where's my daughter? Rona! I want to go —

MISS EVELYN (*very firmly*). Mrs. Halpern said to tell you that she will phone you this evening. Now let us make you comfortable, dear, in your little nook.

JENNY (*as she is pushed along by Miss Evelyn*). Berney! Berney! (*But Berney is in the hall calling after Mrs. Compton, who has disappeared.*)

BERNEY. I demand to have your name and address. I warn you I will go to a lawyer. You must repay me for this wanton destruction. *Madame!* I am speaking to you —

JENNY'S VOICE. Berney, take me in the subway home —

BERNEY (*as the lights dim, he looks around, can't find her*). I'll come and see you every day. Grandma, make that old lady fix my camera —

(*The lights go up in the office of the Florentine Shoe Corporation. Herman is onstage.*)

HERMAN (*calling*). Tonio! Tonio! Stop the machines! Look at this shoe! Stop! For Christ's sake!

TONIO (*coming in*). Herman, for twenty years I ask you not to do that Christ talk. Everybody's not a Jew. You know I'm an altar boy when the altar boy don't show up.

HERMAN. You got pretty worries. I envy you. Pretty worries. (*He holds up the shoe he is carrying. It is very odd*) Look.

TONIO. You stop the religious stuff, I stop. (*He takes the shoe, stares at it*) A shoe?

HERMAN. Is this a shoe for a human foot? Is the human heel part of the human toe? Macy's ain't gonna take that shoe. Not when the last ones melted. (*Going through the desk*) Where's the bicarbonate? Did you hock the bicarbonate?

TONIO. They'll never accept, and if they don't accept, we'll be bankrupt —

HERMAN. Don't say it. Last time you said it, it happened. It's bad luck, that word. There are days when bicarbonate don't do much anymore. I could always count on bicarbonate when I was young.

TONIO. Well, we ain't young anymore. And bankrupt twice. Three times is out.

HERMAN. Is that Internal Revenue guy still here? That stinker —

KELLY (*looking at a ledger as he enters*). Yes, I'm still here. August, 1960. Check deposited to Frank James' account. September, one thousand withdrawn by Frank James. December, two thousand deposited, twenty-five hundred withdrawn. Thirty-seven of these entries. Who is Frank James?

HERMAN. Mr. Kelly, it's lunch time. Come and have a bottle of champagne, a little caviar —

KELLY. I hate caviar. I got ulcers.

TONIO (*nervous giggle*). Everybody's sick. My wife is preparing a hysterectomy. Right this minute, a hysterectomy is coming.

KELLY. Frank James doing the operation? (*Reads from ledger*) Frank James, for publicity releases. Frank James, a trip to Cincinnati to christen a ship. Cincinnati for a ship. Frank James, for attending leather auction in Newark. Five hundred is a lot of money for a trip to Newark. Now, gentlemen, the affairs of Florentine Shoes, Inc., are not my business, but —

HERMAN. Believe me, I wish they were. Believe me. Take the business and don't say thank you. (*In a whisper*) We are right on top of bankrupt.

KELLY. I regret to hear it. My business concerns only your income tax reports. Who is Frank James?

HERMAN. Over and over, we say he's died. Last year he died. People die.

KELLY. When and where did he die?

HERMAN. He drowned last August.

TONIO. No, *Christmas.* Christmas night. I was in church when the news came. It was sad —

HERMAN. Mr. Kelly, it's time to tell you the truth. Frank James is my son. The junior partner. You got a son? Ever heard of one? An employee. A college man. The new brains.

KELLY. Changed his name?

HERMAN. Yes, changed his name. In America, the land of the free and no classes, it seems a poet should not be called Bernard Halpern. My son's a poet. (*Hastily*) I mean at night. When he isn't here working.

KELLY. What's your bookkeeper's name?

HERMAN. *Mrs.* Sophronia Knopf. Nice name?

KELLY (*calling*). Mrs. Knopf!

HERMAN. Not here. Poor woman's been sick for a week.

(*Mrs. Knopf enters.*)

MRS. KNOPF. What's the matter now? I'm listening to the war.

KELLY. What war?

MRS. KNOPF. Place called Biannina. We can't allow a foreign power to menace our people. It's in Africa or Asia.

HERMAN. What are you talking about?

MRS. KNOPF (*to Herman*). Your country. Why don't you listen to the radio?

HERMAN. We can't afford one.

MRS. KNOPF. Three Senators enlisted, Prince Radziwill, Serge Obelensky, and the butler in the Moroccan embassy. Isn't that nice?

KELLY. Very nice. Now let's get down to business. This your handwriting?

MRS. KNOPF. Yep. I put it down. That don't mean I know anything about it.

KELLY. Certainly not. But perhaps you can help. Now before Frank James died last Christmas in August —

MRS. KNOPF. Mr. Kelly, I don't know anything. I put down what I'm told to put down. You through with me? I want to listen about the war. I got three daughters.

(*She exits.*)

TONIO. War. Good thing *we* ain't got sons.

HERMAN. What's the matter with you? I got Berney.

TONIO. They ain't going to take Berney.

HERMAN. Why not?

TONIO. The country ain't that bad off. Last war we made a little dough. But planes and bombs don't wear shoes, I guess.

HERMAN. Planes, bombs. They're always going to need men to do the dying, trudging in the mud, don't I remember. (*After a second*) Trudging in the mud. Trudging in the mud! (*Sudden energy, in a new voice*) Mr. Kelly, did you hear the news? Did you hear our country might be at war?

KELLY. I heard. What do you want me to do, call it off?

HERMAN. Mr. Kelly, we haven't time to waste. What is it you want to know? Just come out and say frankly and let us get on with our business. Tonio, call Walter Copside. Remind him of the army shoes last time. Ask him how much leather —

KELLY. Who is Frank James?

HERMAN. Look here. You can't go on disturbing two legitimate businessmen. How's it going to look when people come around with war orders and Internal Revenue is sitting here, sitting in the way of our army?

KELLY. I don't know. Who is Frank James?

HERMAN. A nagger you are. A nagger.

TONIO (*into the phone*). Copside? Herman wants to talk.

HERMAN. Mr. Kelly, that's enough for today. Make an appointment with our secretary — (*On the phone*) Copside? Listen to the news? Yeah. Yeah. Remember last time you were late with the leather? The war started without you, Copside, and remember your tears?

(*The lights go down in Herman's office and go up in Berney's bedroom. Berney is listening to the radio. Styron, a colored man, is putting together Berney's camera. Hannah is sitting near Styron.*)

VOICE. To this end the Sixth of Michigan, the Ninth Airborne and the atom-powered battleship *Clara* have been ordered to the scene. . . . A New Jersey spinach grower, Fred Moncey, today killed and dismembered his inamorata, long claimed as his wife. . . . The University of Alabama students rioted when Charlie Lee Stimpson, a twenty-five-year-old Negro, said he did not believe in war. He was reported still unconscious in the hospital. . . .

STYRON. That's where I was born. Little old Tuscaloosa, Alabama.

BERNEY. Must be a fine joint.

STYRON. No worse than others.

BERNEY. Your folks couldn't stand it?

STYRON. They still there.

BERNEY. Why don't they leave?

STYRON. Why don't anybody leave anyplace?

BERNEY. You left.

STYRON. No, I didn't. I liked Tuscaloosa, Alabama. I got put out.

BERNEY. *Liked it? Liked it?* What kind of man are you, Styron?

HANNAH. He's a man. He's a man okay. (*Styron and Hannah both laugh in intimate pleasure*) You a man, Berney? You one?

BERNEY (*to Styron*). I wish I had been born a black man. I wish I had a chance to raise up a downtrodden people.

STYRON. Ain't you a Jew, Mr. Berney?

BERNEY. Yes, but nobody does anything to us anymore.

STYRON. Well, pretend you a nigger. Lot of people do now.

BERNEY. I tell you those black men speaking out are heroes, the way nobody else in this country has ever had a chance to be. War. Bah! You're protected in a war. The conception of man as hero had disappeared. But suddenly here are those black boys and the dream of the hero has returned —

STYRON. Ain't it so? Fine fellows. Three of 'em.

BERNEY. I sent ten dollars last week. All I had.

HANNAH. Better you pay me what you owe me from last Christmas.

STYRON. Ten dollars's always nice, but it ain't going to fix that boy's head. Ain't that a disgrace? Hit him in the head he got to use to get through college?

BERNEY. Styron, how could you have left a land where you were needed? Why don't you go back? Think what that would mean. A black man coming down from the North, returning to help his people? You'd walk right up, followed by thousands of admiring people. You'd be a great man, a noble man —

STYRON. Yeah. I wouldn't mind. I like the South. I got a wife in Montgomery. Nice little woman. Only about twenty-one years old still. But I don't want no trouble with my head.

BERNEY. There wouldn't be. This time they got troops. White troops. You'd go right up, say, "Here I am, I've come to take Charlie Lee Stimpson's place. I'm a man and a patriot." Styron, I'll go with you. I'll go right along. I'll walk right through those crowds by your side —

(Hannah rises, goes to the living room, picks up the silver coffee pot.)

STYRON. I would like to see my folks, my little wife.

BERNEY. Your little wife will be right by your side. Styron, let's go.

STYRON. All right, kid. Let's have a drink and take us a train. There's a good old train at eight P.M. We'll walk right up and I'll say, "I'm a man, a right noble black man" —

HANNAH (*calls*). Bye, Styron, noble bunny.

STYRON (*rises*). What you cutting up for? Be right with you.

BERNEY. Styron! You said —

HANNAH (*to Berney*). Now, listen here, boy. I want you to give your Ma a message. I want you to tell her she owes me two weeks' wage, overdue, like always. I want you to tell her I had enough of you, all of you. I want you to tell her I'm taking this Altman silver pot and I'll be glad to give it back the day she mail me my wages. (*To Styron*) Styron, bunny, let's go and have us a nice drink and you just spend the rest of the night telling me about your twenty-one-year-old little wife.

STYRON. Yeah, I wanted to do that for a long time, Hannah. It's a good story.

(The lights go down and come up in Katz's office. Katz is lying

on the couch, a telephone at his side. Rona is standing at the desk, sobbing.)

DR. KATZ. Now, now, now, dearest girl. Now, now, now.

RONA. We did such things. Such things. I never did such things before, Zatz. Terrible things —

DR. KATZ. There is no terrible thing in the passion of a man and woman. All is clean. (*There is a rumbling in the phone. He speaks into the box*) Evelyn? Yes, I'm resting, dear. Give her a nice aspirin.

RONA. Zatz, how will I sleep tonight? How will I face Herman and my son? Tell them, confess — ?

DR. KATZ. Dearest girl, dearest girl, dearest girl.

RONA. We didn't even talk first, Zatz. We didn't even exchange our dreams, our hopes —

DR. KATZ. Life is ahead. Life is ahead.

RONA (*in a gasp*). Have you a wife?

DR. KATZ (*sad*). Yes.

RONA (*lets out a pained cry*). Oh, Zatz. Do you do our things with her?

DR. KATZ. No, dear girl, no, dear girl.

RONA. With other women, ever?

DR. KATZ. No, dear girl, no.

RONA (*crying*). But then it's unusual, what we did. You said it wasn't, Zatz.

DR. KATZ. The Kinsey Institute shows that eighty-five percent of Americans —

RONA. But my *mother's* in the building.

DR. KATZ. And you must go and see her now, dear.

RONA. Do you love me, Zatz?

DR. KATZ. Dear girl, we will share our dreams. *I* have a large dream, and you will help me and aid me —

RONA. But, Zatz, we should have dreamed first, before we — (*Cries*) My husband, my son, my mother!

(*The phone buzzes.*)

DR. KATZ (*deep, dignified voice*). Why, yes. Yes, she's here. Unfortunately, I had to keep her waiting. Yes, all details will, I am sure, be to your liking. I have given her the lowest possible rate — (*To Rona*) Your husband wishes to speak to you. (*Rona screams. Deep voice*) Nurse, is Mrs. Halpern still here? Her husband wishes to speak to her.

RONA (*gasping whisper*). *I can't. I can't.* He would guess. He —

DR. KATZ (*softly*). No, sex doesn't show on the phone. (*Loud, near the telephone, motions wildly to Rona to come to the phone*) Say good-bye to your mother, Mrs. Halpern. She is in loving hands and there is no need for a daughter's tears.

RONA (*into the phone*). Yes, Herman. (*Crying*) But why not? Oh. (*Gives shriek of disbelief, then giggles with pleasure*) Oh, Herman! Oh, Herman! I knew something would turn up. Now, really, won't you ever learn? (*To Katz, very happy*) There's a little war started. God takes care of his own. (*To Herman*) See you later, dear. (*She hangs up, rushes to button her blouse, grabs her coat*) Oh, Zatz. Tell Mama I'll see her tomorrow. I'm so relieved for Herman. Supplies are going to be very short and I have a family, you know —

DR. KATZ (*as she flies out of the door*). Good-bye, dearest girl. I'm so glad about Mr. Halpern's good luck. It will be eighty a week —

RONA. Zatz! You said seventy.

DR. KATZ. No, dear, *you* said seventy.

(*The lights go down in Dr. Katz's office and go up in a bedroom in the Golden Age Nursing Home. Mrs. Compton, Mrs. Lazar, Mrs. Kaufman are smoking, eating candy and reading. Mr. Lazar comes to the door, stares at the ladies, salutes smartly.*)

MR. LAZAR. Up. Up. On the ready. All hands needed. (*Nobody answers him*) Out. Out. Civil Defense. Where do they keep the toilet here?

MRS. LAZAR. Milton, don't start that.

(*Miss Evelyn appears wheeling Jenny.*)

MR. LAZAR (*peers at Jenny, starts to unzip his pants*). Now what pretty lady is this? A war victim?

MISS EVELYN. Move, Mr. Lazar.

MRS. LAZAR (*shrieks*). Milton, go to your room.

(*Mr. Lazar exits.*)

MISS EVELYN. Ladies, Mrs. Jenny Stern.

MRS. COMPTON. Well, just go get Dr. Katz. Just go get him. This room is for three, not for four. We pay for three —

(*Dr. Katz appears, very cheerful.*)

DR. KATZ. Now I hope none of you is too exercised about the war news. No trouble will ever reach our little home. (*To Mrs. Kaufman*) Put up the cigarette, dear. You know it's bad for you. (*He takes away the candy from Mrs. Lazar*) Tsh, tsh.

MRS. COMPTON. I pay for a room for three ladies —

DR. KATZ. I know, dear. Just for a few days. Now be nice, old dears. We all need love.

MRS. COMPTON. I don't need it four in a room.

MRS. KAUFMAN (*reading from her newspaper*). Mrs. Whittemore cooks dinner in a ten-year-old Mainbocher dress. If you amortize the cost, she says, it is cheaper than — Amortize, amortize, amortize. All my life that's all I hear. Amortize. You live your life that way. Amortize. We come here, amortize the expense, Mama, and it comes to less than giving you an apartment. So here we are. Amortize, amortize.

DR. KATZ. *I* amortize my *life* for you.

MR. LAZAR (*reappears. He is carrying a book. He moves to Mrs. Lazar*). Good night.

MRS. LAZAR. Good night twice.

MR. LAZAR (*reads from the book*). The erotic life of the people of antiquity laid stress upon the sexual instinct *itself,* whereas *we* emphasize the *object.* Therefore, they honored even an inferior object, whereas we — (*He pinches Miss Evelyn*) Freud. *Quotations from Great Men.* Nice book. (*Reads*) During our fourth day in the Hebrides we were told of a man, ninety-one, who had fathered a baby boy —

(*He pinches Miss Evelyn.*)

MISS EVELYN. Mr. Lazar, knock it off.

MR. LAZAR. Good night. (*To Mrs. Lazar*) Good night, darling.

MRS. LAZAR (*shrieks*). So amortize the good nights. Good night.

MRS. KAUFMAN. A father at ninety-one. That's good? Who wants children?

DR. KATZ. Now, dear, they'll visit you this week. Don't worry. Anyway, *I'm* your son, and *I'm* your father, and *I'm* your doctor — (*Mr. Lazar is now unbuttoning his belt. Dr. Katz takes him by the arm, ushers him out*) Good night, darlings. Good night.

MRS. LAZAR. Good night, good night, good night, good night, good night.

MRS. KAUFMAN (*to Miss Evelyn, pointing to Jenny*). What's the matter with her? What disease?

JENNY. Who's got one disease? (*To Miss Evelyn*) How much does it cost here? How much do they pay for me?

MRS. LAZAR. How rich did your children say they weren't? No less than seventy. Maybe a hundred. Depends.

JENNY. My God. (*She tries to rise*) I think I go, Miss Evelyn. You tell the doctor I come and talk tomorrow —

MISS EVELYN (*pushes her back*). Now, Mrs. Stern. No nonsense. You're a very sick lady.

MRS. KAUFMAN. It's night. Rest yourself. There's no place to go. If anybody wanted you, you wouldn't be here. You have to pay anyway for a week. Maybe you pay for yourself like Mrs. Compton?

JENNY. No.

MRS. KAUFMAN. Ach. That's bad. Poor lady. Children, terrible. Terrible.

JENNY. Not if you're lucky.

MRS. KAUFMAN. Who's lucky?

MISS EVELYN. Good night, ladies. Do try to sleep through. I'm very tired. No smoking, no candy —

(*She exits. Mrs. Compton takes out her newspaper. Mrs. Kaufman takes out her box of candy. Mrs. Lazar takes out her cigarettes.*)

MRS. KAUFMAN. No smoking, no salt, no candy — (*To Jenny*) You know why? So we'll live longer. Have a piece. Don't talk too much, don't eat too much, don't cry too much, no spices. You know why?

(*Jenny takes a piece of candy, holds it in her hand.*)

MRS. LAZAR. So you'll live longer.

MRS. KAUFMAN. Button up your throat in winter, don't sweat in summer, don't think so much, no fats, no starches — You know why?

MRS. COMPTON (*roaring with laughter*). So you'll live longer.

MRS. LAZAR. Take the pills, come for the vitamins, rest after lunch. Lunch, fine lunch, tablespoon tuna fish — You know why?

MRS. COMPTON, LAZAR, KAUFMAN (*they are now noisy and uproarious*). So you'll live longer.

MRS. KAUFMAN. But someday soon I am going to die. No more for my sons to fight who pays.

MRS. COMPTON. Me, too. Me, too. But first I'll lie on my back and I'll pretend to be gone and my children will talk thinking I can't hear. They will have quite a time finding the safe-deposit boxes. I fixed it that way. May take years.

MRS. LAZAR. Fix another safe box and you'll live longer.

MRS. COMPTON. Clauses and clauses and clauses I put in the will. And I made up people to leave things to. I put the bonds in St. Louis and the cash in Newark in another name. Not Compton. MacCompton.

(*Mr. Lazar appears.*)

MR. LAZAR. Know what's the matter in here? Freud could have told you. The sexual instinct begins with the moment of birth and lasts until the moment of death.

MRS. LAZAR. God forbid.

(*Mr. Lazar crosses to Jenny.*)

MR. LAZAR. New little lady, I want to show you something.

(*He starts to untie his pajamas. Jenny gives him the piece of candy she has been holding. Mrs. Lazar shouts at Mr. Lazar. Miss Evelyn comes running in.*)

MISS EVELYN. Mr. Lazar! I will not allow you —

MR. LAZAR (*to Miss Evelyn*). Don't get so jealous, dear. I got plenty for everybody.

MISS EVELYN. Out! Out! Immediately! Mrs. Lazar, this cannot go on. You must talk to him tomorrow —

MRS. LAZAR. I don't want to.

MISS EVELYN (*to Jenny*). You encouraged him. I saw you offer him a piece of candy.

JENNY. Poor old man. Poor old fool. (*Miss Evelyn puts out the lights, exits. After a second, Mrs. Compton puts on her light, continues reading the stock-market page. The others are in darkness*) I never been in a hospital in my whole life. Never. I'll keep you ladies awake.

MRS. KAUFMAN. Take your sleeping pill.

(*She hands it to her.*)

JENNY. I ain't never taken a sleeping pill.

MRS. COMPTON. Never taken a sleeping pill! I never heard of such a thing. Are you poor?

JENNY. Yes.

MRS. LAZAR. Ssh, please. I'm sleeping.

MRS. KAUFMAN. Good night. Don't be scared.

JENNY. Good night.

(*The lights dim down and go up in a bar with a small jazz band of two black men and one white man. The white man plays the sax; the two Negroes play bass and drums. There are customers at the bar. Berney is sitting at the bar. He is drunk. He is carrying a portable radio.*)

BERNEY (*to bartender*). Don't they know there's a war on? Don't they? (*The bartender doesn't answer. Berney speaks to the man and woman next to him*) Don't *you* know there's a war on?

WOMAN. Where?

BERNEY. Where there's a war on.

WOMAN. Outside?

BERNEY. That's America for you. Sitting here, waiting like doped pigeons for the bomb, knowing nothing, caring less, drinking, sexing —

WOMAN. Sexing? Look, kid, I don't say you always got to lie down, but I do say you got to come closer together than sitting on a bar stool.

BERNEY (*shouts*). Listen, you moldy figs, there's a war on. You haven't been out of this joint in so long —

(*He turns on his portable radio.*)

THE RADIO VOICE. The right to defend ourselves in Africa. The God-given right, never to be surrendered by free men — (*The jazz band plays. Berney turns the radio louder. The band stops*) For our children's future and their children's, across unknown seas and uncharted deserts —

BERNEY. The last night on earth. Tomorrow the seas will run into the land, fire will top the mountains, a stone from the Australian seas will hit the body of a mourning Indian in Montana — (*To the woman next to him*) You will lie on top of your fat friend, colon merging into colon, guts entwined in guts —

WOMAN. Ah, look here. That ain't nice.

BERNEY (*shouting*). All of you. You're looking into death. *Death.*

JAZZ PLAYER (*to bartender*). Take out the nutty fay.

BARTENDER. Screw, boy.

WOMAN (*puts her arm around Berney*). Nobody's going to touch a Greek. Not while I'm around. He wants his Mama.

BERNEY. I don't want my Mama. I don't want her. My Grandma's dying —

WOMAN (*she takes a balloon from her companion, gives it to Berney*) Here, dear.

(*Berney holds the balloon, rests his head on the bar. The band starts to play. The customers listen with great attention. The jazz is good. Berney gets down from the bar stool, wanders over to the musicians, listens.*)

BERNEY (*to the White Sax Player*). Man, man. I got something to say. You got to be black to play good. No way out. Give up. (*The White Sax Player ignores him. Berney plucks at his coat*) Did you hear me? You white boy, you can't make it. I'm telling you. *I* tried. This ain't the age for white boys. Africa is moving on the move. The Chinks will run over Europe. The American Indian will rise and the white man will be a flea in the pelvis of the black race. (*The Sax Player quits. The other two dribble off. The Sax Player stares at Berney*) Twelve-tone scale! You got to play better than that — and you can't. You're a moldy fig, boy. The last night of the world and I wanted to hear better jazz than this — (*All three players rise. The Bartender moves toward Berney. Berney is crying now*) The last night of the world and this is the way it ends, not with a bang but a whimper. Know who said that? Thomas Stearns Eliot. Blow that cool. The world will end not with a bang but a whimper. (*To the Sax Player*) And you whimper, boy. That sax whimpers.

(*As the men close in on Berney the lights go out. There is a crash. Then the jazz band begins again. The lights go up in the waiting room of the Golden Age Nursing Home. Mrs. Lazar is reading the Bible. Mr. Lazar is holding her hand. After a minute Mrs. Lazar frees her hand in order to turn a page.*)

MR. LAZAR. Miriam, for a minute put up the Bible. (*Takes her hand again*) When Mr. and Mrs. Finney depart this life — Mr. Finney couldn't eat his breakfast — I have applicated for their room. For you and me.

MRS. LAZAR. Applicate for yourself.

MR. LAZAR. A nice room.

MRS. LAZAR. I know. *You* have it.

MR. LAZAR. (*after a second*). Miriam, on desertion a divorce can be gotten.

MRS. LAZAR. A lot of trouble, a lot of money.

(*Mrs. Kaufman enters.*)

MRS. KAUFMAN. I used to like to take a bath. I don't anymore.

MRS. LAZAR. Yes, lots of things go. I used to like to tell nice lies. When I was very young, I said to myself, if you tell the truth about people you got to talk bad but I don't like to talk bad about people. So I decided never to tell the truth again.

MR. LAZAR. Oh, you never talked bad about anybody and you never will.

MRS. LAZAR (*pats the Bible*). Yes, I will. I been saving up the truth for years. Saving it for Abraham.

MR. LAZAR. Who?

MRS. LAZAR. Abraham in the Bible. What's the matter with you?

MR. LAZAR. Oh. Abraham.

MRS. LAZAR. I'm going to find him in heaven, where he don't belong, and when I do, I'm going to say, so you go into Egypt and you're afraid they'll kill you, so you tell Sarah to say she's your sister, not your wife, and so Pharaoh fucks her and treats you fine. Then you and the Lord decide *that* ain't kosher all of a sudden, so the Lord sends plagues to poor Pharoah, and poor Pharoah done nothing but fuck what he thought was a sister. Abraham, you tricked Pharaoh, you old shit.

(*Mrs. Kaufman flees in shock.*)

MR. LAZAR (*shocked*). Miriam, I never knew you knew such words.

MRS. LAZAR. I didn't know I knew them, either. You and Sarah. Stinkers, both of you. I hate you both.

MR. LAZAR. Oh, Miriam. It's water over the dam.

MRS. LAZAR. Not for me.

(*Mrs. Compton enters.*)

MRS. COMPTON. The stock market is in some trouble.

(*Jenny enters, a paper in her hand, and goes toward the phone booth.*)

MR. LAZAR. Here's that new pretty lady.

MRS. COMPTON. Mrs. Stern, I must ask you not to use the phone. I am waiting for a call from my broker.

MR. LAZAR (*Jenny, weak, is having difficulty with coins, with dialing*). Pretty lady, can an admirer help you?

(*Miss Evelyn passes by and Mr. Lazar exits skipping after her.*)

JENNY (*into the phone*). Is this the Shamus Benevolent Association? Yes? This is Mrs. Samuel Jenny Stern, formerly of two-o-o-five Simpkins Avenue. I want to speak about my funeral benefit paper. The five hundred dollars. I don't want a funeral. I'd like to have it now, today, please. Yes, this is me. Who else? (*Amazed, annoyed*) No, I'm not my daughter. No, I'm not my son. I'm not my mother. I'm me. If I was dead how could I be in a phone booth? It's hot in here. Would it be all right if I signed a paper? It's *my* money. I saved it — I don't want no letter. (*She hangs up, looks sad and weak, sits down. To Mrs. Lazar*) I wanted it today.

MRS. LAZAR. You in trouble?

JENNY. I wanted it today. (*Mrs. Lazar points to Mrs. Compton, whispers to Jenny. Jenny approaches Mrs. Compton*) I got five hundred dollars coming for my funeral expenses. I don't want no funeral.

MRS. COMPTON. You don't? I do. I've fixed the will so that before they inherit a cent they're going to have to take the Madison Avenue Church, bank it with yellow flowers —

JENNY. I hear you lend a little money sometimes. If I signed the funeral paper to you —

MRS. COMPTON. Absolutely not. Mrs. Lazar, I don't want you to tell people I lend money. I *give* to certain friends. (*The phone rings, she sprints to it*) Hello. Mr. Warkins? Where is he? I don't want secretaries. What right has he got to use my losses to pay for secretaries. Well, find him and tell him — Hello. What's the latest news? IBM? (*Listens*) My God. Polaroid? My God. Texas Instruments? (*Bangs the phone, returns to her chair*) I never before heard of a war sending stocks down. A new kind of war. I don't like it. (*After a second, to Jenny*) What is it you wanted, dear?

JENNY. I wanted to sign funeral paper so you get five hundred dollars when I die. But I wanted the money today.

MRS. COMPTON. What's the nature of your disease?

JENNY. All over me.

MRS. COMPTON. Heart?

JENNY. Lungs. (*Mrs. Compton shakes her head, goes back to her paper. Jenny waits a minute*) Heart, too. Very bad, Mrs. Compton. (*Mrs. Lazar whispers to Jenny*) I'd pay good interest. You could take fifty dollars.

MRS. COMPTON. No, sorry, Mrs. Stern. (*Jenny rises, sighs, stumbles. Mrs. Compton watches with great interest*) You're weak, Mrs. Stern. Shall I ring for Evelyn?

JENNY. No.

MRS. COMPTON. I'd like to help you, if I could. How would three seventy be?

JENNY. Three seventy what?

MRS. COMPTON. Three hundred and seventy dollars.

JENNY. I give you the five hundred paper and you give me three hundred and seventy? (*Sadly*) Tsh.

MRS. COMPTON. Mrs. Stern, if you live for ten years I'm out three hundred and seventy that could be earning at least fourteen dollars and eighty cents a year.

JENNY. I ain't going to live for ten years. Maybe not for ten days. If I promise you I won't live for ten days —

MRS. COMPTON. If you go in ten days, I'll give you back fifty dollars, making four twenty in all. Fair?

JENNY (*after a second*). Can I have it now?

(*Mrs. Compton hands her a pen and paper. Jenny begins to write as Mrs. Compton opens her purse. The lights dim down and come up in Dr. Katz's office. Rona is lying on the couch. Dr. Katz is pacing up and down.*)

DR. KATZ. Within our time, human life has been prolonged one point zero six. Within the next ten years — anything can happen. We will possibly live to be a hundred, maybe two hundred. But there will never be, in my opinion, a solution for the young and vigorous not wishing to be burdened with the old, no matter how beloved. Therefore —

RONA. What is your wife like, Zatz?

DR. KATZ. A mistake. Therefore, the increasing need, the *demand* for nursing homes for senior citizens. A fortune to be made. A chain of nursing homes all over the country; tie-ups with chain markets, tie-ups with chain laundries, chain drug supplies. The happy problem of our time — longer life. What nobler goal for a man of medicine? At this very minute, Rona, I am working with a scientist at Revlon Products —

RONA (*yawns*). When we talk like this, when you tell me your aims in life, I don't feel so guilty about the sex things we do.

DR. KATZ. All over the country. Nursing homes in the desert, at the seashore. Special homes in special places for those who can afford it. At this minute, there is a fine brownstone on East Eighty-second Street — many children don't want their parents on the West Side — but I haven't the money. I've got to get it. Chances have to be taken. Have to be taken, Rona, darling.

RONA. Zatz, no matter how I act, I want you to know I have affection for Herman. I want you to know that.

DR. KATZ. Of course, dear. And *I* want to do him a favor. I want you to go to him, Rona, today —

RONA (*rises, throws herself in his arms; he looks bewildered, but embraces her*). I must wait for Berney to find himself. Herman couldn't afford a divorce settlement now, but if the war goes on —

DR. KATZ. I'm thirty-eight, Rona. I must move fast or else —

RONA. I'm a little older than you are, darling. When I'm seventy you'll be sixty-eight —

DR. KATZ. Now I must tell you my brilliant idea. Sit down, dear. (*She lies down*) I think you'd better sit up.

RONA (*annoyed*). Why? Why? I've been lying here for an hour and now you tell me to sit up.

DR. KATZ (*mildly embraces her*). When you lie down, I cannot talk, cannot think, cannot do anything but want you —

(*She grabs him.*)

RONA. I said to myself last night, how can I do without him for a day, a night? (*Looks at her watch*) Zatz, it's late. I must think of my family. The war scare. I must supply them with supplies. I *want* to stay here, darling, but you've wasted an hour, with me lying here doing nothing —

DR. KATZ (*held tight, but trying not to be*). Now listen carefully. Death comes to every man —

RONA (*shrieks*). I'm not sick. What are you saying? You haven't examined me. I mean, not that way.

DR. KATZ (*kisses her, laughs pulls away*). Darling, darling girl. You are the picture of health and desire. I mean desirability.

RONA. Zatz, I've been on this couch for an hour. The stores close at five and I have my family to think of —

DR. KATZ. *You* interrupted *me,* darling. Now. There we are eighty, ninety, a hundred years old, but finally the worms are ready for us.

RONA. Worms! Worms! What do you mean? What kind of love-making is this? There are things I won't do even for you, Zatz —

DR. KATZ. Darling, darling, darling, please don't scream. There are ladies in this place. Your own mother. Your hair is so beautiful, a nest of swans. Now. When death comes, under our present economy, the family sends the best clothes of the beloved deceased to the undertaker. This is a waste and God does not like waste. In short order, the worms come, and pouf. Now fine clothes can be sold or given away for a tax deduction. The beloved deceased should be outfitted in fresh, *cheap* raiment. Shoes, for example. I believe that your husband and I could make a fortune on a two-dollars, maybe two-fifty, death shoe. We could call it the "Honor" shoe because it would be in honor of the dead and because the dead would want their beloved ones to keep the expensive shoes and benefit from them. Take my word, I know about these things and when I first saw you, I thought — Now, I could go to Mr. Halpern myself, but I thought that in the light of our relationship, and our future, perhaps it would be more delicate —

RONA (*rises, buttons her blouse, hitches her skirt, takes her coat, looks at her watch*). I will go and see my dear mother now. I will see my husband tonight. I will not tell him of the Honor shoe. *Honor* shoe. But I will tell him that you tried to rape me in your office in order to reach up his factory. I cannot prophesy what will happen. Good-bye, Zatz.

DR. KATZ. Rona, Rona, darling. I have loved you. I wished only to have money for you and I to live in divorce —

(*But she has turned, passing Miss Evelyn as Miss Evelyn enters.*)

RONA (*to Miss Evelyn*). Nurse, tell my mother that I will return early in the morning. I have found a new nursing home more in conformity with her needs.

(*She sweeps out. Miss Evelyn closes the door, stares at Katz.*)

DR. KATZ. I don't do anything right anymore. Nothing. Brilliant idea and it blows up in my face.

MISS EVELYN. You must learn to be patient.

(*He takes her in his arms.*)

DR. KATZ. I can't be patient. It's not my nature. Never was. Even in City College.

(*The lights go down and come up in the Halpern living room. Rona appears dragging bundles and packages and boxes. Berney's room is dark, but we can see Berney lying on the bed.*)

RONA. Herman? (*No answer. She crosses to Berney's door, opens it, sees Berney on the bed*) Come help me, dear. For the first time in my life, I feel old. (*Returns to the hall, brings in more packages*) We grow frightened, women, I mean, Berney, and we reach out — I've learned a bitter lesson, but I can't tell you about it. Someday when I'm very old and you and I are living in Athens or Florence, with the flowers — It's a madhouse downtown. And the meat market. Posito's didn't want to charge this side of beef. How do you like that after all these years? I said to them that I would have them persecuted, prosecuted, for war profiteers unless — I do wish your father would pay the bills, but now thank God — Good thing your Grandmother's in the hospital. Don't know where we'd store this stuff — (*Calls out to Berney, as she begins to pull things toward Jenny's room*). All I thought of was you. What you'd like best when famine comes. Too many canned peaches they made me take in order — I got you two dozen cans of those truffle things, dear. Berney, am I still pretty? I need a compliment, dear. (*Herman enters. He looks awful.*

He goes immediately to pour himself a drink. Rona moves toward him) Herman, I must talk to you alone. A man, a *man,* attempted — (*She hits her foot against a large package*) Do help me with the canned goods. I can't tell you what this day's been like. There's panic buying. I bought you woolen underwear, I had to take any size I could get. And a hood for Berney. Berney, come see your bomb hood. (*Takes out a foolish-looking hood. Points to a box*) I've never liked mink and you know it, Herman. Never wanted it. I bought it for the vicuna lining. It's warm. God knows how much time we'll all have to spend out of doors. (*Holds up a large package*) Sterno cans. I had to fight for them, believe me. Herman, pay attention.

HERMAN. I'm paying attention. You had to fight for Sterno cans.

RONA (*drags in a giant package*). You'll never guess. A massage table. Can be an outdoor bed. You know, just in case.

HERMAN. I like an outdoor bed. Just in case.

RONA. Two fresh salmon. Into the freezer. Just for you, Herman. I hate salmon.

HERMAN. I do, too.

RONA. You do? I never knew that.

HERMAN. I've always hated salmon.

RONA. Why are you so proud of it?

HERMAN. What else did you buy, Rona?

RONA. A picnic kit. They had a sale. We're going to have to go to the country, probably quite a lot, Herman. We're going to have to go where our President orders us. A set of Thomas Hardy, the novelist. For Berney, you know. And a sable duster. They had a sale on the strangest things today.

HERMAN (*he has a second drink*). Sometimes strange things turn out the most practical. What did you use for money?

RONA. Herman, I've become very suspicious of Zatz — Dr. Katz, I mean. We must move Mama to a better place, and —

HERMAN. Ah. (*After a second*) What did you use for money, Rona? (*She unpacks a fur automobile robe*) What's that? Your cousin?

RONA (*comes to him, flirtatious*). Mr. Parker. The market fell. I think Mr. Parker's in some kind of crooked scandal and they're going to Mexico. Isn't that terrible? She wanted me to have it, she just threw it in — with — What's the matter with you, Herman?

HERMAN. You know damn well I never eat salmon. When did you ever see me eat salmon?

RONA. Always, that's when. On our honeymoon, I think it was. I never heard such a fuss about salmon. You'd be better off using your aggressions on something more worthwhile than hating little salmons.

HERMAN. I'm going to try. What did you use for money, Rona?

RONA (*hauls out a rubber boat. The boat inflates itself*). A boat, dear. For escape over water.

HERMAN. For escape over water.

RONA. And an oxygen tank —

HERMAN (*softly*). An oxygen tank. (*Screams*) What did you use for money?

(*Berney appears. He is carrying a valise and his head is entirely covered in a bandage. Rona screams.*)

BERNEY. It's all right. Just my head. And who needs that?

RONA. What happened? Berney —

BERNEY (*to Herman*). Could you let me have fifty dollars? I won't be asking you again. I'm going to enlist.

RONA (*screams*). Enlist! Are you crazy? Last week you marched in a peace parade. Today you're a warmonger.

HERMAN. Which side are you going to enlist on? If I knew, I might make a little dough on a bet —

RONA. Fine talk from a father. Berney, this afternoon I put down a deposit on two tickets to Greece. Greece. You and me — and you, too, Herman, when you can spare the time.

HERMAN. I can spare the time. *Where'd you get the money, Rona?*

BERNEY. Could I have twenty-five? I tell you, I am going away for good, and won't ask you again.

RONA. Berney, I have sleeping pills. Hidden. I will go and get them now and kill myself —

HERMAN. I hope you have enough for me.

RONA. Berney, you know what else I did for you? I arranged to buy Mr. Parker's — Did I tell you? He's off to Mexico, the crook — sports Mercedes (*Holds up the fur rug*) — and the rug for me in winter —

HERMAN (*shouts*). *Answer me.* What did you use for money?

RONA. Herman, I've had a very hard day. A man tried to rape me.

HERMAN. I didn't know people paid for rape.

RONA. Fine talk in front of our child.

HERMAN. Where did you get the money?

RONA. Well, I thought to myself, we've *got* to have food, and there was a run on the stores such as you wouldn't believe. Well, I went into Stopes and Surly's jewelry store and there was that man. Would you believe it, Herman, twenty-seven years ago? He's old now, of course. I guess it was the last thing you ever paid for because he couldn't have been nicer, and there was my engagement ring still on my finger, and he recognized me, and he recognized the ring —

HERMAN. I know it's hard, but get to the point, Rona. What were you doing in Stopes and Surly's jewelry store?

RONA. I charged a string of small pearls. I still don't like big pearls. The man couldn't have been nicer and kept asking where we'd been all these years —

HERMAN (*looks at his watch*). Give me the pearls, Rona.

RONA. Oh, Herman, how could I have bought the food and the things with pearls? People don't like even me that much and you've ruined our credit. So I took the pearls around to that pawnshop where you took all your mama's stuff, and the man asked about you, and where had you been lately, and I got money and — you think a woman likes to go to a pawnshop?

BERNEY. Papa, I'd like to go now. Could I have twenty dollars?

HERMAN. Rona, my friends tell me that federal jails are cleaner than local jails. Of course you stay there a little longer, but — You've pawned jewelry that didn't belong to you, I'm bankrupt, and there's a man called Frank James.

RONA (*angry*). I don't know what you're talking about. I think you talk this way just to keep me miserable. Bankrupt! There's a war on and you made plenty of money in the last one.

HERMAN. No. The war is over. It never began.

(*There is a long pause.*)

RONA (*softly*). How dare they? How dare they? The dirty little cowards —

BERNEY. Could I have twenty dollars?

HERMAN. I heard you, Berney. I've got three dollars and that's all I've got in the world, so I'd go back and lie down if I were you while the bed is still there.

(*As Berney slowly walks back to his room, the lights go down in the Halpern living room and come up in a corner of the*

Nursing Home bedroom. We see only Jenny's bed and Berney sitting next to the bed.)

BERNEY. So Mama said they were dirty little cowards for not having a war, and she cried, and I went back to bed, Grandma, and that's how Berney Halpern didn't leave home. (*No answer*) You asleep?

JENNY. Sure. Better to sleep than to hear.

BERNEY. I'll go someday soon, Grandma, you'll see.

JENNY. No.

BERNEY. There's a boy I went to school with. He makes jewelry. Tomorrow I'll go around and see him. Takes a little time to find yourself in this stinking world —

JENNY. Find yourself. What do you find when you find yourself? Go away. Like I say. Like I always said.

BERNEY. You can't go far on the subway.

JENNY. You're not much good, Berney. You're not much good.

BERNEY (*shocked, very softly, desperately*). I try. I try.

JENNY. No, you don't. Would you go away if you could? Would you? Tell the truth.

BERNEY. Yes. And you and I know just where I'd go.

(*Jenny reaches under her pillow, hands him a roll of bills.*)

JENNY. Three hundred and seventy dollars. I got it kosher. It's mine, okay, and now it's yours.

BERNEY (*stares at the money*). You don't understand what I said. Papa's going to jail.

JENNY. So. He'll have a rest.

BERNEY. Grandma, *Mama's* going to jail, too.

JENNY. So write her once a week.

BERNEY (*shocked*). You don't understand. I said *jail.* They can't pay for you here anymore. You'll need this money and more —

JENNY. Mind your business about me, Berney.

BERNEY (*puts the money next to her*). Awfully good of you, Grandma, really. But I guess I ought to stick around when they're in trouble. You know. When summer comes, I can bum a ride out West — you'll see.

JENNY (*lifts her head in great anger*). Don't talk no more, Berney. Don't come and see me again. Get out now.

(*She turns in the bed so that she will not see him. After a long pause Berney takes the money from her hand, presses her shoulder. She nods and the scene blacks out. The lights come up on Berney in a small tent. The tent is furnished for living — a small stove, a pot on the stove, books, an Indian headdress, a tomahawk. Berney is sitting at a group of crates which have been made into a table. He is speaking into his tape recorder.*)

BERNEY. Chapter Forty-four. My grandmother lived for seven months past that day. She even got better for a while and worked in the kitchen. Then one day she disappeared and months later a letter came from the Belmont Free Hospital. I wrote to her and she said she was proud of me. This book, and maybe all my books, all my life, will be dedicated to her. The Sit Down Press, to whom I sent a chapter, wrote a nice letter and said they wished me the best of luck. My mother and father didn't go to jail, I guess business people don't go much, and they are living in Cleveland now. I don't know how he did it, but my father is back in the shoe business and seems to be doing all right with what he calls an "Honor" shoe, a shoe to be buried in, a shoe in honor of the dead. He wrote me once and said he'd give me a hundred dollars if I published my book under the name of Frank James. I'm not going to do that, I'm not ashamed of Halpern. My mother was wild when I left and made all kinds of threats of suicide and all. She once sent me a postcard and there was a motto on it that said the eye that mocks the father and does not obey the mother, the ravens shall pick it out, and the young eagles shall eat it. (*Giggles*) There are plenty of ravens and eagles here, but nothing's happened. Last Christmas I sent her a nice silver bracelet I made and she sent me two cans of truffles and said she cried every day for me, but I haven't heard from her since. Funny. Well, I guess that about ends the notes on my mother, my father and me. I'm getting together a volume of poetry. It will be called *You Find Jerusalem Where You Find Her*. This is the first, or lead, poem.

You find Jerusalem where you find her
Many a lonely night
Considered I the crossing of the water
To join my people
In the building of Israel.
But then, decided I, in Jerusalem, Israel,
There is muscle and strength.
Here the muscle and strength have gone.
Here I am needed
Here they are weak

And I must teach them to rise again,
Rise again.

(There is the sound of a train. Quickly Berney rises, picks up an Indian headdress, puts on a poncho, takes his tom-tom, and steps outside. An old Indian, dressed in a well-tailored suit, joins him, carrying blankets that will be for sale. A pretty girl, dressed in the latest model from the local store, comes along with a tray of silver jewelry. A middle-aged Indian lady, her hair carefully done in the latest fashion, follows, carrying children's toys, leather book-marks, baskets. Dolly, the dog, wanders on, sits near Berney. The train noise sounds again. The young girl finishes arranging the displays and starts off.)

INDIAN WOMAN (*to Berney*). The kids are going to the Y to swim in the pool. Why don't you go?

BERNEY. No, thank you.

INDIAN WOMAN. I've made roast beef and spaghetti for dinner. Want to come?

BERNEY. Mama Suni, you would do better to make a batch of the maize cakes, and boil the sorrel and wild arrow root. I cannot say often enough that little will be accomplished until we return to the ways of our ancestors —

(We hear the sound of a train approaching.)

INDIAN WOMAN (*points off*). Here come the suckers. Play, play.

(Berney begins on the tom-tom. The old man frowns in pain at the noise, shakes his head, puts a fixed smile on his face as the curtain falls.)

Curtain